An Introduction to the
Law *of* Contracts
FOURTH EDITION

An Introduction to the
Law *of*
Contracts

FOURTH EDITION

Martin A. Frey
Professor Emeritus
The University of Tulsa
College of Law

Phyllis Hurley Frey
Attorney at Law
Tulsa, Oklahoma

DELMAR
CENGAGE Learning™

Australia • Brazil • Japan • Korea • Mexico • Singapore • Spain • United Kingdom • United States

DELMAR
CENGAGE Learning

**An Introduction to the Law of Contracts,
Fourth Edition**
Martin A. Frey, Phyllis Hurley Frey

Career Education Strategic Business Unit

Vice President: Dawn Gerrain

Director of Learning Solutions: John Fedor

Acquisitions Editor: Shelley Esposito

Managing Editor: Robert Serenka, Jr.

Senior Product Manager: Melissa Riveglia

Editorial Assistant: Melissa Zaza

Director of Content & MediaProduction:
   Wendy A. Troeger

Senior Content Project Manager:
   Betty L. Dickson

Art Director: Joy Kocsis

Director of Marketing: Wendy Mapstone

Marketing Manager: Gerard McAvey

Marketing Coordinator: Jonathan Sheehan

Cover Design: Joseph Villanova

For product information and technology assistance, contact us at
Cengage Learning Customer & Sales Support, 1-800-354-9706

For permission to use material from this text or product,
submit all requests online at **www.cengage.com/permissions**
Further permissions questions can be emailed to
permissionrequest@cengage.com

Library of Congress Control Number: 2007025338

ISBN-13: 978-1-4018-6471-2

ISBN-10: 1-4018-6471-6

Delmar
Executive Woods
5 Maxwell Drive
Clifton Park, NY-12065
USA

Cengage Learning is a leading provider of customized learning solutions with office locations around the globe, including Singapore, the United Kingdom, Australia, Mexico, Brazil, and Japan. Locate your local office at **international.cengage.com/region**

Cengage Learning products are represented in Canada by Nelson Education, Ltd.

For your lifelong learning solutions, visit **delmar.cengage.com**

Visit our corporate website at **www.cengage.com**

Printed in the United States of America
4 5 6 7 11

Contents

PART II

Step Two: Contract Formation   47

INTRODUCTION   A TRANSACTIONAL GUIDE TO CONTRACT FORMATION / **48**

CHAPTER 2
The Offer Phase   49

CHAPTER 3
The Post-Offer/Pre-Acceptance Phase

CHAPTER 4
The Acceptance Phase
153

CHAPTER 5
The Post-Acceptance Phase
195

PART III
Step Three: Contract Enforceability 235

 CONTRACTS THAT ARE NOT ENFORCEABLE / **236**

CHAPTER 7
Contract Enforceability: Protecting Members of a Class 237

CHAPTER 13
The Defendant's *No Breach–Justification* Response to the Plaintiff's Allegation of Breach

417

CHAPTER 14
The Defendant's *No Breach–Terminated Duty* Response to the Plaintiff's Allegation of Breach

447

PART VII

Third-Party Interests   519

INTRODUCTION BEYOND THE TWO CONTRACTING PARTIES / **520**

CHAPTER 17
Third-Party Interests   521

Table of Exhibits

Table of Cases

Preface

The paralegal profession continues to grow dramatically. Each year more attorneys rely on the services of paralegals, and each year attorneys expect more sophisticated work from their paralegals. As attorney expectations increase, paralegal training becomes more demanding and more advanced.

As with all relatively new programs, paralegal teaching materials have lagged behind the demand. Often instructors have not had materials specifically designed for their needs. This has been true for the field of contract law where the materials used were often borrowed from business law or law school programs rather then designed especially for paralegal programs. This text, originally titled *Introduction to Contracts and Restitution* when published in 1988, was written specifically to meet the needs of paralegal education.

This is the fourth edition of our contracts text. Although the title has been changed to *An Introduction to the Law of Contracts* and the restitution material has been deemphasized, this edition retains the contract's "road map" along with other features that our readers from the earlier editions have found helpful.

A Well-Organized, Functional Approach to the Law of Contracts

An Introduction to the Law of Contracts provides students with a well organized, functional approach to the law of contracts. Students learn an approach for analyzing contracts problems. They can readily transfer what they learn in class to what they need for their professional assignments. Our former students tell us that they remember and use the analysis in practice. This functional approach takes the form of a six-step paradigm.

Step One: What law applies to this transaction?

Step Two: Has a contract been formed?

Step Three: Is the contract enforceable?

Step Four: What is the plaintiff's allegation of breach?

Step Five: Does the defendant have a viable response to the plaintiff's allegation of breach?

Step Six: What remedies are available to the plaintiff for the defendant's breach of contract?

For those students who find visual aids reinforce their learning, the paradigm is presented as a "road map" for the law of contracts.

Organization of the Textbook

This text introduces the law of contracts to paralegal students. It is written with the basic premise that the law of contracts need not be a jumble of unrelated rules. To remove the mystery, we developed the road map for analyzing breach of contract actions. The text follows the road map found in the Introduction.

An Introduction to the Law of Contracts is divided into seven parts. Each of the first six takes students through a step in the road map analysis. The seventh goes beyond the original two contracting parties and explores third-party interests in the contract.

Part I. Step One:	Determining the Applicable Law (Choice of Law)
Part II. Step Two:	Contract Formation
Part III. Step Three:	Contract Enforceability
Part IV. Step Four:	Plaintiff's Allegation of Defendant's Breach of Contract
Part V. Step Five:	Defendant's Response to the Plaintiff's Allegation of Breach
Part VI. Step Six:	Plaintiff's Remedies for the Defendant's Breach of Contract
Part VII:	Third-Party Interests

The fourth edition reintroduces the road map at the beginning of each chapter. The material covered in the chapter is highlighted on the road map. This will help students relate the chapters to one another.

Students learn that the rules of law are not unrelated rules that must be memorized in the abstract but are related and form a cohesive structure. A change of one rule may, therefore, have an impact on the other rules of the structure.

Primary Pedagogical Features

The primary pedagogical features of this text are the contracts paradigm, the active involvement of students in learning the rules and how they work, the comparative approach between a common law and a code solution, the straightforward use of terms and concepts, and drafting exercises.

The Contracts Paradigm (the Road Map)

The Introduction is devoted to presenting the contracts paradigm and its visual model, the road map. Thus the Introduction presents a summary of the course and is intended to be used as a review tool as the course evolves. The Introduction should be revisited as each chapter is begun.

The Development of the Rules of Law by Actively Involving Students

A rule of law is presented in three stages. Students first see the rule discussed in the abstract. Thus students acquire the "black letter rule." The rule will be followed by a clearly designated "Example." The example demonstrates how the rule relates to a concrete set of facts. The rule is no longer merely an abstraction but becomes a tool for resolving a dispute. Finally, students will be asked to actively participate in a "Paralegal Exercise" by relating a given set of facts to the rule or by analyzing a short judicial opinion that demonstrates how a court relates a set of facts to the rule. The Paralegal Exercise is provided to enable students to develop their skills by applying what they have learned. It is a practical method of immediately reinforcing newly acquired knowledge. By actively participating in either a Paralegal Exercise or by analyzing a case, students gain an understanding of the dynamics of the rules and how the rules relate to each other.

Problem Resolution under the Common Law and under a Code

This text also teaches students how to analyze a contracts transaction using a case law approach and a code approach (Articles 1 and 2 of the Uniform Commercial Code). The code analysis is not only important in the abstract but is an essential tool now because contracts for the sale of goods are governed by code.

Straightforward Use of Terms and Concepts

The text approaches the law of contracts pragmatically. An attempt is made to cut through excess verbiage (e.g., consideration rather than adequate consideration; contract rather than valid contract); and outdated doctrine (e.g., manifestation of assent rather than meeting of the minds). This approach enables students to gain an understanding of the rules rather than merely parrot obsolete and often misleading terms and phrases.

Extrapolating Analytical Techniques to Other Fields of Law

Students learn that if a paradigm (road map) can be developed for this area of law, a paradigm can be designed for other areas as well.

Review and Study Materials

Every chapter ends with materials that reinforce the rules of the chapter. Chapter-ending materials include a "Paralegal Checklist" and a test bank of "Review Questions."

Paralegal Checklist

The "Paralegal Checklist" provides students with a brief, but detailed review of each chapter and is a most effective method of summarizing what was learned in the chapter.

Review Questions

Following the Paralegal Checklist for each chapter is a test bank of "Review Questions." Review Questions have five sections: (1) a list of new terms and phrases; (2) true/false questions; (3) fill-in-the-blank questions; (4) multiple-choice questions; and (5) short-answer questions. These questions are designed to test the student's knowledge of the basic concepts discussed in the chapter. The answers are found in the *Instructor's Manual.*

Additional Pedagogical Features

We have included in *An Introduction to the Law of Contracts* a number of additional pedagogical features, including an introductory paragraph on chapter objectives and a chapter road map, multiple exhibits, definitions of new terms and phrases, extensive examples, numerous paralegal exercises, selected edited cases, and drafting problems.

Chapter Objectives and Chapter Road Map

Each chapter begins with a paragraph orienting the student to the objectives of that chapter. Following the chapter's orientation paragraph is a road map that places the topic of the chapter in the context of the contracts road map. By learning how concepts relate, students develop an approach to analyzing a contract transaction.

Exhibits

Exhibits may be found throughout the text. They are designed to present material in a logical and easy-to-understand manner.

Definitions of New Terms and Phrases

New terms and phrases are in bold. This is designed to capture the students' attention. Care has been taken to define terms and phrases as they first appear in the text. All boldfaced terms and phrases are defined in the margin of the pages where they first appear and in the Glossary at the end of the text.

Extensive Examples

Each rule is illustrated with one or more Examples. The Examples demonstrate how the rule is used for resolving a dispute.

Numerous Paralegal Exercises

After the rule and its Example, students are asked to apply the rule to a new set of facts. These brief Paralegal Exercises give students an opportunity to explore the rule and its application.

Selected Edited Cases

At times, a rule and its example are followed by a judicial opinion. The cases have been edited to highlight the rule being discussed.

Drafting Problems

A chapter on drafting a contract follows the chapters on contract formation. This chapter provides a change of pace for those who have the time and the desire to include some drafting exercises in their course. Also, several short drafting exercises are sprinkled throughout the text. As with other pedagogical devices that are used through the text, the drafting exercises are designed to give students a "hands on" experience with the material.

Appendix and Other Back Matter

The back matter is divided into a glossary, comments on briefing cases and analyzing statutes, and an index.

Glossary

The Glossary of 200 terms and phrases provides not only a quick reference for the definition of terms and phrases but a source for review prior to tests.

Briefing Cases and Analyzing Statutes

The Appendix discusses how to brief a case and how to analyze a statute. The briefing techniques presented in this appendix can be applied to the cases found in the text.

Index

The extensive index at the end of the book assists students in quickly finding the location of materials within the text.

New Features of the Fourth Edition

Among the changes and new features of the fourth edition are:

- The road map has been expanded from five to six parts (choice of law, contract formation, contract enforceability, plaintiff's allegation of defendant's breach, defendant's response to the plaintiff's allegation of breach, and plaintiff's remedies for the defendant's breach), thus emphasizing the plaintiff's allegation of the defendant's breach, an essential step in focusing the issues of the dispute and in maintaining a breach of contract action.
- Each of the four defendant responses to the plaintiff's allegation of breach (no breach–compliance, no breach–excuse, no breach–justification, and no breach–terminated duty) now has its own chapter. This places more emphasis on the individual response. Each response also has its own end-of-chapter paralegal checklist and review questions.
- The no breach–compliance discussion has been expanded and reorganized to include the issues concerning contract terms that had previously been found in the discussion of contract formation. The chapters on contract formation now deal with offer and acceptance and leave whether a term is in the contract to the no breach–compliance discussion.
- The no breach–excuse material has been redrafted for clarity. Several Restatement sections have been added for emphasis.
- The single chapter that, in previous editions, discussed remedies has now been subdivided into two chapters— common law remedies and UCC Article 2 remedies. Each will begin with an exhibit depicting the available remedies.
- The chapter on choice of law has been expanded to include international transactions where one party has a business in the United States and the other party has a business in another country. The use of arbitration in international disputes is also discussed. Several Paralegal Exercises have been added— each requiring the use of the Internet.
- Some cases have been deleted and others added.
- In the third edition, key terms were boldfaced at first mention. In the fourth edition, the definition for each term also appears in the margin of the page where the term is first mentioned.

Supplemental Teaching Materials

- The **Instructor's Manual** is available online at
  http://www.paralegal.delmar.cengage.com in the Instructor's Lounge
  under Resource. Written by Martin and Phyllis Frey, the
  Instructor's Manual contains suggested syllabi, answers to the
  text questions, useful Web sites, and a test bank.

- **Online Companion**™—The Online Companion™ Web site
  can be found at **http://www.paralegal.delmar.cengage.com** in the
  Resource section of the Web site. The Online Companion™
  contains the following:
    - Chapter Commentaries (including additional primary
      and secondary authority)
    - Exhibits
    - Paralegal Checklists
    - Review Questions
    - WebLinks

- **Web page**—Come visit our Web site at
  http://www.paralegal.delmar.cengage.com where you will find
  valuable information specific to this book as well as other
  Delmar Cengage Learning products.

- **Westlaw®**—West's online computerized legal research
  system offers students "hands-on" experience with a system
  commonly used in law offices. Qualified adopters can receive
  10 free hours of Westlaw®. Westlaw® can be accessed with
  Macintosh and PC.

Please note that Internet resources are of a time-sensitive nature and
URL addresses may often change or be deleted.

Contact us at delmar.help@cengage.com

Acknowledgments

We have been fortunate to have a number of very fine people encourage and assist us in preparing the four editions of this book. We appreciate the comments from our students who used the first three editions. Many of their suggestions have been incorporated into the fourth edition. We are also grateful for the valuable observations made by the reviewers.

Erin Calkins
College of Saint Mary
Omaha, NE

Mimi Flaherty
RETS Technical Center
Centerville, OH

Diane Pevar
Manor College
Jenkintown, PA

Jill Bush Raines
University of Oklahoma
Norman, OK

Randi Ray
Des Moines Area Community
  College
Des Moines, IA

Simone Wong
University of California
  Riverside
Riverside, CA

Rebecca Zanetti
North Idaho College
Coeur d'Alene, ID

The idea for the first edition of this text began with a suggestion by Terry H. Bitting, a practitioner who was teaching in a paralegal program at the time. Once the development of the manuscript began, Terry served as a co-author and did so for the first three editions. Several years ago, Terry was appointed a Special District Court Judge for Tulsa County. We enjoyed working with Terry and wish her all the best as a member of the judiciary.

Thanks go out to Michelle Gaudreau, our copyeditor, and Naman Mahisauria, our Project Manager, both at ICC Macmillan. Special thanks to Shelley Esposito, our Acquisitions Editor, Melissa Riveglia, our Senior Product Manager, Melissa Zaza, our Editorial Assistant, Betty L. Dickson, our Senior Content Project Manager, and to all those at Delmar Cengage Learning whose efforts have made this book possible.

Selected sections of the following Restatements have been reprinted with permission of The American Law Institute:

Restatement of Contracts. Copyright © 1932 by The American Law Institute. Reprinted with permission. All rights reserved.

Restatement (Second) of Contracts. Copyright © 1979 by The American Law Institute. Reprinted with permission. All rights reserved.

Restatement of Restitution. Copyright © 1937 by The American Law Institute. Reprinted with permission. All rights reserved.

Selected sections of the Uniform Commercial Code have been reprinted with the permission of The American Law Institute and the National Conference of Commissioners on Uniform State Laws:

A Road Map for Analyzing the Law of Contracts

This introduction is the most important section in this text. It gives an overview of the analytical process for evaluating a dispute involving a contract and is a reference point for all topics discussed in the text. If students review this section as they work through each subsequent section, they will have an analytical process firmly in mind for evaluating a transaction involving a contract.

There are six steps for analyzing the law of contracts. Within each step, issues of major importance are identified and discussed. Because each step is the foundation for the next, it is important to understand each step before going on to the next.

The six steps and the chapters in which each will be examined in depth are:

Step One: Determining the Applicable Law (Choice of Law)
  • Chapter 1
Step Two: Contract Formation
  • Chapters 2 through 6
Step Three: Contract Enforceability
  • Chapters 7 through 9
Step Four: Plaintiff's Allegation of Defendant's Breach of Contract
  • Chapter 10
Step Five: Defendant's Response to the Plaintiff's Allegation of Breach
  • Chapters 11 through 14
Step Six: Plaintiff's Remedies for the Defendant's Breach of Contract
  • Chapters 15 and 16

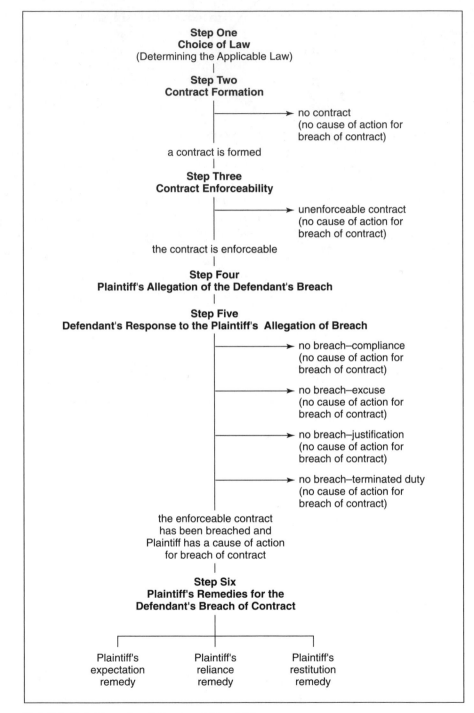

Exhibit I–1 Breach of Contract Road Map

Sixteen chapters are necessary to cover the six steps in the analysis. The Introduction, therefore, provides only an overview of the issues in each step of the Road Map. Do not attempt to memorize the Introduction but return to it often for an overview of the course (see Exhibit I–1).

STEP ONE: DETERMINING THE APPLICABLE LAW (CHOICE OF LAW)

Choice of law is the selection of the legal rules under which the dispute will be resolved. Choice of law, therefore, is the threshold step in any contract analysis. Choice of law questions arise in a number of settings: conflicting laws of different countries; conflicting federal and state laws; conflicting laws of two different states; conflicting laws within a state.

If the contracting parties are from different countries, three issues may arise: whether any dispute arising from the contract should be resolved through arbitration or litigation; if litigation is chosen, whether the law of country A or the law of country B should apply; and which court will be the forum court.

choice of law
Choice of law is the determination of which law applies where more than one state is involved in a transaction, where conflicting laws exist within a state, or where federal law may preempt state law.

Example

A Florida citrus grower contracts to sell 100 carloads of oranges to a Russian buyer. In the contract the parties provide a mandatory arbitration provision. The Russian wants to avoid litigating in an American court and the American wants to avoid litigating in a Russian court. They also want the adjudicator to have expertise in the commercial citrus market.

Before the oranges can be shipped, a Category 5 hurricane moves through Florida, destroying the grower's orange crop. The buyer believes that the seller breached by not delivering the oranges. The seller believes that it was excused from delivering due to an act of God.

By including the mandatory arbitration provision in their contract, the parties will present their dispute to an arbitrator for adjudication.

Example

If the parties in the previous example had not included a mandatory arbitration provision in their contract, and if, at the time of the dispute, they could not agree on arbitration, the dispute would be resolved through litigation.

The question is whether Russian law or Florida law governs the transaction. Since one party has a business in Florida (and the United States is a contracting state for the Commission on the International Sale of Goods, or CISG), the parties will find it necessary to determine whether Russia is a contracting state as well. If it is, then CISG applies to the transaction unless the parties have opted out. If the parties have opted out, then their choice of law would apply (if compatible with the law of the forum) unless they have not chosen which law applies. In that case, the choice of law rules of the forum would be applied to determine the appropriate law.

Example

If the parties in the previous example litigate, will the litigation take place in Russia or Florida (or in a third location)? Did the parties discuss choice of forum in their contract and, if so, will the court acquiesce to the forum selected? If the parties did not discuss choice of forum, the plaintiff would select the location of the court and the defendant could challenge this location. (Note that at times the court in one state or one country will use the law of another state or country.)

A conflict may exist between federal and state law. Federal law, for example, may preempt or override state law in some aspects of a consumer transaction.

Example

Buyer purchases a VCR for home use from a department store. The Seller of a consumer product, in making a written warranty, must follow the requirements set forth in the federal Magnuson-Moss Warranty–Federal Trade Commission Improvement Act. This Act establishes federal minimum standards for written warranties, limitations on disclaimers of implied warranties, and remedies that are separate and apart from state remedies. The Buyer, therefore, acquires rights under federal law that exceed those rights acquired under state law.

If state law applies, geographic considerations raise choice of law questions. In a transaction spanning several states, which state's law governs must be determined at the outset. An **interstate transaction** (also known as a multistate transaction) is a transaction spanning several states. Does the law of State A or the law of State B govern the transaction?

interstate transaction

A transaction spanning several states. Also known as a multistate transaction.

Example

A New Yorker owns a yacht that she is interested in selling. The New Yorker mails a letter to a potential Buyer in California promising to sell the yacht for $175,000. After sending this letter but before receiving a response from the California Buyer, the Seller sells the yacht to someone else for $200,000. Upon completing this sale, the Seller mails a letter to the California Buyer revoking her offer. After the Seller's letter of revocation has been sent but before it has been received, the California Buyer mails a letter to the Seller accepting the Seller's offer. Upon receiving the California Buyer's letter of acceptance, the Seller notifies the California Buyer that she has sold the yacht to someone else. (See Exhibit I–2.)

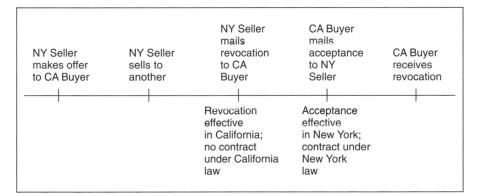

Exhibit I–2 Timeline for NY Seller/CA Buyer

Under both New York and California law, an offer sent by mail is effective when sent. New York and California, however, have different rules as to when revocation is effective. In New York revocation is effective when received. In California revocation is effective when sent. If California law applies, the Seller's revocation of her offer was effective (when sent) before the Buyer's acceptance was effective (when sent). If New York law applies, the Buyer's acceptance is effective (when sent) before the Seller's revocation is effective (when received). Therefore, the choice between New York and California laws will determine whether a contract between the New York Seller and the California Buyer has been formed.

Once the appropriate state is determined, the investigation considers whether a special body of law within that state applies to the transaction. If the transaction is a sale of goods, for example, the appropriate state's version of Article 2 of the Uniform Commercial Code (UCC) will govern the transaction rather than the state's common law. If the transaction is a lease of goods, Article 2A of the UCC will govern. The **Uniform Commercial Code** is a comprehensive compilation of rules drafted by the American Law Institute (ALI) and the National Conference of Commissioners on Uniform State Laws (NCCUSL). The UCC becomes the law of a given state upon enactment by that state's legislature and signature of the governor. The **common law** is the body of law derived from judicial decisions (i.e., court-made law).

Uniform Commercial Code

A comprehensive compilation of rules drafted by the American Law Institute and the National Conference of Commissioners on Uniform State Laws that includes a number of topics including sale of goods and which becomes the law of a given state upon enactment by that state's legislature and signature of the governor.

common law

Common law has several meanings. The common law is the body of law and jurisprudential theory that originated and developed in England. Common law, as distinguished from law created by legislative enactment, is derived from custom and usage and from judicial decisions recognizing and enforcing custom and usage.

Example

Owner takes her car to Garage for repair. The car needs new parts, body work, and painting. The bill is itemized at $300 labor and $300 parts. After three months, the paint blisters. If the transaction is governed by Article 2 of the UCC (sale of goods), there will be an implied warranty that the paint would be fit for the ordinary purpose, and Owner could recover. If, however, the transaction is not viewed as a sale of goods but only as a sale of services, the transaction is not governed by Article 2 of the UCC, no implied warranty attaches to the transaction, and Owner could not recover for the blistering paint job unless Garage expressly warranted that the paint would not blister.

While this example illustrates the impact of Article 2 of the UCC on contract law, the UCC is not the only body of specialized state law that affects contracts. Another illustration involves identifiable groups of contracting parties who may be unable to protect themselves. A state legislature may enact special rules to protect consumers, minors, and the mentally incapacitated. The legislature may change other court-made rules of contract law as well.

Once choice of law issues have been resolved, the next and one of the most important questions in the analysis must be raised—"Has a contract been created?"

STEP TWO: CONTRACT FORMATION

The second step in the analysis focuses on the two components of contract formation: the offer and the acceptance.

The Offer

An **offer** is a manifestation of willingness to enter into a bargain, which justifies another person in understanding that his or her assent to that bargain is invited and will conclude it. What constitutes an offer and when an offer has been made are basic inquiries at this stage. The **offeror** is the party who makes the offer. The **offeree** is the party who receives the offer and is asked to accept it and thus form a contract.

What constitutes an offer is determined by the components of the offer. An offer may be for a bilateral contract or for a unilateral contract. When the **offer** is **for a bilateral contract**, the offeror makes a promise to entice the offeree to make a promise (a promise for a promise). If the offeree accepts by promising, a contract is formed. The offeree's performance of his or her promise will occur after contract formation.

Example

"I promise to pay you $1,000 for your promise to paint my house."

When the **offer** is **for a unilateral contract**, the offeror makes a promise to entice the offeree to perform (a promise for a performance). The offeror does not want the offeree's promise. The offeror only wants the offeree's performance. If the offeree accepts by performing, a contract is formed. The offeree's performance occurs before contract formation. The vast majority of contracts are bilateral. Unilateral contracts are very rare.

Example

"I promise to pay you $1,000 for your painting my house."

Consideration is what the promisor wants in exchange for his or her promise. If the promisor makes a promise without demanding something in return, the promisor's promise is "not supported by consideration" and there is "no offer." The promisor has only made a promise to make a future gift.

offer
An offer is a manifestation of willingness to enter into a bargain, which justifies another person in understanding that his or her assent to that bargain is invited and will conclude it.

offeror
An offeror is the party who extends the offer to the offeree.

offeree
An offeree is the party whom the offeror invites to accept the offer.

offer for a bilateral contract
In an offer for a bilateral contract, the offeror makes a promise to entice the offeree to make a promise (a promise for a promise).

offer for a unilateral contract
In an offer for a unilateral contract, the offeror makes a promise to entice the offeree to perform (a promise for a performance).

consideration
A contract has two "considerations"—consideration for the promisor's promise and consideration for the promisee's promise or performance. Consideration is the "price" sought by the promisor for his or her promise and the "price" sought by the promisee for his or her promise or performance.

We have chosen to include the concept of consideration as a crucial element of both offer and acceptance. Often, the concept of consideration is treated as a third element of contract formation: offer, acceptance, and consideration. If consideration is treated as a separate element and not a part of the offer, the conclusion might very well be "offer, but no consideration." Although this difference may appear to be semantic, it goes to the heart of what an offer is: a promise for consideration.

Even if the promisor has made a promise and has stated a consideration for his or her promise, the promise and consideration must be connected. The promisor must make his or her promise to induce the promisee to give what the promisor says he or she is seeking. Thus, the sequence of events is important.

Example

When Henrietta returned John's lost dog, Toby, John promised to pay Henrietta $50 for her efforts. Since Henrietta had already returned Toby to John when he made his promise to pay her, John's promise was not intended to induce her to act. Thus, there was no consideration for John's promise, and it was only a gift promise. If John refuses to pay Henrietta, she has no contract upon which to sue him.

Once the promisor makes a promise in exchange for the promisee's promise or performance *and* communicates his or her intentions to the promisee, the offer is created. At this time, the promisor becomes the offeror and the promisee becomes the offeree.

The Acceptance

acceptance
An acceptance is the offeree's manifestation of assent to the terms of the offer.

Once an offer has been made, attention focuses on acceptance. An **acceptance** is the offeree's manifestation of assent to the terms of the offer. The basic questions are: What constitutes acceptance and when does an attempt to accept become an effective acceptance? The components of acceptance parallel those of an offer. If the offer was for a bilateral contract (a promise for a promise), the acceptance is the offeree's promise that is made to secure the offeror's promise.

Example

Offer: "I promise to pay you $1,000 for your promise to paint my house."
Acceptance: "I promise to paint your house for your promise to pay $1,000."

If the offer was for a unilateral contract (a promise for a performance), the acceptance is the offeree's performance that was made to secure the offeror's promise.

Example

Offer: "I promise to pay you $1,000 for your painting my house."
Acceptance: Painting the house (i.e., painting the house for your
promise to pay $1,000).

The consideration for the offeree's promise or performance is the offeror's promise. If consideration for the offeree's promise or performance is lacking, the conclusion is "no acceptance" and not "acceptance but no consideration."

The fact that an attempt to accept an offer has taken place does not always lead to the conclusion that a contract has been formed. One of the following events may have occurred and rendered the attempted acceptance ineffective:

- The offer may have lapsed because it was not accepted within the time stated in the offer or, if no time was stated, within a reasonable time.
- The offeror may have revoked the offer.
- The offeree may have rejected the offer before attempting to accept it.
- The offeror or offeree may have died or become incapacitated.

If none of these events has occurred, the attempted acceptance of the offer is effective, and a contract is formed.

STEP THREE: CONTRACT ENFORCEABILITY

Once a contract is formed, the next step is determining whether the contract is enforceable. The focus shifts from "freedom of contract" (i.e., the parties' power to create their own contract terms and structure their relationship as they choose) to the governmental regulation of contract. A number of policy considerations, resulting in legislative enactment or judicial decision, may preclude enforcement of the contract. These policy grounds may be grouped into three categories. The legislature or the judiciary may seek the following goals:

- To protect a selected class of people unable to protect themselves (e.g., minors and those who are mentally incapacitated)

- To protect a contracting party from overreaching by the other contracting party (e.g., unconscionability, fraud, duress)
- To protect the integrity of the judicial process (e.g., potential perjury due to a lack of writing [Statute of Frauds], illegality, and inappropriate forum selection)

rescission

A rescission is the abrogation of a contract. Rescission usually involves returning the parties to their pre-contract positions.

reformation

Reformation is a judicial remedy designed to revise a writing to conform to the real agreement or intention of the parties.

If unenforceable, the contract may be rescinded, or depending on the nature of the problem, the contract may be reformed, thereby eliminating the obstacle precluding its enforcement. **Rescission** is revocation (termination) of the contract. Unlike the revocation of an offer that has not been accepted (no contract has been formed), rescission is the revocation (termination) of an existing contract. **Reformation** is the revision of a writing to conform to the true agreement or intention of the parties.

STEP FOUR: PLAINTIFF'S ALLEGATION OF DEFENDANT'S BREACH OF CONTRACT

When the conclusion at Step Three is that the contract is enforceable, the analysis focuses on the plaintiff's allegation of the defendant's breach of the contract. Who is complaining and what is the complaint?

promisor

A promisor is the party who makes the promise.

promisee

A promisee is the party to whom a promise is made.

In a bilateral contract, the promises are reciprocal: the offeror promises the offeree and the offeree promises the offeror. The offeror, by promising the offeree, has a duty to the offeree to perform; the offeree, by being the recipient of the offeror's promise, has a right to receive the offeror's promised performance. The offeror, by having the duty, is the promisor. A **promisor** is the party who makes the promise. The offeree, by having the right, is the promisee. A **promisee** is the party to whom a promise is made. Therefore, when the offeror says "I promise to sell you my car," the offeror (promisor) has the duty to sell the car to the offeree, and the offeree (promisee) has the right to receive the car from the offeror.

The offeree, by promising the offeror, also has a duty to perform; the offeror, by being on the receiving end of the offeree's promise, has a right to receive the offeree's promised performance. The offeree, by having the duty, is the promisor; the offeror, by having the right, is the promisee. Therefore, when the offeree says "I promise to pay you $5,000," the offeree (promisor) has the duty to pay the offeror $5,000, and the offeror (promisee) has the right to receive $5,000 from the offeree (see Exhibit I–3).

Because the offeror is both promisor and promisee and the offeree is both promisor and promisee in a bilateral contract, the label *promisee* refers to the party claiming the unperformed right, and the label *promisor* refers to the party who owes the duty associated with the right. Therefore, the complainant is the promisee.

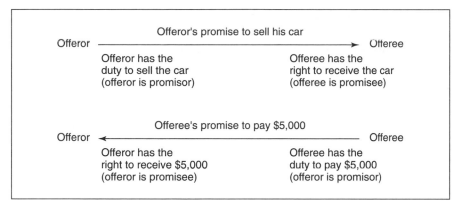

Exhibit I–3 Reciprocal Promises with Offeror Being Both Promisor and Promisee and Offeree Being Both Promisor and Promisee

The promisee, as complainant, will allege that the promisor has breached a contractual duty by either notifying the promisee that the promise will not be performed when the performance is due (breach by anticipatory repudiation) or by having not performed when the performance was due.

STEP FIVE: DEFENDANT'S RESPONSE TO THE PLAINTIFF'S ALLEGATION OF BREACH

The promisor has five responses to the promisee's allegation of breach.

1. **No breach–compliance**: "I am complying with the terms of the contract, and therefore I have not breached the contract."

no breach–compliance
The defendant responds to the plaintiff's allegation of breach—"I am complying with the terms of the contract."

Example

A homeowner's insurance policy provides that Insurance Company will pay Insured for all losses due to fire. When Insured's valuable art collection is stolen, she files a claim, and Insurance Company rejects the claim on the ground that the loss was not due to fire. If Insured sues Insurance Company for breach of contract alleging that her claim was not paid, Insurance Company will respond, "No breach–compliance." Insurance Company is in compliance with the terms of the contract because it does not become obligated to pay until Insured has a loss by fire. Because no fire loss has occurred, the contract has not been breached, and Insured has no cause of action for breach of contract.

2. **No breach–excuse:** "Although I am not complying with the terms of the contract, my nonperformance was excused, and therefore I have not breached the contract."

This response combines the promisor's admission of nonperformance under the contract with the promisor's claim that this nonperformance was excused and therefore was not a breach. "It is true that I didn't do what the promisee said I didn't do, but I was excused from doing it."

Example

Singer contracts to perform for a week for a Las Vegas hotel. After the first performance, Singer becomes seriously ill and cannot perform for the remainder of the engagement. If the hotel sues Singer for breach of contract alleging that Singer breached by not performing, Singer could respond, "No breach–excuse. Although I am not complying with the terms of the contract, I am excused from performing due to my serious illness." Unlike the first response ("No breach–compliance"), the condition (serious illness) was not an express term in the contract. Even though this condition (an act of God) was not an express term, it may excuse Singer's nonperformance. If Singer is excused, she is not in breach, and the hotel cannot maintain a cause of action for breach of contract.

3. **No breach–justification:** "Although I am not complying with the terms of the contract, my nonperformance was justified by your breach of this contract, and therefore I have not breached the contract."

This response to the plaintiff's allegation of breach joins the promisor's admission of nonperformance with the promisor's claim that his or her nonperformance was justified because the party alleging breach had breached the contract.

Example

Builder contracts to build a house for Owner. Owner promises to pay every 30 days as the work progresses. Builder begins to build, but Owner does not pay. After two months, Builder stops work. If Owner sues Builder for breach of contract alleging that Builder breached by stopping work, Builder would respond, "No breach–justification. My stopping work was justified because you did not pay me." Builder's nonperformance is not a breach; it is a justified nonperformance. Because Owner rather than Builder is the breaching party, Owner's action for breach of contract against Builder cannot be maintained.

---

4. **No breach-terminated duty**: "Although I am not complying with the terms of the contract, my duty to perform the contract has been terminated, and therefore I have not breached the contract."

This response contains both the promisor's admission of nonperformance and a claim that the promisor's contractual duty has ended either by agreement or by law, and therefore the promisor has not breached the contract.

no breach-terminated duty

The defendant responds to the plaintiff's allegation of breach—"Although I am not complying with the terms of the contract, my duty to perform the contract has been terminated, and therefore I have not breached the contract."

Example

Employer and Employee have a contract whereby Employer is to pay Employee "a reasonable wage." After Employee works for a month, a dispute arises between the parties about the meaning of "a reasonable wage." Employer gives Employee a check that carries the notation "Payment in Full." Employee cashes the check and then demands still more money from Employer. The Employer refuses. If Employee sues Employer for breach of contract alleging that Employer breached by not paying him a reasonable wage, Employer would respond, "No breach, my duty has been terminated." Employer's duty to pay "a reasonable wage" is terminated by the subsequent contract in the form of Employer's check with the notation "Payment in Full" and by Employee's cashing the check. Because Employer is not a breaching party, Employee cannot maintain a breach of contract action.

accord

An accord is a contract to pay a stated amount to discharge a prior obligation that is either uncertain as to its existence or amount. Satisfaction (performance) of the accord contract is required before the duties under the original contract are terminated.

satisfaction

Satisfaction is the performance of the accord contract. Once the accord contract has been performed, the original contractual duties are terminated.

The previous example demonstrates an accord and satisfaction. An **accord** is a contract to pay a stated amount to discharge an obligation which is uncertain either as to its existence or amount. The **satisfaction** is the performance of the accord contract. Employer's tendering the check is the offer for an accord contract ("I promise to pay you this amount for your promise to take this amount as full payment of my obligation to you"). Employee's cashing the check implies the Employee's "promise to take the check as full payment for Employer's promise to pay the stated amount" and therefore is the acceptance of the offer for the accord contract. Employee's cashing the check is also the "satisfaction" or the performance of the accord contract.

The terminating event may be unilateral—such as a release. A **release** is the intentional relinquishment of a right.

release
A release is the intentional relinquishment of a right.

Example

Abner hires Rachel to work for him as an assistant manager for one year. After six months, Abner wrongfully fires Rachel. Rachel may release her right to recover under the contract, thus terminating Abner's duty.

Mutual release terminates both parties' duties to perform. After a release, the party who released the other cannot successfully assert that the other has breached his or her duty. That duty to perform has been terminated.

The terminating event may occur by operation of law. A **Statute of Limitations** provides for a specified period of time within which a cause of action may be brought.

Statute of Limitations
A Statute of Limitations provides for a specified period of time within which a cause of action must be brought.

Example

Martina entered into a written lease of a store front from Ricardo Realty Corporation. Prior to the time when Martina was to occupy the store front, Ricardo Realty told Martina that the property was no longer available. Three years and two days later, Martina brought a breach of contract action against Ricardo Realty. If the Statute of Limitations was three years, Ricardo Realty's duties under the contract terminated two days before Martina brought her breach of contract action.

5. Breach: "I admit I have breached the contract."

The fifth and final response to the plaintiff's allegation of defendant's breach is an admission by the defendant. Whether the defendant's breach is intentional or unintentional is irrelevant. The law of contracts does not evaluate the mental state accompanying nonperformance. The only question is whether the defendant has not performed his or her duty under the terms of the contract.

If the defendant is unable to maintain his or her response to the plaintiff's allegation of breach (the defendant is unable to prove "no breach–compliance," "no breach–excuse," "no breach–justification," or "no breach–terminated duty"), or if the defendant admits breach, the plaintiff has established a cause of action for breach of contract. A **cause of action** is the theory upon which relief should

cause of action
A cause of action is the theory upon which relief should be granted. The cause of action should be distinguished from the remedy sought if the cause of action could be maintained. Breach of contract is a cause of action; damages is a remedy for breach of contract.

be granted. The plaintiff can now proceed to Step Six and pursue his or her remedies for the defendant's breach. A **remedy** is the relief sought if a cause of action can be maintained.

STEP SIX: PLAINTIFF'S REMEDIES FOR THE DEFENDANT'S BREACH OF CONTRACT

The nonbreaching party may maintain an action for breach of contract and is entitled to a remedy if the conclusion at Step Five is that the contract has been breached. The remedies for breach of contract are designed to protect not only the nonbreaching party's expectation interest but that party's reliance and restitution interests as well.

When parties enter into a contract, both have expectations regarding what the net economic gain will be once the contract has been fully performed. Protecting the nonbreaching party's **expectation interest** places him or her in as good a position as if both parties had fully performed the contract according to its terms. The nonbreaching party may receive damages. **Damages** are compensation awarded by a court to a party who has suffered loss or injury to rights or property. In the unusual case when money damages would be inadequate compensation and the subject of the contract is unique, the court may award specific performance. **Specific performance** is a remedy whereby a court directs the breaching party to deliver the subject of the contract to the nonbreaching party. In some cases, an appropriate remedy may be an injunction. An **injunction** is an order issued by a court directing the breaching party to refrain from doing specified acts.

When parties contract, each party's performance may rely on the other's promise to perform. Protecting the nonbreaching party's **reliance interest** places that party in the position that he or she was in before relying on the other's promise. The nonbreaching party is compensated, not on the basis of expectation, but for the injury suffered as a result of reliance on the other's promise. The measure of damages is the reasonable value to the nonbreaching party for the injury suffered by relying on the other's promise.

When parties contract, one party, while performing under the contract, may confer a benefit on the other party. Protecting the nonbreaching party's **restitution interest** will place that party in the position he or she was in before conferring the benefit on the other. The nonbreaching party is compensated, not on the basis of either expectation or reliance on the other's promise, but for the value of the benefit conferred. The measure of damages is the reasonable value of the benefit to the party receiving the benefit.

remedy
A remedy is the relief sought if a cause of action can be maintained.

expectation interest
Protecting the nonbreaching party's expectation interest places the nonbreaching party in the position he or she would have been in had the contract been fully performed by both parties according to the contract.

damages
Damages are compensation awarded by a court to a party who has suffered loss or injury to rights or property.

specific performance
Specific performance is a remedy whereby a court directs a party to do a specified act.

injunction
An injunction is an order issued by a court directing a party to refrain from a specified act.

reliance interest
Protecting the nonbreaching party's reliance interest places the nonbreaching party back to the position he or she was in prior to relying on the breaching party's promise.

restitution interest
Protecting the nonbreaching party's restitution interest places the breaching party back to the position he or she was in prior to receiving the benefit conferred upon him or her by the nonbreaching party.

THIRD-PARTY INTERESTS

Although they are not involved as a step in the contracts analysis, three other groups of parties who were not parties to the original contract (third parties) may have or may acquire an interest in the contract. The first type of third party is the third-party beneficiary to the contract. A **third-party beneficiary** is a party who will be benefited by the performance of a contract and may be a creditor, donee, or incidental beneficiary. The creditor and donee beneficiaries are intended beneficiaries. Incidental beneficiaries, on the other hand, do not have a court-protected interest. The third-party beneficiary acquires rights as a result of the contract but never acquires duties.

third-party beneficiary
A third-party beneficiary is a party who will be benefited by the performance of a contract. A third-party beneficiary may be a donee, creditor, or incidental beneficiary. An incidental beneficiary has no enforceable rights under the contract.

Example

On Wednesday Jane borrowed $100 from Caroline promising to repay her on Monday. On Friday Agnes borrowed $100 from Jane promising to pay Caroline on Monday for Jane. Caroline is a creditor beneficiary of the Agnes/Jane contract.

Example

Mary, wishing to leave her estate to her niece Sarah, contracts with an attorney to draft her will. Sarah is the donee beneficiary of the attorney/client contract.

Example

The City, in preparing for the Fourth of July, hires the Stars and Stripes Fireworks Company to supply the fireworks for the celebration. John Q. Public is only an incidental beneficiary of the City/Stars and Stripes contract.

assignment
An assignment is the transfer of a contractual right.

delegation
A delegation is the empowering of another by the obligor to perform the obligor's contractual duty.

The second type of third party consists of assignees and delegatees. An **assignment** is the transfer of a contractual right to a third party who was not a party to the original contract. A **delegation** is the empowerment of a party who was not a party to the original contract to perform that party's contractual duty. Neither an assignee nor a delegatee was a party to the original contract. By an assignment, a third party (an assignee) acquires rights in the original contract. By a delegation, a third party (a delegatee) agrees to perform a duty of one of the original contracting parties.

Example

Sally borrowed $1,000 from Friendly Finance. Friendly transferred its right to receive Sally's repayment to Easy Credit Company. Friendly's transfer of its right to receive Sally's money is an assignment of that right.

Example

The Six Flags Coal Company contracted to sell 300,000 carloads of coal to the Ever Ready Power Company. The contract provided that the coal was to be mined at Six Flags mine no. 6. Six Flags sold its mine no. 6 and its contract to deliver coal to Ever Ready to A-1 Coal Company. A-1 is the delegatee of the Six Flags/Ever Ready contract.

The third type of third party neither has a right under the original contract nor has subsequently acquired a right or duty relating back to the original contract. This type of third party has committed a wrong by interfering with existing contract rights.

Example

Rinaldo, a tenor, has a one-year contract to sing at the Gotham Opera Company. The Metropolis Opera Company offers Rinaldo more money and thus entices him to breach his contract with the Gotham Opera Company. The Metropolis Opera Company has committed a wrong by interfering with the Rinaldo/Gotham contract.

KEY TERMS

Acceptance	Injunction
Accord	Interstate transaction
Assignment	No breach–compliance
Cause of action	No breach–excuse
Choice of law	No breach–justification
Common law	No breach–terminated duty
Consideration	Offer
Damages	Offer for a bilateral contract
Delegation	Offer for a unilateral contract
Expectation interest	Offeree

Offeror   Rescission
Promisee   Restitution interest
Promisor   Satisfaction
Reformation   Specific performance
Release   Statute of Limitations
Reliance interest   Third-party beneficiary
Remedy   Uniform Commercial Code

REVIEW QUESTIONS

TRUE/FALSE QUESTIONS (CIRCLE THE CORRECT ANSWER)

1. T   F   The first step in the contract analysis is to determine the applicable law.

2. T   F   The second step in the contract analysis is to determine whether a contract has been formed.

3. T   F   The third step in the contract analysis is to determine the enforceability of the contract.

4. T   F   The fourth step in the contract analysis is to determine the plaintiff's allegation of the defendant's breach.

5. T   F   The fifth step in the contract analysis is to evaluate the defendant's response to the plaintiff's allegation of breach.

6. T   F   The sixth step in the contract analysis is to determine the plaintiff's remedies for the defendant's breach of contract.

7. T   F   The following is an offer for a unilateral contract: "I promise to sell you my watch for your promise to pay $500."

8. T   F   The following is an offer for a bilateral contract: "I promise to sell you my watch for your paying $500."

9. T   F   A bilateral contract has not just one consideration but has consideration for both the offeror's promise and the offeree's promise.

10. T   F   Both the offeror and the offeree may breach a unilateral contract.

11. T   F   In a bilateral contract, the offeror is both a promisor and promisee and the offeree is both a promisor and promisee.

12. T   F   In a unilateral contract, the offeror is both a promisor and promisee and the offeree is both a promisor and promisee.

13. T   F   In a bilateral contract, the breaching party may be either the offeror or offeree.

14. T   F   In a unilateral contract, the breaching party may only be the offeror.

15.   T   F   A "no breach–compliance" response is distinguished from the "no breach–excuse," "no breach–justification," and "no breach–terminated duty" responses in that the "no breach–compliance" response denies noncompliance with the terms of the contract while the other three responses admit noncompliance.

16.   T   F   If a defendant in a breach of contract action responds to the plaintiff's allegation of breach by stating "no breach–justification," the defendant is saying my breach was justified by your breach.

17.   T   F   Whether a defendant's breach in a breach of contract action is intentional or unintentional is irrelevant.

18.   T   F   If the plaintiff succeeds in maintaining a breach of contract action against a defendant, the plaintiff may select among the expectation, reliance, and restitution remedies available in a breach of contract action.

19.   T   F   Specific performance is always available as a remedy in a breach of contract action.

FILL-IN-THE-BLANK QUESTIONS

1.   _____.   Determining the set of rules under which the alleged cause of action will be resolved.

2.   _____.   A manifestation of willingness to enter into a bargain, which justifies another person in understanding that his or her assent to that bargain is invited and will conclude the bargain.

3.   _____.   The party making the offer.

4.   _____.   The party receiving the offer.

5.   _____.   The shorthand phrase for an offer for a bilateral contract.

6.   _____.   The shorthand phrase for an offer for a unilateral contract.

7.   _____.   The shorthand phrase for the defendant's response: "I am complying with the terms of the contract."

8.   _____.   The shorthand phrase for the defendant's response: "Although I am not complying with the terms of the contract, my nonperformance was excused, and therefore I have not breached the contract."

9.   _____.   The shorthand phrase for the defendant's response: "Although I am not complying with the terms of the contract, my nonperformance was justified by your breach of this contract, and therefore I have not breached the contract."

10.   _____.   The shorthand phrase for the defendant's response: "Although I am not complying with the terms of the

contract, my duty to perform the contract has been terminated, and therefore I have not breached the contract."

11. _____. The shorthand phrase for the defendant's response: "I admit I have breached the contract."

12. Protecting the nonbreaching party's "_____" places that party in as good a position as if both parties had fully performed the contract according to its terms.

13. Protecting the nonbreaching party's "_____" places that party in the position that he or she was in before relying on the other's promise.

14. Protecting the nonbreaching party's "_____" places the breaching party in the position he or she was in before receiving the benefit.

MULTIPLE-CHOICE QUESTIONS (CIRCLE ALL THE CORRECT ANSWERS)

1. Emma Smythe, a California sculptor, was hired by the City Council of New York City to create a sculpture for Central Park. The offer was sent by mail to Smythe in California. She accepted by mail. The preliminary work on the sculpture was to be done in California, the casting in Oregon, and the final assembly in New York. After Smythe completed the design, the City Council canceled the contract due to lack of funds.

   Identify the choice of law problem(s):
   (a) Whether the law of California, Oregon, or New York governs this transaction
   (b) Whether Article 2 of the UCC or the state's common law governs this transaction
   (c) Whether federal or state law governs this transaction
   (d) Whether CISG applies to this transaction
   (e) This transaction does not involve a choice of law problem.

2. A Florida Buyer purchased a video camera from a Vermont Seller through a shopping channel on cable TV. The Buyer did not leave his home in Florida but telephoned his order to a telephone number in Georgia. When the Buyer received shipment of the camera, it was packaged along with a written warranty. The writing, however, disclaimed all implied warranties. The camera proved to be defective. The defect was not within the written warranty but was within an implied warranty of merchantability, had it not been disclaimed.

   Identify the choice of law problem(s):
   (a) Whether the law of Florida, Georgia, or Vermont governs this transaction
   (b) Whether Article 2 of the UCC or the state's common law governs this transaction
   (c) Whether federal or state law governs this transaction
   (d) Whether CISG applies to this transaction
   (e) This transaction does not involve a choice of law problem.

3. What constitutes acceptance of an offer for a unilateral contract?
   (a) The offeree's promise
   (b) The offeree's promise to perform
   (c) The offeree's preparing to perform
   (d) The offeree's partial performance
   (e) The offeree's full performance

4. Bart Cartright purchased an automobile insurance policy from
   Guarantee Insurance Company. The policy covered damage to the
   vehicle due to collision but excluded damage due to natural disasters
   such as hail and flood. Cartright's automobile was heavily damaged
   by volcanic ash when Mt. St. Helens erupted. Cartright filed a claim
   with Guarantee, and Guarantee refused to pay.
      If Cartright sued Guarantee for breach of contract alleging that
   Guarantee breached the contract by not paying his claim, Guarantee
   would respond
   (a) no breach–compliance.
   (b) no breach–excuse.
   (c) no breach–justification.
   (d) no breach–terminated duty.
   (e) breach.

5. Ronald Redcloud entered into a contract with Universal Publishers
   for his memoirs. Redcloud died when he had completed about half
   of the project. If Universal sued Redcloud's estate for breach of
   contract alleging that Redcloud had failed to deliver a completed
   manuscript, the estate would respond
   (a) no breach–compliance.
   (b) no breach–excuse.
   (c) no breach–justification.
   (d) no breach–terminated duty.
   (e) breach.

6. Gotham University contracted with Educational Excellence, a
   consulting corporation, for a thorough study of the University. The
   contract provided that Educational would be paid a consulting fee
   and expenses. The contract provided that the consulting fee would
   be paid in four quarterly payments and the expenses would be paid
   monthly. After working on the project for four months (project
   expected to last about a year), Educational refused to continue
   because it had been paid neither the first quarterly payment nor its
   expenses for the past three months.
      If Gotham sued Educational for breach of contract alleging that
   Educational had breached by notifying Gotham that it would not
   complete the work, Gotham would respond
   (a) no breach–compliance.
   (b) no breach–excuse.
   (c) no breach–justification.
   (d) no breach–terminated duty.
   (e) breach.

7. Mary Lou Webster was hired by Gotham University as an assistant
   professor. Dr. Webster was given a three-year contract that would be
   automatically renewed for another three years unless Dr. Webster

desired not to have the contract renewed or the University had cause not to renew. The contract defined cause for nonrenewal. Dr. Webster's contract was not renewed after the initial three-year term expired. The nonrenewal was not based on cause as was required by her contract.

Four years after her nonrenewal, Dr. Webster brought a breach of contract action against Gotham University alleging that Gotham breached the contract by not offering her a new three-year contract and that its refusal was not based on cause. Gotham responded with the Statute of Limitations. Gotham's response is

(a) no breach–compliance.
(b) no breach–excuse.
(c) no breach–justification.
(d) no breach–terminated duty.
(e) breach.

SHORT-ANSWER QUESTIONS

1. List the six steps in the Road Map for the law of contracts.

2. List four different settings in which a choice of law question may arise.

3. List the elements that constitute an offer for a bilateral contract.

4. Distinguish an offer for a bilateral contract from an offer for a unilateral contract.

5. Why does this text consider that a contract consists of two elements, an offer and an acceptance, rather than three elements, an offer, an acceptance, and consideration?

6. List the elements that constitute an acceptance for a bilateral contract.

7. List four events that could occur between the offer and the attempted acceptance that would render the attempted acceptance ineffective.

8. The legislature or the judiciary may seek to protect what three categories of policy grounds by precluding the enforcement of a contract?

9. After the plaintiff alleges that the defendant has breached the contract, the defendant's reply may be divided into what five responses?

PART I

Step One: Determining the Applicable Law (Choice of Law)

FOUR CHOICE OF LAW ISSUES

The threshold step in a contracts problem involves "choice of law." **Choice of law** is the selection of the legal rules under which the dispute will be resolved. Choice of law questions arise in a number of settings. Part I of this book (Chapter 1) introduces four settings: (1) determining the applicable rules when the contracting parties are from different countries; (2) determining the applicable rules when federal and state laws conflict; (3) determining the applicable rules in a multistate transaction where the dispute would be resolved differently under the rules of the different interested states; and (4) determining the applicable rules from among the different conflicting rules within a state.

The subject of choice of law is complex and exceeds the needs of paralegal students in an introductory course in contract law. Our goal in Part I of *Introduction to the Law of Contracts* is simply to have students recognize this issue when it arises. We have, therefore, chosen to provide the limited coverage of choice of law that we deem essential to meet this goal.

choice of law
Choice of law is the determination of which law applies where more than one state is involved in a transaction, where conflicting laws exist within a state, or where federal law may preempt state law.

CHAPTER 1

Determining the Rules Governing the Dispute

Once a dispute ceases to be private and a third party is called upon to resolve the dispute for the parties (as in litigation and arbitration), the disputants lose control over the procedural, evidentiary, and substantive rules that govern the resolution of their dispute. Determining the rules that govern a dispute involves choice of law questions such as the following:

- With increasing globalization, and with international transactions becoming commonplace, if one party is from the United States and the other is from another country, do the domestic procedural, evidentiary, and substantive rules of the United States or of the other party's country govern?
- If the domestic rules of the United States apply, would federal law or state law be used by the adjudicator?
- If state law applies and the transaction has multistate characteristics, would the law of State A or the law of State B be used?

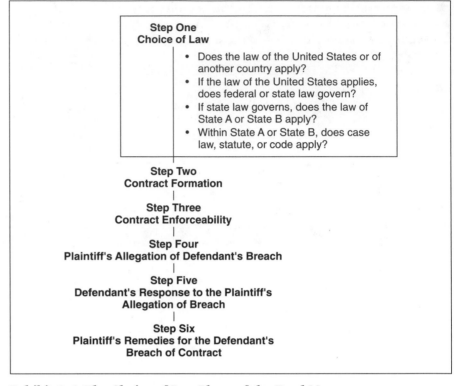

Exhibit 1–1 The Choice of Law Phase of the Road Map

- Once it is determined which state's law will be used, would the case law, statutes, or codes of that state be used to resolve this dispute? (See Exhibit 1–1.)

DETERMINING THE RULES WHEN ONE CONTRACTING PARTY IS FROM THE UNITED STATES AND THE OTHER IS FROM ANOTHER COUNTRY

When one contracting party has a business in the United States and the other party has a business in another country, these countries may have different procedural, evidentiary, and substantive rules. They may also have different legal systems. The United States, with only 4.5 percent of the world's population, has a common law system (with the exception of Louisiana, which has a system that is based on the French civil code). What is the likelihood that the other contracting party will also have a business in a country that has a common law system? Other than the United States, only 2 percent of the world's population resides in a country that has a common law system.

As of 2007, the European Union (EU) had 27 member countries. Only 2 of the 27 countries have common law systems: Ireland and the United Kingdom (England, Scotland, Wales, and Northern Ireland). So if the party having a business in the United States is contracting with a party having a business in an EU country other than the United Kingdom or Ireland, the two countries will have different legal systems.

⫾ PARALEGAL EXERCISE 1.1

On the Internet, use a search engine to find "World Legal Systems." This leads you to the University of Ottawa's Web site. Find "Statistics" in the menu and complete the following table:

Legal System	Total Population	% of World's Population
Civil law systems		
Common law systems		
Systems of customary law		
Systems of Muslim law		
Mixed systems of civil law and common law		
Mixed systems of civil law and customary law		
Mixed systems of civil law and Muslim law		
Mixed systems of common law and customary law		
Mixed systems of common law and Muslim law		
Mixed systems of civil law, Muslim law, and customary law		
Mixed systems of common law, Muslim law, and customary law		
Mixed systems of civil law, common law, and customary law		
Mixed systems of common law, Muslim law, and civil law		
Mixed systems of civil law, common law, and Talmudic law ▧		

▥ PARALEGAL EXERCISE 1.2

On the Internet, use a search engine to find a definition for each of the following legal systems:

Common law system

Civil law system

Muslim law system

Customary law system

Talmudic law system ▧

▥ PARALEGAL EXERCISE 1.3

On the Internet, use a search engine to find "Gateway to the European Union." From this Web site, identify the countries in the EU. ▧

With so many differences in legal systems and in procedural, evidentiary, and substantive rules within systems, it is imperative for the contracting parties to choose the following at the time of contract formation:

1. The method of dispute resolution in the event of a subsequent dispute
2. The laws that will apply in the event of a subsequent dispute
3. The location of the forum

Most international transactions provide that subsequent disputes will be resolved by arbitration rather than litigation. They will also select the international arbitration service provider. Arbitration has its advantages.

- The parties select the arbitrator or arbitrators; thus, arbitrators who have expertise may be selected.
- The parties control scheduling.
- The parties determine whether the arbitration will be conducted by document or by hearing.
- If arbitration is conducted by hearing, the parties determine its location.
- The parties can have input into the rules of discovery and into the procedural and evidentiary rules for the hearing (the rules of evidence can be relaxed and evidence can be admitted without live testimony).
- The hearing can be scheduled without interruptions.
- The parties establish a deadline for when the arbitrator must render the award.
- The parties can require the arbitrator to choose between a high and a low award—or can provide a high/low range for the award.

- The arbitrator's decree is final and generally cannot be appealed—so arbitration gives finality to the resolution of the dispute.
- The costs can be controlled and apportioned.
- As a result of the Convention on the Recognition of Enforcement of Foreign Arbitral Awards (i.e., the New York Convention of 1958), a foreign arbitration award is more easily enforced than a foreign court judgment.

Most international transactions include a choice of law provision in the event of a subsequent dispute. If the transaction involves the international sale of goods, the United Nations Convention on Contracts for the International Sale of Goods (CISG) may come into play. This occurs if the sale is between parties whose places of business are in different states (countries) and the states are contracting states (CISG Article 1). The contracting parties, however, are permitted to opt out of CISG (CISG Article 6).

PARALEGAL EXERCISE 1.4

On the Internet, use a search engine to find "UNCITRAL" (United Nations Commission on International Trade Law). Use the menus to find "texts & status," then "CISG," then "CISG" (again), and finally "Status." Return to your list of EU countries in Paralegal Exercise 1.3. Identify the EU countries that are "contracting states." ▮

Once the method of dispute resolution and the choice of law are selected, the final consideration is the choice of location of the forum. If the parties have selected arbitration as their method of dispute resolution, the location of the forum is unlimited because arbitration is a private process. If, however, the parties have selected litigation, their choice of location must conform to the rules of the forum state selected.

DETERMINING THE RULES WHEN FEDERAL AND STATE LAWS CONFLICT

In some instances, **federal preemption** causes state law, whether case law or statute, to be inoperative. Under the federal preemption doctrine, state law must give way to federal law when federal law either expressly regulates the matter or when a particular subject is regarded as being beyond the bounds of state action.

The area of warranties illustrates the federal preemption doctrine.

federal preemption
The doctrine derived from the Supremacy Clause of the United States Constitution ("This Constitution, and the laws of the United States which shall be made in pursuance thereof; and all treaties made, or which shall be made, under the authority of the United States, shall be the supreme law of the land; and the judges in every state shall be bound thereby, anything in the Constitution or laws of any State to the contrary notwithstanding") whereby any federal law takes precedence over any conflicting state law.

All states with the exception of Louisiana have enacted Article 2 of the Uniform Commercial Code (UCC). Article 2 of the UCC applies to transactions involving a sale of goods. Article 2 of the UCC permits a seller who makes an express warranty to disclaim an implied warranty. The United States Congress has enacted the Magnuson-Moss Warranty Act to regulate the sale of consumer goods distributed in commerce. Magnuson-Moss does not permit a seller who makes an express warranty to disclaim an implied warranty. Therefore, if a buyer purchases a product that is consumer goods, and if the seller makes an express warranty but attempts to disclaim an implied warranty granted by state statute, the attempted disclaimer is not effective because the federal statute will preempt the state statute. The buyer therefore purchases the consumer goods with an implied warranty.

DETERMINING THE RULES WHEN MORE THAN ONE STATE HAS AN INTEREST IN THE TRANSACTION

Which state's law applies when the laws of different states conflict? The answer may be provided by the contracting parties. When the contract was formed, the parties may have chosen the state whose laws would apply to the transaction. If the parties did not select the state or made an ineffective selection, then the answer is found in the choice of law rules of the **forum state** (the state where the lawsuit is filed). Unfortunately, several choice of law rules exist, producing different results.

forum state

The forum state is the state in which the case is filed (the state hearing the case).

Selection of the Law by the Parties

Contracting parties can choose the law of a particular state to govern their contractual rights and duties and include their choice as a provision in the contract.

A choice of law provision could take the following form: "This Agreement shall be governed and interpreted in accordance with the laws of the State of Indiana."

Because parties contract to create predictability in their relationship, courts will give effect to the parties' own choice of applicable law. The deference to the parties' own choice of applicable law is known as the **"party autonomy" rule**. The autonomy rule, however, has limitations. If the contracting parties select a state and incorporate it as a provision in their contract, then the court in the forum state will enforce this choice of law provision unless: (1) the chosen state has no substantial relationship to the parties or the transaction; or (2) the result obtained from the applicability of the law of the chosen state would be contrary to the forum state's public policy.

party autonomy rule

The court deference to the parties' own choice of applicable law.

ⅲ PARALEGAL EXERCISE 1.5

In *S. Leo Harmonay, Inc. v. Binks Manufacturing Co.*, General Motors hired Binks, a Delaware corporation with its principal place of business in Illinois, as general contractor to expand its assembly plant in Tarrytown, New York. Binks subcontracted the mechanical piping work to Harmonay, a New York corporation, at a cost of approximately $2 million.

A dispute arose regarding damages for delays, and Harmonay filed a breach of contract action against Binks in the United States District Court for the Southern District of New York.

The subcontract, a standard printed form, provided that the "contract resulting from the acceptance of this order is to be construed according to the law of the state from which this order issues, which is printed on the opposite side hereof." Binks's corporate headquarters' address in Franklin Park, Illinois, was clearly printed on the form, signifying Illinois as the state. Binks argued that Illinois law should govern the dispute.

Harmonay countered that the choice of law provision in the subcontract was unenforceable because Illinois lacked a substantial relationship to the transaction—and therefore New York law, rather than Illinois law, should govern. Under the law of Illinois, a "no damages for delay" clause would be incorporated into the subcontract, and Binks could successfully defend the lawsuit. Under New York law, a "no damages for delay" clause would not be incorporated into the subcontract, and Harmonay could recover.

Review the following excerpt from *S. Leo Harmonay, Inc. v. Binks Manufacturing Co.*, and determine whether the court applied Illinois or New York law and why. ■

CASE

S. Leo Harmonay, Inc. v. Binks Manufacturing Co.
United States District Court, Southern District of New York (1984)
597 F.Supp. 1014, 1024–25

I. CHOICE OF LAW

Jurisdiction in this case rests on diversity of citizenship, 28 U.S.C. § 1332, and therefore the Court must apply the substantive law of the forum state, including the conflict of law rules. See Klaxon v. Stentor Elec. Mfg. Co., 313 U.S. 487, 61 S.Ct. 1020, 85 L.Ed. 1477 (1941). Thus, New York law applies to the conflicts question raised herein. See La Beach v. Beatrice Foods Co., 461 F.Supp. 152 (S.D.N.Y. 1978); Business Incentives Co., Inc. v. Sony Corp. of America, 397 F.Supp. 63 (S.D.N.Y. 1975).

While it is true that some jurisdictions give determinative effect to a choice of law clause and thereby follow the so-called "autonomy rule," see Note, Effectiveness of Choice of Law Clauses in Contract Conflicts of Law: Party Autonomy or Objective Determination?, 82 Colum.L.Rev. 1659, 1660 (1982), New York is not one of them. See La Beach, supra; Southern Intern. Sales Co. v. Potter & Brumfield, 410 F.Supp. 1339 (S.D.N.Y. 1976); Business Incentives Co., supra; Fricke v. Isbrandtsen Co., 151 F.Supp. 465 (S.D.N.Y. 1957).

A better rule, suggested by Judge Learned Hand, is that such clauses are prima facie valid and will be upheld absent a showing that they result from fraud or overreaching, that they are unreasonable or unfair, or that enforcement would contravene a strong public policy of the forum. See Krenger v. Pennsylvania R. Co., 174 F.2d 556, 560–61 (2d Cir.) (L. Hand, Ch. J., concurring), cert. denied, 338 U.S. 866, 70 S.Ct. 140, 94 L.Ed. 531 (1949); Bense v. Interstate Battery System of America, Inc., 683 F.2d 718, 721–22 (2d Cir. 1982); Richardson Greenshields Securities, Inc. v. Metz, 566 F.Supp. 131, 133 (S.D.N.Y. 1983).

The "substantial relationship" approach followed in New York, which parallels Judge Hand's rule, is stated succinctly in Restatement (Second) of Conflicts of Law § 187. See Nakhleh v. Chemical Construction Corp., 359 F.Supp. 357 (S.D.N.Y. 1973). In relevant part, that section states:

> "(2) The law of the state chosen by the parties to govern their contractual rights and duties will be applied, even if the particular issue is one which the parties could not have resolved by an explicit provision in their agreement directed to that issue (i.e., questions of validity, formalities and capacity) unless either
> (a) the chosen state has no substantial relationship to the parties . . . or
> (b) application of the law of the chosen state would be contrary to a fundamental policy of a state which has a materially greater interest than the chosen state . . . "

Thus, although New York does recognize the choice of law principle that parties to a contract have a right to choose the law to be applied to their contract, see Compania de Inversiones Internacionales v. Industrial Mortgage Bank of Finland, 269 N.Y. 22, 198 N.E. 617 (1935), this freedom of choice on the part of the parties is not absolute. See Nakhleh, supra.

With respect to the substantial relationship test, the New York Court of Appeals has held that while the parties' choice of law is to be given considerable weight, the law of the jurisdiction with the "most significant contacts" is to be applied. Haag v. Barnes, 9 N.Y.2d 554, 559–60, 175 N.E.2d 441, 216 N.Y.S.2d 65 (1961); see La Beach, supra, at 155–56; Southern Intern., supra, at 1341.

Under this analysis, the parties' "choice" of Illinois law in the Binks standard printed form diminishes when viewed against the facts of the case. The only Illinois contact is that it is the principal place of defendant's business. The contract itself was executed in Michigan. On the other hand and most impressive are these factors: the place of performance of the work was in New York, all negotiations for the extra work and other claims occurred in New York, the prime contract is governed by the law of New York, and plaintiff, a New York corporation, has its principal place of business in New York. Illinois has no substantial relationship to the parties and New York would seem to have a materially greater interest in the application of its law. In light of the foregoing, the rights and duties of the parties to the contract are to be governed by the law of New York, despite the "agreement" of the parties to the contrary.

III PARALEGAL EXERCISE 1.6

Ryder Truck Lines, Inc. v. Goren Equipment Co. involved a contract for the sale of 75 used diesel engines. Ryder, a Florida corporation with its headquarters in Florida, sold the engines to Goren, a Georgia corporation with its principal place of business in Georgia. Goren buys used truck engines and engine parts from companies such as Ryder for resale to other trucking industry companies in the United States and internationally.

Upon receiving the 75 engines, Goren became dissatisfied and fell behind in its payments. Ryder sued Goren in the United States District Court for the Northern District of Georgia, alleging a breach of contract. Goren responded with allegations of duress, fraud, and the unenforceability of the liquidated damages provision. The contract stated that Florida law would apply to any dispute between the parties.

Review the following excerpt from *Ryder Truck Lines, Inc. v. Goren Equipment Co.*, and determine whether the court applied Georgia or Florida law and why. ■

CASE

Ryder Truck Lines, Inc. v. Goren Equipment Co.
United States District Court, Northern District of Georgia (1983)
576 F.Supp. 1348, 1354

A. CHOICE OF LAW

In resolving the various claims presented in this diversity action, the federal court must follow the Georgia conflict of laws rules. Klaxon Co. v. Stentor Electric Manufacturing Co., 313 U.S. 487, 61 S.Ct. 1020, 85 L.Ed. 1477 (1941). Georgia's conflicts rule states that the law of the state where the contract is made and performed will govern the validity and interpretation of the contract, unless the parties have chosen the law of a particular state to govern their contractual rights and responsibilities. In that event, the choice of law provision in the contract will be applied, except where the chosen state has no substantial relationship to the parties or the transaction, or the result obtained from the applicability of the law of the chosen state would be contrary to Georgia's public policy. See, 5 Encyclopedia of Georgia Law, Conflict of Laws §§ 27, 11; Restatement (Second) of Conflict of Laws § 187 (1971). Cf. Nasco v. Gimbert, 239 Ga. 675, 238 S.E.2d 368 (1977).

In the case at bar, paragraph 9 of the January contract provides that the agreement shall be governed by the laws of Florida. The issues of fraud and duress, however, relate to the validity of the contract as a result of alleged pre-contract misrepresentations, and are matters outside the contract. Furthermore, contracts procured by fraud and/or duress are contrary to the fundamental policy of the state of Georgia, as is a damages provision in a contract which purports to be liquidated damages, but instead is a penalty to deter a person from breaching the contract. As these issues involve matters of public policy in Georgia, the court will apply Georgia law in resolving the issues of fraud, duress, and the enforceability of the liquidated damages provision, notwithstanding the parties' choice of Florida law provision in the contract. On the other hand, the court does not find the questions of interest and attorney's fees to be matters of important public policy where such items are provided for in the contract. These issues are governed by the agreement, and therefore Florida law will be applied in deciding these issues.

The Law in the Absence of an Effective Choice by the Parties

The following is a general discussion of several conflict of law rules used in the field of contracts when the parties have not included a choice of law provision in their contract. The choice of law rule specified by the forum state determines which state's law will govern.

Example 1-3

A Texas Buyer, in preparation for a Fourth of July program, contracted to purchase 1,000 cases of fireworks from an Oklahoma Manufacturer-Seller. Seller shipped the cases to Buyer in Texas. As Buyer was unloading and storing the fireworks, they exploded, severely injuring Buyer. Four years and two months after the explosion, Buyer filed a breach of contract action in a Texas court seeking damages for breach of an implied warranty of merchantability under Oklahoma's version of Article 2 of the Uniform Commercial Code. The contract did not include a choice of law provision.

Seller contended that the Texas court should apply Texas rather than Oklahoma law. Under the Texas version of the UCC (§ 2–725), "An action for breach of any contract for sale must be commenced within *four* years after the cause of action has accrued" (emphasis added). "A cause of action accrues when the breach occurs, regardless of the aggrieved party's lack of knowledge of the breach. A breach of warranty occurs when tender of delivery is made . . ." Under the Oklahoma version of the UCC, the Statute of Limitations has been extended to *five* years. Therefore, if Oklahoma law applies, the suit is timely. If Texas law applies, the suit is barred by the Statute of Limitations.

Because the lawsuit was filed in a Texas court, Texas is the forum state. The Texas court will use the Texas choice of law rules to resolve whether the Texas court should use Texas or Oklahoma law.

Which choice of law rule applies is often a complex question. Jurisdictions do not share a uniform solution. One choice of law rule applies the law of the place of the making of the contract. Generally, the place of the making of the contract is the place where the last act necessary to form the contract occurs. The place of the last act may be the place of acceptance, the place of delivery of a document, or the regular place of business of the party who accepts the offer.

Another choice of law rule applies the law of the place of performance of the contract. This would be the place where the contract specifies that the performance is to occur.

A third choice of law rule is proposed by the Restatement (Second) of Conflicts. The **Restatements of the Law**, drafted by the American Law Institute (an organization composed of judges, practitioners, and academicians) are an attempt to codify the common law of the various states into black letter law with commentary and examples. At times, the Restatements exceed codification and propose what the law ought to be. The Restatements cover a number of areas including the Restatement of Conflicts, the Restatement (First) of Contracts, the Restatement (Second) of Contracts, and the Restatement of Restitution. The Restatement rule applies the law of the state with the most significant contacts or relationship with the transaction. This rule is called the "center of gravity," "grouping of contacts," or "most significant relationship theory." This Restatement rule gives effect to the stated intent of the parties. If the contract fails to express the intent of the parties, the Restatement looks at the following list of contacts:

- Place of contracting
- Place of negotiation of the contract
- Place of performance
- Location of the subject matter of the contract
- Domicile, residence, nationality, place of incorporation, and place of business of the parties

If the place of the making of the contract and the place of negotiating are the same, courts will tend to use the law of that place.

The following example illustrates the application of these basic conflict of law rules.

Restatements of the Law

The Restatements are an attempt by the American Law Institute (ALI) to codify the common law of the various states into black letter law with commentary and examples. At times, the Restatements go beyond the common law and present the ALI's view of what the law should be.

Example 1–4

Gary, a resident of State A, purchased a BMW. Gary, while in State A, mailed an offer to Barbara in State B to sell her his BMW. Gary's offer stated that the car would be delivered to Barbara in State C. On the following Tuesday, Gary, having second thoughts about his offer to Barbara, mailed a letter to her revoking his offer.

On Wednesday, Barbara received Gary's offer and not knowing that Gary had sent a letter of revocation, mailed a letter to Gary accepting his offer. On Thursday, Barbara received Gary's letter of revocation. On Friday, Gary received Barbara's letter of acceptance. When Barbara telephoned Gary demanding the car, Gary refused.

Under the laws of States A, B, and C, acceptance of an offer sent by mail is effective when the letter of acceptance is sent. Therefore, Barbara's letter of acceptance would be effective on Wednesday, the date it was mailed.

State B and State A, however, have different rules governing revocation of the offer. Under State B's law, revocation is effective when sent. Therefore, Gary's letter of revocation would be effective on Tuesday, the day it was sent. Gary's offer no longer existed for Barbara to accept, and a contract was not formed because under State B's law, the revocation was effective before the attempted acceptance was effective. Because a contract was never formed in the first place, Gary's failure to deliver the BMW could not constitute a breach under State B's law.

Under State A's law, revocation is effective when received. Because the attempted revocation was effective on Thursday and the acceptance was effective on Wednesday, Gary's offer was accepted, and his attempted revocation arrived too late to be effective. Gary's failure to deliver the BMW constituted a breach of contract.

Does the law of State B or State A apply? Could the law of State C, whatever it is, apply because the car was to be delivered in State C?

Under the law of the place of the making of the contract, the law of State B would probably apply because Barbara mailed her acceptance in State B.

Under the place of performance rule, the law of State C will probably govern because delivery was to be made there.

Under the Restatement's most significant relationship theory, the place of contracting is State B, where Barbara accepted. The place of negotiating could be both State B and State A, especially if negotiations were made by mail. The place of performance would be State C where delivery was to be made; and the domiciles and residences of the parties are State B and State A. Under the Restatement rule, it is difficult to predict which law will be applied since it depends on how the forum jurisdiction will view the contacts.

Gary mails offer from State A to Barbara in State B to sell a BMW located in State C	Gary mails revocation from State A to Barbara in State B	Barbara in State B receives Gary's offer sent from State A and mails an acceptance from State B	Barbara in State B receives Gary's letter of revocation sent from State A	Gary in State A receives Barbara's letter of acceptance sent from State B
	Tuesday	Wednesday	Thursday	Friday

Exhibit 1-2 Timeline for Example 1-4

PARALEGAL EXERCISE 1.7

Your supervising attorney is drafting a contract between the firm's client, a manufacturer of computer equipment, and its foreign supplier of computer components. She has asked you whether the contract should include a choice of law provision. She has also asked you to draft a choice of law provision for the contract. She has given you the following sample choice of law provisions to assist you in drafting.

> Florida law shall govern this agreement.
>
> This agreement shall be governed by and construed in accordance with the law of the State of Arkansas.
>
> The laws of the State of California govern and control this document and all actions in conjunction with the enforcement of this document.
>
> The construction and performance of this agreement shall be governed by the laws of the Commonwealth of Pennsylvania, United States of America. If any provision of this agreement is held to be invalid or unenforceable, this agreement shall be considered divisible as to all such provisions, and the balance of this agreement shall continue in full force and effect as though such invalid or unenforceable provisions were not included in this agreement. ■

DETERMINING THE RULES WHEN A STATE HAS SEVERAL SETS OF RULES

The previous section explored the various choice of law rules used in determining the rules for resolving a dispute when more than one state has an interest in the transaction. Once the appropriate state has been determined, attention focuses on the laws within that state. The law of contracts within a state comes from two primary sources: the legislature and agencies (statutes, codes, and regulations) and the courts (case law).

When the legislature enacts a statute addressing a specific issue, the law has been codified. Courts are not free to ignore the legislative mandate and create their own law.

Example 1–5

A general rule under case law (court-made law) is that a person who enters into a contract while a minor may disaffirm the contract while still a minor or within a reasonable time after reaching majority. Suppose that Mary Smith purchases a DVD player when she is 17 years old. Six months after turning 18, Mary decides that she no longer wants the VCR and wants her money back. She therefore seeks to disaffirm the contract. Under the court-made law, Mary has a reasonable time after reaching majority (age 18) to disaffirm. If the merchant resists Mary's attempt to disaffirm, the court will be asked to determine whether six months after reaching 18 was a reasonable time within which to disaffirm under the facts of this case. If, however, the legislature has enacted a statute that states that one year after reaching majority is a reasonable time to disaffirm, the statutory rule applies, rather than the case law. The courts cannot ignore a statute. The courts, however, have the duty to interpret the statute in light of the facts of the case before them.

When dealing with a code, such as the UCC, the paralegal's approach should differ from the approach involving an isolated statute and case law. First, the paralegal should review the relevant documents made by the parties. Next, the paralegal should consult relevant code law, not case law. The code is the primary, principal, and often preemptive source of law. Do not disregard the code. The code is an integrated document with interrelated sections. It includes definitions as well as rules.

Article 2 of the UCC, dealing with the sale of goods, provides 104 interrelated sections on the law of contracts pertaining to the sale of goods. Therefore, as a threshold question, one must determine whether the transaction is controlled by Article 2 of the UCC or by some other law of the jurisdiction. If the UCC applies, the rules in the case law are irrelevant, unless the case law interprets the UCC or the UCC is silent on the issue. UCC §1–103 provides:

> Unless displaced by the particular provisions of this Act, the principles of law and equity, including the law merchant and the law relative to capacity to contract, principal and agent, estoppel, fraud,

misrepresentation, duress, coercion, mistake, bankruptcy, or other validating or invalidating cause shall supplement its provisions.

The name "Uniform Commercial Code" is a misnomer. The code is not limited to commercial transactions. For example, the Uniform Commercial Code controls the contract between two neighbors for the sale of a used lawn mower as well as the contract between two large corporations for the sale of steel beams.

Article 2 of the UCC is limited, however, to "transactions in goods." The term "transactions," although not defined in the code, has generally been limited to sales. Therefore, Article 2, as its short title indicates, is the law of sale of goods. Because Article 2 is generally limited to sales, it does not govern transactions that are pure leases. Article 2A covers leases of goods.

Article 2 applies to transactions in "goods," a term that is defined to mean all things that are movable at the time of identification to the contract for sale, other than the money in which the price is to be paid, investment securities, and things in action. Whether a particular sales transaction is governed by Article 2 instead of other statutory or case law rules may, therefore, depend on whether the subject of the sale was within the UCC's definition of "goods."

⚏ PARALEGAL EXERCISE 1.8

Which of the following transactions are controlled by Article 2 of the UCC?

1. An employment contract
2. A contract to sell natural gas (after it has been extracted from a well)
3. A contract to sell electricity
4. A contract to sell advertising time on the radio
5. A contract to sell an airplane ticket
6. A contract to sell a cow with her calf
7. A contract to sell the Empire State Building
8. A contract to sell an automobile
9. A contract to sell timber standing in a forest
10. A contract to sell a business ▓

Because Article 2 governs transactions for the sale of goods but not for the sale of services, a difficult question is posed when the sale is a mixed or hybrid transaction. **Hybrid transactions** are contracts for both goods and services. Examples include the sale and installation of an air conditioning system, the repair of an automobile, the construction of a bridge, the charge for a blood transfusion, and the charge for a beauty treatment. When faced with a hybrid transaction, courts most frequently use the rule that Article 2 is applicable if the sales aspect predominates and is inapplicable if the service aspect predominates. This is known as the **predominant factor test.**

hybrid transactions
Contracts that are for both the sale of goods and the sale of services.

predominant factor test
The test used to resolve whether a hybrid transaction should be treated under Article 2 of the UCC (sale of goods) or under the common law (sale of a service).

PARALEGAL CHECKLIST

Determining the Rules Governing the Dispute

❏ ALTHOUGH questions of choice of law (selecting the rules governing the dispute) are complex and well beyond an introductory course in contract law, paralegals should be able to identify when a choice of law problem exists. If a choice of law question goes undetected, the wrong set of rules may be applied to a given set of facts, resulting in an inaccurate solution and loss of valuable time. Choice of law is the threshold question, and its existence can be discovered using the following analysis.

1. Does the transaction involve one party who has a business in the United States and another party who has a business in another country? If so, answer the following:

   a. Did the parties contract as to the method of dispute resolution? Most parties will select arbitration rather than litigation in a foreign court. If the parties have not selected arbitration at the time of contracting, then unless they agree on arbitration at the time of the dispute, their dispute will be litigated.

   b. Did the parties contract as to choice of law?

      1) If one party has a business in the United States and the other party has a business in a country that is a contracting state, then CISG will apply to the dispute unless the parties have opted out at the time of contract formation.

      2) If one party has a business in the United States and the other party does not have a business in a contracting state, CISG will not apply.

         a) If the parties have a choice of law provision in their contract, that provision should apply if it is consistent with the rules of the forum state.

         b) If the parties have not included a choice of law provision in their contract, then the choice of law rules of the forum state will apply.

   c. Did the parties contract as to choice of forum?

      1) If the parties have a choice of forum provision and it is consistent with the rules of the forum state, then their choice of forum will govern.

      2) If the parties have not contracted as to choice of forum, then the plaintiff, by filing the petition or complaint, selects the forum, and that forum will retain jurisdiction unless the defendant could establish that another forum would be more appropriate.

2. Does federal law apply to any issue in the dispute? If both federal law and state law address the same issue, federal law will preempt state law.

3. Does the transaction relate to multiple states (whether by the parties, offer and acceptance, or the performance of the contract)? If more than one state is involved, a choice of law question may exist.

   a. Did the parties contract as to which state's law would govern their dispute? Under the "party autonomy" rule, a court in the forum state (the state where the legal action is brought) will enforce the parties' choice unless

      • the chosen state has no substantial relationship to the parties or to the transaction, or

      • the parties' choice would result in a decision contrary to the forum state's public policy.

b. If the parties have not included a choice of law provision in their contract, the forum state's choice of law rule determines which state's law will govern. Because states do not share the same choice of law rules, the answer may vary depending on where the action was filed (i.e., which state was the forum state). The following list illustrates the variation in choice of law rules:

- The law of the place of making the contract
- The law of the place of performance of the contract
- The law of the state with the most significant contacts with the transaction

4. Is there more than one rule within the state that could apply to this dispute? When case law and statutes conflict, statutes control. For example, Article 2 of the state's version of the Uniform Commercial Code will prevail over case law.

KEY TERMS

Choice of law

Federal preemption

Forum state

Hybrid transactions

Party autonomy rule

Predominant factor test

Restatements of the Law

REVIEW QUESTIONS

TRUE/FALSE QUESTIONS (CIRCLE THE CORRECT ANSWER)

1. T   F   Thirty-two percent of the world's population is in countries that use a common law system.

2. T   F   Most countries in the European Union are civil law countries.

3. T   F   Most international disputes are resolved through arbitration rather than litigation.

4. T   F   Court judgments are more easily enforced in a foreign court than are arbitration awards.

5. T   F   CISG applies to all international sales transactions if each contracting party has a business in a country that is a member of the United Nations.

6. T   F   The contracting parties may opt out of CISG.

7. T   F   The court in the forum state may apply the law of one state to one issue and the law of another state to another issue.

8. T   F   The law of contracts is generally a creation of federal law.

9. T   F   Contracting parties can choose the law of a particular state to govern their contractual rights and duties.

10.	T	F	Choice of law rules do not vary from state to state.
11.	T	F	Hybrid transactions are contracts for labor (services) only.
12.	T	F	Under the federal preemption doctrine, state law must always give way to federal law when federal law either expressly regulates the matter or when a particular subject is regarded as being beyond the bounds of state action.
13.	T	F	When the legislature of a state has enacted a statute addressing a specific issue, courts may not ignore this statute or create their own law.
14.	T	F	When a section of Article 2 of the UCC and those sections of Magnusen-Moss that deal with warranties conflict, the state's UCC provisions will apply.
15.	T	F	A choice of law question may exist if the offer was made in one state, accepted in another state, and the contract performed in a third state.
16.	T	F	The state hearing the case is called the forum state.
17.	T	F	The following statement is an illustration of a forum selection provision: "This agreement shall be governed and interpreted in accordance with the law of the State of Maine."
18.	T	F	If the parties have not included a choice of law provision in their contract, the choice of law rule of the forum state will determine which state's law will govern.
19.	T	F	Article 2 of the UCC applies only to merchants.
20.	T	F	The Uniform Commercial Code is divided into Chapters, Parts, and Sections.
21.	T	F	Article 2 of the UCC applies to leases and sales of goods.
22.	T	F	Although the title to Article 2 of the UCC is "Transactions in Goods," it deals exclusively with the "Sale of Goods."

FILL-IN-THE-BLANK QUESTIONS

1. _____. The preferred dispute resolution method if a third party is called upon to adjudicate an international business dispute.

2. _____. The United Nations convention that applies to some international sales of goods.

3. _____. The convention that makes arbitration awards more easily enforceable than litigation judgments in foreign courts.

4. _____. The article of CISG that authorizes contracting parties to opt out.

5. _____. The determination of which law applies where more than one state is involved in a transaction, where conflicting laws within a state exist, or where federal law may preempt state law.

6. _____. Law derived from custom and usage and from judicial decisions recognizing and enforcing custom and usage.

7. _____. Law enacted by a state legislature.

8. _____. The Code that includes an article on the sale of goods.

9. _____. The article of the UCC that deals with the sale of goods.

10. _____. Contracts for parts and labor.

11. _____. Under this doctrine, state law must give way to federal law when federal law either expressly regulates the matter or when a particular subject is regarded as being beyond the bounds of state action.

12. _____. The state in which the case is filed.

13. _____. Deference given by the courts to the parties' own choice of applicable law.

14. _____. The name of the choice of law rule proposed by the Restatement (Second) of Conflicts.

15. _____. The article in the UCC that deals with lease of goods.

MULTIPLE-CHOICE QUESTIONS (CIRCLE ALL THE CORRECT ANSWERS)

1. Which of the following is the convention that makes arbitration awards more easily enforceable than litigation judgments in foreign courts?
   (a) CISG
   (b) The New York Convention of 1958
   (c) The Uniform Commercial Code
   (d) The Restatement of Judgments
   (e) The Uniform Arbitration Act

2. Which of the following legal systems is most prevalent in the world?
   (a) Common law
   (b) Civil law
   (c) Customary law
   (d) Muslim law
   (e) Talmudic law

3. Which two countries in the European Union have common law systems?
   (a) England
   (b) Ireland
   (c) France
   (d) Scotland
   (e) Wales
   (f) United Kingdom

4. Which legal system is most prevalent in the European Union?
   (a) Common law
   (b) Civil law
   (c) Customary law

(d) Muslim law

(e) Talmudic law

5. The forum state is
   (a) the state hearing the case.
   (b) the state that has the governing law.
   (c) the state where the parties are located.
   (d) the state in which the case is filed.
   (e) the state where performance takes place.

6. The following are known choice of law questions:
   (a) Selecting the rules when more than one state has an interest in the transaction
   (b) Selecting the rules when federal and state laws conflict
   (c) Selecting the rules when the parties dispute whether a law is applicable
   (d) Selecting the rules when the parties dispute whether the forum state has jurisdiction
   (e) Selecting the rules when a state has several sets of rules

7. Buyer (offeror) is located in Oregon and Seller (offeree) is located in Florida. The goods that will be the subject of this contract will be manufactured in Ohio and shipped by the Seller to the Buyer's warehouse in California. Under the party autonomy rule, which state or states could the parties select for their choice of applicable law?
   (a) Oregon
   (b) New Mexico
   (c) Ohio
   (d) California
   (e) Florida

8. Buyer (offeror) is located in Oregon and Seller (offeree) is located in Florida. The goods that will be the subject of this contract will be manufactured in Ohio and shipped by the Seller to the Buyer's warehouse in California. The parties have not included a choice of law provision in their contract. Seller fails to deliver the goods to Buyer and Buyer brings a breach of contract action against the Seller in Oregon. The Oregon court will use the choice of law rule of which state to determine which state's law will govern?
   (a) Florida
   (b) Ohio
   (c) California
   (d) Oregon
   (e) New Mexico

9. The following choice of law rules may apply to contracts:
   (a) The law of the plaintiff's domicile
   (b) The law of the place of the making of the contract
   (c) The law of the place of performance of the contract
   (d) The law of the state with the most significant contacts or relationship with the transaction
   (e) The location of the forum court

SHORT-ANSWER QUESTIONS

1. Why would parties to an international transaction prefer arbitration to litigation, and is there a way that parties can express their preference?

2. What is CISG, to whom does it apply, and can parties opt out?

3. Describe the five basic legal systems in the world.

4. Buyer is located in Oregon and Seller is located in Florida. The goods that will be the subject of this contract will be manufactured in Ohio and shipped by the Seller to the Buyer's warehouse in California. Draft a choice of law provision for the parties.

5. Although courts will give effect to the parties' own choice of applicable law, this deference is not without limitations. If the contracting parties select the state with the applicable law and incorporate this selection into their contract for their choice of law, then the court in the forum state will enforce this choice of law provision unless _____ .

6. Adam hired Quality to paint his house. Quality promised to do a turn-key job, that is, to supply the paint as well as apply the paint. The contract was oral. Quality failed to complete the work and Adam sued Quality for breach of contract. If this transaction is a sale of goods, Article 2 of the UCC applies, and the contract must satisfy the Statute of Frauds provision of the UCC and be in writing to be enforceable. If this transaction is not a sale of goods, Article 2 is inapplicable, and the contract is enforceable regardless of whether it was oral or written. Does Article 2 of the UCC or state common law apply?

7. Describe the federal preemption doctrine.

PART II

Step Two: Contract Formation

A TRANSACTIONAL GUIDE TO CONTRACT FORMATION

Part II investigates the three phases of contract formation (offer, post-offer/pre-acceptance, and acceptance); the modification of an existing contract (the post-acceptance phase); and drafting a contract.

Evaluating whether the parties have formed a contract follows the transaction's evolution from beginning to end. In the offer phase, the parties become acquainted with each other. They begin negotiating. When one party has enough information and is ready to enter into a binding transaction, that party makes an offer requesting an exchange. "I will do this if you will do that." The offeror states what he or she will do in exchange for what the other party, the offeree, must do. Implicit in the offer is the offeror's statement, "I will be bound by the terms that I have stated if you say yes."

The second phase, post-offer/pre-acceptance, may last no longer than an instant or may extend for hours, days, weeks, or even months. This post-offer/pre-acceptance phase is a waiting period for the offeror. The offeror waits for the offeree to either accept or reject the offer. The longer the wait, the greater the opportunity for the transaction to go awry.

A number of events can occur that will cause the offer to terminate before an attempted acceptance:

- The offeror may reconsider the wisdom of the offer and revoke it, in which case the offeree no longer has an offer to accept.
- The offeree may decide that a contract on the offeror's terms would not be in his or her best interest and therefore rejects the offer. A rejection extinguishes the offer. Because an offer no longer exists, the offeree may assume the role of offeror and propose an alternative offer (known as a counteroffer) with more favorable terms.
- The offer may have stated a time limit within which it must be accepted. If not accepted within this time, the offer ceases to exist (lapses).
- If the offer does not state how long the offeree has to accept, the offer will cease to exist (lapse) after the offeree has had a reasonable time to accept.
- Finally, the offeror or offeree could die or become incapacitated or the subject matter of the offer could be destroyed before the offer was accepted.

If the offer continues to exist, the offeree can accept the offer. To accept the offer, the offeree agrees to the terms the offeror has proposed. Because the offeror has control of the offer ("the offeror is the master of his or her offer"), the offer is made on a "take it or leave it" basis. If the offeree accepts the offeror's offer, the offeree's acceptance concludes the transaction, and a contract is formed on the offeror's terms. If the offeree finds the terms of the offer unacceptable, he or she can reject the offer and propose his or her own offer (a counteroffer). The offeree now has control over the terms of the offer and the original offeror must either "take it or leave it." If the offeror accepts the offeree's offer, the offeror's acceptance concludes the transaction, and a contract is formed on the offeree's terms.

Sometimes, the parties wish to change the terms of the existing contract or to correct an error in the written contract. They are now in the post-acceptance phase of contract formation, and they do not have the same flexibility that existed during prior phases. Although the relationship of the parties can be changed after a contract has been formed, they have surrendered their "freedom to contract" and now must follow the often intricate rules imposed upon them by the law.

The Offer Phase

Chapter 2, "The Offer Phase," is the first chapter of Part II— "Contract Formation." A contract consists of an offer and an acceptance. An **offer** is made when the **offeror** (**promisor**) creates the power in the **offeree** (**promisee**) to accept the offer, thereby forming a contract. This power is created when the promisor (offeror) *manifests* a willingness to enter into a contract by inviting the promisee (offeree) to agree to the promisor's (offeror's) terms. Acceptance of the offeror's terms by the offeree forms the contract.

A synonym for *manifestation* is *demonstration*. A "manifestation of willingness" or a "demonstration of willingness" refers to the outward actions of the negotiating parties as understood by a third person watching the parties. This hypothetical third-party observer is referred to as the **reasonable person**, and the measure used by

offer

An offer is a manifestation of willingness to enter into a bargain, which justifies another person in understanding that his or her assent to that bargain is invited and will conclude it.

offeror

An offeror is the party who extends the offer to the offeree.

promisor

A promisor is the party who makes the promise.

offeree

An offeree is the party whom the offeror invites to accept the offer.

promisee

A promisee is the party to whom a promise is made.

reasonable person

A reasonable person is a hypothetical (not one of the contracting parties), rational person who can objectively interpret a set of facts.

reasonable person's standard (reasonable man's standard)

The reasonable person's standard is an objective rather than a subjective standard. The inquiry is how a reasonable person, having observed the transaction, perceived the transaction. The inquiry is not whether the parties mentally viewed the transaction in a common fashion. For example, if the parties dispute whether an offer was made, the legal conclusion will be that an offer was made if a reasonable person would conclude from the disputants' manifestations that an offer was made. The reasonable person's standard is used in modern contracts law.

objective standard

The objective standard is the reasonable person's standard. It is based on manifestations that could be reasonably interpreted by hypothetical third persons watching the transaction.

subjective standard

The subjective standard refers to a party's thinking or mental state rather than manifestations. The subjective standard is commonly referred to as the meeting of the minds.

meeting of the minds

Meeting of the minds is an outdated phrase that refers to the subjective theory of contract law.

this unbiased nonparticipating hypothetical observer is the **reasonable person's standard**.

The reasonable person's standard is an objective standard. Objectivity focuses on taking the transaction at face value. If strangers observe the negotiations, their conclusions would be objective. The strangers would possess only those facts appearing on the face of the negotiation and would not be aware of underlying motivations or intent. The manifestation of willingness is evaluated by this **objective standard**—the reasonable person's standard.

Both the Restatement (First) and the Restatement (Second) of Contracts use an objective standard for the law of contracts. Early contracts cases, however, used a subjective standard. The **subjective standard** evaluated communications by asking how the person making the communications would interpret them and not how a reasonable person would interpret them. The **"meeting of the minds"** concept depends on subjective evaluations by both parties to the contract. The subjective "meeting of the minds" has been replaced by the objective "manifestation of assent." Unfortunately, old phraseology dies hard. Although the standard in the Restatement's definition of contract is clearly objective, many current cases parrot subjective language. Care must be taken when reading cases that use "meeting of the minds" language (see Exhibit 2–1).

The Facts:	"We will sell peas at 35¢ a pound."	
The Offeror's perception of the facts	offer	offer
The Offeree's perception of the facts	offer	not an offer
Conclusion	offer	not an offer

Offer vs. Non-Offer Using a Subjective Standard

The Facts:	"We will sell peas at 35¢ a pound."		
The Offeror's perception of the facts	offer	offer	offer
The Offeree's perception of the facts	offer	not an offer	not an offer
The Reasonable Person's perception of the facts	if offer	if offer	if not an offer
Conclusion	offer	offer	not an offer

Offer vs. Non-Offer Using an Objective Standard

Exhibit 2–1 Offer vs. Non-Offer Using a Subjective or an Objective Standard

The manifestation by the offeror must be sufficient to justify an understanding by the offeree that his or her assent to that bargain is invited and will conclude it. A contract will be formed, and the offeror will be bound by the contract when the offeree assents. After the offeree accepts the offer, it will be too late for the offeror to unilaterally add, delete, or modify the terms of the offer (see Exhibit 2–2).

Chapter 2 begins with a study of the classical contract law definition of offer—the promisor's promise and consideration for the promisor's promise—and then explores two alternatives to classical consideration. The first involves legislative and judicial tinkering with classical doctrine. The second introduces **reliance** as an alternative to consideration.

Finally, if a classical contract "promise" (unequivocal assurance) is lacking, an alternative cause of action may exist. Depending on the circumstances—detrimental reliance or unjust enrichment (benefit conferred)—courts have recognized a **reliance cause of action** and a **restitution cause of action** (see Exhibit 2–2).

THE CLASSICAL OFFER—THE OFFEROR'S PROMISE AND CONSIDERATION FOR THAT PROMISE

A communication may appear to be an offer, but this conclusion may be premature. The communication must have the essential elements of an offer to be an offer. Simply stated, an offer consists of the following:

- The promisor's promise
- The consideration for the promisor's promise (commonly referred to as the "price" for the promisor's promise)

The consideration for the promisor's promise itself has two elements:

- The promisee's promise or performance, depending on which the promisor demands
- The fact that the promisor is using his or her promise to induce the promisee to promise or perform

The promisor is the party making the promise. The offeror is the party making the offer. The promisor does not become an offeror until the two elements of offer (the promisor's promise and the consideration for the promisor's promise) are satisfied.

Although every offer begins with a promisor's promise, the consideration for the promisor's promise may be either a promise or a performance. The promisor may want the promisee to promise now and perform later ("promise for a promise") or to perform and not promise to perform ("promise for a performance"). The offeror, who is the master of the offer, controls whether the offer is a promise for a promise or a promise for a performance.

reliance

Reliance may be a cause of action (the basis of a claim), a remedy (the relief sought) for a breach of contract or a reliance cause of action, or a tool to circumvent an obstacle to a breach of contract cause of action (e.g., reliance may circumvent a lack of consideration, a lack of an express option contract, and a lack of a writing required by the Statute of Frauds. Reliance are based on the aggrieved party reasonably relying on the promisor.)

reliance cause of action

A reliance cause of action uses reliance as the basis of the plaintiff's complaint (or claim).

restitution cause of action

A restitution cause of action uses unjust enrichment as the basis of the plaintiff's complaint (or claim).

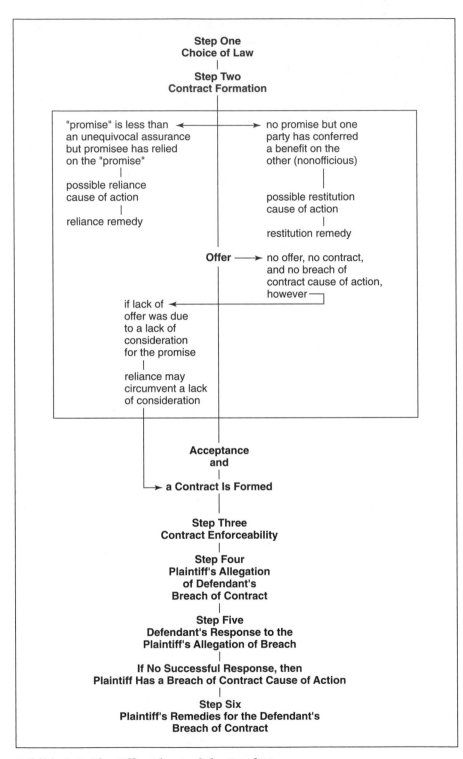

Step One
Choice of Law

Step Two
Contract Formation

"promise" is less than
an unequivocal assurance
but promisee has relied
on the "promise"

no promise but one
party has conferred
a benefit on the
other (nonofficious)

possible reliance
cause of action

possible restitution
cause of action

reliance remedy

restitution remedy

Offer → no offer, no contract,
and no breach of
contract cause of action,
however

if lack of
offer was due
to a lack of
consideration
for the promise

reliance may
circumvent a lack
of consideration

Acceptance
and

a Contract Is Formed

Step Three
Contract Enforceability

Step Four
Plaintiff's Allegation
of Defendant's
Breach of Contract

Step Five
Defendant's Response to the
Plaintiff's Allegation of Breach

If No Successful Response, then
Plaintiff Has a Breach of Contract Cause of Action

Step Six
Plaintiff's Remedies for the Defendant's
Breach of Contract

Exhibit 2–2 The Offer Phase of the Road Map

An offer that is "a promise for a promise" is an **offer for a bilateral contract**. *Bi* is the Latin prefix meaning two; thus two promises: "promise for a promise." The offeror makes a promise to entice the offeree to promise. For example, an offer for a bilateral contract for the sale of a car would be "I promise to sell you my 1976 VW camper bus for your promise to pay me $5,000." The consideration for the offeror's promise to sell the camper bus is the offeree's "promise to pay $5,000" (see Exhibit 2–3).

When the offeror makes an offer for a bilateral contract, the offeree accepts the offer by promising to do, or not do, what the offeror requested, thus forming a bilateral contract. Contract formation occurs when the offeree promises and not when the offeree performs. Once the contract is formed, each party has a duty to perform his or her promise, and each has a right to receive the other party's performance. Since both the offeror and the offeree have duties toward the other, both are promisors and promisees and either (by being a promisor) could be the breaching party (see Exhibit 2–4).

An offer that is "a promise for a performance" is an **offer for a unilateral contract**. *Uni* is the Latin prefix meaning one; thus one promise (the offeror's promise). The offeror makes a promise to entice the offeree to perform (and not promise). For example, an offer for a unilateral contract would be "I promise to sell you my 1976 VW camper bus for your paying me $5,000." The consideration for the offeror's promise to sell the camper bus is the offeree's "paying $5,000." The offeror is not asking the offeree to promise to pay. The offeror is asking the offeree to actually pay in return for the offeror's promise to sell (see Exhibit 2–5).

An offer for a unilateral contract does not become a contract until the offeree has fully performed. Once the offeree has fully

offer for a bilateral contract

In an offer for a bilateral contract, the offeror makes a promise to entice the offeree to make a promise (a promise for a promise).

offer for a unilateral contract

In an offer for a unilateral contract, the offeror makes a promise to entice the offeree to perform (a promise for a performance).

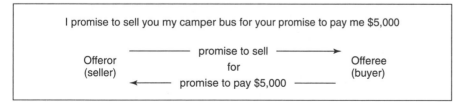

Exhibit 2–3 An Offer for a Bilateral Contract

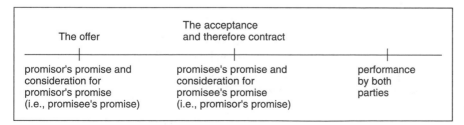

Exhibit 2–4 Timing of Acceptance of an Offer for a Bilateral Contract

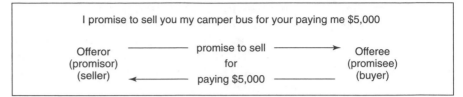

Exhibit 2–5 An Offer for a Unilateral Contract

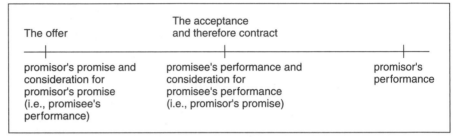

Exhibit 2–6 Timing of Acceptance of an Offer for a Unilateral Contract

performed and a unilateral contract is formed, only the offeror has a duty to perform. The offeror is the only party who has made a promise and therefore has a duty upon contract formation. Only the offeror could be the breaching party (see Exhibit 2–6).

Most offers are for bilateral contracts. "I promise to work for you for one year for your promise to pay me $1000 a week." "I promise to paint your house for your promise to pay me $1,500." "I promise to build you a house for your promise to pay me $225,000." "I promise to sell you my yacht for your promise to pay me $25,000."

Most people do not speak or write in the formal "I promise for your promise." Usually, the offer takes the form "I'll sell you my car for $5,000." "I'll sell" translates to "I promise to sell," and "for $5,000" translates to "for your promise to pay $5,000." Because the formal designation provides clarity in legal analysis, common usage will be upgraded for our purposes to the formal "I promise."

Only in an unusual transaction, often in a family, friend, or reward setting or in a situation where the likelihood of success is uncertain, will an offeror make an offer for a unilateral contract. "I promise to give you Blackacre if you care for me for the remainder of my life." "I promise to pay you $10,000 if you provide information leading to the conviction of Scarface Jones, a known criminal." "I promise to pay you $100 if you win the race tomorrow." "I promise to give you a half-interest in Greenacre if you discover gold." In each of these offers, the offeree cannot accept by promising but must fully perform what the offeror has requested—"caring for the offeror for the remainder of the offeror's life," "providing information leading to the conviction of Scarface Jones," "winning the race," and "discovering gold."

Had the offeror created an offer for a bilateral contract, the offeree could accept by making the promise. "I promise to give you Blackacre if you promise to care for me for the remainder of my life." "I promise to pay you $10,000 if you promise to provide information leading to the conviction of Scarface Jones." "I promise to pay you $100 if you promise to win the race tomorrow." "I promise to give you a half-interest in Greenacre if you promise to discover gold." Note that in each of these offers, the offeree cannot accept by performing but must expressly promise to do or not to do what the offeror has requested—"a promise to care for the offeror for the remainder of the offeror's life," "a promise to provide information leading to the conviction of Scarface Jones," "a promise to win the race," and "a promise to discover gold." (Whether a promise can be implied from performance is a question that will be discussed later in this text.) As a rule, an offer will be presumed to be an offer for a bilateral contract unless the offeror clearly articulates that it is the offeree's performance and not the offeree's promise that is the consideration for the promisor's promise.

What the offeror is asking for in return for his or her promise is known as "the consideration for the promisor's promise." "Consideration for the promisor's promise" is the price the promisor is charging the promisee for his or her promise. If the offer were for a unilateral contract, the consideration for the promisor's promise would be "caring for the offeror for the remainder of the offeror's life," "providing information leading to the conviction of Scarface Jones," "winning the race," or "discovering gold." If the offer were for a bilateral contract, the consideration for the promisor's promise would be "a promise to care for the offeror for the remainder of the offeror's life," "a promise to provide information leading to the conviction of Scarface Jones," "a promise to win the race," or "a promise to discover gold."

The consideration in the offer must be *for* the promisor's promise. The promisor's promise and the consideration for the promisor's promise are tied together. The promisor is making his or her promise to get the promisee to promise, if the offer is for a bilateral contract, or to perform, if the offer is for a unilateral contract. When the offeror makes a promise for a promise or a promise for a performance, one-half of "a bargained-for exchange" is made. When the offeree responds with the promise requested by the offeror for the offeror's promise, or with the requested performance for the offeror's promise, the second half of the bargained-for exchange takes place (see Exhibit 2–7).

An Offer Begins with the Offeror's (Promisor's) Promise

An offer for a bilateral contract consists of the promisor's promise and the consideration for the promisor's promise; moreover, the

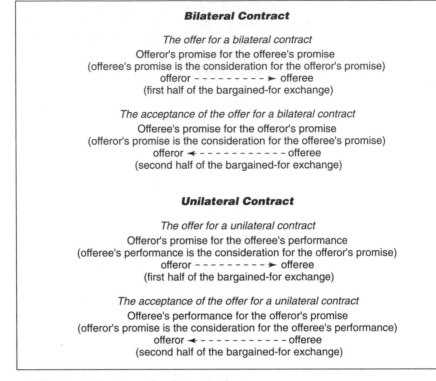

Exhibit 2–7 The Bargained-For Exchange

promisor's promise must be made to induce the promisee to promise. Consider the first element—the promisor's promise. A promise is an unequivocal assurance that something will or will not be done. Anything less, such as an inquiry, an invitation to make a promise, a "promise" that is subject to the promisor's subsequent approval, a joke, an illusory "promise," or an indefinite "promise," is not the grade of promise required for an offer.

Courts often use the phrase "offer" when the focus is on the "promisor's promise" and not on the "consideration for the promisor's promise." For example, the question is posed as "offer or **preliminary negotiation**" rather than "promisor's promise or inquiry." Without the promisor's promise there can be no offer.

Offer (Promise) or Inquiry?

An inquiry is a request for information. An party who makes an inquiry does not make an unequivocal assurance that something will or will not be done but rather seeks information upon which to determine whether to make such a promise. An inquiry may or may not be the forerunner to an offer. Inquiries are often referred to as preliminary negotiation.

Fairmount Glass Works v. Grunden-Martin Woodenware Co., although an old case, provides an excellent set of facts upon which

preliminary negotiation

Preliminary negotiations include all discussions of the parties that occur prior to the offer.

THE OFFER PHASE 57

to determine whether a communication is an offer or merely an inquiry (preliminary negotiation). The opinion begins by describing the various communications between Grunden-Martin, the potential buyer, and Fairmount Glass, the potential seller. While reading through the opinion, place each communication in chronological order. Next, begin with the first communication and determine whether it was a promise or merely preliminary negotiation. Consider the following:

Did Grunden-Martin intend to be bound by its letter if Fairmount Glass responded yes without stating any additional or different terms, or did Grunden-Martin want Fairmount Glass to make the offer (promise with consideration) so Fairmount Glass could evaluate the terms and would be the party that responded by saying yes?

If the first Grunden-Martin letter was not the offer, was Fairmount's letter in reply the offer, or was it still only preliminary negotiation?

Did Fairmount Glass intend to be bound by its letter if Grunden-Martin responded yes without stating any additional or different terms?

If the Fairmount letter was not the offer but still only preliminary negotiations, then evaluate the remaining communications, in order, until an offer has been found or all the communications have been exhausted.

In reading *Fairmount Glass,* determine whether the judge's evaluation of each communication is based on a subjective or an objective standard. Was the judge concerned with what each party thought it was saying (subjective) or how the communication would be understood by a reasonable person (objective)?

Finally, is the issue in *Fairmount Glass* one of "offer" or "promisor's promise"?

CASE

Fairmount Glass Works v. Grunden-Martin Woodenware Co.
Court of Appeals of Kentucky (1899)
106 Ky. 659, 51 S.W. 196

HOBSON, J.

On April 20, 1895, appellee wrote appellant the following letter:

"St. Louis, Mo., April 20, 1895. Gentlemen: Please advise us the lowest price you can make us on our order for ten car loads of Mason green jars, complete, with caps, packed one dozen in a case, either delivered here, or f.o.b. cars your place, as you prefer. State terms and cash discount. Very truly, Grunden-Martin W. W. Co."

To this letter appellant answered as follows:

"Fairmount, Ind., April 23, 1895. Grunden-Martin Wooden Ware Co., St. Louis, Mo.–Gentlemen: Replying to your favor of April 20, we quote you Mason fruit jars, complete, in one-dozen boxes, delivered in East St. Louis, Ill.: Pints $4.50, quarts $5.00, half gallons $6.50, per gross, for immediate acceptance, and shipment not later than May 15, 1895; sixty days' acceptance, or 2 off, cash in ten days. Yours truly, Fairmount Glass Works."

. . . .

For reply thereto, appellee sent the following telegram on April 24, 1895: "Fairmount Glass Works. Fairmount, Ind.: Your letter twenty-third received. Enter order ten car loads as per your quotation. Specifications mailed. Grunden-Martin W. W. Co."

In response to this telegram, appellant sent the following: "Fairmount, Ind., April 24, 1895. Grunden-Martin W. W. Co., St. Louis, Mo.: Impossible to book your order. Output all sold. See letter. Fairmount Glass Works."

Appellee insists that, by its telegram sent in answer to the letter of April 23d, the contract was closed for the purchase of 10 car loads of Mason fruit jars. Appellant insists that the contract was not closed by this telegram, and that it had the right to decline to fill the order at the time it sent its telegram of April 24. This is the chief question in the case. The court below gave judgment in favor of appellee, and appellant has appealed, earnestly insisting that the judgment is erroneous.

We are referred to a number of authorities holding that a quotation of prices is not an offer to sell, in the sense that a completed contract will arise out of the giving of an order for merchandise in accordance with the proposed terms. There are a number of cases holding that the transaction is not completed until the order so made is accepted. 7 Am. & Eng. Enc. Law (2d Ed.) p. 138; Smith v. Gowdy, 8 Allen, 566; Beaupre v. Telegraph Co., 21 Minn. 155. But each case must turn largely upon the language there used. In this case we think there was more than a quotation of prices, although appellant's letter uses the word "quote" in stating the prices given. The true meaning of the correspondence must be determined by reading it as a whole. Appellee's letter of April 20th, which began the transaction, did not ask for a quotation of prices. It reads: "Please advise us the lowest price you can make us on our order for ten car loads of Mason green jars. * * * State terms and cash discount." From this appellant could not fail to understand that appellee wanted to know at what price it would sell it 10 car loads of these jars; so when, in answer, it wrote: "We quote you Mason fruit jars * * * pints $4.50, quarts $5.00, half gallons $6.50, per gross, for immediate acceptance; * * * 2 off, cash in ten days,"–it must be deemed as intending to give appellee the information it had asked for. We can hardly understand what was meant by the words "for immediate acceptance," unless the latter was intended as a proposition to sell at these prices if accepted immediately. In construing every contract, the aim of the court is to arrive at the intention of the parties. In none of the cases to which we have been referred on behalf of appellant was there on the face of the correspondence any such expression of intention to make an offer to sell on the terms indicated. In Fitzhugh v. Jones, 6 Munf. 83, the use of the expression that the buyer should reply as soon as possible, in case he was disposed to accede to the terms offered, was held sufficient to show that there was a definite proposition, which was closed by the buyers acceptance. The expression in appellant's letter, "for immediate acceptance," taken in connection with appellee's letter, in effect, at what price it would sell it the goods, is, it seems to us, much stronger evidence of a present offer, which, when accepted immediately, closed the contract. Appellee's letter was plainly an inquiry for the price and terms on which appellant would sell it the goods, and appellant's answer to it was not a quotation of prices, but a definite offer to sell on the terms indicated, and could not be withdrawn after the terms had been accepted. . . .

Judgment affirmed.

Offer (Promise) or Invitation to Make an Offer (Promise)?

The issue of offer or invitation to make an offer also arises in advertisements, auctions, and what appear to be offers—except for the fact that they are subject to the "promisor's promise." An offer consists of the promisor's promise and consideration for that promise. Is the advertisment the offer that is accepted by the customer or is the customer the offeror? Is the auctioneer the offeror and the bidders the offerees or are the bidders offerors? Is a document signed by the traveling salesperson the offeror or is the customer with whom the salesperson deals the offeror? As you read the following material on advertisements, auctions, and offers subject to approval, should the question be whether an offer—or a promise—has been made? Without a promisor's promise there can be no offer.

The Advertisement   All offers discussed thus far have been directed to a specific party. Advertisements, by contrast, are made to the general public. Simply because an advertisement is directed to the general public, however, does not preclude it from being an offer. Offers need not be made to a specific party. The offer of a reward, for example, is an offer made to the general public.

The general rule followed in most states is that advertisements are not offers, but merely invitations to bargain. Exceptions to this general rule do exist.

⫿ PARALEGAL EXERCISE 2.1

Compare the following two advertisements. Are both advertisements offers, or are they simply invitations to negotiate?

Saturday 9 A.M. Sharp 3 Brand New Fur Coats Worth to $100.00 First Come First Served $1 Each

Saturday 9 A.M. 1 Black Lapin Stole Beautiful, Worth $139.50 . . . $1.00 First Come First Served

What factors did the Supreme Court of Minnesota use in *Lefkowitz v. Great Minneapolis Surplus Store, Inc.,* to determine whether these advertisements were offers or only invitations to negotiate (preliminary negotiations)? ■

CASE

Lefkowitz v. Great Minneapolis Surplus Store, Inc.
Supreme Court of Minnesota (1957)
86 N.W.2d 689

Kitchen MURPHY, Justice.

This is an appeal from an order of the Municipal Court of Minneapolis denying the motion of the defendant for amended findings of fact, or, in the alternative, for a new trial. The order for judgment awarded the plaintiff the sum of $138.50 as damages for breach of contract.

This case grows out of the alleged refusal of the defendant to sell to the plaintiff a certain fur piece which it had offered for sale in a newspaper advertisement. It appears from the record that on April 6, 1956, the defendant published the following advertisement in a Minneapolis newspaper:

> *"Saturday 9 A.M. Sharp*
> *3 Brand New Fur Coats*
> *Worth to $100.00*
> *First Come*
> *First Served*
> *$1 Each"*

On April 13, the defendant again published an advertisement in the same newspaper as follows:

> *"Saturday 9 A.M.*
> *2 Brand New Pastel*
> *Mink 3-Skin Scarfs*
> *Selling for $89.50*
> *Out They Go*
> *Saturday, Each . . . $1.00*
> *1 Black Lapin Stole*
> *Beautiful,*
> *Worth $139.50 . . . $1.00*
> *First Come*
> *First Served"*

The record supports the findings of the court that on each of the Saturdays following the publication of the above-described ads the plaintiff was the first to present himself at the appropriate counter in the defendant's store and on each occasion demanded the coat and the stole so advertised and indicated his readiness to pay the sale price of $1. On both occasions, the defendant refused to sell the merchandise to the plaintiff, stating on the first occasion that by a "house rule" the offer was intended for women only and sales would not be made to men, and on the second visit that plaintiff knew defendant's house rules.

The trial court properly disallowed plaintiff's claim for the value of the fur coats since the value of these articles was speculative and uncertain. The only evidence of value was the advertisement itself to the effect that the coats were "Worth to $100.00," how much less being speculative especially in view of the price for which they were offered for sale. With reference to the offer of the defendant on April 13, 1956 to sell the "1 Black Lapin Stole * * * worth $139.50 * * *" the trial court held that the value of this article was established and granted judgment in favor of the plaintiff for that amount less the $1 quoted purchase price.

1. The defendant contends that a newspaper advertisement offering items of merchandise for sale at a named price is a "unilateral offer" which may be withdrawn without notice. He relies upon authorities which hold that, where an advertiser publishes in a newspaper that he has a certain quantity or quality of goods which he wants to dispose of at certain prices and on certain terms, such advertisements are not offers which become contracts as soon as any person to whose notice they may come signifies his acceptance by notifying the other that he will take a certain quantity of them. Such advertisements have been construed as an invitation for an offer of sale on the terms stated, which offer, when received, may be accepted or rejected and which therefore does not become a contract of sale until accepted by the seller; and until a contract has been so made, the seller may modify or revoke such prices or terms. Montgomery Ward & Co. v. Johnson, 209 Mass. 89, 95 N.E. 290; Nickel v. Theresa Farmers Co-op. Ass'n, 247 Wis. 412, 20 N.W.2d 117; Lovett v. Frederick Loeser & Co. Inc., 124 Misc. 81, 207 N.Y.S. 753; Schenectady Stove Co. v. Holbrook, 101 N.Y. 45, 4 N.E. 4; Georgian Co. v. Bloom, 27 Ga.App. 468, 108 S.E. 813; Craft v. Elder & Johnston Co., 38 N.E.2d 416, 34 Ohio L.A. 603; Annotation, 157 A.L.R. 746.

. . . .

There are numerous authorities which hold that a particular advertisement in a newspaper or circular letter relating to a sale of articles may be construed by the court as constituting an offer, acceptance of which would complete a contract. J. E. Pinkham Lumber Co. v. C. W. Griffin & Co., 212 Ala. 341, 102 So. 689; Seymour v. Armstrong & Kassebaum, 62 Kan. 720, 64 P. 612; Payne v. Lautz Bros. & Co., City Ct., 166 N.Y.S. 844, affirmed, 168 N.Y.S. 369, affirmed, 185 App.Div. 904, 171 N.Y.S. 1094; Arnold v. Phillips, 1 Ohio Dec. Reprint 195, 3 West. Law J. 448; Oliver v. Henley, Tex.Civ.App., 21 S.W.2d 576; Annotation, 157 A.L.R. 744, 746.

The test of whether a binding obligation may originate in advertisements addressed to the general public is "whether the facts show that some performance was promised in positive terms in return for something requested." 1 Williston, Contracts (Rev. ed.) § 27.

The authorities above cited emphasize that, where the offer is clear, definite, and explicit, and leaves nothing open for negotiation, it constitutes an offer, acceptance of which will complete the contract. The most recent case on the subject is Johnson v. Capital City Ford Co., La.App., 85 So.2d 75, in which the court pointed out that a newspaper advertisement relating to the purchase and sale of automobiles may constitute an offer, acceptance of which will consummate a contract and create an obligation in the offeror to perform according to the terms of the published offer.

Whether in any individual instance a newspaper advertisement is an offer rather than an invitation to make an offer depends on the legal intention of the parties and the surrounding circumstances. Annotation, 157 A.L.R. 744, 751; 77 C.J.S., Sales, § 25b; 17 C.J.S., Contracts, § 389. We are of the view on the facts before us that the offer by the defendant of the sale of the Lapin fur was clear, definite, and explicit, and left nothing open for negotiation. The plaintiff having successfully managed to be the first one to appear at the seller's place of business to be served, as requested by the advertisement, and having offered the stated purchase price of the article, he was entitled to performance on the part of the defendant. We think the trial court was correct in holding that there was in the conduct of the parties a sufficient mutuality of obligation to constitute a contract of sale.

2. The defendant contends that the offer was modified by a "house rule" to the effect that only women were qualified to receive the bargains advertised. The advertisement contained no such restriction. This objection may be disposed of briefly by stating that, while an advertiser has the right at any time before acceptance to modify his offer, he does not have the right, after acceptance, to impose new or arbitrary conditions not contained in the published offer. Payne v. Lautz Bros. & Co., City Ct., 166 N.Y.S. 844, 848; Mooney v. Daily News Co., 116 Minn. 212, 133 N.W. 573, 37 L.R.A., N.S., 183.

Affirmed.

▥ PARALEGAL EXERCISE 2.2

Find three different types of advertisements in your local newspaper, and determine whether each is an offer or only an invitation to negotiate (preliminary negotiation). ▪

The Auction   An auction may be either "with reserve" or "without reserve." Whether the auction is with or without reserve is the key to whether the auctioneer (acting as agent for the seller) or the bidder is the offeror.

In an **auction with reserve**, the auctioneer may withdraw the property at any time until he or she announces the completion of the sale. Therefore, the auctioneer, rather than being the offeror, is asking potential bidders to make an offer. The auctioneer evaluates the bidder's offer and either accepts it by the fall of the hammer or in another customary manner (thus concluding the sale) or rejects it by withdrawing the property from the auction. Since the seller may withdraw the property from the auction, the seller may also bid.

auction with reserve

In an auction with reserve, the auctioneer may withdraw the property at any time until he or she announces the completion of the sale. The potential bidders are the offerors.

Example 2-1

In an auction with reserve on Greenacre, the auctioneer asked whether anyone would open the bid at $200,000. The bidding, however, began at $10,000 and ended at $100,000. The auctioneer could reject the $100,000 bid and withdraw Greenacre from the auction or bring the hammer down and accept the bid.

Since the auction was with reserve, the bidders were the offerors and the auctioneer, as offeree, had the power to either accept or reject the highest offer.

In an **auction without reserve** (an absolute auction), the auctioneer is the offeror and the bidders are the offerees. After the auctioneer calls for bids on the property, the auctioneer cannot withdraw the property if a bid is made within a reasonable time. Each bid is an acceptance conditioned on there being no higher bidder. Therefore, the auctioneer must sell to the highest bid. Since the auctioneer (acting for the seller) is the offeror, the seller cannot bid.

auction without reserve

In an auction without reserve, the auctioneer is the offeror and the bidders are the offerees.

Example 2-2

In an auction without reserve on Greenacre, the auctioneer asked whether anyone would open the bid at $200,000. The bidding, however, began at $10,000 and ended at $100,000. The auctioneer could not reject the $100,000 bid and withdraw Greenacre from the auction, but had to bring the hammer down and conclude the sale.

Since the auction was without reserve, the auctioneer was the offeror and each bidder exercised the power to accept the auctioneer's offer to sell.

An auction is with reserve unless a contrary intention is apparent from a statute, court order, or advertisement or by an announcement at the beginning of the auction. A statement in an advertisement, however, "that the property will be offered to the highest bidder" does not mean that the auction will be conducted without reserve. Such a statement is considered only preliminary negotiation.

▥ PARALEGAL EXERCISE 2.3

Sam Brown, the auctioneer, presented a Louis XV ormolu clock to the potential bidders at the auction. Susan Sanchez, the owner of the valuable antique clock, had told Sam not to sell it for less than $5,000. In spite of Sam's best efforts, the highest bid was $2,500.

Could Sam withdraw the clock from the auction? ▪

At times in an auction with reserve, the seller does not give the auctioneer authority to conclude the sale. Rather, the seller reserves the power to accept or reject the highest bid (i.e., the bidder's offer). In *Cuba v. Hudson & Marshall,* consider whether the auction is with or without reserve. If the auction is with reserve, does the auctioneer or the seller have the power to accept the bidder's offer? What facts did you consider when making this decision?

CASE

Cuba v. Hudson & Marshall
Court of Appeals of Georgia (1994)
213 Ga. App. 639, 445 S.E.2d 386

POPE, Chief Judge,

Defendants are auctioneers who conducted an auction of real estate for the Resolution Trust Corporation ("RTC"). Plaintiffs attended the auction and were the high bidder for a particular parcel, Property No. 230. After the bidding was ended by the fall of the auctioneer's hammer, however, plaintiffs were told that the RTC rejected their bid. Plaintiffs sued defendants for damages, and after discovery, plaintiffs and defendants filed crossmotions for summary judgment. The trial court denied plaintiffs' motion and granted defendants', and plaintiffs appeal from both rulings.

The parties essentially agree on the facts. Defendants prepared an auction brochure listing and describing the various RTC properties to be auctioned. Some of the properties were listed with the word "absolute" next to them; others, including Property No. 230, were not. On the back cover, under the heading "AUCTION INFORMATION & TERMS," the brochure stated that properties without "absolute" next to them were being sold with reserve, and that "[f]or property being sold 'With Reserve,' the highest bid is subject to the approval of the seller." (Emphasis supplied.) Defendant Asa Marshall, who conducted the actual auction, stated in his introductory remarks that with respect to those properties being auctioned with reserve, "I can assure you you're not wasting your time. We have officials from RTC all over the country here. The only thing they want to make sure of is that they do have active bidding on those properties auctioned on reserve, and if they do they are going to sell them. I can assure you of that. They are not here to waste your time or to get this property appraised." Immediately following Asa Marshall's introductory remarks, however, another employee of defendant Hudson & Marshall, Inc. got up and pointed out to the audience that the terms of the auction were set forth on the back cover of the brochure. He held up a brochure and showed the audience exactly where the terms and conditions were and then said they would abide by those terms.

1. Plaintiffs first argue that a contract for the sale of Property No. 230 was formed at the time the auctioneer's hammer fell, and that defendant auctioneers are liable for the breach of that contract. As a general rule, even if an auction is with reserve (and all auctions are presumed to be with reserve unless they are expressly stated to be without reserve), the seller must exercise his right to withdraw the property from sale before the auctioneer accepts the high bid by letting his hammer fall; immediately after the hammer falls, an irrevocable contract is formed. See Stanley v. Whitmire, 233 Ga. 675, 212 S.E.2d 845 (1975); Tillman v. Dunman, 114 Ga. 406, 409(1), 40 S.E. 244 (1901); Coleman v. Duncan, 540 S.W.2d 935, 937-938 (Mo.Ct.App. 1976). Compare also OCGA § 11-2-328.[1] Yet at the same time, the seller has the right to establish any terms and conditions for the sale he wishes, and where the seller explicitly reserves the right to reject any bid made, the contract for sale is not formed until the seller actually accepts the bid. Rountree v. Todd, 210 Ga. 226, 78 S.E.2d 499 (1953). We think the only way to reconcile these cases is to recognize, as other courts have, that there is a distinction between auctions which are merely conducted with reserve and those

in which the seller explicitly reserves the right to approve, confirm, or reject the high bid. Coleman, 540 S.W.2d at 938. ("[S]uch a reservation sets a sale apart from the garden variety of auctions with reserve.") See also Continental Can Co. v. Commercial Waterway Dist., 56 Wash.2d 456, 347 P.2d 887 (1959); Moore v. Berry, 40 Tenn.App. 1, 288 S.W.2d 465 (1955); New York v. Union News Co., 222 N.Y. 263, 118 N.E. 635 (1917). Where the seller explicitly reserves the right to reject or approve, the auctioneer is without authority to accept for the seller. Thus, the fall of the hammer in such auctions merely ends the bidding, and no contract is formed until the seller actually accepts the high bid. See Continental Can, 347 P.2d at 888–889; Moore, 288 S.W.2d at 467–468; Union News, 118 N.E. at 636–637.

The seller in this case explicitly reserved the right to reject or approve the high bid in the brochure. And Asa Marshall's "assurance" that all properties would be sold as long as the bidding was active did not modify this reservation since it was immediately followed by the announcement of another speaker who called the bidders' attention to the terms in the brochure and stated that "we will abide by those terms." Accordingly, the fall of the auctioneer's hammer merely ended the bidding and no enforceable contract was formed.

. . . .

Judgment affirmed.
McMURRAY, P.J., and SMITH, J., concur.

---

1. This statute is part of our codification of Article 2 of the Uniform Commercial Code and thus does not directly apply to auctions of real property.

See OCGA § 11-2–102. Courts in other states have recognized that this portion of the Article reflects common law principles applicable to land auctions as well as auctions of goods, however, and have borrowed rules from it or applied it to land auctions by analogy. See, e.g., Chevalier v. Sanford, 475 A.2d 1148 (Me. 1984); Hoffman v. Horton, 212 Va. 565, 186 S.E.2d 79 (1972).

"Offer (Promise)" or "Offer (Promise)" Subject to the Promisor's Subsequent Approval   The timing of the offer also comes into question when what purports to be an offer contains a "subject to approval" clause. At times, a party may not want to give the other party the power to accept and thereby form a contract. Rather, that party may want the other to be the offeror and by doing so receive the power to accept and form a contract.

These situations arise, for example, when a merchant does not directly deal with a potential customer but rather employs an agent. The merchant provides the agent with a form that appears to be an offer—except that the writing provides that the offer is subject to the approval of the merchant. Neither the merchant nor the agent is the offeror. Rather, the customer becomes the offeror—although the customer makes the offer in the terms on the form and in the terms provided by the merchant. The agent returns the form to the merchant who determines whether to accept the customer's offer. By including the "subject to approval" clause, the merchant is able to control the agent so the agent does not deviate from the merchant's terms.

Example 2-3

The ABC Roofing Company has a number of salespeople working door-to-door selling ABC roofs. The company has provided each salesperson with a preprinted form. When the salesperson finds a homeowner who wants to buy an ABC roof, the salesperson completes the form and has the homeowner sign.

The ABC Roofing Company does not want its salespeople to change any of the terms in the form and therefore has included in the form the phrase "this offer is subject to the approval of the President of ABC Roofing Company." By including the "subject to approval" provision, the homeowner makes the promise (and since the promise is with consideration, the homeowner becomes the offeror).

When Is an Offer (Promise) Really an Offer (Promise)?

The previous section discussed the question of the timing of an offer. An offer was forthcoming—but when? Was the offer the first, second, or third communication? Generally, a contract was ultimately formed. The question is when was the offer made—and therefore who was the offeror?

The focus in this section is quite different. The question is not when an offer comes into existence but whether an offer exists at all. Three situations are explored in this section: the offer (promise) or the joke, the promise or the illusory promise, and the promise or the indefinite promise.

A **promise** is an unequivocal assurance that something will or will not be done. "I may sell my car to you" is not unequivocal and therefore is less than a promise. On the other hand, "I will sell you my car" is an unequivocal assurance and is a promise. The unequivocal assurance could be to refrain from doing something as well as to do something. Thus, "I will not sell my car to Marylou" is as much a promise as "I will sell my car to Marylou."

Offer (Promise) or Joke?   What people say and what they actually mean may be entirely different. The outward expression (objective) rather than the secret or unexpressed intent (subjective) determines whether a statement is intended as an offer. Thus, the objective intent rather than the subjective intent determines whether an offer has been extended.

A graphic illustration of this principle is the joke. In *Lucy v. Zehmer*, A. H. and Ida Zehmer, owners of the Ferguson farm, operated a local restaurant. One evening their old friend W. O. Lucy met

promise

A promise is a manifestation of intention to act or refrain from acting in a specified way, which justifies a promisee's understanding that the promisor has made a commitment. A promise is an unequivocal assurance that something will or will not be done.

them at the restaurant, and after a few drinks and a lot of talk, the Zehmers signed a writing that said that they promised to sell W. O. Lucy the Ferguson farm for $50,000 cash.

Consider the following questions when reading the case. As each question is answered, complete the two charts below.

1. Did A. H. Zehmer believe that his writing was an offer or a joke?
2. Did W. O. Lucy believe that Zehmer's writing was an offer or a joke?
3. Would a reasonable person, viewing the events at the restaurant, believe that the writing was an offer or a joke?
4. Did the court use an objective or subjective standard to resolve whether Zehmer's writing was an offer or a joke?
5. What facts were useful in reaching your conclusions?

The Facts: Zehmer's Writing	
Zehmer's perception of his writing	offer or joke?
Lucy's perception of Zehmer's writing	offer or joke?
Conclusion	offer or joke?

The Facts: Zehmer's Writing	
Zehmer's perception of his writing	offer or joke?
Lucy's perception of Zehmer's writing	offer or joke?
Reasonable Person's perception of Zehmer's writing	offer or joke?
Conclusion	offer or joke?

CASE

Lucy v. Zehmer
Supreme Court of Appeals of Virginia (1954)
196 Va. 493, 84 S.E.2d 516

Before EGGLESTON, BUCHANAN, MILLER, SMITH and WHITTLE, JJ.
BUCHANAN, Justice.

This suit was instituted by W. O. Lucy and J. C. Lucy, complainants, against A. H. Zehmer and Ida S. Zehmer, his wife, defendants, to have specific performance of a contract by which it was alleged the Zehmers had sold to W. O. Lucy a tract of land owned by A. H. Zehmer in Dinwiddie county containing 471.6 acres, more or less, known as the Ferguson farm, for $50,000. J. C. Lucy, the other complainant, is a brother of W. O. Lucy, to whom W. O. Lucy transferred a half interest in his alleged purchase.

The instrument sought to be enforced was written by A. H. Zehmer on December 20, 1952, in these words: "We hereby agree to sell to W. O. Lucy the Ferguson Farm complete for $50,000.00, title satisfactory to buyer," and signed by the defendants, A. H. Zehmer and Ida S. Zehmer.

The answer of A. H. Zehmer admitted that at the time mentioned W. O. Lucy offered him $50,000 cash for the farm, but that he, Zehmer, considered that the offer was made in jest.

. . . .

Depositions were taken and the decree appealed from was entered holding that the complainants had failed to establish their right to specific performance, and dismissing their bill. The assignment of error is to this action of the court.

W. O. Lucy, a lumberman and farmer, thus testified in substance: He had known Zehmer for fifteen or twenty years and had been familiar with the Ferguson farm for ten years. Seven or eight years ago he had offered Zehmer $20,000 for the farm which Zehmer had accepted, but the agreement was verbal and Zehmer backed out. On the night of December 20, 1952, around eight o'clock, he took an employee to McKenney, where Zehmer lived and operated a restaurant, filling station and motor court. While there he decided to see Zehmer and again try to buy the Ferguson farm. He entered the restaurant and talked to Mrs. Zehmer until Zehmer came in. He asked Zehmer if he had sold the Ferguson farm. Zehmer replied that he had not. Lucy said, "I bet you wouldn't take $50,000.00 for that place." Zehmer replied, "Yes, I would too; you wouldn't give fifty." Lucy said he would and told Zehmer to write up an agreement to that effect. Zehmer took a restaurant check and wrote on the back of it, "I do hereby agree to sell to W. O. Lucy the Ferguson Farm for $50,000 complete." Lucy told him he had better change it to "We" because Mrs. Zehmer would have to sign it too. Zehmer then tore up what he had written, wrote the agreement quoted above and asked Mrs. Zehmer, who was at the other end of the counter ten or twelve feet away, to sign it. Mrs. Zehmer said she would for $50,000 and signed it. Zehmer brought it back and gave it to Lucy, who offered him $5 which Zehmer refused, saying, "You don't need to give me any money, you got the agreement there signed by both of us."

The discussion leading to the signing of the agreement, said Lucy, lasted thirty or forty minutes, during which Zehmer seemed to doubt that Lucy could raise $50,000. Lucy suggested the provision for having the title examined and Zehmer made the suggestion that he would sell it "complete, everything there," and stated that all he had on the farm was three heifers.

Lucy took a partly filled bottle of whiskey into the restaurant with him for the purpose of giving Zehmer a drink if he wanted it. Zehmer did, and he and Lucy had one or two drinks together. Lucy said that while he felt the drinks he took he was not intoxicated, and from the way Zehmer handled the transaction he did not think he was either.

December 20 was on Saturday. Next day Lucy telephoned to J. C. Lucy and arranged with the latter to take a half interest in the purchase and pay half of the consideration. On Monday he engaged an attorney to examine the title. The attorney reported favorably on December 31 and on January 2 Lucy wrote Zehmer stating that the title was satisfactory, that he was ready to pay the purchase price in cash and asking when Zehmer would be ready to close the deal. Zehmer replied by letter, mailed on January 13, asserting that he had never agreed or intended to sell.

Mr. and Mrs. Zehmer were called by the complainants as adverse witnesses. Zehmer testified in substance as follows:

He bought this farm more than ten years ago for $11,000. He had had twenty-five offers, more or less, to buy it, including several from Lucy, who had never offered any specific sum of money. He had given them all the same answer, that he was not interested in selling it. On this Saturday night before Christmas it looked like everybody and his brother came by there to have a drink. He took a good many drinks during the afternoon and had a pint of his own. When he entered the restaurant around 8:30, Lucy was there and he could see that he was "pretty high." He said to Lucy, "Boy, you got some good liquor, drinking, ain't you?" Lucy then offered him a drink. "I was already high as a Georgia pine, and didn't have any more better sense than to pour another great big slug out and gulp it down, and he took one too."

After they had talked a while Lucy asked whether he still had the Ferguson farm. He replied that he had not sold it and Lucy said, "I bet you wouldn't take $50,000.00 for it." Zehmer asked him if he would give $50,000 and Lucy said yes. Zehmer replied, "You haven't got $50,000.00 in cash." Lucy said he did and Zehmer replied that he did not believe it. They argued "pro and con for a long time," mainly about "whether he had $50,000 in cash that he could put up right then and buy that farm."

Finally, said Zehmer, Lucy told him if he didn't believe he had $50,000, "you sign that piece of paper here and say you will take $50,000.00 for the farm." He, Zehmer, "just grabbed the back off of a guest check there" and wrote on the back of it. At that point in his testimony Zehmer asked to see what he had written to "see if I recognize my own handwriting." He examined the paper and exclaimed, "Great balls of fire, I got 'Firgerson' for Ferguson. I have got satisfactory spelled wrong. I don't recognize that writing if I would see it, wouldn't know it was mine."

After Zehmer had, as he described it, "scribbled this thing off," Lucy said, "Get your wife to sign it." Zehmer walked over to where she was and she at first refused to sign but did so after he told her that he "was just needling him [Lucy], and didn't mean a thing in the world, that I was not selling the farm." Zehmer then "took it back over there * * * and I was still looking at the dern thing. I had the drink right there by my hand, and I reached over to get a drink, and he said, 'Let me see it.' He reached and picked it up, and when I looked back again he had it in his pocket and he dropped a five dollar bill over there, and he said, 'Here is five dollars payment on it.' * * * I said, 'Hell no, that is beer and liquor talking. I am not going to sell you the farm. I have told you that too many times before.' "

Mrs. Zehmer testified that when Lucy came into the restaurant he looked as if he had had a drink. When Zehmer came in he took a drink out of a bottle that Lucy handed him. She went back to help the waitress who was getting things ready for next day. Lucy and Zehmer were talking but she did not pay too much attention to what they were saying. She heard Lucy ask Zehmer if he had sold the Ferguson farm, and Zehmer replied that he had not and did not want to sell it. Lucy said, "I bet you wouldn't take $50,000.00 cash for that farm," and Zehmer replied, "You haven't got $50,000 cash." Lucy said, "I can get it." Zehmer said he might form a company and get it, "but you haven't got $50,000.00 cash to pay me tonight." Lucy asked him if he would put it in writing that he would sell him this farm. Zehmer then wrote on the back of a pad, "I agree to sell the Ferguson Place to W. O. Lucy for $50,000.00 cash." Lucy said, "All right, get your wife to sign it." Zehmer came back to where she was standing and said, "You want to put your name to this?" She said "No," but he said in an undertone, "It is nothing but a joke," and she signed it.

She said that only one paper was written and it said: "I hereby agree to sell," but the "I" had been changed to "We". However, she said she read what she signed and was then asked, "When you read 'We hereby agree to sell to W. O. Lucy,' what did you interpret that to mean, that particular phrase?" She said she thought that was a cash sale that night; but she also said that when she read that part about "title satisfactory to buyer" she understood that if the title was good Lucy would pay $50,000, but if the title was bad he would have a right to reject it, and that that was her understanding at the time she signed her name.

On examination by her own counsel she said that her husband laid this piece of paper down after it was signed; that Lucy said to let him see it, took it, folded it and put it in his wallet, then said to Zehmer, "Let me give you $5.00," but Zehmer said, "No, this is liquor talking. I don't want to sell the farm, I have told you that I want my son to have it. This is all a joke." Lucy then said at least twice, "Zehmer, you have sold your farm," wheeled around and started for the door. He paused at the door and said, "I will bring you $50,000.00 tomorrow. * * * No, tomorrow is Sunday. I will bring it to you Monday." She said you could tell definitely that he was drinking and she said to her husband, "You should have taken him home," but he said, "Well, I am just about as bad off as he is."

. . . .

If it be assumed, contrary to what we think the evidence shows, that Zehmer was jesting about selling his farm to Lucy and that the transaction was intended by him to be a joke, nevertheless the evidence shows that Lucy did not so understand it but considered it to be a serious business transaction and the contract to be binding on the Zehmers as well as on himself.

Not only did Lucy actually believe, but the evidence shows he was warranted in believing, that the contract represented a serious business transaction and a good faith sale and purchase of the farm.

In the field of contracts, as generally elsewhere, "We must look to the outward expression of a person as manifesting his intention rather than to his secret and unexpressed intention. 'The law imputes to a person an intention corresponding to the reasonable meaning of his words and acts.'" First Nat. Exchange Bank of Roanoke v. Roanoke Oil Co., 169 Va. 99, 114, 192 S.E. 764, 770.

At no time prior to the execution of the contract had Zehmer indicated to Lucy by word or act that he was not in earnest about selling the farm. They had argued about it and discussed its terms, as Zehmer admitted, for a long time. Lucy testified that if there was any jesting it was about paying $50,000 that night. The contract and the evidence show that he was not expected to pay the money that night. Zehmer said that after the writing was signed he laid it down on the counter in front of Lucy. Lucy said Zehmer handed it to him. In any event there had been what appeared to be a good faith offer and a good faith acceptance, followed by the execution and apparent delivery of a written contract. Both said that Lucy put the writing in his pocket and then offered Zehmer $5 to seal the bargain. Not until then, even under the defendants' evidence, was anything said or done to indicate that the matter was a joke. Both of the Zehmers testified that when Zehmer asked his wife to sign he whispered that it was a joke so Lucy wouldn't hear and that it was not intended that he should hear.

The mental assent of the parties is not requisite for the formation of a contract. If the words or other acts of one of the parties have but one reasonable meaning, his undisclosed intention is immaterial except when an unreasonable meaning which he attaches to his manifestations is known to the other party.

. . . .

An agreement or mutual assent is of course essential to a valid contract but the law imputes to a person an intention corresponding to the reasonable meaning of his words and acts. If his words and acts, judged by a reasonable standard, manifest an intention to agree, it is immaterial what may be the real but unexpressed state of his mind. 17 C.J.S., Contracts, § 32, p. 361; 12 Am. Jur., Contracts, § 19, p. 515.

So a person cannot set up that he was merely jesting when his conduct and words would warrant a reasonable person in believing that he intended a real agreement. 17 C.J.S., Contracts, § 47, p. 390; Clark on Contracts, 4 ed., § 27, at p. 54.

Whether the writing signed by the defendants and now sought to be enforced by the complainants was the result of a serious offer by Lucy and a serious acceptance by the defendants, or was a serious offer by Lucy and an acceptance in secret jest by the defendants, in either event it constituted a binding contract of sale between the parties.

. . . .

The complainants are entitled to have specific performance of the contract sued on. The decree appealed from is therefore reversed and the cause is remanded for the entry of a proper decree requiring the defendants to perform the contract in accordance with the prayer of the bill.

Reversed and remanded.

Promise or Illusory Promise? The phrase **"illusory promise"** is a misnomer because an illusory promise is not a promise. It is less than a promise and does not create the power in the offeree to accept an offer. An illusory promise is not an unequivocal assurance that something will or will not be done.

illusory promise
An illusory promise is a statement that is less than a commitment to do or refrain from doing something. Therefore, an illusory promise is a misnomer because it is not a promise.

Example 2–4

"I may sell you my car" is an illusory promise. It is not the unequivocal statement "I will sell you my car." The same is true for the statement "I will work for you next Monday if I feel like it." There is no commitment to do or to refrain from doing something.

⫶ PARALEGAL EXERCISE 2.4

Is the term in the writing in *Rosenberg v. Lawrence* a promise or an illusory promise? What specific language is used by the court to distinguish a promise from an illusory promise? ▪

CASE

Rosenberg v. Lawrence
District Court of Appeal of Florida (1988)
541 So.2d 1204

Before NESBITT, DANIEL S. PEARSON, and JORGENSON, JJ.

ON MOTION FOR CLARIFICATION AND REHEARING

NESBITT, Judge.

We grant the appellant's motion for clarification and deny the appellee's motion for rehearing; vacate our previous opinion and replace it with the following:

Charles and Cynthia divorced in 1976 and in 1978 entered into an agreement to provide for the support of their sons. In pertinent part, the agreement provided:

> The parties are equally desirous of providing for the health, education, maintenance and support of their four sons, notwithstanding that three of their sons have reached majority. To that end, each of Charles and Cynthia, promises the other, and each of the children, to share on an equal basis, the expenses of educating, maintaining, supporting and providing health care for each of their four children. In an effort to encourage consistent attitudes toward their children, the parties shall encourage the love and affection of the children for each other and shall consult one another before incurring a material expense which would be governed hereby.

Various disputes arose under this agreement. During earlier litigation, the parties entered into a modification of the agreement, which was incorporated into an amended final judgment entered on June 3, 1982, which provides in part:

> This will confirm the understanding of both parties and their counsel that paragraph 8 of the Final Judgment, as it relates to Howard's conferring with both Plaintiff and Defendant before incurring, material, unusual or extraordinary expenses, means that neither Plaintiff nor Defendant will be obligated for any material, unusual or extraordinary expense to which he or she does not consent.

When the 1982 agreement was made, son Howard was enrolled in college. Subsequently, he withdrew from school, returned to Miami and began working. In September 1984, he commenced his college career anew at a different university. Without previous consultation, negotiation, or any consent from the father, Howard's mother paid all of his expenses in connection with his education, boarding, lodging, and maintenance from September 1984 through November 17, 1985, exclusive of a summer term, in an aggregate amount of $43,616.38. Thereafter, the mother demanded that the father reimburse her for one-half of those expenses. The father's defense to payment was that he had never been consulted, nor had he consented to the educational plan or any of the expenses. The trial court entered the money judgment against the father from which he appeals.

· · · ·

Under the initial contract, the parties exchanged mutual promises to each defray one-half of son Howard's college education. The specific details of payment were to be implemented by [reasonable] negotiation. The 1982 amendment attempted to change the method by which the son was to obtain needed funds. Our initial opinion held that the failure of Cynthia to negotiate the plan and costs with Charles rendered the contract unenforceable. Charles's motion for clarification represented that the duty of consultation and negotiation was removed from the original agreement in order to avoid further acrimony between the parties. Cynthia conceded this point in her motion for rehearing. Due to the language employed and the parties' own interpretation of the agreement, we agree that the 1982 amendment terminated the duty of negotiation between the ex-spouses.

Where one party retains to itself the option of fulfilling or declining to fulfill its obligations under the contract, there is no valid contract and neither side may be bound. Miami Coca-Cola Bottling Co. v. Orange-Crush Co., 291 F. 102 (D.C.Fla. 1923), aff'd, 296 F. 693 (5th Cir. 1924). "One who in words promises to render a future performance, if he so wills and desires when the future time arrives, has made no real promise at all." 1 Corbin on Contracts § 149 (1963). See also Port Largo Club, Inc. v. Warren, 476 So.2d 1330 (Fla. 3d DCA 1985) (vendor's contract obligation wholly illusory where he could breach contract with impunity); Young v. Johnston, 475 So.2d 1309 (Fla. 1st DCA 1985) and cases cited therein (where one party retains to itself the option of fulfilling or declining to fulfill its obligations under the contract, there is no valid contract and neither side may be bound); Spooner v. Reserve Life Ins. Co., 47 Wash.2d 454, 287 P.2d 735 (1955) (statement by insurance company that sales bonus was voluntary and could be withheld with or without notice rendered promise illusory and unenforceable). "An illusory promise is no promise at all as that term has been . . . defined. If the expression appears to have the form of a promise, this appearance is 'an illusion.' " 1 Corbin on Contracts § 16 (1963). "As a matter of course, no action will lie against the party making the illusory promise. Having made no promise, it is not possible for him to be guilty of a breach." 1 Corbin on Contracts § 145 (1963).

Under the 1982 modification, the parties were not "obligated for any material, unusual or extraordinary expense to which he or she does not consent." Because payment was contingent upon each parent's consent to undertake an obligation, Charles and Cynthia's "promise" represented no more than an illusion which did not obligate either party to act. The illusory nature of each parent's promise made that promise void and the mother has no right to seek reimbursement based on that illusory commitment, either by way of direct action for breach or under an estoppel theory. See 1A Corbin on Contracts § 201 (1963) (action in reliance on a supposed promise creates no obligation on a man whose only promise is wholly illusory). Their "obligation" meant nothing more than, "I will if I want to."

. . . .

For the foregoing reasons, the trial court's order finding the father responsible for one-half of the son's expenditures is reversed and the cause remanded with directions for the mother to receive payment for the outstanding allowance funds only.

NESBITT and JORGENSON, JJ., concur.

DANIEL S. PEARSON, J., concurs in the result only.

Promise or Indefinite Promise? The phrase "indefinite promise" is also a misnomer because an indefinite promise is not a promise. An **indefinite promise** omits terms essential for enabling the court to determine an appropriate remedy in the event that the promise is breached.

Example 2–5

Seller says "I promise to sell you a cow for your promise to pay $750." When Seller owns a Holstein herd and does not designate a specific animal, Seller has made an indefinite promise. The animals vary in value; some are worth substantially more than $750 and some substantially less. If Seller does not deliver a cow, how will the court determine the appropriate remedy for Seller's refusal to deliver? Even if Seller does deliver a cow but Buyer complains that this was not the cow she wanted, how will the court determine whether the promise to deliver has been breached and, if breached, the appropriate remedy?

ⅲ PARALEGAL EXERCISE 2.5

What makes the following promise indefinite? "I promise to pay you if you promise to work for me." ▪

If the transaction involves a sale of goods, Article 2 of the Uniform Commercial Code governs. Section 2–204(3) provides the following statement as to indefiniteness:

> (3) Even though one or more terms are left open a contract for sale does not fail for indefiniteness if the parties have intended to make a contract and there is a reasonably certain basis for giving an appropriate remedy.

Under section 2–204(3), the parties must "[intend] to make a contract." If the parties do not intend to make a contract, there is no contract. Also there must be "a reasonably certain basis for giving an appropriate remedy." Without a reasonably certain basis for giving an appropriate remedy, there is no contract. If the parties have intended to make a contract but have failed to supply key terms, Article 2 may supply these terms. **Gap fillers** are those terms supplied by Article 2 of the UCC that supplement the terms supplied by the contracting parties. The gap fillers are generally found in Part 3 (2–300s) of Article 2 of the UCC. The gap fillers include provisions as to price (§ 2–305), place of delivery (§ 2–308), time for shipment or delivery (§ 2–309), payment or running of credit (§ 2–310), warranty of title (§ 2–312), warranty against infringement (§ 2–312), implied warranty of merchantability (§§ 2–314(1), (2)), implied warranty of usage of trade (§ 2–314(3)), and implied warranty of fitness for a particular purpose (§ 2–315).

Example 2-6

Uniform Commercial Code § 2–305. Open Price Term.

(1) The parties if they so intend can conclude a contract for sale even though the price is not settled. In such a case the price is a reasonable price at the time for delivery if
   (a) nothing is said as to price; or
   (b) the price is left to be agreed by the parties and they fail to agree; or
   (c) the price is to be fixed in terms of some agreed market or other standard as set or recorded by a third person or agency and it is not so set or recorded.

PARALEGAL EXERCISE 2.6

Apex Oil Co., a manufacturer and seller of petroleum products, including asphalt used in paving, and Mathy Construction Co., a road builder, discussed by telephone the possibility of Mathy purchasing 30,000 barrels of asphalt, to be picked up at Apex's Wood River, Illinois, plant for shipment up the Mississippi River to La Crosse, Wisconsin, during the week of July 30th. Apex and Mathy agreed on a price of $75 a ton and Apex assured Mathy that 30,000 barrels could be available. At this time, Mathy was uncertain whether it needed 120–150 pen-grade product or 85–100 pen-grade product. The parties did not reach an agreement as to the type and grade of asphalt and whether any agreement was contingent on the availability of barge transportation to move the barrels from Wood River to La Crosse. Mathy could not secure a barge and did not pick up the asphalt. If Apex sues Mathy alleging breach of contract, consider the following:

1. Does Article 2 of the UCC govern this transaction (i.e., is this a contract for the sale of goods under § 2–102)?
2. Were one or more terms left open?
3. Did the parties intend to make a contract?
4. Could a court find a reasonably certain basis for giving an appropriate remedy?
   a. Are these terms essential for enabling the court to determine an appropriate remedy in the event the promise is breached?
   b. Are any of these open terms supplied in the gap fillers of Part 3 of Article 2 (the 2–300s)?

Consideration for the Offeror's (Promisor's) Promise

The second element of an offer is the **consideration for the promisor's promise**. In the offer "I promise to sell you my car for your promise to pay me $5,000," the phrase "I promise to sell you my car" is the promisor's promise and "your promise to pay me $5,000" is the consideration for the promisor's promise.

Consideration is the "price" that the offeror demands for his or her promise. "Price" has been placed in quotation marks to emphasize that the term "price" is not limited to dollars and cents. It can be anything that the law recognizes as consideration. It could be a promise to barter. "I promise to sell you my car for your promise to roof my house." The consideration for the offeror's promise can easily be found by asking "what is the price for the offeror's promise"? In this example, the "price" for the offeror's promise to sell the car is the offeree's return promise to roof the offeror's house.

Every contract has two considerations. If the contract is bilateral, the first consideration is the "price" in the offer for the offeror's promise, and the second consideration is the "price" in the acceptance for the offeree's promise.

Offer: "I promise to sell you my car for your promise to pay me $5,000."
Offeror's promise: "I promise to sell you my car."
Consideration for the offeror's promise: "Your promise to pay me $5,000."

Acceptance of the offer: "I promise to pay you $5,000 for your promise to sell me your car."
Offeree's promise: "I promise to pay you $5,000."
Consideration for the offeree's promise: "Your promise to sell me your car."

If the contract is unilateral, the first consideration is the "price" in the offer for the offeror's promise and the second consideration is the "price" in the acceptance for the offeree's performance.

Offer: "I promise to sell you my car for your paying me $5,000."
Offeror's promise: "I promise to sell you my car."
Consideration for the offeror's promise: "Your paying me $5,000."

Acceptance of the offer: "My paying you $5,000 for your promise to sell me your car."
Offeree's performance: "My paying you $5,000."
Consideration for the offeree's performance: "Your promise to sell me your car."

For clarity, these two considerations will be distinguished by referring to "consideration for the offeror's (promisor's) promise" and **"consideration for the offeree's (promisee's) promise"** (if the offer is for a bilateral contract) or **"consideration for the offeree's (promisee's) performance"** (if the offer is for a unilateral contract). The term "consideration" standing alone, will be used only when a general reference to consideration is made.

We have just made the point that "consideration" is an element in the offer and an element in the acceptance. An offer does not exist without "consideration for the offeror's promise" and an acceptance does not exist without "consideration for the offeree's promise or performance." It is not uncommon, however, to find judicial opinions and texts that describe a contract as consisting of an offer, an acceptance, and consideration. Viewing consideration as a separate element is redundant since the concept of consideration has already been addressed—not once but twice—once when evaluating the offer and once when evaluating the acceptance. Therefore, this text will describe a contract as consisting of only an offer and an acceptance.

consideration for the promisee's promise or performance
Consideration for the promisee's promise or performance is the "price" sought by the promisee for his or her promise.

The Consideration for the Promisor's Promise Must Be at Least a Peppercorn (Adequacy of Consideration Is Irrelevant)

Early in the evolution of contract law, judges decided that some promises should be enforced while others should not. The promise of a future gift fell in the latter category. The only promise to make a gift that would be enforced would be that where the gift had already been made. That is, if a donor changed his or her mind and wanted the gift returned, the court would not require the gift already conveyed to be returned. On the other hand, a person who promised to make a gift in the future but who had not yet conveyed the gift would not be forced by the court to follow through with his or her promise.

A promise to make a future gift is a one-sided promise since it requests nothing in return for the promisor's promise. An offer, on the other hand, is more than a one-sided promise. An offer requires "something" in return for the promisor's promise. This "something" is the consideration or the "price" for the offeror's promise.

Example 2-7

Gift Promise: "I promise to give you $15,000."
Offer: "I promise to give you $15,000 for your promise to give me your car."

In a commercial setting, most promisors seek something in exchange for their promises. If the transaction involves sale of goods, construction, or employment, there is always an exchange. Neither party to the transaction promises to give something for nothing. The promisor's motivation in making a promise may be quite different in the commercial world than it is in a family or interpersonal setting. In the family or interpersonal setting, the promisor may make a promise and not seek something in return. When a parent promises a child a weekly allowance of $4 (with no strings attached) or use of the car for the spring dance, the parent is making nothing more than a promise of a future gift.

The law of contracts does not concern itself with the size or value of the consideration. The court will not investigate whether the consideration sought by the offeror is "adequate." Adequacy of consideration is irrelevant. What is relevant is that there be some consideration, no matter how small. Consideration may be as small as a peppercorn, if that is what the offeror is bargaining to receive in exchange for his or her promise.

Example 2–8

The following are offers since the adequacy of the consideration is irrelevant.

"I promise to sell you my car for your promise to pay me $15,000."
"I promise to sell you my car for your promise to pay me $5,000."
"I promise to sell you my car for your promise to pay me $500."
"I promise to sell you my car for your promise to pay me one peppercorn."

As we all know, promises are not made to get peppercorns. Most contracts are performed, and the parties are satisfied with the results (or are not so dissatisfied that they will do anything more than grumble). In some cases, one party may feel that he or she has paid too much or received too little. At the time of contracting, the parties were free to design the contract to their own specifications. If, after the fact, one party feels dissatisfied with the terms to which he or she agreed, this is not the concern of the court. A judge will not evaluate whether one party received more under the contract than the other and therefore will not evaluate the adequacy of the consideration.

Although the law recognizes something the size of a peppercorn as consideration, it does not recognize everything as potential consideration. "Love and affection" cannot serve as consideration. If "love and affection" were to be consideration, the entire concept of consideration would crumble because the distinction between a promise to make a future gift and a contract promise would no longer exist. All promises would have legal significance and could be enforceable regardless of whether they were intended as gifts.

Example 2-9

The following is a gift promise and not an offer.

"I promise to give you my car since you are a loving niece."

The following sections discuss six consideration-related problems:

- The Price for the Promisor's Promise or a Joke?
- The Price for the Promisor's Promise or an Illusory Promise?
- The Price for the Promisor's Promise or an Indefinite Promise?
- The Price for the Promisor's Promise or the Promisor's Motive for Making the Promise?
- The Price for the Promisor's Promise or the Promisor's Satisfaction of a Moral Obligation?
- The Price for the Promisor's Promise or a Sham?

The Price for the Promisor's Promise or a Joke? Although in *Lucy v. Zehmer,* the promisor's promise ("I promise to sell you the farm") was found to be a promise, it could have as easily been found to have been a joke. Taking this one step further, there is no reason why the joke could not be the consideration for the promisor's promise rather than the promisor's promise itself.

PARALEGAL EXERCISE 2.7

In *Lucy v. Zehmer,* Zehmer said "I promise to sell you my farm for your promise to pay me $50,000." What if Zehmer had said instead "I promise to sell you my farm for your promise to pay me $50,000,000,000." Would the consideration for Zehmer's promise to sell be consideration or a joke? ■

The Price for the Promisor's Promise or an Illusory Promise? The statement "I promise to sell you my pig, if I feel like it" is an illusory promise by the promisor. The illusory promise could just as well be the consideration for the promisor's promise.

Example 2-10

In the statement "I promise to sell you my pig for your promise to pay me $250, if you feel like it," the "if you feel like it" has been moved from the promisor's promise to the consideration for the promisor's promise. The consideration for the promisor's promise has now become illusory.

The Price for the Promisor's Promise or an Indefinite Promise? Just as a promisor's promise could be an indefinite promise, so could the consideration for the promisor's promise.

Example 2–11

In *Fairmount Glass,* the offer was to sell 10 railroad car loads of glass jars. The jars came in pints, quarts, and half gallons. The offer neither specified the quantity of each size nor the exact date of delivery ("ship no later than May 15th"). Had the parties not been merchants in the glass jar trade, the court might have found the consideration for the promisor's promise to ship 10 car loads no later than May 15th an indefinite promise (i.e., "promise to accept and pay for 10 railroad car loads of glass jars"). The parties were, however, merchants in the glass jar trade and the court held the following:

> Appellant also insists that the contract was indefinite, because the quantity of each size of the jars was not fixed, that 10 car loads is too indefinite a specification of the quantity sold, and that appellee had no right to accept the goods to be delivered on different days. The proof shows that "10 car loads" is an expression used in the trade as equivalent to 1,000 gross, 100 gross being regarded a car load. The offer to sell the different sizes at different prices gave the purchaser the right to name the quantity of each size, and, the offer being to ship not later than May 15th, the buyer had the right to fix the time of delivery at any time before that.

Fairmount Glass Works v. Grunden-Martin Woodenware Co., 51 S.W. 196, at 198 (Ky. Ct. App. 1899).

The Price for the Promisor's Promise or the Promisor's Motive for Making the Promise? Motive cannot be consideration for a promise. The promisor's motive must be separated from the consideration for his or her promise.

Consider the following statement: "I promise to sell you my car for your promise to pay me $5,000." The promisor's motive for promising to sell her car might be to buy a newer car, to take a trip to Europe, to bury $5,000 in a tin can in the backyard, to pay a hospital bill, or to bet on a horse. Whatever the motive or motives, and no matter how interesting or unique, motives are irrelevant. Although motive may explain why the promisor is doing or not doing something, what is relevant is that there be consideration for the promisor's promise—what will be received by the promisor in return for his or her "promise to sell the car."

In the following problems, identify the motive and determine whether consideration exists separate and apart from motive.

▥ PARALEGAL EXERCISE 2.8

A budding sculptor, seeking public exposure for her work, promises to lend a large sculpture to First Bank if First Bank will promise to exhibit it in its foyer for one year.

1. What is the sculptor's motive or motives for promising to lend the sculpture to the Bank?
2. What is the consideration for the sculptor's promise to lend the sculpture to the Bank? ▦

▥ PARALEGAL EXERCISE 2.9

A grandmother promises to pay her granddaughter's tuition if the grand-daughter will go to college.

1. What is the grandmother's motive for her promise to pay her granddaughter's tuition?
2. What is the consideration for the grandmother's promise to pay the tuition? ▦

▥ PARALEGAL EXERCISE 2.10

Mary lost her wedding ring and placed an advertisement in the personal column of the local newspaper: "I promise to pay a $400 reward to the person who finds and returns my diamond ring."

1. What is Mary's motive for making the promise to pay $400?
2. What is the consideration for Mary's promise to pay $400? ▦

The Price for the Promisor's Promise or the Promisor's Satisfaction of a Moral Obligation?   The fact that someone feels morally obligated to make a promise cannot be consideration for a promise. Moral obligation is not consideration. It is synonymous with motive and, as discussed in the preceding section, motive is not consideration.

Example 2–12

Shortly after Allen became estranged from his mother, Allen's sister, Linda, promised him that if he were disinherited by their mother, Linda would give him half of their mother's estate. Prior to their mother's death, the mother executed a will that left her entire estate to Linda. When Allen sought to enforce Linda's promise to share their mother's estate, the court in *In re Estate of Poncin,* 1998 WL 8470 (Minn. App.) discussed whether Linda's promise suffered from a lack of consideration.

> Appellant [Allen] concedes that there was no consideration given for respondent's [Linda's] statement. Consideration insures that a promise enforced as a contract is not "accidental, casual, or gratuitous" but has been made with "some deliberation, manifested by reciprocal bargaining or negotiation." . . . Promises that lack any consideration are "bare moral obligations, binding only on the conscience, a breach of which is not redressible in the courts."

▥ PARALEGAL EXERCISE 2.11

Mills nurses Wyman's emancipated son who is seriously ill. After Wyman's son dies, Wyman promises to reimburse Mills for any expenses incurred by Mills for this care. Because Wyman's son was emancipated, Wyman is under no legal obligation to reimburse Mills. Wyman has a change of heart and subsequently refuses to pay Mills. Mills claims that Wyman made an offer.

1. What was Wyman's motive in making his promise to reimburse Mills?
2. What was the consideration that Wyman requested in exchange for his promise to pay Mills? ▪

sham consideration

Sham consideration is feigned or pretended consideration.

The Price for the Promisor's Promise or a Sham? **Sham consideration** is feigned or pretended consideration. A promise or performance that is purported to be consideration but is a sham is not consideration. The stated consideration for a promise may be a sham when the promisor is attempting to disguise the promise, which is intended as a future gift, as a contract offer.

Example 2–13

A father, intending to give his son a car as a gift, says to his son, "I promise to sell you my car for your promise to pay me $5,000." Because the father had no intention of receiving the $5,000 payment but had disguised his promise of a future gift as an offer, the stated consideration for the father's promise ("your promise to pay me $5,000") is a sham and does not count as consideration.

Sham consideration relates to both adequacy of consideration and motive. Although a court will not investigate whether the consideration for a promise is adequate, the court might investigate whether the stated consideration is a sham. While motive will not be consideration, motive may play a role in determining whether the consideration stated is a sham.

The Promisor's Promise Must Be Made to Induce the Consideration

Not only must the consideration for the promisor's promise be at least a pcppcrcorn, the promisor must be making his or her promise to induce the promisee to either promise or perform, depending on which of these the promisor is requiring. The promisor's promise and the consideration for that promise are therefore bound together. The two elements of offer are connected.

The promisor's promise anticipates a "bargained-for exchange." The phrase "bargained-for exchange" does not require hard bargaining with protracted negotiation. The requirement is that the promisor, by his or her promise, must be seeking the promisee's promise or performance (the consideration). The promisor's promise must be made to induce (entice) the consideration.

The following material explores three inducement problems: past consideration, preexisting duty, and condition vs. consideration.

Past Consideration   The past consideration problem is a timing issue. In an offer the offeror must make his or her promise to induce the offeree to promise or to perform. If the offeree has already promised or performed, the offeror would not be making his or her promise to induce the offeree to promise or perform.

The issue of past consideration more often occurs when the offeror is asking the offeree to perform rather than to promise. Therefore, a past consideration issue occurs when the offer is for a unilateral contract rather than for a bilateral contract.

⛉ PARALEGAL EXERCISE 2.12

Several months after Stan Hall was injured in an automobile accident, Stan learned that Mary Little had rendered first aid and that Mary's quick action probably saved his life.

Acting upon this information, Stan promised to pay Mary $2,000 for saving his life.

1. What is the consideration for Stan's promise to pay Mary $2,000?
2. Did Stan make his promise to induce Mary to render the consideration for his promise? ▪

Ⅲ PARALEGAL EXERCISE 2.13

At his granddaughter's graduation, Granddad promises to pay her $5,000 for graduating with honors.

1. What is the consideration for Granddad's promise to pay $5,000?
2. Did Granddad make his promise in order to induce his granddaughter to render the consideration for his promise? ■

Preexisting Duty   Consideration for the promisor's promise must be free from obligation already owed to the promisor. If the promisee has a duty to perform that which the promisor is currently seeking to induce, the duty previously owed cannot be used as consideration for the promisor's new promise. The promisee is already committed to perform that duty.

Example 2–14

Ron Armstrong has a three-year contract to play football for the Chicago Bears at $1 million a year. Ron's performance during the first year under the contract was outstanding, and the Bears decided to increase his salary for the remaining two years of the contract. The Bears promised to pay Ron $1,200,000 a year for his promise to play for them for the next two years. The consideration for the Bears' promise to pay Ron $1,200,000 a year is his promise to play for them for the next two years. This promise to play for the Bears for the next two years is a promise to which Ron is already committed in his original contract. Therefore, his promise to play for the Bears for the next two years cannot be consideration for the Bears' promise to pay him $1,200,000 a year.

Original contract:
Offer: "We promise to pay $1 million a year for *your promise to play for the Bears for three years.*"
Acceptance: "I promise to play for the Bears for three years for your promise to pay $1 million a year."

The attempt at renegotiating the contract:
Attempted offer: "We promise to pay $1.2 million a year for *your promise to play for the Bears for the remaining two years.*"

preexisting duty

A preexisting duty is that which is already owed to a party before a promise is made to perform that duty to that party.

If the source of the **preexisting duty** comes from a contract and if the parties enter into a contract for mutual releases of their contractual duties, the parties no longer have preexisting duties and may contract.

Example 2-15

Original contract:

Offer: "We promise to pay $1 million a year for *your promise to play for the Bears for three years.*"

Acceptance: "I promise to play for the Bears for three years for your promise to pay $1 million a year."

Release contract:

Offer: "I promise to release you from your duty to pay $1 million a year for your promise to release me from my duty to play for the Bears for the remaining two years of my contract."

Acceptance: "We promise to release you from your duty to play for the Bears for the remaining two years of your contract for your promise to release us from our duty to pay $1 million a year."

Renegotiated contract:

Offer: "We promise to pay $1.2 million a year for *your promise to play for the Bears for the remaining two years.*"

Acceptance: "I promise to play for the Bears for the remaining two years for your promise to pay $1.2 million a year."

At the time of entering into the renegotiated contract, the player did not have a duty to play for the Bears for what would be the remaining two years of the original three-year term. Therefore, the promise to play for the Bears for the remaining two years could be consideration for the Bears' promise to pay $1.2 million a year.

PARALEGAL EXERCISE 2.14

Singleton, a clothing designer, contracted to work for J. Smyth, Inc., a clothing manufacturer, for one year at $1,000 a week. A short time later, Singleton was offered $1,500 a week to work for a competitor. Upon hearing that they may be losing Singleton's services, J. Smyth promised to increase Singleton's salary to $1,300 a week for the remainder of the contract term. Singleton turned down the other offer and stayed with J. Smyth. Three months later, J. Smyth fired Singleton without cause. Singleton brought a breach of contract action against J. Smyth seeking damages based on $1,300 a week. Answer the following questions. Assume J. Smyth made the original offer.

1. What was the original offer made by J. Smyth?
2. What was the consideration for J. Smyth's promise in that offer?
3. What was the new promise made by J. Smyth?
4. What was the consideration for J. Smyth's new promise?
5. Was the consideration for J. Smyth's new promise the same as the consideration for J. Smyth's original promise?
6. Has J. Smyth made a new offer or is the consideration for J. Smyth's new promise lacking due to Singleton's preexisting duty?

⚏ PARALEGAL EXERCISE 2.15

Singleton, a clothing designer, contracted to work for J. Smyth, Inc., a clothing manufacturer, for one year at $1,000 a week. A short time later, Singleton was offered $1,500 a week to work for a competitor. Upon hearing that they may be losing Singleton's services, J. Smyth promised to rescind Singleton's original contract and to increase Singleton's salary to $1,300 a week for the remainder of the contract term. Three months later, J. Smyth fired Singleton without cause. Singleton brought a breach of contract action against J. Smyth seeking damages based on $1,300 a week. Answer the following questions. Assume J. Smyth made the original offer.

1. What was the original offer made by J. Smyth?
2. What was the consideration for J. Smyth's promise in that offer?
3. Did J. Smyth make a promise to rescind the original contract?
4. What was the consideration for J. Smyth's promise to rescind?
5. Was the consideration for J. Smyth's promise the same as the consideration for J. Smyth's original promise?
6. Have the parties entered into a rescission contract?
7. What was the third promise made by J. Smyth?
8. What was the consideration for J. Smyth's third promise?
9. Was the consideration for J. Smyth's third promise the same as the consideration for J. Smyth's original promise?
10. Has J. Smyth made a new offer or is the consideration for J. Smyth's third promise lacking due to Singleton's preexisting duty? ▨

---

condition

A condition is a contingency.

Condition vs. Consideration   The **condition** vs. consideration problem will occur only in situations when the offer is for a unilateral contract (promise for a performance) and not when the offer is for a bilateral contract (promise for a promise). Unlike the past consideration and preexisting duty problems that are timing issues, the condition vs. consideration problem is a question of pure inducement. "Why did the promisor make his or her promise?" Was the promisor's motive to induce the promisee to perform or was the promisor's motive only to make the promisee a gift—and the promisee had to put himself or herself into a position to receive the gift? In the former, the promisor is using his or her promise to entice the promisee's performance. Since the promisor's promise is being used to induce the promisee's performance, the promisee's performance is the consideration for the promisor's promise and the promisor is making an offer. In the latter, the promisor is not using his or her promise to entice the promisee's performance. The promisee, however, must perform in order to be in a position to receive the promisor's gift. Since the promisor's promise is *not* being used to induce the promisee's performance, the promisee's performance is *not* the consideration for the promisor's promise and the promisor is not making an offer. The promisor's motive, therefore, is the key to resolving the condition vs. consideration issue.

Example 2–16

"I promise to give you $5,000 if you refrain from smoking for one year." Why did the promisor make her promise? If the promisor is making her promise to get the promisee to stop smoking, the promisor is using her promise to induce the promisee to stop smoking. The "not smoking for one year" is the consideration for the promisor's promise to pay.

Example 2–17

"I promise to give you a place to live if you move here." Why did the promisor make her promise? If the promisor was trying to get the promisee to move, then "if you move here" is consideration for the promisor's promise to give her a place to live. The promisor is using "the place to live" to induce the promisee to move there. If, however, the promisor did not care whether the promisee moved there or not but would provide her with a place to live if she did move, then "if you move here" is only a condition that the promisee must fulfill before she can partake in the promisor's gift promise.

▥ PARALEGAL EXERCISE 2.16

Professor Williston, in his treatise on Contracts (1 Williston on Contracts 445 (Jaeger 3d ed. 1957)), used the following illustration to demonstrate the difference between consideration and a condition: "[A] benevolent man says to a tramp,—'If you go around the corner to the clothing store there, you may purchase an overcoat on my credit.'"

1. What is the benevolent man's promise?
2. What was required of the tramp?
3. What was the benevolent man's motivation in asking the tramp to "go around the corner to the clothing store"?
4. Was the benevolent man asking for an exchange (a promise to purchase a coat in exchange for the tramp's walking), or did the benevolent man not seek an exchange but only that the tramp be in a position to receive the gift? ▦

▥ PARALEGAL EXERCISE 2.17

A father told his son that if the son would move back to town, the father would start him in business.

1. What was the father's promise?
2. What did the father require the son to do?
3. Why did the father require the son to do this?
4. Is the father using his promise to induce the son to perform or does the father not really care whether the son performs? ▦

ALTERNATIVES TO CLASSICAL CONSIDERATION

Under classical contract law, consideration for the promisor's promise is an essential element of an offer. Without consideration, the promisor's promise is merely a promise to make a future gift and is unenforceable in court. Rigid adherence to this consideration doctrine often led to unnecessarily harsh results. Modern contract law employs several methods to rectify this. The first involves legislative and judicial tinkering with the classical doctrine. The second introduces reliance as an alternative to consideration. Both lead to the conclusion of offer and contract.

Tinkering with the Classical Doctrine

Both legislatures and courts tinker with the classical consideration doctrine. A legislature, by statute, may substitute a writing for consideration. A statute could take one of the following forms:

> A written promise signed by the person promising is not unenforceable for lack of consideration.

> A written promise signed by the person promising is not unenforceable for lack of consideration if the writing contains an express statement, in any form of language, that the signer intends to be legally bound.

Rather than substitute a writing, the legislature may alter the rule about which party has the burden of proving consideration. Traditional contract law required the party introducing the contract to prove offer and acceptance, including the element of consideration for the promisor's promise. The following pair of statutes shifts the burden of proof from the party introducing the contract to the party challenging the contract. A number of states have this statutory pattern.

> A written instrument is presumptive evidence of a consideration.

> The burden of showing a want of consideration sufficient to support an instrument lies with the party seeking to invalidate or avoid it.

These illustrative statutes apply to all transactions. A legislature may, however, write with a finer pen. Consideration may be eliminated in a specific type of transaction rather than in all transactions. Article 2 of the Uniform Commercial Code, which has been enacted by the legislatures of all states except Louisiana, provides a good example. Article 2 deals with transactions involving a sale of goods. UCC § 2–209(1) provides:

> (1) An agreement modifying a contract within this Article needs no consideration to be binding.

🏛 PARALEGAL EXERCISE 2.18

Describe how the legislature is tinkering with the classical consideration doctrine in the following statute. Does the statute apply to all types of contracts or only to a specific type of transaction? Does the statute dispense with the need for consideration, or does it merely substitute something in its place?

> Every contract in writing hereafter made shall import a consideration in the same manner and as fully as sealed instruments have heretofore done. ■

🏛 PARALEGAL EXERCISE 2.19

Describe how the legislature is tinkering with the classical consideration doctrine in the following statute. Does the statute apply to all types of contracts or only to a specific type of transaction? Does the statute dispense with the need for consideration, or does it merely substitute something in its place?

> An offer by a merchant to buy or sell goods in a signed writing which by its terms gives assurance that it will be held open is not revocable, for lack of consideration, during the time stated or if no time is stated for a reasonable time, but in no event may such period of irrevocability exceed three months; but any such term of assurance on a form supplied by the offeree must be separately signed by the offeror. ■

The legislatures have not been the only tinkerers with the classical consideration doctrine. The courts, at times, also have been active. The following case, *Webb v. McGowin,* presents an excellent illustration. On August 3, 1925, Joe Webb, an employee of the W. T. Smith Lumber Company, was clearing the upper floor of a company mill by dropping the wood on that floor to the ground below. While Webb was in the act of dropping a 75-pound pine block from the upper floor to the ground below, he saw J. Greeley McGowin standing on the ground below. Webb knew that he could remain safely on the upper floor of the mill and allow the block to drop, but the block would fall on McGowin and cause him serious injury or death. Webb chose to hold on to the block as it fell to the ground, thus diverting it from McGowin's direction. McGowin was saved, but Webb suffered serious bodily injuries that left him crippled for life. On September 1, 1925, McGowin promised to pay Webb $15 every two weeks for the remainder of Webb's life for Webb's having prevented McGowin from sustaining death or serious bodily harm and for the injuries Webb received. The payments, made for over eight years, were discontinued when McGowin died.

Webb sued McGowin's estate for breach of contract, and the estate responded by claiming a lack of consideration for McGowin's promise to pay. Webb's injury and saving of McGowin's life occurred before McGowin made his promise to pay Webb $15 every two weeks. McGowin's promise to pay did not induce Webb to act.

The Court of Appeals of Alabama found in favor of Webb. In reading *Webb v. McGowin,* consider:

1. How does the court tinker with the classical consideration doctrine to resolve the timing problem? The problem with the classical consideration doctrine was that the consideration was performed before the promisor promised; therefore, the promisor's promise could not have been made to induce the promisee to perform.
2. Is the court's attempted analogy between a physician and a patient sound? Was relief in the physician-patient situation based on breach of contract?

We have discussed the inability of a moral obligation to serve as consideration. In *Webb v. McGowin,* the court linked moral obligation with a material benefit received by the offeror. The court stated that the moral obligation was the consideration for the promisor's promise (see paragraph number 2 in the court's opinion). Is this rationale acceptable?

The court referred to an alternative solution involving a prior legal or equitable obligation, which has become unenforceable, followed by subsequent promise to pay (see paragraph number 3). Is this rationale applicable to this case? Did McGowin have either a legal or equitable obligation to pay Webb before he made his promise to Webb?

Is the outcome acceptable? Is either rationale acceptable? If the outcome is acceptable but the rationale is not, suggest a better rationale. Could the promise to pay have occurred by implication when McGowin looked up and saw the block with his name on it, teetering on the edge of the upper floor of the mill?

CASE

Webb v. McGowin
Court of Appeals of Alabama (1935)
27 Ala. App. 82, 168 So. 196 certiorari denied,
Supreme Court of Alabama (1936)
232 Ala. 374, 168 So. 199

1. The averments of the complaint show that appellant saved McGowin from death or grievous bodily harm. This was a material benefit to him of infinitely more value than any financial aid he could have received. Receiving this benefit, McGowin became morally bound to compensate appellant for the services

rendered. Recognizing his moral obligation, he expressly agreed to pay appellant as alleged in the complaint and compiled with this agreement up to the time of his death; a period of more than eight years.

Had McGowin been accidentally poisoned and a physician, without his knowledge or request, had administered an antidote, thus saving his life, a subsequent promise by McGowin to pay the physician would have been valid. Likewise, McGowin's agreement as disclosed by the complaint to compensate appellant for saving him from death or grievous bodily injury is valid and enforceable.

Where the promisee cares for, improves, and preserves the property of the promisor, though done without his request, it is sufficient consideration for the promisor's subsequent agreement to pay for the service, because of the material benefit received. . . .

In Boothe v. Fitzpatrick, 36 Vt. 681, the court held that a promise by defendant to pay for the past keeping of a bull that had escaped from defendant's premises and been cared for by plaintiff was valid, although there was no previous request, because the subsequent promise obviated that objection; it being equivalent to a previous request. On the same principle, had the promisee saved the promisor's life or his body from grievous harm, his subsequent promise to pay for the services rendered would have been valid. Such service would have been far more material than caring for his bull. Any holding that saving a man from death or grievous bodily harm is not a material benefit sufficient to uphold a subsequent promise to pay for the service, necessarily rests on the assumption that the saving of life and preservation of the body from harm have only a sentimental value. The converse of this is true. Life and preservation of the body have material, pecuniary values, measurable in dollars and cents. Because of this, physicians practice their profession charging for services rendered in saving life and curing the body of its ills, and surgeons perform operations. The same is true as to the law of negligence, authorizing the assessment of damages in personal injury cases based upon the extent of the injuries, earnings, and life expectancies of those injured.

In the business of life insurance, the value of a man's life is measured in dollars and cents according to his expectancy, the soundness of his body, and his ability to pay premiums. The same is true as to health and accident insurance.

It follows that if, as alleged in the complaint, appellant saved J. Greeley McGowin from death or grievous bodily harm, and McGowin subsequently agreed to pay him for the service rendered, it became a valid and enforceable contract.

2. It is well settled that a moral obligation is a sufficient consideration to support a subsequent promise to pay where the promisor has received a material benefit, although there was no original duty or liability resting on the promisor. . . . In the case of State ex rel. Bayer v. Funk, 105 Or. 134, 199 P. 592, 209 P. 113, 25 A.L.R. 625, 634, the court held that a moral obligation is a sufficient consideration to support an executory promise where the promisor has received an actual pecuniary or material benefit for which he subsequently expressly promised to pay.

The case at bar is clearly distinguishable from that class of cases where the consideration is a mere moral obligation or conscientious duty unconnected with receipt by promisor of benefits of a material or pecuniary nature. Park Falls State Bank v. Fordyce, 206 Wis. 628, 238 N.W. 516, 79 A.L.R. 1339. Here the promisor received a material benefit constituting a valid consideration for his promise.

3. Some authorities hold that, for a moral obligation to support a subsequent promise to pay, there must have existed a prior legal or equitable obligation, which

for some reason had become unenforceable, but for which the promisor was still morally bound. This rule, however, is subject to qualification in those cases where the promisor, having received a material benefit from the promisee, is morally bound to compensate him for the services rendered and in consideration of this obligation promises to pay. In such cases the subsequent promise to pay is an affirmance or ratification of the services rendered carrying with it the presumption that a previous request for the service was made. . . .

Under the decisions above cited, McGowin's express promise to pay appellant for the services rendered was an affirmance or ratification of what appellant had done, raising the presumption that the services had been rendered at McGowin's request.

4. The averments of the complaint show that in saving McGowin from death or grievous bodily harm, appellant was crippled for life. This was part of the consideration of the contract declared on. McGowin was benefited. Appellant was injured. Benefit to the promisor or injury to the promisee is a sufficient legal consideration for the promisor's agreement to pay. . . .

5. Under the averments of the complaint the services rendered by appellant were not gratuitous. The agreement of McGowin to pay and the acceptance of payment by appellant conclusively shows the contrary.

From what has been said, we are of the opinion that the court below erred in the ruling complained of; that is to say, in sustaining the demurrer, and for this error the case is reversed and remanded.

Reversed and remanded.

SAMFORD, Judge (concurring).

The questions involved in this case are not free from doubt, and perhaps the strict letter of the rule, as stated by judges, though not always in accord, would bar a recovery by plaintiff, but following the principle announced by Chief Justice Marshall in Hoffman v. Porter, Fed.Cas. No. 6,577, 2 Brock. 156, 159, where he says, "I do not think that law ought to be separated from justice, where it is at most doubtful," I concur in the conclusions reached by the court.

Reliance as an Alternative to Consideration

Legislative and judicial tinkering have produced results in a crazy quilt fashion. Sometimes judicial tinkering has resolved only the dispute between a specific plaintiff and defendant. Legislative tinkering has been limited to certain types of transactions, such as sale of goods, or has distinguished written from unwritten promises. This tinkering has not produced a solution applicable to all transactions.

A solution that applies to all transactions is currently emerging in the courts. It is based on reliance as an alternative to consideration. The Restatement (Second) of Contracts § 90, entitled "Promise Reasonably Inducing Action or Forbearance," has become the focus for this movement:

> (1) A promise which the promisor should reasonably expect to induce action or forbearance on the part of the promisee or a third person and which does induce such action or forbearance is binding

if injustice can be avoided only by enforcement of the promise. The remedy granted for breach may be limited as justice requires.

The four elements of reliance as an alternative to consideration are the following:

- A promise by the promisor
- That the promisor should reasonably expect the promisee to induce action or forbearance on the part of the promisee
- That the promise does induce such action or forbearance
- That injustice can be avoided only by enforcement of the promise

The Restatement (Second) of Contracts § 90 makes the point that the "remedy granted for breach may be limited as justice requires." Since reliance substitutes for consideration, justice may require the remedy for breach of the offeror's promise be limited to compensation for the injury induced by the promisee's reliance on the promisor's promise. Courts, however, have paid little attention to this limitation and have given the promisee an expectation remedy. That is, the courts have given the remedy that would place the promisee in the position he or she would have been in had the contract been fully performed.

Example 2-18

A father promised his 22-year-old son $20,000 when his son became 25. The father knew that if he made the promise his son would probably purchase a new car. In anticipation of receiving $20,000 at age 25, the son spent $17,000 on a new car, a purchase he would not have made if his father had not promised him the gift. When the son became 25, the father refused to pay. Because the father's promise was for a future gift, there was no consideration for the father's promise, and it would not constitute an offer.

Since reliance is a substitute for consideration and the father's promise is enforceable, the question remains—to what extent is the father's promise enforceable? Under § 90, the son would be entitled to a remedy that "may be limited as justice requires." Because the son's recovery is based on reliance, his remedy should be based on reliance as well. Therefore, the son's reliance interest should be protected, and he should recover for his injury suffered by relying—$17,000 or less. In practice, however, the courts will tend to protect the son's expectation interest and place the son in the position he would have been in had the father's promise been fully performed—$20,000.

The following two cases, *Ricketts v. Scothorn* and *Feinberg v. Pfeiffer Co.,* illustrate the use of reliance before and after the promulgation of Restatement of Contracts § 90. In *Ricketts,* a case involving the early evolution of the reliance doctrine, Miss Scothorn had been given a $2,000 note by her grandfather. When her grandfather died and his executor refused to pay, Miss Scothorn sued to enforce the note.

1. Was the grandfather's promise really without consideration?
2. In looking for precedent, does the court agree with the rationale of the church and college cases that "the expenditure of money or assumption of liability by the donee on the faith of the promise constitutes a valuable and sufficient consideration"?
3. What rationale did the *Ricketts* court prefer?

The court used the phrase "equitable estoppel." Compare the elements for "equitable estoppel" in *Ricketts* with those set forth previously for reliance. In this context, equitable estoppel means the party challenging the lack of consideration for his or her promise is precluded from doing so because his or her promise induced the other party to rely to his detriment. If equitable estoppel is taken to its logical conclusion, the preclusion of the lack of consideration argument leaves the promise as if it had consideration and thus an offer. The offer forms a contract, and the contract is enforced as are all other contracts. Thus the nonbreaching party would be entitled to protection of his or her expectation, reliance, or restitution interests and not just his or her reliance interest. What interest did the *Ricketts* court protect?

CASE

Ricketts v. Scothorn
Supreme Court of Nebraska (1898)
57 Neb. 51, 77 N.W. 365

SULLIVAN, J.

In the district court of Lancaster county the plaintiff, Katie Scothorn, recovered judgment against the defendant, Andrew D. Ricketts, as executor of the last will and testament of John C. Ricketts, deceased. The action was based upon a promissory note, of which the following is a copy: "May the first, 1891. I promise to pay to Katie Scothorn on demand $2,000, to be at 6 per cent. per annum. J. C. Ricketts."

The material facts are undisputed. They are as follows: John C. Ricketts, the maker of the note, was the grandfather of the plaintiff. Early in May—presumably on the day the note bears date—he called on her at the store where she was working. What transpired between them is thus described by Mr. Flodene, one of the plaintiff's witnesses: "A. Well, the old gentleman came in there one morning about nine o'clock, probably a little before or a little after, but early in the morning, and he unbuttoned his vest, and took out a piece of paper in the shape of a note; that is the way it looked to me; and he says to Miss Scothorn, 'I have fixed out something that you have not got to work any more.' He says, none of my grandchildren work, and you don't have to. Q. Where was she? A. She took the piece of paper and kissed him, and kissed the old gentleman, and commenced to cry." It seems Miss Scothorn immediately notified her employer of her intention to quit work, and that she did soon after abandon her occupation. The mother of the plaintiff was a witness, and testified that she had a conversation with her father, Mr. Ricketts, shortly after the note was executed, in which he informed her that he had given the note to the plaintiff to enable her to quit work; that none of his grandchildren worked, and he did not think she ought to. For something more than a year the plaintiff was without an occupation, but in September, 1892, with the consent of her grandfather, and by his assistance, she secured a position as bookkeeper with Messrs. Funke & Ogden. On June 8, 1894, Mr. Ricketts died. He had paid one year's interest on the note, and a short time before his death expressed regret that he had not been able to pay the balance. In the summer or fall of 1892 he stated to his daughter, Mrs. Scothorn, that if he could sell his farm in Ohio he would pay the note out of the proceeds. He at no time repudiated the obligation. We quite agree with counsel for the defendant that upon this evidence there was nothing to submit to the jury, and that a verdict should have been directed peremptorily for one of the parties. The testimony of Flodene and Mrs. Scothorn, taken together, conclusively establishes the fact that the note was not given in consideration of the plaintiff pursuing, or agreeing to pursue, any particular line of conduct. There was no promise on the part of the plaintiff to do, or refrain from doing, anything. Her right to the money promised in the note was not made to depend upon an abandonment of her employment with Mayer Bros., and future abstention from like service. Mr. Ricketts made no condition, requirement, or request. He exacted no quid pro quo. He gave the note as a gratuity, and looked for nothing in return. So far as the evidence discloses, it was his purpose to place the plaintiff in a position of independence, where she could work or remain idle, as she might choose. The abandonment of Miss Scothorn of her position as bookkeeper was altogether voluntary. It was not an act done in fulfillment of any contract obligation assumed when she accepted the note. The instrument in suit, being given without any valuable consideration, was nothing more than a promise to make a gift in the future of the sum of money therein named. Ordinarily, such promises are not enforceable, even when put in the form of a promissory note. Kirkpatrick v. Taylor, 43 Ill. 207; Phelps v. Phelps, 28 Barb. 121; Johnston v. Griest, 85 Ind. 503; Fink v. Cox, 18 Johns. 145. But it has often been held that an action on a note given to a church, college, or other like institution, upon the faith of which money has been expended or obligations incurred, could not be successfully defended on the ground of a want of consideration. Barnes v. Perine, 12 N.Y. 18; Philomath College v. Hartless, 6 Or. 158; Thompson v. Board, 40 Ill. 379; Irwin v. Lombard University, 56 Ohio St. 9, 46 N.E. 63. In this class of cases the note in suit is nearly always spoken of as a gift or donation, but the decision is generally put on the ground that the expenditure of money or assumption of liability by the donee on the faith of the promise constitutes a valuable and sufficient consideration. It seems to us that the true reason is the preclusion of the defendant, under the doctrine of estoppel, to deny the consideration. Such seems to be the view of the matter taken by the supreme court of Iowa in the case of Simpson Centenary College v. Tuttle, 71 Iowa, 596, 33 N.W. 74, where Rothrock, J., speaking for the court, said: "Where a note, however, is based on a promise to give for the support of the objects referred to, it may still be open to this defense [want of consideration], unless it shall appear that the donee has, prior to any revocation, entered into engagements, or made expenditures based on such promise, so that he must suffer loss or injury if the note is not paid. This is based on the equitable principle that, after allowing the donee to incur obligations on the faith that the note would be paid, the donor would be estopped from pleading want of consideration."

According to the undisputed proof, as shown by the record before us, the plaintiff was a working girl, holding a position in which she earned a salary of $10 per week. Her grandfather, desiring to put her in a position of independence, gave her the note, accompanying it with the remark that his other grandchildren did not work, and that she would not be obliged to work any longer. In effect, he suggested that she might abandon her employment, and rely in the future upon the bounty which he promised. He doubtless desired that she should give up her occupation, but, whether he did or not, it is entirely certain that he contemplated such action on her part as a reasonable and probable consequence of his gift. Having intentionally influenced the plaintiff to alter her position for the worse on the faith of the note being paid when due, it would be grossly inequitable to permit the maker, or his executor, to resist payment on the ground that the promise was given without consideration. The petition charges the elements of an equitable estoppel, and the evidence conclusively establishes them. If errors intervened at the trial, they could not have been prejudicial. A verdict for the defendant would be unwarranted. The judgment is right, and is affirmed.

In *Feinberg v. Pfeiffer Co.,* Mrs. Feinberg, a longtime employee of the Pfeiffer Company, was promised retirement income when she retired. Eighteen months later, Feinberg, relying on Pfeiffer's promise, retired. When Pfeiffer Company changed management and subsequently refused to pay, Mrs. Feinberg sued to enforce the company's promise.

1. Was the Pfeiffer Company's promise really without consideration?
2. Why does the court use the phrase "promissory estoppel" rather than "equitable estoppel"? Should the term "estoppel" even be used? Would "reliance" or "detrimental reliance" be a better term? Does the Restatement of Contracts § 90 use the term "estoppel"?
3. What is the rationale used by the *Feinberg* court to resolve the dispute? Does Feinberg's recovery protect her expectation or reliance interest?

CASE

Feinberg v. Pfeiffer Co.
St. Louis Court of Appeals, Missouri (1959)
322 S.W.2d 163

DOERNER, Commissioner.

This is a suit brought in the Circuit Court of the City of St. Louis by plaintiff, a former employee of the defendant corporation, on an alleged contract whereby defendant agreed to pay plaintiff the sum of $200 per month for life upon her retirement. A jury being waived, the case was tried by the court alone. Judgment below was for plaintiff for $5,100, the amount of the pension claimed to be due as of the date of the trial, together with interest thereon, and defendant duly appealed.

The parties are in substantial agreement on the essential facts. Plaintiff began working for the defendant, a manufacturer of pharmaceuticals, in 1910, when she was but 17 years of age. By 1947 she had attained the position of bookkeeper, office manager, and assistant treasurer of the defendant.

. . . .

On December 27, 1947, the annual meeting of the defendant's Board of Directors was held at the Company's offices in St. Louis, presided over by Max Lippman, its then president and largest individual stockholder. The other directors present were George L. Marcus, Sidney Harris, Sol Flammer, and Walter Weinstock, who, with Max Lippman, owned 5,007 of the 6,503 shares then issued and outstanding. At that meeting the Board of Directors adopted the following resolution, which, because it is the crux of the case, we quote in full:

"The Chairman thereupon pointed out that the Assistant Treasurer, Mrs. Anna Sacks Feinberg, has given the corporation many years of long and faithful service. Not only has she served the corporation devotedly, but with exceptional ability and skill. The President pointed out that although all of the officers and directors sincerely hoped and desired that Mrs. Feinberg would continue in her present position for as long as she felt able, nevertheless, in view of the length of service which she has contributed provision should be made to afford her retirement privileges and benefits which should become a firm obligation of the corporation to be available to her whenever she should see fit to retire from active duty, however many years in the future such retirement may become effective. It was, accordingly, proposed that Mrs. Feinberg's salary which is presently $350.00 per month, be increased to $400.00 per month, and that Mrs. Feinberg would be given the privilege of retiring from active duty at any time she may elect to see fit so to do upon a retirement pay of $200.00 per month for life, with the distinct understanding that the retirement plan is merely being adopted at the present time in order to afford Mrs. Feinberg security for the future and in the hope that her active services will continue with the corporation for many years to come. After due discussion and consideration, and upon motion duly made and seconded, it was—

"Resolved, that the salary of Anna Sacks Feinberg be increased from $350.00 to $400.00 per month and that she be afforded the privilege of retiring from active duty in the corporation at any time she may elect to see fit so to do upon retirement pay of $200.00 per month, for the remainder of her life."

At the request of Mr. Lippman, his sons-in-law, Messrs. Harris and Flammer, called upon the plaintiff at her apartment on the same day to advise her of the passage of the resolution. Plaintiff testified on cross-examination that she had no prior information that such a pension plan was contemplated, that it came as a surprise to her, and that she would have continued in her employment whether or not such a resolution had been adopted. It is clear from the evidence that there was no contract, oral or written, as to plaintiff's length of employment, and that she was free to quit, and the defendant to discharge her, at any time.

Plaintiff did continue to work for the defendant through June 30, 1949, on which date she retired. In accordance with the foregoing resolution, the defendant began paying her the sum of $200 on the first of each month. Mr. Lippman died on November 18, 1949, and was succeeded as president of the company by his widow. Because of an illness, she retired from that office and was succeeded in October, 1953, by her son-in-law, Sidney M. Harris. Mr. Harris testified that while Mrs. Lippman had been president she signed the monthly pension check paid plaintiff, but fussed about doing so, and considered the payments as gifts. After his election, he stated, a new accounting firm employed by the defendant questioned the validity of the payments to plaintiff on several occasions, and in the spring of 1956, upon its recommendation, he consulted the Company's then attorney, Mr. Ralph Kalish. Harris testified that both Ernst and Ernst, the accounting firm, and Kalish told him there was no need of giving plaintiff the money. He also stated that he had concurred in the view that the payments to plaintiff were mere gratuities rather than amounts due under a contractual obligation, and that following his discussion with the Company's attorney plaintiff was sent a check for $100 on April 1, 1956. Plaintiff declined to accept the reduced amount, and this action followed. Additional facts will be referred to later in this opinion.

Appellant's next complaint is that there was insufficient evidence to support the court's findings that plaintiff would not have quit defendant's employ had she not known and relied upon the promise of defendant to pay her $200 a month for life, and the finding that, from her voluntary retirement until April 1, 1956, plaintiff relied upon the continued receipt of the pension installments. The trial court so found, and, in our opinion, justifiably so. Plaintiff testified, and was corroborated by Harris, defendant's witness, that knowledge of the passage of the resolution was communicated to her on December 27, 1947, the very day it was adopted. She was told at that time by Harris and Flammer, she stated, that she could take the pension as of that day, if she wished. She testified further that she continued to work for another year and a half, through June 30, 1949; that at that time her health was good and she could have continued to work, but that after working for almost forty years she thought she would take a rest.

. . . .

We come, then, to the basic issue in the case. . . .

". . . whether plaintiff has proved that she has a right to recover from defendant based upon legally binding contractual obligation to pay her $200 per month for life."

It is defendant's contention, in essence, that the resolution adopted by its Board of Directors was a mere promise to make a gift, and that no contract resulted either thereby, or when plaintiff retired, because there was no consideration given or paid by the plaintiff. It urges that a promise to make a gift is not binding unless supported by a legal consideration; that the only apparent consideration for the adoption of the foregoing resolution was the "many years of long and faithful service" expressed therein; and that past services are not a valid consideration for a promise. Defendant argues further that there is nothing in the resolution which made its effectiveness conditional upon plaintiff's continued employment, that she was not under contract to work for any length of time but was free to quit whenever she wished, and that she had no contractual right to her position and could have been discharged at any time.

. . . .

By the terms of the resolution defendant promised to pay plaintiff the sum of $200 a month upon her retirement. . . .

Section 90 of the Restatement of the Law of Contracts states that: "A promise which the promisor should reasonably expect to induce action or forbearance of a definite and substantial character on the part of the promisee and which does induce such action or forbearance is binding if injustice can be avoided only by enforcement of the promise." This doctrine has been described as that of "promissory estoppel," as distinguished from that of equitable estoppel or estoppel in pais, the reason for the differentiation being stated as follows:

> "It is generally true that one who has led another to act in reasonable reliance on his representations of fact cannot afterwards in litigation between the two deny the truth of the representations, and some courts have sought to apply this principle to the formation of contracts, where, relying on a gratuitous promise, the promisee has suffered detriment. It is to be noticed, however, that such a case does not come within the ordinary definition of estoppel. If there is any representation of an existing fact, it is only that the promisor at the time of making the promise intends to fulfill it. As to such intention there is usually no misrepresentation and if there is, it is not that which has injured the promisee. In other words, he relies on a promise and not on a misstatement of fact; and the term 'promissory' estoppel or something equivalent should be used to make the distinction." Williston on Contracts, Rev.Ed., Sec. 139, Vol. 1.

In speaking of this doctrine, Judge Learned Hand said in Porter v. Commissioner of Internal Revenue, 2 Cir., 60 F.2d 673, 675, that ". . . 'promissory estoppel' is now a recognized species of consideration." . . .

Was there such an act on the part of plaintiff, in reliance upon the promise contained in the resolution, as will estop the defendant, and therefore create an enforceable contract under the doctrine of promissory estoppel? We think there was. One of the illustrations cited under Section 90 of the Restatement is: "2. A promises B to pay him an annuity during B's life. B thereupon resigns a profitable employment, as A expected that he might. B receives the annuity for some years, in the meantime becoming disqualified from again obtaining good employment. A's promise is binding."

. . . .

At the time she retired plaintiff was 57 years of age. At the time the payments were discontinued she was over 63 years of age. It is a matter of common knowledge that it is virtually impossible for a woman of that age to find satisfactory employment, much less a position comparable to that which plaintiff enjoyed at the time of her retirement.

. . . .

As the trial court correctly decided, such action on plaintiff's part was her retirement from a lucrative position in reliance upon defendant's promise to pay her an annuity or pension. In a very similar case, Ricketts v. Scothorn, 57 Neb. 51, 77 N.W. 365, 367, 42 L.R.A. 794, the Supreme Court of Nebraska said:

> ". . . According to the undisputed proof, as shown by the record before us, the plaintiff was a working girl, holding a position in which she earned a salary of $10 per week. Her grandfather, desiring to put her in a position of independence, gave her the note accompanying it with the remark that his other grandchildren did not work, and that she would not be obliged to work any longer. In effect, he suggested that she might abandon her employment, and rely in the future upon the bounty which he promised. He doubtless desired that she should give up her occupation, but, whether he did or not, it is entirely certain that he contemplated such action on her part as a reasonable and probable consequence of his gift. Having intentionally influenced the plaintiff to alter her position for the worse on the faith of the note being paid when due, it would be grossly inequitable to permit the maker, or his executor, to resist payment on the ground that the promise was given without consideration."

The Commissioner therefore recommends, for the reasons stated, that the judgment be affirmed.

PER CURIAM.

The foregoing opinion by DOERNER, C., is adopted as the opinion of the court. The judgment is, accordingly, affirmed.

WOLFE, P.J., and ANDERSON and RUDDY, JJ., concur.

⫿ PARALEGAL EXERCISE 2.20

Marylou Maxwell, an honors student in high school, was offered a full tuition scholarship by Utopia College. Marylou turned down partial scholarships from other colleges so she could attend Utopia. After the second week of classes, Marylou was informed that Utopia could not honor its commitment to give her a full scholarship.

Did Utopia College make an offer to Marylou? What were the promisor's promise and the consideration for the promisor's promise?

If Utopia college did not extend an offer to Marylou because its promise lacked consideration, could Marylou satisfy the four elements of reliance? Would she be entitled to protection of her expectation or reliance interest? ▪

ALTERNATIVE CAUSES OF ACTION IF THERE IS NO OFFER

An offer requires a promisor's promise—an unequivocal assurance that something will or will not be done. Without this unequivocal assurance, there can be no offer, no contract, no breach of contract action, and no remedy for breach of contract. If the parties walk away without there being a promise (an unequivocal assurance), neither could successfully maintain a breach of contract cause of action and claim injury to an expectation interest. A breach of contract action, however, is not the only action. A reliance or restitution action may at times be available even if neither party made an unequivocal assurance.

The Role of Reliance as a Cause of Action When There Is No Promise (No Unequivocal Assurance)

If a party acts or refrains from acting because he or she is relying on the other party's encouragement, a reliance interest comes into being even though no contract caliber promise (unequivocal assurance) has been made.

Example 2-19

New World Corporation and Green Construction Company are negotiating for construction of a new production plant for New World. At this time, although neither has made an offer, New World says to Green, "Although I am not ready to make you an offer, you should buy a large earthmover so you can start work as soon as we contract." If Green buys the earthmover but New World never makes an offer, Green has suffered an injury by relying on New World's encouragement.

Although traditional contract law emphasizes expectation interests, several cases in recent years have permitted recovery although the transaction never reached the promise (unequivocal assurance) phase. Because a contract had not been formed, recovery was based on reliance on statements made during preliminary negotiations rather than on the breach of a "contract promise."

The most famous case in this area, *Hoffman v. Red Owl Stores, Inc.*, was decided by the Wisconsin Supreme Court in 1965. Joseph Hoffman owned and operated a bakery in Wautoma, Wisconsin, where his success led him to consider expanding his operations to include a grocery store. With this in mind, he bought a small grocery store in Wautoma. A short time later, Hoffman contacted a Red Owl Representative to discuss establishing a Red Owl franchise store. After their initial negotiations, the following events took place:

- June 6, 1961: Hoffman sold his grocery store in Wautoma.
- Hoffman bought an option to buy a building site in Chilton.
- September 15, 1961: Hoffman exercised his option to buy the building site in Chilton by paying $1,000 down.

- November 6, 1961: Hoffman sold his bakery business and bakery building in Wautoma.
- November 1961: Hoffman moved to Neenah and obtained employment at an Appleton bakery.

The first half of the following appellate court opinion chronicles the negotiations between Hoffman and various Red Owl representatives. Analyze this part of the opinion as follows:

1. Create a timeline for the Hoffman/Red Owl negotiations by listing in chronological order each request made by the Red Owl representatives and each response made by Hoffman.
2. Beginning with the first request listed on the timeline, decide whether that request constitutes an offer for the franchise.
3. When the parties walked away from each other had an offer for the franchise already been made or were the parties still in the preliminary negotiation phase of the transaction?

In the second half of the opinion, focus on Chief Justice Currie's statements for the court and answer the following questions:

1. When Hoffman was awarded a judgment against Red Owl, did the court base recovery on a breach of contract or on promissory estoppel?
2. Under the theory of recovery used by the court, was recovery intended to compensate Hoffman for an injury based on his expectation or for an injury suffered as a result of his reliance?
3. What did Hoffman need to prove to be entitled to a recovery under the cause of action used by the court?

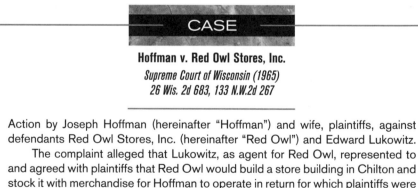

CASE

Hoffman v. Red Owl Stores, Inc.
Supreme Court of Wisconsin (1965)
26 Wis. 2d 683, 133 N.W.2d 267

Action by Joseph Hoffman (hereinafter "Hoffman") and wife, plaintiffs, against defendants Red Owl Stores, Inc. (hereinafter "Red Owl") and Edward Lukowitz.

The complaint alleged that Lukowitz, as agent for Red Owl, represented to and agreed with plaintiffs that Red Owl would build a store building in Chilton and stock it with merchandise for Hoffman to operate in return for which plaintiffs were to put up and invest a total sum of $18,000; that in reliance upon the abovementioned agreement and representations plaintiffs sold their bakery building and business and their grocery store and business; also in reliance on the agreement and representations Hoffman purchased the building site in Chilton and rented a residence for himself and his family in Chilton; plaintiffs' actions in reliance on the representations and agreement disrupted their personal and business life;

plaintiffs lost substantial amounts of income and expended large sums of money as expenses. Plaintiffs demanded recovery of damages for the breach of defendants' representations and agreements.

The action was tried to a court and jury. The facts hereafter stated are taken from the evidence adduced at the trial. Where there was a conflict in the evidence the version favorable to plaintiffs has been accepted since the verdict rendered was in favor of plaintiffs.

Hoffman assisted by his wife operated a bakery at Wautoma from 1956 until sale of the building late in 1961. The building was owned in joint tenancy by him and his wife. Red Owl is a Minnesota corporation having its home office at Hopkins, Minnesota. It owns and operates a number of grocery supermarket stores and also extends franchises to agency stores which are owned by individuals, partnerships and corporations. Lukowitz resides at Green Bay and since September, 1960, has been divisional manager for Red Owl in a territory comprising Upper Michigan and most of Wisconsin in charge of 84 stores. Prior to September, 1960, he was district manager having charge of approximately 20 stores.

In November, 1959, Hoffman was desirous of expanding his operations by establishing a grocery store and contacted a Red Owl representative by the name of Jansen, now deceased. Numerous conversations were had in 1960 with the idea of establishing a Red Owl franchise store in Wautoma. In September, 1960, Lukowitz succeeded Jansen as Red Owl's representative in the negotiations. Hoffman mentioned that $18,000 was all the capital he had available to invest and he was repeatedly assured that this would be sufficient to set him up in business as a Red Owl store. About Christmastime, 1960, Hoffman thought it would be a good idea if he bought a small grocery store in Wautoma and operated it in order that he gain experience in the grocery business prior to operating a Red Owl store in some larger community. On February 6, 1961, on the advice of Lukowitz and Sykes, who had succeeded Lukowitz as Red Owl's district manager, Hoffman bought the inventory and fixtures of a small grocery store in Wautoma and leased the building in which it was operated.

After three months of operating this Wautoma store, the Red Owl representatives came in and took inventory and checked the operations and found the store was operating at a profit. Lukowitz advised Hoffman to sell the store to his manager, and assured him that Red Owl would find a larger store for him elsewhere. Acting on this advice and assurance, Hoffman sold the fixtures and inventory to his manager on June 6, 1961. Hoffman was reluctant to sell at that time because it meant losing the summer tourist business, but he sold on the assurance that he would be operating in a new location by fall and that he must sell this store if he wanted a bigger one. Before selling, Hoffman told the Red Owl representatives that he had $18,000 for "getting set up in business" and they assured him that there would be no problems in establishing him in a bigger operation. The makeup of the $18,000 was not discussed; it was understood plaintiff's father-in-law would furnish part of it. By June, 1961, the towns for the new grocery store had been narrowed down to two, Kewaunee and Chilton. In Kewaunee, Red Owl had an option on a building site. In Chilton, Red Owl had nothing under option, but it did select a site to which plaintiff obtained an option at Red Owl's suggestion. The option stipulated a purchase price of $6,000 with $1,000 to be paid on election to purchase and the balance to be paid within 30 days. On Lukowitz's assurance that everything was all set plaintiff paid $1,000 down on the lot on September 15th.

On September 27, 1961, plaintiff met at Chilton with Lukowitz and Mr. Reymund and Mr. Carlson from the home office who prepared a projected financial statement. Part of the funds plaintiffs were to supply as their investment in the venture were to be obtained by sale of their Wautoma bakery building.

On the basis of this meeting Lukowitz assured Hoffman: " * * * [E]verything is ready to go. Get your money together and we are set." Shortly after this meeting Lukowitz told plaintiffs that they would have to sell their bakery business and bakery building, and that their retaining this property was the only "hitch" in the entire plan. On November 6, 1961, plaintiffs sold their bakery building for $10,000. Hoffman was to retain the bakery equipment as he contemplated using it to operate a bakery in connection with his Red Owl store. After sale of the bakery Hoffman obtained employment on the night shift at an Appleton bakery.

The record contains different exhibits which were prepared in September and October, some of which were projections of the fiscal operation of the business and others were proposed building and floor plans. Red Owl was to procure some third party to buy the Chilton lot from Hoffman, construct the building, and then lease it to Hoffman. No final plans were ever made, nor were bids let or a construction contract entered. Some time prior to November 20, 1961, certain of the terms of the lease under which the building was to be rented by Hoffman were understood between him and Lukowitz. The lease was to be for 10 years with a rental approximating $550 a month calculated on the basis of 1 percent per month on the building cost, plus 6 percent of the land cost divided on a monthly basis. At the end of the 10-year term he was to have an option to renew the lease for an additional 10-year period or to buy the property at cost on an installment basis. There was no discussion as to what the installments would be or with respect to repairs and maintenance.

On November 22nd or 23rd, Lukowitz and plaintiffs met in Minneapolis with Red Owl's credit manager to confer on Hoffman's financial standing and on financing the agency. Another projected financial statement was there drawn up entitled, "Proposed Financing For An Agency Store." This showed Hoffman contributing $24,100 of cash capital of which only $4,600 was to be cash possessed by plaintiffs. Eight thousand was to be procured as a loan from a Chilton bank secured by a mortgage on the bakery fixtures, $7,500 was to be obtained on a 5 percent loan from the father-in-law, and $4,000 was to be obtained by sale of the lot to the lessor at a profit.

A week or two after the Minneapolis meeting Lukowitz showed Hoffman a telegram from the home office to the effect that if plaintiff could get another $2,000 for promotional purposes the deal could go through for $26,000. Hoffman stated he would have to find out if he could get another $2,000. He met with his father-in-law, who agreed to put $13,000 into the business provided he could come into the business as a partner. Lukowitz told Hoffman the partnership arrangement "sounds fine" and that Hoffman should not go into the partnership arrangement with the "front office." On January 16, 1962, the Red Owl credit manager teletyped Lukowitz that the father-in-law would have to sign an agreement that the $13,000 was either a gift or a loan subordinate to all general creditors and that he would prepare the agreement. On January 31, 1962, Lukowitz teletyped the home office that the father-in-law would sign one or other of the agreements. However, Hoffman testified that it was not until the final meeting some time between January 26th and February 2nd, 1962, that he was told that his father-in-law was expected to sign an agreement that the $13,000 he was advancing was to be an outright gift. No mention was then made by the Red Owl representatives of the alternative of the father-in-law signing a subordination agreement. At this meeting the Red Owl agents presented Hoffman with the following projected financial statement:

"Capital required in operation:

"Cash	$ 5,000.00
"Merchandise	20,000.00
"Bakery	18,000.00
"Fixtures	17,500.00
"Promotional Funds	1,500.00
"TOTAL:	$62,000.00

"Source of funds:

"Red Owl 7-day terms	$ 5,000.00
"Red Owl Fixture contract (Term 5 years)	14,000.00
"Bank Loans (Terms 9 years Union State Bank	
"of Chilton)	8,000.00
"(Secured by Bakery Equipment)	
"Other loans (Term No-pay) No interest	13,000.00
"Father-in-law	
"(Secured by None)	
"(Secured by Mortgage on	2,000.00
"Wautoma Bakery Bldg.)	
"Resale of Land	6,000.00
"Equity Capital: $5,000.00-Cash	
"Amount owner has 17,500.00-Bakery Equip.	
"to invest:	22,500.00
"TOTAL:	$70,500.00"

Hoffman interpreted the above statement to require of plaintiffs a total of $34,000 cash made up of $13,000 gift from his father-in-law, $2,000 on mortgage, $8,000 on Chilton bank loan, $5,000 in cash from plaintiff, and $6,000 on the resale of the Chilton lot. Red Owl claims $18,000 is the total of the unborrowed or unencumbered cash, that is, $13,000 from the father-in-law and $5,000 cash from Hoffman himself. Hoffman informed Red Owl he could not go along with this proposal, and particularly objected to the requirement that his father-in-law sign an agreement that his $13,000 advancement was an absolute gift. This terminated the negotiations between the parties.

The case was submitted to the jury on a special verdict with the first two questions answered by the court. This verdict, as returned by the jury, was as follows:

"Question No. 1: Did the Red Owl Stores, Inc. and Joseph Hoffman on or about mid-May of 1961 initiate negotiations looking to the establishment of Joseph Hoffman as a franchise operator of a Red Owl Store in Chilton? Answer: Yes. (Answered by the Court.)

"Question No. 2: Did the parties mutually agree on all of the details of the proposal so as to reach a final agreement thereon? Answer: No. (Answered by the Court.)

"Question No. 3: Did the Red Owl Stores, Inc., in the course of said negotiations, make representations to Joseph Hoffman that if he fulfilled certain conditions that they would establish him as a franchise operator of a Red Owl Store in Chilton? Answer: Yes.

"Question No. 4: If you have answered Question No. 3 'Yes,' then answer this question: Did Joseph Hoffman rely on said representations and was he induced to act thereon? Answer: Yes.

"Question No. 5: If you have answered Question No. 4 'Yes,' then answer this question: Ought Joseph Hoffman, in the exercise of ordinary care, to have relied on said representations? Answer: Yes.

"Question No. 6: If you have answered Question No. 3 'Yes' then answer this question: Did Joseph Hoffman fulfill all the conditions he was required to fulfill by the terms of the negotiations between the parties up to January 26, 1962? Answer: Yes.

"Question No. 7: What sum of money will reasonably compensate the plaintiffs for such damages as they sustained by reason of:

"(a) The sale of the Wautoma store fixtures and inventory?
    "Answer: $16,735.00.
"(b) The sale of the bakery building?
    "Answer: $2,000.00.
"(c) Taking up the option on the Chilton lot?
    "Answer: $1,000.00.
"(d) Expenses of moving his family to Neenah?
    "Answer: $140.00.
"(e) House rental in Chilton?
    "Answer: $125.00."

Plaintiffs moved for judgment on the verdict while defendants moved to change the answers to Questions 3, 4, 5, and 6 from "Yes" to "No", and in the alternative for relief from the answers to the subdivisions of Question 7 or a new trial. On March 31, 1964, the circuit court entered the following order:

"IT IS ORDERED in accordance with said decision on motions after verdict hereby incorporated herein by reference:

"1. That the answer of the jury to Question No. 7(a) be and the same is hereby vacated and set aside and that a new trial be had on the sole issue of the damages for loss, if any, on the sale of the Wautoma store, fixtures and inventory.

"2. That all other portions of the verdict of the jury be and hereby are approved and confirmed and all after-verdict motions of the parties inconsistent with this order are hereby denied."

Defendants have appealed from this order and plaintiffs have cross-appealed from paragraph 1. thereof.

CURRIE, Chief Justice.

The instant appeal and cross-appeal present these questions:

1. Whether this court should recognize causes of action grounded on promissory estoppel as exemplified by sec. 90 of Restatement, 1 Contracts?
2. Do the facts in this case make out a cause of action for promissory estoppel?
3. Are the jury's findings with respect to damages sustained by the evidence?

RECOGNITION OF A CAUSE OF ACTION GROUNDED ON PROMISSORY ESTOPPEL

Sec. 90 of Restatement, 1 Contracts, provides (at p. 110):

"A promise which the promisor should reasonably expect to induce action or forbearance of a definite and substantial character on the part of the promisee and which does induce such action or forbearance is binding if injustice can be avoided only by enforcement of the promise."

. . . .

Many courts of other jurisdictions have seen fit over the years to adopt the principle of promissory estoppel, and the tendency in that direction continues. As Mr. Justice McFADDIN, speaking in behalf of the Arkansas court, well stated, that the development of the law of promissory estoppel "is an attempt by the courts to keep remedies abreast of increased moral consciousness of honesty and fair representations in all business dealings." Peoples National Bank of Little Rock v. Linebarger Construction Company (1951), 219 Ark. 11, 17, 240 S.W.2d 12, 16. For a further discussion of the doctrine of promissory estoppel, see 1A Corbin, Contracts, pp. 187, et seq., secs. 193–209; 3 Pomeroy's Equity Jurisprudence (5th ed.), pp. 211, et seq., sec. 808b; 1 Williston, Contracts (Jaeger's 3d ed.), pp. 607, et seq., sec. 140; Boyer, Promissory Estoppel: Requirements and Limitations of the Doctrine, 98 University of Pennsylvania Law Review (1950), 459; Seavey, Reliance Upon Gratuitous Promises or Other Conduct, 64 Harvard Law Review (1951), 913; Annos. 115 A.L.R. 152, and 48 A.L.R.2d 1069.

The Restatement avoids use of the term "promissory estoppel," and there has been criticism of it as an inaccurate term. See 1A Corbin, Contracts, p. 232, et seq., sec. 204. On the other hand, Williston advocated the use of this term or something equivalent. 1 Williston, Contracts (1st ed.), p. 308, sec. 139. Use of the word "estoppel" to describe a doctrine upon which a party to a lawsuit may obtain affirmative relief offends the traditional concept that estoppel merely serves as a shield and cannot serve as a sword to create a cause of action. See Utschig v. McClone (1962), 16 Wis.2d 506, 509, 114 N.W.2d 854. . . . We have employed its use in this opinion not only because of its extensive use by other courts but also since a more accurate equivalent has not been devised.

Because we deem the doctrine of promissory estoppel, as stated in sec. 90 of Restatement, 1 Contracts, is one which supplies a needed tool which courts may employ in a proper case to prevent injustice, we endorse and adopt it.

APPLICABILITY OF DOCTRINE TO FACTS OF THIS CASE

The record here discloses a number of promises and assurances given to Hoffman by Lukowitz in behalf of Red Owl upon which plaintiffs relied and acted upon to their detriment.

Foremost were the promises that for the sum of $18,000 Red Owl would establish Hoffman in a store. After Hoffman had sold his grocery store and paid the $1,000 on the Chilton lot, the $18,000 figure was changed to $24,100. Then in November, 1961, Hoffman was assured that if the $24,100 figure were increased by $2,000 the deal would go through. Hoffman was induced to sell his grocery store fixtures and inventory in June, 1961, on the promise that he would be in his new store by fall. In November, plaintiffs sold their bakery building on the urging of defendants and on the assurance that this was the last step necessary to have the deal with Red Owl go through.

We determine that there was ample evidence to sustain the answers of the jury to the questions of the verdict with respect to the promissory representations made by Red Owl, Hoffman's reliance thereon in the exercise of ordinary care, and his fulfillment of the conditions required of him by the terms of the negotiations had with Red Owl.

There remains for consideration the question of law raised by defendants that agreement was never reached on essential factors necessary to establish a contract between Hoffman and Red Owl. Among these were the size, cost, design, and layout of the store building; and the terms of the lease with respect to rent, maintenance, renewal, and purchase options. This poses the question of whether the promise necessary to sustain a cause of action for promissory estoppel must embrace all essential details of a proposed transaction between promisor and promisee so as to be the equivalent of an offer that would result in a binding contract between the parties if the promisee were to accept the same.

Originally the doctrine of promissory estoppel was invoked as a substitute for consideration rendering a gratuitous promise enforceable as a contract. See Williston, Contracts (1st ed.), p. 307, sec. 139. In other words, the acts of reliance by the promisee to his detriment provided a substitute for consideration. If promissory estoppel were to be limited to only those situations where the promise giving rise to the cause of action must be so definite with respect to all details that a contract would result were the promise supported by consideration, then the defendants' instant promises to Hoffman would not meet this test. However, sec. 90 of Restatement, 1 Contracts, does not impose the requirement that the promise giving rise to the cause of action must be so comprehensive in scope as to meet the requirements of an offer that would ripen into a contract if accepted by the promisee. Rather the conditions imposed are:

1. Was the promise one which the promisor should reasonably expect to induce action or forbearance of a definite and substantial character on the part of the promisee?
2. Did the promise induce such action or forbearance?
3. Can injustice be avoided only by enforcement of the promise?

We deem it would be a mistake to regard an action grounded on promissory estoppel as the equivalent of a breach of contract action. As Dean Boyer points out, it is desirable that fluidity in the application of the concept be maintained. 98 University of Pennsylvania Law Review (1950), 459, at page 497. While the first two of the above listed three requirements of promissory estoppel present issues of fact which ordinarily will be resolved by a jury, the third requirement, that the remedy can only be invoked where necessary to avoid injustice, is one that involves a policy decision by the court. Such a policy decision necessarily embraces an element of discretion.

We conclude that injustice would result here if plaintiffs were not granted some relief because of the failure of defendants to keep their promises which induced plaintiffs to act to their detriment.

DAMAGES

Defendants attack all the items of damages awarded by the jury.

. . . .

Plaintiffs never moved to Chilton because defendants suggested that Hoffman get some experience by working in a Red Owl store in the Fox River Valley. Plaintiffs, therefore, moved to Neenah instead of Chilton. After moving, Hoffman worked at night in an Appleton bakery but held himself available for work in a Red Owl store. The $140 moving expense would not have been incurred if plaintiffs had not sold their bakery building in Wautoma in reliance upon defendants' promises. We consider the $140 moving expense to be a proper item of damage.

We turn now to the damage item with respect to which the trial court granted a new trial, i.e., that arising from the sale of the Wautoma grocery store fixtures and inventory for which the jury awarded $16,735. The trial court ruled that Hoffman could not recover for any loss of future profits for the summer months following the sale on June 6, 1961, but that damages would be limited to the difference between the sales price received and the fair market value of the assets sold, giving consideration to any goodwill attaching thereto by reason of the transfer of a going business. There was no direct evidence presented as to what this fair market value was on June 6, 1961. The evidence did disclose that Hoffman paid $9,000 for the inventory, added $1,500 to it and sold it for $10,000 or a loss of $500. His 1961 federal income tax return showed that the grocery equipment had been purchased for $7,000 and sold for $7,955.96. Plaintiffs introduced evidence of the buyer that during the first 11 weeks of operation of the grocery store his gross sales were $44,000 and his profit was $6,000 or roughly 15 percent. On cross-examination he admitted that this was gross and not net profit. Plaintiffs contend that in a breach of contract action damages may include loss of profits. However, this is not a breach of contract action.

The only relevancy of evidence relating to profits would be with respect to proving the element of goodwill in establishing the fair market value of the grocery inventory and fixtures sold. Therefore, evidence of profits would be admissible to afford a foundation for expert opinion as to fair market value.

Where damages are awarded in promissory estoppel instead of specifically enforcing the promisor's promise, they should be only such as in the opinion of the court are necessary to prevent injustice. Mechanical or rule of thumb approaches to the damage problem should be avoided. In discussing remedies to be applied by courts in promissory estoppel we quote the following views of writers on the subject:

. . . .

"The wrong is not primarily in depriving the plaintiff of the promised reward but in causing the plaintiff to change position to his detriment. It would follow that the damages should not exceed the loss caused by the change of position, which would never be more in amount, but might be less, than the promised reward." Seavey, Reliance on Gratuitous Promises or Other Conduct, 64 Harvard Law Review (1951), 913, 926.

. . . .

At the time Hoffman bought the equipment and inventory of the small grocery store at Wautoma he did so in order to gain experience in the grocery store business. At that time discussion had already been had with Red Owl representatives that Wautoma might be too small for a Red Owl operation and that a larger city might be more desirable. Thus Hoffman made this purchase more or less as a temporary experiment. Justice does not require that the damages awarded him, because of selling these assets at the behest of defendants, should exceed any actual loss sustained measured by the difference between the sales price and the fair market value.

Since the evidence does not sustain the large award of damages arising from the sale of the Wautoma grocery business, the trial court properly ordered a new trial on this issue.

Order affirmed. Because of the cross-appeal, plaintiffs shall be limited to taxing but two-thirds of their costs.

The *Hoffman* court derived the elements for promissory estoppel from section 90 of the Restatement (First) of Contracts (1932):

> A promise which the promisor should reasonably expect to induce action or forbearance of a definite and substantial character on the part of the promisee and which does induce such action or forbearance is binding if injustice can be avoided only by enforcement of the promise.

After *Hoffman v. Red Owl* was decided, the American Law Institute, the drafters of the Restatements, revised the Restatement of Contracts. Restatement (Second) of Contracts includes section 90 in a slightly revised form:

> (1) A promise which the promisor should reasonably expect to induce action or forbearance on the part of the promisee or a third person and which does induce such action or forbearance is binding if injustice can be avoided only by enforcement of the promise. The remedy granted for breach may be limited as justice requires.

How does the revision of section 90 change the four elements for promissory estoppel?

⫼ PARALEGAL EXERCISE 2.21

Pursuant to its decision to begin distributing its beer in Missouri, Adolph Coors Company, a Colorado corporation, created a distribution plan that divided Missouri into 13 separate geographical areas. In August 1977, Coors released news reports requesting any person interested in becoming a Coors distributor to write the company requesting an application. Coors mailed formal applications and copies of Coors' "Basic Distributor Selection Guidelines" to Burst and approximately 1,600 other prospective applicants. Three hundred and seventy-nine applications were completed and returned to Coors of which 35, including Burst's, were for the Area No. 10 distributorship. Burst was one of four applicants selected for a field interview for Area No. 10 and the only one asked to Coors' headquarters for an in-house interview. However, on February 7, 1978, Burst received a letter notifying him that his application to become a Coors distributor had been rejected. Coors found none of the original applicants for Area No. 10 satisfactory and did not award the distributorship to any of them. Instead, Coors had Coors Distributing Company, a subsidiary, handle the distribution of its products until early 1979, when Coors awarded United City Distributors, which had not been one of the original 35 applicants, the distributorship for a part of original Area No. 10. Coors Distributing Company retained the remainder.

Based on the three elements for promissory estoppel (update the requirements so they relate to the Restatement (Second) of Contracts), should Burst prevail if he sues Coors? *Burst v. Adolph Coors Co.,* 650 F.2d 930 (8th Cir. 1981). ▪

The Role of Restitution as a Cause of Action
When There Is No Promise

Even though classical contract law emphasizes the expectation interest, it also recognizes a restitution interest. The courts protect the restitution interest by granting an injured party a restitution remedy in a breach of contract action. The courts also have created a cause of action for restitution, separate from an action for breach of contract.

A restitution cause of action is not based on a contract—neither one that is express (stated) nor one implied in fact (implied from the facts)—but on the court's imagination. It is important to understand that the phrase "restitution cause of action" has been selected to encompass all *actions* based on unjust enrichment. Over the years, the restitution cause of action has been referred to by various names such as "action in quasi-contract," "implied contract" (implied by law), "constructive contract," "assumpsit," ***"quantum meruit"***, and ***"quantum valebant"***. To add to the confusion, a breach of contract cause of action also masquerades as an action for assumpsit, *quantum meruit,* or *quantum valebant*. What the cause of action is labeled is unimportant. What is important are the requirements necessary for the cause of action. For a breach of contract cause of action, the requirements are a contract (offer and acceptance) that is enforceable, and that has been breached.

Restitution, the cause of action, is based on the policy of preventing "unjust enrichment." A restitution action requires

- that there is a benefit (the enrichment) conferred by one party on another, and
- that the retention of the benefit without compensating the party conferring the benefit would be unjust.

Finding the enrichment is often relatively easy. The difficult question is determining whether it would be unjust to allow the benefit to be retained without compensating the party conferring the benefit.

A person who interferes in the affairs of another by conferring an unnecessary or unwanted benefit cannot successfully seek compensation for his or her interference. Such a person is officious; that is, a meddler.

The Comments to the Restatement explore the concept of officiousness:

> a. Officiousness means interference in the affairs of others not justified by the circumstances under which the interference takes place. Policy ordinarily requires that a person who has conferred a benefit either by way of giving another services or by adding to the value of his land or by paying his debt or even by transferring property to him should not be permitted to require the other to pay therefore, unless the one conferring the benefit had a valid reason

quantum meruit

Quantum meruit is a common count (a standard allegation) in an action of assumpsit for work and labor. It is based on an implied assumpsit or promise on the part of the defendant to pay the plaintiff as much as is reasonably deserved for his or her labor.

quantum valebant

Quantum valebant is a common count (a standard allegation) in an action of assumpsit for goods sold and delivered. It is based on an implied assumpsit or promise on the part of the defendant to pay the plaintiff as much as the goods sold by the plaintiff and delivered to the defendant were reasonably worth.

for so doing. A person is not required to deal with another unless he so desires and, ordinarily, a person should not be required to become an obligor unless he so desires.

The principle stated in this Section is not a limitation of the general principle stated in § 1 ["A person who has been unjustly enriched at the expense of another is required to make restitution to the other."]; where a person has officiously conferred a benefit upon another, the other is enriched but is not considered to be unjustly enriched. The rule denying restitution to officious persons has the effect of penalizing those who thrust benefits upon others and protecting persons who have had benefits thrust upon them (see § 112). . . . Restatement of Restitution § 2, comment a (1937).

In *Gould v. American Water Works Service Co.*, Gould, the landowner, sought to entice The Bernards Water Company to purchase his land by drilling a productive water well on the land. An offer and a series of counteroffers followed. When the parties failed to reach an agreement, The Bernards Water Company, now knowing that the land in that area would produce the water required, purchased land adjacent to Gould's since that land could be purchased at a better price.

Gould brought a restitution cause of action against The Bernards Water Company, claiming unjust enrichment. Did Gould confer a benefit (an enrichment) on The Bernards Water Company? Was The Bernards Water Company *unjustly* enriched?

CASE

Gould v. American Water Works Service Co.
Supreme Court of New Jersey (1958)
52 N.J. 226, 245 A.2d 14

PER CURIAM.

The issue here is whether plaintiff, Jasper C. Gould, has a cause of action for damages against defendant The Bernards Water Company in *quasi* or implied contract based upon alleged unjust enrichment resulting from defendant's appropriation and use of information developed through plaintiff's efforts and skill in locating underground water wells. The trial court decided that the evidence created a jury question on the subject and the jury found for plaintiff Jasper Gould. The complaint against defendant American Water Works Service Co., Inc. was dismissed and has not been appealed. The Appellate Division, in an unreported opinion, reversed, holding that plaintiff was a mere volunteer and that no legal basis existed for imposing a *quasi*-contractual liability on defendant. We granted certification. 51 N.J. 182, 238 A.2d 469 (1968).

Plaintiff Jasper C. Gould is an experienced well digger. Defendant is a public utility engaged in the business of selling water to the public in Bernards Township and other localities. In 1953 plaintiff learned from a friend of many years standing, one Burd, who was in defendant's employ as a superintendent, that the company was interested in developing an additional water supply. Upon Gould's inquiry, Burd indicated the company's interest was in wells which would yield 200 to 225 gallons of water a minute. Gould asked also what the company would be willing to pay for such a well. Burd replied he was not the "boss" but he knew it would pay a fair price. Nothing further was said. The friendship between Gould and Burd was purely social. They had had no business relationship. Some time later Burd asked Gould if he would be gracious enough to talk with defendant's geologist. Gould agreed and spent two days with the geologist showing him wells Gould had dug on his own property and discussing conditions he encountered in doing so.

Thereafter, in the latter part of 1953 or early 1954, Gould spent some time drilling a well on five acres of land he owned in Bernards Township. At a depth of 365 feet the well delivered only 60 gallons a minute, so he abandoned it. He moved his equipment 80 feet farther in on his property and began to drill again. This time, after going down 670 feet, he located water and the well yielded over 200 gallons per minute. A short time later, at a social gathering, Gould told Burd he had a very good well and inquired as to whether the company would be interested in seeing a pump test on it. Burd said he would find out from his superiors, and a few days later he advised Gould his superiors would like to have such a test. In April 1954 the test was made. It revealed the well was yielding over 300 gallons a minute. In another conversation with Gould, Burd said the well was not large enough to admit defendant's pumping equipment and asked what it would cost to enlarge it from 6 to 10 inches. It is undisputed that Gould never furnished a figure. Instead he proceeded to ream the well to a 10-inch diameter for a depth of 250 feet. He admitted that nobody connected with the water company asked him to do so.

Later in 1954, how much later does not appear, Gould met with Burd's superiors who offered $12,000 for the well. There was no discussion about whether the offer was for title to the land or an easement. The conference was a short one because Gould asked for $100,000. About a year later defendant offered $12,000 to $13,000. It was again rejected. Some time later in 1955 or in 1956 Gould reduced his asking price to $50,000, but defendant was not interested. Finally about five years later, in 1960 or 1961, defendant offered $16,000 and Gould lowered his figure to $35,000. The negotiations ended on that note and no agreement was ever reached.

Gould conceded that no representative of defendant asked or authorized him to dig a well or to prospect for water in its behalf, or ever agreed that if he dug a well which produced water at the rate of 200 gallons a minute the company would buy it from him.

· · · ·

In August 1961 defendant acquired property on the south side of Route 202 opposite Gould's acreage and began to dig 490 feet from Gould's well. In March 1962, eight years after completion of Gould's second well, defendant's digging reached 1,450 feet in depth and produced sufficient water to move defendant to obtain a permanent diversionary permit from the State Division of Water Policy and Supply to divert up to 500,000 gallons of water a day from the well. About a year later plaintiff brought this action seeking damages from the water company. He alleged that defendant had been unjustly enriched as the result of plaintiff's well-digging activity and the knowledge defendant acquired thereby that water was to be found in the immediate area to an extent which defendant, as a seller of water to the public, was interested in locating and acquiring. More specifically, plaintiff claimed that defendant had encouraged him to dig wells to locate water of the volume desired. Thus when he dug such a well, and informed defendant of the location, defendant's failure to buy it coupled with the subsequent use of the information as the incentive for acquiring nearby property and digging a sufficiently productive well of its own, unjustly enriched defendant at plaintiff's expense. Therefore, plaintiff contended, in order to do justice the law ought to impose an obligation on defendant to pay plaintiff for the expenses and losses resulting from defendant's inequitable conduct.

After consideration of the entire record, we agree with the Appellate Division that plaintiff's proof fails to establish a claim upon which relief can be granted. We concur in its declaration:

> "The evidence is uncontradicted that what the plaintiff did was not done at the request of Bernards nor with any expectation at that time that he would be reimbursed by Bernards for his well digging expenses. Plaintiff * * * [Gould] dug the two wells on his property on his own initiative in the hope that if he were successful in finding an adequate water supply, he would be able to negotiate for a sale of the well or an interest in his property to the water company. The fact that the drawn-out negotiations were unsuccessful because the parties did not agree on a price affords no basis for imposing a *quasi*-contractual liability on defendant, nor is such basis to be found in the fact that defendant thereafter dug its own well approximately 500 feet away to a depth almost twice that of plaintiff's well. See Restatement, Restitution § 2, p. 15; § 112, p. 461; § 41, p. 162 (1937)."

In our judgment the plaintiff occupied the status of a volunteer who hoped that if his efforts produced a result which would interest defendant, an agreement to sell that result to defendant could be consummated. The fact that plaintiff knew defendant was interested generally in locating an additional water supply in the area would not transform his status from volunteer into an obligee when he found a source which defendant could use. Nor would the fact that defendant offered to buy the well at its price make it an obligor.

. . . .

When the negotiations broke off, it meant that plaintiff's speculative venture had failed to achieve its ultimate purpose. If it is assumed that defendant had learned from plaintiff's unsolicited efforts that there was substantial underground water in the area, and to that extent was the recipient of a benefit, such enrichment should not be regarded as unjust enrichment creating a liability for plaintiff's expenses and losses simply because defendant, encouraged by plaintiff's experience, acquired nearby property, dug a well about 500 feet from that of plaintiff and more than twice as deep, and located an acceptable additional supply of water.

Accordingly the judgment of the Appellate Division is affirmed.

For affirmance: Chief Justice WEINTRAUB and Justices JACOBS, FRANCIS, PROCTOR, HALL, SCHETTINO and HANEMAN–7.

For reversal: None.

Using the following two steps, analyze Paralegal Exercises 2.22 through 2.28:

1. Focus on the benefit (the enrichment) and identify:
   a. What was the benefit conferred?
   b. Who conferred the benefit?
   c. Upon whom was the benefit conferred?
2. Consider whether it would be unjust to permit the party receiving the benefit to retain it without compensating the party who conferred the benefit.

⫼ PARALEGAL EXERCISE 2.22

Last Christmas, Aunt Jane gave her niece Sylvia $1,000 as a gift. Aunt Jane had hoped that Sylvia would use this money to further her education. Shortly after Christmas, Sylvia squandered $600. Should Aunt Jane be entitled to restitution of the $600 Sylvia spent? Should Aunt Jane be entitled to restitution of the remaining $400? ■

⫼ PARALEGAL EXERCISE 2.23

When business was slow for the Quality Paving Company, employees would cruise neighborhoods in search of vacant houses with "For Sale" signs. If the driveway was in a state of disrepair, Quality would repave the drive and send a bill to the owner. Should Quality be entitled to restitution for the new driveway? ■

⫼ PARALEGAL EXERCISE 2.24

Under state statute, a father is required to provide support for his minor children. When Mr. Stephens failed to provide his minor son, Tommy, with adequate food and clothing, a neighbor fed and clothed the child. Is this neighbor entitled to restitution? ■

⫼ PARALEGAL EXERCISE 2.25

Would your answer to this problem be the same if a store instead of a neighbor had supplied the food and clothing? ■

⫼ PARALEGAL EXERCISE 2.26

Would your answer be the same if Mr. Stephens had been out of town and did not know that his son was improperly fed and clothed? ■

⫼ PARALEGAL EXERCISE 2.27

Would your answer be the same if the state had neither a common law nor a statutory rule requiring a father to support his minor children? ▪

⫼ PARALEGAL EXERCISE 2.28

How should the following case be resolved?

The streetcar in which Harrison was riding was involved in an accident. Harrison was thrown from the streetcar with such force that he hit his head on the sidewalk and was rendered unconscious. A spectator summoned Dr. Wisdom, who had an office down the street. In an effort to save Harrison's life, Dr. Wisdom performed a difficult operation, but Harrison died without regaining consciousness.

Should Dr. Wisdom be entitled to recover in a restitution action against Harrison's estate?

If Dr. Wisdom should be compensated for the injury to his restitution interest, what factors are relevant in determining how much he should recover? ▪

PARALEGAL CHECKLIST

The Offer Phase

❏ After all of the communications and events have been placed on a timeline, the paralegal and the supervising attorney can use the following checklist to determine whether an offer under classical contract law has been made.

1. Is the first communication an offer?
   a. Use an objective (reasonable person) standard.
   b. Has the promisor (offeror) created the power of acceptance in the promisee (offeree) by making a promise and demanding consideration (a "price") for that promise?
      1) Begin with the promisor's promise.
         a) Is the promisor's statement a promise or an inquiry? A promise is an unequivocal assurance that something will or will not be done.
         b) Is the promisor's statement a promise or an invitation to make a promise (offer)?
            (1) If the promisor's statement is an advertisement, is the ad a promise or an invitation to make a promise?
            (2) If the promisor's statement is by an auctioneer at an auction, is the auctioneer's statement a promise or an invitation to the audience to make a promise?
            (3) If the promisor's statement is in a preprinted form, is the statement in the form a promise or is the purported promise subject to the promisor's subsequent approval?
         c) Is the promisor's statement really a promise?
            (1) Is the promisor's statement a promise or a joke?
            (2) Is the promisor's statement a promise or an illusory

promise? An illusory promise is not a promise because it is uncertain—something may or may not be done depending on whether the promisor feels like doing it.

(3) Is the promisor's statement a promise or an indefinite promise? An indefinite promise is not a promise because it omits terms that the court must consider when determining an appropriate remedy for breach of contract.

2) Next, focus on the consideration for the promisor's promise. The consideration for the promisor's promise is the promisee's *performance* if the offer is for a unilateral contract or the promisee's *promise* if the offer is for a bilateral contract. The fact that the promisee's promise ultimately involves the promisee's performance does not change the promise into a performance. An offer for a unilateral contract is rarely made.

a) Is what purports to be the consideration for the promisor's promise at least a peppercorn? Courts will not be concerned with the size or value of the consideration. Something as small as a "peppercorn" can be consideration.

(1) Is the promisor asking for a price for his or her promise and only for something that is a joke?

(2) Is the promisor asking for a price for his or her promise or is the promisor asking for an illusory promise?

(3) Is the promisor asking for a price for his or her promise or is the promisor asking for an indefinite promise?

(4) Is the promisor asking for a price for his or her promise or is the promisor merely stating his or her motive for making the promise? Consideration is *what* the promisor wants to get in return for his or her promise and not *why* the promisor wants to get it.

(5) Is the promisor asking for a price for his or her promise or is the promisor merely trying to satisfy a moral obligation? Consideration is what the promisor wants to get in return for his or her promise and not the fact that the promisor feels an obligation to promise.

(6) Is the promisor asking for a price for his or her promise or is the promisor merely stating a price as a sham to feign consideration? Sham consideration is pretended or phony consideration—the "price" the promisor never intends to collect.

b) Has the promisor made his or her promise to attempt to induce the promisee to promise (if the offer is for a bilateral contract) or to perform (if the offer is for a unilateral contract)?

(1) Has the promisee already performed the requested price for the promisor's promise? Past consideration—a timing problem—cannot be consideration for the promisor's promise because the promisor's promise cannot be used to get

something that already
occurred.

(2) Does the promisee already
have the duty to perform
(preexisting duty to perform
what the promisor is asking
for)? A duty the promisee
has already committed to
perform cannot be consid-
eration for the promisor's
promise because the
promisor's promise is not
being used to entice the
promisee to perform. The
promisee is already
obligated to perform.

(3) Is the promisor stating a
price for his or her promise
or merely stating a
condition that the promisee
must satisfy to receive a gift?
The promisor's motive
distinguishes whether the
promisor is attempting to
entice the promisee's
performance by using his or
her own promise or whether
the promisee must perform
to put himself or herself in
the position to receive the
promisor's performance of a
gift promise.

❏ If the first communication is not an offer,
is the next communication an offer? Continue down the timeline until a communication that is an offer is found.

❏ If no classical offer is found due to a lack of
consideration for the promisor's promise,
check the alternatives for consideration.

1. Determine whether the legislature has
   a. substituted a writing for consideration;
   b. altered the rule about which party has
      the burden of proving consideration;
      or
   c. eliminated the consideration
      requirement in specific types of
      transactions.

2. Analyze whether the courts have:
   a. implied a promise—thereby supplying
      consideration;
   b. implied a promise to correct a timing
      problem; or
   c. recognized the doctrine of
      detrimental reliance (promissory
      estoppel) (Restatement (Second) of
      Contracts § 90(1)) to enforce a
      promise that lacks consideration. The
      elements of detrimental reliance are
      the following:
      1) That there is a promise by the
         promisor
      2) That the promisor should have
         reasonably expected his or her
         promise to induce action or
         forbearance on the part of the
         promisee
      3) That the promise did induce such
         action or forbearance
      4) That injustice could be avoided
         only by the enforcement of the
         promise

❏ If the lack of a "contract" quality promise prevents an offer from being formed
(lack of an unequivocal assurance), check
whether a detrimental reliance or a restitution *cause of action* exists.

1. Determine whether your court recognizes
   a detrimental reliance cause of action.
   The elements are the same as for
   detrimental reliance as a substitute for
   consideration (see Restatement (Second)
   of Contracts § 90(1)), except that the
   "promise" may be less than an
   unequivocal assurance.

2. Determine whether your court recognizes
   a restitution (unjust enrichment) cause
   of action if no offer exists. (See
   Restatement of Restitution §§ 112–117).
   The general elements for a restitution
   cause of action are the following:
   a. That there is a benefit conferred by
      one party on the other
   b. That the retention of the benefit
      without compensation would be unjust

KEY TERMS

Auction with reserve

Auction without reserve

Condition

Consideration

Consideration for the Promisee's promise or performance

Consideration for the Promisor's promise

Gap fillers

Illusory promise

Indefinite promise

Meeting of the minds

Objective standard

Offer

Offeree

Offer for a bilateral contract

Offer for a unilateral contract

Offeror

Preexisting duty

Preliminary negotiation

Promise

Promisee

Promisor

Quantum meruit

Quantum valebant

Reasonable person

Reasonable person's standard

Reliance cause of action

Restitution cause of action

Sham consideration

Subjective standard

REVIEW QUESTIONS

TRUE/FALSE QUESTIONS (CIRCLE THE CORRECT ANSWER)

1. T   F   The pre-offer phase of a transaction is also known as preliminary negotiation.

2. T   F   Preliminary negotiation takes place after an offer has been made.

3. T   F   The Restatement (Second) of Contracts § 24 defines an offer as: the manifestation of willingness to enter into a bargain, so made as to justify another person in understanding that his assent to that bargain is invited and will conclude it.

4. T   F   Offer, as defined in the Restatement (Second) of Contracts § 24, is based on an objective standard rather than on a subjective standard.

5. T   F   The offeror, to create the power of acceptance in the offeree, must state the terms of the contract so nothing remains for the offeror to negotiate once the offeree assents to these terms.

6. T   F   An offer is a promise made by one party to another in exchange for the other's promise or performance.

7. T   F   An offeror must make a promise for there to be an offer.

8.   T   F   The consideration for the offeror's promise is also called the "price" for the offeror's promise and is part of a "bargained-for exchange."

9.   T   F   Consideration for the offeror's promise may be either the offeree's promise or performance, depending on which the offeror prefers.

10.   T   F   An offer which is a "promise for a promise" is an offer for a unilateral contract.

11.   T   F   A "manifestation of willingness" or a "demonstration of willingness" refers to the outward actions of the negotiating parties as understood by an impartial third person watching the parties.

12.   T   F   The third person who is evaluating the outward actions of the negotiating parties is referred to as "the reasonable person."

13.   T   F   The reasonable person's standard is a subjective standard.

14.   T   F   Early contracts cases used an objective standard.

15.   T   F   Both the Restatement (First) and the Restatement (Second) of Contracts use an objective standard for the law of contracts.

16.   T   F   An advertisement made to the general public may be an offer.

17.   T   F   An advertisement may never be an offer.

18.   T   F   An offer must always be made to a specific party.

19.   T   F   In an auction "with reserve," the auctioneer is the offeror.

20.   T   F   In an auction "with reserve," the auctioneer may withdraw the property at any time until he or she announces the completion of the sale.

21.   T   F   Once a bidder had made a bid in an auction, he or she may not retract this bid.

22.   T   F   A statement in an advertisement for an auction that says "the property will be offered to the highest bidder" means that the auction will be conducted "without reserve."

23.   T   F   An auction is with reserve unless a contrary intention is apparent from a statute, court order, or advertisement or by an announcement at the beginning of the auction.

24.   T   F   Sam Brown, the auctioneer, presented a Louis XV ormolu clock to the potential bidders at an auction. Susan Sanchez, the owner of this valuable antique clock, had told Sam not to sell it for less than $5,000. In spite of Sam's best efforts, the highest bid was $2,500. Sam could withdraw the clock from the auction.

25.   T   F   A person with a secret (subjective) intent to make a joke while outwardly expressing (objective) intent to make an offer will be judged on his or her subjective intent.

26.   T   F   Contract formation occurs upon acceptance of the offer.

27.   T   F   If the offeror proposes a unilateral contract, the offeree must fully perform to accept the offer.

28. T   F   An illusory promise is an unequivocal assurance that something will or will not be done.

29. T   F   An indefinite promise contains all essential terms to allow the court, in the event of breach, to fashion a remedy.

30. T   F   Consideration is the "price" that the offeror demands in return for his or her promise.

31. T   F   Every contract has not one but two considerations: one for the offeror's promise and one for the offeree's promise or performance.

32. T   F   The consideration for the offeror's promise in the offer is the same as the offeree's promise or performance in the acceptance.

33. T   F   The consideration for the offeree's promise or performance in the acceptance is the same as the offeror's promise in the offer.

34. T   F   The promisor's promise to make a future gift lacks consideration and therefore cannot be an offer.

35. T   F   If a donor of a gift changes his or her mind, a gift that has already been made must be returned.

36. T   F   For an offer to exist, the consideration for the promisor's promise must be adequate.

37. T   F   A "peppercorn" cannot be consideration for the promisor's promise.

38. T   F   "I promise to pay you $1,000 for your love and affection" is an offer.

39. T   F   "I promise to paint your barn for $10" is an offer.

40. T   F   Motive can be consideration for a promise.

41. T   F   Moral obligation may be consideration for a promise.

42. T   F   An obligation already owed to the promisor (a preexisting duty) may be consideration for the promisor's promise.

43. T   F   If the promisee has already promised or performed (past consideration), the promisor would not be making his or her promise to induce a promise or performance and there would be no "bargained-for exchange."

44. T   F   Modern contract law allows a less rigid adherence to the classical consideration doctrine.

45. T   F   Reliance can never be an alternative to consideration.

46. T   F   Gloria VanFleet had a five-year contract to coach the Springfield Volunteers, a professional football team. During Gloria's second year as coach, her team won its league championship. The owners were so delighted that they offered to replace Gloria's contract with a new five-year contract at a 50 percent increase in salary. Gloria's promise to coach for five years would be consideration for the owner's promise to pay 50 percent more.

47.   T   F   The restitution cause of action is based on the policy of preventing unjust enrichment.

48.   T   F   The restitution cause of action is based on the fact that the promisee relied on the promisor's promise to his or her detriment.

49.   T   F   A restitution cause of action is based on a contract.

50.   T   F   A restitution remedy in a breach of contract action is the same as a restitution cause of action.

51.   T   F   *Quantum meruit* means "as much as it is worth."

52.   T   F   Under the Restatement of Restitution § 2 (1937), an officious person is one who is entitled to receive compensation for a benefit conferred upon another while serving in an official capacity.

53.   T   F   An officious person is a meddler.

54.   T   F   Restitution actions are often called contracts implied by law.

55.   T   F   When negotiations end without one party making an offer, the parties are *always* free to walk away from each other without any obligation.

56.   T   F   Restitution may be both a cause of action and a remedy.

57.   T   F   Reliance may be both a cause of action and a remedy.

58.   T   F   The elements for the reliance cause of action come from Restatement of Contracts § 90.

59.   T   F   An express contract and an implied in fact contract are real contracts and may form the basis for a breach of contract action. A contract implied by law is not a real contract but rather a judicial construct and may form the basis for a restitution cause of action.

60.   T   F   A person who is officious can recover in a restitution action for a benefit that he or she has conferred on another party.

61.   T   F   When business was slow for the Quality Paving Company, employees would cruise neighborhoods in search of vacant houses with "For Sale" signs. If the driveway was in a state of disrepair, Quality would repave the drive and send a bill to the owner. Quality could not successfully maintain a restitution cause of action for compensation for the new driveway because Quality was officious.

FILL-IN-THE-BLANK QUESTIONS

1.   _____.   A third person who is evaluating the outward actions of the negotiating parties.

2.   _____.   The reasonable person's standard.

3.   _____.   Standard used in early contracts cases.

4.   _____.   An auction in which the auctioneer is the offeror.

5. _____. An auction in which the bidder is the offeror.

6. _____. A contract that results from a promise for a performance.

7. _____. A contract that results from a promise for a promise.

8. _____. The "price" that the promisor expects to receive for his or her promise.

9. _____. May sometimes be an alternative to consideration under modern contract law.

10. _____. An unequivocal assurance that something will or will not be done.

11. _____. An equivocal assurance that something will or will not be done.

12. _____. "I promise to sell you my car if I feel like it."

13. _____. A promise that omits terms essential for the court to determine an appropriate remedy in the event the promise is breached.

14. _____. Feigned or pretended consideration.

15. _____. An obligation already owed to the promisor by the promisee.

16. _____. A cause of action based on the policy of preventing unjust enrichment.

17. _____. Preclusion of an assertion by the promisor that is inconsistent with a previously made promise upon which the promisee has relied.

18. _____. A figment of the court's imagination.

19. _____. A Latin expression meaning "as much as it is worth."

20. _____. A term used to describe what takes place when the plaintiff has conferred a benefit on the defendant and it would be unfair to permit the defendant to retain this benefit without compensating the plaintiff.

21. _____. A promise that is neither express nor implied in fact but is a legal fiction which represents the court's label attached to a set of facts to reach a desired result.

22. _____. A promise that is inferred from conduct rather than expressed orally or in writing.

MULTIPLE-CHOICE QUESTIONS (CIRCLE ALL THE CORRECT ANSWERS)

1. The following statements are preliminary negotiation:
   (a) "What will you take for your car?"
   (b) "I will give you $1,500 for your car."
   (c) "Will you take $1,500 for your car?"

(d) "Quote me a price for your car."

(e) "I will pay you no more than $1,500 for your car."

2. Identify the offer in the following sequence of events.

(a) Please advise us of the lowest price you can make on our order for 10 car loads of Mason green jars, complete, with caps, packed one dozen in a case, either delivered here, or f.o.b. cars your place, as you prefer. State terms and cash discount.

(b) Replying to your letter, we quote you Mason fruit jars, complete, in one-dozen boxes, delivered to your place: pints $4.50, quarts $5.00, half gallons $6.50, per gross, for immediate acceptance. Credit 60 days' trade acceptance or 2 percent off if cash in 10 days. Your order subject to the approval of our executive officer.

(c) Your letter received. Enter order for 10 car loads as per your quotation.

(d) Replying to your letter, price now pints $5.00, quarts $5.50, half gallon $6.50, per gross, for immediate acceptance.

(e) Seller ships 10 car loads to the Buyer.

3. Identify which of the following are offers for a unilateral contract.

(a) "I promise to pay $500 for your promise to sell me your gold watch."

(b) "I promise to pay $500 for your selling me your gold watch."

(c) "I promise to sell you my gold watch for your promise to pay $500."

(d) "I promise to sell you my gold watch for your paying me $500."

(e) "I promise to pay you $500 for your refraining from smoking for five years."

4. Identify which of the following is an offer.

(a) "I may sell you my car for $5,000."

(b) "I will sell you my car for $5,000."

(c) "I will sell you one of my cars for $5,000."

(d) "I might sell you my car for $5,000."

(e) "I will consider selling you my car for $5,000."

5. Identify which of the following is an offer.

(a) "I promise to sell you my car."

(b) "I will sell you my car for your promise to pay $5."

(c) "I promise to give you my car if you roof my house."

(d) "I will give you my car for your having roofed my house."

(e) "I will give you $1,000 for your having taken care of me while I was ill."

6. Under classical contract law, the court will investigate the following:

(a) Whether there is consideration for the promisor's promise

(b) Whether what appears to be consideration is really a sham

(c) Whether there is mutuality of obligation

(d) Whether the promisor's motive is appropriate

(e) Whether the consideration is adequate

7. A restitution cause of action has also been known as a cause of action based upon which of the following?

(a) A contract implied by law

(b) A constructive contract

(c)   An express contract
(d)   Quasi-contract
(e)   An implied contract

8.   When may a cause of action for reliance occur?
(a)   When the parties have not negotiated
(b)   When the parties have negotiated, but no offer has been made
(c)   After an offer has been revoked
(d)   After an offer has been rejected
(e)   After an offer has been accepted

9.   A restitution cause of action requires:
(a)   a promise by the promisor.
(b)   a benefit being conferred by one party on another.
(c)   that the promisor reasonably expected to induce action or forbearance on the part of the other party.
(d)   that the retention of the benefit without compensating the party conferring the benefit would be unjust.
(e)   that injustice could be avoided only by enforcement of the promise.

10.   Anderson's car skidded off the highway during an ice storm and hit a tree. Anderson was knocked unconscious by the impact. McGill, a doctor of internal medicine, came upon the accident scene on her way home from making rounds at the local hospital. Dr. McGill rendered first aid at the scene and later sent Anderson a bill for her services. Anderson refused to pay, claiming that he did not request her services.
(a)   Dr. McGill could not successfully maintain either a breach of contract or a restitution cause of action against Anderson.
(b)   Dr. McGill could successfully maintain a breach of contract action against Anderson but not a restitution cause.
(c)   Dr. McGill could successfully maintain a restitution cause of action against Anderson but not a breach of contract cause of action.
(d)   Dr. McGill could successfully maintain both a breach of contract cause of action and a restitution cause of action against Anderson.

SHORT-ANSWER QUESTIONS

1.   Describe the difference between evaluating a communication using an objective standard rather than a subjective standard.

2.   Discuss the practical significance between an offer for a unilateral contract and an offer for a bilateral contract.

3.   Discuss why past services cannot be consideration for the promisor's promise.

4.   A father told his son that if the son would move back to town, the father would start him in business. Is the son's moving back to town consideration for the father's promise or only a condition?

5.   Discuss several ways legislatures have tinkered with the classical consideration doctrine.

6. Discuss several ways courts have tinkered with the classical consideration doctrine.

7. List the four elements of the reliance doctrine necessary to enable it to be used as an alternative to consideration.

8. List the four elements for a cause of action for reliance.

9. Grandpa Jones sent his 18-year-old granddaughter, Katie, a letter in which he promised to give her $10,000 when she became 25. In the meantime, he would pay her 6 percent interest annually on the $10,000 so she could stop working. Upon receiving this letter, Katie quit her job. Could Katie successfully sue Grandpa Jones's estate if after he died his estate discontinued paying her the annual interest?

10. Describe the role of expectation when negotiations fail to produce an offer.

11. Describe the role of reliance when negotiations fail to produce an offer.

12. Describe the role of restitution when negotiations fail to produce an offer.

13. Are implied by law, implied in fact and implied contracts really contracts?

14. When is a person officious?

The Post-Offer/
Pre-Acceptance Phase

Chapter 3 focuses on the time after the offer is made but before it is accepted. If the offer is accepted, a contract is formed. If, however, the offeree does not accept the offer within the time specified in the offer, or if no time is specified and a reasonable time passes, the offer lapses. The offer ceases to exist if the offeror revokes the offer or the offeree rejects the offer. The death or incapacity of the offeror or offeree also ends the offer.

   An offer is kept open through a second contract called an option contract. Classical contract law recognized a subsidiary contract called an express option contract. Modern contract law extends the option contract concept to recognize an implied option contract if the offeree to the main contract offer relies on the offer (see Exhibit 3–1).

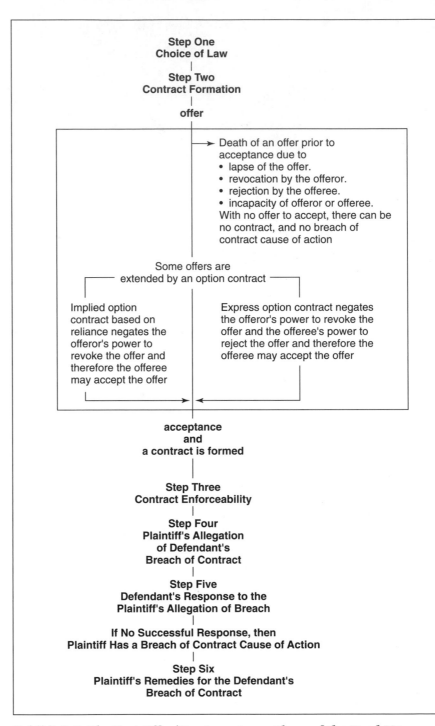

Exhibit 3–1 The Post-Offer/Pre-Acceptance Phase of the Road Map

THE DEATH OF AN OFFER PRIOR TO ACCEPTANCE

After the offeror has made an offer, thereby conferring the power of acceptance on the offeree, the offeree's power can be terminated in several ways:

- By the offeree's inaction so the offer lapses
- By the offeror's revocation of the offer
- By the offeree's rejection of the offer
- By death or incapacity of the offeror or offeree

The Offeree's Inaction (Lapse)

An offer may state an expiration time: "This offer will end at noon on Saturday, July 16th." Unless the offeree accepts by that time, the offer ceases to exist. A provision of this type gives the parties some certainty. The offeror knows that if the offeree fails to accept the offer before the specified time, the offeror is free to make other plans without informing the offeree. The offeree, on the other hand, knows there is only a limited time to accept the offer. The offeree knows the offer will lapse at the stated termination time and the offeror may revoke the offer prior to that time.

ⅲ PARALEGAL EXERCISE 3.1

Describe a situation where the offeror would find it desirable to have an express termination date in the offer. ▪

If the offer does not state a time by which the offer must be accepted, the offer lapses if the offer is not accepted within a reasonable time. **Lapse**, therefore, is the termination of the offer through the offeree's failure to accept it within the time specified in the offer or if no time is specified then within a reasonable time. What is "a reasonable time" varies with the transaction. The subject matter of the contract is an important factor in determining reasonable time.

lapse
Lapse is the termination of the offer through the offeree's failure to accept it within the time specified in the offer or, if no time is specified, then within a reasonable time.

Example 3–1

An offeree should have a substantially shorter time to accept an offer to sell grapes than an offer to sell an encyclopedia.

ⅲ PARALEGAL EXERCISE 3.2

Arrange the following four situations in time from the shortest to the longest "reasonable time." None of the offers contains an express expiration time.

- An offer to sell Blackacre (100 acres of undeveloped farmland)
- An offer by the Ringling Brothers Circus to sell Sally, a trained elephant, to the Bumbling Brothers Circus
- An offer to sell a truckload of vine-ripened tomatoes to Safeway Stores
- An offer to buy a used automobile from the automobile's current owner ■

Revocation of the Offer

revocation

Revocation is the offeror's manifestation to withdraw the offer.

As master of the offer, the offeror may terminate the power to accept. **Revocation** is the offeror's manifestation to withdraw the offer. As a general rule, revocation is effective when received by the offeror.

Revocation requires no special language. The offeror need not say "revoke" to achieve a revocation. The only requirement for revocation is that it be clear to the offeree that the offer is revoked.

The offeror may directly communicate to the offeree that the offer is revoked. *Hoover Motor Express Co. v. Clements Paper Co.* is an example of direct communication. Analyze *Hoover Motor Express* as follows:

1. Record each event on a timeline.
2. Determine whether the first event on the timeline is an offer.
3. Evaluate each subsequent event on the timeline until the offer is reached.
4. Evaluate each subsequent event on the timeline until the acceptance is reached.
5. Change the facts to weaken Hoover's assertion that its statement was a revocation.

CASE

Hoover Motor Express Co. v. Clements Paper Co.
Supreme Court of Tennessee (1951)
193 Tenn. 6, 241 S.W.2d 851

TOMLINSON, Justice.
[On November 19, 1949, the Hoover Motor Express Company delivered to the Clements Paper Company a written offer to purchase certain real estate. Although Williams, a Vice President at Clements, had been authorized in December to accept Hoover's offer, Williams believed that he would accept the offer unless he could negotiate a better deal. Williams did not, however, contact Hoover until January 13, 1950, when he spoke to Hoover by telephone. On January 20, 1950, Clements made a written acceptance of Hoover's offer. Hoover refused to perform claiming that it had revoked its offer on January 13. Clements claimed that Hoover did not revoke its offer on January 13 but rather Clements had accepted Hoover's offer on January 20.

Clements sued Hoover for breach of contract and asked the Chancellory Court for specific performance or damages. The Chancellor sided with Clements in holding that Hoover's offer had not been revoked on January 13. Hoover appealed to the Court of Appeals and that court affirmed the Chancellor's decree. Hoover petitioned for certiorari before the Supreme Court of Tennessee.

We join the Supreme Court of Tennessee's opinion as the court discusses Williams' testimony before the Chancellor.]

Mr. Williams testified that he got Mr. Hoover on the phone on January 13 and "told him that we were ready to go through with it and I would like to discuss it with him." The matter which he testifies that he wanted to discuss with Mr. Hoover was whether Hoover would permit Clements to retain an easement for certain purposes through the property which Hoover had offered to buy.

Williams testifies that in reply to Williams' statement that he, Williams, wanted to discuss the offer with Hoover that Hoover replied "Well, I don't know if we are ready. We have not decided, we might not want to go through with it."

Williams made several other statements in his testimony as to what Hoover said in this phone conversation. The following are quotations from Williams' testimony: "He said he thought they might not go through with it."

"Q. After you had talked to him on January 13, on the telephone, that is Mr. Eph Hoover, Jr., he indicated to you that he had made other plans or in some way 'indicated' to you that the company had made other plans?

A. Yes."

. . . .

"Q. You had been told that they had made other plans? A. No, I had not been told. He said that he didn't think they were going through with the proposal and that he would call me on January 17."

(Hoover did not call Williams after the January 13 phone conversation.)

. . . .

"A. That they had other plans in mind and he would let me know. He was not sure if he was going through with the original proposition."

"Q. Did he definitely refuse to positively commit himself on January 13 that he would go through with it? A. That is right."

. . . .

"It was a very short discussion. Frankly, I was very much shocked when I heard from him that they didn't plan to go through with it. I had made my plans and had gone to the extent of having this elevation made."

The interpretation which Mr. Williams placed upon what Hoover said to him in the phone conversation of January 13 is stated in Clements' bill of complaint as follows: "This was the first information, suggestion or intimation that complainant had received that the defendant would not or might not carry out its agreement or offer."

Our problem is reduced to answering the question as to whether there can reasonably be placed upon the above quoted testimony of Williams a construction that prevents the statement of Hoover, as testified to by Williams, from amounting to a withdrawal on January 13 of the offer before it was attempted on January 20 to accept it. This is true because "the continued existence of the offer until acceptance is, however, necessary to make possible the formation of the contract." 12 American Jurisprudence, page 531.

Although there is no Tennessee case deciding the point, in so far as we can find, the general rule is that express notice, in so many words, of withdrawal before acceptance of an offer of the character we have here is not required. In 55 American

Jurisprudence, page 488, under a discussion of "Termination of Offer", there appears in the text, supported by reference to decisions, this statement: "It is sufficient to constitute a withdrawal that knowledge of acts by the offerer inconsistent with the continuance of the offer is brought home to the offeree."

. . . .

Restatement of the Law of Contracts, Section 41, page 49, has this to say: "Revocation of an offer may be made by a communication from the offeror received by the offeree, which states or implies that the offeror no longer intends to enter into the proposed contract, if the communication is received by the offeree before he has exercised his power of creating a contract by acceptance of the offer."

. . . .

Applying to the undisputed testimony as furnished by Williams the rule clearly stated in all the authorities from which we have above quoted—and we find none to the contrary—we think it must be concluded that Hoover's written offer of November 19 was withdrawn on January 13 thereafter prior to its attempted acceptance on January 20, and that the concurrent finding of the Chancellor and the Court of Appeals to the contrary is not supported by any material evidence. There can be no doubt as to it being a fact that on January 13 knowledge was brought home to Williams that Hoover no longer consented to the transaction. There was, therefore, no offer continuing up to the time of the attempted acceptance on January 20.

The decree of the Court of Appeals and of the Chancellor will be reversed and the cause remanded for entry of a decree in keeping with this opinion. All costs in all Courts will be adjudged against Clements Paper Company.

Revocation may also be indirectly communicated to the offeree if the offeror takes action inconsistent with her intention to enter into the proposed contract with the offeree and this information is "brought home" to the offeree before the offeree attempts to accept the offer.

Example 3-2

On Monday, Mary offers to sell her house to Ted for $250,000. The offer provides that it shall remain open until Saturday at noon. On Thursday, Ted learns from a reliable source that Mary has accepted Seymour's offer to pay $275,000 for the house. Although Mary has not directly communicated to Ted that her offer to him has been revoked, the revocation has been indirectly communicated to Ted. Mary's offer to Ted has been revoked.

Although Mary said that her offer to Ted would "remain open until Saturday at noon," Mary's statement was no more than a time when the offer would lapse. Mary retained the power to revoke her offer and this power could be exercised at anytime prior to the time Ted accepted Mary's offer.

Rejection of the Offer

The offer ceases to exist when the offeree rejects it. **Rejection** is the offeree's manifestation of nonacceptance of the offer. The offeree may reject without making a new offer.

rejection

Rejection is the offeree's manifestation of nonacceptance of the offer.

Example 3–3

A–1 Used Cars does not post prices on its cars but has a big sign that reads: "Make us an offer." Tommy Thomas found a car that he liked on A–1's lot and made A–1 the following offer: "I promise to pay you $1,200 for that red convertible." A–1 responded: "You must be kidding." A–1 has rejected Tommy's offer, and the parties no longer have an offer pending before them.

In addition to being a rejection, the offeree's rejection could include a new offer. In this case, the offeree's rejection contains a counteroffer. A **counteroffer** is an offer made by the offeree to the offeror that deals with the subject matter of the original offer but with some variation in terms. With a counteroffer the whole process of offer and acceptance begins again. The original offeree is now the offeror.

counteroffer

A counteroffer is an offer made by the offeree to the offeror that deals with the subject matter of the original offer but with some variation in terms.

Example 3–4

Consider the A–1/Tommy Thomas hypothetical again. This time A–1 responded: "No, but we will sell it to you for $1,500." A–1 has rejected Tommy's offer and has made its own offer, now known as a counteroffer. A–1 is now the offeror.

Once the offeree rejects an offer, the offeree cannot accept the offer. The original offer can only be accepted if one of the parties resubmits the original offer and the other accepts it. Even though the original and the new offer are identical, the offeree technically accepts the new, not the original offer.

⫼ PARALEGAL EXERCISE 3.3

On December 5, the B & O Railroad wrote the following letter to Baltimore Rolling Mill: "Please quote me prices for 500 to 3,000 tons 50–pound steel rails and for 2,000 to 5,000 tons 50–pound iron rails."

On December 8, the Mill sent the following letter to B & O: "We do not make steel rails. For iron rails, we will sell 2,000 to 5,000 tons of 50–pound rails for $54 per ton."

On December 16, B & O sent a letter to the Mill: "Please enter our order for 1,200 tons 50–pound iron rails."

On December 18, the Mill telegraphed B & O: "We cannot book your order at present at that price."

On December 19, B & O telegraphed the Mill: "Please enter an order for 2,000 tons 50–pound iron rails."

The Mill did not respond to B & O's telegram nor did it ship the rails. Answer the following:

1. Was B & O's letter of December 5th preliminary negotiation or an offer?
2. Was the Mill's letter of December 8th preliminary negotiation, an offer, a rejection with a counteroffer, or an acceptance?
3. Was B & O's letter of December 16th preliminary negotiation, an offer, a rejection with a counteroffer, or an acceptance?
4. Was the Mill's telegram of December 18th preliminary negotiation, an offer, a rejection, a rejection with a counteroffer, an acceptance, or of no significance?
5. Was B & O's telegram of December 19th preliminary negotiation, an offer, a rejection, a rejection with a counteroffer, an acceptance, or of no significance?
6. Based on your answers, did B & O and the Mill have a contract and, if so, for what? ▪

As a general rule, a rejection sent by the offeree is effective as a rejection when *received* by the offeror. The same is *not* true for an acceptance. An acceptance sent by the offeree is effective when *sent* by the offeree. When the offeree sends one letter, has a change of mind and then sends the other letter, the offeror may not necessarily receive the letters in the order in which they were sent. Which letter is effective—the rejection or the acceptance? The Restatement (Second) of Contracts § 40 provides a partial solution:

> Rejection . . . by mail . . . does not terminate the power of acceptance until received by the offeror, but limits the power so that a letter . . . of acceptance started after the sending of an otherwise effective rejection . . . is only a counteroffer unless the acceptance is received by the offeror before he receives the rejection . . . .

Example 3–5

On February 1st, Dan promised to sell his 1966 Mustang to Sara for Sara's promise to pay him $20,000. On February 5th, Sara sent Dan a letter stating that she was not interested. On February 6th, Sara sent Dan a second letter, this time accepting his offer. Dan received the letter of February 6th (the acceptance) the day before he received the letter of February 5th (the rejection). Sara's letter of February 6th is an effective acceptance. Although the acceptance was sent after the rejection was sent, the acceptance was received first. (Dan would have seen the acceptance first, thought a contract was formed, and could have relied on there being a contract.)

▥ PARALEGAL EXERCISE 3.4

Would the answer in Example 3–5 change if Dan received the rejection first? ▨

▥ PARALEGAL EXERCISE 3.5

Would the answer in Example 3–5 change if Sara had sent Dan the letter of acceptance on February 5th and the letter of rejection on February 6th— and Dan had received the letter of February 5th (the acceptance) before the letter of February 6th (the rejection)? ▨

▥ PARALEGAL EXERCISE 3.6

Would the answer in Example 3–5 change if Sara had sent Dan the letter of acceptance on February 5th and the letter of rejection on February 6th— and Dan had received the letter of February 6th (the rejection) before he received the letter of February 5th (the acceptance)? ▨

Often when the offeror has made an offer, the offeree may want to investigate whether the terms of the offer are negotiable. Can the offeree strike a better deal with the offeror? Once the offeror makes an offer, the offeree must use great care when probing for better terms. The offeree's probing may signal to the offeror that the offer is rejected. The test is not whether the offeror or the offeree perceives the offeree's response to be a rejection and counteroffer. What is important is whether a reasonable person would perceive the offeree's response to be a rejection and counteroffer.

Example 3-6

Seller states to Buyer "I promise to sell you my car for $15,000." Buyer responds, "I will pay $12,000 for your car." Buyer is rejecting Seller's offer and making a counteroffer.

𝚰𝚰𝚰 PARALEGAL EXERCISE 3.7

Seller states to Buyer "I promise to sell you my car for $15,000." In each of the following, is Buyer rejecting Seller's offer and making a counteroffer?

1. Buyer responds, "Would you take $12,000 for your car"?
2. Buyer responds, "I am considering your offer to sell me your car for $15,000, but would you take $12,000"?
3. Buyer responds, "I am not rejecting your offer to sell me your car for $15,000, but would you take $12,000"? ▮

The Death or Incapacity of the Offeror or the Offeree

After an offer is made but before the offeree is accepted (that is, before contract formation), either the offeror or the offeree may die or become legally incapacitated. Does the offeree's power to accept the offer come to an end with the death or incapacity of the *offeror*? Does the offeree's power to accept the offer come to an end with the death or incapacity of the *offeree*? The Restatement (Second) of Contracts § 48 answers both questions:

> An offeree's power of acceptance is terminated when the offeree or offeror dies or is deprived of legal capacity to enter into the proposed contract.

𝚰𝚰𝚰 PARALEGAL EXERCISE 3.8

Mary Randolph, an artist of some renown, told Joan Scott: "I will sell you my latest landscape for $25,000. Let me know by next Friday." On Wednesday, while vacationing in the Caribbean, Mary was involved in a boating accident. Although Mary died that evening in a local hospital, the news of her death was not reported in the United States until the following Saturday. Meanwhile Joan, not knowing that Mary had died the previous evening, mailed a letter "accepting" Mary's offer. Joan even enclosed a $25,000 check.

Has Joan effectively accepted Mary's offer? Must the offeree know that the offeror is dead for the attempted acceptance to be ineffective? ▮

option contract

An option contract is a contract that negates the promisor's power to revoke the offer. An option contract has the same requirements as the main contract— promisor's promise, consideration for the promisor's promise, promisee's promise or performance, and consideration for the promisee's promise or performance.

THE OFFER THAT REFUSES TO DIE

The offeree's power of acceptance need not be terminated by the offeror's attempted revocation, the offeree's attempted rejection, or the death or incapacity of the offeror or offeree. Some offers refuse to die. These offers are supported by a subsidiary contract called an option contract. An **option contract** is a contract that negates the offeror's power to revoke during the term of the option contract. An option contract may be express or implied by law.

The Classical (Express) Option Contract

When an offeror makes an offer that creates in the offeree the power to accept, the offeror retains the power to revoke the offer. Under classical contract law, the offeror may exercise this power at any time prior to acceptance by the offeree.

At times, it is important for the offeree to have time to evaluate the offer without being concerned that the offeror may revoke.

Example 3-7

A real estate developer needs several months to evaluate whether a certain location now for sale would be well suited for commercial development.

Example 3-8

An apartment tenant needs an apartment for a year and possibly for longer if she decides not to buy a house.

Example 3-9

A professional soccer team wants to play in a stadium for a season and will want to play there for the following season if the team is successful at the gate.

⫶ PARALEGAL EXERCISE 3.9

Describe three additional situations where the offeree might want time to evaluate the offeror's offer, without having to be concerned with whether the offer may be revoked. ▇

The offeree solves this dilemma by buying the offeror's power to revoke. The offeree does this with an option contract. The option contract is subsidiary to the main contract offer. Because the option contract is a contract, the option contract offer must have both a promise and consideration for that promise. The offeror of the option contract may be either the offeror or the offeree of the main contract offer.

If the offer for the option contract comes from the offeror of the main contract offer, the promise in the option offer is "I promise not

```
Main contract                    Option contract
                                 (subsidiary contract)

Offer                            Offer
    "I promise to sell               "I promise not to revoke my offer
    you my car for your              to sell you my car for $15,000
    promise to pay me                for your promise to pay me $100"
    $15,000"
                                 Acceptance
                                     "I promise to pay you $100
                                     for your promise not to revoke
                                     your offer to sell me your car
                                     for $15,000"
```

**Exhibit 3–2 Option Contract Where the Offeror of the Main Contract
Offer Is the Offeror of the Option Contract**

to revoke my main contract offer." The consideration for this promise may be either the main contract offeree's promise or performance: "for your promise to pay . . ." or "for your paying. . . ." The
option contract offer would be "I promise not to revoke my main
contract offer for your promise to pay . . ." or "I promise not to revoke
my main contract offer for your paying me . . ." (see Exhibit 3–2).

If the offer for the option contract comes from the offeree of the
main contract offer, the promise in the option offer is "I promise to
pay. . . ." The consideration for this promise is the main contract
offeror's "promise not to revoke his or her main contract offer." The
option contract offer would be "I promise to pay . . . for your promise not to revoke your main contract offer" (see Exhibit 3–3).

Although a main contract offer and an option contract offer
are often made at the same time, the consideration in the option

```
Main contract                    Option contract
                                 (subsidiary contract)

Offer                            Offer
    "I promise to sell               "I promise to pay you $100 for
    you my car for your              your promise not to revoke your
    promise to pay me                offer to sell me your car for
    $15,000"                         $15,000"

                                 Acceptance
                                     "I promise not to revoke my offer
                                     to sell you my car for $15,000
                                     for your promise to pay me $100"
```

**Exhibit 3–3 Option Contract Where the Offeree of the Main Contract
Offer Is the Offeror of the Option Contract**

contract offer and acceptance must not be the same as the consideration in the main contract offer. If the main contract offer is "I promise to sell you my car for your promise to pay $15,000," and the option contract offer is "I promise not to revoke my main contract offer for your promise to pay $100," the offeree's promise to pay $100 in the option contract offer must not be a part of the offeree's promise to pay $15,000 in the main contract offer. The need for unrelated consideration is apparent when the offer for the option contract is spelled out in full: "I promise not to revoke my offer to sell you my car for your promise to pay $15,000 for your promise to pay me $100." Because the purpose of the option contract is to provide the offeree time to evaluate the main contract offer, it is only the offer for the option contract that is accepted at this time. It is "the promise to pay $100" and not "the promise to pay $15,000."

What at first may appear to be an offer for an option contract may only be the time after which the offer will lapse.

Example 3–10

The main contract offer is "I promise to sell you my car for your promise to pay $15,000 and I will not revoke my offer for 15 days." There is no consideration for the promise not to revoke for 15 days and therefore the 15 days is the time when the offer will lapse. Without an option contract, the offeror retains the power to revoke the offer at any time.

Example 3–11

"I promise to sell you my car for your promise to pay $15,000 and I will not revoke my offer for 15 days for your promise to pay $100." The promise to pay $100 is consideration for the offeror's promise not to revoke for 15 days. If the offeree promises to pay $100 for the offeror's promise not to revoke, an option contract is created and the offeror cannot revoke the main contract offer for 15 days. The 15 days no longer represents the time when the offer lapses. The offer lapses after a reasonable time, with the minimum being 15 days.

Once the offer for the option contract is accepted and the option contract formed, the offeror of the main contract offer no longer has the power to revoke the main contract offer.

Example 3-12

Main contract offer

> I promise to sell you Blackacre for your promise to pay $250,000.

Option contract offer

> I promise not to revoke my offer to sell you Blackacre for $250,000 for 30 days for your promise to pay me $100.

Option contract acceptance

> I promise to pay you $100 for your promise not to revoke for 30 days your offer to sell me Blackacre for $250,000.

For the next 30 days, the offeror may not revoke the offer to sell Blackacre to the offeree for $250,000.

▥ PARALEGAL EXERCISE 3.10

David promised to sell his *Mad* magazine collection to Mary Jane for $200. When can David sell his *Mad* magazine collection to Darron for $300 without being in breach of contract with Mary Jane? ▪

▥ PARALEGAL EXERCISE 3.11

David promised to sell his *Mad* magazine collection to Mary Jane for $200. Mary Jane paid David $10 for a three-month option contract. When can David sell his *Mad* magazine collection to Darron for $300 without being in breach of contract with Mary Jane? ▪

An express option contract not only negates the offeror's power to revoke but it also continues the offeree's power to accept the main contract offer after an attempted rejection or the death or incapacity of the offeror.

Example 3-13

On June 1st, Seller offers to sell her car to Buyer for $15,000. Also on June 1st, Seller promises not to revoke her offer to sell for 30 days for Buyer's promise to pay $100. Buyer promises to pay $100, thus forming an option contract.

On June 15th, Buyer offers to buy Seller's car for $12,000.

On June 20th, Seller rejects Buyer's counteroffer.

On June 25th, Buyer accepts Seller's offer of June 1st.

Because of the option contract, Buyer's counteroffer of June 15th did not reject Seller's offer of June 1st. Therefore, on June 25th when Buyer accepts Seller's offer of June 1st, a contract is formed.

Example 3-14

On June 1st, Seller offers to sell her car to Buyer for $15,000. Also on June 1st, Seller promises not to revoke her offer to sell for 30 days for Buyer's promise to pay $100. Buyer promises to pay $100, thus forming an option contract.

On June 15th, Seller dies.

On June 25th, Buyer accepts Seller's offer of June 1st.

Because of the option contract, Seller's death does not terminate Buyer's power of acceptance, so on June 25th when Buyer accepts Seller's offer of June 1st, a contract is formed.

PARALEGAL EXERCISE 3.12

If the offeror and offeree to the main contract offer have an express option contract—thus giving the offeree the power to accept the main contract offer after the offeror's death or incapacity—should not the offeree (through his or her estate) have the same power after his or her death or incapacity? ■

Unlike an offer for the main contract that is accepted when the acceptance is sent by the offeree, an offer for an option contract is accepted when received by the offeror of the option contract.

The Implied Option Contract

If the offeror enters into an express option contract, the offeror may not revoke the main contract offer for the duration of the option contract. This protects the offeree from the offeror's change of heart. But what if the offeror and offeree have not entered into an express option contract? It is common for the offeree, without having accepted the offeror's main contract offer, to change his or her conduct in reliance on that offer. Will this reliance create an implied option contract? The analysis differs depending on whether the main contract offer is for a unilateral or bilateral contract.

An offer for a unilateral contract ("I promise for your performance") can only be accepted by the offeree's performance. Because the offeror is asking the offeree to accept by performing (and not by promising), a promise by the offeree is ineffective as acceptance.

To accept the offer, the offeree must perform in full. Neither beginning the performance nor almost completing the performance is full performance. If the offeror has the power to revoke and may exercise this power at any time prior to acceptance, the offeree may begin the requested performance only to have the offeror revoke the offer prior to the offeree's full performance. Therefore, all offers for a unilateral contract would place the offeree at risk.

Example 3-15

Farmer Jones promises to pay Simon $1,000 for painting his barn. Simon begins to paint and completes three sides of the barn when Jones walks up to Simon and says, "Mighty nice job, Simon, but I revoke my offer." Because the offer is a promise for a performance, Simon could accept only by performing in full, that is, painting all four sides of the barn. Painting three sides is not full performance, and the offeror can revoke prior to Simon's having fully performed. Simon does not have an express option contract that prevents Farmer Jones from revoking his offer. Without an offer and an acceptance, Simon could not successfully sue Farmer Jones under classical contract theory for a breach of contract.

The Restatement (Second) of Contracts § 45 came to the aid of the Simons of the world with an implied option contract:

> (1) Where an offer invites an offeree to accept by rendering a performance and does not invite a promissory acceptance, an option contract is created when the offeree tenders or begins the invited performance or tenders a beginning of it.
> (2) The offeror's duty of performance under any option contract so created is conditional on completion or tender of the invited performance in accordance with the terms of the offer.

Under section 45, when the offeree begins the performance requested by the offeror under the main contract offer, an implied option contract is created that deprives the offeror of the power to revoke the main contract offer. Technically, the offeree's beginning of the performance is the consideration for the offeror's implied promise not to revoke. The implied option contract exists long enough for the offeree to have an opportunity to complete the performance requested in the main contract offer. By completing the performance, the offeree accepts the main contract offer, and a contract is formed.

If section 45 is operative in the Farmer Jones illustration, Farmer Jones's attempted revocation is ineffective. When Simon begins to paint the barn, an implied option contract comes into being. During the life of the option contract, the offeror is powerless to revoke the main contract offer. If Simon paints the last side of the barn, he completes the requested performance and thus accepts the offer. He could successfully maintain a breach of contract action if Farmer Jones refuses to pay the contract price.

An offer for a bilateral contract ("I promise for your promise") can only be accepted by the offeree's promise to do or not do what the offeror requests. The offeree's promise may be express or implied from the offeree's conduct. Unlike the offer for a unilateral contract, which requires full performance by the offeree to constitute acceptance of the offer, the offeree in an offer for a bilateral contract has a rapid and easy method of acceptance—simply promise. If the offeree begins performing without expressly promising the offeror, a promise implied from the offeree's performance constitutes acceptance of the offer. The problem generally is not with the offeree's beginning the performance requested by the offeror but preparing to begin the performance.

Example 3-16

Consider Farmer Jones again. This time, Jones promises to pay Simon $1,000 if Simon promises to paint Jones's barn. Simon does not respond to Farmer Jones but buys paint and brushes for the job. Before Simon tells Jones that he promises to paint and before he starts painting, Jones writes Simon stating, "I revoke my offer." Because the offer has not been accepted and because Simon does not have an express option contract, Jones could revoke because the attempted revocation occurs prior to Simon's attempted acceptance. Without an acceptance, Simon could not successfully sue Farmer Jones in classical contract theory for breach of contract.

Section 45 of the Restatement (Second) of Contracts was not designed to give the Simons of the world any help in this situation. Section 45 only applies to an offer for a unilateral contract. Farmer Jones's offer is for a bilateral contract. The Restatement (Second) of Contracts § 87(2) was created to address the offer for a bilateral contract:

(2) An offer which the offeror should reasonably expect to induce action or forbearance of a substantial character on the part of the offeree before acceptance and which does induce such action or

forbearance is binding as an option contract to the extent necessary to avoid injustice.

Section 87(2) provides that once the offeree either begins preparation or begins performance as defined by the terms of the offer, an implied option contract is created.

Example 3–17

When Simon buys the paint and brushes, an implied option contract is created with the beginning of the preparation acting as the consideration for the offeror's implied promise not to revoke. Simon now has a reasonable time to promise Farmer Jones and thus accept the main contract offer.

The language of section 87(2) is not limited to the offer for a bilateral contract. Its language encompasses both offers for bilateral and unilateral contracts. By using preparation as the time for implying the option contract, section 87(2) creates the option contract at an earlier point than section 45.

Example 3–18

Under section 87(2), Simon's purchase of paint brushes acts as consideration for the offeror's implied promise not to revoke. If the main contract offer is for a unilateral contract, Simon has the opportunity to fully perform; if the main contract offer is for a bilateral contract, Simon has the opportunity to promise to perform.

▥ PARALEGAL EXERCISE 3.13

Aunt Martha wrote her niece Ellen, "I promise to leave you Blackacre in my will if you live with and care for me for the remainder of my life." Aunt Martha attempts to revoke her offer while Ellen is preparing to move so she could live with and care for Aunt Martha (i.e., Ellen is preparing to perform the requested performance but has not begun to perform the requested performance). Could Ellen successfully maintain a breach of contract action against Aunt Martha using

1. classical contract theory (requires an express option contract to negate Aunt Martha's power to revoke her offer);
2. Restatement (Second) of Contracts § 45; or
3. Restatement (Second) of Contracts § 87(2)? ■

⫛ PARALEGAL EXERCISE 3.14

Aunt Martha wrote her niece Ellen, "I promise to leave you Blackacre in my will if you live with and care for me for the remainder of my life." Aunt Martha attempts to revoke her offer after Ellen has begun to live with and care for her (i.e., Ellen is performing the requested performance). Could Ellen successfully maintain a breach of contract action against Aunt Martha using

1. classical contract theory (requires an express option contract to negate Aunt Martha's power to revoke her offer);
2. Restatement (Second) of Contracts § 45; or
3. Restatement (Second) of Contracts § 87(2)? ▪

⫛ PARALEGAL EXERCISE 3.15

Aunt Martha wrote her niece Ellen, "I promise to leave you Blackacre in my will if you promise to live with and care for me for the remainder of my life." Aunt Martha has changed her offer from an offer for a unilateral contract to an offer for a bilateral contract. Aunt Martha attempts to revoke her offer while Ellen is preparing to move so she could live with and care for Aunt Martha but before Ellen has promised to live with and care for Aunt Martha for the remainder of her life (i.e., Ellen is preparing to perform the requested performance but has neither begun to perform the requested performance nor has promised to perform). Could Ellen successfully maintain a breach of contract action against Aunt Martha using

1. classical contract theory (requires an express option contract to negate Aunt Martha's power to revoke her offer);
2. Restatement (Second) of Contracts § 45; or
3. Restatement (Second) of Contracts § 87(2)? ▪

⫛ PARALEGAL EXERCISE 3.16

Aunt Martha wrote her niece Ellen, "I promise to leave you Blackacre in my will if you promise to live with and care for me for the remainder of my life." Aunt Martha attempts to revoke her offer after Ellen has begun to live with and care for her but before Ellen has expressly promised Aunt Martha to live with and care for her for the remainder of her life (i.e., Ellen is performing the requested performance although has not expressly promised). Could Ellen successfully maintain a breach of contract action against Aunt Martha using

1. classical contract theory (requires an express option contract to negate Aunt Martha's power to revoke her offer);
2. Restatement (Second) of Contracts § 45; or
3. Restatement (Second) of Contracts § 87(2)? ▪

🏛 PARALEGAL CHECKLIST

The Post-Offer/Pre-Acceptance Phase

❏ After all the communications and events have been placed on a timeline and the paralegal and his or her supervising attorney have determined an offer has been made, has the offeree's power to accept the offer expired during the period between the offer and the attempted acceptance?

1. Does the offer state an expiration date that would have ended the offer prior to the offeree's attempted acceptance? If the offer states an expiration date, the offer will expire at the expiration date unless something occurs that causes the offer to expire earlier.

2. If the offer did not state an expiration date, has a reasonable time expired since the time the offer was made so the offer has lapsed? A "reasonable time" will vary with each transaction.

3. Has the offer been revoked by the offeror? Revocation may be by either a direct or an indirect communication from the offeror. Revocation requires no specific language but does require a clear understanding (from a reasonable person's standpoint) that the offer has been revoked.

4. Has the offer been rejected by the offeree? The offeree may merely reject the offer or may substitute its own offer, which is called a counteroffer. The same tests apply for a counteroffer as for an offer. Once the offeree has rejected an offer, the offeree cannot accept the offer unless the offeror makes a new offer. The new offer may even be identical to the original offer, but must be made anew.

5. Has either the offeror or the offeree died or become incapacitated? When either the offeror or the offeree has died or has become incapacitated, the offeree's power to accept is terminated.

❏ Is there an option contract that would keep the offer open even though the offeror has attempted to revoke the offer, the offeree has attempted to reject the offer, or the offeror has died or become incapacitated?

1. Is there an express option contract? An express option contract ("I promise not to revoke my offer for your promise to pay . . .") is known as a subsidiary contract (the original offer is known as the offer for the main contract) and requires an offer and an acceptance (which includes consideration for the offeror's promise and consideration for the offeree's promise or performance).

2. If there is no express option contract, is there an implied (by law) option contract? Determine whether the offer for the main contract was an offer for a unilateral or a bilateral contract.

   a. If the offer for the main contract was an offer for a unilateral contract, follow Restatement (Second) of Contracts § 45, which creates an option contract "when the offeree tenders or begins the invited performance or tenders a beginning of it." The offeree must then complete the performance to accept the offer for the main contract. It should be noted that Restatement (Second) of Contracts § 87(2) also applies to an offer for a unilateral contract and may create an option contract at an earlier time than section 45.

   b. If the offer for the main contract was an offer for a bilateral contract, follow Restatement (Second) of Contracts § 87(2), which states that an option contract is created to the extent necessary to avoid injustice when "an offer which the offeror should reasonably expect to induce action or forbearance of a substantial character on the part of the offeree before acceptance and which does induce such action or forbearance."

❏ Continue the analysis with the acceptance if the offer has not been terminated or if a terminating event has occurred but an option contract has prevented the terminating event from being effective.

KEY TERMS

Counteroffer

Lapse

Option contract

Rejection

Revocation

REVIEW QUESTIONS

TRUE/FALSE QUESTIONS (CIRCLE THE CORRECT ANSWER)

1. T   F   An offer must state a termination date.
2. T   F   If an offer states a termination date, the offer ceases to exist after that date.
3. T   F   An offer that states "this offer will be held open until Wednesday, March 3d," cannot be revoked prior to that date.
4. T   F   An offer that does not state a termination date will end after "a reasonable time."
5. T   F   "A reasonable time" is a period set by statute.
6. T   F   The offeror may reject the offer and the offeree may revoke the offer.
7. T   F   An offer can be revoked through a direct communication between the offeror and offeree.
8. T   F   An offer will cease to exist when the offeree rejects it.
9. T   F   An offeree's rejection can include a new offer.
10. T   F   A counteroffer is a new offer by the offeree who then becomes the offeror.
11. T   F   Even after an offeree has rejected an offer, he or she can still accept it.
12. T   F   Samantha offers to sell Rollo, a polo pony, to Jorge for $4,000. Jorge tells Samantha that he would pay $3,500 for the pony. Samantha rejects Jorge's counteroffer. When Jorge promises to pay Samantha $4,000 for the pony, a contract is formed.
13. T   F   An offer dies when either the offeror or offeree dies or becomes legally incapacitated—unless an option contract exists.

14. T   F   An offer cannot be accepted after the offeree or offeror dies or becomes legally incapacitated.

15. T   F   An option contract is a contract subsidiary to the main contract offer.

16. T   F   Option contracts must be express. They may not be implied by law.

17. T   F   An option contract eliminates the risk that the offeror will revoke the offer before the offeree has an opportunity to accept the offer.

18. T   F   Modern contract law may imply an option contract when there has been reliance by the offeree.

19. T   F   An option contract will keep the power of acceptance alive in spite of the death or incapacity of the offeror or offeree.

20. T   F   Josephine promises to pay Rolfe $200 if Rolfe paints her portrait. Rolfe begins to paint but before he could complete his work, Josephine decides that she no longer wants her portrait painted. Under classical contract law, Josephine's revocation is effective.

21. T   F   Josephine promises to pay Rolfe $200 if Rolfe paints her portrait. Rolfe begins to paint but before he could complete his work, Josephine decides that she no longer wants her portrait painted. Under modern contract law (Restatement (Second) of Contracts § 45), Josephine's revocation is effective.

22. T   F   Josephine promises to pay Rolfe $200 if Rolfe paints her portrait. Rolfe begins to paint but before he could complete his work, Josephine decides that she no longer wants her portrait painted. Under modern contract law (Restatement (Second) of Contracts § 45), Rolfe must complete his performance to accept the offer.

FILL-IN-THE-BLANK QUESTIONS

1. _____. The time at which an offer ceases to exist if there is no stated time limit for accepting or rejecting the offer.

2. _____. Termination of the offer by the offeror.

3. _____. Termination of the offer by the offeree.

4. _____. The new offer that is made by the offeree after the offeree has rejected the offeror's offer.

5. _____. A contract that is subsidiary to the main contract offer and negates the offeror's power to revoke.

6. _____. A contract implied by law when the offeree relies on the offeror's offer but has not as yet accepted the offer.

7. _____. A contract that allows the offeree to buy the offeror's power to revoke.

8. _____. Under this section of the Restatement (Second) of Contracts, an offer for a unilateral contract cannot be revoked "when the offeree tenders or begins the invited performance or tenders a beginning of it."

9. _____. Under this section of the Restatement (Second) of Contracts, an offer for a bilateral contract cannot be revoked if the offeree either begins preparation or begins performance as defined by the terms of the offer.

10. _____. Under this section of the Restatement (Second) of Contracts, an offer for a unilateral contract cannot be revoked if the offeree begins preparation for the performance as defined by the terms of the offer.

MULTIPLE-CHOICE QUESTIONS (CIRCLE ALL THE CORRECT ANSWERS)

1. The offeree's power to accept an offer may be terminated by which of the following?
   (a) The offeree's inaction
   (b) The offeror's revocation of the offer
   (c) The offeree's rejection of the offer
   (d) The death or incapacity of the offeror or offeree
   (e) The sale of the subject matter to a third person when the offeree has no notice of the sale

2. An offer that states that it shall be held open until "Sunday, noon"
   (a) cannot be revoked prior to Sunday, noon.
   (b) will cease to exist on Sunday, noon.
   (c) must be held open until Sunday, noon.
   (d) can be rejected and then accepted prior to Sunday, noon.
   (e) is not an option contract.

3. Which offer has the longest life span?
   (a) An offer to sell 10 acres of real estate in an area that is being developed rapidly
   (b) An offer to sell a puppy
   (c) An offer to sell a truckload of peaches currently being harvested
   (d) An offer to buy a new automobile from a dealer
   (e) An offer to buy 180 acres of undeveloped farmland

4. On March 1, the Katy Railroad sent a letter to the A-1 Steel Company asking the price of 50,000 tons of steel rails.
   On March 5, A-1 responded by letter offering to sell Katy 50,000 tons of steel rails for $75 a ton and stating that this offer would remain open for 30 days.
   On March 10, Katy wrote that it would buy 100,000 tons at $75 a ton.
   On March 15, A-1 responded that it could not fill an order for 100,000 tons.
   On March 20, Katy wrote back stating that it would buy 50,000 tons at $75 a ton.
   On March 25, A-1 responded that it could not fill Katy's order.

(a) A contract was formed for 50,000 tons when Katy accepted A-1's offer to sell 50,000 tons at $75 a ton.

(b) No contract was formed because Katy's letter offering to buy 100,000 tons was a rejection of A-1's offer and once rejected, A-1's offer could not be accepted.

(c) A contract was formed for 50,000 tons since the express option contract precluded A-1 from revoking its offer.

(d) A contract was formed for 50,000 tons since the express option contract kept A-1's offer open even though Katy attempted to reject it.

(e) The transaction ended with Katy making an offer to buy 50,000 tons and A-1 rejecting this offer.

5. An option contract may be which of the following?
(a) Express
(b) Implied by law
(c) Either express or implied by law
(d) Express only
(e) Implied by law only

6. An offer for an express option contract
(a) may be proposed by the party who proposed the offer for the main contract.
(b) may be proposed by the party who is the offeree in the main contract.
(c) may be proposed by either the offeror or the offeree in the main contract.
(d) must be proposed when the offer for the main contract is proposed.
(e) may be proposed at any time after the offer for the main contract has been proposed (contemporaneous or subsequent).

7. An offer for an express option contract may be proposed
(a) prior to the offer of the main contract.
(b) contemporaneous with the offer of the main contract.
(c) subsequent to the offer of the main contract.
(d) after the offer of the main contract has been rejected.
(e) after the offer of the main contract has been accepted.

8. An implied contract is implied
(a) by law.
(b) from the facts.
(c) by the offeree.
(d) by the offeror.
(e) by the courts.

9. Under modern contract law, an option contract
(a) may be implied by law.
(b) may be expressly agreed upon by the parties.
(c) no longer exists.
(d) may be implied where the offer in the main contract is for a unilateral contract or for a bilateral contract.
(e) not only negates the offeror's power to revoke his or her offer but also applies where the offeree has previously attempted to reject the offer.

10. Restatement (Second) of Contracts § 87(2) applies to the following offers:

   (a) Offer for a unilateral contract only

   (b) Offer for a bilateral contract only

   (c) Offer for either a unilateral or bilateral contract

   (d) Neither an offer for a unilateral nor a bilateral contract

   (e) Offer for the sale of goods

SHORT-ANSWER QUESTIONS

1. The City of Metropolis intends to build an expressway along the river. To acquire the property needed for the expressway, the City has made offers to various property owners. What factors should be considered to determine how long a property owner has to accept the City's offer?

2. On March 1, the Katy Railroad sent a letter to the A-1 Steel Company asking the price on 50,000 tons of steel rails.

   On March 5, A-1 responded by letter offering to sell Katy 50,000 tons of steel rails for $75 a ton and that this offer would remain open for 30 days.

   On March 10, Katy wrote that it would buy 100,000 tons at $75 a ton.

   On March 15, A-1 responded that it could not fill an order for 100,000 tons.

   On March 20, Katy wrote back stating that it would buy 50,000 tons at $75 a ton.

   On March 25, A-1 responded that it could not fill Katy's order.

   Analyze each communication and determine whether a contract has been formed.

3. Martha Jennings wrote a letter to her nephew, John, promising to pay him $5,000 if he would perform the duties of executor of her estate when she died. After Martha died, John acted as her executor, but the court refused to recognize the existence of a contract between Martha and John. Has a contract been formed?

4. Charles made a written offer to sell Blackacre to Mary for $250,000. In addition to Charles's promise to sell Blackacre to Mary, Charles promised not to revoke his offer for 60 days for Mary's promise to pay him $1,000. Mary promised to pay Charles the $1,000. Several days later, Mary sent Charles a check for $1,000.

   Thirty days later, Charles wrote Mary stating he was revoking his offer and returning her $1,000 check. Mary wrote Charles that she had decided to accept his offer to sell her Blackacre and she was returning her $1,000 check.

   Has a contract to sell Blackacre been formed?

5. Martina promised to pay Rachael $450 if Rachael would teach Martina's daughter, Erica, French during the summer. Rachael spent June and July teaching Erica French. On August 1st, Martina told Rachael that she was revoking her offer.

Analyze whether a contract has been created between Martina and Rachael.

6. Martina promised to pay Rachael $450 if Rachael would promise to teach Martina's daughter, Erica, French during the summer. Prior to the beginning of summer vacation, Rachael spent time purchasing French books and preparing her lesson plan. Late in May, Martina notified Rachael that she had changed her mind and was not interested in having Erica learn French. Rachael wrote Martina attempting to accept Martina's offer.

Analyze whether a contract has been created between Martina and Rachael.

The Acceptance Phase

Chapter 4 explores the acceptance. The elements of an acceptance depend on whether the offer is for a bilateral or unilateral contract. If the offer is for a bilateral contract (offeror's promise for the offeror's promise), the acceptance is the offeree's promise for the offeror's promise. If the offer is for a unilateral contract (offeror's promise for the offeree's performance), the acceptance is the offeree's performance (full performance) for the offeror's promise. Chapter 4 explores a number of problems that may surface when investigating the elements of an acceptance (see Exhibit 4–1).

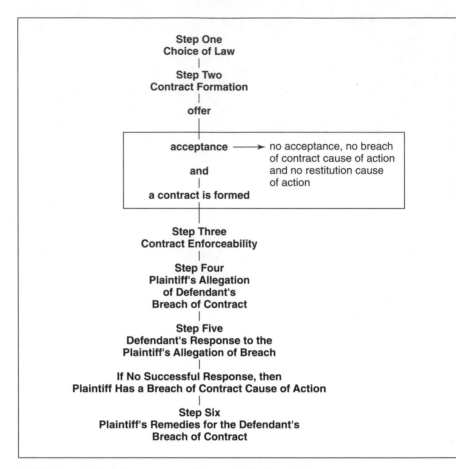

Exhibit 4–1 The Acceptance Phase of the Road Map

- Must acceptance be in response to the offer (must the offeree have knowledge of the offer prior to attempting to accept the offer)?
- Must the offeror's promise not be subject to a preexisting duty?
- Must the terms of the acceptance mirror the offer?
- Does acceptance occur when the attempted acceptance reflects a miscommunication between the parties?
- Is the offeree required to notify the offeror that the offer has been accepted?
- May the offeror limit who may accept the offer?

In addition to problems inherent with the elements of an offer, Chapter 4 also considers several problems that may preclude an acceptance from being effective:

- What method of acceptance must the offeree follow?
- When is acceptance effective?

The final topic in Chapter 4 involves the restitution cause of action.

- Is a restitution cause of action available when the offeror, after making the offer, confers a benefit on the offeree, and the offeree *rejects* the offer but retains the benefit?
- Is a restitution cause of action available when the offeror, after making the offer, confers a benefit on the offeree, and the offeree *accepts* the offer and retains the benefit?

THE CLASSICAL ACCEPTANCE—THE OFFEREE'S PROMISE AND CONSIDERATION FOR THAT PROMISE *OR* THE OFFEREE'S PERFORMANCE AND CONSIDERATION FOR THAT PERFORMANCE

An offeror, as master of the offer, can propose to the offeree that the contract be bilateral or unilateral. If the offeror proposes that the contract be bilateral, the offeror's offer will be a promise for a promise. The offeror is seeking to exchange his or her promise for the offeree's promise. "I promise to pay you $5,000 for your promise to walk from New York to San Francisco." The "price," the "exchange," or the "consideration" for the offeror's promise is the offeree's promise (promise to walk from New York to San Francisco) (see Exhibit 4–2).

If the offeror proposes that the contract be unilateral, the offeror's offer will be a promise for a performance. The offeror is seeking to exchange his or her promise for the offeree's performance. "I promise to pay you $5,000 for walking from New York to San Francisco." The "price," the "exchange," or the "consideration" for the offeror's promise is the offeree's performance (walking from New York to San Francisco) (see Exhibit 4–3).

The offeree's acceptance must be responsive to the offeror's offer. If the offer is a promise for a promise (bilateral contract), the acceptance must also be a promise for a promise. The promises in

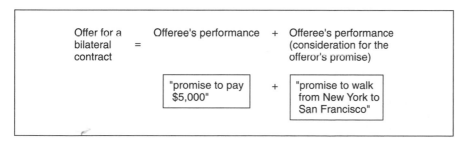

Exhibit 4–2 Offeree's Promise Is the Consideration for the Offeror's Promise

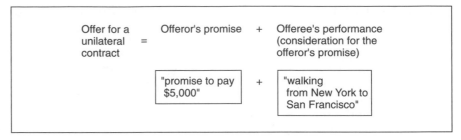

Exhibit 4–3 Offeree's Performance Is the Consideration for the Offeror's Promise

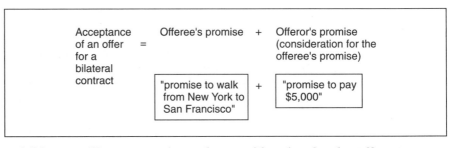

Exhibit 4–4 Offeror's Promise Is the Consideration for the Offeree's Promise

the acceptance are the mirror image of the promises in the offer. In other words, the promises are reversed in order. The offeree is exchanging his or her promise for the offeror's promise. If the offeror says "I promise to pay you $5,000 for your promise to walk from New York to San Francisco," the offeree, by responding "OK," "I'll do it," or "I promise to walk," is in fact responding "I promise to walk from New York to San Francisco for your promise to pay $5,000." The "price," the "exchange," or the "consideration" for the offeree's promise is the offeror's promise to pay $5,000 (see Exhibit 4–4).

If the offer is a promise for a performance (offer for a unilateral contract), the acceptance must be a performance for a promise. The promise and performance are reversed from the offer. The performance and promise in the acceptance are the mirror image of the promise and performance in the offer. The offeree is exchanging a performance for the offeror's promise. If the offeror proposes "I promise to pay you $5,000 for walking from New York to San Francisco," the offeree would respond *not* by promising since a promise is not what the offeror is seeking in exchange for his or her promise, but by actually walking from New York to San Francisco. The "price," the "exchange," or the "consideration" for the offeree's performance is the offeror's promise to pay $5,000 (see Exhibit 4–5).

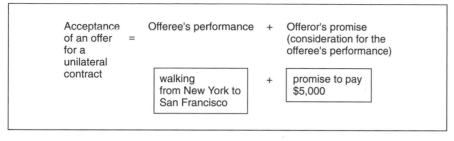

Exhibit 4–5 Offeror's Promise Is the Consideration for the Offeree's Performance

The Acceptance Must Be in Response to the Offer

The offeror, when making the offer, makes a promise to entice the offeree to promise (offer for a bilateral contract) or to perform (offer for a unilateral contract). The offeree, when making the acceptance, must promise (if the offer is for a bilateral contract) or perform (if the offer is for a unilateral contract). It is not enough that the offeree's promise or performance happens by coincidence.

Knowledge of the Offer

If the offer is for a bilateral contract, the offeree must have knowledge of the offer before responding with a promise. Otherwise, the offer is not inducing the offeree's response, and the offeree's response is ineffective as an acceptance.

▥ PARALEGAL EXERCISE 4.1

David, who lives in Texas, is the original owner of a 1966 Mustang, which is in mint condition. His cousin Susan, who lives in Georgia, has often stated that she would like to buy it. David has always said his Mustang was not for sale.

On March 1st, David wrote Susan that he was now ready to sell her his Mustang for $8,000. On March 2nd, Susan, *not* knowing that David was ready to sell, decided to press David on the issue of the Mustang. She wrote him saying that she would pay $8,000 for the Mustang. Susan received David's letter on March 4th.

David received Susan's letter on March 8th but has had second thoughts about selling his Mustang. From the postmark on Susan's letter, he knows that she could not have received his letter before writing hers. If Susan does not write a second letter to David, has Susan accepted David's offer? ◼

If the offer is for a unilateral contract, the offeree's performance often requires time to complete. "Walking from New York to San Francisco" could take months. "Refraining from drinking until 21" could take years. When must the offeree learn of the offeror's promise? Must the offeree have knowledge of the offer before beginning the requested performance, or would having knowledge before completing performance be sufficient?

The Restatement of Contracts has changed its stance over the years. The Restatement (First) of Contracts § 53 (1932) affirmed the rigid common law position that the offeree was required to have knowledge of the offer before beginning the requested performance.

> The whole consideration requested by an offer must be given after the offeree knows of the offer.

The Restatement (Second) of Contracts § 51 (1979) took a more tolerant stance by requiring the offeree to have knowledge of the offer prior to completing the requested performance.

> Unless the offeror manifests a contrary intention, an offeree who learns of an offer after he has rendered part of the performance requested by the offer may accept by completing the requested performance.

▥ PARALEGAL EXERCISE 4.2

Bonney, a convicted murderer, escaped from the county jail. The City Council offered a $50,000 reward to any person who captured and returned Bonney to jail.

Bonney fled to another county and before the news of the reward spread to that county, Oliver, a private detective, captured Bonney. As Oliver was driving Bonney back to the county jail, he learned about the reward on his car radio.

If Oliver does not release Bonney and recapture him, is he contractually entitled to the reward? Would your answer be the same under the Restatement (First) or Restatement (Second) of Contracts? ▪

Preexisting Duty. While exploring the components of offer, we discussed the requirement that consideration for the offeror's promise be "new" consideration and not something already required of the offeree. If the offeror requested the offeree to promise or perform some act or forbearance that the offeree already had a duty to perform, the offeree's promise or performance violates the "preexisting duty" rule, and the offeror's promise would lack consideration. The offeror's attempt to make an offer fails.

Example 4-1

Under state law a law enforcement officer is required to apprehend escaped convicts. Bonney, a convicted murderer, escaped from the city jail. The City Council promised a $50,000 reward to any law enforcement officer who promised to capture and return Bonney to jail. The City Council is attempting to make *an offer for a bilateral contract* that states: "We promise to pay $50,000 if you promise to capture and return Bonney to jail." Because law enforcement officers have a preexisting duty to apprehend escaped convicts, the City Council's promise to pay lacks consideration and therefore is not an offer as far as law enforcement officers are concerned.

Example 4-2

Under state law a law enforcement officer is required to apprehend escaped convicts. Bonney, a convicted murderer, escaped from the city jail. The City Council promised a $50,000 reward to any law enforcement officer who captures and returns Bonney to jail. The City Council is attempting to make *an offer for a unilateral contract* that states: "We promise to pay $50,000 for your capturing and returning Bonney to jail." Because law enforcement officers have a preexisting duty to apprehend escaped convicts, the City Council's promise to pay lacks consideration and therefore is not an offer as far as law enforcement officers are concerned.

The "preexisting duty" rule also applies to acceptance. If the offeror was already obligated to do what his or her promise entailes, the offeror's promise violates the "preexisting duty" rule and could not be consideration for the offeree's promise or performance. Since the offeree's promise or performance lacks consideration, the offeree's attempt to accept the offer fails.

Example 4-3

Under state law, a law enforcement officer is required to apprehend escaped convicts. Bonney, a convicted murderer, escaped from the city jail. A law enforcement officer promised to capture and return Bonney to jail if the City Council would promise to pay him a $50,000 reward. The officer's *offer for a bilateral contract* was: "I promise to capture and return Bonney for your promise to pay $50,000." The attempted acceptance would be the mirror image of the offer: "We promise to pay $50,000 for your promise to capture and return

Bonney." The officer has a preexisting duty to capture and return escapees, which means there could be no consideration for the City Council's promise to pay, no acceptance of the offer, and no contract.

Example 4–4

Under state law a law enforcement officer is required to apprehend escaped convicts. Bonney, a convicted murderer, escaped from the city jail. A law enforcement officer promised to capture and return Bonney to jail if the City Council pays him a $50,000 reward. The officer's *offer for a unilateral contract* was: "I promise to capture and return Bonney for your paying me $50,000." The attempted acceptance would be the mirror image of the offer: "Paying $50,000 for the officer's promise to capture and return Bonney." The officer has a preexisting duty to capture and return escapees, which means there could be no consideration for the City Council's paying and therefore no acceptance and no contract.

It is important to consider "preexisting duty" when evaluating both the attempted offer and the attempted acceptance. The offer may not involve a preexisting duty problem in its consideration, but the attempted acceptance may.

⫼ PARALEGAL EXERCISE 4.3

William was the sole heir under his father's will. When William's father died, the executor said to William, "I promise to pay you your inheritance, if you promise to donate 10 percent to charity." William responded, "I promise to donate 10 percent to charity if you promise to pay me my inheritance." Does the attempted offer suffer from a lack of consideration due to the preexisting duty rule? Does William's attempted acceptance lack consideration due to the preexisting duty rule? ■

The Offeree Must Agree to All of the Offeror's Terms

The offeror, by being the master of the offer, controls the terms of the contract.

mirror image
Mirror image means that the offeree must accept the offer without changing it.

Common Law Mirror Image Rule

The common law mirror image rule leaves the parties in an all-or-nothing situation. **Mirror image** means that the offeree must accept the offer without changing it. If the attempted acceptance mirrors the offer, a contract is formed, and the terms are those of the offer.

Example 4–5

If a homeowner promises to pay a painter $1,500 to paint his house white, the painter must respond that she will paint the owner's house white for $1,500. If the painter responds with either $1,600 or gray, the attempted acceptance does not mirror the offer and is treated as a rejection of the offer. If the rejection meets the requirements of an offer, it would be considered a counteroffer, and it would be up to the original offeror (by counteroffer, the original offeror becomes the offeree), the homeowner, to accept the counteroffer.

⫯ PARALEGAL EXERCISE 4.4

PG Studios, a motion picture company, promised to pay Cynthia $5 million if she promises to star in PG's new picture, with filming to begin on August 1st. Cynthia writes PG that she accepts the offer but cannot begin filming until August 10th. PG does not respond to Cynthia's letter. PG begins filming on August 1st but uses another actress. Is there a contract between PG Studios and Cynthia? ■

Example 4–6

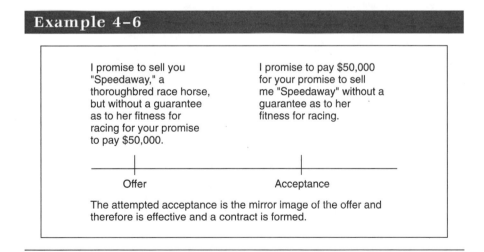

I promise to sell you "Speedaway," a thoroughbred race horse, but without a guarantee as to her fitness for racing for your promise to pay $50,000.

I promise to pay $50,000 for your promise to sell me "Speedaway" without a guarantee as to her fitness for racing.

Offer   Acceptance

The attempted acceptance is the mirror image of the offer and therefore is effective and a contract is formed.

If the attempted acceptance is not the mirror image of the offer, the offer is not accepted but is rejected, and the attempted acceptance becomes a counteroffer.

Example 4-7

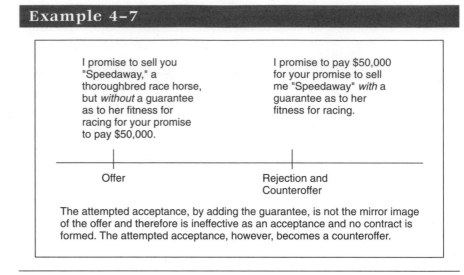

I promise to sell you "Speedaway," a thoroughbred race horse, but *without* a guarantee as to her fitness for racing for your promise to pay $50,000.

I promise to pay $50,000 for your promise to sell me "Speedaway" *with* a guarantee as to her fitness for racing.

Offer

Rejection and Counteroffer

The attempted acceptance, by adding the guarantee, is not the mirror image of the offer and therefore is ineffective as an acceptance and no contract is formed. The attempted acceptance, however, becomes a counteroffer.

If the original offeror takes no further action, the parties are without a contract. If the original offeror accepts the counteroffer, a contract is formed with the terms being those of the counteroffer. This is known as the **last shot doctrine.** The "last shot" is the last offer and it dictates all the terms.

last shot doctrine

A common law doctrine that provides where the acceptance of an express offer is implied from the offeree's performance (e.g., acceptance of the shipment and paying), the offeree, by performance, has accepted the offeror's terms.

Example 4-8

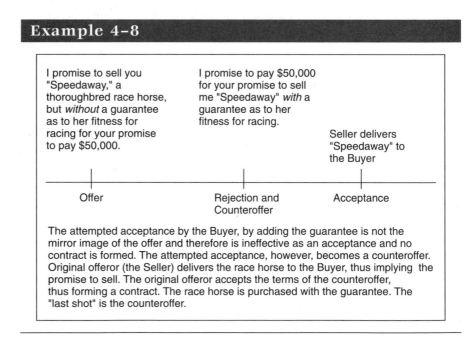

I promise to sell you "Speedaway," a thoroughbred race horse, but *without* a guarantee as to her fitness for racing for your promise to pay $50,000.

I promise to pay $50,000 for your promise to sell me "Speedaway" *with* a guarantee as to her fitness for racing.

Seller delivers "Speedaway" to the Buyer

Offer

Rejection and Counteroffer

Acceptance

The attempted acceptance by the Buyer, by adding the guarantee is not the mirror image of the offer and therefore is ineffective as an acceptance and no contract is formed. The attempted acceptance, however, becomes a counteroffer. Original offeror (the Seller) delivers the race horse to the Buyer, thus implying the promise to sell. The original offeror accepts the terms of the counteroffer, thus forming a contract. The race horse is purchased with the guarantee. The "last shot" is the counteroffer.

In most commercial transactions that are based on an exchange of written forms, the preprinted terms on the forms neither agree nor are read before the seller delivers or the buyer accepts delivery.

Under the common law "last shot" doctrine, if the seller sends the last form (counteroffer) and delivers the goods, and the buyer accepts the delivery and pays for the goods (acceptance of the counteroffer), a contract is formed and the terms are those found in the seller's form, regardless of whether they are in the fine print and the buyer has never read them.

Example 4–9

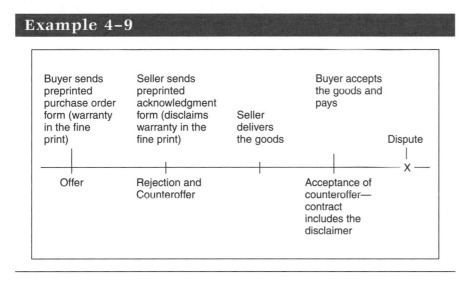

If the buyer sends the last form (counteroffer) and the seller delivers the goods (acceptance of the counteroffer), a contract is formed and the terms are those found in the buyer's form, even if they are in the fine print and the seller has never read them.

Example 4–10

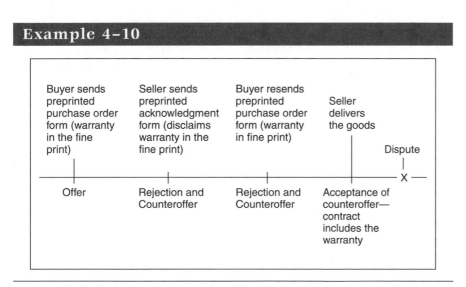

The Uniform Commercial Code § 2–207

The drafters of the Uniform Commercial Code sought to change the common law's mirror image rule in those transactions involving sale of goods. The drafters set up the following scheme:

> Section 2–207. Additional Terms in Acceptance or Confirmation
>
> (1) A definite and seasonable expression of acceptance or a written confirmation which is sent within a reasonable time operates as an acceptance even though it states terms additional to or different from those offered or agreed upon, unless acceptance is expressly made conditional on assent to the additional or different terms.
>
> (2) The additional terms are to be construed as proposals for addition to the contract. Between merchants such terms become part of the contract unless:
>
> (a) the offer expressly limits acceptance to the terms of the offer;
>
> (b) they materially alter it; or
>
> (c) notification of objection to them has already been given or is given within a reasonable time after notice of them is received.
>
> (3) Conduct by both parties which recognizes the existence of a contract is sufficient to establish a contract for sale although the writings of the parties do not otherwise establish a contract. In such case the terms of the particular contract consist of those terms on which the writings of the parties agree, together with any supplementary terms incorporated under any other provisions of this Act.

While the common law "last shot" doctrine may, at times, have given harsh results, the section 2–207 scheme creates an almost unworkable maze with often unpredictable results. The Decision Tree in Exhibit 4–6 will provide the routes through section 2–207. These steps must be followed carefully and in order.

Before discussing these steps, it is important to look at sample preprinted forms (Buyer's Purchase Order and Seller's Acknowledgment Form) (see Exhibits 4–7 and 4–8).

The forms have variables terms (price, quantity, subject matter, and delivery) and fixed terms (often the small print). The **"bargained-for" terms** are the variable terms. The **"boilerplate" terms** are the fixed terms. The boilerplate terms may be either substantive terms (warranty, disclaimer, credit, arbitration, risk of loss, choice of law, and choice of forum) or procedural terms ("only my terms shall apply" and "this is not an acceptance unless you agree to all of our terms").

The section 2–207 analysis begins with subsection (1). The initial phrase "A definite and seasonable expression of acceptance or a written confirmation which is sent within a reasonable time" establishes that 2–207(1) deals with two very different types of factual situations. The first is the traditional offer and acceptance, an initial form (an offer) and a response form (an acknowledgment form). The second is an oral contract followed by a written confirmation. For our purposes, we will focus only on the first situation.

---

bargained-for terms

The bargained-for terms in a preprinted form are those terms that are supplied by the party on the form and have not been preprinted.

boilerplate terms

Boilerplate terms are the fixed terms in a preprinted form and are not bargained-for. Boilerplate terms may be either substantive terms (warranty, disclaimer, credit, arbitration, risk of loss, choice of law, and choice of forum) or procedural terms ("only my terms shall apply" and "this is not an acceptance unless you agree to all of our terms").

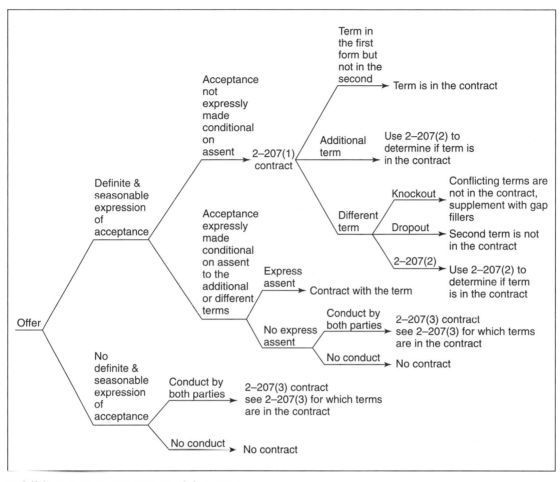

Exhibit 4–6 UCC § 2–207 Decision Tree

"A definite and seasonable expression of acceptance" assumes that the first form is an offer. Therefore focus on the second form which is the attempted acceptance. The **"definite . . . expression of acceptance"** refers to the "bargained-for" terms in the forms. "Bargained-for" terms are not preprinted terms and must be supplied by the parties on the forms. If the bargained-for terms in the second form are not the mirror image of the bargained-for terms in the first form, the second form is not a "definite . . . expression of acceptance." If the parties by their conduct recognize the existence of a contract, a contract is formed under subsection (3), sentence 1. Subsection (3), sentence 2 provides for the terms. "In such case the terms of the particular contract consist of those terms on which the writings of the parties agree, together with any supplementary terms incorporated under any other provision of this Act." Under sentence 2, the substantive boilerplate

definite expression of acceptance

When the offeree responds to the offeror's preprinted form with his or her own preprinted form, the offeree manifests a definite expression of acceptance when the offeree's form accepts the offeror's "bargained-for" terms.

PURCHASE ORDER			
Seller's Name:		**Buyer's Name:**	
Address:		**Address:**	
Telephone No. ( )		**Telephone No.** ( )	
FAX: ( )		**FAX:** ( )	
E-Mail:		**E-Mail:**	
Description	Quantity	Price/Unit	Total Price
Shipping Terms:			
Payment Terms:			
Additional Terms:			
This Purchase Order is subject to the terms on the back of this form.			
Signatures			
Buyer: **Date:** **Title:**			
Seller: **Date:** **Title:**			
This Purchase Order does not become effective until it is signed by both the Buyer and the Seller, or unless accepted by the Seller in accordance with Section 1 on the back of this Purchase Order.			

Exhibit 4–7 Buyer's Purchase Order

Additional Terms

1. **Acceptance** (Governed by UCC § 2–207)
This Purchase Order must be signed and returned to the Buyer within ten (10) business days. Any additional terms suggested by the Seller are declined unless expressly agreed to by the Buyer. Any delivery or beginning of delivery of either part or all of the goods listed on this Purchase Order will constitute an acceptance by the Seller of all of the terms listed on this form.

2. **Choice of Law** (Governed by UCC § 1–105)
This Purchase Order and any other additions to this Purchase Order shall be governed by the state where the Buyer is located.

3. **Choice of Forum**
Any dispute that arises from this transaction shall be resolved in the state where the Buyer is located.

4. **Choice of Dispute Resolution**
Any dispute that arises from this transaction shall be resolved by mediation. If the parties cannot resolve their dispute through mediation, then the dispute shall be resolved by arbitration.

5. **Changes** (Governed by UCC §§ 2–202, 2–209)
Buyer has the opportunity to change the following items without being in violation of the terms of this Purchase Order:
   a. Method of shipment;
   b. Time or place of delivery;
   c. Quantity of items purchased as long as it does not exceed 5% of the original order.

6. **Delivery** (Governed by UCC §§ 2–503, 2–601)
Any failure of the Seller to follow the terms regarding delivery as stated in this Purchase Order will constitute a breach of contract.

7. **Warranty** (Governed by UCC §§ 2–312 thru 2–314)
The Buyer reserves all of the express and implied warranties under Article 2 of the Uniform Commercial Code.

8. **Remedies** (Governed by UCC §§ 2–711 thru 2–717)
In the event of the Seller's breach of contract, the Buyer reserves all of its remedies under Article 2 of the Uniform Commercial Code.

Exhibit 4-7 (*Continued*)

ACKNOWLEDGMENT FORM

This Acknowledgment Form confirms the receipt of your
order of _____ for:

        Month   Day   Year

Description: _____

Quantity: _____

Price per unit: _____

Total price: _____

To be shipped on: _____

To: _____

Shipment arrangements: _____

Payment arrangements: _____

This Acknowledgment Form must be signed and returned to the Seller within 10 business days. Any acceptance of delivery of either a part or all of the goods listed in this Acknowledgment Form will constitute an acceptance by the Buyer and all the terms listed in this Acknowledgment Form shall apply to this transaction.

The following terms apply to this contract for sale:

1. **Terms.** Only the terms stated in this Acknowledgment Form apply to this contract for sale. Any additional terms suggested by the Buyer are declined unless expressly agreed to by the Seller.
2. **Choice of Law Provision.** The law of Seller's state shall apply to this contract for sale.
3. **Payment.** Any failure of the Buyer to follow the terms regarding payment as stated in this Acknowledgment Form will constitute a breach of contract.
4. **Warranty.** The Seller disclaims all express and implied warranties with the exception that the Seller warrants that the goods shall not be defective. Any claim that the goods are defective must be made in writing within 30 days of receipt. If goods are defective, the Seller has the option to repair or replace the goods.
5. **Dispute Resolution.** All disputes shall be resolved by litigation in the state where the Seller is located.
6. **Breach.** Any failure of the Buyer to comply with the terms of this Acknowledgment Form as supplemented by Article 2 of the Uniform Commercial Code shall constitute a breach.
7. **Remedies.** In the event of the Buyer's breach of contract, the Buyer reserves all of its remedies under the Uniform Commercial Code.

_____

(Seller)   (Title)   (Date)

_____

(Buyer)   (Title)   (Date)

Exhibit 4–8 Seller's Acknowledgment Form

terms of the two forms are compared. The terms will sort into three patterns: those that agree, those that disagree, and those that are only in one form. Those boilerplate terms that are the same are terms of the contract. Those terms that are different or those that appear in only one form are not terms of the contract. The final step is to check the Uniform Commercial Code for terms that the Code supplies if the contract is silent. Many of these terms, know as "gap filler" terms, are found in Part 3 of Article 2 (the 2–300s). For example, section 2–305 supplies a price term and section 2–314 supplies implied warranties.

For the following example, assume that the "bargained-for" terms do not agree between the Buyer's purchase order and the Seller's acknowledgment form. A **purchase order** is the buyer's offer form. The **acknowledgment form** is the seller's acceptance form.

purchase order

The purchase order is the buyer's offer form.

acknowledgment form

The acknowledgment form is the seller's acceptance form.

Example 4–11

▥ PARALEGAL EXERCISE 4.5

If, in the previous example, the Buyer's purchase order did not contain the warranty term, would the contract be with or without an implied warranty? ▪

ⅲ PARALEGAL EXERCISE 4.6

If, in the previous example, the Seller's acknowledgment form did not contain the disclaimer of warranty term, would the contract be with or without an implied warranty? ▪

ⅲ PARALEGAL EXERCISE 4.7

If, in the previous example, the Seller's acknowledgment form contained a mandatory arbitration term and the Buyer's purchase order was silent on this issue, would the contract be with or without a mandatory arbitration term? ▪

If the bargained-for terms in the second form are the mirror image of the bargained-for terms in the first form, the second form is a "definite . . . expression of acceptance." The second form, however, must be a "definite and *seasonable* expression of acceptance. **"Seasonable . . . expression of acceptance"** refers to the fact that the second form must have been sent within a reasonable time after receiving the first form.

Subsection (1) continues by stating that the second form "operates as an acceptance even though it states terms additional to or different from those offered." The additional or different terms are boilerplate terms. At this point section 2–207(1) deviates from the common law mirror image rule. Under the common law, the second form with additional or different terms in the boilerplate would operate as a rejection of the offer and would become a counteroffer. Under 2–207(1), the second form operates as an acceptance regardless of the additional or different terms in the boilerplate. An **additional term** is a substantive boilerplate term that appears in the second form but not in the first form. A **different term** is a substantive boilerplate term that appears in both forms but one is not the mirror image of the other.

One issue remains under section 2–207(1). Subsection (1) ends with the phrase "unless acceptance is expressly made conditional on assent to the additional or different terms." This statement requires us to focus on the procedural terms in the boilerplate. We are looking for a term that states "this is not an acceptance unless you agree to all of our terms." A term that states "all of our terms govern" will be insufficient because it does not withhold acceptance. If an "unless acceptance" term is found in the second form, the form does not act as an acceptance but is a counteroffer and the party who sent the first form must assent to the terms in the second form. If the party who sent the first form expressly assents to the fact that all of the second form terms govern, a contract is formed and the terms are those in the counteroffer (the second form). If there is no express assent by the party who sent the first form, assent may be implied by the conduct of the parties under subsection (3). If the parties by their conduct do not recognize the existence of a contract, no contract is formed.

seasonable expression of acceptance

When preprinted forms are exchanged, a seasonable expression of acceptance refers to the fact that the second form must have been sent within a reasonable time after receiving the first form.

additional term

When two forms are exchanged, an additional term is a substantive boilerplate term that appears in the second form but not in the first form.

different term

When two forms are exchanged, a different term is a substantive boilerplate term that appears in both forms—but one is not the mirror image of the other.

If no "unless acceptance" term is found in the second form, the form acts as an acceptance and a contract is formed under subsection (1). It is important to note that subsection (1) only creates the contract. It does not discuss which terms are in the contract.

In the following examples, assume that the "bargained-for" terms agree between the Buyer's purchase order and the Seller's acknowledgment form.

Example 4-12

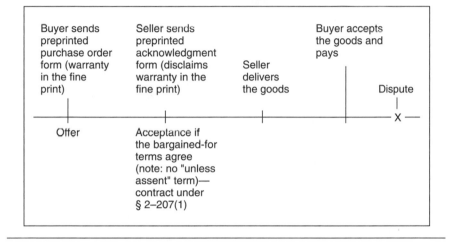

Example 4-13

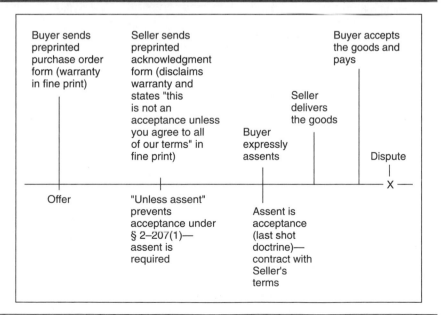

Example 4-14

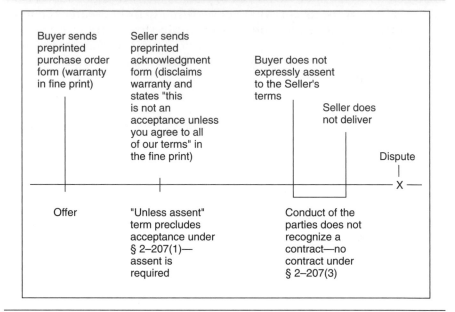

Example 4-15

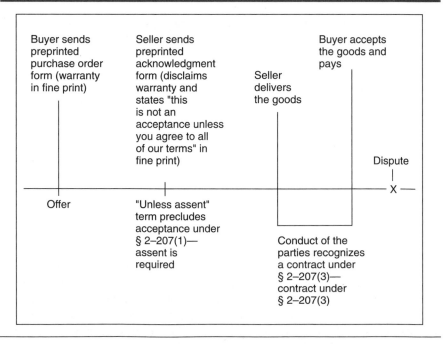

Now that a contract has been formed under subsection (1), it is necessary to determine what boilerplate terms are in this contract. The substantive boilerplate terms of the two forms are compared. The terms will sort into four patterns: those that agree, those that are in the first form but not in the second, those that are in the second form but not in the first, and those that disagree. The boilerplate terms that match are terms of the contract. The boilerplate terms that are in the first form but not in the second are in the contract. The party who issued the second form had an opportunity to object to the first form's term but did not and therefore accepted that term. The boilerplate terms that are in the second form but not in the first form are known as "additional terms" and are discussed in subsection (2). The boilerplate terms that conflict are known as "different terms."

If a term is an additional term, then under the first sentence of subsection (2), it becomes a "proposal for addition to the contract." If the term is accepted, it becomes a part of the contract.

Example 4–16

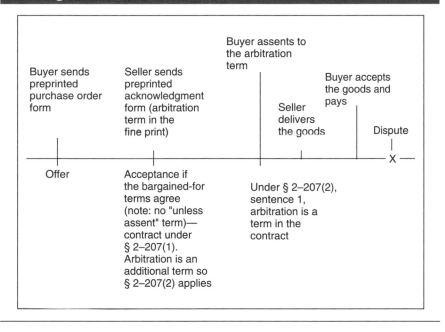

If no action is taken as to the additional term under the first sentence of subsection (2), the second sentence of subsection (2) will come into play. The additional term will become a part of the contract if the contract is "between merchants" and the offer has not expressly limited acceptance to the terms of the offer, the additional term does not materially alter the contract, and notification of objection to the additional term has not already been given or is given within a reasonable time after notice of the additional term is received.

Example 4–17

Assume the Buyer and Seller are members of a trade that routinely does business by sending preprinted purchase order forms and preprinted acknowledgment forms and therefore are considered "merchants" for section 2–207(2), sentence 2, purposes. **"Merchant"** and **"between merchants"** are defined in section 2–104 and in its comment 2. Also assume that the Buyer's purchase order did not have a term in its boilerplate limiting acceptance to its terms, that the arbitration term did not materially alter the contract since arbitration was the normal method of dispute resolution in that trade, and that the Buyer did not object to the arbitration term until after the dispute arose.

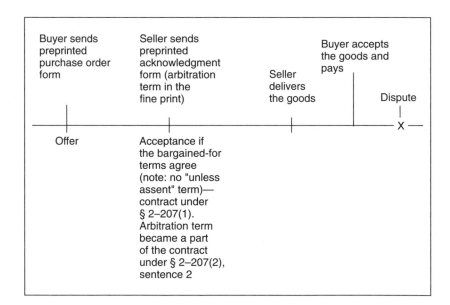

The final step is to check the Uniform Commercial Code for terms that the Code supplies (i.e., gap fillers) if the contract is silent.

---

merchant

A merchant as used in Article 2 of the UCC is defined in section 2–104 and its comment 2 and may be either a merchant who has specialized knowledge as to the goods, specialized knowledge as to the business practices, or specialized knowledge as to both the goods and the business practices. The business practices are those practices discussed in a specific code section. Therefore, a party may have specialized knowledge as to some business practices but not others—or may have specialized knowledge as to the goods but not as to specialized business practices and therefore may be a merchant for one Code section but not another.

between merchants

Between merchants means that both parties to the transaction (the buyer and the seller) are chargeable with the knowledge or the skill required to be a merchant for a particular Code section.

If a substantive boilerplate term in the acceptance is a different term (conflicts with a substantive boilerplate term in the offer), courts are divided in their approach to resolving the issue. Should subsection (2) apply, although subsection (2) does not expressly apply to different terms? Comment 3 to § 2–207 suggests subsection (2) be read "additional or different." Should the terms knock each other out so neither is in the contract and the terms of the contract are supplemented by the Code's gap fillers? Comment 6 to § 2–207 suggests this result. Should the term in the acceptance drop out because the offeree had an opportunity to object to this term and did not do so?

ⅲ PARALEGAL EXERCISE 4.8

The ABC Company sent its purchase order to the Quality Brick Company for 6 million bricks at $10 per 100. ABC's purchase order form was silent as to warranty.

Quality responded by sending its acknowledgment form, which stated 6 million bricks at $10 per 100. Preprinted on Quality's form was the statement "all bricks warranted for 90 days as to defects in materials or workmanship. All other express and implied warranties are disclaimed."

Quality sent the bricks, and ABC accepted the shipment and paid. A year later and after a winter's use, ABC noticed that some bricks were cracking because they were improperly dried during manufacture.

Under UCC § 2–207(1), is there a contract for the sale of the bricks? If there is a contract, then under 2–207(2), is the contract with or without the limited warranty expressed in Quality's acknowledgment form? ▪

ⅲ PARALEGAL EXERCISE 4.9

The ABC Company sent its purchase order to the Quality Brick Company for 6 million bricks at $10 per 100. ABC's purchase order form was silent as to warranty.

Quality responded by sending its acknowledgment form, which stated 6 million bricks at $12 per 100. Preprinted on Quality's form was the statement "all bricks warranted for 90 days as to defects in material or workmanship. All other express and implied warranties are disclaimed."

Although the forms did not agree as to price, Quality sent the bricks, and ABC accepted the shipment and paid the higher price. A year later and after a winter's use, ABC noticed that some bricks were cracking because they were improperly dried during manufacture.

Under UCC § 2–207(1), is there a contract for the sale of the bricks? If not, is there a contract for the sale of the bricks under 2–207(3)? If there is a contract under 2–207(3), then, under 2–207(3), is the contract with or without the limited warranty expressed in Quality's acknowledgment form? ▪

Miscommunication between the Offeror and the Offeree

An interesting problem occurs when the offeror and offeree say the same thing but mean different things.

Example 4–18

Imagine a situation where the buyer and seller of chickens used the term "chickens" but the seller was thinking of "stewing chickens" and the buyer was thinking of "frying chickens." The seller ships chickens to the buyer, and the buyer is surprised to discover that the chickens are "stewing chickens."

This miscommunication can be resolved by considering what a reasonable person would have meant had that person been placed in this situation. It is important to note that the plaintiff has the burden of proving the reasonable person's meaning by a preponderance of the evidence. The defendant need not prove anything—but only cast enough doubt on the plaintiff's assertion so that the plaintiff's proof does not rise to the preponderance-of-the-evidence level.

Assume the plaintiff is the offeror. If the offeror proves by a preponderance of the evidence that a reasonable person would have meant what the offeror had meant, there would be a contract and the offeror's meaning governs. The offeree's meaning would be disregarded as unreasonable.

If the offeror fails to prove by a preponderance of the evidence that a reasonable person would have meant what the offeror had meant, there would be a contract and the offeree's meaning governs by default since the offeror's meaning does not govern. The offeror's meaning would be disregarded as unreasonable and the result would be judgment for the defendant on this issue.

Return to the chickens and assume the buyer is the plaintiff. If the buyer proves by a preponderance of the evidence that the reasonable person would have meant "frying chickens" when using the word "chicken," the reasonable meaning is "frying chickens" and the buyer prevails in a breach of contract action. If the buyer is not able to prove by a preponderance of the evidence that "frying chickens" is the reasonable meaning, the seller prevails on this issue and is not in breach of contract.

Assume now that the seller is the plaintiff because the buyer rejected the shipment on the ground that "frying chickens" were ordered. Seller must prove by a preponderance of the evidence that the reasonable meaning of "chicken" is not limited to "frying chickens." If the seller is unable to prove by a preponderance of the evidence that the reasonable meaning of "chicken" is not limited to "frying chickens," the buyer prevails on this issue and is not in breach of contract (see Exhibit 4–9).

What the parties said: "chicken"			
What the plaintiff offeree (buyer) meant	frying chickens	frying chickens	frying chickens
What the defendant offeror (seller) meant	stewing chickens	stewing chickens	stewing chickens
What the reasonable person would have meant	if frying chickens	if not necessarily frying chickens	if either frying chickens or not necessarily frying chickens
Conclusion	contract for frying chickens	contract for not necessarily frying chickens	no contract

Exhibit 4–9 Miscommunication between the Offeror and Offeree Using an Objective Standard

☰ PARALEGAL EXERCISE 4.10

In June, Mary planned a dinner party for 28 people and had it catered by Le Gourmet, a French restaurant that specializes in catering dinner parties. In discussing the menu, Mary discovered that Le Gourmet had a "special" that consisted of roast duckling with all the trimmings for $60 per person. She chose "the special" and the party was a success.

The next month, Mary planned a second dinner party, again for 28 people, and telephoned Le Gourmet and ordered "the special." Much to Mary's surprise, when dinner was served, it was pheasant under glass for $100 per person.

While both Mary and Le Gourmet agreed on "the special," Mary meant the roast duckling at $60 per person, while Le Gourmet meant the July special of pheasant under glass at $100 per person. Has a contract been formed between Mary and Le Gourmet and, if so, was it for the duckling or the pheasant? ■

The Parties Who Can Accept the Offer

The offeror, by being master of the offer, controls who may accept the offer. An offer made to a specific party can only be accepted by that party. The offeree may not empower someone else to accept, thereby making the other person the offeree.

An offer need not, however, be limited to one party. A number of offers are made to the public in general.

Example 4-19

A reward for information leading to the arrest and conviction of the perpetrator of a violent crime is an offer to anyone who supplies the information.

Example 4-20

The auctioneer who announces that the auction will be without reserve makes an offer to all those present.

Example 4-21

An advertisement that contains the elements of offer is an offer to anyone who reads the ad.

It should be noted that in all of these situations, the offer, while it may be accepted by any party, can be accepted by only one party. Only one party can supply the information, make the highest bid, or purchase each individual item advertised.

THE METHOD FOR ACCEPTING AN OFFER AND NOTICE OF ACCEPTANCE

The offeror, by being the master of the offer, not only establishes the terms of the contract but also establishes how the offeree must accept the offer (method of acceptance) and whether notice of acceptance is required. These two concepts, method of acceptance and notice of acceptance, often are achieved by the same act. In some situations, however, the method of acceptance will not provide notice of acceptance.

The Method of Acceptance

The Restatement (Second) of Contracts § 50(1) defines acceptance of an offer as:

> a manifestation of assent to the terms thereof made by the offeree in a manner invited or required by the offer.

The offer may be silent as to the method of acceptance, may suggest a method, or may mandate a method. If the offer mandates a method, then that method is how the offer must be accepted.

If the offer does not mandate a method of acceptance, the general rules of contract law apply, and this takes the discussion back to offers for unilateral and bilateral contracts. If the offer is for a unilateral contract—a promise for a performance—the offer must be accepted by performance. A promise will not do; nor can a promise be used to imply the required performance. Beginning or nearly completing performance is also inadequate as the method of acceptance. Full performance is the method of acceptance unless the offeror has dictated another method.

If the offer is for a bilateral contract—a promise for a promise—it must be accepted by a promise. Full performance is not the method of acceptance. Full performance or even part performance, however, may *imply* the required promise. Implying a promise from performance is not the same as stating that the method of acceptance of an offer for a bilateral contract is performance. The method is a promise, although the promise may be implied from performance.

▥ PARALEGAL EXERCISE 4.11

The Black Forest, a Bavarian restaurant, promised to pay Media International, an advertising agency, $40,000 for Media's promise to plan and execute a three-month advertising campaign for Black Forest. Media telephoned Black Forest to say that it "accepted" the offer.

Has Media accepted the Black Forest offer? ▦

▥ PARALEGAL EXERCISE 4.12

Same facts as Paralegal Exercise 4.11 but instead of Media telephoning Black Forest to say it "accepted" the offer, Media began planning the campaign.

Has Media accepted the Black Forest offer? Can this question be answered without additional facts? What would these facts be, and why are they essential? ▦

▥ PARALEGAL EXERCISE 4.13

Same facts as Paralegal Exercise 4.11 but instead of Black Forest promising to pay Media for Media's promise to plan and execute a three-month advertising campaign for Black Forest, Black Forest promised to pay for Media's planning and executing a three-month advertising campaign for Black Forest. Media telephoned Black Forest to say it "accepted" the offer.

Has Media accepted the Black Forest offer? ▦

ⅢPARALEGAL EXERCISE 4.14

Same facts as Paralegal Exercise 4.13 but instead of Media telephoning Black Forest to say it "accepted" the offer, Media began planning the campaign.
Has Media accepted the Black Forest offer? ▪

When an offeror specifies a method of acceptance, care should be exercised to determine whether the method stated is the only method or an optional method.

Example 4–22

The offer for a bilateral contract states, "This offer may be accepted by beginning performance." Since the offer is in terms of "may," the offeree could accept either by complying with the method stated in the offer (beginning performance) or by following the traditional method for accepting an offer for a bilateral contract (a promise).

ⅢPARALEGAL EXERCISE 4.15

The Black Forest promised to pay Media $40,000 for Media's promise to plan and execute a three-month advertising campaign. The offer stated that Media could accept by either notifying Black Forest or by beginning the advertising campaign. Black Forest first learned that Media was working on a campaign when a Black Forest advertisement appeared in a local newspaper. Has Media accepted Black Forest's offer? ▪

Notice to the Offeror That the Offer Has Been Accepted

When an offer is accepted, the offeror must notify the offeree of the acceptance unless the offer states that the offeree need not notify the offeror. The notice will be different depending on whether the offer is for a bilateral or a unilateral contract.

If the offeror proposes a bilateral contract, the offeree must communicate his or her promise to the offeror. If the parties are standing face-to-face or are communicating by telephone, this communication may be oral. If the parties are not in voice contact, then another form of communication, such as a letter, telegram, fax, e-mail, or messenger, could provide the notice.

If the offeror proposes a unilateral contract, the offeree must communicate that his or her performance to the offeror has been completed. If the performance, by its very nature, is known to the offeror as it occurs, then the offeree's act of performance is itself notice to the offeror. If, however, the performance occurs at a distant location so that the offeror would not know about it, the offeree must, in some fashion, communicate the completion of performance to the offeror.

WHEN AN ATTEMPTED ACCEPTANCE IS EFFECTIVE

An attempted acceptance is effective when it gives notice to the offeror that the offeree has accepted. If the parties are dealing face-to-face or are in voice contact, such as by telephone, the offeree has the opportunity to give the offeror instant notification.

If, however, the parties are dealing at a distance and are not in voice contact, then each party will be unaware of the other's actions. The offeror will not know that the offeree has mailed an acceptance, nor will the offeree know that the offeror has received the mailed acceptance. Each party operates in the dark for at least a part of the time.

At which point will the mailed acceptance be effective?

1. When the offeree posts her acceptance
2. When the offeror receives the offeree's acceptance
3. When the offeror posts his notice to the offeree that he has received her acceptance
4. When the offeree receives the offeror's notice
5. When the offeree posts her notice to the offeror that she has received his notice that he has received her acceptance

The judges, who shaped the law, selected the least complicated approach—when the offeree posts the acceptance if posting is a medium reasonable in the circumstances (see Exhibit 4–10). This rule has become known as the **"posting"** or **"mailbox" rule.**

posting (mailbox) rule
The rule of determining when an acceptance sent from a distance is effective. Under the posting (mailbox) rule, acceptance is effective when sent.

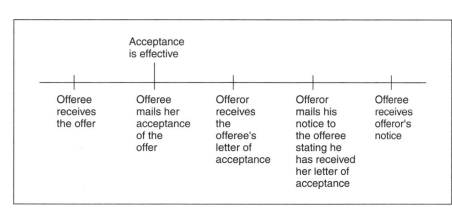

Exhibit 4–10 Acceptance by Post

The Restatement (Second) of Contracts § 63 (a) follows the mailbox rule:

> Unless the offer provides otherwise,
> (a) an acceptance made in a manner and by a medium invited by an offer is operative and completes the manifestation of mutual assent as soon as put out of the offeree's possession, without regard to whether it ever reaches the offeror . . . .

When the offeror sends the offeree an offer and does not specify a specific method of acceptance, the offeror builds in the risk that the offer may be accepted before the offeror learns of the acceptance. The offeror has the opportunity to create an offer that would minimize these risks. If the offeror chooses not to take advantage of this opportunity, the offeror assumes the risk.

Example 4-23

- May 1–the Apex Fireworks Company sends a purchase order to the Zippy Chemical Company to buy all of its requirements of potassium nitrate (saltpeter) for one year at $100 a ton.
- May 5–Zippy receives Apex's purchase order of May 1st.
- May 15–Zippy mails a letter of acceptance of Apex's May 1st purchase order.
- June 1–Apex enters into a requirements contract with Megga Chemical Company for one year at $90 a ton.
- June 2–Apex receives Zippy's letter of May 15th.

Since Apex did not specify a method of acceptance that would insure immediate notice of acceptance, Apex now has two contracts to buy all of its requirements of saltpeter: one with Zippy and one with Megga.

Just when an attempted acceptance is effective becomes more complicated when the offeror attempts to revoke the offer. The Restatement (Second) of Contracts § 42 provides the following rule:

> An offeree's power of acceptance is terminated when the offeree receives from the offeror a manifestation of an intention not to enter into the proposed contract.

Example 4-24

- May 25–Seller sends a letter to Buyer offering to sell Buyer a computer for $2,000.
- June 1–Buyer receives Seller's letter of May 25th.

- June 5—Seller sends a letter to Buyer revoking her offer.
- June 6—Buyer sends a letter of acceptance to Seller.
- June 7—Buyer receives Seller's letter attempting to revoke the offer.
- June 8—Seller receives Buyer's letter of June 6th.

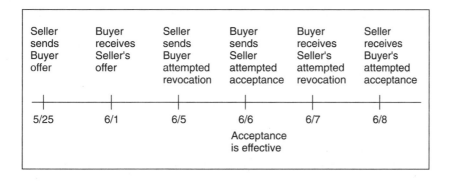

Seller sends Buyer offer	Buyer receives Seller's offer	Seller sends Buyer attempted revocation	Buyer sends Seller attempted acceptance	Buyer receives Seller's attempted revocation	Seller receives Buyer's attempted acceptance
5/25	6/1	6/5	6/6	6/7	6/8
			Acceptance is effective		

Under the Restatement (Second) of Contracts § 63(a), the Buyer's acceptance was effective on June 6th, the date when the acceptance was sent. Under the Restatement (Second) of Contracts § 42, the Seller's attempted revocation was effective on June 7th, the date when the attempted revocation was received. Since the Buyer's acceptance was effective before the Seller's attempted revocation, the contract was formed.

ⅲ PARALEGAL EXERCISE 4.16

- May 25—Seller sends a letter to Buyer offering to sell Buyer a computer for $2,000.
- June 1—Buyer receives Seller's letter of May 25th.
- June 5—Buyer sends a letter to Seller accepting the offer.
- June 6—Seller sends a letter of revocation to Buyer.

Seller sends Buyer an offer	Buyer receives Seller's offer	Buyer sends Seller an attempted acceptance	Seller sends Buyer an attempted revocation	Seller receives Buyer's attempted acceptance	Buyer receives Seller's attempted revocation
5/25	6/1	6/5	6/6	6/7	6/8

- June 7—Seller receives Buyer's letter attempting to accept the offer.
- June 8—Buyer receives Seller's letter of June 6th.

Has the Buyer accepted the Seller's offer? ▨

Just when an attempted acceptance is effective becomes even more complicated when the offeree attempts to reject the offer. If the offeree sends an acceptance before sending a rejection, the general rule is that a rejection is not effective until it is received by the offeror.

▥ PARALEGAL EXERCISE 4.17

If an acceptance is effective when sent and a rejection is effective when received, has a contract been formed in the following two situations?

Seller sends Buyer an offer	Buyer receives Seller's offer	Buyer sends Seller an attempted acceptance	Buyer sends Seller an attempted rejection	Seller receives Buyer's attempted acceptance	Seller receives Buyer's attempted rejection
5/25	6/1	6/5	6/6	6/7	6/8

Seller sends Buyer an offer	Buyer receives Seller's offer	Buyer sends Seller an attempted acceptance	Buyer sends Seller an attempted rejection	Seller receives Buyer's attempted rejection	Seller receives Buyer's attempted acceptance
	6/1	6/5	6/6	6/7	6/8

▨

If, however, the offeree sends the rejection before sending the acceptance, the rule reaches a new level of complexity. The Restatement (Second) of Contracts § 40 formulates the rule as follows:

> Rejection . . . by mail . . . does not terminate the power of acceptance until received by the offeror, but limits the power so that a letter . . . of acceptance started after the sending of an otherwise effective rejection . . . is only a counteroffer unless the acceptance is received by the offeror before he receives the rejection. . . .

⏚ PARALEGAL EXERCISE 4.18

Using Restatement (Second) of Contracts §§ 40 and 63(a), has a contract been formed in the following two situations?

Seller sends Buyer an offer	Buyer receives Seller's offer	Buyer sends Seller an attempted rejection	Buyer sends Seller an attempted acceptance	Seller receives Buyer's attempted acceptance	Seller receives Buyer's attempted rejection
	6/1	6/5	6/6	6/7	6/8

Seller sends Buyer an offer	Buyer receives Seller's offer	Buyer sends Seller an attempted rejection	Buyer sends Seller an attempted acceptance	Seller receives Buyer's attempted rejection	Seller receives Buyer's attempted acceptance
	6/1	6/5	6/6	6/7	6/8

A final problem remains. If an offer is made that is followed by an option contract negating the offeror's power to revoke its offer and the offeree's power to reject the offer, the time when the attempted acceptance of the original offer shifts from the time when the attempted acceptance is sent (Restatement (Second) of Contract § 63(a)) to the time when the attempted acceptance is received (Restatement (Second) of Contracts § 63(b)).

> Unless the offer provides otherwise,
> (a) an acceptance made in a manner and by a medium invited by an offer is operative and completes the manifestation of mutual assent as soon as put out of the offeree's possession, without regard to whether it ever reaches the offeror; but
> (b) an acceptance under an option contract is not operative until received by the offeror.

Example 4–25

- May 25–Seller sends a letter to Buyer offering to sell Buyer a computer for $2,000.
- June 1–Buyer receives Seller's letter of May 25th.
- June 5–Seller and Buyer enter into an option contract whereby Seller promises not to revoke her offer for 10 days.

- June 12—Buyer sends a letter attempting to accept Seller's offer.
- June 16—Seller notifies Buyer that her offer is revoked.
- June 17—Buyer receives Seller's letter of June 12th attempting to accept Seller's offer.

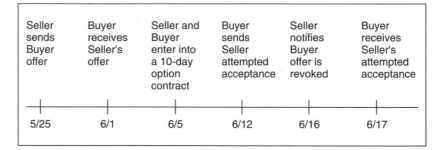

Under the Restatement (Second) of Contracts § 63(a), Buyer's acceptance was effective on June 12th, the date when the acceptance was sent. The option contract, however, changes the rules. Under the Restatement (Second) of Contracts § 63(b), Buyer's acceptance is not effective until it is received. Since Buyer's acceptance was not received until June 17th, a day after Seller revoked her offer, Buyer's attempted acceptance was ineffective and no contract was formed.

ⅢPARALEGAL EXERCISE 4.19

- May 25—Seller sends a letter to Buyer offering to sell Buyer a computer for $2,000.
- June 1—Buyer receives Seller's letter of May 25th.
- June 5—Seller and Buyer enter into an option contract whereby Seller promises not to revoke her offer for 10 days.
- June 10—Seller notifies Buyer that her offer was revoked.
- June 12—Buyer sends a letter attempting to accept Seller's offer.
- June 17—Buyer receives Seller's letter of June 12th attempting to accept Seller's offer.

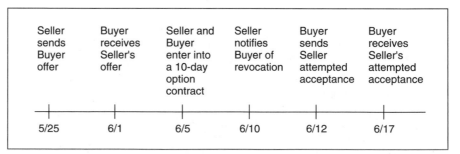

Has a contract been formed? ▪

COULD A RESTITUTION ACTION
BE AN ALTERNATIVE TO ACCEPTANCE?

If the offer is not accepted, no contract is formed and neither party may maintain a cause of action for breach of contract. Is another cause of action, a restitution cause of action, available?

In Chapter 2, we explored the availability of a restitution cause of action if no offer has been made and if one party conferred a benefit on another party and it would be unjust to permit the party with the benefit to retain it without compensating the party who conferred the benefit. This was a restitution cause of action based on unjust enrichment and not a breach of contract action (see Exhibit 4–11).

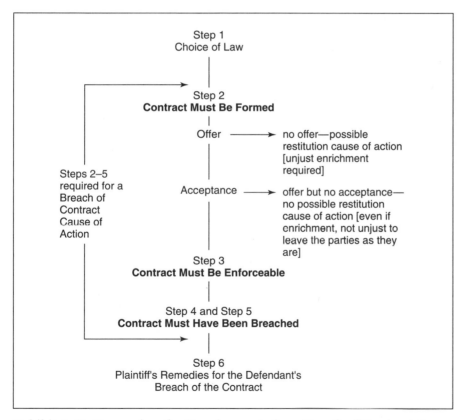

Exhibit 4–11 Comparing the Requirements for a Breach of Contract Cause of Action with the Requirements for a Restitution Cause of Action

PARALEGAL CHECKLIST

The Acceptance Phase

❑ If the offer has not been revoked by the offeror, rejected by the offeree, or lapsed, check whether the offer has been accepted. Evaluate the following:

1. Does the apparent acceptance have the necessary elements to be an acceptance?
   - If the offer was for a bilateral contract, the acceptance is: (1) the offeree's promise and (2) consideration for the offeree's promise (i.e., the offeror's promise and the offeree must be promising in order to obtain the offeror's promise).
   - If the offer was for a unilateral contract, the acceptance is: (1) the offeree's full performance and (2) consideration for the offeree's full performance (i.e., the offeror's promise and the offeree must have fully performed in order to obtain the offeror's promise).
     a. The acceptance must be in response to the offer.
       (1) If the offer is for a bilateral contract, the offeree must have knowledge of the offer before responding with a promise. Otherwise the offeror's promise is not inducing the offeree to respond and, therefore, the offeree's response is not an effective acceptance.

          If the offer is for a unilateral contract, the Restatement (First) of Contracts § 53 would require the offeree to have knowledge of the offer before beginning the requested performance. The Restatement (Second) of Contracts § 51 requires only that the offeree learn of the offer sometime

       prior to completing the requested performance.
       (2) The offeror's promise must not be subject to a preexisting duty. Otherwise, the offeror's promise cannot be consideration for the offeree's promise or performance.
     b. The offeree must agree to the offeror's terms.
       (1) Under the common law mirror image rule, the offeree must agree to all of the offeror's terms. Any deviation constitutes a rejection of the offeror's offer and is a counteroffer by the offeree. If the offeree's response is a counteroffer and the offeror begins performance of its promise, the performance may constitute an implied (in fact) promise to accept all of the offeree's terms and the contract is formed under the offeree's terms. This is known as the "last shot" doctrine. The party who makes the last express offer prior to performance by the other party is the party whose terms control the transaction.
       (2) If the transaction is a sale of goods, Article 2 of the Uniform Commercial Code applies and a contract may be formed if the bargained-for terms (the variable terms) coincide. An application of UCC § 2–207 determines what other terms, if any, are a part of the contract.
       (3) If the offeror and offeree say the same thing but mean

different things, the outcome is determined by the reasonable person's perception of what the parties said. The plaintiff has the burden of proving the reasonable meaning by a preponderance of the evidence. If the plaintiff can prove by a preponderance of the evidence that the reasonable person's perception coincides with his or her meaning, a contract is formed and the meaning is the plaintiff's meaning. If the defendant can cast enough doubt so the plaintiff cannot prove the reasonable person's perception by a preponderance of the evidence, the plaintiff's meaning does not prevail.

2. Who may accept the offer? The offeror controls who may accept the offer. An offer made to a specific party can be accepted only by that party. An offer, however, made to the general public can be accepted by anyone.

3. Who sets the terms of the contract and establishes the method by which the offer must be accepted? The offeror, as the master of the offer, not only sets the terms of the contract but also establishes the method by which the offeree must accept the offer.
   a. If the offeror mandates the method of acceptance, that method is the appropriate method.
   b. If the offeror does not mandate a method of acceptance and the offer is for a bilateral contract, the offer is accepted by a promise. The promise can, however, be implied from performance.
   c. If the offeror does not mandate a method of acceptance and the offer is for a unilateral contract, the offer must be accepted by full performance.
   d. When an offeror specifies a method of acceptance, care must be exercised to determine whether the method stated is an optional method or the only method.

4. Did the offeree notify the offeror that the offer has been accepted?
   a. If the offer was for a bilateral contract, the offeree must communicate acceptance to the offeror. The communication need not follow a special method unless the offeror has required a special method in the offer.
   b. If the offer was for a unilateral contract, the offeree's communication of acceptance is normally obvious to the offeror by the offeree's performance. Where, however, the offeror would not see the offeree's performance, the offeree must communicate acceptance (the completion of performance) to the offeror.

5. When will the mailed acceptance be effective? If the offeror and offeree are dealing at a distance and are not in voice contact, each party will be unaware of the other's actions. If the offeree mails an acceptance, the acceptance is effective when posted.

6. Could the offeree be liable in a restitution cause of action for a benefit conferred by the offeror after the offer has been made (but not accepted)? If the offeror confers a benefit on the offeree after making the offer but the offeree does not accept the offer, the offeree will not be liable in a restitution cause of action for the benefit received.

KEY TERMS

Acknowledgment form	Last shot doctrine
Additional term	Merchant
Bargained-for terms	Mirror image
Between merchants	Posting (Mailbox) rule
Boilerplate terms	Purchase order
Definite expression of acceptance	Seasonable expression of acceptance
Different term	

REVIEW QUESTIONS

TRUE/FALSE QUESTIONS (CIRCLE THE CORRECT ANSWER)

1. T   F   An offeror can propose either a unilateral or bilateral contract.

2. T   F   The offer for a unilateral contract is a promise.

3. T   F   If the offer is for a bilateral contract, the offeree must have knowledge of the offer before responding with a promise.

4. T   F   If an offer is for a unilateral contract, the offeree's performance is acceptance of the offer even though the offeree performed without learning of the offer until after completing the requested performance.

5. T   F   The "preexisting duty" rule, which applies to consideration for the promisor's promise, does not apply to consideration for the promisee's promise or performance.

6. T   F   Under the common law, the offeree may accept the offer without agreeing to all of the offeror's terms.

7. T   F   Alfred sent a letter promising to purchase Jan's 1965 T-Bird for Jan's promise to sell for $5,500. Jan wrote Alfred that she would sell for $5,500 if Alfred would let her drive it in one more road rally. Under the common law, the offer has been accepted.

8. T   F   The offeror is master of the offer and controls the terms of the contract.

9. T   F   Under the common law mirror image rule, the offeree cannot change the terms of the offer without rejecting the offer.

10. T   F   The preprinted terms on the forms used in commercial transactions are called "armor plate."

11. T   F   When the offeror and the offeree say the same thing but mean different things, the party proving by a

preponderance of the evidence that his or her meaning coincides with the reasonable person's perception prevails.

12. T   F   A mistake in understanding the terms of the offer can be resolved by considering what the average person would have meant if he or she had been placed in this situation.

13. T   F   The seller wrote the buyer that she would sell her bean crop to him for $3 a bushel. The buyer wrote back that he would be happy to buy her bean crop for $3 a bushel. The seller has a crop of Kentucky Wonders. The buyer thinks the seller has a crop of Blue Lakes. The buyer has never seen the seller's crop. If both the buyer's and the seller's perception of the manifestation "bean" were reasonable, the buyer's letter would not be an acceptance of the seller's offer.

14. T   F   As a general rule, the offeree does not need to notify the offeror that the offer has been accepted.

15. T   F   If the offeree decides not to accept the offer, he or she may empower someone else to accept it.

16. T   F   An offer may not be directed to the general public.

17. T   F   The offeror may establish the method by which the offeree must accept the offer.

18. T   F   If the offeror does not mandate the method of acceptance, the general rules of contract law apply.

19. T   F   The "mailbox" rule is also known as the "posting" rule.

20. T   F   Under the "mailbox" rule, an acceptance is effective when it is received in the mail by the offeror.

21. T   F   If after an offer has been created, the offeror confers a benefit on the offeree and the offeree subsequently rejects the offer but retains the benefit, the offeror could successfully maintain a restitution cause of action against the offeree for unjust enrichment.

FILL-IN-THE-BLANK QUESTIONS

1. _____. The phase after the transaction passes through the post-offer/pre-acceptance phase.

2. _____. The type of contract that results when the offer is a promise for a performance.

3. _____. The type of contract that results when the offer is a promise for a promise.

4. _____. A common law rule that prevents the offeree from changing the terms of the offer in his or her acceptance.

5. _____. A rule that prevents a prior obligation from being consideration for a promise or performance.

6. _____. The master of the offer.

7. _____. Preprinted terms on the forms used in commercial transactions.

8. _____. A rule that provides that acceptance is effective when the offeree posts his or her acceptance.

9. _____. An action that may be available but only when a breach of contract action cannot be maintained.

10. _____. The doctrine where the last form under the common law mirror image rule is the offer.

11. _____. The problem that occurs when the offeror and offeree say the same thing but mean different things.

12. _____. The party controlling who may accept the offer.

13. _____. A manifestation of assent to the terms of the offer.

MULTIPLE-CHOICE QUESTIONS (CIRCLE ALL THE CORRECT ANSWERS)

1. One evening, Harry, a chimpanzee, escaped from the local zoo. WGAB, a local radio station, offered a reward of $500 for the capture and return of Harry. That evening Carlos found a chimpanzee in his garage. Since it was too late to call the animal shelter, Carlos thought he would try to take the chimp to the zoo. Maybe they could take care of him. Carlos put the chimp in his van and began to drive to the zoo. As he drove he happened to hear an announcement on WGAB about Harry's escape and the information concerning the reward. Carlos continued to the zoo, left Harry, and then demanded his reward from WGAB.

   (a) Carlos is not entitled to the reward because rewards are not offers.

   (b) Carlos is not entitled to the reward because he did not call WGAB to promise to capture Harry.

   (c) Carlos is not entitled to the reward because under Restatement (First) of Contracts § 53 (1932) he must have knowledge of the offer before beginning the requested performance.

   (d) Carlos is entitled to the reward because under Restatement (Second) of Contracts § 51 (1979) he must have knowledge of the offer only before completing the requested performance.

   (e) Carlos is not entitled to the reward because as a good citizen, he had a preexisting duty to capture and return Harry to the zoo.

2. ABC Company sent the XYZ Company a purchase order for 50,000 metal bracelets at $.50 each. ABC's purchase order contained the following provision in its fine print: "all disputes will be settled by arbitration."

   XYZ sent its acknowledgment form to ABC and subsequently shipped the bracelets. XYZ's form stated in its fine print: "all disputes will be settled by mediation-arbitration."

   ABC accepted the shipment and paid.

    (a)   Under common law, XYZ's acknowledgment form constitutes the acceptance.

    (b)   Under common law, XYZ's shipment constitutes the acceptance.

    (c)   Under common law, ABC's acceptance of the shipment and payment constitutes the acceptance.

    (d)   Under UCC § 2–207(1), XYZ's acknowledgment form constitutes the acceptance.

    (e)   Under UCC § 2–207(3), ABC's acceptance of the shipment and payment constitutes the acceptance.

3. ABC Company sent the XYZ Company a purchase order for 50,000 metal bracelets at $.50 each. ABC's purchase order contained the following provision in its fine print: "all disputes will be settled by arbitration."

    XYZ sent its acknowledgment form to ABC and subsequently shipped the bracelets. XYZ's form stated in its fine print: "all disputes will be settled by mediation-arbitration." XYZ's form also stated "this is not an acceptance unless the buyer assents to all of the seller's terms."

    ABC accepted the shipment and paid.

    (a)   Under common law, XYZ's acknowledgment form constitutes the acceptance.

    (b)   Under common law, XYZ's shipment constitutes the acceptance.

    (c)   Under common law, ABC's acceptance of the shipment and payment constitutes the acceptance.

    (d)   Under UCC § 2–207(1), XYZ's acknowledgment form constitutes the acceptance.

    (e)   Under UCC § 2–207(3), ABC's acceptance of the shipment and payment constitutes the acceptance.

4. ABC Company sent its purchase order form to XYZ Company for the purchase of 4,000 valves at $32 each. ABC's form stated in its boilerplate "ABC reserves all express and implied warranties."

    XYZ responded with its acknowledgment form which stated in its boilerplate "all express and implied warranties are disclaimed." XYZ shipped the valves.

    ABC accepted the shipment and paid.

    (a)   Under UCC § 2–207(1), XYZ's acknowledgment form is the acceptance of ABC's offer, even though it states terms different from those in the offer.

    (b)   Under UCC § 2–207(3), a contract has been formed by the conduct of the parties.

    (c)   XYZ's disclaimer is a term in the first form but not in the second and therefore is a term in the contract.

    (d)   XYZ's disclaimer is an additional term and under UCC § 2–207(2) may or may not be a term in the contract.

    (e)   XYZ's disclaimer is a different term and may or may not be a term in the contract depending on whether the knockout, dropout, or the UCC § 2–207(2) approach is used.

5. ABC Company sent its purchase order to XYZ Company for the purchase of 5,000 steel rods at $1 each.

    XYZ sent its acknowledgment form which stated 4,500 steel rods at $1 each. In the boilerplate of XYZ's acknowledgment form, XYZ disclaimed all express and implied warranties. XYZ shipped the rods.

ABC accepted the shipment and paid.
(a)   Under UCC § 2–207(1), XYZ's acknowledgment form was the acceptance.
(b)   Under UCC § 2–207(2), XYZ's acknowledgment form was the acceptance.
(c)   Under UCC § 2–207(3), the shipping and accepting shipment and paying constituted a contract.
(d)   Under UCC § 2–207(3), the contract contains all implied warranties.
(e)   Under UCC § 2–207(3), all express and implied warranties are excluded from the contract.

6.   Alex wrote a letter to Sally promising to pay for a trip to Europe if Sally would promise to take Alex's daughter with her. When is this offer accepted?
(a)   When Sally posts her acceptance
(b)   When Alex receives Sally's acceptance
(c)   When Alex posts his notice to Sally stating that he has received her acceptance
(d)   When Sally posts her notice to Alex stating that she has received his notice that he has received her acceptance
(e)   When she takes Alex's daughter to Europe

SHORT-ANSWER QUESTIONS

1.   On March 1st, Bernadette mailed her cousin Agnes a letter stating that she would pay Agnes $100 if Agnes would promise to sell her grandmother's antique cake stand.

On March 2nd, Agnes wrote to her cousin Bernadette stating that she would sell Bernadette her grandmother's cake stand if Bernadette would promise to pay $100.

Agnes received Bernadette's letter on March 4th. Bernadette received Agnes's letter on March 5th.

Has a contract been formed?

2.   Jose wrote Charlene, an artist, promising to pay her $2,500 if she painted his daughter's portrait. As it happened, Charlene had already begun to paint the portrait when she received Jose's letter. Charlene completed the portrait.

Has Jose's offer to pay $2,500 been accepted by Charlene?

3.   John had a statutory duty to support his daughter, Anne, until she became 18. John wrote his father promising to support Anne until she became 18 if his father would promise to leave her the family farm. John's father wrote John promising to leave the family farm to John's daughter for John's promise to support her until she became 18. At the time John's father made his promise, Anne was 7.

Has John's father accepted John's offer?

4.   When Sam was 17, Uncle Bob promised Sam, his nephew, that if Sam would refrain from smoking and drinking until he was 21, Uncle Bob would pay Sam $5,000.

Was a contract formed when Sam promised Uncle Bob that he would refrain?

The Post-Acceptance Phase

Chapter 5 focuses on the contract after it comes into existence.

After the creation of a contract but before full performance, the needs of the contracting parties may change. The parties may attempt to modify their contract.

The parties may want to go beyond modification and terminate their contractual relationship without completing their contractual duties. Four topics are investigated: terminating a contractual duty when neither party has fully performed; terminating a contractual duty when one party has fully performed; terminating a noncontractual duty; and terminating a contractual or noncontractual duty with a "payment in full" check (the accord and satisfaction) (see Exhibit 5–1).

MODIFYING A CONTRACT

After the creation of a contract but before full performance, the needs of the contracting parties may change and they may desire to modify the terms of their contract. A **modification** of a contract

modification

Under classical contract theory, modification of a contract is itself a contract and must follow the same rules of contract formation required for the original contract.

195

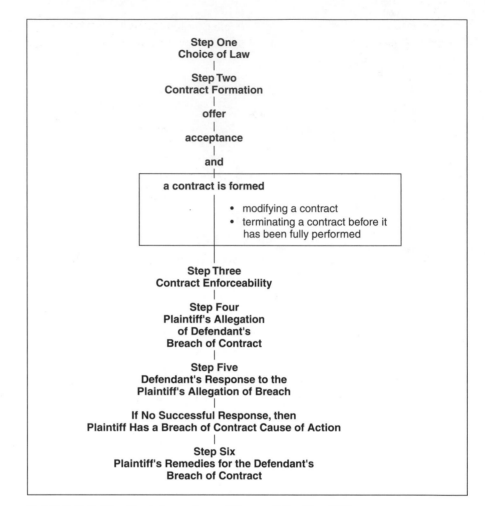

Exhibit 5–1 The Post-Acceptance Phase of the Road Map

is itself a contract and follows the same rules of contract formation required for the original contract. If the offer to modify is an offer for a bilateral contract, it must have a promisor's promise and consideration for that promise. The acceptance of the offer to modify must have the promisee's promise and consideration for that promise. Under classical contract law, a preexisting duty rule problem may arise as regards either the consideration for the promisor's promise or the consideration for the promisee's promise.

Example 5–1

"I promise to sell you Blackacre for your promise to pay $500,000 cash." "I promise to pay $500,000 cash for your promise to sell me Blackacre." Buyer's promise to pay $500,000 in cash is consideration for Seller's promise to sell Blackacre; Seller's promise to sell Blackacre is consideration for Buyer's promise to pay $500,000 in cash.

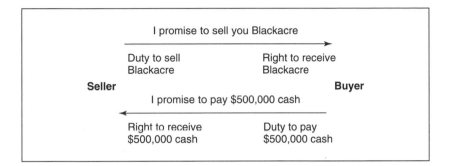

Assume Buyer becomes a little short on cash and would like to modify the contract so she can pay $300,000 cash and $200,000 plus 5 percent interest in one year. Seller, knowing that $500,000 is a good price, is willing to modify the contract so Buyer has more time to pay. The dialogue, translated into offer format, might be something like this:

"I promise to sell you Blackacre for your promise to pay me $300,000 cash and $200,000 plus 5 percent interest in one year."

The consideration for Seller's promise to sell Blackacre is Buyer's promise to pay $300,000 cash and $200,000 plus 5 percent interest in one year.

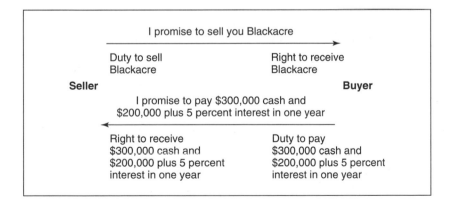

Under the original contract, Buyer had the duty to pay $500,000. Buyer's new promise adds the duty to pay 5 percent interest on $200,000 to the promise to pay $500,000. Seller is asking for new consideration from Buyer. Seller has made a new offer.

Now analyze Buyer's attempted acceptance: "I promise to pay $300,000 cash and $200,000 plus 5 percent interest in one year for your promise to sell me Blackacre." The consideration for Buyer's promise to pay $300,000 cash and $200,000 plus 5 percent interest in one year is Seller's promise to sell Blackacre. Under the original contract, Seller had the duty to sell Blackacre to Buyer. In the attempted modification, Buyer is not asking for a new consideration from Seller. Seller has a preexisting duty to sell Buyer Blackacre. Because the offer to modify cannot be accepted (preexisting duty precludes consideration), the attempt at modification fails.

⫿ PARALEGAL EXERCISE 5.1

The Bon Appetit Bakery Company contracted with Samantha Mills to host a 15-episode TV cooking show sponsored by Bon Appetit. The contract provided that Mills would receive $200,000 per episode. Filming would take place at the WFUN studios in Boston.

1. Before the filming began, Mills demanded that Bon Appetit increase her salary to $250,000 an episode. Bon Appetit agreed. Bon Appetit paid Mills $250,000 for the first 14 episodes but only $200,000 for the 15th. Was the contract successfully modified, thus entitling Mills to an additional $50,000 for the last episode?
2. Same facts except in addition to increasing Mills's salary to $250,000 an episode, Mills agreed to a 16th episode. Bon Appetit paid Mills $250,000 for the first 15 episodes but only $200,000 for the 16th. Was the contract successfully modified, thus entitling Mills to an additional $50,000 for the last episode?
3. Same facts except instead of adding an episode, Mills agreed to reduce the number to 14. Bon Appetit paid Mills $250,000 for the first 13 episodes but only $200,000 for the 14th. Was the contract successfully modified, thus entitling Mills to an additional $50,000 for the last episode?
4. Same facts as (1) except the attempted modification also called for the filming to be in southern France rather than in Boston. Bon Appetit paid Mills $250,000 for the first 14 episodes but only $200,000 for the 15th. Was the contract successfully modified, thus entitling Mills to an additional $50,000 for the last episode? ▧

Recently, state legislatures have addressed the modification issue. The Uniform Commercial Code makes the most uniform and sweeping change for the sale of goods. Section 2–209(1) provides:

An agreement modifying a contract within this Article needs no consideration to be binding.

ⅲ PARALEGAL EXERCISE 5.2

The Quality Glue Company contracted to sell to the Heirloom Furniture Company all of its glue requirements for the next year at $10 a barrel. Three months into the contract, Quality raised its price to $11 a barrel with Heirloom's consent. Has the contract price been successfully modified from $10 to $11 a barrel? Assume that this jurisdiction has enacted Article 2 of the UCC. ▪

TERMINATING A CONTRACT BEFORE IT HAS BEEN FULLY PERFORMED

After a bilateral contract has been created but before it has been fully performed by both parties, the contracting parties may find that their needs have changed and that full performance of the contract is no longer in their best interests. They may want to terminate their contractual duties before the contract is fully performed.

Terminating a Contractual Duty When Neither Party Has Fully Performed

The desire to end a contractual relationship may occur when *both* parties have duties to perform. Neither may have begun to perform, one may have begun to perform, or both may have begun to perform. **Mutual releases** will terminate the parties' duties to perform their contractual duties. To create a mutual release, the parties must follow the same rules of contract law used when they formed the original contract. The release has an offer and an acceptance. The offer consists of the offeror's promise and the consideration for the offeror's promise. "I promise to release you from your contractual duties to me for your promise to release me from my contractual duties to you." The acceptance consists of the offeree's promise and the consideration for the offeree's promise (the mirror image of the offer). "I promise to release you from your contractual duties to me for your promise to release me from my contractual duties to you." When the offeree promises, the offer is accepted and the release contract is formed. A mutual release absolves both parties from their future contractual obligations. The duties of both parties under the original contract are terminated (see Exhibit 5–2).

mutual releases
Mutual releases will terminate the parties' duties to perform their contractual duties.

ⅲ PARALEGAL EXERCISE 5.3

Tom, a stand-up comic, contracted with the Village Theatre of Victor, New York, to perform during the first two weeks of August. In mid-July, Tom received an offer to perform at a Las Vegas hotel that would substantially benefit his career. The Village Theatre does not want to lose Tom.

Can Tom rescind the contract? ▪

Offer for a Release

I promise to release you from
your contractual duties to me

Offeror   for   **Offeree**

Your promise to release me from
my contractual duties to you

———————————————————▶

Acceptance for a Release

I promise to release you from
your contractual duties to me

Offeror   for   **Offeree**

Your promise to release me from
my contractual duties to you

◀———————————————————

Exhibit 5–2 Mutual Release

▥ PARALEGAL EXERCISE 5.4

Susan, an interior decorator, contracts to work for Design Today for one year at a salary of $1,000 a week. After working for three months, Susan is invited to join another interior decorating firm with an increase in salary. Design Today has encouraged Susan to accept the new position because business at Design Today has been rather slow.

Draft a rescission that will free both Susan and Design Today from their duties under their contract. ▥

Terminating a Contractual Duty When One Party Has Fully Performed

When one party has fully performed while the other party has either not begun to perform or has only partially performed, the party who has fully performed may want to release the other from his or her contractual duties. This release cannot follow contract form because the offeror has fully performed and no longer owes a duty to the offeree. Without a duty owed by the offeror, consideration for the offeror's promise to release is missing. "I promise to release you from your contractual duty for your promise to release me from my contractual duty" becomes "I promise to release you from your contractual duty." Without consideration for the offeror's promise, the attempted offer fails. Without an offer, the attempted release contract fails (see Exhibit 5–3).

▥ PARALEGAL EXERCISE 5.5

Roberta, an artist, sold Jim a bronze sculpture for $2,500. Roberta delivered the sculpture to Jim, and he paid her $1,500. The next month Jim paid Roberta $500.

Attempted Offer for a Release

Offeror	I promise to release you from your contractual duties to me for [since offeror has already fully performed, offeror cannot ask offeree to promise to release the offeror from his or her contractual duty] →	**Offeree**

Therefore there is no offer for a release contract.

Exhibit 5–3 Failed Release

Upon reflection, Jim decided $2,500 was too high a price for the sculpture and he wanted to be released from his duty to pay the outstanding $500. Jim presented Roberta with a writing that said, "I, Roberta, promise to release Jim from his duty to pay me $500 for Jim's promise to release me from my duties to him." The writing also stated, "I, Jim, promise to release Roberta from her duties to me for her promise to release me from my duty to pay her $500."

If both parties sign the writing, has Roberta contracted to release Jim? ■

If one party has fully performed, that party can unilaterally release the other party. The transaction would not be a contract because the promise to release would lack consideration. The party who has fully performed can, however, confer a gift on the party who has contractual duties. The subject of the gift would be the right to that performance. The promisor's statement would be "I give you my right." The law of gifts would apply to the promisor's promise.

PARALEGAL EXERCISE 5.6

Could Roberta, in Paralegal Exercise 5.5, release Jim from his duty to pay $500? Should the failed attempt to contract be treated as a gift? ■

Terminating a Noncontractual Duty

Not all duties arise from contract. A number of duties are noncontractual. Parties may release noncontractual duties by using a release that meets the requirements of contract law. The release consists of an offer and an acceptance. The offer has the offeror's promise and consideration for the offeror's promise.

Example 5–2

"I promise to pay you $1,000 for your promise to release your claim against me." The "promise to release" is the consideration for the promisor's "promise to pay $1,000."

ⅢPARALEGAL EXERCISE 5.7

Stephanie was walking on the sidewalk in a downtown business district when a bucket suddenly struck her head. A window washer on the 20th floor of a local office building had been using the bucket. Pedestrians were not warned that someone was washing windows. Stephanie spent four days in the hospital and missed six weeks of work.

The window washer promised to pay Stephanie $3,000 for her promise to release her claim against him.

Have they formed a contract? ■

ⅢPARALEGAL EXERCISE 5.8

While eating at the Pink Penguin, a local bar and grill, Erma began to choke on a piece of meat. A patron dislodged the obstruction and saved Erma's life. Erma threatened to sue the Pink Penguin, although she thought that her own carelessness could have caused the incident.

The Pink Penguin promises to pay Erma $1,500 if she promises not to sue. Erma promises.

Have the parties formed a contract? ■

Terminating a Contractual or Noncontractual Duty with a "Payment in Full" Check—The Accord and Satisfaction

accord

An accord is a contract to pay a stated amount to discharge a prior obligation that is either uncertain as to its existence or amount. Satisfaction (performance) of the accord contract is required before the duties under the original contract are terminated.

"Accord and satisfaction" is another variation on the theme of ending a contract before it has been fully performed. Although an accord and satisfaction can operate without a check, generally it does involve a check. In an accord and satisfaction, one party (the drawer) writes a check to the other (the payee) and states on the bottom or back of the check, "This check is taken in full payment of my obligation to you." The **"accord"** is a contract to pay a stated amount to discharge a prior obligation.

Because the accord is simply a contract, the traditional rules of offer and acceptance, including the rules of consideration, apply. For an offer to exist under classical contract law, there must be consideration for the drawer's promise. The consideration for "the drawer's promise to pay the stated amount" would be "the payee's promise to take the amount as full payment." The situation gives

Offer for an Accord Contract

**Offeror
(drawer)**

I promise to pay $_____
for
Your promise to take this amount as
full payment of my obligation to you

**Offeree
(payee)**

→

Acceptance for the Accord Contract

**Offeree
(payee)**

I promise to take this amount as
full payment of your obligation to me
for
Your promise to pay $_____

**Offeror
(drawer)**

←

Exhibit 5–4 An Accord Contract

rise to an offer. For an acceptance to exist, there must be consideration for the payee's promise. The consideration for the "payee's
promise to take the amount as full payment" would have to be
(under the mirror image rule) "the drawer's promise to pay the
amount" (see Exhibit 5–4).

If either the existence or the amount of the drawer's obligation
is in dispute, the notation "payment in full" is significant. When
either the existence or the amount of the drawer's duty under the
original contract is in dispute, the drawer's promise to pay a stated
amount, by not reaffirming a preexisting duty, can be consideration for the payee's promise to take the stated amount as full
payment. With this acceptance of the offer, an accord contract is
created. **Satisfaction** is the performance of the accord contract. In
the case of a check, satisfaction is the payee's exercising dominion
over the check which normally takes place when the payee cashes
or deposits the check. Upon satisfaction, the original contractual
duty to pay is discharged.

satisfaction
Satisfaction is the
performance of the accord
contract. Once the accord
contract has been
performed, the original
contractual duties are
terminated.

Example 5–3

The Quality Nursery contracted to landscape the Rainbow Mall to
Rainbow's specifications. The contract provided that the price would
be "a reasonable price."

After Quality landscaped the Mall according to Rainbow's
specifications, Quality sent Rainbow a bill for $20,000. Rainbow
sent Quality a check for $18,000. The check carried the notation
"payment in full."

Rainbow's offer in the original contract was: "I promise to pay you a reasonable price for your promise to landscape the Mall according to my specifications." Quality's acceptance was: "I promise to landscape your Mall according to your specifications for your promise to pay me a reasonable price."

By sending the check for $18,000, Rainbow made an offer for an accord contract: "I promise to pay you $18,000 for your promise to accept this amount as full payment of my disputed obligation to you." The amount is in dispute because Quality claims the reasonable amount is $20,000 and Rainbow claims the reasonable amount is $18,000. If Quality cashes the check, it accepts the offer of the accord. Quality's actions would amount to saying, "I promise to accept $18,000 as full payment of your disputed obligation to me for your promise to pay me $18,000." (See Exhibit 5–5.)

Exhibit 5–5 The Original Contract and the Accord Contract

If neither the existence nor the amount of the drawer's obligation is in dispute, the drawer has a preexisting duty to pay the undisputed higher amount. An attempt to promise to pay only a part of the undisputed amount cannot be a promise in the contractual sense. The attempted promise is not an unequivocal assurance that something will or will not occur. An unequivocal assurance already exists so the drawer has a preexisting duty. Therefore, although the drawer has attempted a promise to pay, no offer for an accord contract is created. Also, the drawer's attempted promise to pay only a part of the undisputed amount will not be consideration for the payee's promise to take this amount as full payment. The drawer has a preexisting duty. Therefore, the drawee's attempted acceptance is not an acceptance of an accord offer.

Without acceptance and thus without an accord contract, the drawer's notation on the check, "payment in full," is irrelevant, and the payee may exercise dominion over the check without losing his or her right to enforce the drawer's original promise to pay.

Example 5-4

The Quality Nursery contracted to landscape the Rainbow Mall to Rainbow's specifications. The contract provided that the price would be $20,000.

After Quality landscaped the Mall according to Rainbow's specifications, Quality sent Rainbow a bill for $20,000. Rainbow sent Quality a check for $18,000. The check carried the notation "payment in full."

Rainbow's offer in the original contract was: "I promise to pay you $20,000 for your promise to landscape the Mall according to my specifications." Quality's acceptance was: "I promise to landscape your Mall according to your specifications for your promise to pay me $20,000."

Although Rainbow sent a check for $18,000, it did not make an offer for an accord contract. Neither Rainbow's obligation to pay nor the amount that it was obligated to pay was in dispute. The contract clearly established the amount of the obligation as $20,000. Rainbow had a preexisting duty to pay $20,000, and therefore its promise to pay less could not be consideration for Quality's promise to take $18,000 as full payment.

The Original Contract
  Offer
                    I promise to pay $20,000
Rainbow   for   **Quality**
              your promise to landscape the Mall
              _____→

  Acceptance
              I promise to landscape the Mall
Quality   for   **Rainbow**
              your promise to pay $20,000
              ←_____

The Attempted Accord Contract

  Attempted offer for the Accord Contract

                    I promise to pay $18,000
Rainbow   for   **Quality**
(drawer)   (payee)
              your promise to take $18,000 as
              full payment of my obligation to pay
                        you $20,000
              _____→

  Attempted acceptance for the Accord Contract

              I promise to take $18,000 as
              full payment of your obligation
                to pay me $20,000
Quality   for   **Rainbow**
(payee)   (drawer)
              your promise to pay $18,000
              ←_____

Exhibit 5–6 The Original Contract and the Attempted Accord

If Quality cashes the $18,000 check, Rainbow is still obligated to Quality for $2,000. An accord and satisfaction has not been made. (See Exhibit 5–6.)

Even if the drawer's obligation is in dispute, new consideration for the payee's promise to do something that the drawer was not legally obligated to do already is consideration for the payee's promise to take the lesser amount as full payment. If, for example, the payee required the drawer to promise to pay a day or even an hour before the debt is due, pay at a different place, pay a third person, or pay in personal property or anything other than money, then the drawer's promise would be consideration for the payee's promise to take the lesser amount as full payment.

Example 5-5

Jane borrowed $2,000 from Sally and promised to repay her in one year at 6 percent interest. The amount due would be $2,120. A week before the loan was due, Jane sent Sally a check for $2,100 with the notation "payment in full." If Sally accepts the check, she has accepted Jane's offer for an accord contract. Although neither the existence of Jane's obligation nor the amount of it was in dispute, Jane's promise to pay before the due date would be consideration to support Sally's promise to accept the lesser amount as full payment.

PARALEGAL EXERCISE 5.9

The Quality Print Company ordered 10,000 reams of paper from Excel Paper, Inc., at $2 a ream. After the paper was delivered, Quality sent Excel a check for $15,000 with the notation "payment in full." If Excel cashes the check, does Excel still have a claim against Quality for $5,000? ■

PARALEGAL EXERCISE 5.10

The Evertite Pool Company contracted to seal Jones's leaking swimming pool for "a reasonable price." After sealing the pool, Evertite sent Jones a bill for $800. Jones, believing that a reasonable price was $500, sent Evertite a check for $500 with the notation "payment in full." If Evertite cashes the check, does it still have a claim against Jones for $300? ■

When a dispute exists, classical contract law prevents the payee from rejecting the offer for the accord by altering the notation on the check. The payee, however, may negotiate the check without discharging the drawer if an accord cannot be proven or the payee does not see the obscure "payment in full" notation.

PARALEGAL CHECKLIST

The Post-Acceptance Phase

❏ Have the parties sought to modify the terms of the contract after it has been formed?

1. Analyze whether the modification involves an offer and an acceptance. As a general rule, the modification is itself a contract and requires an offer (a promise with consideration for that promise) and an acceptance (a promise or performance and consideration for that promise or performance).

2. Find out if the transaction involves a sale of goods. If it does, the Uniform Commercial Code provides that a modification can be effective without consideration.

❏ Have the parties attempted to terminate the contract after it has been formed but before it has been fully performed?

1. If neither party has fully performed, a rescission contract may be made using the rules of contract formation (offer and acceptance).
2. If one party has fully performed, that party can unilaterally release the other party.
3. Parties may settle noncontractual claims by using a release, if the release consists of an offer and an acceptance.
4. One contracting party may attempt to terminate a contractual or noncontractual duty with a "payment in full" check (an accord and satisfaction). The existence or the amount of the claim must be in dispute for an accord contract to be created. The satisfaction is the performance of the accord contract. Once the accord contract has been performed, the original duty is terminated.

KEY TERMS

Accord

Modification

Mutual releases

Satisfaction

REVIEW QUESTIONS

TRUE/FALSE QUESTIONS (CIRCLE THE CORRECT ANSWER)

1. T F Once a contract has been created it may not be modified.
2. T F Under classical contract law, a modification is a contract and must follow the same rules of contract formation required for the original contract.
3. T F Under Article 2 of the UCC, an agreement modifying a contract for the sale of goods needs no consideration.
4. T F Parties may agree to end their contractual duties when the contract has not been fully performed by either party.
5. T F If parties want to rescind a contract that has not been fully performed by either party, they must follow the same rules of contract law used to form the original contract.
6. T F The rescission of a contract has an offer and an acceptance.
7. T F When one party has fully performed but the other party has only partially performed, the party who has fully performed cannot unilaterally release the other party from its contractual duties.
8. T F The release parties use for terminating a noncontractual duty need not meet the requirements of contract law.
9. T F An "accord and satisfaction" generally involves a check, written by one party to the other, stating, "This check is taken in full payment of the obligation."
10. T F An "accord and satisfaction" can be used to discharge an obligation regardless of whether the existence of the obligation or the amount of the obligation is in dispute.

11. T F Constance Brown contracted to pay $800 to Harvey Elliott for Harvey's promise to paint her house. After Harvey completed painting, Constance had second thoughts about the price and sent him a check for $500 with the notation "Acceptance of this check constitutes payment in full." By accepting the check, Harvey has no recourse against Constance for the remaining $300.

12. T F An "accord and satisfaction" is a contract to pay a stated amount to discharge a prior obligation that is in dispute.

13. T F The traditional rules of offer and acceptance do not apply to the accord.

14. T F The "satisfaction" is the performance of the accord contract and discharges the original contractual duties.

FILL-IN-THE-BLANK QUESTIONS

1. _____. The process whereby the terms of a contract are changed to meet the changing needs of the parties.

2. _____. The relinquishment of a right.

3. _____. A contract to pay a stated amount to discharge a prior obligation that is in dispute and the performance of that contract.

4. _____. A notation used on a check in an accord and satisfaction.

MULTIPLE-CHOICE QUESTIONS (CIRCLE ALL THE CORRECT ANSWERS)

1. The Quality Glue Company contracted to sell to the Heirloom Furniture Company all of its glue requirements for the next year at $10 a barrel. Three months into the contract, Quality raised its price to $11 a barrel with Heirloom's consent.
   (a) Under classical contract law, the modification is ineffective since there is no new consideration for Heirloom's promise to pay $11 a barrel.
   (b) Under classical contract law, the modification is ineffective since a contract cannot be modified.
   (c) Under classical contract law, the modification requires a peppercorn for Heirloom's promise to pay more per barrel.
   (d) Under Article 2 of the UCC, the modification is ineffective since there is no new consideration for Heirloom's promise to pay $11 a barrel.
   (e) Under Article 2 of the UCC, the modification is ineffective since there is no new consideration for Quality's promise to continue to deliver.

SHORT-ANSWER QUESTION

1. Describe the accord and satisfaction process.

Drafting a Contract

Chapters 2, 3, 4, and 5 have taken you through the evolution of a contract: offer, post-offer/pre-acceptance, acceptance, and post-acceptance. We now have a contract. Some types of contracts must be in writing to be enforceable (see Chapter 9). Others are enforceable without a writing. Even contracts that do not need to be in writing often are written. A writing preserves the agreement of the parties and is the best evidence in the event of a subsequent dispute. Chapter 6 briefly discusses the art of drafting a well-written contract.

DRAFTING A BETTER CONTRACT

Drafting contracts involves skills that the paralegal can develop and hone. The ability to write well is the most valuable tool a paralegal can acquire. The following material provides some suggestions for drafting a well-written contract. These suggestions also apply to drafting well-written memoranda and briefs. Reflect upon your own writing and determine whether some of these tips could be useful.

When we discuss drafting a well-written contract, we are not suggesting that it is always necessary or even desirable to begin with a blank sheet of paper. Rather, our comments in this chapter can be used to either customize and improve existing writings—or, if no such writing exists, then to draft material from scratch. Check out *West's Legal Forms* online at *http://www.Westlaw.com* for a wealth of information on contract writing. Also, a variety of forms can be accessed over the Internet; have your search engine look for "legal forms." Naturally, a more descriptive entry will target more relevant forms (e.g., lease v. apartment lease). The files of a supervising attorney are another excellent source of previously prepared documents. Often these documents are in an electronic format that will facilitate the editing process.

Planning

Planning is the key to any well-drafted contract. Begin by considering the following:

- The format of the contract (formal or informal?)
- The purpose of the contract (offer, acceptance, or written confirmation of an existing contract?)
- The subject of the contract (narrow or broad topic, in-depth or summary coverage?)
- The sources of information available to you (interviews, personal knowledge, legal and nonlegal research, similar documents?)
- The audience for whom the document will be drafted (client, attorney, yourself, or a court?)
- The limitations on the project (length restrictions, deadlines, the balancing of other projects?)
- The involvement of others (critiques by others?)
- The opportunity to edit and redraft

Draft from an Outline

Before drafting, develop an outline for the contract. An outline helps the drafter present the terms of the contract in a logical, orderly fashion. An outline prevents the omission or duplication of essential terms.

Begin the outlining process by defining the purpose of the contract. Next, following the organizational structure of the road map (see the Introduction to this text), develop a checklist of items that the contract might or should address. A review of similar contracts (many in form format) will provide ideas as to items that should be included in your contract.

Example 6–1

The following is the beginning of a checklist.

1. Choice of law
   The applicable state law if the parties decide to select the applicable state law (that is, choice of law provision)

2. Contract formation
   a. The offeror's duties
   b. The offeree's duties
   c. The timing and dependence of the performance of the duties
      to one another
   d. Events or conditions necessary to create the duty
   e. Events or conditions necessary to terminate the duty
   f. Whether all the terms of this contract will be set forth in this
      writing and, if so, whether the writing should so state (i.e.,
      merger clause)
3. Enforcement
   a. If the type of contract must be in writing to be enforceable,
      the terms the writing should contain and who must sign
   b. If the contract could be held unenforceable, the alternative
      course of action of the parties
4. Breach—Definition of breach
5. Significance of breach
6. Remedies for the aggrieved party
   a. The aggrieved party's remedies
   b. Alternative methods of dispute resolution in lieu of litigation
      (e.g., mediation or arbitration)
   c. The forum in which litigation would take place
   d. A statement relating to costs and attorneys' fees

▥ PARALEGAL EXERCISE 6.1

Relate the items in the checklist in the previous example to the terms of the
following contract. What would you change in the contract to improve it?

LEASE

This contract is between _____, the Lessor, and
_____, the Lessee, for the rental of a residential house located at
_____. The lease term will begin on _____
and will end on _____.

The Lessor promises:

1. to have the property available and ready for occupancy at the
   beginning of the lease term;
2. to have the appliances in good working order and to reimburse
   Lessee for any repairs made to the appliances during the lease
   term;
3. to pay all taxes on the property during the lease term;
4. to insure the physical structure and the Lessor's personal
   property within the structure during the lease term;

5. to provide exterior maintenance, including yard maintenance service, during the lease term; and
6. to refund the Lessee's deposit, less deductions for damage, within 10 days after the Lessee vacates the property.

The Lessee promises:

1. to pay the Lessor $_____ monthly by the fifth of the month during the term of the lease;
2. to have the property available and ready for occupancy by the Lessor, or the Lessor's designee, at the end of the lease term;
3. to leave the property clean when vacating the property;
4. to maintain the appliances in good working order and to notify the Lessor in the event repairs are necessary;
5. to insure the Lessor's personal property within the structure during the lease term;
6. to notify the Lessor when exterior maintenance, including yard maintenance service, is needed;
7. to maintain the decorum of the neighborhood;
8. to not have pets on the premises unless with written consent of the Lessor;
9. to not sublease the property without written consent by the Lessor; and
10. to be responsible for up to and exceeding the deposit all damage to the property, beyond normal wear and tear.

Failure of the Tenant to pay the monthly rent on time or breach of any other promise by the Tenant shall be a breach of this agreement and shall entitle the Lessor to evict the Lessee. Eviction of the Lessee does not terminate the Lessee's duty to pay the remaining monthly payments.

In the event of a dispute between Landlord and Tenant, the parties will attempt to resolve their dispute through mediation. In the event the parties cannot resolve their dispute through mediation, then the dispute shall be resolved by arbitration using the _____ Arbitration Services.

With the signing of this lease, the Lessee has paid $_____ as a deposit.

In the event a part of this lease is deemed void, the remainder of the lease shall be enforceable.

This writing incorporates the terms agreed to by the parties. Terms not in this writing are not terms of the lease.

This lease shall be governed by the laws of _____ .

_____   _____
Lessor   Lessee

_____   _____
Address   Address

_____   _____
Date   Date

Be Brief

Omit surplus words. State the meaning clearly and concisely. More words do not make a better contract. Wordiness only creates an opportunity for ambiguity and confusion. Eliminate unnecessary paragraphs, sentences, phrases, and words. Good writing is concise.

A single word can often substitute for a verbose phrase:

afford an opportunity	allow, let
and/or	or
as to whether	whether
at that point in time	then
due to the fact that	because
during the period when	when
during the time that	during, while
file an action against	sue
force and effect	force, effect
for the reason that	because
free and clear	free, clear
full and complete	full, complete
from the point of view	from, or
good consideration	consideration
have an impact on	affect
have a tendency to	tend
insofar as . . . is concerned	(omit entirely and start with the subject)
null, void, and of no further effect	void
point in time	time
prior to	before
subsequent to	after
suffer and permit	permit
sufficient consideration	consideration
there is no doubt but that	doubtless, no doubt
the question as to whether	whether, the question whether
this is a topic that	this topic
void contract	no contract
written document	document
written instrument	instrument

Example 6–2

The following paragraph contains unnecessary and verbose phrases. They are in brackets.

[By this written document,] the seller, [the party of the first part,] for [good and sufficient] consideration, [hereby] gives [and grants to] the buyer[, the party of the second part,] her ownership interest in Blackacre. If [for any reason] this [written] document is held [null,] void, [and of no further effect,] the seller[, the party of the first part,] shall return the [good] consideration [paid by the party of the second part] to the buyer[, the party of the second part].

By either omitting unnecessary phrases or by substituting a single word for a verbose phrase, this paragraph could read:

The seller, for consideration, gives the buyer her ownership interest in Blackacre. If this document is held void, the seller shall return the consideration to the buyer.

Many such phrases are compound prepositions:

by means of	by
by reason of	because of
by virtue of	by, under
for the period of	for
for the purpose of	to
in accordance with	by, under
inasmuch as	since, because
in connection with	with, about, concerning
in favor of	for
in instances in which	when
in lieu thereof	instead
in order to	to
in regard to	about
in relation to	about, concerning
in spite of the fact that	although
in terms of	in
in the nature of	like
in view of	because
on the basis of	by, from
on the part of	by
until such time as	until
with the exception of	except
with reference to	about, concerning
with regard to	about, concerning
with respect to	on, about

Example 6-3

The following sentence contains two compound prepositions. They are indicated by brackets.

> [In spite of the fact that] the prisoner implicated his co-conspirators, the jury found that [inasmuch as] the prisoner was the instigator, he could not be acquitted.

By substituting one word for each compound preposition, the sentence becomes

> *Although* the prisoner implicated his co-conspirators, the jury found that *because* the prisoner was the instigator, he could not be acquitted.

▥ PARALEGAL EXERCISE 6.2

Remove the unnecessary verbiage from the following paragraph.

1. The lessor, party of the first part, agrees
2. to lease, rent, and/or otherwise allow the lessee,
3. party of the second part, to use, occupy, and
4. hereafter during the term of this lease, make use
5. of lessor's, said party of the first part's, premises.
6. The lessee, said party of the second part, shall
7. compensate, pay and/or remit to the lessor, said
8. party of the first part, for and in consideration
9. of the said agreement of lease, rent, and/or
10. otherwise use lessor's, said party of the first
11. part's, premises, the dollar sum of Two Thousand
12. Dollars ($2,000.00). ▪

Simplify the Language

Use clear, concise terms. Avoid synonyms. If writers mean "rooster," they should use "rooster." If they mean "hen," they should use "hen." If writers mean "rooster" but use "chicken," a synonym, the reader might believe they mean "hen." Do not confuse the reader by using different words to refer to the same object or idea.

Avoid legalese. Legalese does not make a writing "legal." Legalese only makes a writing pompous and confusing.

Example 6-4

Said Jack and said Jill went up the said hill to fetch a said pail of said water.

When paralegals remove "said" from their writing, they should also remove "heretofore," "one," "whereas," and any other legalese that they might find.

Remove the following:

aforementioned

aforesaid

forthwith

hereafter

hereby

herein

hereinafter

heretofore

herewith

one

said

thence

whereas

Minimize confusion by referring to parties by name rather than designating them "the party of the first part" and "the party of the second part."

Avoid indefinite pronouns such as "it, they, this, who, and which." An indefinite pronoun only adds confusion. When possible, substitute a noun for a pronoun.

▥ PARALEGAL EXERCISE 6.3

Rewrite the following sentences to eliminate the indefinite pronouns:

1. In this law review article, it states that paralegals are real assets.
2. They say that the program for legal assistants is one that benefits students.
3. This text is written so that it can be put together one chapter after another.
4. There is a house, it stands on a hill. ▪

Avoid "etc."; it gives the reader no new information.

Example 6–5

"The bride received gifts from New York, Florida, California, etc."
Rewrite: "The bride received gifts from many states, including New York, Florida, and California."

Paralegals can simplify their drafting style by grouping similar terms together.

Example 6-6

The seller shall deliver the goods to buyer's store. The buyer shall pay the seller upon delivery. The seller will pay the cost of shipping. The buyer will inspect the goods upon delivery. The goods are sold "as is." The buyer shall insure the goods during transit.

The seller shall

1. sell the goods "as is";
2. deliver the goods to the buyer's store; and
3. pay the cost of shipping.

The buyer shall

1. pay the seller upon delivery;
2. inspect the goods upon delivery; and
3. insure the goods during transit.

⚊ PARALEGAL EXERCISE 6.4

Redraft the following by deleting the legalese and grouping the lessor's duties and lessee's duties.

1.   WITNESSETH: that the party of the first
2. part, for and in consideration of the rents,
3. covenants and agreements hereinafter contained,
4. docs, and by these presents, demise, lease, and
5. rent, for a period of six months from the first
6. day of June, 2007, to the party of the second
7. part, the following described property, to wit:
8.   The party of the second part, for and in
9. consideration of the use and possession of said
10. premises for said period, does hereby agree to pay
11. unto the party of the first part, the sum of Three
12. Thousand Dollars ($3,000.00), said sum to be paid
13. in the following amounts and at the time herein
14. designated, to wit:
15.   On the first day of June, 2007, the sum of
16. Five Hundred Dollars ($500.00), and on the first
17. day of each and every month thereafter the sum of
18. Five Hundred Dollars ($500.00), until the total
19. sum of Three Thousand Dollars ($3,000.00) shall
20. have been fully paid.
21.   THE PARTY OF THE SECOND PART further agrees to
22. keep and maintain all portions of the building let
23. to him by the terms of this contract in as good
24. state of repair as the same are turned over to him.

25.   THE SECOND PARTY further agrees to be
26. responsible for and pay for the repair of any damage
27. done to any of the buildings or grounds by any of
28. his family or guests.
29.   THE SECOND PARTY agrees to hold said first
30. party free from any and all expenses for lights,
31. heat, or any other expense incident to the
32. occupant of said property.
33.   THE PARTY OF THE SECOND PART shall not engage in,
34. or allow any other person, pet, or animal to engage
35. in, any conduct that will disturb the quiet and
36. peaceful enjoyment of the other tenants, the party
37. of the first part, or the neighbors of second
38. party, or use the premises for any purpose
39. whatsoever which violates the laws of the
40. United States, the State of New Hampshire, or the
41. City of Concord. ■

Use Base Verbs and the Active Voice

Write in the active voice, replacing nouns with verbs. The purest verb form is the base verb (for example, collide, decide, pay). Verbs give sentences movement and life. Nouns do not. Use the base verb rather than its derivative noun.

collision	collide
decision	decide
payment	pay

▥ PARALEGAL EXERCISE 6.5

Identify four additional base verbs and their derivative nouns. ■

▥ PARALEGAL EXERCISE 6.6

Write four sentences, each using one of the four derivative nouns from Paralegal Exercise 6.5. Then rewrite each sentence, changing the noun to a verb. ■

Replace forms of the verb "to be" (is, are, be) with active verbs (run, skip, jump).

Example 6–7

"The ruling was made by the trial judge" becomes "The trial judge ruled."

The active voice energizes the paralegal's writing. Substitute active for passive verbs. With the active voice, the subject of the sentence acts.

Example 6-8

"Tom called the police."

With the passive voice, the subject of the sentence is acted upon.

Example 6-9

"The police were called by Tom."

The passive voice usually requires more words than the active voice. In our illustration, the passive voice requires a supporting verb (were) and a preposition (by).

The passive voice creates detached abstraction within the sentence. With the active voice, the reader readily understands who is doing what to whom. With the passive voice, who is doing what to whom is often unclear.

Avoid Sexist Language

"Every man for himself" is history. Paralegals should delete sexist language from their writing. Several tips are useful:

1. Avoid expressions that imply value judgments based on gender.

Example 6-10

"Are you a man or a mouse?"
"A difficult task is a man's work."
"Don't be such a weak sister."
"He refused to do woman's work."

2. Change the wording of male-oriented expressions to include both men and women.

Example 6-11

"reasonable man" becomes "reasonable person"
"gentlemen of the jury" becomes "members of the jury"
"Dear Sir" becomes "Dear Madam or Sir"

3. Replace gender-based descriptions and titles with non-gender-based descriptions and titles.

Example 6-12

"workman" becomes "worker"
"newsman" becomes "journalist"
"fireman" becomes "firefighter"

4. Use parallel construction when referring to both men and women.

Example 6-13

"man and wife" becomes "husband and wife."

5. Avoid masculine singular pronouns when not referring to a male. While "he or she" can be used in moderation, it is often best to rewrite the sentence.
   a. Omit the pronoun if it is unnecessary.

Example 6-14

"The average citizen feels that he is doing his duty by voting" becomes "The average citizen feels a duty to vote."

Example 6-15

"Every person has his constitutional rights" becomes "Every person has constitutional rights."

   b. Use the second person rather than the third person.

Example 6-16

"Each voter must cast his own ballot" becomes "As a voter, you must cast your own ballot."

   c. Use the plural rather than the singular.

Example 6-17

"Every spring the farmer plows his fields" becomes "Every spring farmers plow their fields."

Example 6-18

"The policeman risks his life on a daily basis" becomes "Police officers risk their lives daily."

Check Spelling, Punctuation, and Grammar

Eliminate common spelling errors. Do not expect a secretary to correct the mistakes. Errors will reflect on the paralegal and not the secretary. Paralegals should keep a list of words they tend to misspell.

Example 6-19

The following are common spelling errors:

accommodate	not accomodate
coming	not comming
defendant	not defendent
demurrer	not demurer
judgment	not judgement
occurred	not ocurred or occured

Check punctuation.

Eliminate grammatical errors. A common error is to write "it's" for "its" and "its" for "it's." "It's" is a contraction, meaning "it is." "Its" is a possessive pronoun.

Example 6-20

"It's February 2d and the groundhog saw its shadow."

A similar error is to write "your" for "you're". "You're" is a contraction meaning "you are." "Your" (like "its"), is possessive pronoun. Don't make the common mistake of writing sentences like this: "Your cordially invited to attend . . . ."

Another increasingly common error is substituting the word "less" for the word "fewer." "Less" is an adjective used to modify collective nouns that are "uncountable." "Fewer" is used to modify non-collective, "countable" nouns: "I may earn less money than you do, but at least I have fewer expenses."

Irregardless is improper. Use *regardless.* Use *could have* and *should have* rather than *could of* and *should of.* Check *to, too,* and *two,* as well as *accept* and *except, advice* and *advise, affect* and *effect, between* and *among,* and *principal* and *principle,* and *ensure* and *insure.*

Revising

Schedule yourself time to revise your draft. If possible, let the draft rest for a while before you revise. Your fresh eyes will see your draft in a new light and you will be more objective. Remember, you are writing not for yourself but for another reader. Consider how the other reader will view your final product.

The revision process has two parts: the first is "macro"; the second is "micro." A "macro" revision evaluates the writing as a whole. Does the writing do what it was intended to do? Is the organization strong or should the paragraphs be reorganized? Does the document stay on track or does it wander? Are all the paragraphs necessary or are some redundant? Are all the sentences necessary or are some redundant or irrelevant? Which sentences could be eliminated?

The "micro" revision involves the internal elements of the sentence. Are all sentences clear and concise or do some need to be rewritten? Are surplus words present? Are some words ambiguous? Has all the legalese been deleted? Is the active voice used or are sentences noun driven rather than verb driven? Has all sexist language been avoided? Have commonly misspelled words, improper punctuation, and grammatical errors been corrected?

A well-written product often requires multiple drafts.

These suggestions are but a brief introduction to better drafting. A number of helpful books are available. They include

G. Block, *Effective Legal Writing: For Law Students and Lawyers* (Foundation Press 5th ed. 1999)

P. Butt & R. Castle, *Modern Legal Drafting: A Guide to Using Clear Language* (Cambridge University Press 2001)

A. Enquist & L. C. Oats, *Just Writing: Grammar, Punctuation, and Style for the Legal Writer* (Aspen Law & Business 2d ed. 2005)

B. Garner, *The Elements of Legal Style* (Oxford University Press 2d ed. 2002)

D. Hacker, *A Writer's Reference* (Bedford/St. Martin's 6th ed. 2006)

C. Miller & K. Swift, *The Handbook of Nonsexist Writing* (iUniverse 2d ed. 2001)

L. C. Oates & A. Enquist, *Legal Writing Handbook* (Aspen Law & Business 4th ed. 2006)

M. B. Ray & B. J. Cox, *Beyond the Basics, A Text for Advanced Legal Writing* (West Group 2d ed. 2003)

H. V. Samborn & A. B. Yelin, *Basic Legal Writing for Paralegals* (Aspen Publishers 2d ed. 2004)

W. Strunk & E. B. White, *The Elements of Style* (Longman 4th ed. 1999)

P. R. Tepper, *Basic Legal Writing* (McGraw-Hill Companies 2d ed. 2006)

University of Chicago Press Staff, *Chicago Manual of Style* (15th ed. 2003)

R. Wydick, *Plain English for Lawyers* (Carolina Academic Press 5th ed. 2005)

DRAFTING EXERCISE

ⅲ PARALEGAL EXERCISE 6.7

Your supervising attorney has a client, Sarah Delbarton, who has four children (Amy, age 12; Clara, age 8; Reginald, age 6; and Hugo, age 5). Ms. Delbarton, a single mother, travels extensively on business. Ms. Delbarton is in the process of hiring a tutor to teach her children. The tutor will receive room and board, a salary, and insurance benefits. The tutor will have a three-month probationary period, after which will begin a one-year term. Ms. Delbarton would like an option to renew for an additional year. After the renewal year, the parties will be free to renegotiate the contract. The household staff includes a housekeeper, a nanny, a cook, and a gardener. Ms. Delbarton would like your law firm to identify the appropriate person, conduct the initial interview to screen applicants, complete the necessary background check, and prepare the necessary documents. Ms. Delbarton, however, would conduct the final interview and make the selection. Ms. Delbarton would like to remain anonymous until the final interview.

1. Draft an advertisement for your local newspaper. Should this advertisement be an offer or only preliminary negotiation?
2. Draft an offer in letter form. Do you want this offer to be a total integration of the terms of the proposed contract or only a partial integration so some terms will be in the writing and others will be supplied orally?

    You may want to explore various form books or the internet for sample employment contracts. They may give you ideas about format and content. You may want to check out such Web sites as "Legal Forms," "Lectric Law Library's Legal Form Room," and "Sample Employment Contract." Also check *West's Legal Forms* at *http://www.Westlaw.com*. When using such material, a number of points must be remembered. First, the forms may not be accurate in spite of the drafters' best efforts. Second, the forms may not be current because the law is always changing. Third, the forms may be accurate for one situation but not for another.
3. Assume that Ms. Delbarton has interviewed and selected Gwenneth Lloyd-Jones for the position and your firm has, on Ms. Delbarton's behalf, sent Ms. Lloyd-Jones an offer. Ms. Lloyd-Jones, however, has responded with the following letter:

Thank you for your letter of June 5th. While I find the position and the terms of your letter very enticing, I have been advised to request that the following be added to the contract.

1. In the event of a dispute, I would like us to attempt to resolve the dispute by negotiation. If that fails, I would like us to try mediation. Only if negotiation and mediation fail, would we resort to arbitration. Disputes would not be resolved by litigation. Also, disputes will be resolved in this state using the laws of this state.

2. Although this contract is for a stated term, I would like the opportunity to terminate the contract upon four weeks' notice.

3. I would like the option to include an automatic increase in compensation of 10 percent.

4. I would also like to be assured that during the first and each successive year of my employment, a two-week paid vacation is provided.

Please let me hear from you at your earliest convenience if these requests are satisfactory. I have another offer and need to make a decision within the next two weeks.

Is Ms. Lloyd-Jones's letter an acceptance, a rejection and counteroffer, or merely an inquiry? Draft a response.

4. It is now six months later. Ms. Lloyd-Jones has accepted Ms. Delbarton's offer as you have drafted it in part (3) and has begun work. Ms. Delbarton and Ms. Lloyd-Jones have discussed modifying their contract in the following manner: (1) increasing the term of the option to five years; (2) adding a week of vacation for each two years of service; and (3) decreasing compensation by 15 percent as each child graduates from high school and leaves the family estate.

Draft a modification of the contract that you drafted in part (3). Remember to provide the appropriate consideration for both the offeror's promise and the offeree's promise.

If additional facts are necessary for any part of this question, you may create these facts (including compensation) as you draft. ■

PARALEGAL CHECKLIST

Drafting a Contract

❑ Paralegals can develop their drafting skills by using the following ideas:

1. Construct an outline for the contract before drafting.
   a. Begin the outlining process by defining the purposes of the contract.
   b. Prepare a checklist of items that the contract should address by following the organizational structure of the road map.

2. Be brief when drafting. Omit surplus words.
   a. Can a single word substitute for a verbose phrase?

b. Can a compound preposition be eliminated?
3. Simplify the language. Use clear, concise terms.
   a. Avoid synonyms.
   b. Avoid legalese.
   c. Refer to the parties by name rather than by the phrase "the party of the first part."
   d. Avoid indefinite pronouns.
   e. Avoid "etc."
   f. Simplify the drafting style by grouping similar terms together.
4. Use base verbs and the active voice.
   a. Write in the active voice by replacing nouns with verbs.
   b. Replace forms of the verb "to be" (is, are, be) with active verbs (run, skip, jump).
   c. Substitute active for passive verbs.

5. Avoid sexist language.
   a. Avoid expressions that imply value judgments based on gender.
   b. Change the wording of male-oriented expressions to include both men and women.
   c. Replace gender-based descriptions and titles with non-gender-based descriptions and titles.
   d. Use parallel construction when referring to both men and women.
   e. Avoid masculine singular pronouns when not referring to a male.
      (1) Avoid pronouns if unnecessary.
      (2) Use second person rather than third person.
      (3) Use plural rather than singular.
6. Review for errors of spelling, punctuation, and grammar.

REVIEW QUESTIONS

TRUE/FALSE QUESTIONS (CIRCLE THE CORRECT ANSWER)

1. T F Preparing an outline before drafting a contract is a waste of time.
2. T F Begin the outlining process by defining the purpose of the contract.
3. T F Good writing stresses conciseness.
4. T F Never use a single word when an important-sounding phrase has the same meaning.
5. T F The longer the contract, the better the contract.
6. T F The use of "legalese" makes a contract look professional.
7. T F Avoid the use of synonyms in drafting a contract.
8. T F Indefinite pronouns make writing less confusing.
9. T F Always use the base verb rather than its derivative noun.
10. T F Do not worry about sexist language. Everyone knows that male-oriented expressions include both men and women.
11. T F Paralegals are responsible for correct spelling, punctuation, and grammar.
12. T F The use of "etc." gives the reader no new information.

13.   T   F   Synonyms add interest to an otherwise dull contract.

14.   T   F   The use of ambiguous terms will add clarity and precision to a contract.

15.   T   F   Always use "party of the first part" and "party of the second part" to distinguish between the parties.

16.   T   F   Using different words to refer to the same object or idea will confuse the reader.

FILL-IN-THE-BLANK QUESTIONS

1. Substitute a single word for the verbose phrase.

   a. _____. afford an opportunity

   b. _____. and/or

   c. _____. as to whether

   d. _____. at that point in time

   e. _____. due to the fact that

   f. _____. during the period when

   g. _____. during the time that

   h. _____. file an action against

   i. _____. force and effect

   j. _____. for the reason that

   k. _____. free and clear

   l. _____. full and complete

   m. _____. from the point of view

   n. _____. good consideration

   o. _____. have an impact on

   p. _____. have a tendency to

   q. _____. insofar as . . . is concerned

   r. _____. null, void, and of no further effect

   s. _____. point in time

   t. _____. prior to

   u. _____. subsequent to

   v. _____. suffer and permit

   w. _____. sufficient consideration

   x. _____. the question as to whether

   y. _____. this is a topic that

   z. _____. void contract

2. Change each compound preposition to a single word.

    a. _____. by means of

    b. _____. by reason of

    c. _____. by virtue of

    d. _____. for the period of

    e. _____. for the purpose of

    f. _____. in accordance with

    g. _____. inasmuch as

    h. _____. in connection with

    i. _____. in favor of

    j. _____. in instances in which

    k. _____. in lieu thereof

    l. _____. in order to

    m. _____. in regard to

    n. _____. in relation to

    o. _____. in spite of the fact that

    p. _____. in terms of

    q. _____. in the nature of

    r. _____. in view of

    s. _____. on the basis of

    t. _____. on the part of

    u. _____. until such time as

    v. _____. with the exception of

    w. _____. with reference to

    x. _____. with regard to

    y. _____. with respect to

3. Change each noun to its base verb.

    a. _____. collision

    b. _____. decision

    c. _____. payment

    d. _____. elimination

    e. _____. rejection

    f. _____. disapproval

    g. _____. isolation

h. _____. possession

i. _____. affiliation

j. _____. application

k. _____. abduction

4. Correct the spelling of these words:

a. _____. acomodate

b. _____. comming

c. _____. defendent

d. _____. demurer

e. _____. ocurred

f. _____. definate

g. _____. existance

h. _____. seperate

i. _____. suprise

j. _____. truely

k. _____. untill

l. _____. writting

m. _____. writen

n. _____. payroll evidence

o. _____. Statue of Frauds

SHORT-ANSWER QUESTIONS

1. Rewrite the following sentences, replacing forms of the verb "to be" (is, are, be) with active verbs (run, skip, jump). The subject of an active verb is the doer of the action. A passive verb generally has two parts. The first part is a form of "be"—such as *be, been, is, are, was, were,* and *am.* The second part is a past participle (a verbal generally ending in *d, ed, n, en,* or *t*)— such as *discussed* and *broken.* Therefore, *was discussed* and *were broken* are passive verbs. All other verb forms are active.

a.   The ruling was made by the trial judge.

_____

_____

b.   The race was won by Stacey Jackson.

_____

_____

c.   The biggest lie was told by my brother.

_____

_____

d. The bus was towed by the wrecker.

_____

_____

e. The game was won by a shot at the buzzer.

_____

_____

f. The work had been done by the same few people.

_____

_____

2. Rewrite the following sentences using clear, concise terms.

a. The aforementioned clock, hereinafter referred to as said clock, is a valuable antique.

_____

_____

b. The aforesaid lessor will furnish all utilities to said lessee.

_____

_____

c. Whereas said plumber, the party of the first part, had performed services heretofore on behalf of the customer, the party of the second part, the party of the first part presented a bill to the party of the second part.

_____

_____

d. Please respond to all inquiries hereafter forthwith.

_____

_____

e. We hereby request your cooperation in this matter.

_____

_____

f. Your timely response will afford an opportunity to file an action against the breaching party.

_____

_____

g. Please let us know as to whether you wish to pursue aforesaid matter.

_____

_____

h. You had problems at that point in time due to the fact that you failed to complete the work.

_____

_____

i. During the period when the aforesaid problems arose, they were ignored for the reason that all of the parties were out of town.

_____

_____

j.   The promisee's promise was good consideration for the promisor's promise.

_____

_____

_____

k.   What you do at this point in time will have an impact on the entire case.

_____

_____

_____

l.   There is no doubt but that small problems have a tendency to grow larger until such time as they are resolved.

_____

_____

_____

m.   In connection with your letter in regard to the written instrument enclosed herein, please call our office for an appointment.

_____

_____

n.   We received further information in relation to the matter subsequent to the time that we thought there had been full and complete disclosure.

_____

_____

o.   It will be unnecessary for you to contact us until such time as we notify you of further developments in the case inasmuch as there is nothing that can be done at this point in time.

_____

_____

_____

_____

3.   Rewrite the following sentences using nonsexist language.

a.   The cook served man-sized portions.

_____

_____

b.   Now is the time for all good men to come to the aid of their country.

_____

_____

c.   Newsmen fly around the world covering interesting stories.

_____

_____

d.   Men and their wives often share a similar sense of humor.

_____

_____

e.   Firemen wear highly specialized protective clothing.

_____

_____

f.   Policemen directing traffic use reflective vests for safety.

_____

_____

g.   The gentlemen of the jury often engage in lengthy
      deliberations.

_____

_____

h.   The reasonable man will consider a question in an objective
      manner.

_____

_____

i.   Nursing is a job for compassionate women.

_____

_____

j.   Ordinary men may perform heroic actions under stress.

_____

_____

PART III

Step Three: Contract Enforceability

CONTRACTS THAT ARE NOT ENFORCEABLE

Although parties are free to create contracts, public interest may override the parties' freedom to contract. When this occurs, a court will refuse to enforce the contract brought before it. A balance must be struck between freedom *to* contract and freedom *from* contract. The identification of overriding public interest may come from the legislatures through statute or from the courts through the evolution of common law.

When contractual duties are not enforced by the courts, the overriding public interest may be classified into three categories depending on whether a member of a class is being protected, a party is being protected against overreaching, or the judicial process is being protected.

Chapter 7 considers precluding enforcement of a contract to protect members of a class, such as minors, the mentally incapacitated, and persons incapacitated due to alcohol or other drugs. Chapter 8 explores precluding enforcement of a contract to protect a party against another's overreaching through unconscionability, fraud, duress, or mistake in a basic assumption of fact. Chapter 9 investigates precluding enforcement of a contract to protect the judicial process from involvement in nonjudicial type activity, such as illegality, perjury, and inappropriate forum shopping.

CHAPTER 7

Contract Enforceability: Protecting Members of a Class

At times either the legislature or the court will find the members a class of people particularly vulnerable. Without some protection, members of these classes may contract when it is not in their own best interest. Rather than deal with each transaction as it arises, the law protects all members of the class in all their contract transactions. Instead of the members of the vulnerable class being precluded from contracting, they are permitted to contract as are others who are not members of these classes. The members of the protected class, however, are given the power to unilaterally **disaffirm** their contracts. When a contracting party disaffirms a contract, the party **repudiates** the contract.

Chapter 7 investigates three protected classes, the minor (infant), the mentally incapacitated, and the person lacking capacity due to alcohol or other drugs (see Exhibit 7–1).

disaffirm

A contracting party disaffirms a contract when that party notifies the other contracting party that he or she will no longer be bound by the contract's terms.

repudiation

Repudiation is the refusal to accept a right or to perform a duty.

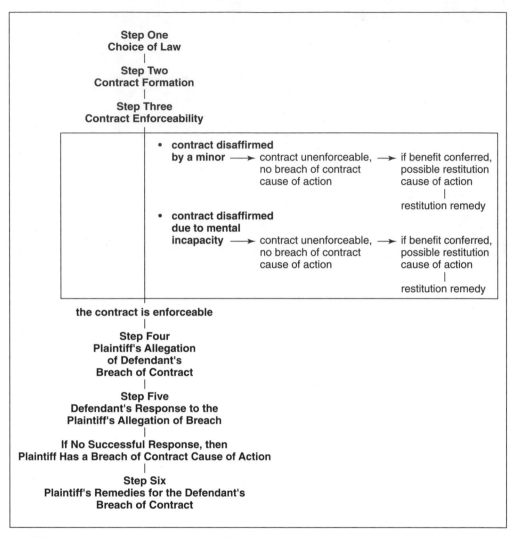

Exhibit 7–1 The Contract Enforceability (Protecting a Class) Phase of the Road Map

MINORITY (INFANCY)

Minors have long been a protected class. Early contract law, which was based on the *meeting of the minds,* viewed minors as mindless and, therefore, unable to contract. Their "contracts" were "void." Modern contract law, which is based on the *manifestation of assent,* gives minors the power to contract and the power to disaffirm a contract, even after the other party has fully performed. Early contract law established the age of protection for minority as under 21, but most modern statutes have rolled this age back to 18.

Minority as a Defense to a Breach of Contract Action (Minority as a Shield)

As a general rule, a minor may disaffirm a contract made during minority if the disaffirmance occurs during minority or within a reasonable time after reaching the age of majority. The power to disaffirm is one-sided; only the minor has the power to disaffirm. Disaffirmance terminates the minor's duty to perform. Once the minor exercises the power to disaffirm, the other party may not enforce the contract. Minority, therefore, acts as a shield to an action of breach of contract.

Example 7-1

When Charlene was 16, she entered into a four-year contract to model for Universal Modeling, Inc. Under the contract, Charlene promised to give Universal the exclusive rights to her services as a model. The contract also provided that in the event Charlene breached the contract, she would pay Universal $5,000. It is now a year later and Charlene has been approached by Super Modeling, Inc., to model for them.

Since Charlene is still a minor (under 18), she has the power to disaffirm her contract with Universal. If Charlene exercises her power and disaffirms, she no longer has a duty to perform. When Charlene disaffirms, the contract becomes unenforceable against her. Therefore, when she does not perform, she is not in breach and Universal could not successfully sue her for breach of contract.

A minor need not disaffirm a contract during minority but may disaffirm within a reasonable time after reaching the age of majority. A reasonable time varies depending on the circumstances. Some factors that may shed light on "reasonable time" include performance by either side, the nature of that performance, the ability of the minor to disaffirm, and the prejudice suffered by the minor's delay in disaffirming.

▥ PARALEGAL EXERCISE 7.1

Just before going to college, Belinda, age 17, entered into three contracts. Should she have the same length of time after reaching majority (age 18) to disaffirm each?

1. Belinda contracts to model for an agency after she graduates from college.
2. Belinda buys a 20-inch LCD HDTV from Quality Electronics and takes it to college.
3. Belinda buys a registered setter from Doctor Pets and takes it to college.

In each of these situations, would it matter whether Belinda was going to college near home or far away? ■

When a minor disaffirms a contract, whether during minority or within a reasonable time after reaching the age of majority, the contract is unenforceable and the other party has no cause of action for breach of contract.

If the minor does not disaffirm the contract within a reasonable time after reaching the age of majority, the court will conclude that the minor, who has now reached the age of majority, has ratified the contract. **Ratification** is the confirmation of the contract.

The fact that the minor willfully misrepresented his or her age at the time of contract formation does not preclude the minor from disaffirming. The minor may, however, be liable in a separate tort action for misrepresentation.

ratification

Ratification is the confirmation (affirmation) of the contract.

Example 7–2

When Alexander was 16, he purchased a Harley from Over-the-Road Motors. At the time of the purchase, Alexander represented his age as 18. When Alexander was 17, he disaffirmed the contract and discontinued his payments. Over-the-Road Motors could not successfully sue Alexander for breach of contract since the contract is not enforceable. Over-the-Road Motors could successfully sue Alexander for misrepresentation.

Could Restitution Be a Cause of Action When a Minor Disaffirms a Contract? (Minority as a Sword)

Minority may be the shield in an action for breach of contract brought by the other party against the minor. Minority may also act as a sword if the minor seeks to be returned to the time when the contract was formed. The minor must not only disaffirm the contract but must also seek a restitution cause of action for the return of what he or she has given the other party under the contract. As has been discussed previously, a restitution cause of action is based on unjust enrichment. The enrichment is the benefit conferred by the minor on the other party.

Example 7–3

The minor may disaffirm the contract and seek a restitution cause of action for the reasonable value of the benefit conferred on the other party if

- the minor has paid for the item (the benefit conferred is the payment).
- the minor has conveyed real or personal property (the benefit conferred is the real or personal property).

If the minor disaffirms the contract and seeks a restitution cause of action, the minor must return to the other party *only* what the minor received under the contract *and* still has in his or her possession. The minor need not compensate the other person for something that he or she no longer has.

▥ PARALEGAL EXERCISE 7.2

Lucy, aged 16, contracted to buy an encyclopedia from the publisher for $1,000. Lucy paid the purchase price and received her encyclopedia. Six months later, Lucy decided that she did not want the encyclopedia.

Could Lucy disaffirm the contract, return the used encyclopedia, and get her money back? ▪

▥ PARALEGAL EXERCISE 7.3

Jennifer, aged 16, contracted to buy a gold pendant from Sly's Jewelry Store for $200. She paid the purchase price and received the pendant. Over the next six months, the price of gold increased dramatically, and the pendant increased in value. Could Sly disaffirm the contract, return Jennifer's $200, and get the pendant back?

If the price of gold decreased dramatically and the pendant decreased in value, could Jennifer disaffirm the contract, return the pendant, and get her $200 back? ▪

Upon disaffirmance, the minor is entitled to be restored to his or her pre-contract position (before the minor conferred the benefit on the other contracting party). Therefore, a minor who has partially or fully performed his or her duty to pay is entitled to the return of what he or she has paid. If the minor has given personal property other than money, the minor is entitled to its return as well, assuming that the other party still has what the minor gave.

A minor-seller may trace real property from the original contracting party (buyer) to a subsequent bona fide purchaser for value (the subsequent buyer who has purchased in good faith and without notice of the fact that the original seller was a minor). A minor, however, cannot reclaim personal property that has been sold by the original contracting party (buyer) to a subsequent bona fide purchaser for value.

Ⅲ PARALEGAL EXERCISE 7.4

Jeremy, aged 17, purchased a used Ford Truck from Friendly Motors for $1,500. He paid for his truck with $1,000 in cash and the trade-in of his old Chevy. Shortly after delivering his Chevy to Friendly, paying the money, and taking delivery of the truck, Jeremy was involved in an accident in which his truck was totaled.

Can Jeremy disaffirm the contract and recover $1,000 from Friendly? Can he recover the Chevy from Friendly?

If Friendly has sold the Chevy to Alice, who purchased it for value, in good faith, and without notice that it had been previously owned by a minor, can Jeremy recover his Chevy from her? ■

A Minor's Liability for Necessaries

A minor is liable for necessaries. Although the term necessaries generally consists of food, clothing, shelter, medical services, and education, the term necessaries varies with the facts. What may be considered necessaries for one minor may not be considered necessaries for another. **Necessaries**, as defined by the courts, are those articles that the minor actually needs and must supply for himself or herself because the person who has the duty to provide these articles either cannot or will not provide them.

In *Webster Street Partnership, Ltd. v. Sheridan,* two minors signed a lease, paid a security deposit, and paid rent for a period of time. After the landlord brought an action against the two minor tenants for back rent, one minor cross-petitioned seeking return of the security deposit, and the other minor cross-petitioned seeking return of all monies paid to the landlord. The landlord claimed that the minors could not disaffirm the lease since the contract was for a necessary.

necessaries

Necessaries are those articles that the minor actually needs and must supply for himself or herself because the person who has the duty to provide these articles either cannot or will not provide them.

CASE

Webster Street Partnership, Ltd. v. Sheridan
Supreme Court of Nebraska (1985)
220 Neb. 9, 368 N.W.2d 439

KRIVOSHA, C. J., and BOSLAUGH, WHITE, HASTINGS, CAPORALE, SHANAHAN, and GRANT, JJ.

KRIVOSHA, Chief Justice.

. . . .

Just what are necessaries, however, has no exact definition. The term is flexible and varies according to the facts of each individual case. In Cobbey v. Buchanan, 48 Neb. 391, 397, 67 N.W. 176, 178 (1896), we said: " 'The meaning of the term "necessaries" cannot be defined by a general rule applicable to all cases; the question is a mixed one of law and fact, to be determined in each case from the particular facts and circumstances in such case.' " A number of factors must be considered before a court can conclude whether a particular product or service is a necessary. As stated in Schoenung v. Gallet, 206 Wis. 52, 54, 238 N.W. 852, 853 (1931):

> "The term 'necessaries,' as used in the law relating to the liability of infants therefor, is a relative term, somewhat flexible, except when applied to such things as are obviously requisite for the maintenance of existence, and depends on the social position and situation in life of the infant, as well as upon his own fortune and that of his parents. The particular infant must have an actual need for the articles furnished; not for mere ornament or pleasure. The articles must be useful and suitable, but they are not necessaries merely because useful or beneficial. Concerning the general character of the things furnished, to be necessaries the articles must supply the infant's personal needs, either those of his body or those of his mind. However, the term 'necessaries' is not confined to merely such things as are required for a bare subsistence. There is no positive rule by means of which it may be determined what are or what are not necessaries, for what may be considered necessary for one infant may not be necessaries for another infant whose state is different as to rank, social position, fortune, health, or other circumstances, the question being one to be determined from the particular facts and circumstances of each case."

(Citation omitted.) This appears to be the law as it is generally followed throughout the country.

In Ballinger v. Craig, 95 Ohio App. 545, 121 N.E.2d 66 (1953), the defendants were husband and wife and were 19 years of age at the time they purchased a house trailer. Both were employed. However, prior to the purchase of the trailer, the defendants were living with the parents of the husband. The Court of Appeals for the State of Ohio held that under the facts presented the trailer was not a necessary. The court stated:

> "'To enable an infant to contract for articles as necessaries, he must have been in actual need of them, and obliged to procure them for himself. They are not necessaries as to him, however necessary they may be in their nature, if he was already supplied with sufficient articles of the kind, or if he had a parent or guardian who was able and willing to supply them. The burden of proof is on the plaintiff to show that the infant was destitute of the articles, and had no way of procuring them except by his own contract.'"

(Citation omitted.) Id. at 547, 121 N.E.2d at 67. Under Ohio law the marriage of the parties did not result in their obtaining majority.

In 42 Am.Jur.2d Infants § 67 at 68–69 (1969), the author notes:

> Thus, articles are not necessaries for an infant if he has a parent or guardian who is able and willing to supply them, and an infant residing with and being supported by his parent according to his station in life is not absolutely liable for things which under other circumstances would be considered necessaries.

The undisputed testimony is that both tenants were living away from home, apparently with the understanding that they could return home at any time. Sheridan testified:

> Q. During the time that you were living at 3007 Webster, did you at any time, feel free to go home or anything like that?
> A. Well, I had a feeling I could, but I just wanted to see if I could make it on my own.
>
> Q. Had you been driven from your home?
> A. No.
>
> Q. You didn't have to go?
> A. No.
>
> Q. You went freely?
> A. Yes.
>
> Q. Then, after you moved out and went to 3417 for a week or so, you were again to return home, is that correct?
> A. Yes, sir.

It would therefore appear that in the present case neither Sheridan nor Wilwerding was in need of shelter but, rather, had chosen to voluntarily leave home, with the understanding that they could return whenever they desired. One may at first blush believe that such a rule is unfair. Yet, on further consideration, the wisdom of the rule is apparent. If, indeed, landlords may not contract with minors, except at their peril, they may refuse to do so. In that event, minors who voluntarily leave home but who are free to return will be compelled to return to their parents' home—a result which is desirable. We therefore find that both the municipal court and the district court erred in finding that the apartment, under the facts in this case, was a necessary.

. . . .

Even when a minor is liable for necessaries, the question remains whether the minor's liability is in a breach of contract action or in a restitution action. The courts are divided on this issue.

If the minor's liability is in a breach of contract action, the doctrine of necessaries becomes an exception to the general rule that a minor has the absolute power to disaffirm a contract. The other party may seek expectation damages in a breach of contract action. **Expectation damages** places the nonbreaching party in the position he or she would have been in had the contract been fully performed. This means that the other party would receive the full contract price.

If, however, the minor's liability is in a restitution action, the general rule that a minor has the power to disaffirm remains absolute. The minor may disaffirm a contract made for necessaries but, once the contract is disaffirmed, the other party may pursue a cause of action in restitution for unjust enrichment. The other party will seek restitution damages for the restitution cause of action. **Restitution damages**, in the case of a minor's disaffirmance of a contract for necessaries, returns the minor to the position he or she was in prior to the time when the minor received the benefit conferred under the contract (i.e., the minor disgorges the benefits received as measured by the reasonable value to the minor).

This distinction may be important to the minor. Under the contract, the minor is liable for the contract price. Under a restitution action, the minor is only liable for the reasonable value to him or her. While the contract price and the reasonable value to the minor are often the same, instances may exist when they differ.

PARALEGAL EXERCISE 7.5

Donald, aged 16, was involved in an automobile accident and was charged with leaving the scene of an accident. Donald hired the law firm of Ambrose & Pete to defend him. Through the firm's efforts, the charge was reduced to failure to yield the right of way, and Donald pleaded guilty, paying a small fine. The bill from Ambrose & Pete was $1,000. After discovering that most other law firms charge $700 for this service, Donald disaffirmed the contract and refused to pay.

Are the services of the law firm necessaries?

If the services are not necessaries, does Donald have the power to disaffirm the contract?

What damages will Ambrose & Pete recover if Donald disaffirms the contract and the services are not necessaries?

If the services are necessaries, does Donald have the power to disaffirm the contract?

What damages will Ambrose & Pete recover if Donald cannot disaffirm the contract even though the services are necessaries?

What damages will Ambrose & Pete recover if Donald can disaffirm the contract and the services are necessaries? ▮

expectation remedies (including expectation damages)

Expectation remedies (including expectation damages) place the nonbreaching party in the position he or she would have been in had the contract been fully performed.

restitution remedies (including restitution damages)

Restitution remedies (including restitution damages) place the breaching party back to the position he or she was in prior to the time the breaching party received the benefit conferred upon him or her by the nonbreaching party. The measure of damages is the reasonable value of the benefit conferred to the breaching party.

Is a Minor Liable for Depreciation Prior to Disaffirmance?

Prior to the time a minor disaffirms a contract and seeks restitution for the benefit he or she has conferred on the other contracting party, the minor may have used what the other contracting party has exchanged and it may have depreciated. Should the minor compensate the other contracting party for the value of the use and the depreciation of what the minor has received prior to the time of disaffirmance? Courts are divided on this issue. Some reason that the minor's right to disaffirm would no longer be absolute if the minor was required to compensate the other party for use and depreciation. Other courts reason that the minority doctrine should protect minors but not go so far as to give them a windfall.

offset

An offset is a deduction of the amount awarded to the defendant from the amount awarded to the plaintiff.

If a minor is liable for the use and depreciation of what he or she received, the charge will be in the form of an offset. An **offset** is a deduction of the amount awarded to the defendant from the amount awarded to the plaintiff. In the case of a minor's disaffirmance, the offset is the deduction of the amount awarded to the defendant (nonminor) for use and depreciation from the amount of restitution awarded to the plaintiff (minor).

Example 7–4

Teresa, a minor, purchased a motorcycle from Quality Motors for $1,500. When Teresa disaffirmed the contract and returned the motorcycle to Quality, the motorcycle had depreciated $500.

Teresa is entitled to restitution of $1,500 less an offset of $500.

ⅢPARALEGAL EXERCISE 7.6

In the following two situations, is there a difference in whether the minor should be restored to the position she was in before contracting? If so, how much should she receive?

1. Mary Alice, aged 16, purchased a used Pinto from Friendly Ford for $1,500. She took delivery of the Pinto and financed it over 24 months. After driving the Pinto for a year, Mary Alice disaffirmed the contract, ceased making payments, and returned the Pinto to Friendly Ford. Friendly Ford sued Mary Alice for breach of contract, claiming that she breached the contract by not continuing to pay her installments.

   What, if anything, should be restored to Mary Alice?

2. Using the same facts, assume that instead of financing the car, Mary Alice paid cash. Mary Alice sued Friendly Ford in a restitution action, seeking the return of her money.

   What, if anything, should be restored to Mary Alice?

   Should the answers to these problems be the same or different? Why? ■

Statutory Variations

Although the minority doctrine began as a judicially recognized doctrine, a number of states now have statutes that deal with the minor's right to disaffirm a contract. Some statutes may establish the time after reaching majority in which the minor must disaffirm.

Example 7-5

In all cases other than those specified herein, the contract of a minor may be disaffirmed by the minor himself, either before his majority or within one (1) year's time afterwards.

Some statutes address the issue of necessaries.

Example 7-6

(a) Contracts not disaffirmable. A contract, otherwise valid, entered into during minority, cannot be disaffirmed upon that ground either during the actual minority of the person entering into such contract, or at any time thereafter in the following cases:

1. Necessaries. A contract to pay the reasonable value of things necessary for his support, or that of his family, entered into by him when not under the care of a parent or guardian able to provide for him or them; provided, that these things have been actually furnished to him or to his family.

Other statutes may provide for judicially determined emancipation that includes the loss of the right to disaffirm. **Emancipation** means that the court no longer considers a person a minor even though the minor's chronological age would fall within the definition of a minor.

emancipation
Emancipation occurs when a court no longer considers the person a minor even though the person's chronological age would fall within the definition of a minor.

Example 7-7

A minor ordered emancipated under this Act shall have the right to enter into valid legal contracts, and shall have such other rights and responsibilities as the court may order that are not inconsistent with the specific age requirements of the State or federal constitution or any State or federal law.

In any event, when an issue of minority arises, the paralegal must check the appropriate state statutes to determine whether the governing state has codified or modified the common law rules.

MENTAL INCAPACITY

Early contract law, under the meeting of the minds theory, denied the power to contract to the mentally incapacitated. A "contract" by a party who was mentally incapacitated was "void." Modern contract law (manifestation of assent) gives the mentally incapacitated the power to contract and the power to disaffirm the contract. Only the mentally incapacitated party has the power to disaffirm. The other party to the contract does not have this power.

Although a person suffering from mental incapacity may disaffirm the contract, the definition of what constitutes mental incapacity varies from state to state. Traditionally, the legislatures and courts measured contractual mental capacity by what is largely a "cognitive" test. Under the **cognitive test**, the court inquired whether the mind was so affected as to render the contracting party wholly and absolutely unable to understand the nature of the transaction. This standard governing competency to contract evolved when psychiatric knowledge was primitive. This standard failed to account for those who by reason of mental illness were unable to control their conduct even though their cognitive ability seemed unimpaired.

Some courts and the drafters of the Restatement of Contracts have modernized the standard. The Restatement (Second) of Contracts § 15 provides the following version:

> (1) A person incurs only voidable contractual duties by entering into a transaction if by reason of mental illness or defect
> (a) he is unable to understand in a reasonable manner the nature and consequence of the transaction, or
> (b) he is unable to act in a reasonable manner in relation to the transaction and the other party has reason to know of his condition.
> (2) Where the contract is made on fair terms and the other party is without knowledge of the mental illness or defect, the power of avoidance under Subsection (1) terminates to the extent that the contract has been so performed in whole or in part or the circumstances have so changed that avoidance would be unjust. In such a case a court may grant relief as justice requires.

Subsection (1)(a) retains the cognitive test, the inability to understand. Subsection (1)(b) includes a "volitional" test. The **volitional test** recognizes an inability to act in a reasonable manner. The cognitive and volitional tests are alternatives. A person can disaffirm if by reason of mental illness or defect that person cannot understand OR cannot act in a reasonable manner. This permits people who understand but cannot control their actions to disaffirm their contracts. It should be noted that the power to disaffirm under subsection (1)(b) is limited to those situations where the other party had reason to know of the mental disease or defect.

cognitive test
The traditional common law test whereby a contracting party may disaffirm a contract if his or her mind was so affected by mental disease or defect as to render him or her wholly and absolutely unable to comprehend and understand the nature of the transaction.

volitional test
The more modern test which supplements the cognitive test so a person may disaffirm a contract when, due to mental disease or defect, he or she is unable to act in a reasonable manner and the other party had reasons to know of the mental disease or defect.

Example 7-8

Napoleon Westerville suffered from an insane delusion that he was Napoleon Bonaparte. During one of his delusionary episodes, Napoleon, dressed as Napoleon Bonaparte, purchased a Citroen from Import Motors and paid in cash.

Under the Restatement (Second) of Contracts § 15, Napoleon will be able to disaffirm the contract, return the Citroen, and recover his money. His demeanor and dress will establish that he contracted while he was suffering from mental illness—the delusion. If he cannot prove that he was "unable to understand in a reasonable manner the nature and consequences of the transaction," because of the delusion, he could prove that he was "unable to act in a reasonable manner in relation to the transaction" because of the delusion. For the latter, Napoleon must also prove that Import Motors had reason to know of his condition, which could be established by his demeanor and dress.

ⅲ PARALEGAL EXERCISE 7.7

Thelma Simmons, a 60-year-old Medville schoolteacher, suffered a nervous breakdown and was placed on medical leave. Her illness was diagnosed as involving involutional psychosis, melancholia type, and her psychiatrist suspected that she suffered from cerebral arteriosclerosis. While on disability, she contracted with her teachers' retirement system to provide her the maximum retirement benefits during her lifetime with no benefits to her beneficiaries upon her death. She did not tell her husband, who was relying on the continuation of her retirement benefits as his sole means of support if she predeceased him.

Four months after contracting with the retirement system, Mrs. Simmons died, leaving her husband penniless.

Can Mrs. Simmons's executor disaffirm her contract with the retirement system? ■

INCAPACITY DUE TO ALCOHOL OR OTHER DRUGS

The degree of incapacity due to alcohol or other drugs may vary. A person who is totally incapacitated due to alcohol or other drugs may, from an objective standard (the reasonable person), not even have the capacity to assent. In these instances, without a "manifestation of assent," a contract cannot be formed.

A person who suffers from compulsive alcoholism or drug addiction may have diminished capacity to contract. Such a condition may constitute mental illness, and therefore, mental incompetency as grounds for disaffirmance of the contract may be available. If the mental illness test of the Restatement (Second) of Contracts § 15 is followed, the person must, to incur only voidable contractual duties by reason of mental illness, be unable "to understand in a reasonable manner the nature and consequence of the transaction" or "to act in a reasonable manner in relation to the transaction and the other party has reason to know of his condition." Even if a person qualifies under this test for the power to disaffirm a contract, the Restatement (Second) of Contracts § 15(2) places limitations on the power to disaffirm.

> (2) Where the contract is made on fair terms and the other party is without knowledge of the mental illness or defect, the power of avoidance . . . terminates to the extent that the contract has been so performed in whole or in part or the circumstances have so changed that avoidance would be unjust. In such a case a court may grant relief as justice requires.

A person who voluntarily diminished his or her capacity to contract through the use of alcohol or other drugs may not be considered to have a mental illness. The Restatement (Second) of Contracts § 16, however, provides such a party with grounds to disaffirm a contract. Although the Restatement's language is in terms of intoxication, it could be argued that the use of other drugs should be similarly treated.

> A person incurs only voidable contractual duties by entering into a transaction if the other party has reason to know that by reason of intoxication
>
> (a) he is unable to understand in a reasonable manner the nature and consequences of the transaction, or
>
> (b) he is unable to act in a reasonable manner in relation to the transaction.

Under the Restatement's test, if the intoxication does not constitute mental illness, an intoxicated person's power to disaffirm is severely restricted. The other contracting party must have had reason to know that he or she was intoxicated and that, by reason of the intoxication, was unable "to understand in a reasonable manner the nature and consequences of the transaction" or "to act in a reasonable manner in relation to the transaction."

⫸ PARALEGAL EXERCISE 7.8

In the case of *Lucy v. Zehmer,* the Zehmers, owners of the Ferguson Farm, operated a local restaurant. One evening, their old friend Lucy met them at the restaurant, and after a few drinks and a lot of talk, the Zehmers signed a writing saying they promised to sell Lucy the Ferguson Farm for $50,000 cash. Review *Lucy v. Zehmer,* pages 67–71, in light of the incapacity due to alcohol and other drugs. Did Zehmer have the power to claim an incapacity and preclude the enforcement of the contract? ▪

PARALEGAL CHECKLIST

Unenforceable Contracts—Protecting a Class

❏ The fact that a contract has been formed does not necessarily lead to the conclusion that it can be enforced in court by a nonbreaching party. The paralegal must evaluate whether one of the parties has the power to disaffirm the contract making it unenforceable. The supervising attorney will, of course, always make the final determination in all such matters and will advise the client. Enforcement problems can be divided into three broad categories:

1. Precluding enforcement of a contract to protect members of a class, such as minors, the mentally incapacitated, and persons incapacitated due to alcohol and other drugs.

2. Precluding enforcement of a contract to protect a party against another party's overreaching through unconscionability, fraud, duress, or mistake in a basic assumption of fact.

3. Precluding enforcement of a contract to protect the judicial process from involvement in nonjudicial type activity, such as illegality, perjury, and inappropriate forum shopping.

❏ Chapter 7 deals with the first category—protecting members of a class.

1. Was one of the parties a member of a protected class? If, at the time of contract formation, one of the parties was a minor, suffered from a mental disease or defect, or was under the influence of alcohol or other drugs, that party may be a member of a protected class and could possibly have the power to disaffirm the contract and claim unjust enrichment for any benefit conferred on the other.

2. Was the party a minor at the time of contract formation? If so, he or she may disaffirm the contract during minority or within a reasonable time thereafter.

   a. Determine whether the minor has exercised the power to disaffirm. To do so, the minor must return to the other party only what the minor received under the contract and still has in his or her possession.

   b. Find out if the minor has been restored to the position he or she was in before contracting. Upon disaffirmance, the minor is entitled to be restored to that position.

   c. Evaluate whether the minor is liable for necessaries. Courts are divided over the question of whether a minor could disaffirm if the contract was for necessaries. If the minor may disaffirm a contract for necessaries, he or she is still liable for the necessaries in a restitution action (reasonable value to the minor and not necessarily the contract price). If the minor may not disaffirm, the minor is liable in a breach of contract cause of action.

   d. Check whether what the minor has received has depreciated prior to disaffirmance.

   e. Check whether these general rules have been altered by statute or judicial decision.

3. Was the party suffering from a mental illness or defect at the time of contract formation? If so, he or she may (if the Restatement (Second) of Contracts § 15 is followed by your court) disaffirm the contract if by reason of the mental illness or defect he or she was unable to understand in a reasonable manner the nature and consequence of the transaction or to act in a reasonable manner in relation to the transaction and the other party had reason to know of his or her condition. If the contract was made on fair terms and the other party was without knowledge of the

mental illness or defect, the power to disaffirm may cease to the extent that the contract has been performed or the circumstances have changed causing disaffirmance to be unjust. In such a case, a court could grant relief as justice requires.

4. Was the party incapacitated due to alcohol or another drug at the time of contract formation?

a. Determine whether the party was totally lacking the capacity to assent (using an objective standard). If so, the party may assert that the contract was not formed (no manifestation of assent).

b. Check whether the party was suffering diminished capacity due to compulsive alcoholism or drug addiction. If so, the party may assert the condition constitutes mental illness, thus rendering the contract unenforceable under the mental illness test.

c. Analyze whether the party was suffering voluntarily diminished capacity due to alcohol or other drugs. If so, the party may assert that the contract was unenforceable (1) if the other contracting party had reason to know of his or her condition; and (2) that by reason of the alcohol or other drugs, he or she was unable to understand in a reasonable manner the nature and consequences of the transaction or to act in a reasonable manner in relation to the transaction.

KEY TERMS

Cognitive test	Offset
Disaffirm	Ratification
Emancipation	Repudiation
Expectation damages	Restitution damages
Necessaries	Volitional test

REVIEW QUESTIONS

TRUE/FALSE QUESTIONS (CIRCLE THE CORRECT ANSWER)

1. T   F   Certain classes of people are protected by law in their contract transactions.

2. T   F   The members of a protected class are given the power to unilaterally rescind their contracts.

3. T   F   Modern contract law prevents minors from entering into contracts and thus their "contracts" are void.

4. T   F   Minors may disaffirm contracts made during minority if they disaffirm while still in minority or within a reasonable time after reaching majority.

5. T   F   Both parties involved in a contract in which one is a minor have the power to disaffirm.

6. T   F   A minor has the power to decide not to disaffirm a contract and may continue to perform and demand performance under the contract.

7. T   F   The minor who willfully misrepresents his or her age at the time of contract formation may not disaffirm.

8. T   F   Once a minor disaffirms a contract, the minor no longer has outstanding duties to perform and the other party may not enforce the contract against him or her.

9. T   F   The minor who willfully misrepresents his or her age at the time of contract formation may be liable in a tort action for misrepresentation.

10. T   F   A minor who disaffirms a contract will be restored to the position he or she was in before contracting.

11. T   F   A minor who disaffirms a contract may reclaim personal property but not real property from a subsequent bona fide purchaser for value.

12. T   F   The minor must restore to the other party what the minor received under the contract. If the minor no longer has what was given, then he or she cannot disaffirm the contract.

13. T   F   If the minor disaffirms the contract, discontinues performing, and files a restitution action to recover the benefit conferred on the other contracting party, some courts will charge the minor for the use and depreciation of what he or she received.

14. T   F   A minor who disaffirms a contract for necessaries may still be liable for the reasonable value of the necessaries.

15. T   F   A minor who disaffirm a contract for necessaries will be liable in a breach of contract cause of action.

16. T   F   Under a restitution action a minor is only liable for the reasonable value of the necessaries to him or her rather than the contract price.

17. T   F   A minor's liability for necessaries is based on a restitution cause of action rather than breach of contract.

18. T   F   Early contract law, based on the meeting of the minds theory, denied the mentally incapacitated the power to contract.

19. T   F   Modern contract law allows both the mentally incapacitated party and the other party to disaffirm.

20. T   F   A person who is totally incapacitated due to alcohol or other drugs may not have the capacity to assent that is necessary to contract formation.

21. T   F   A person who suffers from mental illness due to compulsive alcoholism or drug addiction has an unlimited power to disaffirm a contract.

22. T   F   If voluntary intoxication does not constitute mental illness, the intoxicated person has no power to disaffirm a contract.

FILL-IN-THE-BLANK QUESTIONS

1. _____. A class of people protected by law in their contract transactions because of their age.

2. _____. The action that may be brought in some courts to allow the other contracting party to collect from a minor for necessaries.

3. _____. The inability to understand or the inability to act in a reasonable manner due to mental illness or defect.

4. _____. A measure of contractual mental capacity to determine if a person is unable to understand the nature of the transaction.

5. _____. A measure of contractual mental capacity to determine if a person is unable to act in a reasonable manner.

MULTIPLE-CHOICE QUESTIONS (CIRCLE ALL THE CORRECT ANSWERS)

1. A minor who enters into a contract has the power
   (a) to disaffirm the contract during minority.
   (b) to disaffirm the contract within a reasonable time after reaching majority.
   (c) to disaffirm the contract only if he or she still has what was received under the contract.
   (d) to disaffirm the contract and continue to retain what he or she received under the contract.
   (e) to ratify the contract after reaching majority.

2. A minor who has exercised his or her right to disaffirm the contract, cannot successfully maintain a restitution action to be restored to the position he or she was in before contracting if
   (a) the minor has ratified the contract.
   (b) the minor conferred no benefit on the other party.
   (c) the minor has conveyed real property, and the other contracting party had already conveyed the property to a subsequent purchaser who purchased in good faith and without notice of the fact that the preceding vendor was a minor.
   (d) the minor no longer has what was given to him or her.
   (e) the subject of the contract was necessaries.

SHORT-ANSWER QUESTIONS

1. Albert, aged 17, contracted to buy an automobile from Friendly Motors for $4,500. Albert paid $1,500 down and promised to pay the balance in monthly installments over three years. Two months after Albert turned 18, he was involved in an automobile accident and his car received $4,000 in damage.
   Could Albert disaffirm the contract and recover the money that he paid?

2. How might a minor use minority (disaffirmance of a contract) as a defensive as well as an offensive weapon?

Contract Enforceability: Protecting a Party Against Overreaching

- Adhesion and Unconscionability
  Unconscionability under Common Law
  Unconscionability under Article 2 of the UCC (UCC § 2–302)
- Fraud and Misrepresentation
- Duress and Undue Influence
- Mistake in a Basic Assumption of Fact

Chapter 8, the second of three chapters dealing with contract enforceability, discusses governmental regulations (legislative and judicial) when one party overreaches another during contract formation. Rather than define a class and uniformly protect every member of the class (Chapter 7), the approach here protects one contracting party from the other contracting party's overreaching on a transaction-by-transaction basis. Chapter 8 explores four situations of overreaching: adhesion and unconscionability; fraud and misrepresentation; duress and undue influence; and mistake in a basic assumption of fact (see Exhibit 8–1).

ADHESION AND UNCONSCIONABILITY

An **adhesion contract** is a contract that is offered on a "take it or leave it" basis. The terms of a contract of adhesion are not negotiable. An offeree who receives such an offer has two choices: accept or reject the offer. If the offeree rejects, the offeror will not be interested in a counteroffer. Adhesion contracts are commonplace and are found, for example, in the standardized forms produced by

adhesion contract

An adhesion contract (contract of adhesion) is a contract formed by one party imposing his or her will upon an unwilling or even unwitting party.

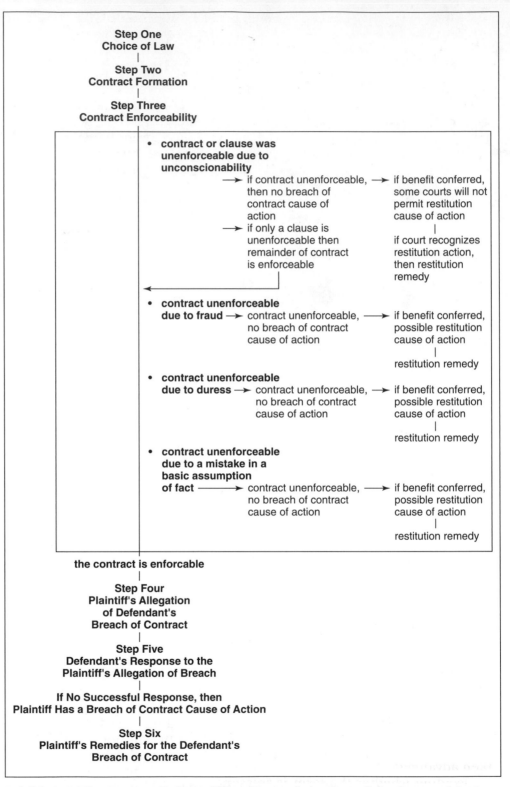

Step One
Choice of Law
|
Step Two
Contract Formation
|
Step Three
Contract Enforceability

- **contract or clause was
  unenforceable due to
  unconscionability**
  → if contract unenforceable, → if benefit conferred,
  then no breach of   some courts will not
  contract cause of   permit restitution
  action   cause of action
  → if only a clause is
  unenforceable then   if court recognizes
  remainder of contract   restitution action,
  is enforceable   then restitution
                                            remedy

- **contract unenforceable
  due to fraud** → contract unenforceable, → if benefit conferred,
                          no breach of contract   possible restitution
                          cause of action   cause of action
                                                                |
                                                           restitution remedy

- **contract unenforceable
  due to duress** → contract unenforceable, → if benefit conferred,
                            no breach of contract   possible restitution
                            cause of action   cause of action
                                                                  |
                                                             restitution remedy

- **contract unenforceable
  due to a mistake in a
  basic assumption
  of fact** ⟶ contract unenforceable, ⟶ if benefit conferred,
                    no breach of contract   possible restitution
                    cause of action   cause of action
                                                        |
                                                   restitution remedy

the contract is enforcable
|
Step Four
**Plaintiff's Allegation
of Defendant's
Breach of Contract**
|
Step Five
**Defendant's Response to the
Plaintiff's Allegation of Breach**
|
**If No Successful Response, then
Plaintiff Has a Breach of Contract Cause of Action**
|
Step Six
**Plaintiff's Remedies for the Defendant's
Breach of Contract**

**Exhibit 8-1 The Contract Enforceability (Protecting a Party from Overreaching)
Phase of the Road Map**

insurance companies, automobile dealerships, shipping companies, and airlines. As with any other document, an adhesion contract is strictly construed against its drafter.

While standardized contracts illustrate adhesion contracts, nonstandardized contracts can be adhesion contracts as well. Nonstandardized contracts could involve a party with superior bargaining power who dictates the terms on a take-it-or-leave-it basis.

Although adhesion contracts are one-sided and offered on a take-it-or-leave-it basis, not all adhesion contracts are unenforceable. An adhesion contract or a clause in an adhesion contract may be unenforceable if it is unconscionable.

The contract or contract term must be unconscionable at the time of contract formation. If events subsequent to contract formation make the performance of the contract a severe hardship, the contract cannot be challenged as unconscionable.

Unconscionability under Common Law

Courts generally recognize **unconscionability** as an absence of meaningful choice on the part of one of the parties together with contract terms that are unreasonably favorable to the other party. Whether the first element, "an absence of meaningful choice on the part of one of the parties," is present in a particular case can only be determined once all the circumstances surrounding the transactions are considered. Absence of meaningful choice has two components: the imbalance in bargaining power and a lack of knowledge of the terms. A gross inequality of bargaining power will lead to the conclusion of absence of meaningful choice even if the other party had knowledge of the terms. If, however, the inequality of bargaining power is not gross, there still might be an absence of meaningful choice if the other party had little or no knowledge of the contract's terms. This lack of knowledge may occur when the terms are hidden in a maze of fine print or minimized by deceptive sales practices. Even with a term that is clearly set forth, a party must be given a reasonable opportunity to become acquainted with the term (see Exhibit 8–2).

For example, a contract written in English does not inform a buyer who can read only Spanish.

Absence of meaningful choice alone does not produce an unconscionable contract. The absence of meaningful choice must be coupled with a contract term that unreasonably favors the other party. If the term is not unreasonably favorable, it is not unconscionable even though there was a gross inequality of bargaining power, because the party with superior bargaining power has not taken advantage of that power.

Deciding whether the term is "reasonable" or "fair" cannot be done in a vacuum. The term must be considered in light of the

unconscionability

A contract or contract term is unconscionable if, at the time of contract formation, one party imposed an unreasonably favorable contract or term on the other party who lacked a meaningful choice.

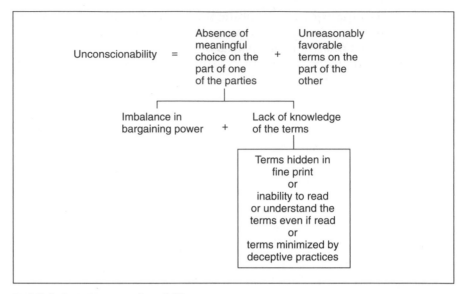

Exhibit 8–2 Unconscionability

circumstances existing when the contract was made. The general commercial background and the commercial needs of the particular trade or case shed light on reasonableness.

Unconscionability as a Shield

Unconscionability may be used as either a shield or a sword. Consider the following case, *Garrett v. Hooters-Toledo*, where unconscionability was used as a shield. Garrett brought a gender discrimination case against her former employer, Hooters-Toledo. Hooters responded with a motion to compel arbitration and to stay the litigation proceedings, claiming Garrett signed a mandatory arbitration agreement. Garrett defended on the ground that the arbitration agreement was unconscionable.

CASE

Garrett v. Hooters-Toledo
United States District Court, Northern District of Ohio (2003)
295 F. Supp.2d 774

ORDER

CARR, District Judge.
This is a gender discrimination case in which the plaintiff, Rachel Garrett, alleges that her former employer, a Hooters restaurant in Toledo, Ohio, wrongfully discharged her after she disclosed to her manager that she was pregnant. Plaintiff

has filed suit against defendants Hooters-Toledo, R.M.D. Corporation, and Chris Reil. This court has jurisdiction pursuant to 28 U.S.C. § 1331.

Pending is defendants' motion to compel arbitration and stay these proceedings. For the following reasons, defendants' motion shall be denied.

BACKGROUND

A. Alternative Dispute Resolution Agreement

Plaintiff began working at Hooters restaurant in April, 1999. The restaurant did not require plaintiff to sign an arbitration agreement at that time. A couple of months thereafter Hooters adopted a policy that required any employee who wished to be considered for any job change, bonus, promotion, or transfer to accept the terms and conditions of Hooter's "Agreement to Mediate and Arbitrate Employment-Related Disputes" ("ADR Agreement").

On June 27, 1999, defendant Chris Reil, plaintiff's manager at Hooters, gave plaintiff a copy of the ADR Agreement and a binder entitled "Rules and Procedures for Alternative Resolution of Employment-Related Disputes." Plaintiff claims that she did not understand the materials, but carried them around with her in her bag for several weeks. Defendants claim that Reil offered to answer employees' questions about the agreement, but neither plaintiff nor any other employee asked any questions of him.

Plaintiff alleges that when she arrived at work on August 9, 1999, she was told that she had to sign the agreement, or she could not work another shift at Hooters. She signed the agreement. Defendants' motion seeks to enforce the agreement's mediation and arbitration provisions.

Those provisions require an employee first to file a request for mediation to resolve a claim or dispute against Hooters. Once mediation has been requested, the employee can then "initiate a resolution," which triggers the agreement's arbitration provisions. The mediation procedure, while mandatory, is not binding. The outcome of arbitration is binding.

B. Plaintiff's Pregnancy and Termination

Plaintiff worked at Hooters for over three years, until she was terminated on July 17, 2002. Plaintiff alleges that she was terminated by defendants because she became pregnant in June, 2002.

Plaintiff told defendant Reil that she was pregnant on June 18, 2002. She alleges that Reil did not speak to her for several days after this disclosure, and he reduced the number of shifts to which she was assigned to work.

Plaintiff also alleges that she requested permission to wear a modified maternity uniform, but Reil denied her request. She claims that when she complained that other employees' similar requests had been granted, Reil responded "Not while I have been here" and ordered her to go home early. Plaintiff alleges that Reil had harassed other employees who asked to wear pants during their pregnancies.

Additionally, plaintiff claims that Reil permitted plaintiff's co-workers to "harass plaintiff and make crude comments about her pregnancy." Plaintiff claims that she received a phone call from Hooters management on July 16, 2002, asking her to come to a meeting the next morning. At this meeting, plaintiff was terminated. She alleges that her position was filled by a non-pregnant person.

Defendants deny plaintiff's allegations and claim that she was assigned to the same number of shifts she had been before she disclosed her pregnancy. Defendants also assert that plaintiff did not ask for permission to wear the approved

Hooters maternity uniform, but instead requested to wear sweatpants. Defendants assert that Reil told her she could not wear sweatpants without a doctor's note and deny that Reil made any harassing comments to plaintiff. Defendants claim that all pregnant servers are allowed to wear the maternity uniform, but that plaintiff never asked to do so. Defendants admit that plaintiff was asked to go home after Reil denied her request to wear a modified uniform, but allege that she was asked to leave because "she threw a tantrum over being denied the right to wear sweatpants."

Defendants assert that other Hooters employees have become pregnant, worked throughout their pregnancies, and returned to work at Hooters after giving birth.

STANDARD OF REVIEW

Through the Federal Arbitration Act ("FAA"), 9 U.S.C. § 1 et seq., Congress has declared a national policy favoring arbitration. Southland Corp. v. Keating, 465 U.S. 1, 10, 104 S.Ct. 852, 79 L.Ed.2d 1 (1984). The FAA's purpose is "to reverse the longstanding judicial hostility to arbitration agreements . . . and to place arbitration agreements upon the same footing as other contracts." Gilmer v. Interstate/Johnson Lane Corp., 500 U.S. 20, 24, 111 S.Ct. 1647, 114 L.Ed.2d 26 (1991). Accordingly, "the [FAA] establishes that, as a matter of Federal law, any doubts concerning the scope of arbitrable issues should be resolved in favor of arbitration . . . ." Moses H. Cone Memorial Hosp. v. Mercury Constr. Corp., 460 U.S. 1, 24–25, 103 S.Ct. 927, 74 L.Ed.2d 765 (1983).

Notwithstanding this policy, "arbitration is a matter of contract and a party cannot be required to submit to arbitration [in] any dispute which he has not agreed so to submit." AT&T Techs. v. Communications Workers of America, 475 U.S. 643, 648, 106 S.Ct. 1415, 89 L.Ed.2d 648 (1986). Under § 2 of the FAA, an arbitration agreement is "valid, irrevocable, and enforceable, save upon such grounds as exist at law or in equity for the revocation of any contract." 9 U.S.C. § 2.

When considering a motion to stay proceedings and compel arbitration under the Act, a court has four tasks:

> first, it must determine whether the parties agreed to arbitrate; second, it must determine the scope of that agreement; third, if federal statutory claims are asserted, it must consider whether Congress intended those claims to be nonarbitrable; and fourth, if the court concludes that some, but not all, of the claims in the action are subject to arbitration, it must determine whether to stay the remainder of the proceedings pending arbitration. Stout v. J. D. Byrider, 228 F.3d 709, 714 (6th Cir. 2000).

"In determining whether the parties have made a valid arbitration agreement, 'state law may be applied if that law arose to govern issues concerning the validity, revocability,' and enforceability of contracts generally, although the FAA preempts 'state laws applicable to only arbitration provisions.'" Great Earth Cos. v. Simons, 288 F.3d 878, 889 (6th Cir. 2002) (quoting Doctor's Assocs., Inc. v. Casarotto, 517 U.S. 681, 686–87, 116 S.Ct. 1652, 134 L.Ed.2d 902 (1996)). Thus, "[s]tate law governs 'generally applicable contract defenses [to an arbitration clause], such as fraud, duress, or unconscionability.'" Id. at 889 (quoting Casarotto, 517 U.S. at 687, 116 S.Ct. 1652).

In this case, the question whether the ADR Agreement is an enforceable arbitration agreement is resolved by basic, generally applicable precepts of Ohio contract law. The federal policy favoring arbitration, however, is taken into consideration even in applying ordinary state law. Inland Bulk Transfer Co. v. Cummins Engine Co., 332 F.3d 1007, 1014 (6th Cir. 2003) (quoting Great Earth, 288 F.3d at 887).

DISCUSSION

Plaintiff argues that the ADR Agreement is "revocable because it is unconscionable" according to Ohio common law.

Under Ohio law, a contract is unconscionable where one party has been misled as to its meaning, where a severe imbalance of bargaining power exists, or where the specific contractual clause is outrageous. Cross v. Carnes, 132 Ohio App.3d 157, 170, 724 N.E.2d 828 (1998) (citing Orlett v. Suburban Propane, 54 Ohio App.3d 127, 129, 561 N.E.2d 1066 (1989)). Unconscionability is generally recognized to include an absence of meaningful choice on the part of one of the parties to a contract, combined with contract terms that are unreasonably favorable to the other party. Collins v. Click Camera & Video, Inc., 86 Ohio App.3d 826, 834, 621 N.E.2d 1294 (1993).

The unconscionability doctrine embodies two separate components: "(1) substantive unconscionability, i.e., unfair and unreasonable contract terms, and (2) procedural unconscionability, i.e., individualized circumstances surrounding each of the parties to a contract such that no voluntary meeting of the minds was possible." Jeffrey Mining Prods. L.P. v. Left Fork Mining Co., 143 Ohio App.3d 708, 718, 758 N.E.2d 1173 (2001). A certain "quantum" of both substantive and procedural unconscionability must be present to find a contract unconscionable. Collins, 86 Ohio App.3d at 834, 621 N.E.2d 1294.

A. Substantive Unconscionability

"Substantive unconscionability involves those factors which relate to the contract terms themselves and whether they are commercially reasonable. Because the determination of commercial reasonableness varies with the content of the contract terms at issue in any given case, no generally accepted list of factors has been developed for this category of unconscionability." Dorsey v. Contemporary Obstetrics & Gynecology, Inc., 113 Ohio App.3d 75, 80, 680 N.E.2d 240 (1996) (citing Collins, 86 Ohio App.3d at 834, 621 N.E.2d 1294).

1. Cost-Splitting Provision of ADR Agreement

Plaintiff claims that the cost-splitting provision of the ADR Agreement prevents plaintiff and other potential claimants from vindicating their statutory rights. Plaintiff argues that the expenses she would incur under the ADR Agreement's Rules and Procedures would deter her from pursuing her claim. She points to the provision requiring her to pay the lesser of one half of the expenses or the equivalent of one week's average gross compensation as cost-prohibitive because she is supporting an infant and has experienced long periods of unemployment. She also argues that the rule requiring any claims filed under the ADR Agreement to be adjudicated in Jefferson County, Kentucky, would prohibitively increase her costs because it would require her to arrange for and pay child care while she traveled out of the state.

Under current law, there is no clear standard to determine if or when arbitration can be so cost prohibitive for an individual seeking to resolve a dispute with a business that the arbitration agreement becomes unenforceable.

When federal rights are at issue, the Supreme Court has recognized that "the existence of large arbitration costs could preclude a litigant . . . from effectively vindicating her federal statutory rights in the arbitral forum." Green Tree Financial Corp. v. Randolph, 531 U.S. 79, 90, 121 S.Ct. 513, 148 L.Ed.2d 373 (2000). The Court went on to hold, though, that "where . . . a party seeks to invalidate an arbitration agreement on the ground that arbitration would be prohibitively expensive, that party bears the burden of showing the likelihood of incurring such costs." Id. at 92, 121 S.Ct. 513.

The Court in Green Tree did not, however, provide a standard for determining how detailed the showing of prohibitive expenses must be to find an arbitration agreement unenforceable. The Sixth Circuit, in Morrison v. Circuit City Stores, Inc., 317 F.3d 646 (6th Cir. 2003), created its own test, concluding:

> [I]f the reviewing court finds that the cost-splitting provision would deter a substantial number of similarly situated potential litigants, it should refuse to enforce the cost-splitting provision in order to serve the underlying functions of the federal statute. In conducting the analysis, the reviewing court should define the class of such similarly situated potential litigants by job description and socioeconomic background. It should take the actual plaintiff's income and resources as representative of this larger class's ability to shoulder the costs of arbitration.
> Id. at 663.

As the court stated in *Morrison*, the costs plaintiff would incur if this claim were to be arbitrated "must be considered from the vantage point of the potential litigant . . . . Recently terminated, the potential litigant must continue to pay for housing, utilities, transportation, food, and other necessities of life . . . ." 317 F.3d at 669. Defendants argue that the ADR Agreement's cost-splitting provision is fair because it requires plaintiff to pay for the *lesser* of one half of the expenses or one week's compensation toward the costs of arbitration. This argument, however, assumes that one week's compensation can and should readily be sacrificed by a plaintiff who has experienced long periods of unemployment and who must provide for herself and a child. Plaintiff's brief does not disclose her income, but she does assert that her job at Hooter's provided her substantially more money than she had ever earned. One week's compensation, therefore, imposes a high burden on a single mother experiencing intermittent periods of unemployment, and who earns less than she had while employed at defendants' restaurant.

Additionally, the ADR Agreement requires the employee to pay a one hundred dollar "Resolution Fee" to arbitrate her claim. There is no indication in the agreement that this fee is waivable if the employee cannot afford this fee. Defendants liken the fee to the filing fee required to bring a claim in court, but courts routinely waive filing fees on submission of an *in forma pauperis* applications.

Plaintiff has not estimated the amount for which she would be liable if this court were to enforce the ADR Agreement. She presumes that the cost will exceed one week's average gross cash compensation in her case (meaning that she will be liable for the equivalent of one week's compensation), and asserts that this amount will deter her, and others similarly situated, from pursuing her claim under the ADR Agreement. Plaintiff also has not provided information about the comparative costs of litigating and arbitrating her claims.

Although I find plaintiff's arguments generally persuasive, they are insufficient, in light of the present record, to establish a factual basis for substantive unconscionability of the cost-splitting provision. See Rickard, 279 F.Supp.2d at

918; Garcia v. Wayne Homes, L.L.C., No. 01 CA 53, 2002 WL 628619, at 13 (Ohio Ct.App. Apr.19, 2002) (holding that "proof of costs alone will not invalidate an arbitration clause" and stating that, because the plaintiffs did not produce evidence of the expected cost differential between arbitration and litigation in court, the plaintiffs "failed to produce sufficient facts or allegations . . . that the undisclosed costs of arbitration rendered the provision unconscionable.").

I would, if necessary, grant plaintiff leave to provide a detailed showing of the costs associated with arbitrating her claim and her personal financial record, reflecting her inability to pay those costs (and the inability of others similarly situated, according to the *Morrison* test). Because, however, I find the ADR Agreement to be substantively unconscionable on other grounds, such supplementation of the record is unnecessary.

2. Time Limit for Filing a Claim

The ADR Agreement states that all claims against Hooters should be filed within 10 days from the last day on which the claim arose. Claimants are required first to file a request for mediation, which is nonbinding and from which lawyers are excluded from participating. Once mediation is initiated, the claimant must "initiate a resolution" (request arbitration) within 180 days from the last day on which the claim arose, or within the time limit set forth by the appropriate government agency if the claimant has a right to file with such agency. Even if the parties are still mediating the dispute under that provision of the agreement, the claim for resolution must be filed within the arbitration time limit or it is forfeited.

These time limits are an essential part of the ADR Agreement which plaintiff was told she must accept if she wished to be eligible for any promotion, bonus, raise, or transfer. According to the agreement, if a claimant does not file a request for mediation, the claimant is expressly prohibited from bringing that claim against Hooters. Although the agreement provides that requests for mediation submitted after the 10-day time limit will be considered, it is not clear on what basis such late claims will be evaluated and processed. Also, abrogation of the 10-day limit does not toll the time for filing a request for arbitration, which must be done, in any event, after the request for mediation is filed.

The 10-day time limit for bringing a claim is unreasonable and unfair. Few, if any, potential claimants would be able to assess their situation, with or without consulting an attorney, within such time period. As a practical matter, this 10-day period would be too short to enable a terminated worker to locate and meet with an attorney. This extreme limitation has no apparent justification, and, even if defendants tried to justify this draconian term, the severely adverse impact on a claimant's ability meaningfully to assess and assert her rights would greatly outweigh such justification. The sole purpose—and, in any event, the clear effect—of this limitation is to eliminate the likelihood that discharged employees will challenge their terminations, even if the ADR Agreement otherwise is reasonable and fair.

Support for this conclusion is found in the Third Circuit's recent decision in Alexander v. Anthony Int'l, L.P., 341 F.3d 256, 266 (3d Cir. 2003), in which the court held that a 30-day time limit in an arbitration agreement was substantively unconscionable because it was "clearly unreasonable and unduly favorable to [the employer]." In the instant case, the time limit is only 10 days, 20 days shorter than the limit in Alexander, and is even more substantively unconscionable than the limitations period in that case.

3. Mediation Requirement

Even aside from the 10-day limitation, the mediation requirement has other substantively unconscionable aspects. Plaintiff alleges that she was presented with a "take it or leave it" demand to sign the agreement. At the very least, this combination of coerciveness coupled with the fundamental inequality of bargaining power that exists between a lone former employee and a large, sophisticated, nationwide employer gives rise to a need to scrutinize the ADR Agreement with particular care to ensure that the mediation requirement is not an effective barrier to redress.

A claimant's inability to be represented by counsel unfairly disadvantages her and favors the defendants. The agreement simply refers, moreover, to mediation between "the parties": there is no indication of the extent to which the parties can call witnesses, or who their representatives may be. Though defendants likewise forego representation, an imbalance may arise if the participants include company representatives, such as human relations personnel, who have experience in dealing with claims of unfair or improper treatment.

Mediation is to be conducted in Jefferson County, Kentucky, before two mediators, one of whom is to be selected by the plaintiff and the other by the defendants from a list of purportedly neutral mediators provided by the company. The likelihood that a claimant would have any basis on which to choose a mediator who might be open to her contentions is slight, if nonexistent. She would probably be as well off throwing a dart at the company's list as she would be to attempt any other method of choosing a mediator. This "trust us" aspect of the method by which mediators are selected supports the finding of unconscionability of the mediation process.

Forum selection clauses generally are presumed to be *prima facie* valid, but "a forum selection clause may be unconscionable if the place or manner in which arbitration is to occur is unreasonable taking into account the respective circumstances of the parties." Comb v. PayPal, Inc., 218 F.Supp.2d 1165, 1177 (N.D.Cal. 2002) (internal citations omitted) (citing an unfair forum selection clause as one of several reasons to find an arbitration agreement substantively unconscionable). In the instant case, there appears to be little justification for the requirement that mediation and arbitration be conducted in Jefferson County (i.e., Louisville), Kentucky. If the term "the parties" were to be given a limited meaning, and include only the plaintiff and the defendants, no reason appears not to have the mediation conducted in Toledo.

The obligation to travel to Kentucky becomes more onerous if plaintiff were to desire to have witnesses appear on her behalf. Whether she or the company could do so is not clear from the ADR Agreement, which simply provides that the mediators would determine the format. If the parties could call witnesses, it is likely that, as a practical matter, only the company would be in a position to do so at a mediation held in Kentucky.

There can be no doubt that the mediation requirement and the ADR Agreement as a whole are written to discourage potential claimants from pursuing their claims; the agreement's rules impose burdens and barriers that would routinely deter former employees from vindicating their rights. Even if a former employee were able successfully to overcome these barriers, it appears to be very unlikely that she could prevail.

On balance, the agreement is unreasonable and unfair because it require claimants to participate in a process designed to be, and which is, excessively and unjustifiably favorable to Hooters. The requirement to mediate, which must be undertaken before arbitration can be sought, is substantively unconscionable. The unconscionability of this precondition to arbitration renders the balance of the ADR Agreement unconscionable and unenforceable.

B. Procedural Unconscionability

In determining procedural unconscionability, Ohio courts look to "factors bearing on the relative bargaining position of the contracting parties, including their age, education, intelligence, business acumen and experience, relative bargaining power, who drafted the contract, whether the terms were explained to the weaker party, and whether alterations in the printed terms were possible." Cross v. Carnes, 132 Ohio App.3d 157, 170, 724 N.E.2d 828 (1998). "The crucial question is whether 'each party to the contract, considering his obvious education or lack of it, [had] a reasonable opportunity to understand the terms of the contract, or were the important terms hidden in a maze of fine print . . . ?'" Ohio Univ. Bd. of Trs. v. Smith, 132 Ohio App.3d 211, 724 N.E.2d 1155 (1999) (quoting Williams v. Walker-Thomas Furniture Co., 350 F.2d 445, 449 (D.C.Cir. 1965)).

The ADR Agreement signed by plaintiff in this case is procedurally, as well as substantively, unconscionable. Defendants wrote the ADR Agreement, which I have already decided is unreasonable and unfair, and presented it to plaintiff after she had been working for defendants for approximately three months. Plaintiff claims that she earned more money working for defendants than she had at any previous job she had held, and that she would have done anything to keep her position. Defendants told plaintiff that she must sign and accept the agreement in order to be eligible for any job change, including promotions, bonuses, or job transfers. Defendants did not explain the agreement and its implications to employees, including plaintiff, but merely suggested that they read it and ask questions if they did not understand. Plaintiff claims that she tried to read it, but did not understand either its terms or its future ramifications. Later, after plaintiff had possession of the agreement for about a month, defendants, according to the plaintiff, told her that she had to sign it or she could not work another shift. Plaintiff, accordingly, signed and accepted the agreement, though she states that she still did not understand what it meant.

Plaintiff had no opportunity to negotiate the terms of the ADR Agreement. Surely, had she been able to understand the impact of the rights she was giving up and the limitations to which she was acquiescing, plaintiff and any other person in her position would have objected to many of the provisions of the agreement. Even if she had done so, however, it is clear that plaintiff would not have been able to continue working at Hooters for very long if she had declined to accept the ADR Agreement as written and presented to her. Even if defendants had allowed her to continue working shifts as a waitress, she would have been ineligible for any raise, promotion, or transfer.

Therefore, my conclusion that the ADR Agreement is procedurally unconscionable is not reliant, as defendants claim, on whether plaintiff would certainly have lost her job had she not accepted the agreement. The unequal bargaining power between the parties, coupled with plaintiff's lack of sophistication and the clearly demonstrated pressures on her to accept the agreement, no matter what it said, make defendants' motion and its supplemental memorandum in support of its motion unpersuasive. Plaintiff's acceptance of the agreement was not freely given, and the agreement is procedurally unconscionable.

CONCLUSION

Because it is both substantively and procedurally unconscionable, the ADR Agreement violates Ohio common law and is unenforceable.

It is therefore ORDERED THAT defendants' motion to compel arbitration and stay these proceedings be, and hereby is, denied. A scheduling conference is set for December 12, 2003 at 8:30 a.m.

So ordered.

Unconscionability as a Sword

Unconscionability becomes a sword when a contracting party brings an action to reform an unconscionable term in a contract. In *Vockner v. Erickson,* the seller of an apartment building sued the purchaser, seeking reformation and payment of accrued interest on the ground that the contract was unconscionable.

CASE

Vockner v. Erickson
Supreme Court of Alaska (1986)
712 P.2d 379

Before RABINOWITZ, C.J., and BURKE, MATTHEWS, COMPTON and MOORE, J.J.

OPINION

RABINOWITZ, Chief Justice.
This appeal arises from the superior court's ruling that the contract between Bernd Vockner and Leo Erickson, concerning the purchase of Erickson's apartment house, was unconscionable.

I. FACTS

In the spring of 1975, Erickson, then 73 years of age, ran an advertisement offering a 12-person boarding house for sale. Bernd Vockner, a real estate agent, answered the advertisement and arranged to meet with Erickson. When Vockner arrived at the boarding house on the evening of April 30, 1975, Erickson informed him that the boarding house was not for sale, but that she desired to sell her 12 unit apartment house located on East 13th Avenue in Anchorage.

After discussing the possible purchase of the apartment house, Vockner took Erickson with him to inspect the building. Upon returning to the boarding house, Vockner prepared an earnest money agreement with forms he had brought with him, detailing the terms of the sale.

Although Erickson initially asked for $265,000, they settled on a sale price of $250,000. Vockner agreed to assume Erickson's existing deed of trust to the Small Business Administration for approximately $90,000, and to make a down payment of $10,000. Additionally, Vockner promised to execute a second deed of trust in favor of Erickson for $153,365.46 with 8-½% interest, payable at the rate of $500 per month commencing on August 13, 1976. The earnest money agreement also provided for a balloon payment in the amount of $15,000 on

August 13, 1976. The parties signed the earnest money agreement that evening, and Vockner delivered to Erickson an earnest money check for $1,000.

Subsequently, Erickson became dissatisfied with the agreement for two reasons: another purchaser had offered her $265,000, and she realized that the $500 a month payment would not even cover the interest as it accrued on the note. She expressed her dissatisfaction with the purchase price in a letter to Vockner on May 23, 1975, and returned the $1,000 earnest money. Vockner responded, informing Erickson that he expected performance. Erickson continued to resist complying with the earnest money agreement. Consequently, Vockner filed a complaint for specific performance and in the alternative for damages. Erickson believed that she had to comply because an attorney had informally advised her that Vockner would win and because of her husband's ill health, so she filed a *pro per* answer stating that she was ready to perform the earnest money agreement.

The earnest money agreement was then forwarded to Alaska Title Guarantee for preparation of the closing documents. Paul Nangle, the attorney retained to prepare the closing documents, discovered that the earnest money agreement did not contain a payoff date. Nangle called Vockner's attorney, who suggested that Nangel insert a 30-year term. The superior court found that Erickson was never asked whether she agreed to the 30-year term.

Vockner and Erickson then proceeded to close the sale. The promissory note provided in part for a 30-year term with a $311,000 balloon payment at the end. The closing agent specifically remembered explaining all of the terms of the contract to Erickson. Four-and-a-half years later, Erickson filed a *pro per* complaint seeking reformation and payment of accrued interest, or return of the property. This complaint, later amended, also named as a defendant the then owner of the apartment house, as Vockner had sold the property within three or four months of purchase.

The case proceeded to trial with the 30-year term as one of the primary issues. Vockner testified that he discussed the 30-year term with Erickson before drawing up the agreement. Erickson testified that she did not know about the 30-year term until she signed the documents at the closing. The superior court found that Erickson was never asked if she agreed to the term, but that she was informed about it before signing the closing papers.

The superior court held that Erickson was not under duress sufficient to invalidate the transaction. In so deciding, the court concluded that Erickson had viable alternatives to bowing under to any duress that the filing of the specific performance action might have generated.

The superior court rejected the contention that Vockner or his attorney had committed an intentional misrepresentation. In so holding, the court disagreed with the argument that there was an implicit false representation arising from the insertion of the 30-year term into the closing documents. The court found that the closing agent apprised Erickson as to the existence of the 30-year term and that Erickson was capable of reading the contract documents.

Overall, however, the superior court ruled that under the standards of § 208 of the Restatement (Second) of Contracts the contract was "clearly unconscionable." In so holding the superior court articulated the following reasons for its conclusion: Erickson is an elderly woman; it made no sense for someone her age to enter into a 30-year agreement that would not even pay the interest as it accrued; the security for the loan would diminish as the building deteriorated over time; and elements of "quasi-coercion" constituted indicia of unconscionability.

These elements included Vockner's filing of the specific performance and damages action, the fact that Vockner had counsel in that litigation and Erickson did not, and Vockner's greater experience in real estate matters.

. . . .

Based upon the foregoing rulings the superior court reformed the parties' agreement and entered judgment against Vockner for the principal amount of $52,559.72, an amount sufficient to amortize the principal and interest from June 1975 to June 1983, and $126,894.54, with 8-½% interest, due in monthly installments of $1,075.36, an amount that would amortize the principal and interest over the term of the 30-year note.

Lastly, the superior court ordered Vockner to execute a deed of trust in favor of Erickson, encumbering other real property in an amount at least 10% greater than the total amount of judgment. In return for this second deed of trust, the court ordered Erickson to convey her interest in the deed of trust and promissory note of June 30, 1975 to Vockner.

II. THE SUPERIOR COURT DID NOT ERR IN HOLDING THAT THE CONTRACT BETWEEN VOCKNER AND ERICKSON WAS UNCONSCIONABLE.[1]

In ruling that the contract was unconscionable, the superior court relied in part on § 208 of the Restatement (Second) of Contracts. Section 208 provides that:

> If a contract or term thereof is unconscionable at the time the contract is made a court may refuse to enforce the contract, or may enforce the remainder of the contract without the unconscionable term, or may so limit the application of any unconscionable term as to avoid any unconscionable result.[2]

The Restatement does not provide an explicit definition of unconscionability. It does identify factors, however, that support a finding of unconscionability. Additionally, it contains the following significant comment:

> Theoretically it is possible for a contract to be oppressive taken as a whole, even though there is no weakness in the bargaining process and no single term which is in itself unconscionable. Ordinarily, however, an unconscionable contract involves other factors as well as an overall imbalance.

Id. comment c at 108. Concerning these "other factors," in comment b the Restatement quotes § 2–302 of the UCC, comment 1, which states: "[t]he principle is one

---

1. In her complaint and at trial, Erickson advanced theories of misrepresentation, duress, mistake, and unconscionability as grounds for invalidating the 30-year term in the promissory note.
2. Restatement (Second) of Contracts § 208 at 107 (1981). Comment a indicates the scope of this provision:

> [T]he policy against unconscionable contracts or terms applies to a wide variety of types of conduct. The determination that a contract . . . is or is not unconscionable is made in light of its setting, purpose, and effect. Relevant factors include weakness in the contracting process like those involved in more specific rules as to contractual capacity, fraud, and other invalidating causes. . . .
> Id. at 107.

of the prevention of oppression and unfair surprise and not of disturbance of allocation of risks because of superior bargaining power." (Citation omitted.)[3]

As we indicated at the outset, the superior court articulated numerous factors
relating to the parties' respective circumstances and to the terms of the agreement
that led it to the conclusion that the contract was unconscionable. The court considered determinative that: Erickson is elderly and would be 103 years old when the
large balloon payment was due; the balloon payment at the end of 30 years would
have been $311,000; and the value of the security would decrease over the course
of this 30-year term.[4] In addition the superior court also considered several indicia
of unconscionability, which it termed "quasi-coercion". These were that Vockner
filed suit for specific performance and damages; that Vockner hired counsel while
Erickson was unrepresented in that suit; and that Vockner had an advantage over
Erickson due to his real estate training. The superior court observed that, "They did
not approach this transaction on an equal level of knowledge[;] [t]he cards were
stacked in favor of Vockner with respect to making the particular bargain."[5]

Based upon our review of the record and in part for the reasons articulated by
the superior court, we hold that the superior court's determination of unconscionability under section 208 of the Restatement (Second) of Contracts should
be affirmed.[6] Additionally, we affirm because Vockner rather than Erickson retained

---

3. In Morrow v. New Moon Homes, Inc., 548 P.2d 279, 292 n. 43 (Alaska 1976) we said
that "unconscionability":

> ... has generally been recognized to include an absence of meaningful choice on
> the part of one of the parties together with contract terms which are unreason-
> ably favorable to the other party.

> Section 208, comment c to the Restatement states, "Inadequacy of considera-
> tion does not of itself invalidate a bargain, but gross disparity in the values
> exchanged may be an important factor in a determination that a contract is
> unconscionable. . . ." § 208 comment c at 108 (1981).

Section 208, comment d to the Restatement states:

> A bargain is not unconscionable merely because the parties to it are unequal in
> bargaining position, nor even because the inequality results in an allocation of
> risks to the weaker party. But gross inequality of bargaining power, together with
> terms unreasonably favorable to the stronger party, may confirm indications that
> the transaction involved elements of deception or compulsion, or may show that
> the weaker party had no meaningful choice. . .

> Id. § 208 comment d at 109.

4. In regard to the deteriorating security factor, the superior court further observed that it was
"[c]ertainly a situation approaching that of near insanity for anyone to enter into a deal like this."

5. See Cambell Soup Co. v. Wentz, 172 F.2d 80, 84 (3d Cir. 1948) where the court held
that although the contract in question was legal, the contract taken as a whole drove too
harsh a bargain for a court of conscience to assist. One commentator, in discussing
§ 2–302 of the UCC stated that:

> Comment 1 goes to some lengths to establish a climate in which courts will feel
> emboldened to strike directly at contracts . . . which appear too heavily weighted
> in favor of one of the parties; that is to act, in some measures at least, as a tribu-
> nal of constitutional review applying "bill-of-rights" prescriptions to the parties'
> private legislation.

M. P. Ellinghaus, *In Defense of Unconscionability,* 78 Yale L.J. 757, 773 (1969).

6. A determination of unconscionability is made as a matter of law. Restatement (Second)
Contracts § 208 comment f at 111 (1981).

the interest on the $6,000 annual interest that was due but not payable under the terms of the promissory note. Erickson should be the party earning interest on the interest. By depriving her of this interest, she would have lost approximately $600,000 over the 30 years, assuming 8% interest compounded monthly. Given the fact that $600,000 in 30 years is worth approximately $55,000, the promissory note had an actual fair market value of only $98,000.[7] This fact, in addition to those factors relied upon by the superior court, persuades us that the superior court's determination of unconscionability should be sustained.[8]

---

7. Erickson argues in part, on appeal, that were interest to accrue and be compounded annually, the balloon payment due in the year 2005 would be $568,498. Erickson further persuasively argues that:

> If the note is construed so as not to require compounding of interest—i.e., payment of interest in year 29 on the accrued unpaid interest of years 1 through 28— then the balloon would "only" be $311,000 in 2005. While this "mitigates" the problem concerning the diminishing collateral, it creates an additional shocking abuse. Without compounding of interest, the actual present value of the note Mrs. Erickson received, even assuming the 8-½% interest rate is and was fair market, was some $50,000 less than its face value of $153,000. (The present value of $311,000 to be received in 30 years is some $24,000, rather than the $75,000 or so that the balloon should be worth at present value if the $153,000 note were to represent $153,000 in present value . . . . Thus, Mrs. Erickson lost 1/3 of her equity the instant she "accepted" the 30-year note as closing.

> . . . .

> If the note does not require compounding the interest accrued, the actual effective rate of interest declines each year. That is, while the $12,000 annual interest (paid or accrued) is 8-½% of the balance in year 1, it is something less than 4% in year 29 ($12,000 interest paid on accrued balance of $300,000+). Not only is Erickson thereby deprived of the interest rate for which she bargained, but the decreasing interest rate works as a powerful disincentive for future owners to refinance the property; refinancing was, effectively, the only hope that Erickson had of actually securing in her lifetime the benefits of the bargain she thought she was making—present and future payments with a present value of $250,000.

8. Inherent in this holding is our rejection of Vockner's argument that the superior court erred in finding unconscionability where there is no procedural unconscionability in the contract. In support of this contention Vockner argues that the trial court must find both procedural and substantive abuses before decreeing a contract unconscionable. See J. White & R. Summers, Uniform Commercial Code §§ 4-3-4-7 (1972); Leff, *Unconscionability and the Code—The Emperor's New Clause*, 115 U.Pa.L.Rev. 485 (1967); Johnson v. Mobil Oil Corp., 415 F.Supp. 264 (E.D.Mich. 1976).

However, not all commentators agree that the court must find both procedural and substantive unconscionability. See e.g., 1 Corbin on Contracts § 128 (1984 Supp.); M. P. Ellinghaus, *In Defense of Unconscionability,* 78 Yale L.J. 757, 777 (1969). Even Williston, *who adheres to* the concept, states:

> Essentially a sliding scale is invoked which disregards the regularity of the procedural process of the contract formation, that creates the terms, in proportion to the greater harshness or unreasonableness of the substantive terms themselves.

15 S. Williston, Law of Contracts § 1763A at 226–27 (Jaeger Ed.1972).

Adopting Williston's analysis we think the superior court's conclusions that both procedural and substantive unconscionability were proven, if indeed both are required, are not erroneous on the facts of this record.

III. THE SUPERIOR COURT'S REFORMATION OF THE CONTRACT

As noted at the outset, the superior court reformed the contract to provide that Vockner was to pay $1,075.36 in monthly installments, the amount that would amortize the principal and interest over the duration of the 30-year note. Vockner contends that the superior court erred in reforming the agreement, based upon its finding of unconscionability, because "there was no finding of fraud, mistake, or overreaching, and because the contract represented the true intentions of the parties."[9] We hold that the superior court did not err in its judgment that partially reformed the contract between Vockner and Erickson.

Courts have reformed contracts to avoid unconscionable results. J. White & R. Summers, Uniform Commercial Code § 4–1 at 112, ¶4–8 at 131 (1972). Professor Dobbs states that "[t]he unconscionable contract may be reformed to limit the unconscionable clause and then enforced as reformed." D. Dobbs, Law of Remedies § 10.1 at 654 (1973). Professor Dobbs further observes that "[I]f it is understood that this does not mean reformation to a true agreement, but reformation to minimum legal standards, then remedy seems entirely suitable." Id. § 10.7 at 707.

In the case at bar, the superior court found unconscionable payment terms that did not pay accrued interest and that would require a balloon payment of over $300,000 in 30 years, secured by an aging building. Under these circumstances, the court ordered the contract reformed so that Vockner had to pay all the interest accrued to the date of judgment and amortize the principal, thereby eliminating the significant balloon payment due after 30 years. The superior court's actions, in our view, comport with Professor Dobbs' analysis that the aim of reformation in these circumstances is to bring the contract in conformity with minimal standards of conscionability.[10]

. . . .

AFFIRMED.

---

9. In the usual situation unconscionability is raised as an affirmative defense. The normal remedy when the court finds unconscionability is for the court to refuse specific performance. D. Dobbs, Law of Remedies § 10.1 at 654 (1973); Restatement (Second) Contracts § 208 comment g at 111 (1981).
10. Within a few months of his purchase of the property from Erickson, Vockner resold the property for $290,000. Thus Vockner is not losing the benefit of what he bargained for and the nonpunitive nature of the remedy noted in the Restatement (Second) Contracts § 206 comment g, is served.

Unconscionability under Article 2 of the UCC (UCC § 2–302)

When a transaction involves a sale of goods, the Uniform Commercial Code simplifies the court's inquiry when the issue of unconscionability arises. Section 2–302 provides:

> (1) If the court as a matter of law finds the contract or any clause of the contract to have been unconscionable at the time it was made the court may refuse to enforce the contract, or it may enforce the remainder of the contract without the unconscionable clause, or it may so limit the application of any unconscionable clause as to avoid any unconscionable result.

(2) When it is claimed or appears to the court that the contract or any clause thereof may be unconscionable the parties shall be afforded a reasonable opportunity to present evidence as to its commercial setting, purpose and effect to aid the court in making the determination.

Unconscionability as a Shield

When the transaction involves a sale of goods, the defendant may under section 2–302 assert that the contract or a clause in the contract is unenforceable due to unconscionability. The court, upon a finding of unconscionable, may refuse to enforce the contract, delete the unconscionable term and enforce the remainder of the contract, or reform the unconscionable term so it no longer produces unconscionable results. Under section 2–302(2), the court may, of its own accord, raise the issue of unconscionability. Also, if the issue of unconscionability is raised, the court *must* hold a hearing to determine the issue. Unconscionability is a question for the court (the judge) to resolve. It is not a question for the jury.

Nowhere in the UCC, including section 2–302, is unconscionability defined. Rather, the common law definition of unconscionability (absence of meaningful choice coupled with unreasonably favorable terms) developed in *Williams v. Walker-Thomas Furniture Co.*, 350 F.2d 445 (D.C. Cir. 1965), is used.

▥ PARALEGAL EXERCISE 8.1

Homer and Felicia Oakley, who are welfare recipients, contracted to purchase a used Chevy Suburban from A-1 Used Cars for $7,000. With the addition of the time credit charges, credit life insurance, credit property insurance, and sales tax, the purchase price totaled $12,300. After the Oakleys paid $6,000, they ceased paying. A-1 brought a breach of contract action against the Oakleys seeking the remaining contract price. The Oakleys claimed that since the Suburban had a blue book price of $3,500 at the time of contract formation, the contract price was unconscionable.

Should the court reform the contract price to the amount paid so the Oakley's will not be in breach of contract? ▪

Unconscionability as a Sword

The previous discussion portrayed unconscionability as a shield. The party claiming unconscionability would assert that the contract or clause sought to be enforced against him or her was unconscionable at the time of contract formation and therefore unenforceable. If the contract was unenforceable, the plaintiff could not maintain a cause of action for breach. If only a term in the contract was unconscionable, that term would be unenforceable.

If the unenforceable term went to the substantive basis for the allegation of breach (source of the duty), there could be no breach and no breach of contract cause of action. If the unenforceable term went to a procedural issue, such as staying the litigation due to a mandatory arbitration provision, the party asserting unconscionability would prevail on the procedural issue.

Unconscionability also may support an action and therefore become a sword. In *Jones v. Star Credit Corp.*, the Joneses were visited at their home by a sales representative from Your Shop At Home Service, Inc. During the visit, the Joneses purchased a $300 home freezer for $900 plus credit life insurance, credit property insurance, and sales tax. After paying over $600, the Joneses brought an action to reform the contract. In reading *Jones,* answer the following:

1. Who is the plaintiff, who is the defendant, what is the plaintiff's cause of action, and what relief is the plaintiff seeking from the court?
2. Did the Joneses and Your Shop At Home Service create a contract?
3. Could the Joneses seek reformation of the price term by claiming the price term was unconscionable?
   a. Was the price term unreasonably favorable toward the Your Shop At Home Service?
   b. Did the Joneses lack a meaningful choice?
      1. What was the relative bargaining power between the parties?
      2. What knowledge did the Joneses have about the price term?

CASE

Jones v. Star Credit Corp.

Supreme Court, Nassau County, New York (1969)
59 Misc.2d 198, 298 N.Y.S.2d 264

SOL M. WACHTLER, Justice.

On August 31, 1965 the plaintiffs, who are welfare recipients, agreed to purchase a home freezer unit for $900 as the result of a visit from a salesman representing Your Shop At Home Service, Inc. With the addition of the time credit charges, credit life insurance, credit property insurance, and sales tax, the purchase price totaled $1,234.80. Thus far the plaintiffs have paid $619.88 toward their purchase. The defendant claims that with various added credit charges paid for an extension of time there is a balance of $819.81 still due from the plaintiffs. The uncontroverted proof at the trial established that the freezer unit, when purchased, had a maximum retail value of approximately $300. The question is whether this transaction and the resulting contract could be considered unconscionable within the meaning of Section 2–302 of the Uniform Commercial Code which provides in part:

> (1) If the court as a matter of law finds the contract or any clause of the contract to have been unconscionable at the time it was made the court may refuse to enforce the contract, or it may enforce the remainder of the contract without the unconscionable clause, or it may so limit the application of any unconscionable clause as to avoid any unconscionable result. (2) When it is claimed or appears to the court that the contract or any clause thereof may be unconscionable the parties shall be afforded a reasonable opportunity to present evidence as to its commercial setting, purpose and effect to aid the court in making the determination. L.1962, c. 553, eff. Sept. 27, 1964.

There was a time when the shield of "caveat emptor" would protect the most unscrupulous in the marketplace—a time when the law, in granting parties unbridled latitude to make their own contracts, allowed exploitive and callous practices which shocked the conscience of both legislative bodies and the courts.

The effort to eliminate these practices has continued to pose a difficult problem. On the one hand it is necessary to recognize the importance of preserving the integrity of agreements and the fundamental right of parties to deal, trade, bargain, and contract. On the other hand there is the concern for the uneducated and often illiterate individual who is the victim of gross inequality of bargaining power, usually the poorest members of the community.

Concern for the protection of these consumers against overreaching by the small but hardy breed of merchants who would prey on them is not novel. The dangers of inequality of bargaining power were vaguely recognized in the early English common law when Lord Hardwicke wrote of a fraud, which "may be apparent from the intrinsic nature and subject of the bargain itself; such as no man in his senses and not under delusion would make." The English authorities on this subject were discussed in Hume v. United States, 132 U.S. 406, 411, 10 S.Ct. 134, 136, 33 L.Ed. 393 (1889) where the United States Supreme Court characterized (p. 413, 10 S.Ct. p. 137) these as "cases in which one party took advantage of the other's ignorance of arithmetic to impose upon him, and the fraud was apparent from the face of the contracts."

The law is beginning to fight back against those who once took advantage of the poor and illiterate without risk of either exposure or interference. From the common law doctrine of intrinsic fraud we have, over the years, developed common and statutory law which tells not only the buyer but also the seller to beware. This body of laws recognizes the importance of a free enterprise system but at the same time will provide the legal armor to protect and safeguard the prospective victim from the harshness of an unconscionable contract.

Section 2–302 of the Uniform Commercial Code enacts the moral sense of the community into the law of commercial transactions. It authorizes the court to find, as a matter of law, that a contract or a clause of a contract was "unconscionable at the time it was made", and upon so finding the court may refuse to enforce the contract, excise the objectionable clause or limit the application of the clause to avoid an unconscionable result. "The principle", states the Official Comments to this section, "is one of the prevention of oppression and unfair surprise". It permits a court to accomplish directly what heretofore was often accomplished by construction of language, manipulations of fluid rules of contract law and determinations based upon a presumed public policy.

There is no reason to doubt, moreover, that this section is intended to encompass the price term of an agreement. In addition to the fact that it has already been so applied (State by Lefkowitz v. ITM, Inc., 52 Misc. 2d 39, 275 N.Y.S.2d 303; Frostifresh Corp. v. Reynoso, 52 Misc.2d 26, 274 N.Y.S.2d 757, revd. 54 Misc.2d 119, 281 N.Y.S.2d 964; American Home Improvement, Inc. v. MacIver, 105 N.H. 435, 201 A.2d 886, 14 A.L.R.3d 324), the statutory language itself makes it clear that not only a clause of the contract, but the contract in toto, may be found unconscionable as a matter of law. Indeed, no other provision of an agreement more intimately touches upon the question of unconscionability than does the term regarding price.

Fraud, in the instant case, is not present; nor is it necessary under the statute. The question which presents itself is whether or not, under the circumstances of this case, the sale of a freezer unit having a retail value of $300 for $900 ($1,439.69 including credit charges and $18 sales tax) is unconscionable as a matter of law. The court believes it is.

Concededly, deciding the issue is substantially easier than explaining it. No doubt, the mathematical disparity between $300, which presumably includes a reasonable profit margin, and $900, which is exorbitant on its face, carries the greatest weight. Credit charges alone exceed by more than $100 the retail value of the freezer. These alone, may be sufficient to sustain the decision. Yet, a caveat is warranted lest we reduce the import of Section 2–302 solely to a mathematical ratio formula. It may, at times, be that; yet it may also be much more. The very limited financial resources of the purchaser, known to the sellers at the time of the sale, is entitled to weight in the balance. Indeed, the value disparity itself leads inevitably to the felt conclusion that knowing advantage was taken of the plaintiffs. In addition, the meaningfulness of choice essential to the making of a contract, can be negated by a gross inequality of bargaining power. (Williams v. Walker-Thomas Furniture Co., 121 U.S.App.D.C. 315, 350 F.2d 445.)

There is no question about the necessity and even the desirability of instalment sales and the extension of credit. Indeed, there are many, including welfare recipients, who would be deprived of even the most basic conveniences without the use of these devices. Similarly, the retail merchant selling on installment or extending credit is expected to establish a pricing factor which will afford a degree of protection commensurate with the risk of selling to those who might be default prone. However, neither of these accepted premises can clothe the sale of this freezer with respectability.

Support for the court's conclusion will be found in a number of other cases already decided. In American Home Improvement, Inc. v. MacIver, supra, the Supreme Court of New Hampshire held that a contract to install windows, a door and paint, for the price of $2,568.60, of which $809.60 constituted interest and carrying charges and $800 was a salesman's commission was unconscionable as a matter of law. In State by Lefkowitz v. ITM, Inc., supra, a deceptive and fraudulent scheme was involved, but standing alone, the court held that the sale of a vacuum cleaner, among other things, costing the defendant $140 and sold by it for $749 cash or $920.52 on time purchase was unconscionable as a matter of law. Finally, in Frostifresh Corp. v. Reynoso, supra, the sale of a refrigerator costing the seller $348 for $900 plus credit charges of $245.88 was unconscionable as a matter of law.

. . . .

> Having already paid more than $600 toward the purchase of this $300 freezer unit, it is apparent that the defendant has already been amply compensated. In accordance with the statute, the application of the payment provision should be limited to amounts already paid by the plaintiffs and the contract be reformed and amended by changing the payments called for therein to equal the amount of payment actually so paid by the plaintiffs.

FRAUD AND MISREPRESENTATION

Although courts often use the terms "fraud" and "misrepresentation" interchangeably, a distinction exists. The Restatement (Second) of Contracts provides that an assertion does not have to be fraudulent to be a misrepresentation. The Restatement (Second) of Contracts § 159 provides:

misrepresentation

A misrepresentation is an assertion that is not in accord with the facts.

> A **misrepresentation** is an assertion that is not in accord with the facts.

A statement the speaker intends as truthful may be a misrepresentation because of ignorance or carelessness.

Example 8–1

Jerry's Electric Company, seeking to induce Bernard to buy a particular generator, wrote Bernard a letter with the intention of describing its output correctly as "1,200 kilowatts." Due to a typist's error, unnoticed by Jerry's, the letter stated that the generator's output was "2,100 kilowatts." When Bernard accepted Jerry's offer, a contract was formed. After Jerry's shipped the generator and Bernard accepted delivery and paid, Bernard discovered the generator's output was only "1,200 kilowatts." Jerry's statement is a misrepresentation as to the output of the generator. Bernard, the party relying on the misrepresentation, may assert that the contract is unenforceable (disaffirm), return the generator, and seek restitution of his purchase price.

fraud in the factum

Fraud in the factum involves the very character of the proposed contract.

A misrepresentation may be fraudulent. A fraudulent misrepresentation may be either fraud in the factum (fraud in the "essence") or fraud in the inducement. **Fraud in the factum** involves the very character of the proposed contract. If the deceived party neither knows nor has reason to know of the character of the proposed contract, the effect of the misrepresentation is that the parties never contracted.

Example 8-2

Rebecca visited Import Motors, Inc., to look at used BMWs. While there Rebecca noticed that Import Motors was giving a free trip to the Bahamas for the winner of a drawing. Quincy, a salesperson, encouraged Rebecca to sign her name to the entry form without reading the fine print. Had she read the fine print she would have discovered that she had purchased the used BMW on display. Since Rebecca did not know that what she had signed was the acceptance of an Import Motors's offer, the effect of the misrepresentation is that she never accepted the offer.

Fraud in the inducement involves a misrepresentation that entices a party to accept an offer. We will focus our attention on this latter type of fraud, fraud in the inducement. Whenever a party fraudulently induces another to enter into a transaction, the deceived party may disaffirm the contract and, in those cases where the defrauded party has conferred a benefit on the defrauding party, claim restitution. This power to disaffirm protects innocent parties from deliberately dishonest statements.

fraud in the inducement

Fraud in the inducement is a false representation or concealment of fact, that should have been disclosed, that deceives and is intended to deceive another party to the contract.

Example 8-3

Marshall induces Betty to purchase a horse by making a statement that the horse is a stallion, when in fact it is a gelding. Betty can disaffirm the contract. Betty can return the gelding and, in a restitution action, recover the purchase price. She may also recover for food, maintenance, and veterinary care as measured by their reasonable value to Marshall.

The court will find the contract unenforceable when a deceived party can establish the following elements of fraud in the inducement:

1. The misrepresentation must be a statement of fact and must be false.
2. The party making the statement must know or believe the statement to be false and, by making the false statement of fact, must intend to influence the other party to act or refrain from acting.
3. The person to whom the statement is made must believe and rely on the statement.
4. The statement must be sufficiently material to induce the party relying on the statement to accept the offer.

☱ PARALEGAL EXERCISE 8.2

Sylvia, of Sylvia's A-1 Used Cars, while attempting to sell Brad a car made statements to him that a particular used car had only 40,000 miles on it. After Brad expressed concern over a lit dashboard warning light indicating faulty brakes, Sylvia further stated that the brakes had been fixed. Relying on these assurances, Brad purchased the car and later discovered that Sylvia had intentionally changed the odometer reading from its prior reading of 85,000 miles and had disconnected the warning light, making it inoperative.

Can Brad disaffirm the contract on the ground that Sylvia's fraudulent conduct precludes enforcement of the contract? ■

☱ PARALEGAL EXERCISE 8.3

Treeland, Inc., represented to Lynn that its grape vines were healthy, free of disease, and suitable for producing wine grapes. Lynn relied on these representations in deciding to purchase the vines. The vines, however, carried a latent disease that had gone undetected by either party prior to purchase. The disease devastated the grape vines soon after purchase, rendering the grape vines incapable of bearing fruit of adequate quality or quantity for Lynn's commercial wine production. Answer the following:

1. Can Lynn disaffirm the contract on the ground that Treeland's fraudulent conduct precludes enforcement of the contract?
2. Would it make any difference whether Lynn acted as a novice gardener or as the experienced owner of a winery? ■

DURESS AND UNDUE INFLUENCE

duress

Duress is the use of any wrongful act or threat to influence a party to contract. Duress has two forms: duress by actual physical force and duress by threat.

duress by actual physical force

This form of duress occurs when a person using physical force compels a party to assent to the contract, even though that party did not intend to contract.

Duress is the use of any wrongful act or threat as a means of influencing a party to contract. Duress takes away a contracting party's "free will." Duress has two forms: duress by actual physical force and duress by threat. In **duress by actual physical force**, a person using physical force compels a party to "assent" to the "contract," even though that party did not intend to contract.

Example 8–4

George presented a document in contract form to Clint for Clint's signature. When Clint refused to sign, George, who was physically stronger, grabbed Clint by the neck and forced him to sign his name. Clint's signature is an ineffective manifestation of assent, and no contract is formed. Clint literally was no more than a mere "mechanical instrument" at the hands of George.

Assent may be induced by someone who is not a party to the contract. The party subject to the duress may disaffirm the contract when the third party uses duress by physical force.

Duress encompasses more than physical force. In **duress by threat**, one party improperly threatens another party to assent to a contract, and the threatened party has no reasonable alternative but to assent. Duress by threat includes "economic duress." In **economic duress**, a party is wrongfully threatened with severe economic loss if the threatened party does not enter the proposed contract.

duress by threat

This form of duress occurs when a person improperly threatens a party to induce assent to a contract, when the threatened party has no reasonable alternative but to assent. Duress by threat includes "economic duress."

economic duress

A party subjected to economic duress is wrongfully threatened with severe economic loss if he or she does not enter the proposed contract.

Example 8-5

Simmons delivered a large order of merchandise to Barnes under a contract for sale. Barnes, knowing that Simmons was in urgent need of cash and was unable to borrow money, refused to pay unless Simmons reduced the contract price by half. Simmons assented to the modification. Barnes's threat amounts to duress. Simmons may disaffirm the modification.

Duress by threat has the following four elements:

1. There must be a threat.
2. The threat must be improper. Improper threats include threats that are either so shocking that the court will not inquire into the fairness of the resulting exchange, such as the threat of a criminal act or criminal prosecution, or threats that in themselves necessarily involve some element of unfairness, such as a breach of the duty of good faith and fair dealing under a contract (often involved with economic duress).
3. The threat must be sufficiently grave to induce the victim to assent. This requires a subjective determination of the victim's perception of the seriousness of the threat.
4. The threat must induce the victim to assent to the contract. A threat does not induce assent if the threatened party has a reasonable alternative to assenting and fails to take advantage of that alternative. Reasonable alternatives may include legal remedies or the availability of similar goods or services in the market place.

𝕀 PARALEGAL EXERCISE 8.4

Reese, a general contractor, was awarded a contract by the government to extend a runway at a military air base. Reese gave Hawkins a subcontract to supply the concrete. After the foundation for the runway had been prepared, Hawkins refused to deliver the concrete unless Reese not only paid more than the contract price for the concrete but awarded Hawkins a subcontract on another job that Reese had. Reese agreed to modify the price and give Hawkins the second contract.

Could Reese disaffirm the modification of the first subcontract due to duress? In evaluating whether Reese could disaffirm, consider the following:

1. Whether Hawkins threatened Reese
2. Whether the threat was improper
3. Whether the threat was sufficiently grave to induce Reese to assent
4. Whether the threat induced Reese to assent to the contract (whether Reese had a reasonable alternative to assenting) ■

⫼ PARALEGAL EXERCISE 8.5

Jill, who had contracted to sell goods to Ben, threatened to refuse to deliver the goods to him unless he modified the contract to increase the price. Ben did not attempt to purchase the goods elsewhere, although he knew that they were available. Being in urgent need of the goods, he agreed to the modification. Jill shipped the goods.

Could Ben disaffirm the modification due to duress? In evaluating whether Ben could disaffirm, consider the following:

1. Whether Jill threatened Ben
2. Whether the threat was improper
3. Whether the threat was sufficiently grave to induce Ben to assent
4. Whether the threat induced Ben to assent to the contract (whether Ben had a reasonable alternative to assenting) ■

When a third party uses duress by threat, the victim of the duress may disaffirm the contract unless the other contracting party has begun performance in good faith and without reason to know of the duress.

Undue influence involves unfair persuasion by a party who is either in a position of dominance or in a position of trust and confidence. Undue influence differs from duress in two ways.

1. Undue influence requires neither threats nor deception, although often one or the other is present.
2. Undue influence requires a special relationship between the parties.

Undue influence often includes the following:

1. The susceptibility of the party influenced, such as the presence of mental or physical weakness
2. The opportunity to exercise undue influence, such as a confidential relationship (including parent-child, husband-wife, attorney-client, or trustee-beneficiary)
3. A resulting transaction that enriches the party exercising the influence at the expense of the party being influenced

undue influence

Undue influence involves unfair persuasion by a party who is either in a position of dominance or in a position of trust and confidence. Undue influence requires neither threats nor deception, although one or the other is often present.

A victim of undue influence may disaffirm the contract unless a third party induces the assent and the other contracting party has begun performance in good faith and without reason to know of the undue influence.

⚏ PARALEGAL EXERCISE 8.6

Johnson, an elderly and illiterate man, lived with his nephew, Barker, and was dependent on him for support. Barker told Johnson that he would no longer support him unless Johnson sold Barker a tract of land called Greenacre. Johnson signed a contract selling Greenacre to Barker.

Could Johnson disaffirm the contract due to undue influence? In evaluating whether Johnson could dissaffirm, consider the following:

1. Whether Johnson was susceptible to Barker's influence
2. Whether Barker had the opportunity to exercise undue influence over Johnson
3. Whether Barker was enriched at the expense of Johnson

Could Johnson disaffirm the contract due to duress? ■

⚏ PARALEGAL EXERCISE 8.7

Tom, inexperienced in business, had for years relied on his local banker, Samantha, for business advice. Samantha constantly urged Tom to sell Jean, Samantha's business associate, a tract of land called Blackacre at a price well below its fair market value. Based on this advice, Tom contracted to sell Blackacre to Jean.

Could Tom disaffirm the contract due to undue influence? In evaluating whether Tom could disaffirm, consider the following:

1. Whether Tom was susceptible to Samantha's influence
2. Whether Samantha had the opportunity to exercise undue influence on Tom
3. Whether Samantha was enriched at the expense of Tom

Could Tom disaffirm the contract due to duress? ■

MISTAKE IN A BASIC ASSUMPTION OF FACT

A **mistake in a basic assumption of fact** involves a situation where the contracting parties believe they were bargaining for something different from what they actually did contract for. Typically, these mistakes involve the existence or identity of the subject matter of the contract.

A "mistake in a basic assumption of fact" problem can be identified by considering five questions:

- What did the contract say?
- At the time of contract formation, what did the *offeror* perceive the contract to mean?

mistake in a basic assumption of fact

A mistake in a basic assumption of fact involves a situation where the contracting parties believe they were bargaining for something different from what they actually did contract for.

- At the time of contract formation, what did the *offeree* perceive the contract to mean?
- At the time of contract formation, what would the *reasonable person* have perceived the contract to mean?
- What were the true facts?

If the issue is mistake in a basic assumption of fact, the offeror, offeree, and reasonable person will all perceive the contract to mean the same thing at the time of contract formation. Their perceptions will coincide. Their perceptions at the time of contract formation, however, will not coincide with the true facts.

Example 8-6

In the famous case of *Sherwood v. Walker,* 66 Mich. 568, 33 N.W. 919 (1887), the mistake involved the sale of Rose 2d of Aberlone. At the time of contract formation both Walker, the seller, and Sherwood, the buyer, believed that Rose was a sterile cow. Therefore, Rose was sold at a sterile cow price. After the contract but before delivery, Walker discovered that Rose was with calf and worth about 10 times the contract price. Walker, therefore, refused to deliver Rose claiming a mistake in a basic assumption of fact.

The following charts the facts in *Sherwood v. Walker.*

The contract term	Rose, a sterile cow
At the time of contracting, the seller perceived the contract to be for—	Rose, a sterile cow
At the time of contracting, the buyer perceived, the contract to be for—	Rose, a sterile cow
At the time of contracting, the reasonable person would have perceived the contract to be for—	Rose, a sterile cow
The subject of the contract ultimately turned out to be	Rose, a pregnant cow

The comments to the Restatement (Second) of Contracts suggest three requirements a party must meet before disaffirming a contract for a mistake in a basic assumption of fact.

1. The mistake must relate to a "basic assumption on which the contract was made," such as the existence or identity of the subject matter.

2. The party seeking to disaffirm must show how the mistake had a material effect on the agreed exchange of performances.
3. The mistake must not involve a risk that the party seeking relief has agreed to bear (as provided in the contract or by implication arising from the party's greater expertise).

Example 8-7

In *Sherwood v. Walker*, the mistake (whether Rose was sterile or able to conceive) involved the very nature of the thing of the bargain, the subject matter of the contract. The mistake had a material effect on the agreed exchange of performances because Rose with calf was worth about 10 times the contract price. Although Walker assumed the risk of undervaluing Rose, the sterile cow, he did not assume the risk of undervaluing Rose, the cow with calf. Therefore, the court permitted Walker, the seller, to disaffirm the contract.

▥ PARALEGAL EXERCISE 8.8

Kitty contracted to sell Northridge Lumber Company a tract of timberland. The high contract price reflected the quantity and quality of the standing timber. At the time of contracting, both parties believed the timber was standing. Unknown to the parties, the timber had recently been destroyed by fire.

Answer the following:

1. Did a mistake as to a basic assumption of fact exist when the parties contracted?
2. Could Northridge show that the mistake had a material effect on the agreed exchange of performances?
3. Did Northridge agree to bear the risk?
4. Could Northridge disaffirm the contract by claiming a mistake in a basic assumption of fact? ▣

Generally, courts allow disaffirmance of only those contracts in which the mistake involves the "identity" or "existence" of the subject matter, rather than mere "quality" or "value."

Example 8-8

Costello sold Sykes ten shares of stock for $316 a share. In fact, employees of the corporation had altered the corporation's books, and the actual value of the stock was $60 a share, rather than $316 a share. Sykes could not successfully sue Costello for breach of contract to recover the contract price based on a mistake in a basic assumption of fact. The mistake relates to "attributes, quality, or value" and not to the "existence or identity" of the stocks sold.

Attorneys who have worked in this area know that this distinction is not always clear, and the application of the law to a set of facts is often difficult.

⫼ PARALEGAL EXERCISE 8.9

Wood found a pretty stone and offered to sell it to Boynton. The parties expressed their ignorance as to the nature of the stone and guessed it to be a topaz. Wood sold the stone to Boynton for one dollar. Later the stone was identified as an uncut diamond worth $1,000. Could Wood rescind the contract due to a mistake in a basic assumption of fact?

Answer the following:

1. Did the mistake relate to a basic assumption on which the contract was made?
2. Could Wood show that the mistake had a material effect on the agreed exchange of performances?
3. What risks did Wood agree to bear in entering into the contract with Boynton?
4. Would it be surprising to learn that the court in *Wood v. Boynton*, 64 Wis. 265, 25 N.W. 42 (1885), held that Wood could not disaffirm?

> The only reasons we know of for rescinding a sale and revesting the title in the vendor so that he may maintain an action at law for the recovery of the possession against his vendee are (1) that the vendee was guilty of some fraud in procuring a sale to be made to him; (2) that there was a mistake made by the vendor in delivering an article which was not the article sold—a mistake in fact as to the identity of the thing sold with the thing delivered upon the sale. . . . There is no pretense of any mistake as to the identity of the thing sold. It was produced by the plaintiff and exhibited to the vendee before the sale was made, and the thing sold was delivered to the vendee when the purchase price was paid. Kennedy v. Panama, etc., Mail Co., supra., 587; Street v. Blay, 2 Barn. & Adol. 456; Gompertz v. Bartlett, 2 El. & Bl. 849; Gurney v. Womersley, 4 El. & Bl. 133; Ship's Case, 2 De G. J. & S. 544. Suppose the appellant had produced the stone, and said she had been told it was a diamond, and she believed it was, but had no knowledge herself as to its character or value, and Mr. Boynton had given her $500 for it. Could he have rescinded the sale if it had turned out to be a topaz or any other stone of very small value? Could Mr. Boynton have rescinded the sale on the ground of mistake? Clearly not, nor could he rescind it on the ground that there

had been a breach of warranty, because there was no warranty, nor could he rescind it on the ground of fraud, unless he could show that she falsely declared that she had been told it was a diamond, or, if she had been so told, still she knew it was not a diamond. See Street v. Blay, supra.

. . . .

The following cases show that, in the absence of fraud or warranty, the value of the property sold, as compared with the price paid, is no ground for a rescission of a sale. Wheat v. Cross, 31 Md. 99; Lambert v. Heath, 15 Mees. & W. 487; Bryant v. Pember, 45 Vt. 487; Kuelkamp v. Hidding, 31 Wis. 503–511. However unfortunate the plaintiff may have been in selling this valuable stone for a mere nominal sum, she has failed entirely to make out a case either of fraud or mistake in the sale such as will entitle her to a rescission of such sale so as to recover the property sold in an action at law.

5. Can the result in Wood be reconciled with the illustration given about Rose 2d of Aberlone? ■

PARALEGAL CHECKLIST

Unenforceable Contracts—Protecting a Party against Overreaching

❏ The fact that a contract has been formed does not necessarily lead to the conclusion that it can be enforced in court by a non-breaching party. The paralegal and the supervising attorney must evaluate whether one of the parties has the power to disaffirm the contract making it unenforceable. The supervising attorney will, of course, always make the final determination in all such matters and will advise the client. The previous chapter dealt with the first category of enforcement problems—protecting members of a class. This chapter deals with the second category—protecting one party against the other party's overreaching. If at the time of contract formation, one of the parties took unconscionable advantage of the other party, procured a contract through fraud or duress, or entered a contract where there was a mistake in a basic assumption of fact, enforcement of the contract may be precluded.

1. Was the offer presented on a take-it-or-leave-it basis? If so, and the offer is accepted, the contract is a "contract of adhesion." A contract of adhesion may be standardized or nonstandardized. Not all contracts of adhesion are unenforceable. A contract of adhesion may be unconscionable and unenforceable in its entirety or in one term only. If the contract is for a sale of goods, see UCC § 2–302. Otherwise, use common law unconscionability.
   a. Ascertain unconscionability by finding out whether superior bargaining power was used to force unreasonably favorable terms on a party (i.e., absence of meaningful choice on the part of one of the parties together with contract terms that are unreasonably favorable to the other party).
      (1) Check for the two components of absence of meaningful choice:
         (a) The imbalance in bargaining power

(b) Lack of knowledge of the terms (e.g., terms hidden in a maze of fine print or minimized by deceptive sales practices)

(2) Analyze whether the contract term unreasonably favors the other party. The term must be considered in light of the circumstances existing when the contract was made. The general commercial background and the commercial needs of the particular trade or case shed light on reasonableness.

b. Consider whether the court might permit unconscionability as a shield or a sword. As a shield, unconscionability may be used to prevent enforcement of a contract on a term in the contract. As a sword, unconscionability may be used to reform a term in the contract. While courts may permit a party to bring an action using unconscionability as the mechanism for reformation of the contract (so the plaintiff owes no more), some courts are reluctant to permit a party to actually recover in restitution for a benefit conferred by the plaintiff when the contract or term in the contract was unconscionable.

2. How are the terms "fraud" and "misrepresentation" distinguishable? An assertion does not have to be fraudulent to be a misrepresentation.

a. Determine whether there was an assertion that is not in accordance with the facts. A statement intended as truthful may be a misrepresentation if made in ignorance or carelessness.

b. Evaluate whether the misrepresentation was fraudulent. A fraudulent misrepresentation may be either

(1) fraud in the factum (fraud in the essence); or

(2) fraud in the inducement.

c. Find out if a party fraudulently induced another to enter into the transaction. If it did, the deceived party may disaffirm the contract and, in those cases where the defrauded party has conferred a benefit on the defrauding party, claim restitution. The elements of fraud are the following:

(1) The misrepresentation must be a statement of fact and must be false.

(2) The party making the statement must know or believe the statement to be false and, by making the false statement of fact, must intend to influence the other party to act or refrain from acting.

(3) The person to whom the statement is made must believe and rely on the statement.

(4) The statement must be sufficiently material to induce the party relying on the statement to accept the offer.

3. Was there duress? Duress is the use of any wrongful act or threat as a means of influencing a party to contract. Duress takes away a contracting party's "free will." Duress has two forms:

(1) Duress by actual physical force

(2) Duress by threat

a. Find out if there was duress by actual physical force. Did a person using physical force compel a party to "assent" to the "contract," even though that party did not intend to contract? If assent was induced by a third party, the party subject to the duress may disaffirm the contract.

b. Determine if there was duress by threat. Duress by threat (including economic duress) has four elements:

(1) There is a threat.

(2) The threat must be improper.

(3) The threat must be sufficiently grave to induce the victim to assent.

(4) The threat must induce the victim to assent to the contract.

When a third party uses duress by threat, the party subject to the duress cannot disaffirm the contract if the other contracting party begins performance in good faith and without reason to know of the duress.

4. Was undue influence exerted by one of the parties? Undue influence differs from duress in two ways:
   a. Undue influence requires neither threats nor deception, although one or the other is often present.
   b. Undue influence requires a special relationship between the parties.

5. Was there a mistake in a basic assumption of fact during contract formation? Courts allow contracting parties adversely affected by a mistake in a basic assumption of fact to disaffirm the contract. This form of mistake pertains to a situation in which the parties believed they were bargaining for something different from the thing for which they actually contracted. Typically, these mistakes concern the existence or identity of the subject matter of the contract.

The following conditions must be met affirmatively for a party to disaffirm a contract for a mistake in a basic assumption of fact:
   a. Determine whether the mistake relates to a "basic assumption on which the contract was made."
   b. Find out whether the party seeking to disaffirm can show how the mistake had a material effect on the agreed exchange of performances.
   c. Determine whether the mistake involves something other than a risk that the party seeking relief has agreed to bear.

Each party bears the risk of a bad bargain that results from failure to investigate the value of the subject matter.

KEY TERMS

Adhesion contract

Duress

Duress by actual physical force

Duress by threat

Economic duress

Fraud in the factum

Fraud in the inducement

Misrepresentation

Mistake in a basic assumption of fact

Unconscionability

Undue influence

REVIEW QUESTIONS

TRUE/FALSE QUESTIONS (CIRCLE THE CORRECT ANSWER)

1. T F   When a court or legislature protects a class, this protection extends to all members of that class in every contractual transaction.

2. T F   A contracting party who is not in a protected class may still be protected from the overreaching of another party.

3. T   F   The terms of a "contract of adhesion" will be enforced because there was a manifestation of assent.

4. T   F   All contracts of adhesion are unenforceable.

5. T   F   The terms of an "adhesion contract" will not be enforced because of the "imposition of will" by one party upon another party during contract formation.

6. T   F   An adhesion contract may be a nonstandardized contract or a standardized contract.

7. T   F   All adhesion contracts are unconscionable.

8. T   F   To determine whether a contract or a contract term is unconscionable, evaluate it as of the time of the allegation of unconscionability.

9. T   F   Unconscionability has been defined by the UCC as an absence of meaningful choice on the part of one of the parties together with contract terms that are unreasonably favorable to the other party.

10. T   F   Absence of meaningful choice has two components:

    (1) The imbalance in bargaining power
    (2) Lack of knowledge of the terms

11. T   F   A gross inequality of bargaining power will not lead to the conclusion of absence of meaningful choice if the other party had knowledge of the terms.

12. T   F   A party could lack knowledge of the terms of a contract if the contract is written in English and the buyer can read only Spanish.

13. T   F   A contract is unconscionable if one party lacked meaningful choice and the other party had no knowledge of that fact.

14. T   F   Determining whether a contract term is reasonable or fair will be done without considering the circumstances at the time the contract was made.

15. T   F   If a case involves a sale of goods, the court must consider whether or not UCC § 2–302 applies when the issue of unconscionability arises.

16. T   F   If a case does not involve a sale of goods, the court may not consider whether the contract or a term in the contract was unconscionable at the time of contract formation.

17. T   F   Unconscionability is a question for the jury.

18. T   F   Under section 2–302(2) of the UCC, the court may, of its own accord, raise the issue of unconscionability.

19. T   F   Unconscionability may be used both as a defense to a breach of contract action and as an action for breach of contract.

20. T   F   Fraud and misrepresentation are interchangeable terms.

21. T   F   An assertion must be fraudulent to be a misrepresentation.

22. T   F   A misrepresentation is "an assertion that is not in accord with the facts."

23. T F A statement a speaker intends as truthful may be a misrepresentation due to ignorance or carelessness.

24. T F A statement a speaker intends as truthful but which is a misrepresentation due to ignorance or carelessness is still fraud.

25. T F A fraudulent misrepresentation may be either fraud in the "factum" or fraud in the "essence."

26. T F Fraud in the "factum" occurs when one party tricks the other into signing a promissory note that the other believes is merely a receipt.

27. T F A typical case of fraud in the "inducement" involves a seller's misrepresentation of the quality of the goods.

28. T F A party who has relied on a misrepresentation made because of ignorance or carelessness may not disaffirm the contract.

29. T F The power to disaffirm a contract protects innocent parties from misrepresentations that are either careless or fraudulent.

30. T F Duress encompasses more than physical force.

31. T F Duress by threat has two elements:
(1) There must be a threat.
(2) The threat must be sufficiently grave to induce the victim to assent.

32. T F Duress by threat includes "economic duress."

33. T F Duress does not take away a contracting party's "free will."

34. T F Undue influence is the same thing as duress.

35. T F Undue influence requires a special relationship between the parties.

36. T F Undue influence requires threats and deception.

37. T F Undue influence involves unfair persuasion by a party who is in either a position of dominance or a position of trust and confidence.

38. T F A contracting party who has been adversely affected by a mistake in a basic assumption of fact may disaffirm the contract.

39. T F A contracting party may disaffirm a contract in which the mistake in a basic assumption of fact involves "quality" or "value."

40. T F A contracting party may not disaffirm a contract in which the mistake in a basic assumption of fact involves the "identity" or "existence" of the subject matter.

FILL-IN-THE-BLANK QUESTIONS

1. _____. A contract formed by one party imposing his or her will upon an unwilling, or even unwitting, party.

2. _____. Occurs when contract negotiations are not between equals, when there is no opportunity to bargain over

the terms, or when one party is unfamiliar with the terms.

3. _____. The imposition by one party of an unreasonably favorable contract or term on the other party who lacked a meaningful choice.

4. _____. The determiner of unconscionability.

5. _____. The UCC section that pertains to unconscionability.

6. _____. An assertion that is not in accord with the facts.

7. _____. A misrepresentation that is a statement of fact known or believed to be false by the party making the statement with the intent of influencing the other party, who believes and relies on the statement, to act or refrain from acting, and the statement is sufficiently material to induce the relying party to accept the offer.

8. _____. A fraudulent misrepresentation that involves the very character of the proposed contract.

9. _____. A fraudulent misrepresentation that typically involves the quality of the goods.

10. _____. Protects contracting parties from deliberately dishonest statements.

11. _____. The use of any wrongful act or threat as a means of influencing a party to contract.

12. _____. Wrongfully threatening a party with severe economic loss if the threatened party does not enter the proposed contract.

13. _____. Unfair persuasion by a party who is in either a position of dominance or a position of trust and confidence.

14. _____. A mistake that involves a situation where both parties believed they were bargaining for something different from the thing for which they actually contracted.

MULTIPLE-CHOICE QUESTIONS (CIRCLE ALL THE CORRECT ANSWERS)

1. The definition of unconscionable is found in which of the following?
   (a) Article 1 of the UCC
   (b) Article 2 of the UCC
   (c) Case law
   (d) Both Article 2 of the UCC and case law
   (e) Article 2A of the UCC

2. Unconscionability is defined as which of the following?
   (a) Absence of meaningful choice on the part of one of the parties
   (b) Gross inequality of bargaining power

    (c) Unreasonably favorable terms

    (d) Deceptive sales practices

    (e) Absence of meaningful choice on the part of one of the parties coupled with unreasonably favorable terms on the part of the other

3. Under UCC § 2–302, the court may

    (a) refuse to enforce the contract.

    (b) delete the unconscionable term and enforce the remaining terms of the contract.

    (c) reform the unconscionable term so it no longer produces an unconscionable result.

    (d) ask the jury to decide whether the contract was unconscionable.

    (e) award damages.

4. Which of the following are the elements of fraud that must be established for a court to find a contract unenforceable?

    (a) The misrepresentation must be a statement of fact.

    (b) The statement must be false.

    (c) The party making the statement must know or believe the statement to be false and, by making the statement, must intend to influence the other party to act or refrain from acting.

    (d) The person to whom the statement is made must believe and rely on the statement.

    (e) The statement must be sufficiently material to induce the party relying on the statement to accept the offer.

5. Undue influence differs from duress in that

    (a) undue influence requires neither threats nor deception.

    (b) undue influence requires deception but not threats.

    (c) undue influence requires threats and deception.

    (d) undue influence requires a special relationship between the parties.

    (e) undue influence requires the party influenced to be susceptible (i.e., the presence of either a mental or physical weakness).

6. Travers contracted to sell "Come from Behind," a racehorse, to Bishop. At the time of contracting, both parties believed "Come from Behind" to be alive and well. Unknown to the parties, "Come from Behind" had recently been severely injured by a careless groom. Bishop could disaffirm the contract under the following theory:

    (a) Unconscionability

    (b) Fraud in the factum

    (c) Fraud in the inducement

    (d) Undue influence

    (e) Mistake in a basic assumption of fact

7. At birth, Simon suffered a brain injury which resulted in an IQ of 79. He lived with his brother, Larry, on the family farm that had been left to Simon by his parents. Larry told Simon that he would

have to move to a group home if he did not sell the farm to Larry. Simon signed the documents conveying the farm to Larry. Simon could disaffirm the contract under the following theory:

(a) Unconscionability
(b) Fraud in the factum
(c) Fraud in the inducement
(d) Undue influence
(e) Mistake in a basic assumption of fact

SHORT-ANSWER QUESTIONS

1. Unconscionability is defined as an absence of meaningful choice on the part of one party coupled with unreasonably favorable terms on the part of the other. Discuss what constitutes absence of meaningful choice.

2. State the four elements of duress by threat.

Contract Enforceability: Protecting the Judicial Process

Chapter 9, the third of three chapters dealing with contract enforceability, discusses protecting the judicial process. Rather than protecting members of a class (Chapter 7) or protecting a party from overreaching (Chapter 8), a legislature or court may protect the judicial process by not permitting disputants to use the courts to promote nonjudicial activity such as perjury, illegality, and inappropriate forum shopping (see Exhibit 9–1).

STATUTE OF FRAUDS

A common misconception is that a contract does not exist without a writing. Whether a contract is written has nothing to do with the

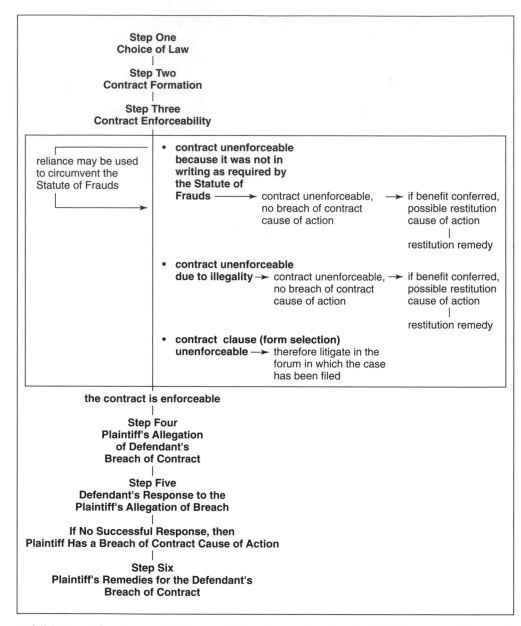

Exhibit 9–1 The Contract Enforceability (Protecting the Judicial Process) Phase of the Road Map

formation of the contract (offer and acceptance) unless the offeror mandates a writing as the method of acceptance.

Although as a general rule a writing is not required for contract formation, written evidence of the contract may be required for the enforcement of the contract.

Example 9-1

Bradley Briggs offered to sell his comic book collection to Kathy Crawford for $200. Bradley's offer also stated that Kathy must accept by registered mail within one week. Bradley has provided a mandatory method of acceptance—registered mail. Therefore, Kathy's written acceptance, sent by registered mail, is the acceptance.

In 1677, the British Parliament enacted a Statute of Frauds that required certain types of contracts to be in writing to be enforceable. The statute had a twofold purpose: cautionary and evidentiary. The necessity of the writing cautioned the parties that this transaction was important and that they should pay attention to what they were doing. This was not a casual transaction without legal significance. The writing also was evidentiary. The terms in the writing were the terms the parties had to follow, even though their memories grew dim. Certainly the opportunity for perjury was reduced by the writing.

In the United States, each state legislature enacted its own Statute of Frauds. Although variations exist from state to state, most are similar. A typical Statute of Frauds may provide:

Promises or Agreements Not Binding Unless in Writing

No action shall be brought upon any of the following agreements or promises, unless the agreement or promise, upon which such action shall be brought or some memorandum or note thereof, shall be in writing, and signed by the party to be charged therewith, or by some other person thereunto by him lawfully authorized:

a. A special promise of an executor or administrator to answer damages out of his own estate;

b. A special promise to answer for the debt, default or mischarge of another person;

c. An agreement made upon consideration of marriage;

d. A contract for the sale of real estate, or any interest in or concerning the same; or

e. An agreement that is not to be performed within one year from the making thereof.

While this Statute of Frauds provides a number of types of contracts that must be in writing to be enforceable, the list is incomplete. The Statute of Frauds dealing with the sale of goods is in Article 2 of the UCC. The Statute of Frauds dealing with the lease of goods is in Article 2A of the UCC. Other Statutes of Frauds may be scattered through a state's statutes.

In 1954, the British Parliament repealed all of its Statutes of Frauds except promises to answer for the debt of another and contracts for the sale of land. American legislatures, however, have been reluctant to follow suit.

This section discusses three types of contracts that must be in writing to be enforceable:

- The contract that cannot be fully performed within one year
- The contract for the transfer of an interest in real property
- The contract for the sale of goods for the price of $500 or more

Contracts That Require a Writing and What Constitutes the Writing

Although not all types of contracts must be in writing to be enforceable, many contracts are written, even though written evidence of the contract was not required for enforcement. A writing addresses a number of problems. The act of writing a contract requires the parties to think about the terms that are to be a part of the writing. Therefore, a written contract may be more definite, refined, and complete than an oral contract, and provides the parties documentation of their promises.

If state statutes require a contract be in writing to be enforceable, what must the writing contain? Different Statutes of Frauds require different writings. The writing required for the contract for the sale of goods for the price of $500 or more differs significantly from the writing for a contract that cannot be fully performed within a year.

Contract Not To Be Performed within One Year

A contract that could not be fully performed within a year from the time of contract formation needs to be in writing to be enforceable. Therefore, a contract whose performance cannot possibly be completed within a year must be in writing. The one-year period runs from the time of contract formation and not from the time when performance begins.

Example 9–2

A contract for a one-day concert recital that will take place 14 months after the date of contracting is within the Statute of Frauds and must be in writing to be enforceable. The fact that the performance will only take one day is irrelevant because the critical time period is between the date of contract formation and the date of full performance. That period is 14 months.

The probability that the contract will be fully performed within the year is irrelevant. What is necessary to bring a contract within the requirements of the Statute of Frauds (requiring a writing) is the lack of any possibility (no matter how slight) that performance will be completed within a year. Whether the contract could or could not be fully performed within a year is not made with 20/20 hindsight. The determination whether the contract could not be fully performed within one year is not made after the parties have performed but as of the date of contract formation.

⚏ PARALEGAL EXERCISE 9.1

The Airport Authority hired the All-Star Construction Company to build a new terminal. Although the normal construction time for such a project was 18 months, All-Star finished the terminal 11 months from the date of contract.

Was this contract under the Statute of Frauds so that a writing was required? Is either the normal construction time or the actual construction time relevant in this determination? At the time of contract formation, was there a possibility that performance could be completed within one year from the date of contract formation? ▨

The Statute of Frauds requires a lack of any possibility of full performance of the contract within one year from the date of contract formation for written evidence of the contract to be necessary. A duty extinguished by full performance is distinguishable from a duty terminated prior to full performance. If a duty to perform is terminated, the duty has not been fully performed. Whether a duty to perform could be terminated within a year of contract formation is irrelevant when determining whether the contract must be evidenced by a writing to be enforceable.

Example 9-3

Pauline Primrose, an actress, contracted to work exclusively for Universal Studios for five years. The contract provided that Universal could waive its rights before one year thus fully performing its contractual duties. Viewing the contract from the time of contract formation, Pauline could die within one year, at which time her contractual duties would terminate. She would not have fully performed. It is also possible that Universal could waive its rights within one year, at which time Universal's contract duties would be fully performed. Since Universal could fully perform within a year, the contract need not be evidenced by a writing to be enforceable by either party.

⫼ PARALEGAL EXERCISE 9.2

Atlas McBee contracts to play football for the Takoma Sasquatch, a professional football team.

1. If the contract is "for five years," must the contract be evidenced by writing to be enforceable?
2. If the contract is "for as long as McBee can play football," must the contract be evidenced by a writing to be enforceable?
3. If the contract is "for five years, but if McBee is injured, the contract is terminated," must this contract be evidenced by a writing to be enforceable? ▪

⫼ PARALEGAL EXERCISE 9.3

Williams, an account executive, entered into a three-year employment contract with the High Profile Advertising Agency. After working for High Profile for six months, Williams was killed in a commercial airplane accident. The employment contract provided that the heirs of any employee would receive $100,000 upon the death of the employee.

Must this contract be in writing to be enforceable? ▪

What must be in the writing to satisfy the Statute of Frauds? The writing must state all the essential terms with reasonable certainty, and the party against whom the contract will be enforced must sign it.

⫼ PARALEGAL EXERCISE 9.4

Anna Aldrich, a realtor, was hired by Metro Realty to sell realty for Metro for two years at $2,000 a month plus commissions. The writing was rather sketchy. While it stated the two-year term, it did not state the salary. The writing was signed by both Aldrich and Metro. In six months, Aldrich is wrongfully (without cause) discharged.

If Aldrich sues Metro for breach of contract, could Metro successfully assert that the contract was unenforceable under the Statute of Frauds? ▪

⫼ PARALEGAL EXERCISE 9.5

Ava, a top model, contracts to pose for a high-fashion magazine for two years at $10,000 a month. The contract was reduced to writing, but only Ava signed it. After six months, Ava is discharged without cause. Ava brings a breach of contract action against the magazine.

Could the magazine successfully claim that the contract was unenforceable under the Statute of Frauds? ▪

⫼ PARALEGAL EXERCISE 9.6

Based on the facts of Paralegal Exercise 9.5, draft a document that would satisfy the Statute of Frauds if Ava were to bring a breach of contract action against the magazine. ▪

Contract for the Transfer of an Interest in Real Property

In addition to the contract for the sale of land, the Statute of Frauds also covers the transfer of a lesser interest in real property. Therefore, to be enforceable, a lease, easement, or mortgage would be within the requirements of the statute and must be evidenced by a writing.

A number of states recognize a "part performance" exception to this category of the Statute of Frauds. If the buyer pays the seller and takes possession of the realty or makes a valuable improvement on the realty with the consent of the seller, a writing is not required. The unequivocal acts of the buyer, in reliance on the seller's promise, leave little doubt that a contract for the sale of the interest in the land has been made. If other remedies are inadequate, it would be unjust to permit the seller to now claim that the contract was unenforceable because it was not in writing.

In *Elizondo v. Gomez*, Elizondo sought to enforce an oral agreement for the sale of real estate. In reading *Elizondo*, consider the following questions:

1. Was there a contract between Elizondo and Gomez?
2. Does the Statute of Frauds require a writing for this contract to be enforceable?
3. Was the writing adequate to satisfy the writing requirement of the Statute of Frauds?
4. Could the contract be enforceable under the part performance doctrine without any written evidence of the contract?

CASE

Elizondo v. Gomez
Court of Appeals of Texas, San Antonio (1997)
957 S.W.2d 862

Before RICKHOFF, LOPEZ and ANGELINI, JJ.
LOPEZ, Justice.
This appeal resulted from appellant's suit raising causes of action . . . for breach of contract. At trial, appellant sought damages and specific performance. Appellant sought to enforce an alleged oral agreement for the sale of real estate based on a "quasi-deed" and partial performance. The trial court found that the statute of frauds barred appellant's claims and ordered appellee to reimburse appellant for the amount of a down payment paid by appellant. . . . We reverse the judgment of the trial court, render in part and remand in part.

FACTS

Appellee, Aida Gomez, holds the deed to property described as three adjacent lots with addresses of 1206 Crystal, 1105 Ferndale, and 1105.5 Ferndale. This property consists of a non-business residence, a retail store, and an adjacent rear apartment, respectively. Appellant, Jesse Elizondo, contends that appellee orally agreed to sell the property for seventy-nine thousand dollars with a five thousand dollar down payment. In support of the oral contract, appellant offered a receipt for the alleged five thousand dollar down payment. The receipt, written on a restaurant "guest check" reads as follows:

> I Jesse Elizondo have paid Mr. & Mrs. Leo Gomez $5000.00 for the Real Estate property located on 1105 Ferndale city of San Antonio, Tex.

The written note contained the alleged signature of Mrs. Leo Gomez.

Appellant never received a deed for the property. At the subsequent trial for specific performance, appellant argued that the "guest check" receipt constitutes a quasi-deed establishing his right to the property as a matter of law. The trial court found the oral contract unenforceable and denied appellant's claims because the oral agreement violates the statute of frauds. However, the trial court ordered appellee to refund the amount of the alleged down payment to appellant.

STATUTE OF FRAUDS

In points of error one through six, appellant argues that the trial court erred in determining that the statute of frauds barred enforcement of appellant's alleged oral agreement for the sale of real estate. The statute of frauds reads in pertinent part that a contract for the sale of real estate "is not enforceable unless the promise or agreement, or a memorandum of it, is (1) in writing; and (2) signed by the person to be charged with the promise or agreement or by someone lawfully authorized to sign for him." Tex. Bus. & Com.Code Ann. § 26.01 (Vernon's 1987). In addition, the writing must adequately describe the property, and the written description must give an amount of information to identify the property with reasonable certainty. Jones v. Kelley, 614 S.W.2d 95, 99 (Tex. 1981); Hebisen v. Nassau Development Co., 754 S.W.2d 345, 351 (Tex.App.–Houston [14th Dist.] 1988, writ denied). Parol evidence may be used to explain or clarify the written agreement, but not to supply the essential terms. Texas Builders v. Keller, 928 S.W.2d 479, 481–82 (Tex. 1996); Morrow v. Shotwell, 477 S.W.2d 538, 541 (Tex. 1972).

Appellant argues that the "guest-check" receipt of an alleged five thousand dollar down payment satisfies the statute of frauds. We disagree. The property in question consists of three parcels of land. Even though the parcels are adjacent to one another, each lot has a separate address; 1105 Ferndale; 1105.5 Ferndale; and 1206 Crystal. The "guest-check" merely identifies the "property located at 1105 Ferndale." Even a most liberal interpretation of the writing, without more, falls short of properly identifying all three lots in question. Therefore, on this basis alone, the writing fails to satisfy the identification requirement of the statute of frauds. Furthermore, the writing fails to properly recite the purchase price of the property. Even if we give the writing full effect, it merely illustrates five thousand dollars of consideration as a down payment. The writing fails to state the full amount of consideration given for the property. Thus, we find the trial court properly found that the writing fails to satisfy the statute of frauds. However, the equitable doctrine of partial performance serves as an exception to the statute of frauds. Leon Ltd. v. Albuquerque Commons Partnership, 862 S.W.2d 693, 702 (Tex.App.–El Paso 1993, no writ); Wiley v. Bertelsen, 770 S.W.2d 878, 882 (Tex.App.–Texarkana 1989, no writ).

In Texas, we may remove an oral contract for the sale of real estate from the statute of frauds when the promisee performs the contract to such a degree that application of the statute would defeat its true purpose. Penwell v. Barrett, 724 S.W.2d 902, 904 (Tex.App.–San Antonio 1987, no writ). The leading case of Hooks v. Bridgewater, 111 Tex. 122, 229 S.W. 1114, 1116 (1921), establishes the three elements required for exemption from the statute of frauds: (1) payment of the consideration, whether it be in money or services; (2) possession by the vendee; and (3) the making by the vendee of valuable and permanent improvements upon the land with the consent of the vendor, or without such improvements, the presence of such facts as would make the transaction a fraud upon the purchaser if it were not enforced. Each of the three elements is indispensable. Penwell, 724 S.W.2d at 904. The alleged oral agreement must unequivocally refer to the agreement and corroborate the fact that a contract actually was made. Chevalier v. Lane's, Inc., 147 Tex. 106, 213 S.W.2d 530, 533–34 (1948). In essence, the performance must supply the key to what was promised. Wiley, 770 S.W.2d at 882.

In the case at bar, the record reveals that in December of 1994, both parties entered into an agreement for the sale of the land in question. The parties agreed to a purchase price of seventy-nine thousand dollars with a five thousand dollar down payment and monthly mortgage payments of seven hundred and ninety-five dollars per month for fifteen years at ten percent interest. On December 24, 1994, appellee delivered the keys to the property to appellant and appellant took possession of all three lots.

In accordance with the terms of the oral agreement, appellant made the agreed monthly payments for April, May, and June. Appellee accepted each payment and made multiple promises to transfer a proper deed. Appellant ceased making the mortgage payments only after appellee interfered with appellant's enjoyment of the property. Appellee misrepresented to the tenants of the property that appellant did not have legal right to the property.

When one party fully performs a contract, the statute of frauds is unavailable to the other who knowingly accepts the benefits and partly performs. Enochs v. Brown, 872 S.W.2d 312, 319 (Tex.App.–Austin 1994, no writ); Estate of Kaiser v. Gifford, 692 S.W.2d 525, 526 (Tex. App.–Houston [1st Dist.] 1985, writ ref'd n.r.e.) (oral installment agreement, payable in 300 monthly installments not barred by statute of frauds because deceased lender made full performance). We find that the facts of the present case fall within the equitable doctrine of partial performance making the oral contract enforceable. Therefore, we affirm appellant's points of error in that the trial court erred in denying appellant's claims based on the application of the statute of frauds.

. . . .

For the reasons recited herein, we reverse the judgment of the trial court, render judgment in favor of appellant, Jesse Elizondo, and remand the case for the determination of damages in accordance with this opinion.

Contract for the Sale of Goods for the Price of $500 or More

Section 2–201(1) of the Uniform Commercial Code mandates:

(1) Except as otherwise provided in this section a contract for the sale of goods for the price of $500 or more is not enforceable by way of action or defense unless there is some writing sufficient to

indicate that a contract for sale has been made between the parties and signed by the party against whom enforcement is sought or by his authorized agent or broker. A writing is not insufficient because it omits or incorrectly states a term agreed upon but the contract is not enforceable under this paragraph beyond the quantity of goods shown in such writing.

To come within the requirements of this Statute of Frauds, there must be a contract for the sale of goods for the price of $500 or more. Therefore, the following are not within *this* Statute of Frauds:

- A transaction for the lease of goods (because it is not a *sale* of goods)
- A transaction for the sale of services (because it is not a sale of *goods*)
- A transaction for the sale of goods for the price of $499.99 (because it is not for the price of $500.00 or more)

⫚ PARALEGAL EXERCISE 9.7

Julius orally contracted with the Apex Door Company for the purchase and installation of overhead doors for his garage. The contract price was $510 less 5 percent if paid by cash or check upon completion of the installation. Prior to commencing work, Julius telephoned the Apex Door Company and canceled the order. Apex Door brought an action for breach of contract against Julius.

Could Julius claim that the contract was unenforceable under UCC § 2–201(1)? ▪

After determining that the contract is for a sale of goods for a price of $500 or more and therefore must be in writing under UCC § 2–201(1), what must the writing contain? Section 2–201(1) states only three requirements:

1. The writing must evidence a contract for the sale of goods.
2. The party against whom enforcement is sought must sign it.
3. The writing must specify a quantity, even though the quantity is inaccurate. Recovery, however, is limited to the quantity stated.

Other terms, although essential to the contract, such as price, time and place of payment or delivery, and warranty, need not be stated in the writing.

⫚ PARALEGAL EXERCISE 9.8

Mom & Pop's Hamburger Haven placed an oral order for 5,000 6-ounce hamburger patties with the delivery person from Quality Meats, Inc. The delivery person completed the purchase order form and gave Mom & Pop's a copy. Mom & Pop's canceled the order before it was delivered.

Could Quality Meats successfully sue Mom & Pop's for breach of contract? Consider whether Mom & Pop's could successfully claim that the contract was unenforceable due to UCC § 2–201(1). What additional facts do you need to determine whether the contract was within the statute? If the contract was within the statute, what additional facts do you need to determine whether the order form would satisfy the writing required by section 2–201(1)? ■

Ⅲ PARALEGAL EXERCISE 9.9

Based on the facts in Paralegal Exercise 9.8, draft a document that would satisfy UCC § 2–201(1) if Quality Meats were to sue Mom & Pop's for breach of contract. ■

Section 2–201(1) begins with the phrase "Except as otherwise provided in *this* section." This means that if a contract must be in writing because it is a contract for the sale of goods for the price of $500 or more, it may still be enforceable even though it does not satisfy the writing requirements of subsection (1). These exceptions are found in subsections (2) and (3) of 2–201:

> (2) Between merchants if within a reasonable time a writing in confirmation of the contract and sufficient against the sender is received and the party receiving it has reason to know its contents, it satisfies the requirements of subsection (1) against such party unless written notice of objection to its contents is given within 10 days after it is received.
>
> (3) A contract which does not satisfy the requirements of subsection (1) but which is valid in other respects is enforceable
>
> (a) if the goods are to be specially manufactured for the buyer and are not suitable for sale to others in the ordinary course of the seller's business and the seller, before notice of repudiation is received and under circumstances which reasonably indicate that the goods are for the buyer, has made either a substantial beginning of their manufacture or commitments for their procurement; or
>
> (b) if the party against whom enforcement is sought admits in his pleading, testimony or otherwise in court that a contract for sale was made, but the contract is not enforceable under this provision beyond the quantity of goods admitted; or
>
> (c) with respect to goods for which payment has been made and accepted or which have been received and accepted (Sec. 2–606).

Subsection (2) addresses the lack of signature in a contract between merchants. In some instances, a written confirmation sent by the party who is not being held liable under the contract may satisfy the signature requirement of the other party.

Example 9-4

The Gotham Zoo telephoned the Pacific Meat Packing Company and placed an order for $10,000 of meat scraps. The scraps were to be delivered in three installments, with the first due one month from the date of the telephone call. Pacific sent the Zoo a written confirmation of the order. The confirmation referenced the telephone call, the quantity, the price, and the delivery date and was signed by Pacific. Pacific sent the first shipment, which was rejected by the Zoo. The shipment was not defective.

Does section 2-201(1) preclude Pacific from enforcing this contract against the Zoo?

Does section 2-201(2) provide relief for Pacific?

Subsection (3)(a) exempts specially manufactured (custom-made) goods from the writing requirement.

Example 9-5

Billy orally contracted to manufacture a neon sign for Steven's bar and grill. When Billy tendered the sign, Steven refused to accept or pay for it.

Is this contract enforceable under section 2-201(1)?

If Billy sues Steven for breach of contract, is the contract enforceable under section 2-201(3)(a)?

Subsection (3)(b) eliminates the UCC § 2-201(1) written evidence of the contract when a party admits in court or in a court document the existence of the contract. The admission of the contract against interest is evidence that a contract did exist.

The contract, however, will not be enforced beyond the admitted quantity.

Example 9-6

Meadowbrook Dairy orally contracted to sell three prize cows and one prize bull to Rolling Hills Farms, a livestock breeder, for $2,500 for each cow and $35,000 for the bull. Several days later, Meadowbrook sold the animals to another breeder for double the price.

Rolling Hills sued Meadowbrook for breach of contract. In its answer to Rolling Hills's petition, Meadowbrook denied the existence of the contract. During the trial, however, Meadowbrook was asked during cross-examination: "Didn't you agree to sell these three prize cows to Rolling Hills for $2,500 each?" Meadowbrook replied: "Yes, sir." The admission of the existence of the oral contract precluded Meadowbrook from asserting the Statute of Frauds. Meadowbrook, however, was not cross-examined about the bull and did not admit the existence of the oral contract as to the bull. Under UCC § 2–201(3)(b), the contract is not enforceable as to the bull.

Subsection (3)(c) eliminates the writing requirement of UCC § 2–201(1) if the seller has accepted payment for the goods or if the buyer accepted shipment of the goods. The actions of the parties evidence the contract.

Example 9–7

Garrison Equipment Company orally contracted to sell a used backhoe to Old McDonald Farms. The price was in excess of $500. Old McDonald Farms sent a cashier's check to Garrison for the agreed purchase price. Garrison deposited the check in its account at First Bank. Several days later, Garrison sold the backhoe to Jonas Higginbotham, a local farmer, for twice the price paid by Old McDonald.

Old McDonald sued Garrison for breach of contract. Although there was no written evidence of the contract as required by UCC § 2–201(1), the fact that Garrison accepted payment evidenced a contract for the sale of the backhoe under UCC § 2–201(3)(c). Garrison could not rely on the Statute of Frauds.

Circumventing the Statute of Frauds through Reliance

Chapter 2 discussed reliance as a cause of action if no offer is made but one party relied on the other's "promise." Chapter 2 also discussed reliance as a tool to circumvent the absence of consideration so the promise could be enforceable in a breach of contract action. Chapter 3 discussed reliance as the basis for creating an implied option contract which in turn would negate the offeror's power to revoke an offer. Once the offeror's power to revoke was negated, the offeree could accept the offer, form a contract, and sue for breach of contract.

This section takes reliance one step further. Could reliance be used to circumvent the lack of a writing as required by the Statute of Frauds? The Restatement (Second) of Contracts § 139 supports using reliance to circumvent the lack of a writing as required by the Statute of Frauds.

§ 139. Enforcement by Virtue of Action in Reliance

(1) A promise which the promisor should reasonably expect to induce action or forbearance on the part of the promisee or a third person and which does induce the action or forbearance is enforceable notwithstanding the Statute of Frauds if injustice can be avoided only by enforcement of the promise. The remedy granted for breach is to be limited as justice requires.

(2) In determining whether injustice can be avoided only by enforcement of the promise, the following circumstances are significant:
   (a) the availability and adequacy of other remedies, particularly cancellation and restitution;
   (b) the definite and substantial character of the action or forbearance in relation to the remedy sought;
   (c) the extent to which the action or forbearance corroborates evidence of the making and terms of the promise, or the making and terms are otherwise established by clear and convincing evidence;
   (d) the reasonableness of the action or forbearance;
   (e) the extent to which the action or forbearance was foreseeable by the promisor.

To circumvent the Statute of Frauds, a party must establish the following:

1. A promise by the promisee
2. That the promisor should reasonably expect the promise to induce action or forbearance on the part of the promisee or a third person
3. That the promise does induce the action or forbearance
4. That injustice can be avoided only by enforcement of the promise notwithstanding the Statute of Frauds

With the exception of the phrase "notwithstanding the Statute of Frauds," the Restatement (Second) of Contracts § 139(1) mirrors § 90(1).

§ 90. Promise Reasonably Inducing Action or Forbearance

(1) A promise which the promisor should reasonably expect to induce action or forbearance on the part of the promisee or a third person and which does induce such action or forbearance is binding if injustice can be avoided only by enforcement of the promise. The remedy granted for breach may be limited as justice requires.

Contract Not To Be Performed within One Year

Whether a contract comes within the one-year Statute of Frauds so that a writing is required is determined by foresight. The determination is made as of the time of contract formation. The determination of whether a writing is required does not depend on hindsight—that is, whether the parties have fully performed within the year. All that is important is whether at the time of contract formation the contract could possibly be fully performed within a year.

Hindsight, however, becomes important when determining whether performance substitutes for the writing after the fact. Part performance, *per se*, does not substitute for the writing. Full performance by one party (hindsight) does take the contract that has been within the Statute of Frauds (foresight) out of the Statute so that the party who fully performs may enforce the contract against the other.

> (1) Where any promise in a contract cannot be fully performed within a year from the time the contract is made, all promises in the contract are within the Statute of Frauds until one party to the contract completes his performance.
>
> (2) When one party to a contract has completed his performance, the one-year provision of the Statute does not prevent enforcement of the promises of other parties. (Restatement (Second) of Contracts § 130 (1981))

As a logical application of this rule, unilateral contracts are taken out of the one-year Statute of Frauds because one party, the offeree, must fully perform to accept the offer and form a contract.

If section 130 is inapplicable because neither party fully performed, then some action or forbearance, although not full performance by one party, may result in the enforcement of the promise if that promise induced the action or forbearance.

> (1) A promise which the promisor should reasonably expect to induce action or forbearance on the part of the promisee or a third person and which does induce the action or forbearance is enforceable notwithstanding the Statute of Frauds if injustice can be avoided only by enforcement of the promise. . . . (Restatement (Second) of Contracts § 139 (1981))

Contract for the Transfer of an Interest in Real Property

If the contract is for the transfer of an interest in real property, part performance may substitute for the writing. Under this "part performance doctrine," one party takes possession of the real property and makes improvements. Judicial relief in the form of specific performance may be ordered when one party relies on the other party's promise to transfer an interest in land. Restatement (Second) of Contracts § 129 (1981) restates the part performance doctrine.

A contract for the transfer of an interest in land may be specifically enforced notwithstanding failure to comply with the Statute of Frauds if it is established that the party seeking enforcement, in reasonable reliance on the contract and on the continuing assent of the party against whom enforcement is sought, has so changed his position that injustice can be avoided only by specific enforcement.

Contract for the Sale of Goods for the Price of $500 or More

The Statute of Frauds provision for the sale of goods is found in section 2–201(1) of the UCC. That section begins:

(1) Except as otherwise provided in this section, a contract for the sale of goods for the price of $500 or more is not enforceable by way of action or defense unless there is some writing sufficient to indicate that a contract for sale has been made between the parties and signed by the party against whom enforcement is sought. . . .

If reliance is to circumvent the Statute of Frauds under section 2–201, one obstacle that must be overcome is the language of section 2–201(1) itself. Subsection (1) begins with the phrase "Except as otherwise provided in this section. . . ." The "in this section" refers to 2–201. Therefore, if the exception is not found in subsection 2–201(2) or (3), the exception does not exist. Since reliance is not found in either subsection (2) or (3), reliance as described in Restatement (Second) of Contracts § 139 (1981) is not an exception to section 2–201(1) for sale of goods.

The following case of *Warder & Lee Elevator, Inc. v. Britten*, illustrates the use of reliance to circumvent the Statute of Frauds. *Warder & Lee* is particularly interesting because it has a strong dissent that illustrates judicial reluctance to use reliance for this purpose. On July 4th, Britten, a farmer, orally contracted to sell 4,000 bushels of corn and 2,000 bushels of beans to the Warder & Lee Elevator for October–November delivery. Warder & Lee, acting in its normal capacity as a broker, immediately sold the corn and beans to a third party. When grain prices increased substantially during July, Britten called Lee and said he wished to "call the deal off." Lee responded, "You cannot call it off. We sold this grain, and we expect delivery this fall." When it became clear that Britten would not deliver, Warder & Lee purchased grain at a higher price to cover its contract with the third person. When Warder & Lee sued Britten for breach of contract, Britten raised the Statute of Frauds as a defense. Identify the reasons that the court and the dissent give for either using or not using reliance to circumvent the Statute of Frauds. Evaluate each reason.

Note in the first paragraph of the court's opinion, Justice McCormick used the phrase "promissory estoppel." Promissory estoppel is an early reference to what we refer to as reliance.

A number of courts continue to use the phrase "promissory estoppel" although the Restatement (Second) of Contracts uses the phrase "reliance" instead. Therefore, the word "reliance" can be substituted for "promissory estoppel."

CASE

Warder & Lee Elevator, Inc. v. Britten
Supreme Court of Iowa (1979)
274 N.W.2d 339

McCORMICK, Justice.

The question in this action for breach of an oral contract to sell grain is whether the trial court erred in holding defendant's statute of frauds defense under the Uniform Commercial Code was defeated by promissory estoppel. We affirm the trial court.

This case was tried to the court at law. The trial court's findings of fact have the effect of a special verdict and we examine the evidence in the light most favorable to the judgment. We are not bound by trial court determinations of law. Kurtenbach v. TeKippe, 260 N.W.2d 53, 54–55 (Iowa 1977).

Plaintiff Warder & Lee Elevator, Inc., operates a grain elevator in the town of Webster. The corporation president, Francis Lee, managed the elevator for many years until he suffered a slight stroke in November 1974. He was succeeded as manager by his son James who had been an elevator employee since 1964. The Lees were the only witnesses at trial.

We recite the evidence in the light most favorable to the judgment. Francis Lee was alone in the elevator office on July 4, 1974. Defendant John W. Britten, a farmer in the area, came to the office during the morning with a friend. The elevator had purchased Britten's grain for years, and he and Lee were well acquainted. At Britten's request Lee quoted him the price the elevator would pay for new-crop corn and soybeans for fall delivery based on market prices of the prior day.

Britten offered to sell and Lee agreed for the elevator to purchase from Britten 4000 bushels of corn at $2.60 per bushel and 2000 bushels of beans at $5.70 per bushel for October–November delivery.

The elevator did not at that time require a seller to sign a memorandum or other writing to show the agreement. Instead, the only writing consisted of notes showing the terms of sale made by Lee for internal bookkeeping purposes. All of the elevator's prior purchases from Britten had been upon oral agreement, and Britten had kept his promises on each occasion. In fact, no seller had previously refused to perform an oral agreement with the elevator.

It was the custom of the elevator not to speculate in grain but to act essentially as a broker. Thus on July 5, 1974, the elevator sold the same quantities of corn and beans as were involved in the Britten purchase for fall delivery to terminal elevators at Muscatine for a few cents more per bushel.

Grain prices increased substantially during July. On July 29, 1974, Britten called Francis Lee and said he wished to "call the deal off". Lee told him: "You cannot call it off. We sold this grain, and we expect delivery this fall." Britten said he would not deliver the grain.

In an effort to mitigate its loss and to enable it to meet its commitment to sell the grain, the elevator purchased appropriate quantities of new-crop corn and beans from other farmers on and shortly after July 29.

In August 1974, James Lee met Britten on a street in Webster. Britten initiated a conversation in which he said he would not fulfill his agreement and offered $500 in settlement. Although counsel for Britten objected to the admissibility of the evidence at trial, the objection was untimely and no motion to strike was made. Lee rejected the offer. He told Britten the elevator had sold the grain and expected him to perform under his contract.

Britten sold his 1974 crop elsewhere.

The elevator brought this action against Britten for breach of the oral agreement, seeking as damages the loss it sustained in covering its delivery obligation under the July 5 contracts by which it sold the quantity of grain purchased from Britten. See § 554.2712, The Code. That loss was $6478.34, which was the amount, plus interest, for which the trial court entered judgment.

Britten offered no evidence at trial. He relied solely on the statute of frauds in § 554.2201, The Code. The elevator urged promissory estoppel in bar of the defense.

The statute of frauds applicable to the sale of crops is § 554.2201. Under this statute an oral contract for the sale of goods for a price of $500 or more is unenforceable, with certain stated exceptions. The elevator does not contend any of those exceptions is applicable. Promissory estoppel is not among them.

Authority for use of promissory estoppel to defeat the statute of frauds, if it exists, must be found under § 554.1103. It provides:

> Unless displaced by the particular provisions of this chapter, the principles of law and equity, including the law merchant and the law relative to capacity to contract, principal and agent, estoppel, fraud, misrepresentation, duress, coercion, mistake, bankruptcy, or other validating or invalidating cause shall supplement its provisions.

We have not had occasion to decide whether the provisions of § 554.2201 displace the doctrine of estoppel which would otherwise be available in accordance with § 554.1103. However, other courts which have considered the question have held the doctrine is available. Several of those decisions involved grain sales in circumstances analogous to those in the present case. See Decatur Cooperative Association v. Urban, 219 Kan. 171, 547 P.2d 323 (1976); Jamestown Terminal Elevator, Inc. v. Hieb, 246 N.W.2d 736 (N.D. 1976); Farmers Elevator Company of Elk Point v. Lyles, 238 N.W.2d 290 (S.D. 1976).

When other courts have refused to apply the doctrine they have done so because of a different view of the doctrine of promissory estoppel rather than because of any perceived statutory bar to its use. See Cox v. Cox, 292 Ala. 106, 289 So.2d 609 (1974); Del Hayes & Sons, Inc. v. Mitchell, 304 Minn. 275, 230 N.W.2d 588 (1975); Farmland Service Coop. v. Klein, 196 Neb. 538, 244 N.W.2d 86 (1976).

We have long recognized promissory estoppel as a means of defeating the general statute of frauds in § 622.32, The Code. See Miller v. Lawlor, 245 Iowa 1144, 66 N.W.2d 267 (1954); Shell Oil Co. v. Kelinson, 158 N.W.2d 724 (Iowa 1968); Johnson v. Pattison, 185 N.W.2d 790 (Iowa 1971). We see nothing in § 554.2201 which purports to require a different rule under the Uniform Commercial Code.

The listing of exceptions to the statute of frauds in § 554.2201 is plainly definitional. The provision does not purport to eliminate equitable and legal principles traditionally applicable in contract actions. Therefore it does not affect the viability of defenses to application of the rule of evidence which it defines. See White and Summers, Handbook of the Law Under the Uniform Commercial Code § 2–6 at 59 (1972) ("There is every reason to believe these remain good law, post-Code.").

If § 554.2201 were construed as displacing principles otherwise preserved in § 554.1103, it would mean that an oral contract coming within its terms would be unenforceable despite fraud, deceit, misrepresentation, dishonesty or any other form of unconscionable conduct by the party relying upon the statute. No court has taken such an extreme position. Nor would we be justified in doing so. Despite differences relating to the availability of an estoppel defense, courts uniformly hold "that the Statute of Frauds, having been enacted for the purpose of preventing fraud, shall not be made the instrument of shielding, protecting, or aiding the party who relies upon it in the perpetration of a fraud or in the consummation of a fraudulent scheme." 3 Williston on Contracts § 553A at 796 (Third Ed. Jaeger, 1960). The estoppel defense, preserved on the same basis as the fraud defense by § 554.1103, developed from this principle. "The Statute was designed as the weapon of the written law to prevent frauds; the doctrine of estoppel is that of the unwritten law to prevent a like evil." Id. at 797–798.

We have found no reported decision in any jurisdiction holding that the statute of frauds in the Uniform Commercial Code, defined as it is in § 554.2201, displaces principles preserved in § 554.1103. We do not believe that our legislature intended for it to do so.

We hold that the provisions of § 554.2201 do not displace the doctrine of estoppel in relation to the sale of goods in Iowa.

We recently discussed the elements of promissory estoppel in Merrifield v. Troutner, 269 N.W.2d 136, 137 (Iowa 1978). Those elements are (1) a clear and definite oral agreement, (2) proof that the party urging the doctrine acted to his detriment in relying on the agreement, and (3) finding that the equities support enforcement of the agreement.

. . . .

Specific circumstances which justify use of the doctrine as a means of avoiding a statute of frauds defense are now expressed in Restatement (Second) of Contracts § 217A (Tent. Draft 1–7, 1973), as follows:

(1) A promise which the promisor should reasonably expect to induce action or forbearance on the part of the promisee or a third person and which does induce the action or forbearance is enforceable notwithstanding the Statute of Frauds if injustice can be avoided only by enforcement of the promise. The remedy granted for breach is to be limited as justice requires.

(2) In determining whether injustice can be avoided only by enforcement of the promise, the following circumstances are significant:

    (a) the availability and adequacy of other remedies particularly cancellation and restitution;

    (b) the definite and substantial character of the action or forbearance in relation to the remedy sought;

    (c) the extent to which the action or forbearance corroborates evidence of the making and terms of the promise, or the making and terms are otherwise established by clear and convincing evidence;

(d) the reasonableness of the action or forbearance;

(e) the extent to which the action or forbearance was foreseeable by the promisor.

This section complements Restatement (Second) of Contracts § 90, the predecessor of which we previously approved. See Miller v. Lawlor, supra. We now approve and adopt the standard in § 217A.

. . . .

In order to obtain the benefit of the doctrine of promissory estoppel to defeat a statute of frauds defense, the promisee must show more than the nonperformance of an oral contract. See 3 Williston on Contracts § 553A (Third Ed. Jaeger, 1960). Under § 217A the defense cannot be overcome, when it is otherwise applicable, unless the promisee proves (1) the promisor should reasonably have expected the agreement to induce action or forbearance, (2) such action or forbearance was induced, and (3) enforcement is necessary to prevent injustice.

In determining whether injustice can be avoided only by enforcement of the promise, the circumstances listed in § 217A(2) must be considered. In this manner, § 217A provides a means of deciding whether the equities support enforcement of the agreement.

We must now decide whether the trial court erred in applying the doctrine of promissory estoppel in this case.

. . . .

Although Britten's second contention presents a closer question, we also find it is without merit. We do so because we believe substantial evidence supports the inference he expected or reasonably should have expected the agreement to induce action by the elevator. It was not necessary for the elevator to prove he actually knew it would rely on his promise. He should have known his prior dealings with the elevator gave the elevator manager every reason to believe he would keep his word. Furthermore, it is reasonable to believe that a farmer who sells grain regularly to country elevators knows they may immediately sell the grain which they purchase. In this case, Britten expressed no surprise when the elevator refused to allow him to rescind because of its sales in reliance on the agreement. Instead he sought to buy his way out of the transaction.

We conclude that the elements of promissory estoppel were supported by substantial evidence. In keeping with the standard in Restatement § 217A, we hold that injustice could be avoided only by enforcement of Britten's promise. The trial court did not err in holding the agreement was enforceable despite the statute of frauds defense.

AFFIRMED.

All Justices concur except REYNOLDSON, C.J., and ALLBEE, J., who dissent.

REYNOLDSON, Chief Justice (dissenting).

I respectfully dissent. The contract in issue falls squarely within the language and intent of the statute of frauds, § 554.2201, The Code 1973. The majority opinion, in my view, misapprehends and misapplies our rules relating to promissory estoppel. Further, the facts in this case do not bring it within the new principles pioneered in this decision.

I. In 1965 the Iowa legislature enacted the "Uniform Commercial Code–Sales." Sixty-First General Assembly, ch. 413, § 2101. It was "a complete revision and modernization of the Uniform Sales Act." D. Stanley & C. Coulter, Iowa Code Comment, 35 I.C.A. § 554.2101 at 118 (1967). Section 554.2201, the UCC's statute of frauds, underwent a substantial liberalizing overhaul designed to eliminate undesirable and overly technical features of the former law. See D. Stanley & C. Coulter, supra, at 145–48; 3 R. Dusenberg & L. King, Sales & Bulk Transfers under the UCC § 2.05 (1978); R. Hudson, *Contracts In Iowa Revisited*, 15 Drake L.Rev. 61, 75–77 (1966); A. Squillante, *Sales Law In Iowa Under The UCC– Article 2*, 20 Drake L.Rev. 1, 61–65 (1970).

At the same time the statute was modified to clarify that its exceptions were limited to those contained in its provisions. Before 1919 the predecessor to § 622.32, our general statute of frauds, covered "sale[s] of personal property." See § 4625, The Code 1897. In 1919 the Uniform Sales Act and its statute of frauds were enacted and the general statute was correspondingly revised. Compare §§ 554.4 and 622.32, The Code 1962. The catch-all exception in § 622.33, "or when there is any other circumstance which, by the law heretofore in force, would have taken the case out of the statute of frauds," ceased to be applicable to sales of goods. Retained as applicable, however, were the "failure to deny" and "oral evidence of the maker" exceptions contained in § 622.34 and .35 respectively. See § 554.5, The Code 1962.

The lead sentence in § 554.2201 now provides:

> Except as otherwise provided *in this section* a contract for the sale of goods for the price of five hundred dollars or more is not enforceable by way of action or defense unless there is some writing sufficient to indicate that a contract for sale has been made between the parties and signed by the party against whom enforcement is sought or by his authorized agent or broker. (Emphasis provided.)

The § 622.34 and .35 exceptions are now incorporated in (3)(b) of the section. The specific limitation of exceptions to those contained "in this section" reflects a marked change from former § 554.4.

With exceptions to the statute of frauds now specifically limited by the terms of the statute to those enumerated in its provisions, the majority's claim that promissory estoppel may be engrafted as simply another exception by virtue of § 554.1103 loses viability. Section 554.1103 permits application of other legal principles, including estoppel, "unless displaced by the particular provisions of this chapter." Plainly, the limiting language of § 554.2201 constitutes such a displacement. Had the legislature intended the concepts of §§ 90 and 217A of the tentative draft of the Restatement (Second) of Contracts to serve as an exception to its statute of frauds, it would have incorporated them as an exception in the act.

Displacing § 554.1103 with the exceptions in § 554.2201 does not render ineffectual the common-law principles contained in the former. First, they supplement other sections of the UCC except those, like § 554.2201, which provide otherwise. Second, the victim of fraud who has no legal remedy because § 554.2201 prevents proof of the oral contract is not left out in the cold. The equitable remedy of restitution is not dependent upon proof of a contract. The basic elements of equitable estoppel and fraud are (1) intentional misrepresentation, (2) innocent, reasonable and foreseeable reliance, and (3) injury. See Walters v. Walters, 203 N.W.2d 376, 379 (Iowa 1973), quoted in Merrifield v. Troutner, 269 N.W.2d 136, 137 (Iowa 1978) (equitable estoppel); Grefe v. Ross, 231 N.W.2d 863, 864 (Iowa 1975) (fraud). Nor is a contract enforced in those situations.

Recovery is based on the injury suffered in the course of reliance. As we stated in *Grefe*, the liability is predicated on the fraud, not on any contract. 231 N.W.2d at 868. With these remedies available, the statute of frauds gives a fraudulent party little protection.

The limiting language of § 554.2201 at least ought to displace a doctrine which would gut the legislative intent of the statute. Distilled to its essence, § 217A, as interpreted by the majority, provides that if one contracting party should know the other contracting party will rely on the contract and injustice will result if the oral contract is not enforced, the statute of frauds will be ignored. It is a rare case when either promisor in a bilateral contract does not rely on the contract. *Del Hayes & Sons, Inc. v. Mitchell,* 304 Minn. 275, 284, 230 N.W.2d 588, 594 (1975). Any party to a contract should realize such reliance occurs. Most situations in which such an oral contract is breached result in injustice.

But the § 554.2201 statute of frauds obviously is designed to suffer these injustices in isolated oral contract cases in favor of the general public policy to reduce fraud and perjury, curtail litigation and controversy, and encourage written contracts in sales of goods for a price of $500 or more. It is significant that by trial time the plaintiff corporation in the case at bar was using written sales contracts with its customers.

Adopting §§ 90 and 217A as an unwritten exception to § 554.2201 will not only encourage oral contracts, it will bring a massive infusion of litigation to our overloaded courts. Trial courts will be compelled to determine, on an *ad hoc* basis, whether there was a contract, whether the promisor could "reasonably expect" the other party to rely on it, whether reasonable action or forbearance resulted, whether "justice requires" a remedy, and otherwise engage in the delicate balancing maneuvers mandated by § 217A(2).

In the final analysis, the majority opinion means written contracts are unnecessary in initial purchases or agricultural products, probably Iowa's largest economic marketplace and involving almost three billion dollars worth of goods each year. We should proceed down that road with great caution.

It is just as clear the majority is moving against a longtime trend:

> This attitude [to extend exceptions to the statute of frauds] has given way gradually, and from quite an early period the statute of frauds has frequently been spoken of as a most beneficial statute which should be liberally construed to effect its object. The wisdom of the statute is a matter within the control of the legislature, not the judiciary, but it has been said to be justified by long experience. The tendency has long been to restrict rather than to enlarge and multiply the cases of exceptions to the statute, and the right to invoke the statute as a defense is no longer regarded with disfavor. The courts should not be tempted to turn aside from its plain provisions merely because of the hardship of the particular case. They should not be controlled by the consequences following upon an application of the statute, or deem obnoxious a law which the legislature has placed in the statutes and allowed to remain for many years, and they cannot disregard the statute. They certainly should refuse to sanction such a construction as would permit the evils that the statute was intended to prevent.

73 Am.Jur.2d Statute of Frauds § 511 (1974).

II. Aside from the above factors, I am convinced promissory estoppel is not an appropriate device to serve as an exception to the statute of frauds.

. . . .

The effect of promissory estoppel on § 554.2201 under the majority opinion is devastating. If the statute is to be repealed the policy decision should be left with the legislature.

III. Finally, it should be noted the facts in this case would not warrant application of § 217A of the Restatement Tentative Draft.

Imposition of § 217A would require proof the defendant seller in this case "should reasonably expect" that the plaintiff corporation would promptly resell the grain. There is no evidence in the transcript in this case to show defendant either knew this was plaintiff's practice or that it was a custom in the industry.

Majority seeks to supply this crucial missing proof by asserting "it is reasonable to believe a farmer who sells grain regularly to country elevators knows they may immediately sell the grain which they purchase."

Majority seems to be judicially noting not only what defendant knew about elevator operations but also the sales practices in a private industry. I doubt these matters qualify for judicial notice as being within common knowledge or capable of certain verification. Motor Club of Iowa v. Department of Transp., 251 N.W.2d 510, 517 (Iowa 1977). Plaintiff corporation's operating officer did not assume defendant had this knowledge. He felt compelled to tell defendant the grain had been resold. This, of course, was long after the event and had no bearing on whether defendant should have "reasonably expect[ed]" such action.

I would reverse and remand for a new trial, during which proof of the alleged contract would be regulated by § 554.2201 undiluted by promissory estoppel.

Could Restitution Be a Cause of Action When the Contract Is Unenforceable Due to the Statute of Frauds?

If one of the parties to an oral contract confers a benefit on the other and the contract is unenforceable by reason of the Statute of Frauds, a restitution cause of action may be available to prevent unjust enrichment.

> A party who would otherwise have a claim in restitution under a contract is not barred from restitution for the reason that the contract is unenforceable by him because of the Statute of Frauds unless the Statute provides otherwise or its purpose would be frustrated by allowing restitution. (Restatement (Second) of Contracts § 375 (1981))

Permitting the restitution cause of action is not the same as enforcing the contract. These restitution actions only occur when the contract is unenforceable due to the Statute of Frauds. The plaintiff in a restitution action proves only an enrichment (benefit conferred by the plaintiff on the defendant)—and that permitting the defendant to retain the benefit without compensating the plaintiff would be unjust. The plaintiff need not allege the defendant's breach of contract nor does the plaintiff need to defend against the defendant's response to the plaintiff's allegation of breach. If a restitution action can be maintained, the plaintiff is not entitled to an expectation remedy (putting the nonbreaching party forward to the position he or she would have been in had the contract been fully performed) since the expectation remedy is only granted in a breach of contract action. The plaintiff in a restitution cause of action is limited to a restitution remedy (reasonable value to the defendant of the benefit the plaintiff conferred on the defendant).

Contract That Cannot Be Fully Performed within a Year

If a contract is unenforceable due to the one-year Statute of Frauds and one party has conferred a benefit on the other without receiving compensation, the party who has conferred the benefit may recover in a restitution action for the reasonable value of the benefit to the recipient.

Example 9–8

Weaver contracted in writing to work for the General Chemical Company for two years at $60,000 a year. His salary was to be paid in monthly installments of $5,000. Shortly after Weaver began work, General Chemical Company became insolvent. Weaver, General Chemical, and General Metals entered into an oral contract whereby Weaver would work for General Metals under the same arrangements he had with General Chemical and General Chemical would be discharged. After working for General Metals for several months, Weaver quit because he was not being paid.

Weaver could successfully sue General Metals in a restitution action. Weaver's recovery would be measured by the reasonable value of his services to General Metals.

Contract for the Transfer of an Interest in Real Property

Courts generally hold that the vendee who pays money, renders services, or transfers personal property under an oral contract to transfer an interest in real property may recover in restitution if the vendor repudiates the agreement.

Example 9-9

A vendee makes a $1,000 down payment to the vendor under an oral contract for the purchase of a farm. Subsequently, the vendee tenders the balance of the purchase price to the vendor, but the vendor refuses to accept the tender of the price and refuses to convey the farm. The vendee may recover the $1,000 down payment in a restitution action.

If the vendor has conferred a benefit on the vendee, the vendor may recover in a restitution action the reasonable value of the benefit conferred.

Example 9-10

If the vendee, who has been in possession of the land, repudiates the oral contract for the sale of the land, the vendor may recover in a restitution action for the use and occupation of the land.

If the vendor has not conferred a benefit on the vendee, the vendor cannot maintain a restitution action.

PARALEGAL EXERCISE 9.10

Sammy orally contracted to sell his hot dog stand on Coney Island to Cassandra for $50,000. Several days later, Cassandra backed out of the deal. Sammy then sold his hot dog stand to Tony for $45,000.

Could Sammy successfully maintain a restitution action against Cassandra?

Contract for the Sale of Goods for the Price of $500 or More

If the contract is for the sale of goods for $500 or more—and therefore under section 2-201(1) a writing is required—and if the buyer has relied on the contract and has paid for the goods and the seller has accepted the payment (or the seller has shipped the goods and the buyer has received and accepted the shipment) the contract is enforceable even though no subsection (1) writing exists. UCC § 2-201(3)(c) provides that:

> (3) A contract which does not satisfy the requirements of subsection (1) but which is valid in other respects is enforceable
>
> . . .
>
> (c) with respect to goods for which payment has been made and accepted or which have been received and accepted (Section 2-606).

Therefore, the cause of action if either the seller does not ship (or ships substandard goods) or the buyer does not pay is breach of contract—and the nonbreaching party is entitled to the appropriate Article 2 expectation remedies.

ILLEGALITY

Illegality as a Defense to a Breach of Contract Action

A contract may be unenforceable due to illegality. The illegality may take different forms. The contract in its entirety may be illegal or the contract may have an illegal term. The contract may be legal but an illegal act may have been used to procure the legal contract or an illegal act may have been committed during the performance of the legal contract.

Example 9-11

- An illegal contract: A contract to commit murder.
- A legal contract with an illegal term: An employment contract that contains an unreasonable covenant not to compete.
- A legal contract procured by an illegal act: A contract for the sale of goods that was procured by the seller bribing the buyer's agent.
- A legal contract performed in an illegal manner: A contract for the sale of real estate where the buyer robs a bank to make the down payment.

Illegal Contract and Illegal Terms

A contract that violates the law is illegal and therefore unenforceable. The court will not aid either party when the contract is illegal, regardless of whether the contract has been performed by one party or both. The court will not become the paymaster for an illegal contract but will leave the parties where it finds them.

Example 9-12

Henry Moran hired Peter Brooks to transport a dozen cases of illegal whiskey from one county in the state to another. The act of transporting was itself illegal. Moran gave Brooks $500 and promised to give him another $500 after the job was done. After Brooks transported the whiskey, Moran refused to pay him the additional $500.

If Brooks were to sue Moran for breach of contract, the court would find the contract unenforceable due to illegality. The purpose of the contract was to perform an illegal act.

⫼ PARALEGAL EXERCISE 9.11

James, an employee of the Calhoun Packing Company, was injured on the job. Shortly after the injury, James and the Packing Company entered into a contract whereby the Packing Company promised James lifetime employment for his promise to waive his worker's compensation claim. Five years later, the Packing Company fired James without cause. A state statute provides, "No agreement by an employee to waive his or her rights to compensation under the worker's compensation law shall be valid."

Could James enforce this contract for lifetime employment against the Packing Company? ■

⫼ PARALEGAL EXERCISE 9.12

Hope, a livestock hauler, entered into a three-year contract with Cox Feedlots that provided Cox would act as a broker, arranging hauling contracts for Hope. In return, Hope would haul all of Cox's livestock to and from the Cox Feedlot, haul all livestock owned by third parties to and from the Cox Feedlot, and pay Cox 10 percent of the gross income for the brokerage services. When Cox discovered that the brokerage fee was, in reality, a rebate in violation of state law, he stopped arranging the hauling contracts with third persons for Hope.

Could Hope enforce this contract against Cox? ■

Because the law of the jurisdiction in which performance of the contract occurs usually governs the contract, the issue of the illegality of a contract is ordinarily determined in accordance with the law of the place where the contract is performed.

⫼ PARALEGAL EXERCISE 9.13

Alex and Carrie contracted in Michigan to sell Michigan lottery tickets in Oklahoma. The contract provided that Alex would buy tickets in Michigan and Carrie would sell them in Oklahoma at a 10 percent markup. The sale of lottery tickets is legal in Michigan but illegal in Oklahoma.

Alex bought the tickets and gave them to Carrie. Having sold them in Oklahoma, Carrie refused to give Alex the proceeds from the sale.

If Michigan law governs, could Alex enforce this contract against Carrie?

If Oklahoma law governs, could Alex enforce this contract against Carrie?

Should the law of Michigan or Oklahoma apply? ■

A covenant not to compete may be illegal as an impermissible restraint on trade when it sweeps too broadly. Parties often use a covenant not to compete in a contract for the sale of a business. This covenant protects the buyer's purchase of the business's goodwill. A covenant may extend only to what is reasonably necessary in terms of subject matter, geography, and duration to protect the buyer's legitimate interest in the enjoyment of the asset purchased.

⚏ PARALEGAL EXERCISE 9.14

Rhodes, a minority shareholder and president of SIS, a security guard business, sold his shares to SIS and left the company. The contract for sale contained the following covenant:

> Covenant by Seller not to Solicit Buyer's Customers. Seller covenants and agrees that for a period of two years from the date of this agreement, Rhodes will not, within a radius of 50 miles of City Hall, Philadelphia, Pennsylvania, directly or indirectly, as a corporation or as an individual, nor will any business entity or corporation of which he is an owner, shareholder, officer, employee, representative, or otherwise, either directly or indirectly, own, manage, operate, control or participate in the ownership, management, operation of or control of or be connected in any manner with or assist others in, the security guard business.

After leaving SIS, Rhodes organized and became associated with Rhodes Investigative Services, a detective agency, and with Hahn Security Service, a security guard business. Both were located in Philadelphia.

Can SIS enforce the covenant against Rhodes as it pertains to his detective agency?

Can SIS enforce the covenant against Rhodes as it pertains to his security guard business? ⬛

An employer hiring a new employee may also use a covenant not to compete when it is either necessary to prevent the disclosure of the employer's trade secrets or confidential lists or the employee's services are special, unique, or extraordinary. In light of the interests the employer is seeking to protect, the covenant must be reasonable in terms of the activities it prohibits the employee from doing, the geographic area in which the employee's activity is prohibited, and the length of time for which the employee is prohibited from doing the activity.

⚏ PARALEGAL EXERCISE 9.15

Apex Sales & Service is in the business of selling and servicing fire protection equipment. When Peters applied for a job with Apex, he executed a written application that contained the following paragraph:

> I further agree that if employed and after working for the company six months or more, I elect to quit, I will not participate in the sale or service of fire protection or safety equipment in the Counties of Harris and Galveston in the State of Texas for a period of two years.

After working for Apex for more than three years, Peters quit and went to work for Delta Safety and Supply Company, a direct competitor of Apex. While at Apex, Peters had been engaged in inspecting, maintaining, testing, and repairing fire protection equipment in various business establishments, particularly in restaurants. At Delta, Peters is the shop manager and oversees Delta's service personnel.

By working at Delta, has Peters breached his covenant not to compete with Apex? Peters will not be in breach of contract if the covenant not to compete is unenforceable. Determining whether the covenant not to compete is unenforceable requires doing the following:

1. Identifying the interest Apex was seeking to protect when it had Peters sign the covenant.
   Was the covenant necessary
   a. to prevent disclosure of Apex's trade secrets or confidential lists; or
   b. to retain the services of a special, unique, or extraordinary employee?
2. Ascertaining, in light of the interest Apex is protecting, whether the covenant is reasonable in terms of
   a. the activities that Peters is prohibited from doing;
   b. the geographic area in which Peters is prohibited from acting; and
   c. the length of time Peters is prohibited from doing such activities. ■

Illegal Conduct to Procure a Legal Contract

Even if the subject of the contract does not involve illegal conduct, illegal conduct may be present in the procurement of the contract. Such cases often involve bribery.

Example 9–13

Sirkin bribed an employee of the Fourteenth Street Store to have the Store purchase merchandise from him. Sirkin delivered the merchandise, but the Fourteenth Street Store refused to pay. When Sirkin sought to use the court to collect on its contract with the Store, the court refused. The illegality—bribery—led to the formation of the legal contract for sale of goods. The court said:

> Nothing could be more corrupting, nor have a greater tendency to lead to disloyalty and dishonesty on the part of servants, agents, and employees, and to a betrayal of the confidence and trust reposed in

them, than these practices which the Legislature has endeavored to stamp out; and I think nothing will be more effective in stopping the growth and spread of this corrupting, and now criminal, custom than a decision that the courts will refuse their aid to a guilty vendor or vendee, or to anyone who has obtained a contract by secretly bribing the servant, agent, or employee of another to purchase or sell property, or to place the contract with him.

Sirkin v. Fourteenth Street Store, 124 A.D. 384, 108 N.Y.S. 830, 834 (N.Y. Sup. Ct. 1908).

Illegal Conduct in the Performance of a Legal Contract

Although a contract may not contemplate illegal activities, one of the parties may act illegally when performing the contract. Not all illegal activity in the performance of a legal contract will preclude the enforcement of the contract. The illegality must be significant and must directly relate to the performance of the contract.

Example 9–14

Commonwealth Pictures wanted the distribution rights to certain Universal films. McConnell promised to get Commonwealth the distribution rights if Commonwealth would promise to pay McConnell a commission on the gross receipts as the films are distributed.

McConnell bribed a representative of Universal to negotiate the Commonwealth/Universal contract. Upon discovering the bribery, Commonwealth refused to pay McConnell the commission.

The Commonwealth/McConnell contract was not illegal at its inception, nor did it contemplate that McConnell would use bribery to procure the Commonwealth/Universal contract. In the performance of the contract, however, McConnell engaged in an act of bribery (committed a significant illegal act) that directly related to his performance of the contract. Therefore, McConnell is not entitled to enforce his contract with Commonwealth for the commission.

Could Restitution Be a Cause of Action When the Contract Is Unenforceable Due to Illegality?

As a general rule, parties who enter into illegal contracts are not only unable to enforce their bargains, they also are unable to obtain restitution for any benefits they have conferred under the contract. Although the courts have created a number of exceptions, judicial opinions are unclear whether they entitle the party who conferred the benefit to a breach of contract or a restitution action.

If an exception circumvents the illegality so that the nonbreaching party could pursue a breach of contract action, that party would have a choice among expectation, reliance, and restitution remedies. An expectation remedy would place the nonbreaching party forward to the position he or she would have been in had the contract been fully performed. An expectation remedy would give the nonbreaching party the "benefit of his or her bargain." A reliance remedy would place the nonbreaching party back in the position he or she was in prior to relying on the other's promise. A reliance remedy would reimburse the nonbreaching party for his or her expenditures that relate to reliance. A restitution remedy would place the breaching party back to the position he or she was in before receiving the benefit from the nonbreaching party. A restitution remedy would require the breaching party to pay what the benefit received was worth to him or her.

If an exception does not circumvent the enforceability issue of illegality so that the nonbreaching party could not pursue a breach of contract cause of action, the exception may permit the party conferring the benefit to pursue a restitution cause of action against the party who received the benefit. As was the case with a restitution remedy for breach of contract, the restitution remedy for a restitution action remedy would place the receiving party back to the position he or she was in before receiving the benefit from the other. Neither party would be a breaching party since the issue of breach is never reached. The breach of contract analysis ends with the contract being unenforceable. A restitution remedy would require the receiving party to pay what the benefit received was worth to him or her. Under the restitution cause of action, neither an expectation nor a reliance remedy would be available.

For the purpose of discussion, the exceptions will be treated as permitting a restitution action, not a breach of contract action. This denies the party who conferred the benefit "the benefit of his or her bargain" and limits recovery to disgorging the benefit from the receiver. Therefore, the receiver who is a wrongdoer does not benefit from the contract.

Three exceptions will be explored: *in pari delicto*, collateral illegality, and repentance. *Pari delicto* means equal fault. When parties are not *in pari delicto*, they do not share fault equally. When the parties are *in pari delicto* (in equal fault), the court will find for the defendant and leave the parties in the position they were in prior to litigating. As between two equally guilty parties, the concept makes sense because there is no reason to shift the loss from one guilty party to the other.

When the parties are not *in pari delicto*, the exception comes into play. A court may allow restitution to the party with less fault.

pari delicto

Pari delicto means equal fault. When parties are not *in pari delicto*, they do not share fault equally.

CASE

Abbott v. Marker
Court of Appeals of Wisconsin (2006)
2006 Wis. App. 174, 722 N.E.2d 162

Before CANE, C.J., HOOVER, P.J., and PETERSON, J.
CANE, C.J.
Dean Abbott appeals a judgment dismissing his claims against attorney Howard Marker. Abbott contends an agreement he had with Marker for client referrals was enforceable. We disagree and affirm.

BACKGROUND

Initially, Marker represented Abbott in a medical malpractice claim with Marker successfully settling the suit for $570,000. Abbott and Marker allegedly entered into an arrangement where Abbott would refer potential clients to Marker.[1] If Marker favorably concluded the cases, Abbott would allegedly receive 25% of any attorney fees Marker collected. Abbott proceeded to refer two cases to Marker, for which Marker paid Abbott pursuant to their agreement.

Subsequently, Abbott referred a case involving the Richardson family. The Richardson case resulted in a recovery of $4 million, including $1.6 million in attorney fees. This amount was much higher than any previous referrals from Abbott, and Marker refused to pay Abbott a percentage of the attorney fees. For the first time, Marker told Abbott it was unethical for him to pay for a referral.

Abbott filed suit against Marker. Abbott made claims of breach of contract and quasi-contract. Marker filed a motion to dismiss. The court dismissed Abbott's promissory estoppel claim. Abbott then amended his complaint to include a legal malpractice claim, and Marker then moved for summary judgment on the remaining claims. After the reconsideration of an earlier motion to dismiss, the circuit court dismissed Abbott's claims, stating that his claims were barred by Wis. Stat. §§ 757.295 and 757.45.[2]

STANDARD OF REVIEW

We review a circuit court's grant of a motion to dismiss for failure to state a claim without deference. See Watts v. Watts, 137 Wis.2d 506, 512, 405 N.W.2d 303 (1987). We evaluate whether the allegations in the complaint, taken as true, are legally sufficient to state a claim for relief. Id. The interpretation of a statute is a question of law that we also review without deference. Barry v. Employers Mut. Cas. Co., 2001 WI 101, ¶ 17, 245 Wis.2d 560, 630 N.W.2d 517.

DISCUSSION

The sole issue is whether the agreement between Marker and Abbott is enforceable, either as a contract or quasi-contract. In Wisconsin, an agreement to compensate

---

1. Although the existence of an agreement is disputed, for this opinion we assume it did exist.
2. All references to the Wisconsin Statutes are to the 2003–04 version unless otherwise noted.

a non-lawyer for a client referral to a lawyer is barred by statute. See Wis. Stat. §§ 757.295 and 757.45. Generally, contractual provisions agreed to by competent parties are valid and enforceable assuming they do not violate statute or public policy. See Kocinski v. Home Ins. Co., 147 Wis.2d 728, 752, 433 N.W.2d 654 (Ct.App. 1988), aff'd as modified, 154 Wis.2d 56, 452 N.W.2d 360 (1990). A contract is considered illegal when its formation or performance is forbidden by civil or criminal statute or where a penalty is imposed for the action agreed to. Hiltpold v. T-Shirts Plus, Inc., 98 Wis.2d 711, 716–17, 298 N.W.2d 217 (Ct.App. 1980). A court generally will not aid an illegal agreement, whether executed or executory, but instead leave the parties where it found them. Venisek v. Draski, 35 Wis.2d 38, 50, 150 N.W.2d 347 (1967). However, Wisconsin courts generally seek to enforce contracts rather than set them aside. See Dawson v. Goldammer, 2003 WI App. 3, ¶ 6, 259 Wis.2d 664, 657 N.W.2d 432.

Wisconsin Stat. § 757.295 states, in pertinent part:

(1) SOLICITING LEGAL BUSINESS. Except as provided under SCR 20:7.1 to 20:7.5, no person may solicit legal matters or a retainer, written or oral, or any agreement authorizing an attorney to perform or render legal services.

(2) SOLICITATION OF A RETAINER FOR AN ATTORNEY. Except as provided under SCR 20:7.1 to 20:7.5, no person may communicate directly or indirectly with any attorney or person acting in the attorney's behalf for the purpose of aiding, assisting, or abetting the attorney in the solicitation of legal matters or the procurement through solicitation of a retainer, written or oral, or any agreement authorizing the attorney to perform or render legal services.

Thus, under this statute, it is illegal for a party to solicit retainers or agreements from another party for an attorney.

Wisconsin Stat. § 757.45, entitled "Sharing of compensation by attorneys prohibited," states in pertinent part:

It is unlawful for any person to divide with or receive from, or to agree to divide with or receive from, any attorney or group of attorneys, whether practicing in this state or elsewhere, either before or after action brought, and portion of any fee or compensation, charged or received by such attorney or any valuable consideration or reward, as an inducement for placing or in consideration of having placed, in the hands of such attorney, or in the hands of another person, a claim or demand of any kind for the purpose of collecting such claim, or bringing an action thereon, or of representing claimant in the pursuit of any civil remedy for the recovery thereof . . . .

Under this statute, then, it is illegal for an attorney to split legal fees with non-attorneys.

Applying these two statutes, the agreement between Marker and Abbott was illegal. Abbott was soliciting clients for Marker in violation of Wis. Stat. § 757.295. Payment of 25% of Marker's attorney fee would violate Wis. Stat. § 757.45. Therefore, requiring Marker to pay Abbott for the Richardson case would violate Wisconsin's prohibition of court enforcement of illegal contracts, and we decline Abbott's invitation to ignore this prohibition.

Though no Wisconsin cases interpret Wis. Stat. §§ 757.295 and 757.45, an Indiana case, with similar facts, discusses the public policy implications upon paid lawyer referrals. In Trotter v. Nelson, 684 N.E.2d 1150, 1151 (Ind. 1997), Trotter was a licensed attorney, and Nelson was a former employee of Trotter. Id. at 1151. Nelson, who was not an attorney, alleged that she and Trotter had an agreement where she received a percentage of any attorney fees for any personal injury or worker's compensation case she referred to Trotter. Id. at 1151–52. Nelson initiated a suit, claiming that Trotter had not fully compensated her per the terms of the agreement. Id. 1152. Trotter contended that no agreement existed, and even if one did, it was unenforceable because it would be against public policy. Id.

The Indiana Supreme Court noted that there are three situations where Indiana's courts have refused to enforce private agreements on public policy grounds, including if the agreement: (1) contravenes a statute; (2) injures the public in some way; or (3) is otherwise contrary to the declared public policy. Id. at 1153. If a contract directly contravenes a statute, then the court must declare the contract void. Id. However, if an agreement might be otherwise contrary to declared public policy, the Indiana Supreme Court set forth five relevant factors to consider: (1) the nature of the subject matter of the agreement; (2) the strength of the public policy underlying the statute; (3) the likelihood the refusal to enforce the bargain will further the applicable public policy; (4) how "serious or deserved" is the forfeiture suffered by the party attempting to enforce the bargain; and (5) the parties' relative bargaining power and freedom to contract. Id.

> The Indiana court concluded:
> To the extent that Nelson's claims for remuneration rely upon the enforcement of the alleged agreement, we instruct the trial court to grant Trotter's motion for partial summary judgment. We do this despite the fact that, if Nelson is correct, Trotter has committed a gross violation of the [Attorney] Conduct Rules and would have essentially entered into a contract which he knew to be unenforceable and now seeks to escape. Nevertheless, when a court determines that a contract must be declared void as against public policy, it does so on the grounds that the good of the public as a whole must take precedence over the circumstances of the individual, no matter the hardship or inequities that may result.

Id. at 1155. The court held that the referral agreement alleged by Nelson was void and unenforceable because it was directly contrary to the Indiana Rules of Professional Conduct, akin to contravening a statute, and against public policy.

Although the fact that the agreement between Marker and Abbott is directly contrary to statute is reason enough for us to decline to enforce the contract as a matter of law, it is also unenforceable on public policy grounds. It is implicitly declared in Wisconsin, through Wis. Stat. §§ 757.295 and 757.45, that referral agreements between an attorney and a non-attorney are contrary to public policy. Thus, like the agreement in *Trotter*, the agreement between Marker and Abbott is unenforceable.

Abbott argues, however, that a party to an otherwise illegal contract may recover in contract or quasi-contract if the parties are not *in pari delicto*.[3] Abbott contends that he and Marker cannot be *in pari delicto* because Marker was an attorney with superior training and legal knowledge. Thus, Abbott contends, the court must enforce the illegal referral agreement.

---

3. "Equally at fault." BLACK'S LAW DICTIONARY 806 (8th ed. 2004).

In pari delicto applies the legal principle that no court shall aid a party whose claim is based on an illegal or immoral act. Evans v. Cameron, 121 Wis.2d 421, 427, 360 N.W.2d 25 (1985). However, *in pari delicto* is not without restriction:

> And indeed in cases where both parties are *in delicto* concurring in an illegal act, it does not always follow that they stand *in pari delicto,* for there may be, and often are, very different degrees in their guilt. One party may act under circumstances of oppression, imposition, hardship, undue influence, or great inequality of condition or age; so that his guilt may be far less in degree than that of his associate in the offense. And besides, there may be on the part of the court itself a necessity of supporting the public interests or public policy in many cases, however, reprehensible the acts of the parties may be.

Id. (citation omitted).

To support his argument that because he is a non-lawyer he should be held less accountable than Marker, Abbott relies heavily on *Evans*. Evans sued her former attorney Cameron for improper legal advice. Id. at 424–25, 360 N.W.2d 25. Evans claimed Cameron advised her to lie under oath in a bankruptcy proceeding, and those lies caused her various damages. Id. Cameron filed a motion to dismiss, which was granted on the grounds of *in pari delicto*. The court of appeals reversed the circuit court. Id. at 425–26, 360 N.W.2d 25.

The Wisconsin Supreme Court reversed the court of appeals and dismissed Evans's claim. With an attorney-client relationship, the supreme court concluded:

> There may be circumstances in which the advice given by an attorney is so complex that the client would be unaware of the wrongfulness involved in following that advice. In such circumstances, more weight may be given to the influence an attorney will have over the client and the amount of reliance which the client can justifiably place in the attorney. The wrongfulness of lying while under oath, however, is apparent. Absent some allegation of special circumstances constituting an exception to the rule of *in pari delicto* independent of the attorney-client relationship, the client's deliberate act of lying under oath places that client *in pari delicto* with the attorney who advised that client to lie.

Id. at 428, 360 N.W.2d 25. Thus, in certain circumstances, advice given by an attorney might be so complex that a client cannot be expected to be aware of the potential impact.

Abbott's reliance on Marker's superior legal knowledge is misplaced. First, unlike in *Evans,* we note that Marker was not acting as Abbott's attorney. It would be improper to impose the unique relationship of attorney-client upon the arrangement between Marker and Abbott. See State v. Meeks, 2003 WI 104, ¶ 59, 263 Wis.2d 794, 666 N.W.2d 859 ("Policy considerations play a fundamental role in protecting the very important relationship between attorney and client. The attorney-client privilege provides sanctuary to protect a relationship based upon trust and confidence."). Further, this situation is not so complex that we should ignore the statutes barring the type of agreement here. Every person in Wisconsin is presumed to know the law, and ignorance of it does not excuse unlawful behavior. See Tri-State Mech., Inc. v. Northland College, 2004 WI App. 100, ¶ 10, 273 Wis.2d 471, 681 N.W.2d 302. Despite Abbott's arguments to the contrary, compliance with the clearly written provisions of Wis. Stat. §§ 757.295 and 757.45 is not something we can only expect of lawyers.

Although Marker disputes having made this referral arrangement with Abbott, if true, Marker has taken an unfair advantage of Abbott and violated his obligations under the statutes and professional ethics. However, to enforce the illegal agreement, we would in effect be nullifying Wisconsin's public policy and statutes prohibiting the sharing of attorney fees with non-attorneys in referral practices.

Next, Abbott contends that he should be awarded a portion of the attorney fees on unjust enrichment grounds. Unjust enrichment is an equitable doctrine. CleanSoils Wisconsin, Inc. v. DOT, 229 Wis.2d 600, 612, 599 N.W.2d 903 (Ct.App. 1999). A circuit court's decision to grant relief due to unjust enrichment is discretionary. Ulrich v. Zemke, 2002 WI App. 246, ¶ 8, 258 Wis.2d 180, 654 N.W.2d 458. A plaintiff may recover through quasi-contract unjust enrichment when the plaintiff confers a benefit on the defendant, the defendant is aware of the benefit, and the retention of the benefit would be inequitable. Halverson v. River Falls Youth Hockey Ass'n, 226 Wis.2d 105, 115, 593 N.W.2d 895 (Ct.App. 1999). Unjust enrichment is grounded upon the moral principle that a party who has received a benefit has a duty to make restitution where retaining such a benefit would be unjust. See Management Comp. Servs. v. Hawkins, Ash, Baptie & Co., 206 Wis.2d 158, 188, 557 N.W.2d 67 (1996).

First, we choose not to enforce an agreement through unjust enrichment when the party cannot enforce the agreement through contract because it is illegal. Second, Marker has not received a benefit from Abbott which requires him to make restitution. Abbott provided Marker with a client referral. Wisconsin Stat. §§ 757.295 and 757.45 make it illegal for an attorney to receive a referral through paying a third party. Thus, Marker has not received a benefit that has a marketable value.

Judgment affirmed.

Collateral illegality is the second exception to the illegality doctrine. **Collateral illegality** arises when the illegality is not closely related to the plaintiff's cause of action. Collateral illegality should not pose an obstacle to either a breach of contract or restitution cause of action.

collateral illegality

Collateral illegality is an illegal act that occurred during the performance of the contract although not contemplated as a part of the performance of the contract when the contract was formed.

Example 9–15

Blackcrow, a Native American, conveyed Blackacre to Smithfield, who was not a Native American. Under state law, Indians could sell tobacco on tribal land without paying state tax. The deed provided that Smithfield could sell tobacco on Blackacre without paying state tax.

The conveyance of Blackacre is legal, although the provision permitting the sale of tobacco without paying state tax is illegal.

The provision permitting the sale of tobacco without paying state tax is collateral to the sale of Blackacre. The court will enforce the contract for sale of the land although the collateral provision is unenforceable.

"Repentance" is the third exception to the illegality doctrine. **Repentance** is a feeling of remorse or regret concerning one's actions. If a contracting party repents before the illegal objective of the contract is accomplished, some courts will permit this party a restitution action to recover the benefit he or she has conferred on the party who has not repented. This encourages a contracting party to back away from the performance of an illegal transaction. Restitution may be available when

repentance

Repentance is a feeling of remorse or regret concerning one's actions.

1. the illegal purpose of the contract has not been accomplished and can be avoided by allowing the repenting party restitution; and
2. the illegality has not been so serious or shamefully wicked in itself that the court regards the mere making of the contract as a substantial offense.

Example 9–16

Mary Melody contracted to sing and play the piano at My Place Lounge for the week of July 1st (Monday through Sunday). Mary sang and played Monday through Saturday but refused to perform on Sunday because state law made it illegal for bars to be open on Sunday. My Place Lounge violates state law and is open on Sundays.

Although the contract between Mary and My Place is illegal, Mary has repented before the illegal purpose has been accomplished (open on Sunday) and the illegality is not an act so serious or shamefully wicked as to make the mere making of the contract a substantial offense. Therefore Mary can maintain an action for restitution to recover the value of her service for Monday through Saturday.

FORUM SELECTION PROVISIONS

At the time of contract formation, the contracting parties may select the forum that will hear any dispute that may arise as the contract is being performed. The parties will actually state their selection in the contract. Because a court is often referred to as a forum, this provision is known as a "forum selection clause."

Example 9–17

The Spanish Mission of Santa Fe, New Mexico, contracted to sell silver jewelry made by Native American artisans to the Old Country Store of Montpelier, Vermont. The contract contained the following forum selection clause: "All disputes arising from this contract shall be decided by the courts of New Mexico." If a dispute arises during the performance of this contract, the dispute will be heard in a New Mexico forum.

The fact that a contract has a forum selection clause does not guarantee that all future disputes will be heard only by the named courts. If the plaintiff files an action in a court other than the court the contract named, the defendant may request the court to enforce the forum selection clause. Enforcement would require the court to transfer the action to the forum named in the contract.

A court will transfer the action only if the selection clause satisfies several criteria.

1. The forum selection provision must not violate the public policy of the named forum.
2. The forum selection provision must not be unjust and unreasonable.
3. The forum selection provision must be free from fraud, undue influence, and unequal bargaining power that subverts the parties' free will at the time of contract formation.
4. The forum selection must be the exclusive forum and not merely a suggested forum for dispute resolution.

A forum selection provision that violates the public policy of the named forum will not be enforced.

Example 9–18

If a breach of contract action is filed in Utah, even though the forum selection provision named New Mexico as the proper state for filing the action, the Utah court will refuse to transfer to New Mexico if the public policy in New Mexico condemns forum selection provisions.

An unjust and an unreasonable forum selection clause will not be enforced. A provision is unjust and unreasonable if a trial in the named forum would create a serious inconvenience to any of the participants. The problems of holding a trial in the selected forum must be so great that they would effectively deny a party his or her day in court. Generally, this degree of inconvenience is extremely difficult to prove.

Example 9–19

Ronar, a New York Corporation, and F & C, a West German corporation, contracted for F & C to manufacture buttons in West Germany and Ronar to distribute them in North America. The contract contained the following forum selection provision:

> The courts at Tirschenreuth, Federal Republic of Germany, shall have jurisdiction and venue.

A dispute arose and Ronar sued F & C in New York. F & C moved to dismiss on the ground that the forum selection provision in their contract conferred venue exclusively on a court in West Germany. The United States District Court for the Southern District of New York, in *Ronar, Inc. v. Wallace,* 649 F. Supp. 319 (S.D.N.Y. 1986) sustained F & C's motion to dismiss.

. . . .

Interpretation of this clause, like that of any other contract provision, begins in familiar territory. The court's goal is to honor the legitimate expectations of the parties to the contract. See The Bremen v. Zapata Off-Shore Co., 407 U.S. 1, 12, 92 S.Ct. 1907, 1914, 32 L.Ed.2d 513 (1972). To do so the court generally must enforce the specific terms that the parties have chosen because those terms reflect the agreement they have freely reached. See id. To be sure, courts are not always bound by contractual language. Most notably, the terms of an agreement are not enforceable when evidence of "fraud, undue influence, or overweening bargaining power" undercuts the premise that the agreement was freely negotiated. Id. But absent a "strong showing" of such impinging circumstances, or some other reason why enforcement would be "unreasonable and unjust," a forum-selection clause is controlling. Id. at 15, 92 S.Ct. at 1916; see Mitsubishi Motors Corp. v. Soler Chrysler-Plymouth, Inc., 473 U.S. 614, _____ , 105 S.Ct. 3346, 3356, 87 L.Ed.2d 444 (1985) (freely negotiated forum-selection clause enjoys a "strong presumption in favor of enforcement").

Ronar does not allege that fraud, undue influence, or overweening bargaining power subverted the parties' free negotiation. Instead it argues simply that enforcement of their agreement would be unfair, unjust, or unreasonable. Ronar explains that it might have difficulty getting personal jurisdiction over the British defendants in West Germany, pretrial discovery would be restricted in a West German proceeding, and many of the parties and prospective witnesses reside in the United States rather than West Germany.

These questions of convenience are hardly different from the ones the Supreme Court considered in *The Bremen,* which like this case involved a dispute between a German corporation and an American one. The Court noted that the inconvenience the plaintiff might suffer by being held to its bargain clearly could have been foreseen. The Bremen, supra, 407 U.S. at 17–18, 92 S.Ct. at 1917–18, and in order to escape the forum-selection provision on the ground that enforcement would be unjust and unreasonable, the American party would have to sustain the heavy burden of showing that "trial in the contractual forum will be so gravely difficult and inconvenient that he will for all practical purposes be deprived of his day in court." Id. at 18–19, 92 S.Ct. at 1917–18.

None of the possible sources of inconvenience mentioned by Ronar strikes the court as grave. See, e.g., Clinton v. Janger, 583 F.Supp. 284, 288 (N.D.Ill. 1984) (plaintiff's inconvenience in suing in multiple forums because one forum does not assert jurisdiction over all defendants is not unreasonable); Karlberg European Tanspa, Inc. v. JK–Josef Kratz Vertriebsgesellschaft mbH, 618 F.Supp. 344, 348 (N.D.Ill. 1985) (neither the restricted scope of discovery in West Germany, nor the fact that most of the witnesses reside in the United States rather than West Germany, is an unreasonable inconvenience). Each inconvenience was foreseeable when the parties agreed to the West German forum. In fact, the court assumes that because Ronar freely entered the agreement, it not only was aware of the potential disadvantages of the German forum but received consideration for them as part of the bargain. See Full-Sight Contact Lens Corp. v. Soft Lenses, Inc., 466 F.Supp. 71, 73 (S.D.N.Y. 1978) (Pierce, J.). Judge Friendly's warning applies here: "There can be nothing 'unreasonable and unjust' in enforcing such an agreement; what would be unreasonable and unjust would be to allow one of the [parties] to disregard it." AVC Nederland B.V. v. Atrium Investment Partnership, 740 F.2d 148, 156 (2d Cir. 1984) (footnote omitted), quoted in Luce v. Edelstein, 802 F.2d 49, 57 (2d Cir. 1986), aff'g in pertinent part and rev'g in part on other grounds, No. 85 Civ. 4064 (S.D.N.Y. Aug. 7, 1985) (Carter, J.).

Unequal bargaining power at the time of contract formation is also a factor. If one party held such a powerful bargaining position that the other was unable to effectively resist the inclusion of the forum selection provision, a court, on the grounds of fairness, may refuse to enforce the clause.

A final criterion is whether the forum selection clause is exclusive. A court will transfer a case to the named forum only if that forum is the exclusive site for litigation.

Example 9-20

Exclusive language is "the courts of Arizona shall have exclusive jurisdiction to hear any and all disputes arising out of this contract." Under this clause, the parties obviously have agreed that the courts of Arizona and no other courts were to hear the action.

Example 9-21

If the clause had read, "The parties, with regard to the resolution of any dispute arising under this agreement, shall submit themselves to the jurisdiction of the courts of Arizona," and if the action were brought in a court outside Arizona, that court could refuse to transfer the action. The clause merely authorized the Arizona courts to hear the claim. The clause did not designate the Arizona courts as the only courts that could hear the case.

PARALEGAL EXERCISE 9.16

Jane and Bill Anderson, residents of Atlantic, Iowa, decided it was time to buy a new car. They found a great deal at Freeway Motors in Omaha, Nebraska, only 50 miles away. They were so excited about the car that they did not notice the clause in the sales contract that said, "All disputes arising from this agreement shall be litigated in the proper court of Nebraska."

Unfortunately, the car was a lemon, and Freeway Motors refused to make the repairs as the warranty required. The Andersons filed a breach of contract action in Iowa.

Should the Iowa court grant Freeway Motors' request to transfer the action to Nebraska? If you were the Iowa judge, what additional facts would you need before you could make your decision and why?

If Freeway Motors had its main office in Kansas City, Missouri, and the contract provided that "all disputes arising from this agreement shall be litigated in the proper courts of Missouri," would the Iowa judge transfer to Missouri? ■

The term "shall," however, does not guarantee that the named forum will be the exclusive forum.

Example 9–22

In *Sterling Forest Associates, Ltd. v. Barnett-Range Corp.*, 643 F. Supp. 530 (E.D.N.C. 1986), the contract between Sterling and Barnett-Range provided:

> This Agreement shall be construed and enforced in accordance with the law of the State of California and the parties agree that in any dispute jurisdiction and venue shall be in California.

A dispute arose and Sterling sued Barnett-Range in North Carolina. Barnett-Range moved to transfer the case to California.

Defendants ask this court to decline to exercise jurisdiction, arguing that plaintiff waived the right to sue in North Carolina when it agreed to the forum-selection clause noted above. Defendants would claim that, instead of establishing California as one possible forum for adjudication, the Agreement creates exclusive jurisdiction over the contract in California. Plaintiff argues that, while the clause assures jurisdiction in California, it tolerates jurisdiction wherever it may otherwise be found by operation of law.

Defendants contend that, even if this court should find that it has jurisdiction, it should use its discretion to transfer the case in the interests of justice and convenience to the parties and witnesses. Plaintiff opposes this contention and asserts that North Carolina is the more convenient situs for this action. This court will first address the interpretation of the forum-selection clause and will then decide which forum offers the greater convenience.

Defendants rely on the Supreme Court decision of The Bremen v. Zapata Off-Shore Co., 407 U.S. 1, 92 S.Ct. 1907, 32 L.Ed.2d 513 (1972). In that case, the Court held that a forum-selection clause which specified the court where cases would be heard would be enforced unless enforcement would be "unreasonable and unjust, or that the clause was invalid for such reasons as fraud or overreaching." 407 U.S. at 15, 92 S.Ct. at 1916. While this court appreciates the considerable impact of the *Bremen* on the validity of forum-selection clauses, it does not find that case to be controlling here.

In *Bremen*, the wording of the forum-selection clause differed in a critical respect from the clause in this case. The contract in *Bremen* stated that "[a]ny dispute arising *must* be treated before the London Court of Justice." 407 U.S. at 2, 92 S.Ct. at 1909 (emphasis added). The disputed clause in this case does not use such mandatory language. The phrase employed here is far more equivocal: "jurisdiction and venue *shall* be in California." (emphasis added). The contract contains no indication as to whether this language is meant to be exclusive or merely permissive. When confronted with a similarly ambiguous clause in Keaty v. Freeport Indonesia, Inc., 503 F.2d 955 (1974), the Fifth Circuit found both interpretations to be reasonable. Faced with two opposing yet reasonable interpretations of the same contract, that court invoked the traditional rule that any ambiguities should be construed against the drafter of the clause. 503 F.2d at 957.

Because the forum-selection clause does not unambiguously give exclusive jurisdiction to California, this court cannot find that the clause is mandatory. Rather, it may fairly be interpreted as having no influence on the appropriateness of other fora where actions could otherwise be properly brought. First National City Bank v. Nanz, Inc., 437 F.Supp. 184, 187 (S.D.N.Y. 1975).

. . . .

No persuasive proof has been offered either that the language of the clause is mandatory or that it is permissive. The defendants, in advancing this choice of forum clause as a bar to proceedings here, have the burden of proving this defense. The defendants have failed on this point. Because the defendants have not shown that their interpretation of the clause is any more plausible than plaintiff's, defendants have not sustained their burden of proof. The court is unable to find that the clause is mandatory and therefore declines to grant relief on this ground.

For the foregoing reasons, it is hereby ORDERED that defendants' motion for change of venue is DENIED.

ⅢPARALEGAL EXERCISE 9.17

Your law firm represents the Panhandle Oil Company, a Texas corporation. Panhandle is negotiating with the Euro ship company, a German corporation, for Euro to tow an oil rig from Galveston, Texas, to Venezuela. Your senior attorney has asked you to draft a forum selection provision so all disputes would be resolved in Texas. She has given you the following forum selection provisions as a starting point.

> Any dispute arising under this contract shall be decided in the state where the Carrier has its principal place of business.
>
> Any action arising out of or relating to any of the provisions of this Agreement may, at the election of the Employer, be brought and prosecuted only in the courts of the Commonwealth of Pennsylvania, and in the event of such election the parties hereto consent to the jurisdiction and venue of said courts.
>
> Any and all claims or causes of action which cannot be mutually settled and agreed to by the parties shall and must be brought or asserted by Purchaser only in the U.S. District Court for the Western District of North Carolina or the Northern Carolina General Court of Justice, Superior Court Division, in Charlotte, North Carolina, and Purchaser hereby expressly agrees, consents and stipulates to the exercise of personal jurisdiction over it and subject matter jurisdiction over any such controversy with respect to such claims or actions being only with such courts. ■

⛪ PARALEGAL CHECKLIST

Contract Enforceability—Protecting the Judicial Process

❑ In addition to protecting members of a class or a party against overreaching, a paralegal must be concerned with aiding the supervising attorney in discovering whether the court will protect itself against nonjudicial activities, such as perjury, illegality, and inappropriate forum shopping.

1. Must the contract be evidenced by a writing to prevent perjury? Many contracts are written even though there is no requirement that they be in writing to be enforceable. Some types of contracts, however, must be evidenced by a writing signed by the person against whom enforcement of the contract is sought. Is this the type of contract that must be evidenced by a signed writing?

   a. Is the contract one that could not be fully performed in less than a year from the time of contract formation? If so, it must be evidenced by a writing to be enforceable.

      (1) Evaluate the possibility of performance. The probability that the contract will be fully performed within the year is irrelevant. What is relevant is whether there is a lack of any possibility (no matter how slight) that performance will be completed within a year from the date of contract formation. The determination is made as of the date of

contract formation and not after the contract has been performed.

(2) Determine whether there could be full performance. The test is full performance, not termination of the duty (which implies something less than full performance).

(3) Check the terms in the writing and the signatures. The writing must state all essential terms of the contract with reasonable certainty, and the party against whom the contract will be enforced must sign it.

b. Is the contract for the transfer of an interest in real property? If so, the contract must be evidenced by a writing to be enforceable. Check the terms in the writing and the signatures. The writing must state all essential terms of the contract with reasonable certainty, and the party against whom the contract will be enforced must sign it.

c. Is the contract for the sale of goods for the price of $500 or more? If so, the contract must be evidenced by a writing to be enforceable. The Statute of Frauds provision is UCC § 2–201.

(1) Determine if the contract satisfies the Statute of Frauds by answering the following questions affirmatively:

(a) Does the writing evidence a contract for the sale of goods?

(b) Has the party against whom enforcement is sought signed it?

(c) Is a quantity specified?

(2) Analyze whether the contract may still be enforceable even if these three requirements have not been met. The contract may still be enforceable if one of the following questions can be answered affirmatively:

(a) If a writing exists but it is not signed by the party against whom enforcement is sought, is it signed by the other party and are the requirements of UCC § 2–201(2) met (between-merchants provision with an oral contract followed by a written confirmation)? or

(b) If no writing exists, is one of the requirements of UCC § 2–201(3) met (i.e., specially manufactured goods; admission in pleading, testimony, or otherwise in court; or payment made by buyer and accepted by seller or goods received and accepted by buyer)?

d. May a party circumvent the Statute of Frauds?

(1) If the writing is required because the contract cannot be fully performed within one year,

(a) full performance by one party will take the contract out of the Statute of Frauds.

(b) some action or forbearance in reliance on a promise may result in the enforcement of the promise notwithstanding the lack of a writing if injustice can be avoided only by enforcement of the promise.

(2) If the writing is required because an interest in real property is transferred,

(a) check for part performance (i.e., possession, payments, and improvements) (a number of states recognize "part performance" as a substitute for the writing).

(b) check for some action or forbearance in reliance on a promise (courts may enforce the promise notwithstanding the lack of a writing if injustice can be avoided only by enforcement of the promise).

e. If the writing is required because the contract cannot be fully performed within a year or is for a transfer of an interest in real property and therefore is unenforceable, check whether a restitution cause of action would be available to prevent unjust enrichment.

2. The paralegal will assist the attorney in determining that a contract may be unenforceable due to illegality by going through the following analysis.
   a. Does the illegality involve the contract?
      (1) Does the contract violate the law? A contract that violates the law is illegal and unenforceable in a breach of contract action. A restitution action is also not available. Some exceptions to the general rule exist.
         (a) Were the parties not *in pari delicto* (in equal fault) at the time of contracting?
         (b) Is the illegality not closely related to the plaintiff's cause of action (collateral illegality)?
         (c) Has the claimant "repented" before the illegal objective was accomplished?
      (2) Does the contract contain a covenant not to compete that may be illegal? A covenant not to compete may be illegal as an impermissible restraint on trade when it sweeps too broadly.
         (a) A sale of a business's goodwill may include a covenant not to compete. Such a covenant may extend only to what is reasonably necessary in terms of subject matter, geography, and duration to protect the buyer's legitimate interest in the enjoyment of the asset purchased.
         (b) An employment contract may include a covenant not to compete. Such a covenant must be evaluated in light of the interests the employer is seeking to protect (either to prevent disclosure of the employer's trade secrets or confidential lists or the employee's special, unique, or extraordinary services). The covenant must be reasonable in terms of the activities it prohibits, the geographic area in which the employee's activities are prohibited, and the length of time during which the employee is prohibited from engaging in those activities.

   b. Did illegal conduct occur in the procurement of a legal contract? Illegal conduct (e.g., bribery) may occur in the procurement of a contract. Such conduct may render the otherwise legal contract unenforceable.
   c. Did illegal conduct occur in the performance of a legal contract? Such conduct may render the otherwise legal contract unenforceable if the illegality is significant and is directly related to the performance of the contract.

3. Does the contract provide a selected forum for hearing future disputes? The

inquiry is *which forum* and not *whose law*. The fact that a contract has a forum selection clause does not guarantee that all future disputes will be heard only by the named courts.

If a case is filed in a forum not named in the contract, that forum will refuse to transfer the action to the forum named in the contract if one of the following questions can be answered affirmatively:

a. Was the forum selection clause unreasonable (e.g., if a trial in the named forum would create a serious inconvenience to any of the participants)?

b. Was the forum selection clause unfair (e.g., if one party held such a powerful bargaining position at the time of contract formation that the other was unable to effectively resist the inclusion of the forum selection provision)? or

c. Was the forum selection clause not exclusive?

KEY TERMS

Collateral illegality

Pari delicto

Repentance

REVIEW QUESTIONS

TRUE/FALSE QUESTIONS (CIRCLE THE CORRECT ANSWER)

1. T F The Statute of Frauds is a judicial doctrine.

2. T F Statutes of Frauds require certain types of contracts to be evidenced by a writing to be enforceable.

3. T F Only three major types of contracts must be evidenced by a writing to be enforceable.

4. T F All contracts must be evidenced by a writing to be enforceable.

5. T F A contract that could be fully performed in less than a year from the time of contract formation does not have to be evidenced by a writing to be enforceable unless it involves a sale of goods.

6. T F The determination of whether a contract could not be fully performed within one year is made after the parties have performed.

7. T F The Statute of Frauds covers a contract for the sale of land but does not apply to the transfer of a lesser interest in land such as a lease, easement, or mortgage.

8. T F Some states recognize a "part performance" exception to the transfer of an interest in the real property category of the Statute of Frauds.

9. T F A "part performance" exception covers unwritten contracts in which the buyer pays the seller and takes possession of the realty or makes a valuable improvement to the realty with the consent of the seller.

10. T F UCC § 2–201(1) provides that a contract for the sale of goods for a price over $500 must be evidenced by a writing to be enforceable.

11. T F Section 2–201(1) of the UCC states that a contract for the sale of goods for the price of $250 or more must be evidenced by a writing to be enforceable.

12. T F Section 2–201(1) of the UCC requires that any transaction for the lease of goods or for the sale of services must be evidenced by a writing to be enforceable.

13. T F Some courts use reliance to circumvent the Statute of Frauds.

14. T F A restitution action may be available to prevent unjust enrichment if an oral contract is unenforceable because of the Statute of Frauds.

15. T F Illegality may be a defense to a breach of contract action.

16. T F Illegality used as a defense to a breach of contract action must involve the subject matter of the contract.

17. T F Illegality used as a defense to a breach of contract action may involve the subject matter of the contract, the procurement of a legal contract, or the performance of a legal contract.

18. T F All contracts that violate the law are unenforceable.

19. T F When the subject matter about which the parties have contracted is illegal, the court will come to the aid of the party who has performed.

20. T F When the subject matter about which the parties have contracted is illegal, the court will leave the parties where it finds them.

21. T F The issue of the illegality of a contract is usually determined in accordance with the law of the place where the contract was formed.

22. T F A covenant not to compete may be illegal as an impermissible restraint on trade when it sweeps too broadly.

23. T F Whether a covenant not to compete is unreasonably broad can only be determined in light of the legitimate interest that the party is seeking to protect with the covenant.

24. T F A covenant not to compete used by an employer hiring an employee must be reasonable in terms of scope, geography, and duration.

25. T F If an employee does not deal with the employer's trade secrets or confidential lists or if the employee's services are not special, unique, or extraordinary, the employee

cannot be the subject of an enforceable covenant not to compete.

26.   T   F   Even if the subject of the contract does not involve illegal conduct, illegal conduct may be present in the procurement of the contract.

27.   T   F   Illegal conduct in the procurement of a contract often involves bribery.

28.   T   F   Any illegal activity in the performance of a legal contract will preclude enforcement of the contract.

29.   T   F   Illegal activity in the performance of a legal contract must be significant and must directly relate to the performance of the contract in order to preclude enforcement.

30.   T   F   The rule that a party who enters into an illegal contract can neither enforce the bargain nor obtain restitution for any benefit conferred has no exceptions.

31.   T   F   As a general rule, a party who enters into an illegal contract is not only unable to enforce the bargain, he or she is also unable to obtain restitution for any benefits conferred under the contract.

32.   T   F   When parties are *in pari delicto* in an illegal contract, the court will not shift the loss from one party to the other.

33.   T   F   When parties are not *in pari delicto* in an illegal contract, the court may allow restitution to the party with less fault.

34.   T   F   As a general rule, collateral illegality (illegality not closely related to the plaintiff's claim) will preclude a restitution claim.

35.   T   F   Collateral illegality is an obstacle to a breach of contract claim.

36.   T   F   Restitution may be available to the plaintiff who has "repented" and wants to back away from performance of an illegal transaction.

37.   T   F   A "forum selection clause" in a contract is a statement naming the courts in which any dispute arising during the performance of the contract will be heard.

38.   T   F   The fact that a contract has a forum selection clause guarantees that all future disputes will be heard only by the named courts.

39.   T   F   A court must enforce a forum selection provision even if it violates the public policy of the named forum.

40.   T   F   A court will refuse to enforce an unreasonable forum selection clause.

41.   T   F   A court may refuse to enforce a forum selection provision on the grounds of fairness if one party held such a powerful bargaining position that the other was unable to resist inclusion of the provision.

42.   T   F   Forum selection clauses do not apply to international contract disputes.

43.   T   F   Contracting parties from different nations may designate the courts of either of their nations or of a third nation to hear their disputes.

FILL-IN-THE-BLANK QUESTIONS

1. _____. Subject matter about which the parties have contracted that makes the contract unenforceable.

2. _____. A type of covenant that may be illegal as an impermissible restraint on trade when it sweeps too broadly.

3. _____. The asset of a business that a new buyer of the business may seek to protect with a covenant not to compete.

4. _____ or _____
The interests that an employer may seek to protect with a covenant not to compete.

5. _____, _____, _____.
Three exceptions to the general rule that a party who enters into an illegal contract is not only unable to enforce the bargain, but is also unable to obtain restitution for any benefits conferred under the contract.

6. _____. A Latin expression meaning in equal fault.

7. _____. Illegality not closely related to the plaintiff's claim.

8. _____. Action by the claimant before accomplishing the illegal objective that may permit a court to give the claimant a remedy.

9. _____. A statute forbidding enforcement of certain types of contracts unless they are evidenced by a writing.

10. _____. A cause of action that may be available to prevent unjust enrichment if an oral contract is unenforceable by reason of the Statute of Frauds.

11. _____. A provision in a contract providing for the forum in which any dispute arising as the contract is being performed will be heard.

MULTIPLE-CHOICE QUESTIONS (CIRCLE ALL THE CORRECT ANSWERS)

1. Christy Carson, when hired by the Gotham Advertising Agency as an account manager, signed a covenant not to compete. The covenant stated that Christy could not work for any advertising agency in the United States for 10 years from the date of her termination of employment with Gotham.

   This covenant not to compete, as applied to Christy Carson, is unenforceable because

   (a) Gotham has no legitimate interest to protect.

    (b) the covenant is unreasonable as to subject matter since there may be positions in an advertising agency that are not related to the legitimate interest that Gotham needs to protect.

    (c) the covenant is unreasonable as to duration because Gotham may not need a 10-year prohibition to protect its legitimate interest.

    (d) the covenant is unreasonable as to geographic inclusion because Gotham may not be doing business in the entire United States but only in a limited regional area.

    (e) the covenant is unreasonable as to duration and geographic inclusion but not as to subject matter.

2. Wilson bribed Amy, a buyer for the Kelleyville Super Store, to have the Store purchase merchandise from him. The Store contracted with Wilson and he shipped the merchandise. The Store accepted the shipment but refused to pay.

    (a) The illegality occurred in the Wilson/Amy contract and not in the Wilson/Store contract and therefore the Wilson/Store contract was enforceable.

    (b) Even though the illegality occurred in the Wilson/Amy contract and not in the Wilson/Store contract, the Wilson/Store contract was unenforceable because it was procured through an illegal act (bribery).

    (c) Even if the Wilson/Store contract was unenforceable under the general rule, Wilson could maintain a cause of action for breach of contract because the parties were not *in pari delicto*.

    (d) Even if the Wilson/Store contract was unenforceable under the general rule, Wilson could maintain a cause of action for breach of contract because of the doctrine of collateral illegality.

    (e) Even if the Wilson/Store contract was unenforceable under the general rule, Wilson could maintain a cause of action for breach of contract because of the repentance doctrine.

SHORT-ANSWER QUESTIONS

1. John Franklin, the owner of the Ben Franklin Print Shop, sold the shop to Ellen Dewey. Could Ellen include a covenant not to compete in the contract for sale and, if so, how should the covenant be drafted to be enforceable?

2. Are all employees subject to an enforceable covenant not to compete?

PART IV

Step Four: Plaintiff's Allegation of Defendant's Breach of Contract

PLAINTIFF'S ALLEGATION OF BREACH

Step one of the analysis requires the finding of the applicable law (foreign vs. domestic, federal vs. state, State A vs. State B, and common law vs. statute or code). Step two concentrates on contract formation (offer and acceptance). Step three raises issues of contract enforceability (minority, mental incapacity, unconscionability, fraud, duress, mistake in a basic assumption of fact, Statute of Frauds, and illegality). Step four focuses attention on the plaintiff's allegation of the defendant's breach of contract.

The allegation of breach is an allegation of breach of a contractual duty. The duty emanates from a contractual promise the promisor has made to the promisee. The promisee (the party who has a right to receive performance of the promisor's promise) alleges that the promisor has breached that duty.

The promisee may allege that the promise has been breached when the promisor (1) has not performed when the performance was due (breach by nonperformance; breach by failure to perform), or (2) has notified the promisee that the performance will not be forthcoming (breach by anticipatory repudiation; anticipatory breach) (see Exhibit IV–1).

A clear and precise identification of the plaintiff's allegation of the defendant's breach is extremely important because the alleged breach distinguishes the promise allegedly breached from all the other promises of the contract. In a bilateral contract, the parties often make a number of promises to each other. Only one or two of these promises, however, may be in issue. The other promises, while important to the contract, become irrelevant for the litigation. Therefore, this step—defining the plaintiff's allegation of the defendant's breach—focuses the lawsuit.

▥ PARALEGAL EXERCISE IV.1

Santa's Workshop in Fairbanks, Alaska, manufactures children's toys, especially for the Christmas season. During the year, Santa's sends its catalogs to

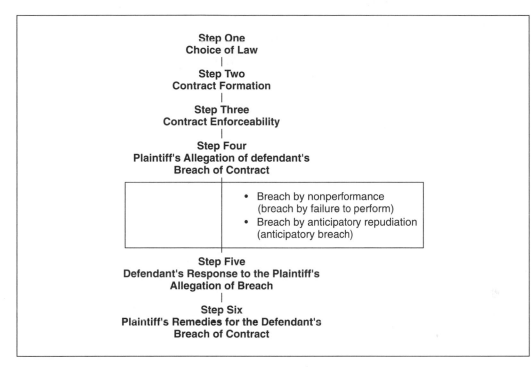

Step One
Choice of Law
|
Step Two
Contract Formation
|
Step Three
Contract Enforceability
|
Step Four
Plaintiff's Allegation of defendant's
Breach of Contract

- Breach by nonperformance
  (breach by failure to perform)
- Breach by anticipatory repudiation
  (anticipatory breach)

Step Five
Defendant's Response to the Plaintiff's
Allegation of Breach
|
Step Six
Plaintiff's Remedies for the Defendant's
Breach of Contract

Exhibit IV–1 The Plaintiff's Allegation of the Defendant's Breach Phase of the Road Map

various retailers across the nation. Each catalog comes with a price list and order form. The price list carries the notations "all prices subject to change without notice," "all orders must be approved by the President of Santa's Workshop," "orders placed before August 1st will receive a 5 percent discount," and "orders placed before August 1st will be shipped by rail within 40 days." The boilerplate in the order form disclaims all express and implied warranties and states, "all disputes shall be settled by arbitration in Fairbanks, Alaska."

Toy Mart has its headquarters in Atlanta, Georgia, and has retail toy stores in six southern states. Toy Mart reviewed Santa's catalog, price list, and order form and sent its order for $2,500,000 worth of toys on July 15th. Rather than use Santa's order form, Toy Mart sent its order on its own purchase order form. Toy Mart's purchase order form differed substantially from Santa's order form. The boilerplate (fine print) of Toy Mart's form called for "a 10 percent discount for all orders over $2,000,000," and "orders to be shipped within 20 working days from the date of receipt." The boilerplate also preserved all express and implied warranties and mandated that "all disputes would be settled by litigation in Georgia."

For some undisclosed reason, Santa's did not receive Toy Mart's order until August 1st. Shipping was delayed until October 1st. Accompanying the shipment was Santa's invoice that was in the format of Santa's order form (and included all of Santa's terms). The toys and the invoice arrived in Atlanta on October 15th. Toy Mart accepted the shipment, wired Santa's bank $2,250,000, and delivered the toys to its various stores.

Santa's wrote Toy Mart demanding an additional $250,000. Toy Mart wrote back that under the contract, Santa had been paid the full amount (contract price less 10 percent).

Because Toy Mart could not deliver the toys to its various stores until after October 15th, it found itself at a competitive disadvantage. Toys needed to be discounted to reduce inventory, so profits wound up being substantially less than anticipated.

After the holiday season, Toy Mart found that the return rate for defective toys was higher than usual, further reducing its profits. Santa's refused to make an adjustment, claiming disclaimer of warranties.

List Santa's duties under the contract.

List Toy Mart's duties under the contract.

If Santa's were to sue Toy Mart, which duty would Santa allege Toy Mart breached?

If Toy Mart were to sue Santa's, which duty would Toy Mart allege Santa's breached? ■

At this step in the analysis, the point must be emphasized that the plaintiff is merely alleging that the defendant has breached a contractual duty (see Exhibit IV–2). The plaintiff has the burden of proving by a preponderance of the evidence that the defendant did in fact breach the duty allegedly breached. The plaintiff may or may not be able to meet this burden of proof. Whether the plaintiff's allegation will be sustained will depend on step five of the analysis (Chapters 11–14)—the defendant's response to the plaintiff's allegation of breach (refer to Exhibit V–1, text p. 360).

IN THE DISTRICT COURT OF [NAME] COUNTY
STATE OF [NAME]

[NAME], dba [Name]	)	
	)	
Plaintiff,	)	
	)	
v.	)	Case No. _____
	)	
[NAME], a [Name of State]	)	
corporation	)	
	)	
Defendant.	)	

COMPLAINT FOR BREACH OF CONTRACT

1. Plaintiff is an individual residing in [Name] County, [Name of State], doing business as [Name].

2. Defendant is a corporation incorporated under the laws of the State of [Name of State].

3. On or about [date], Plaintiff and Defendant entered into a written contract whereby Plaintiff promised to design a marketing plan for Defendant and Defendant promised to pay $ [dollars] and 1 percent of Defendant's net profits earned during the first year after the marketing plan was implemented. The contract also provided that in the event of litigation, reasonable attorney fees could be awarded to the prevailing party. A copy of the contract is attached as Exhibit A.

4. On or about [date], Plaintiff presented the completed marketing plan to the Defendant.

5. All conditions precedent have been performed by Plaintiff or have occurred and Defendant has not been excused from performance.

6. Defendant has breached the contract by failing to pay the Plaintiff for the services rendered.

7. As a result of Defendant's breach of contract, Plaintiff has sustained damages in the sum of $ [dollars].

Accordingly, Plaintiff demands judgment against Defendant for the sum of $ [dollars], interest, and costs, including reasonable attorney fees.

[Attorney's name signed]
[Attorney's name typed]
Attorney for plaintiff
[Bar membership number]
[Address]
[Telephone number]

Exhibit IV-2 Complaint—Plaintiff's Allegation of Defendant's Breach

The Plaintiff's Allegation of the Defendant's Breach

- Breach by Nonperformance (Breach by Failure to Perform When Due)
- Breach by Anticipatory Repudiation (Anticipatory Breach)

The plaintiff (the party having the contractual right) may allege that the defendant (the party having the corresponding contractual duty) has breached the contract by nonperformance or by anticipatory repudiation.

BREACH BY NONPERFORMANCE (BREACH BY FAILURE TO PERFORM WHEN DUE)

A **breach by nonperformance** arises when the time for the promisor's performance has come and gone without the promisor performing.

breach by nonperformance (breach by failure to perform)
A breach by failure to perform is the usual breach and arises when the time for the promisor's performance has come and gone without the promisor performing.

Example 10-1

The House of Gems, a jewelry store, contracted with Quality Printing for the printing of its Christmas catalogs. Quality promised to deliver the catalogs on November 1st. The date passed without the catalogs being delivered. Quality has breached the contract by failing to perform when the performance was due (breach by nonperformance).

In a bilateral contract, either the offeror or the offeree may allege breach. By making the offer, the offeror uses his or her promise to induce the offeree to promise. The offeree accepts with a mirror image of the offer—the offeree's promise for the offeror's promise. Since both the offeror and the offeree promise, both are promisors and both are promisees. As promisors, both have duties—and as promisees, both have rights. The party with the right alleges that the party with the corresponding duty has not performed that duty.

In a unilateral contract, only the offeree may make the allegation of breach. By making the offer, the offeror uses his or her promise to induce the offeree to perform. The offeree accepts by performing. When the contract is formed, the offeree has no duty to perform. The offeror is the only party with a promise. As the promisor, the offeror has a duty and the offeree has a corresponding right.

BREACH BY ANTICIPATORY REPUDIATION (ANTICIPATORY BREACH)

breach by anticipatory repudiation (anticipatory breach)
A breach by anticipatory repudiation is a notice that the promisor will not perform in the future.

The promisee may allege that the promisor has breached a contractual duty by notifying the promisee that performance will not be forthcoming. A **breach by anticipatory repudiation (anticipatory breach)** is a notice that the promisor will not perform in the future. The notice itself is a breach. Some refer to this as an "anticipatory breach." When the promisee receives notice that the promisor will not perform in the future, the promisee need not wait for the date performance is due but may rely on the notification, make other plans, and seek an appropriate remedy in a breach of contract action.

Example 10–2

The House of Gems, a jewelry store, contracted with Quality Printing for the printing of its Christmas catalogs. Quality promised to deliver the catalogs on November 1st. On October 15th, Quality notified the House of Gems that the catalogs could not be delivered on November 1st. Quality's notice that it will not perform on the promised date is a breach by anticipatory repudiation.

The doctrine of breach by anticipatory repudiation presents nonbreaching parties with the opportunity to cease relying on future performances that will never occur and mitigate the damages recoverable in a breach of contract action.

Example 10–3

Amanda Jones, a wealthy oil tycoon, hired Bentley, a professional butler, to accompany her to Monaco for six weeks, beginning

June 1st. On May 1st, Jones notified Bentley that she had decided not to take the trip. By notifying Bentley of her plans, Jones has committed a breach by anticipatory repudiation. Bentley no longer needs to hold himself ready for the trip and may accept other employment for that time period.

A breach by anticipatory repudiation may require the non-breaching party to mitigate (reduce) the damages that would be recoverable in a breach of contract cause of action.

Example 10-4

The county commissioners of the county of Rockford authorized the construction of a bridge over the Arkansas River. The contract to construct was given to Southwest Bridge Builders. When the bridge was still in the planning stage, a new county election occurred and the County Commission changed composition. The new Commission terminated the bridge project and notified Southwest Bridge Builders.

The notification was an anticipatory breach. It required Southwest to stop the project. Southwest was entitled to recover in a breach of contract action the contract price less the cost of labor and materials saved by not constructing.

In an employment contract for a specified term of employment, the employee is selling a specific period of time. When the employer breaches by anticipatory repudiation, the employee's time is not committed. As part of the mitigation doctrine, the employee must make an effort to use this time. Otherwise, the value of this time will be charged to the employee.

Example 10-5

Return to the Jones/Bentley example (Example 10-3). When Jones breached, Bentley was left with six weeks of time that was previously committed to Jones. Bentley must use reasonable efforts to use this time; otherwise, what Bentley could have received from using this time will be charged against Bentley's damage claim.

Therefore, if the Jones contract for the six weeks was $12,000 and Bentley found another job that paid $9,000, Bentley's damages would be $3,000 ($12,000 less $9,000).

Some courts do not apply the doctrine of breach by anticipatory repudiation to unilateral and bilateral contracts where one party has fully performed his or her duties and all that remains for the other to do is to pay money. Courts also are reluctant to apply the doctrine to contracts of indefinite terms such as contracts for lifetime disability payments and annuity contracts. The uncertainty of the duration makes the calculation of damages speculative.

Article 2 of the UCC includes three sections that deal with breach by anticipatory repudiation.

Section 2–609   Right to Adequate Assurance of Performance
Section 2–610   Anticipatory Repudiation
Section 2–611   Retraction of Anticipatory Repudiation

PARALEGAL CHECKLIST

The Plaintiff's Allegation of the Defendant's Breach

❏ Once a contract has been formed and is enforceable, the supervising attorney will want the paralegal to focus on the alleged breach of the contract.

1. What is the plaintiff-promisee alleging the defendant-promisor did wrong?
   a. Did the promisor fail to perform a contractual duty (breach by nonperformance; breach by failure to perform)?
   b. Did the promisor notify the promisee that performance of a contractual duty would not be forthcoming when the performance was due (i.e., breach by anticipatory repudiation; anticipatory breach)?
      1) Does the promisee have reasonable grounds to conclude that the promisor would not perform?
      2) Note that some courts may not recognize breach by anticipatory repudiation as a breach in some situations—such as unilateral or bilateral contract situations where one party has already fully performed or where the only contractual obligation remaining is the payment of money.
      3) If the contract is for the sale of goods, UCC §§ 2–609, 2–610, and 2–611 apply.
2. Sort through all the duties of the parties and focus only on those duties that are in issue and relate to the lawsuit.
3. State the allegation of breach clearly and concisely. The plaintiff's allegation of the defendant's breach defines the lawsuit.

KEY TERMS

Breach by anticipatory repudiation (anticipatory breach)

Breach by nonperformance (breach by failure to perform)

REVIEW QUESTIONS

TRUE/FALSE QUESTIONS (CIRCLE THE CORRECT ANSWER)

1. T   F   The party who is alleged to have breached a contractual duty is the promisee.

2. T   F   Nancy promised to teach Ann a new dance step for Ann's promise to pay Nancy $40. Ann accepted. When the date for the first lesson came and went without Ann showing up for her lesson, Ann committed a breach by anticipatory repudiation.

3. T   F   If the contract involves a sale of goods, breach by anticipatory repudiation is covered by UCC §§ 2–609, 2–610, and 2–611.

4. T   F   In a unilateral contract, only the offeror could be the breaching party.

FILL-IN-THE-BLANK QUESTIONS

1. _____.   The party who alleges the breach of a contractual duty.

2. _____.   When the promisor gives notice that he or she will not perform when the due date for performance arrives.

3. _____.   When the promisor fails to perform his or her contractual duty.

4. _____.   The duty the promisee has when the promisor gives notice of future nonperformance.

5. _____.   Another name for breach by anticipatory repudiation.

MULTIPLE-CHOICE QUESTIONS (CIRCLE ALL THE CORRECT ANSWERS)

1. Robert, a candidate for the U.S. Congress, contracted with the Mid-America Advertising Company to create and manage the publicity for his campaign. The contract provided that Mid-America would charge Robert costs plus 25 percent. After the campaign had just begun, Robert told Mid-America that he would use a different advertising company and would pay whatever Mid-America had spent to date plus 25 percent.
   (a) Mid-America could not sue Robert for breach of contract since he breached no duty.
   (b) Mid-America could sue Robert for breach of contract alleging a breach by anticipatory repudiation.

(c) Mid-America could sue Robert for breach of contract alleging an anticipatory breach.

(d) Mid-America could sue Robert for breach of contract alleging breach by nonperformance.

(e) Mid-America should rely on § 2–610 of the UCC for the basis of its breach of contract cause of action.

SHORT-ANSWER QUESTIONS

1. What is the difference between a breach by anticipatory repudiation and a breach by nonperformance? Give an example of each.

2. What are the policy reasons for having a breach by anticipatory repudiation? Why should the promisee not have to wait until the date of performance?

3. Why should the doctrine of breach by anticipatory repudiation not apply in some situations?

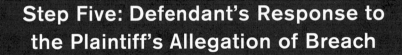

PART V

Step Five: Defendant's Response to the Plaintiff's Allegation of Breach

DEFENDANT'S RESPONSE TO PLAINTIFF'S ALLEGATION OF BREACH

Just because the plaintiff-promisee alleges that the defendant-promisor has breached the contract does not make it so. The defendant has an arsenal of four responses to the plaintiff's allegation of breach, any of which, if successful, will cause the plaintiff's cause of action for breach of contract to fail. These responses can be reduced to shorthand phrases:

1. No breach–compliance
2. No breach–excuse
3. No breach–justification
4. No breach–terminated duty

In the first response ("No breach; I am complying with the terms of the contract"), the defendant denies that he or she is not performing in accordance with the terms of the contract.

> Although the plaintiff alleges that I have breached the contract, I have complied with the terms of the contract. I am not in breach.

If the defendant is in compliance with the terms of the contract, the defendant has not breached the contract, and the plaintiff has no cause of action for breach of contract.

In the second response ("No breach; although I am not complying with the terms of the contract, my nonperformance was excused"), the defendant admits not performing the contract but asserts that this nonperformance was excused by a supervening external event (that is, an event not referenced in the contract) and is therefore not a breach of contract.

> I may not be performing the contract, but there is an outside event that prevents my performance. I am excused from performing, and I am not in breach.

Unlike the first response ("No breach–compliance"), the supervening external event in the second response ("No breach–excuse") was not an express term in the contract. Even though this supervening external event (an act of God or a governmental regulation) was not an express term, it may excuse the defendant's nonperformance. If the defendant's performance is excused, the defendant is not in breach, and the plaintiff cannot maintain a cause of action for breach of contract.

In the third response to the plaintiff's allegation of breach ("No breach; although I am not complying with the terms of the contract, my nonperformance was justified by your breach of this contract"), the defendant admits nonperformance but claims that the nonperformance was justified by a breach by the plaintiff.

> My nonperformance of the contract was justified by your breach of the contract. Therefore, you are the breaching party and not I.

The defendant's nonperformance is not a breach—it is a justified nonperformance much like self-defense in criminal law. Because the plaintiff rather than the defendant is the breaching party, the plaintiff cannot maintain a cause of action for breach of contract against the defendant.

In the fourth response ("No breach; although I am not complying with the terms of the contract, my duty to perform the contract has been terminated"), the defendant admits nonperformance but claims that his or her contractual duty has ended either by agreement or by law and that, therefore, he or she has not breached the contract.

> I no longer have to perform according to the contract. My obligation no longer exists due to some duty terminating occurrence. I am not in breach.

The terminating occurrence may be consensual (substitute contract, accord and satisfaction, or novation), unilateral (release or waiver), or by operation of law (statute of limitations). Because the defendant is not a breaching party, the plaintiff cannot maintain a breach of contract action.

If the defendant's response to the plaintiff's allegation of breach is successful and therefore the plaintiff could not maintain a breach of contract action and if the plaintiff has conferred a benefit on the defendant, the plaintiff may consider a restitution cause of action. A restitution cause of action would be available if it would be unjust to permit the defendant to retain the benefit without compensating the plaintiff.

If the defendant's response to the plaintiff's allegation of breach is unsuccessful, the defendant has breached the contract and the plaintiff has established his or her cause of action for breach of contract. Now the plaintiff is entitled to proceed to the final step in the analysis—the plaintiff's selection of remedies for the defendant's breach of contract (see Exhibit V–1).

Whether the defendant's breach is intentional or unintentional is irrelevant. The law of contracts does not evaluate the mental state accompanying nonperformance. The relevant factor is whether the defendant did not perform his or her contractual duty.

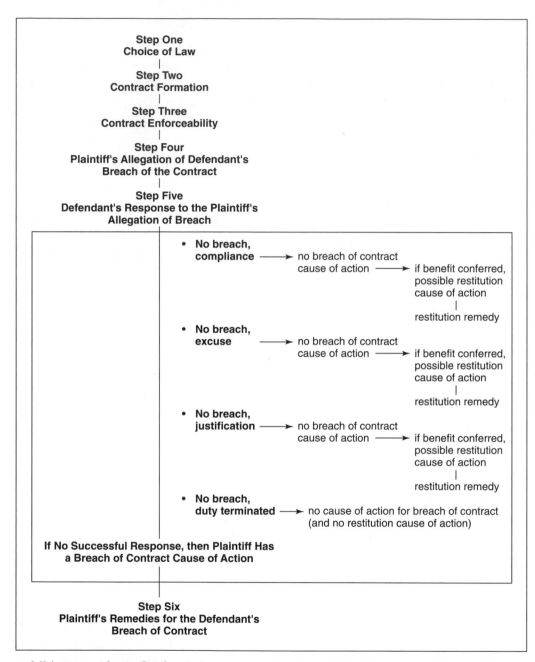

Step One
Choice of Law
|
Step Two
Contract Formation
|
Step Three
Contract Enforceability
|
Step Four
Plaintiff's Allegation of Defendant's
Breach of the Contract
|
Step Five
Defendant's Response to the Plaintiff's
Allegation of Breach

- **No breach,**
  compliance ──────► no breach of contract
  cause of action ──────► if benefit conferred,
  possible restitution
  cause of action
  |
  restitution remedy

- **No breach,**
  excuse ──────► no breach of contract
  cause of action ──────► if benefit conferred,
  possible restitution
  cause of action
  |
  restitution remedy

- **No breach,**
  justification ──────► no breach of contract
  cause of action ──────► if benefit conferred,
  possible restitution
  cause of action
  |
  restitution remedy

- **No breach,**
  duty terminated ──────► no cause of action for breach of contract
  (and no restitution cause of action)

If No Successful Response, then Plaintiff Has
a Breach of Contract Cause of Action

Step Six
Plaintiff's Remedies for the Defendant's
Breach of Contract

Exhibit V–1   The Defendant's Response to the Plaintiff's Allegation of Breach Phase of the Road Map

The Defendant's *No Breach–Compliance* Response to the Plaintiff's Allegation of Breach

The defendant's first response to the plaintiff's allegation of breach is *"No breach; I am complying with the terms of the contract"* (see Exhibit 11–1). With this response, the defendant denies that he or she has failed to comply with the terms of the contract. If the defendant is in compliance, a breach has not occurred, and the plaintiff has no breach of contract cause of action.

When raising the *no breach–compliance* response to the plaintiff's allegation of breach, the defendant can select from a number of contentions.

1. The defendant could contend that the contract does not include the duty the plaintiff alleges the defendant breached.

    (a) If the contract was created through an exchange of forms and the second form does not mirror the first, did the

IN THE DISTRICT COURT OF [NAME] COUNTY
STATE OF [NAME]

[NAME], dba [Name]	)	
	)	
Plaintiff,	)	
	)	
v.	)	Case No. _____
	)	
[NAME], a [Name of State]	)	
corporation	)	
	)	
Defendant.	)	

ANSWER OF DEFENDANT [NAME]

Defendant [name] alleges the following in response to the complaint:

1. Defendant admits the allegations of paragraph 1 of the complaint.

2. Defendant admits the allegations of paragraph 2 of the complaint.

3. Defendant admits the allegations of paragraph 3 of the complaint.

4. Defendant admits the allegations of paragraph 4 of the complaint.

5. Defendant denies that all conditions precedent have occurred as alleged in paragraph 5 of the complaint in that payment was conditioned on the marketing plan improving sales by 50 percent over the next 12 months and 12 months have not yet passed.

6. Defendant denies the allegations of paragraph 6 that it breached the contract.

7. The complaint fails to state a claim against Defendant upon which relief can be granted.

Accordingly, Defendant demands that Plaintiff take nothing by this Action, and that Defendant be awarded costs including reasonable attorney fees.

> [Attorney's name signed]
> [Attorney's name typed]
> Attorney for plaintiff
> [Bar membership number]
> [Address]
> [Telephone number]

Exhibit 11–1 Answer—Defendant's "No Breach–Compliance" Response to the Plaintiff's Allegation of Defendant's Breach

contract include the duty that the plaintiff alleges was breached? The common law ("last shot" doctrine) and Article 2 of the UCC (§ 2–207—battle of the forms) approach this issue differently.

(b) If the contract was reduced to a final writing and the duty alleged to have been breached is in parol communications (oral statements or nonfinal writings) that occurred prior to or contemporaneous with the final writing (the integration), would the contract include the promises in the final writing plus the parol promise or only the promises in the final writing? The parol evidence rule is applied to determine whether the contract consists of the final writing only or of the final writing plus parol.

(c) If the contract does not include an express duty, should the duty be implied? The common law and Article 2 have differing approaches.

2. When raising the *no breach—compliance* response to the plaintiff's allegation of breach, the defendant could contend that when the contract was reduced to a final writing, the writing did not accurately reflect the agreement. Thus, a mistake in integration occurred and the writing should be reformed to correspond to the contract. Under the reformed writing, the defendant may be in compliance with the contract terms.

3. Even if a contract has an express or implied term, is that term from which the defendant's duty eminates susceptible to different interpretations? Does it depend on whether the term has a trade meaning (trade usage)? Does the reasonable person have a role in determining the reasonable interpretation?

4. Just because a duty is in the contract and the plaintiff's alleges that it has been breached does not make it so. Could the nonoccurrence of a condition precedent relieve the defendant from his or her duty to perform at this time?

5. Finally, could restitution be a cause of action when a *no breach–compliance* response negates the plaintiff's breach of contract cause of action?

IDENTIFYING THE TERMS OF THE CONTRACT

The defendant may contend that he or she is complying with the terms of the contract because the contract does not include the duty the plaintiff alleges the defendant has breached. Therefore, the defendant claims that he or she is not a promisor as to that duty.

Whether the contract includes this duty may depend on the battle of the forms, the parol evidence rule, or the recognition of implied terms.

Battle of the Forms

Chapter 4 discussed the common law mirror image rule. The offeror is the master of the offer and the offeree must accept the terms of the offer with no change. Any deviation would be a rejection of the offer and, if it meets the criteria for an offer, a counteroffer.

Chapter 4 also discussed how UCC § 2–207 changed the mirror image rule if the contract is for the sale of goods.

Common Law Last Shot Doctrine

Under the common law last shot doctrine, the last writing is the offer (assuming the last writing qualifies as an offer). If the offeree's subsequent conduct implies the promise sought by the offeror, the offeree accepts the written offer. The offeree's implied promise is taken as the mirror image of the offer and therefore the terms of the contract are those found in the last writing (the last shot).

Example 11–1

Amy, a singer/songwriter, sent a letter to Blue Moon Publishing Company promising to sell the copyright of her latest song (which was number 1 on the country music charts) for Blue Moon's promise to pay $100,000 plus 15 percent royalties. Blue Moon sent Amy a check for $100,000. No letter was enclosed with the check.

When Blue Moon refused to pay Amy royalties, Amy sued Blue Moon for breach of contract, alleging Blue Moon's failure to pay the royalties. Blue Moon responded—*no breach–compliance*—the contract did not include a duty to pay royalties, therefore, I am not in breach.

Blue Moon's conduct (sending the check) implied a promise to pay, thus accepting Amy's offer. Under this contract, all the terms are those found in the last writing, Amy's letter. Since Amy's letter included a promise to pay royalties, Blue Moon's no breach–compliance response fails and Blue Moon has breached the contract.

Example 11–2

Amy, a singer/songwriter, sent a letter to Blue Moon Publishing Company promising to sell the copyright of her latest song (which was number 1 on the country music charts) for Blue Moon's promise to pay $100,000 plus 15 percent royalties. Blue Moon sent Amy a check for $75,000 and a letter offering to pay $75,000 plus 12 percent royalties.

When Blue Moon refused to pay Amy more than 12 percent royalties, Amy sued Blue Moon for breach of contract, alleging Blue Moon's failure to pay the 15 percent royalties. Blue Moon responded—*no breach–compliance*—the contract did not include a duty to pay 15 percent royalties, therefore, I am not in breach.

Blue Moon's letter was not the mirror image of Amy's offer and therefore was a rejection and counteroffer. When Amy deposited Blue Moon's check, her conduct implied a promise to accept the counteroffer. Under this contract, all the terms are those found in the last writing, Blue Moon's letter. Therefore, Blue Moon's no breach–compliance response is good and Blue Moon has not breached the contract. Amy does not have a breach of contract cause of action.

UCC § 2–207

As discussed in Chapter 4, UCC § 2–207 is substantially more complicated than the common law last shot doctrine. UCC § 2–207(1) has two topics: a written offer and a written acceptance, and an oral contract followed by a written confirmation. Both lead to the conclusion of contract.

> (1) **A definite and seasonable expression of acceptance or a written confirmation which is sent within a reasonable time operates as an acceptance even though it states terms additional to or different from those offered or agreed upon,** unless acceptance is expressly made conditional on assent to the additional or different terms. (UCC § 2–207(1))

In the first scenario, the conclusion is acceptance and contract even though the terms of the boilerplate (fine print) in the "acceptance" do not mirror those of the offer. The bargained-for terms in the acceptance must, however, mirror those in the offer.

> (1) **A definite and seasonable expression of acceptance** or a written confirmation which is sent within a reasonable time **operates as an acceptance even though it states terms additional to or different from those offered** or agreed upon. . . . (UCC § 2–207(1))

Example 11–3

The ABC Company sent its purchase order to the Southwest Pottery Company for a number of items listed in the Southwest catalog. In the fine print of its purchase order, ABC reserved all express and implied warranties.

Southwest responded with an acknowledgment form that was the mirror image of ABC's bargained-for terms (price, quantity, subject matter) but not the mirror image of ABC's boilerplate. One difference was that ABC's form reserved all warranties while Southwest's form disclaimed all warranties. A contract was formed even though the boilerplate terms did not agree.

The second scenario involves a bit of double talk. First, a written confirmation refers to an existing contract (which must have had offer and acceptance) that was created orally or through informal correspondence. Although an acceptance to form this contract already exists, the subsequent written confirmation is treated as an acceptance and this is true even though the boilerplate terms in written confirmation do not mirror the terms of the oral contract or the contract created by informal correspondence. The bargained-for terms in the written correspondence must, however, mirror those in the existing contract.

> (1) A definite and seasonable expression of acceptance or **a written confirmation which is sent within a reasonable time operates as an acceptance even though it states terms additional to or different from those** offered or **agreed upon**. . . . (UCC § 2–207(1))

Example 11–4

The ABC Company telephoned its order to the Southwest Pottery Company for a number of items listed in the Southwest catalog. Southwest agreed to ship.

Southwest then sent a form to ABC confirming the contract. The confirmation not only contained the bargained-for terms previously discussed on the telephone but also new terms in the boilerplate, such as a disclaimer of all express and implied warranties. A contract was formed even though the boilerplate terms in the confirmation form added to what was agreed to on the telephone.

Once a contract has been formed under § 2–207(1), the boilerplate term in issue must be classified into one of three categories: (1) a term in the offer but not in the acceptance; (2) a term in the acceptance but not in the offer (i.e., an additional term); and (3) a term that appears in both the offer and the acceptance but that is not the mirror image of the other (i.e., a different term).

Where the term was in the offer but not in the acceptance, it is taken as accepted and therefore is a term of the contract.

Example 11–5

The ABC Company sent its purchase order to the Southwest Pottery Company for a number of items listed in the Southwest catalog. In the fine print of its purchase order, ABC reserved all express and implied warranties.

Southwest responded with an acknowledgment form that was the mirror image of ABC's bargained-for terms but not the mirror image of ABC's boilerplate. One difference was that ABC's boilerplate reserved all warranties while Southwest's boilerplate was silent as to warranties.

Southwest shipped and ABC accepted the shipment and paid. Subsequently, ABC sued Southwest for breach of contract claiming that the goods were not fit for the ordinary purpose for which they were sold (breach of an implied warranty of merchantability under UCC §§ 2–314(1) and (2)(c)). Southwest responded with *no breach–compliance*—the contract did not include warranties and therefore I am not in breach.

The reservation of warranties found in the offer but not in the acceptance was a term of the contract since Southwest raised no objection in its acceptance. Southwest's no breach–compliance response fails and ABC has a breach of contract action.

When the term is only discussed in the acceptance (an additional term), then § 2–207(2) comes into play. If the contract is not between merchants, the first sentence of subsection (2) directs that the additional term is treated as a counteroffer.

> (2) **The additional terms are to be construed as proposals for addition to the contract.** Between merchants such terms become part of the contract unless:
>
> > (a) the offer expressly limits acceptance to the terms of the offer;
> > (b) they materially alter it; or
> > (c) notification of objection to them has already been given within a reasonable time after notice of them is received. (UCC § 2–207(2))

Example 11-6

The ABC Company, a nonmerchant for UCC § 2–207 purposes, sent its purchase order to the Southwest Pottery Company (a merchant for UCC § 2–207 purposes) for a number of items listed in the Southwest catalog. ABC's purchase order was silent as to express and implied warranties.

Southwest responded with an acknowledgment form that was the mirror image of ABC's bargained-for terms but not the mirror image of ABC's boilerplate. One difference was that the Southwest's boilerplate disclaimed all warranties while ABC's boilerplate was silent as to warranties.

Southwest shipped and ABC accepted the shipment and paid. Subsequently, ABC discovered that some of the goods did not conform to an implied warranty of merchantability (UCC §§ 2–314(1), (2)(c)) and sued Southwest for breach of contract, alleging breach of warranty.

Southwest responded with *no breach–compliance,* claiming that the implied warranty was not a term of the contract because ABC had said nothing about warranties while Southwest had disclaimed all warranties.

Since ABC was not a merchant for UCC § 2–207 purposes, the disclaimer of warranties (an additional term) is a counteroffer under the first sentence of § 2–207(2)–and since ABC did not accept this counteroffer, the contract is without the disclaimer and Southwest's no breach–compliance response fails. ABC may maintain its breach of contract action against Southwest.

If the contract is between merchants, the analysis moves beyond the first sentence of subsection (2) and into the second sentence of subsection (2).

(2) The additional terms are to be construed as proposals for addition to the contract. **Between merchants such terms become part of the contract unless:**

    (a) the offer expressly limits acceptance to the terms of the offer;

    (b) they materially alter it; or

    (c) notification of objection to them has already been given within a reasonable time after notice of them is received. (UCC § 2–207(2))

The additional term now becomes a term in the contract unless it is excluded under (a), (b), or (c).

Example 11–7

The ABC Company sent its purchase order to the Southwest Pottery Company for a number of items listed in the Southwest catalog. ABC's purchase order was silent as to express and implied warranties.

Southwest responded with an acknowledgment form that was the mirror image of ABC's bargained-for terms but not the mirror image of ABC's boilerplate. The Southwest's boilerplate disclaimed all warranties (an additional term since ABC's purchase order was silent as to warranties).

Southwest shipped and ABC accepted the shipment and paid. Subsequently, ABC discovered that some of the goods did not conform to an implied warranty of merchantability (UCC §§ 2–314(1), (2)(c)) and sued Southwest for breach of contract, alleging breach of warranty. Both ABC and Southwest are merchants for UCC § 2–207 purposes.

Southwest responded with *no breach–compliance,* claiming that the implied warranty was not a term of the contract because ABC had said nothing about warranties while Southwest had disclaimed all warranties.

Since both ABC and Southwest were merchants for UCC § 2–207 purposes, the disclaimer of warranties (an additional term) is no longer a counteroffer under the first sentence of subsection (2) but becomes a term of the contract under the first half of the second sentence of subsection (2). Southwest's no breach–compliance response is good and ABC cannot maintain its breach of contract action.

If, however, the facts come within one of the (a)–(c) exceptions found at the end of the second sentence to subsection (2), the term returns to its status of counteroffer. Since ABC did not accept the counteroffer, the contract is without the disclaimer and Southwest's response fails. ABC may maintain its breach of contract action against Southwest.

If the term is in the offer and a conflicting term is in the acceptance (i.e., a different term), then courts are divided on how to resolve the problem. Certainly a contract has been formed under § 2–207(1), so the issue is not one of contract formation but one of terms. Courts have ventured in three directions. The language of UCC § 2–207 does not address the different term issue so the courts have become creative in how they resolve this issue. Some courts use § 2–207(2) even though § 2–207(2) references only "additional terms." Other courts knock out both terms and supplement the express terms of the contract with the Code's gap fillers. Still other courts drop the term in the second form, leaving the term in the first form.

Example 11–8

The ABC Company sent its purchase order to the Southwest Pottery Company for a number of items listed in the Southwest catalog. In the boilerplate of ABC's purchase order, all express and implied warranties were reserved.

Southwest responded with an acknowledgment form that was the mirror image of ABC's bargained-for terms but not the mirror image of ABC's boilerplate. The Southwest's boilerplate disclaimed all warranties.

Southwest shipped and ABC accepted the shipment and paid. Subsequently, ABC discovered that some of the goods did not conform to an implied warranty of merchantability (UCC §§ 2–314(1), (2)(c)) and sued Southwest for breach of contract, alleging breach of warranty.

Southwest responded with *no breach–compliance,* claiming that the implied warranty was not a term of the contract because ABC did not object to Southwest's disclaimer.

The first approach to resolving this dispute is the most complicated because it would apply § 2–207(2) by treating the second term (Southwest's disclaimer) as the additional term. The question of merchants must be addressed to determine whether the solution progresses beyond the first sentence of subsection (2). If one party is not a merchant, then Southwest's disclaimer is a counteroffer and the implied warranties are terms in the contract. Southwest's no breach–compliance response fails and ABC has an action for breach of contract.

If both parties are merchants, the analysis progresses to the second sentence of § 2–207(2)–Southwest's disclaimer is in the contract unless the facts satisfy (a), (b), or (c). If the facts satisfy (a), (b), or (c), Southwest's disclaimer returns to the status of counteroffer.

Southwest's no breach–compliance response fails and ABC has a breach of contract action. If the facts do not satisfy (a), (b), or (c), Southwest's disclaimer is a term in the contract and Southwest's no breach–compliance response is good and ABC does not have a breach of contract action.

The second approach would have the implied warranty and disclaimer terms knock each other out (what could be viewed as a double knockout) and the Code would supplement the express contract terms. Article 2 has an implied warranty of merchantability (UCC §§ 2–314(1), (2)(c))–so again, Southwest's no breach–compliance response fails and ABC has a cause of action for breach of contract. (If the Code did not provide for the implied warranty, then Southwest's no breach–compliance response would be good–but not because of the disclaimer which had been knocked out but because ABC's reservation of implied warranties had also been knocked out so that the contract took no position as to implied warranties. Consequently, ABC could not maintain its breach of contract action.)

The third approach, the most simple, would drop Southwest's disclaimer out of the contract because it was second in time; this would leave ABC's reservation of warranties. With this approach, Southwest's no breach–compliance response fails and ABC can maintain its breach of contract action.

Subsection (1) provides a way for the offeree to prevent his or her writing from being the acceptance. The writing must contain a phrase stating in no uncertain terms that it is not an acceptance unless the other party assents to all of its terms. With the other party's assent, the terms become those terms in what would have been the acceptance.

> (1) A definite and seasonable expression of acceptance or a written confirmation which is sent within a reasonable time operates as an acceptance even though it states terms additional to or different from those offered or agreed upon, **unless acceptance is expressly made conditional on assent to the additional or different terms.** (UCC § 2–207(1))

Example 11–9

The ABC Company sent its purchase order to the Southwest Pottery Company for a number of items listed in the Southwest catalog. In the fine print of ABC's purchase order was the reservation of all warranties.

Southwest responded with an acknowledgment form that was not the mirror image of ABC's boilerplate. One difference was that the Southwest form disclaimed all warranties. The Southwest acknowledgment form also stated, *this acknowledgment form is not an acceptance unless ABC assents to all of Southwest's terms.*

Southwest shipped and ABC accepted the shipment and paid. Some courts will consider ABC's conduct as performance that implies assent and that therefore a contract has been formed on Southwest's terms; that is, a contract without the warranties. Other courts will require ABC to expressly assent to Southwest's terms. Therefore, no contract is formed under § 2–207(1) and the analysis proceeds to § 2–207(3)–conduct of the parties that implies a contract.

The first sentence of § 2–207(3) looks to the conduct of the parties to form the contract.

> (3) **Conduct by both parties which recognizes the existence of a contract is sufficient to establish a contract for sale although the writing of the parties do not otherwise establish a contract.** In such case the terms of the particular contract consist of those terms on which the writings of the parties agree, together with any supplementary terms incorporated under any other provisions of this Act. (UCC § 2–207(3))

Example 11–10

The ABC Company sent its purchase order to the Southwest Pottery Company for a number of items listed in the Southwest catalog. ABC listed the prices as found in the Southwest catalog. In the fine print of ABC's purchase order was the reservation of all warranties.

Southwest responded with an acknowledgment form that was not the mirror image of ABC's bargained-for terms or boilerplate. One difference in the bargained-for terms was a price increase. One difference in the boilerplate was that the Southwest form disclaimed all warranties.

When Southwest did not ship, ABC sued for breach of contract. Southwest responded "no contract"—because Southwest did not ship and ABC could not accept the shipment, there was no conduct between the parties that could recognize the existence of a contract. ABC could not maintain its breach of contract action.

If Southwest had shipped and ABC had accepted the shipment and paid, their conduct would have formed a contract under § 2–207(3), sentence 1. The second sentence of § 2–207(3) describes the process for determining the terms of the contract.

---

(3) Conduct by both parties which recognizes the existence of a contract is sufficient to establish a contract for sale although the writing of the parties do not otherwise establish a contract. **In such case the terms of the particular contract consist of those terms on which the writings of the parties agree, together with any supplementary terms incorporated under any other provisions of this Act.** (UCC § 2–207(3))

Example 11–11

The ABC Company sent its purchase order to the Southwest Pottery Company for a number of items listed in the Southwest catalog. ABC listed the prices as found in the Southwest catalog. In the fine print of ABC's purchase order was the reservation of all warranties.

Southwest responded with an acknowledgment form that did not mirror ABC's bargained-for terms or boilerplate. One difference in the bargained-for terms was a price increase. One difference in the boilerplate was that the Southwest form disclaimed all express and implied warranties. Southwest shipped and ABC accepted the shipment and paid the lower price.

Subsequently, ABC discovered that some of the items did not conform to the implied warranty of merchantability and brought a breach of contract action against Southwest.

The bargained-for terms of price do not agree and therefore a contract is not formed under § 2–207(1). Since Southwest shipped and ABC accepted the shipment and paid (although not what Southwest wanted), the conduct of the parties recognized the existence of a contract under § 2–207(3), sentence 1.

The terms are provided by § 2–207(3), sentence 2. "In such case the terms of the particular contract consist of those terms on which the writings of the parties agree, together with any supplementary terms incorporated under any other provisions of this Act." Therefore, the two prices cancel and the gap filler for price (UCC § 2–305) applies. The reservation and disclaimer of warranties cancel and the contract is supplemented with the implied warranties of the Code (UCC §§ 2–314(1), (2)(c)).

Parol Evidence Rule

Although some contracts are created on the spur of the moment, often the contract is a product of negotiations between the parties prior to the actual time of contract formation. These negotiations may be brief or extended. If the parties reduce their agreement to writing (whether the writing is or is not required for the enforcement of the contract), the next question is whether the writing encompasses all the contract terms or only some. The answer is found in the application of the parol evidence rule to the facts.

Under the parol evidence rule, the contract may consist of terms in the final writing and of terms that are parol. **Parol terms** are terms that are oral or, if written, are not in the final writing.

parol terms

Parol terms are terms that are oral or, if written, are not in the final writing.

> In the absence of fraud in the inducement, duress, or mutual mistake of fact, extrinsic evidence, oral or written, made prior to or contemporaneous with the final writing cannot be used to add to or contradict the final writing.

Even though the parol evidence rule is exclusionary, making a certain type of evidence inadmissible, the parol evidence rule is not a rule of evidence. The parol evidence rule is a rule of substantive law. At issue is what are the terms of the contract and not what type of evidence is admissible to demonstrate the terms of the contract. A rule of evidence would not bar the proof of the terms of the contract. It would bar a method of proving the terms of the contract. The fact could be established by a different method.

Example 11–12

The Ventura Dance Company hired Bethany Alexander as its dance director. The contract was for one year and was in writing. After Ventura fired Bethany without cause, Bethany sued Ventura for breach of contract. Bethany attempted to prove the existence of the contract by oral testimony. Under the best evidence rule, the writing is required. The best evidence rule is a rule of evidence. As a general rule, oral testimony cannot be used to provide the existence of a contract when a writing exists. The writing must be produced.

Example 11–13

The Ventura Dance Company hired Bethany Alexander as its dance director. The contract was for one year and was in writing. After Ventura fired Bethany without cause, Bethany sued Ventura for breach of contract. Bethany submitted the writing into evidence and then attempted to prove additional contract terms by oral testimony. Under the parol evidence rule, if these terms were not a part of the contract, the oral testimony is inadmissible. If these terms were a part of the contract, the oral testimony is admissible.

The parol evidence rule does not apply to all transactions, nor does it apply to all parol evidence. First, the parol evidence rule only comes into play when the terms of the contract have been set forth in a final writing. If the parties have a writing but it is not intended as the final writing, the parol evidence rule does not apply. The question that must be asked is "Has the contract been reduced to a final writing?" A final writing is called an **integration** because the final writing brings together the contract terms.

Second, the parol evidence rule does not apply to transactions where there has been fraud in the inducement, duress, or mutual mistake of fact. **Fraud in the inducement** is a false representation or concealment of fact, which should have been disclosed, that is intended to deceive and does deceive another party to the contract. **Duress** is the use of any wrongful act or threat to influence a party to contract. **Mutual mistake of fact** occurs when the parties to a contract have a common intention, but the writing does not reflect that intention due to their misconception of the facts. In those transactions, the parol evidence rule is inapplicable even though the contract has been integrated.

Third, the writing may be a final writing for all the terms of the contract (a total integration) or for only some of the terms (a partial integration). The parol evidence rule will apply to the entire contract if the writing is a total integration. If the writing is a partial integration, the parol evidence rule will apply to only the final writing part of the contract (see Exhibit 11–2).

Fourth, the parol evidence rule only excludes parol evidence made prior to or contemporaneous with (at the same time as) the final writing. The rule does NOT exclude evidence created after the parties entered into the final writing (see Exhibit 11–3).

Fifth, the parol evidence rule only excludes evidence that adds to or contradicts those terms that appear in the final writing. The rule does not exclude evidence intended to clarify or interpret the terms in the final writing (see Exhibit 11–4).

integration
An integration is the final written form of a contract.

fraud in the inducement
Fraud in the inducement is a false representation or concealment of fact, that should have been disclosed, that deceives and is intended to deceive another party to the contract.

duress
Duress is the use of any wrongful act or threat to influence a party to contract. Duress has two forms: duress by actual physical force and duress by threat.

mutual mistake of fact
Mutual mistake of fact occurs when the parties to a contract have a common intention but the writing does not reflect that intention due to their misconception of the facts.

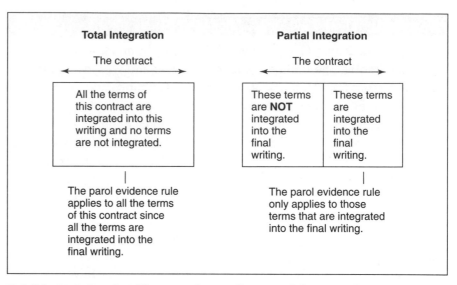

Exhibit 11–2 Parol Evidence Rule: Total vs. Partial Integration

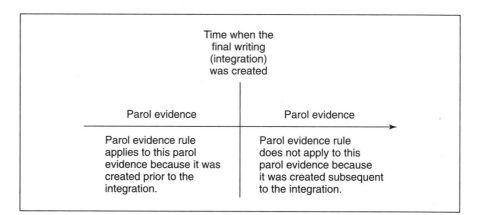

Exhibit 11–3 Parol Evidence: The Timing of the Parol Evidence

Parol evidence that attempts to add to or contradict the terms in the integration	Parol evidence that clarifies or interprets the terms in the integration
This evidence is inadmissible under the parol evidence rule.	This evidence is admissible under the parol evidence rule.

Exhibit 11–4 Parol Evidence That Adds to or Interprets the Final Writing

Example 11–14

Geoquest produced a murder mystery videocassette program, *The Gold Key,* to be sold in home video stores and contacted Embassy, a distributor. The initial negotiations in July produced the following letter by Embassy:

> We will in all likelihood submit a more formal contract letter later, but, in the meantime, I'd like to confirm our agreement regarding Embassy's video distribution of THE GOLD KEY on the following terms . . .

When Geoquest did not sign Embassy's July letter, additional negotiations produced an August letter by Embassy:

> I've revised the July draft along the lines we discussed. This letter now serves to confirm our agreement regarding Embassy's video distribution of THE GOLD KEY on the following terms . . .

When Geoquest did not sign Embassy's August letter, another round of negotiations produced a third Embassy letter. Geoquest signed and returned this letter in September.

> If I've got the essential terms right, please indicate Geoquest's agreement by signing and returning the enclosed copy. . . . Until such time, if ever, that we execute a more formal agreement, this letter will serve to reflect the binding agreement between the parties.

Embassy distributed THE GOLD KEY and sales totaled only 5,700 copies. Geoquest sued Embassy for breach of contract contending that Embassy orally guaranteed minimum sales of 100,000 copies. Embassy has moved to bar this oral evidence under the parol evidence rule.

Step 1. Check for a final writing (an integration). If the contract has not been reduced to a final writing, there is no parol evidence rule problem, even though there may be parol evidence. Although not all writings are intended as final writings, Embassy's September letter was a final writing because it is the last in a series of writings, it states that it incorporates the "essential terms," it notes that there may not be a formal writing, and it is the first writing signed by both parties.

Step 2. Check the final writing for fraud in the inducement, duress, and mutual mistake of fact. None appears here.

Step 3.   Check whether the integration was a final writing for all the terms of the contract (a total integration) or for only some of the terms (a partial integration). Embassy's September letter refers to the "essential terms," and therefore this is a total integration.

Step 4.   Check whether the parol evidence was made prior to, or contemporaneous with, the final writing. If the parol evidence was made subsequent to the final writing, there is no parol evidence rule problem. The alleged oral guarantee was made prior to the final writing in September which means there is a parol evidence rule problem.

Step 5.   Check whether the parol evidence was intended to add to, or contradict, that part of the contract that was reduced to a final writing. If the contract was only partially integrated and if the parol evidence attempts to add to, or contradict, the part of the contract that was *not* reduced to the final writing, there is no parol evidence rule problem. In this situation, the oral guarantee adds to the essential terms found in the final writing and therefore is inadmissible.

Source: *Geoquest Productions, Ltd. v. Embassy Home Entertainment, Inc.*, 593 N.E.2d 727 (IL Ct. App. 1992).

▥ PARALEGAL EXERCISE 11.1

The Eldridge house needed exterior painting, so Eldridge telephoned the Quality Painting Company for an estimate. Quality looked at the house and on several occasions discussed the job with Eldridge by telephone. Finally, Eldridge agreed to pay Quality $2,000 for painting her house. When Quality finished painting the house, Eldridge refused to pay until Quality painted the unattached garage.

Eldridge claims that during the negotiation they discussed the house and the garage and the contract was for both, even though they did not specifically talk about the garage during the final telephone conversation. Quality claims that they did not discuss the garage during the final telephone conversation and therefore the contract was for the house and not the garage.

Is whether the contract includes the garage a parol evidence rule problem? ▪

▥ PARALEGAL EXERCISE 11.2

Same facts as Paralegal Exercise 11.1, except the final telephone conversation was followed by a final writing that spoke of the house but was silent on the garage.

Is whether the contract includes the garage a parol evidence rule problem? ▪

🏛 PARALEGAL EXERCISE 11.3

Same facts as Paralegal Exercise 11.2 but during the negotiation, no mention was made of the garage. The parties only discussed the house for $2,000. After Quality began to paint the house, Eldridge asked Quality how much it would cost to paint the garage. Quality orally responded $500, and they orally agreed.

When Quality finished painting the house and the garage, Eldridge would only pay $2,000 because the writing only stated $2,000.

Is whether the contract can be orally modified to include the garage a parol evidence rule problem? ■

🏛 PARALEGAL EXERCISE 11.4

After extended negotiations, Buyer and Seller contracted for $50,000 of "chickens." Their final writing contained only the term "chickens." Upon uncrating the shipment Buyer was surprised to find "stewing chickens" instead of "fryers."

Should any prior discussion between Seller and Buyer as to the type of chicken be excluded as a violation of the parol evidence rule? ■

Supplying Omitted Terms

Regardless of whether the contract is oral, written, or a bit of both, there are times when a term that the parties never discussed will be added to the contract.

Common Law

Courts have consistently supplied a "good faith" term to contracts. **Good faith** is defined as honesty in fact (subjective honesty) in one's conduct. Therefore, the contracting parties must exercise good faith when performing their contractual duties.

Care, however, should be taken to distinguish the negotiation phase of contract formation from the post-contract formation phase. Although both parties must perform the contract in good faith, neither is required to negotiate the contract in good faith. When the transaction is still in the pre-contract phase, no contractual relationship exists upon which to attach the reciprocal good faith promises.

UCC Article 2 Gap Fillers

If the transaction is a sale of goods, Article 2 of the Uniform Commercial Code will supply some omitted terms. These terms, known as gap fillers, include provisions as to price (§ 2–305), place of delivery (§ 2–308), time for shipment or delivery (§ 2–309),

good faith
Good faith in the case of a merchant means honesty in fact and the observance of reasonable commercial standards of fair dealing in the trade. In the case of a nonmerchant, good faith means honesty in fact in the conduct or transaction concerned.

payment or running of credit (§ 2–310), warranty of title (§ 2–312), warranty against infringement (§ 2–312), implied warranty of merchantability (§§ 2–314(1), (2)), implied warranty from course of dealing or usage of trade (§ 2–314(3)), and implied warranty of fitness for a particular purpose (§ 2–315).

Example 11–15

The Uniform Commercial Code § 2–314. Implied Warranty: Merchantability; Usage of Trade.

(1) Unless excluded or modified (Section 2–316), a warranty that the goods shall be merchantable is implied in a contract for their sale if the seller is a merchant with respect to goods of that kind. Under this section the serving for value of food or drink to be consumed either on the premises or elsewhere is a sale.

(2) Goods to be merchantable must be at least such as

(a) pass without objection in the trade under the contract description; and

(b) in the case of fungible goods, are of fair average quality within the description; and

(c) are fit for the ordinary purposes for which such goods are used; and

(d) run, within the variations permitted by the agreement, of even kind, quality and quality within each unit and among all units involved; and

(e) are adequately contained, packaged, and labeled as the agreement may require; and

(f) conform to the promise or affirmation of fact made on the container or label if any.

(3) Unless excluded or modified (Section 2–316) other implied warranties may arise from course of dealing or usage of trade.

CORRECTING ERRORS IN THE WRITTEN CONTRACT: MISTAKE IN INTEGRATION

Parties may orally contract with the understanding that one of the parties will later draft a writing to reflect the terms of the contract. Ultimately, both parties may sign this written confirmation of their oral contract. The parties may sign the writing without a thorough reading. Later, as the parties perform their duties, one party may be surprised to find that the writing fails to correspond to what he or she thought was agreed upon. A mistake occurred in the integration of the contract. When confronted by this alleged mistake in integration, the drafter may insist that the writing reflects the oral agreement. Can the non-drafting party have the writing reformed (altered) to correspond to the oral agreement?

A court has the power to reform the written evidence of a contract. **Reformation** is a judicial remedy designed to revise a writing to conform to the real agreement or intention of the parties. Reformation is appropriate only if clear and convincing evidence demonstrates the following:

1. The parties' oral agreement expresses their real intentions.
2. The writing fails to express those intentions.
3. The failure is due to a mutual mistake or a unilateral mistake accompanied by the other party's fraudulent conduct.

A **mutual mistake** is a mistake that both parties shared at the time they reduced their agreement to writing. The court will reform a writing only when the parties intended their written agreement to say one thing and, by mistake, it expressed something else. The fact that one party denies that a mistake occurred does not prevent the court from finding a mutual mistake.

In *Bollinger v. Central Pennsylvania Quarry Stripping & Construction Co.,* the Bollingers owned property near the Pennsylvania Turnpike. Central, a contractor working on the Turnpike, orally contracted with the Bollingers for permission to deposit construction waste on the Bollingers' property. Under the oral contract, Central promised to remove the topsoil, deposit the waste, and then replace the topsoil over the waste. Central reduced the oral contract to a writing. At some point in the performance of the contract, Central ceased reclaiming the land but instead began dumping the construction waste over the topsoil. The Bollingers asked the court to reform the writing to include their oral agreement regarding reclamation.

While reading the *Bollinger* case, answer the following:

1. What did the Bollingers allege was the mistake in the final writing (i.e., the integration)?
2. Did Central agree that the writing did not correspond to the oral agreement?
3. Would a reasonable person believe that the writing did not correspond to the oral agreement?
4. What would the reasonable person consider when making this determination?
5. If Central does not agree that a mistake was made in integrating the contract, on what basis does the court conclude that the mistake in integration was mutual?

reformation

Reformation is a judicial remedy designed to revise a writing to conform to the real agreement or intention of the parties.

mutual mistake

Mutual mistake is a mistake that both parties share at the time they reduced their agreement to writing.

CASE

Bollinger v. Central Pennsylvania Quarry Stripping & Construction Co.
Supreme Court of Pennsylvania (1967)
425 Pa. 430, 229 A.2d 741

OPINION OF THE COURT

MUSMANNO, Justice.

Mahlon Bollinger and his wife, Vinetta C. Bollinger, filed an action in equity against the Central Pennsylvania Quarry Stripping Construction Company asking that a contract entered into between them be reformed so as to include therein a paragraph alleged to have been omitted by mutual mistake and that the agreement, as reformed, be enforced.

The agreement, as executed, provided that the defendant was to be permitted to deposit on the property of the plaintiffs, construction waste as it engaged in work on the Pennsylvania Turnpike in the immediate vicinity of the plaintiffs' property. The Bollingers claimed that there had been a mutual understanding between them and the defendant that, prior to depositing such waste on the plaintiffs' property, the defendant would remove the topsoil of the plaintiffs' property, pile on it the waste material and then restore the topsoil in a way to cover the deposited waste. The Bollingers averred that they had signed the written agreement without reading it because they assumed that the condition just stated had been incorporated into the writing.

When the defendant first began working in the vicinity of the plaintiffs' property, it did first remove the topsoil, deposited the waste on the bare land, and then replaced the topsoil. After a certain period of time, the defendant ceased doing this and the plaintiffs remonstrated. The defendant answered there was nothing in the written contract which required it to make a sandwich of its refuse between the bare earth and the topsoil. It was at this point that the plaintiffs discovered that that feature of the oral understanding had been omitted from the written contract. The plaintiff husband renewed his protest and the defendant's superintendent replied he could not remove the topsoil because his equipment for that operation had been taken away. When he was reminded of the original understanding, the superintendent said, in effect, he couldn't help that.

The plaintiffs then filed their action for reformation of the contract, the Court granted the requested relief, and the defendant firm appealed. We said in Bugen v. New York Life Insurance Co., 408 Pa. 472, 184 A.2d 499:

> "A court of equity has the power to reform the written evidence of a contract and make it correspond to the understanding of the parties. * * * However, the mistake must be mutual to the parties to the contract."

The fact, however, that one of the parties denies that a mistake was made does not prevent a finding of mutual mistake. Kutsenkow v. Kutsenkow, 414 Pa. 610, 612, 202 A.2d 68.

Once a person enters into a written agreement he builds around himself a stone wall, from which he cannot escape by merely asserting he had not understood what he was signing. However, equity would completely fail in its objectives if it refused to break a hole through the wall when it finds, after proper evidence, that there was a mistake between the parties, that it was real and not feigned, actual and not hypothetical.

     The Chancellor, after taking testimony, properly concluded:

> "We are satisfied that plaintiffs have sustained the heavy burden placed upon them. Their understanding of the agreement is corroborated by the undisputed evidence. The defendant did remove and set aside the topsoil on part of the area before depositing its waste and did replace the topsoil over such waste after such depositing. It follows it would not have done so had it not so agreed. Further corroboration is found in the testimony that it acted similarly in the case of plaintiffs' neighbor Beltzner."

. . . .

Decree affirmed, costs on the appellant.
BELL, C.J., dissents.
COHEN, J., absent.

Care must be taken to distinguish a parol evidence rule problem from a mistake in integration problem. They share similarities in that both involve parol evidence (oral or nonfinal writings) and both involve an integration (a final writing). In a parol evidence rule problem, the issue is whether the contract consists of the integration and parol or only the integration. No attempt is made to reform the integration to include parol terms. In a mistake in integration problem, the issue is whether the integration should be reformed to include the parol terms. No attempt is made to limit the integration to only some of the terms in the contract. All of the terms of the contract are embodied in the integration.

Example 11–16

Romaro leased space in an office building for the purpose of operating a snack bar. During the negotiations, Romaro agreed to refrain from selling tobacco products in exchange for the exclusive right to sell sandwiches. After the parties orally agreed to all the terms, the landlord drafted a final writing (an integration). Romaro signed the writing without noticing that it did not include his exclusive right to sell sandwiches. Several months later, Romaro noticed that another tenant had a snack bar and was selling sandwiches.

If Romaro wants to enforce his exclusive right to sell sandwiches, he must establish that the parties intended (1) that some contract terms would be in the written lease and some would remain oral and therefore the inclusion of the exclusivity term in the oral part of the contract would not violate the parol evidence rule; or (2) that the exclusivity clause would be in the written lease which means there was a mutual mistake in the integration of the contract since the written lease did not include the exclusivity clause.

INTERPRETING THE LANGUAGE OF THE CONTRACT

If the contract includes the duty alleged to have been breached by the promisor, there remains the question whether this duty was breached. This raises the topic of the interpretation of the contract's language.

Plain Meaning vs. Trade Usage

A term may have two meanings, one used by the general population and the other used in a particular trade.

plain meaning

Plain meaning is the meaning that reasonable people would give to a word or phrase.

Plain meaning is the meaning reasonable people give a term. Because contracts are consensual, the parties may, however, agree to give the term a meaning other than its plain meaning. One party may not secretly attribute a special meaning to that term. If such an attempt is made, the term will be interpreted according to its plain meaning and not the secret meaning.

trade usage

Trade usage gives a word or phrase the meaning of the trade that is different from its plain meaning.

Trade usage is the meaning that reasonable people in the trade give a term. Trade usage is the expected meaning when a term is used in that trade.

If the contracting parties are members of the trade, the term is interpreted according to trade usage. If one party is not a member of the trade, nontrade usage (plain meaning) applies. If one party is a longstanding member of the trade and the other is new to the trade, nontrade usage (plain meaning) will apply unless the new party has actual knowledge of the trade usage or the trade usage is so generally known that actual knowledge could be inferred.

Consider the interpretation of the term "50 percent protein" in *Hurst v. W. J. Lake & Co.* Hurst, the seller of horse meat scraps, contracted to give W. J. Lake & Co., the buyer, a $5 discount for each ton that analyzed less than 50 percent protein. When 140 tons of scraps contained protein varying from 49.53 percent to 49.96 percent, Lake claimed the discount. Hurst objected, asserting that 50 percent was a trade term and that in the trade, 50 percent was really 49.5 percent. Therefore Lake was not entitled to the discount. Should the court use the plain meaning of 50 percent, which is 50 percent, or the trade meaning of 50 percent, which is 49.5 percent? (See Exhibit 11–5.)

What the parties said: Each ton below 50% will receive a $5 discount.		
What the Seller (Hurst) meant	trade usage 50% = 49.5% no discount	trade usage 50% = 49.5% no discount	trade usage 50% = 49.5% no discount
What the Buyer (Lake) meant	plain meaning 50% = 50% $5 discount	plain meaning 50% = 50% $5 discount	plain meaning 50% = 50% $5 discount
What the reasonable person would have meant	if trade usage 50% = 49.5% no discount	if plain meaning 50% = 50% $5 discount	if either plain meaning or trade usage 50% could = either 50% or 49.5%
Conclusion	contract with trade usage 50% = 49.5% no discount	contract with plain meaning 50% = 50% $5 discount	no contract

Exhibit 11–5 Trade Usage or Plain Meaning?

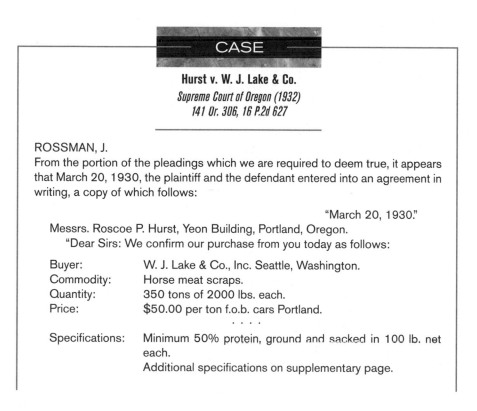

CASE

Hurst v. W. J. Lake & Co.
Supreme Court of Oregon (1932)
141 Or. 306, 16 P.2d 627

ROSSMAN, J.

From the portion of the pleadings which we are required to deem true, it appears that March 20, 1930, the plaintiff and the defendant entered into an agreement in writing, a copy of which follows:

"March 20, 1930."

Messrs. Roscoe P. Hurst, Yeon Building, Portland, Oregon.

"Dear Sirs: We confirm our purchase from you today as follows:

Buyer:	W. J. Lake & Co., Inc. Seattle, Washington.
Commodity:	Horse meat scraps.
Quantity:	350 tons of 2000 lbs. each.
Price:	$50.00 per ton f.o.b. cars Portland.

. . . .

Specifications:	Minimum 50% protein, ground and sacked in 100 lb. net each.
	Additional specifications on supplementary page.

"Yours truly,
        "W. J. Lake & Company, Inc.,
            "By L. E. Branchflower.
"Accepted by:
    "Roscoe P. Hurst.

                                        "March 20, 1930.

"Mr. Roscoe P. Hurst, Yeon Building, Portland, Oregon.
    "Dear Sir: In case any of the Horse Meat Scraps, covered by our purchase order No. 1352, analyzes less than 50% of protein, it is understood that W. J. Lake & Company, Inc., the buyers, are to receive a discount of $5.00 per ton.
                        . . . .

    "Yours very truly,
        "W. J. Lake & Co., Inc.,
            "[Signed] L. E. Branchflower.
"LEB:G   L. E. Branchflower.
"Accepted by:
    "[Signed] Roscoe P. Hurst."

Pursuant to the contract, the plaintiff delivered to the defendant 349.25 tons of horse meat scraps. . . .

Based upon the contention [in] complaint, admitted as true by the defendant, shows that the 140 tons with a protein content of 49.53 per cent. to 49.96 per cent. should have been regarded as within the 50 per cent. protein classification, the plaintiff argues that the circuit court erred when it sustained the defendant's motion for judgment on the pleadings.

It will be observed from the foregoing (1) that there is a group of dealers who trade in the commodity known as horse meat scraps; (2) that both plaintiff and defendant are members of that group; (3) that the terms "minimum 50% protein" and "less than 50% protein" are trade terms to which the group has attached meanings different from their common ones; (4) that this usage, prevalent among this group, demanded that, whenever those terms appeared in a contract for the sale of horse meat scraps, it became the duty of the buyer to accept all scraps containing 49.5 per cent. protein or more, and to pay for them at the rate provided for scraps containing full 50 per cent. protein; and (5) that the defendant was aware of all of the foregoing when it attached its signature to the aforementioned contract.

The flexibility of or multiplicity in the meaning of words is the principal source of difficulty in the interpretation of language. Words are the conduits by which thoughts are communicated, yet scarcely any of them have such a fixed and single meaning that they are incapable of denoting more than one thought. In addition to the multiplicity in meaning of words set forth in the dictionaries, there are the meanings imparted to them by trade customs, local uses, dialects, telegraphic codes, etc. One meaning crowds a word full of significance, while another almost empties the utterance of any import. The various groups above indicated are constantly amplifying our language; in fact, they are developing what may be called languages of their own. Thus one is justified in saying that the language of the dictionaries is not the only language spoken in America. For instance, the word "thousand" as commonly used has a very specific meaning; it denotes 10 hundreds or 50 scores, but the language of the various trades and localities has assigned to it meanings quite different from that just mentioned. Thus in the bricklaying trade a contract which fixes the bricklayer's compensation at "$5.25 a thousand" does not contemplate that he need lay actually 1,000 bricks in order to earn $5.25, but that he should build a wall of a certain size. Brunold v. Glasser, 25 Misc. 285, 52 N.Y.S. 1021; Walker v. Syms, 118 Mich. 183, 76 N.W. 320. In the lumber industry a contract requiring the delivery of 4,000 shingles will be fulfilled by the delivery of only 2,500 when it appears that by trade custom two packs of a certain size are regarded as 1,000 shingles, and that hence the delivery of eight packs fulfills the contract, even though they contain only 2,500 shingles by actual count. Soutier v. Kellerman, 18 Mo. 509. And, where the custom of a locality considers 100 dozen as constituting 1,000, one who has 19,200 rabbits upon a warren under an agreement for their sale at the price of 60 pounds for each 1,000 rabbits will be paid for only 16,000 rabbits. Smith v. Wilson, 3 Barn. & Adol. 728. Numerous other instances could readily be cited showing the manner in which the meaning of words has been contracted, expanded, or otherwise altered by local usage, trade custom, dialect influence, code agreement, etc. In fact, it is no novelty to find legislative enactments preceded by glossaries or brief dictionaries defining the meaning of the words employed in the act. Technical treatises dealing with aeronautics, the radio, engineering, etc., generally contain similar glossaries defining the meaning of many of the words employed by the craft. A glance at these glossaries readily shows that the different sciences and trades, in addition to coining words of their own, appropriate common words and assign to them new meanings. Thus it must be evident that one cannot understand accurately the language of such sciences and trades without knowing the peculiar meaning attached to the words which they use. It is said that a court in construing the language of the parties must put itself into the shoes of the parties. That alone would not suffice; it must also adopt their vernacular.

. . . .

Without setting forth herein our review of the many authorities cited in the briefs, all of which we have read with care, we state our conclusion that members of a trade or business group who have employed in their contracts trade terms are entitled to prove that fact in their litigation, and show the meaning of those terms to assist the court in the interpretation of their language.

Finally, it is suggested that the employment of the terms "minimum 50% protein" and "less than 50% of protein" indicates that the parties rejected the mercantile custom in effecting their contract. It will be recalled that under the state of the record we are compelled to regard these two terms as trade terms possessed of a special significance. We believe that it is safe to assume, in the absence of evidence to the contrary, that, when tradesmen employ trade terms, they attach to them their trade significance. If, when they write their trade terms into their contracts, they mean to strip the terms of their special significance and demote them to their common import, it would seem reasonable to believe that they would so state in their agreement. Otherwise they would refrain from using the trade term and express themselves in other language. We quote from Nicoll v. Pittsvein Coal Co. (C.C.A.) 269 F. 968, 971: "Indeed when tradesmen say or write anything, they are perhaps without present thought on the subject, writing on top of a mass of habits or usages which they take as matter of course. So (with Prof. Williston) we think that any one contracting with knowledge of a usage will naturally say nothing about the matter unless desirous of excluding its operation; if he does wish to exclude, he will say so in express terms. Williston, Contracts, § 653." Nothing in the contract repels the meaning assigned by the trade to the two above terms unless the terms themselves reject it. But, if these terms repel the meaning which usage has attached to them, then every trade term would deny its own meaning. We reject this contention as being without merit. We have considered all other contentions presented by the respondent, but have found no merit in them.

It follows that, in our opinion, the circuit court erred when it sustained the defendant's motion for judgment on the pleadings.

Reversed.

BROWN, BELT, CAMPBELL, and KELLY, JJ., concur.
RAND, J., concurs in the result.
BEAN, C.J., dissents.

Ambiguities

If the terms of the contract are in writing, the parties will refer to the writing to determine each party's obligations. It is helpful when the writing clearly states the duties of the parties and there is no dispute, but writings are seldom perfect.

In 20/20 hindsight, the terms of the writing may not have been as carefully drafted as they should have been. The parties may dispute each other's meaning. They are left with an ambiguity that needs resolution. Ambiguities may be patent or latent. A **patent ambiguity** is apparent from the face of the writing. A **latent ambiguity** is apparent when information beyond the writing demonstrates that the term has a double meaning.

patent ambiguity

A contract term suffers from a patent ambiguity when the ambiguity is apparent from the face of the writing.

latent ambiguity

A latent ambiguity is a miscommunication between the promisor and the promisee and occurs when a term has a double meaning.

Patent Ambiguities

Patent ambiguities are often created by inexact pronoun reference or misleading modifiers.

Example 11-17

The attorney told her client she needs more information. Who needs more information, the attorney or the client?

Example 11-18

I said when I have finished my research, I will write the brief. Does this mean "I have finished my research and I will write the brief" or "I will write the brief when I have finished my research"?

Latent Ambiguities—Miscommunications between the Promisor and the Promisee

An ambiguity may not always be apparent from the face of the writing. Latent ambiguities are often created when the term has a double meaning.

Example 11–19

Buyer purchased 125 bales of cotton from Seller to be shipped from Mumbai (formerly Bombay) to Liverpool on the ship *Peerless.* Buyer met the ship *Peerless* (which sailed from Mumbai) when it docked in Liverpool in October, but there was no cotton. Buyer, believing Seller had breached the contract, purchased substitute cotton on the open market.

In December, a second ship named *Peerless* (which also sailed from Mumbai) docked in Liverpool. Although this ship carried cotton Seller was sending to the Buyer, Buyer no longer needed the cotton and rejected the shipment.

The ambiguity—two ships with the same name sailing from and to the same ports—was not apparent from the face of the contract. The ambiguity became apparent only when Buyer discovered the existence of two ships with the same name. The ambiguity was latent.

Latent ambiguities are resolved by examining what the term means to a reasonable person. If the term is a trade term, the reasonable person will be a reasonable person in the trade (see Exhibit 11–6).

The term: Peerless		
Promisor's perception of the term	October Peerless	October Peerless
Promisee's perception of the term	December Peerless	December Peerless
Reasonable person's perception of the term	If October Peerless	If December Peerless
Conclusion	Then October Peerless	Then December Peerless
Explanation	If the reasonable person's perception is the same as the promisor's perception, the term carries the promisor's meaning.	If the reasonable person's perception is the same as the promisee's perception, the term carries the promisee's meaning.

Exhibit 11-6 Latent Ambiguity

DETERMINING WHETHER THE CONDITION PRECEDENT HAS OCCURRED

Some promises need not be performed until the occurrence of an express condition (**condition precedent**). A condition is a contingency. It is a premise upon which the fulfillment of the promise depends. A condition may be based on the occurrence of an external event.

condition precedent

A condition precedent is a duty-creating event. An event external to the contract can be a condition precedent to the performance of a contracting party. An event internal to the contract, such as the performance by one party, can be a condition precedent to the performance by the other.

Example 11–20

"I promise to come home when the sun goes down." The sun going down is a condition to the promise to come home.

A condition precedent is a duty-creating event.

Example 11–21

"I promise to pay for damages to your home if it is struck by lightning." Being struck by lightning is the event that creates the duty to pay. The promisor has no duty to pay until the event occurs.

Example 11–22

A fire insurance policy presents a classic illustration of a "no breach–compliance" response. Triplett contracted with the Lone Star Insurance Company for homeowner's insurance. Triplett promised to pay the premiums for Lone Star's promise to pay for repairs to Triplett's house for damage caused by natural disaster. Because Triplett's house was located in a flood plain, the policy excluded damage due to flooding. Several months after Triplett paid the premium, his house was damaged by a 100-year flood.

Triplett filed a claim with Lone Star, but Lone Star denied the claim on the ground that the policy did not cover loss by flooding.

If Triplett filed an action against Lone Star for breach of contract, he would allege that Lone Star breached the contract by not paying the claim. Lone Star's response would be "no breach–compliance. Because the contract states that we do not have to pay for losses caused by flooding and because this loss was caused by flooding, we have no duty under the contract to pay for this loss. We are complying with the terms of the contract."

COULD RESTITUTION BE A CAUSE OF ACTION WHEN THE DEFENDANT HAS NOT BREACHED BUT RATHER IS IN COMPLIANCE WITH THE CONTRACT?

The "no breach–compliance" response is a denial of breach. "I am not breaching; I am complying." Without a breach of the contract, a breach of contract action cannot be maintained and the remedies for breach of contract are unavailable.

Some contracts include a condition precedent to one party's full performance. Although that party is required to begin performing before the condition occurs, full performance is not required until after the condition has occurred. If the condition precedent never occurs, the promisee has conferred a benefit on the promisor without being compensated. The promisor has no contractual duty to perform because the condition precedent has not occurred.

The Restatement (Second) of Contracts § 377 (1981) supports a restitution cause of action . . .

> A party whose duty of performance does not arise . . . as a result of . . . non-occurrence of a condition . . . is entitled to restitution for any benefit that he has conferred on the other party by way of part performance. . . .

ⅲ PARALEGAL EXERCISE 11.5

Lewis contracted to purchase Blackacre from Roberts for $85,000. The contract was subject to Lewis's obtaining a 20-year mortgage for $60,000 at 6 percent interest from a lending institution. The contract also called for an $8,500 deposit. The contract does not address who gets the deposit if Lewis makes a good faith attempt to secure financing but is unsuccessful.

Lewis paid Roberts the $8,500 deposit. After exercising due diligence, Lewis was unable to find a 20-year mortgage for $60,000 at 6 percent interest from a lending institution.

Could Lewis maintain a breach of contract action against Roberts for return of the $8,500 deposit?

If Lewis could not maintain a breach of contract action, could Lewis maintain a restitution cause of action against Roberts for return of the $8,500 deposit? ■

🏛 PARALEGAL CHECKLIST

The Defendant's Response to the Plaintiff's Allegation of Breach—No Breach–Compliance

❑ Whether the promisor's breach is intentional or unintentional is irrelevant. The law of contracts does not evaluate the mental state accompanying nonperformance.

The fact that the promisee alleges the promisor breached the contract does not make it so. The promisor may respond to the promisee's allegation of breach with "no breach–compliance"—which says, "no breach; I am complying with the terms of the contract."

Determining whether the defendant is in fact complying with the terms of the contract may depend on (1) whether the contract includes the duty the promisee alleges the promisor has breached (this may lead to a battle of the forms, the parol evidence rule, or issues regarding the supplying of omitted terms), (2) whether a mistake in integration has occurred, (3) whether the contract is interpreted according to the promisee's or promisor's perception (patent and latent ambiguities), or (4) whether the contractual duty has a condition precedent that has yet to occur. If the defendant has not breached the contract, the plaintiff has no cause of action for breach. A restitution action may be available if the plaintiff has unjustly enriched the defendant.

KEY TERMS

Condition precedent

Duress

Fraud in the inducement

Good faith

Integration

Latent ambiguity

Mutual mistake

Mutual mistake of fact

Parol terms

Patent ambiguity

Plain meaning

Reformation

Trade usage

REVIEW QUESTIONS

TRUE/FALSE QUESTIONS (CIRCLE THE CORRECT ANSWER)

1. T F In a no breach–compliance response, the promisor admits to not performing according to the terms of the contract.

2. T F Buyer requested a price list from Seller. Seller complied and sent its price list. Buyer sent an order on its preprinted purchase order form. Seller acknowledged by sending its preprinted acknowledgment form. Seller shipped and Buyer accepted and paid. Subsequently, Buyer claimed that the goods did not comply with an implied warranty of merchantability.

   In the small print of Buyer's form, Buyer reserves all express and implied warranties. In the small print of Seller's form, Seller disclaims all warranties.

   Under common law, Buyer prevails on the warranty issue.

3. T F Same facts as question (2). Under the UCC, Buyer prevails on the warranty issue.

4. T F If the writing is unambiguous it will always reflect the agreed-upon terms.

5. T F If a contract has been reduced to a final writing, prior or contemporaneous parol terms can never be added to the contract.

6. T F The UCC may supply terms (gap fillers) omitted in the offer.

7. T F A mistake made by the drafter in reducing the oral agreement to writing is called a mistake in the integration of the contract.

8. T F The writing should be reformed to reflect the true intent of the parties if their intent is clear and the writing was in error.

9. T F A patent ambiguity becomes apparent only when information beyond the writing demonstrates that the terms have a double meaning.

10. T F A latent ambiguity is apparent from the face of the writing.

11. T F Patent ambiguities are often created by inexact pronoun references or misleading modifiers.

12. T F The two-ship *Peerless* case involved a patent ambiguity.

13. T F A condition precedent is a duty-terminating event.

14. T F Even if there has been no breach of contract, the remedies for breach of contract may still be available in certain situations.

15. T F Even if there has been no breach of contract, restitution remedies in a restitution action may still be available in certain situations.

FILL-IN-THE-BLANK QUESTIONS

1. _____. The defendant's denial that he or she is not complying with the terms of the contract.

2. _____. An ambiguity that is sometimes apparent from the face of the writing.

3. _____. Does the following statement contain a patent or latent ambiguity? "The attorney told her paralegal that she needs more information concerning a certain client's problem."

4. _____. An ambiguity that may become apparent when information beyond the writing demonstrates that the term has a double meaning.

5. _____. Does the following statement contain a patent or latent ambiguity? "I promise to buy 100 hogs from you." (Buyer expected Tamworths but Seller sent Berkshires.)

6. _____. Terms that may be supplied by the UCC when they have been omitted in the contract.

7. _____. A Latin term meaning that the terms of the contract should be strictly construed against the drafter.

8. _____. A rule stating that contract terms should be given their plain meaning.

MULTIPLE-CHOICE QUESTIONS (CIRCLE ALL THE CORRECT ANSWERS)

1. Which of the following are no breach–compliance issues?
   (a) The last shot doctrine
   (b) The parol evidence rule
   (c) The UCC gap fillers
   (d) Latent ambiguities
   (e) Condition precedents

SHORT-ANSWER QUESTIONS

1. Explain the parol evidence rule and provide an illustration.

2. Distinguish between a problem that involves the parol evidence rule and one that involves a mistake in integration.

3. Buyer requested a price list from Seller. Seller complied and sent its price list. Buyer sent an order on its preprinted purchase order form. Seller acknowledged by sending its preprinted acknowledgment form. Seller shipped and Buyer accepted and paid. Subsequently, Buyer claimed that the goods did not comply with an implied warranty of merchantability.

   In the small print of Buyer's form, Buyer reserves all express and implied warranties. In the small print of Seller's form, Seller disclaims all warranties.

   Under common law, should Buyer or Seller prevail on the warranty issue? Provide a full explanation.

4. Same facts as question (3). Under Article 2 of the UCC, should Buyer or Seller prevail on the warranty issue? Provide a full explanation.

5. When should the plain meaning, rather than trade usage, be used to resolve an interpretation dispute? Provide an example.

CHAPTER 12

The Defendant's *No Breach–Excuse* Response to the Plaintiff's Allegation of Breach

- Impossibility and Impracticability
- Frustration of Purpose
- Could Restitution Be a Cause of Action When the Defendant's Nonperformance of a Contractual Duty Is Excused?

The defendant's second response to the plaintiff's allegation of breach is "No breach–excuse."

> Although I have not performed the contract, a supervening external event has prevented my performance and therefore I am excused from performing. I am not in breach.

Unlike the first response ("No breach–compliance") where the defendant claims that he or she *is* performing the contract, in the second response ("No breach–excuse"), the defendant admits that he or she *is not* performing the contract. The defendant, however, claims that a supervening external event (an act of God or a governmental regulation) has excused his or her performance. A **supervening external event** is an event that occurs after contract formation and before full performance of the contract. In the "no breach–excuse" response, the contract does not refer to the occurrence of the supervening external event. Therefore, the risk of the occurrence of the supervening external event is not allocated by contract. If the promisor is excused, the promisor is not in breach, and the promisee cannot maintain a breach of contract action (see Exhibit 12-1).

    The no breach–excuse response has two variations: (1) the supervening external event renders the contract impossible or impracticable to perform; or (2) although the supervening external event does not render the contract impossible or impracticable to perform, it

supervening external event

A supervening external event is an event that occurs after contract formation and before full performance of the contract.

IN THE DISTRICT COURT OF [NAME] COUNTY
STATE OF [NAME]

[NAME], dba [Name]	)	
	)	
Plaintiff,	)	
	)	
v.	)	Case No. _____
	)	
[NAME], a [Name of State]	)	
corporation	)	
	)	
Defendant.	)	

ANSWER OF DEFENDANT [NAME]

Defendant [name] alleges the following in response to the complaint:

1. Defendant admits the allegations of paragraph 1 of the complaint.

2. Defendant admits the allegations of paragraph 2 of the complaint.

3. Defendant admits the allegations of paragraph 3 of the complaint.

4. Defendant admits the allegations of paragraph 4 of the complaint.

5. Defendant alleges that it has been excused from performance as alleged in paragraph 5 of the complaint in that a tornado on [date] destroyed Defendant's offices.

6. Defendant denies the allegations of paragraph 6 that it breached the contract.

7. The complaint fails to state a claim against Defendant upon which relief can be granted.

Accordingly, Defendant demands that Plaintiff take nothing by this Action, and that Defendant be awarded costs including reasonable attorney fees.

> [Attorney's name signed]
> [Attorney's name typed]
> Attorney for plaintiff
> [Bar membership number]
> [Address]
> [Telephone number]

Exhibit 12–1 Answer—Defendant's "No Breach–Excuse" Response to the Plaintiff's Allegation of Defendant's Breach

renders the performance of the contract to be without purpose and therefore the purpose of the contract is frustrated.

IMPOSSIBILITY AND IMPRACTICABILITY

The no breach–excuse response traces its origin to the no breach–compliance response. One form of the no breach–compliance response was the express condition precedent. "I am in compliance with my contractual duties because I am waiting for an express condition precedent to occur." As the no breach–compliance response evolved, the condition precedent was expanded to include implied condition precedents as well. A leading case is *Taylor v. Caldwell,* 3 B. & S. 826, 122 Eng. Rep. 309, 314–15 (K.B. 1863), an old English case. Taylor, an impresario, contracted to rent the Surrey Gardens and Music Hall from Caldwell for four days for the purpose of presenting four "grand concerts" and "day and night fetes" in the hall. Shortly after the parties signed a lease and before the concert dates, fire destroyed the music hall. Taylor brought a breach of contract action against Caldwell, alleging that Caldwell breached the contract by failing to provide the music hall. Caldwell responded that although he did not provide the hall, his not providing the hall was excused due to the fire. The court in *Taylor v. Caldwell,* held that the destruction of the music hall did excuse Caldwell from performing the contract:

> The principle seems to us to be that, in contracts in which the performance depends on the continued existence of a given person or thing, a condition is implied that the impossibility of performance arising from the perishing of the person or thing shall excuse the performance.
>
> In none of these cases is the promise in words other than positive, nor is there any express stipulation that the destruction of the person or thing shall excuse the performance; but that excuse is by law implied, because from the nature of the contract it is apparent that the parties contracted on the basis of the continued existence of the particular person or chattel. In the present case, looking at the whole contract, we find that the parties contracted on the basis of the continued existence of the Music Hall at the time when the concerts were to be given; that being essential to their performance.
>
> We think, therefore, that the Music Hall having ceased to exist, without fault of either party, both parties are excused, the plaintiffs from taking the gardens and paying the money, the defendants from performing their promise to give the use of the Hall and Gardens and other things.

The doctrine of implied conditions ultimately gave way to a more direct analysis of unexpected supervening external events that made full performance of the contract impossible. The response became *no breach–excuse*. Ultimately, the no breach–excuse response was expanded to include impracticability.

> Restatement (First) of Contracts § 454 (1932). *Definition of Impossibility*. In the Restatement of this Subject impossibility means not only strict impossibility but impracticability because of extreme and unreasonable difficulty, expense, injury, or loss involved.

The Restatement (Second) of Contracts discontinues its reference to impossibility and uses *impracticability* exclusively.

> Restatement (Second) of Contracts § 261 (1981). *Discharge By Supervening Impracticability*. Where, after a contract is made, a party's performance is made impracticable without his fault by the occurrence of an event the non-occurrence of which was a basic assumption on which the contract was made, his duty to render that performance is discharged, unless the language or the circumstances indicate the contrary.

Article 2 of the UCC also uses *impracticability* exclusively.

> UCC § 2–615. *Excuse by Failure of Presupposed Conditions*. Except so far as a seller may have assumed a greater obligation and subject to the preceding section on substituted performance:
> (a) Delay in delivery or non-delivery in whole or in part by a seller who complies with paragraphs (b) and (c) is not a breach of his duty under a contract for sale if performance as agreed has been made impracticable by the occurrence of a contingency the non-occurrence of which was a basic assumption on which the contract was made or by compliance in good faith with any applicable foreign or domestic governmental regulation or order whether or not it later proves to be invalid.
> (b) Where the causes mentioned in paragraph (a) affect only a part of the seller's capacity to perform, he must allocate production and deliveries among his customers but may at his option include regular customers not then under contract as well as his own requirements for further manufacture. He may so allocate in any manner which is fair and reasonable.
> (c) The seller must notify the buyer seasonably that there will be delay or non-delivery and, when allocation is required under paragraph (b), of the estimated quota thus made available for the buyer.

The following series of questions focus the impossibility and impracticablility response:

1. Did an unexpected event occur after the contract was formed?
2. Did the occurrence of this event render the promisor's performance of his or her contractual duty impossible or impracticable?
3. Was the risk associated with the occurrence of this event allocated by contract or custom?
4. Was the nonoccurrence of this event a basic assumption on which the contract was made?

If all four questions are answered in the affirmative, the promisor should be excused from performing his or her contractual duty.

1. *Did an unexpected event occur after the contract was formed?* The no breach–excuse response deals with external events and not with something the parties have or should have done. The event must occur after contract formation and before the time full performance of the promisor's contractual duty is due. The event must be unexpected; that is, unpredicted or unanticipated by the parties—for example, an act of God (e.g., fire, flood, and earthquake) or a governmental action (e.g., legislation, executive order, administrative rule, or war).

2. *Did the occurrence of the event render the promisor's performance of the contract impossible or impracticable?* The promisor's performance becomes impossible when the promisor is totally unable to perform. The Restatement (First) of Contracts refers to impossibility as strict impossibility.

The promisor's performance becomes impracticable when the promisor's performance is unreasonably difficult or costly although not strictly impossible. What is reasonably difficult or costly is a question of degree. The difficulty or costs must be significantly more than what would normally be expected.

The occurrence of the event must render the promisor's performance impossible or impracticable. The promisor is totally unable to perform when the subject matter of the contract is destroyed by an unexpected event—as when a fire destroys a theatre and thus makes a ballet company's future use of the theatre impossible. The promisor is totally unable to perform when he or she dies or becomes incapacitated and his or her personal performance is a requirement of the contract—as when the death of an opera singer makes the singer's participation in an upcoming opera production impossible. The promisor is totally unable to perform when legislation prevents performance—as when a federal statute prohibits the importation of lamb pelts from Canada to the United States and thus makes the subsequent delivery of Canadian pelts to Philadelphia impossible. The promisor is totally unable to perform when the outbreak of armed hostilities between two nations leads to the closing of an international waterway and thus makes further shipping through the waterway impossible.

Performance becomes impracticable when it can only be accomplished with great difficulty or through excessive costs. If a theatre was severely damaged by fire after it had been leased to a ballet company for a future production, the lessor's performance may become impracticable when a significant sum of money is necessary to repair the theatre so the ballet could have a forum.

Restatement (Second) of Contracts § 261, comment d, explains the term "impracticability." As previously discussed, the Restatement's definition of impracticability includes impossibility.

Performance may be impracticable because extreme and unreasonable difficulty, expense, injury, or loss to one of the parties will be involved. A severe shortage of raw materials or of supplies due to war, embargo, local crop failure, unforeseen shutdown of major sources of supply, or the like, which either causes a marked increase in cost or prevents performance altogether may bring the case within the rule stated in this Section. Performance may also be impracticable because it will involve a risk of injury to person or to property, of one of the parties or of others, that is disproportionate to the ends to be attained by performance. However, "impracticability" means more than "impracticality." A mere change in the degree of difficulty or expense due to such causes as increased wages, prices of raw materials, or costs of construction, unless well beyond the normal range, does not amount to impracticability since it is this sort of risk that a fixed-price contract is intended to cover. Furthermore, a party is expected to use reasonable efforts to surmount obstacles to performance, and a performance is impracticable only if it is so in spite of such efforts (see Restatement (second) of Contracts § 205 (1979)).

3. *Was the risk of the occurrence of the event allocated by contract or custom?* If the parties allocate the risk of the occurrence of the unexpected (unpredicted or unanticipated) event at the time they contract, the no breach–excuse response is inapplicable. The parties have factored the risk of the external event into their contract, so a no breach–compliance response is more appropriate. Only when the risk is neither expressly allocated by the parties in their contract nor implied by custom is a court called upon to allocate the risk of nonperformance due to impossibility or impracticability.

4. *Was the nonoccurrence of this event a basic assumption on which the contract was made?* The Restatement (Second) of Contracts § 261 and UCC § 2–615 inquire whether the nonoccurrence of the unexpected event was a basic assumption on which the parties made the contract. If the basic assumption of the contracting parties is that the unexpected event would not occur, the promisor is excused from performing when the unexpected event does occur.

Example 12–1

The owner of the Kokomo Comets, a triple-A baseball team, hired Red Kelley to manage the team for three years. The contract was in writing but only signed by Kelley. The contract provided that all litigation would be under Indiana law. During the second season, Kelley was killed in a motorcycle accident. The owner replaced Kelley with another manager at twice Kelley's salary.

The owner of the Comets brought a breach of contract action against Kelley's estate. The breach of contract analysis would be the following:

1.   Choice of law—The contract mandates Indiana law. This contract was for personal services (employment) so common law of Indiana governs.
2.   Contract formation—A personal service contract was formed between the owner of the Comets and Kelley.
3.   Contract enforcement—Since the contract could not be fully performed within a year, the Statute of Frauds required a writing signed by the party against whom enforcement was sought. With Kelley's estate being the defendant, the writing was properly signed and therefore enforceable against Kelley's estate.
4.   Plaintiff's allegation of breach—The owner of the Comets sued Kelley's estate alleging Kelley breached the contract by not coaching for the complete three-year contract term.
5.   The defendant's response—"no breach–excuse."
    (a) An unexpected external event (Kelley's death) occurred after contract formation and before full performance.
    (b) Death rendered Kelley's performance of his personal service contract (managing for three years) impossible.
    (c) The risk associated with the occurrence of Kelley's death was neither allocated by the contract nor by custom.
    (d) The nonoccurrence of this event (Kelley's death) was a basic assumption on which the personal service contract was made since personal service requires the person to be alive to perform.

Therefore, the no breach–excuse response by Kelley's estate is effective, the owner's allegation of Kelley's breach fails, and the owner's breach of contract cause of action should be dismissed.

☷ PARALEGAL EXERCISE 12.1

In the following case, *Di Scipio v. Sullivan,* Sullivan contracted to purchase real estate but died prior to closing. Di Scipio, the seller, brought a breach of contract action against Sullivan for failing to close. Evaluate the *Di Scipio* case using the five steps of the previous example. Is *Di Scipio* correctly decided and why? ■

CASE

Di Scipio v. Sullivan

Supreme Court, Appellate Division, Third Dept., New York (2006)
30 A.D.3d 660, 816 N.Y.S.2d 576

Before: CARDONA, P.J., CREW III, PETERS, SPAIN and MUGGLIN, JJ.
MUGGLIN, J.

Appeal from an order of the Supreme Court (Williams, J.), entered June 1, 2005 in Saratoga County, which granted plaintiff's motion for summary judgment.

Gail A. Sullivan (hereinafter decedent), the purchaser on a real estate contract with plaintiff, died unexpectedly several days before the scheduled closing. Following the appointment of defendant as administrator for decedent's estate, plaintiff declared time to be of the essence and scheduled two closing dates in February 2004. When defendant failed to close, plaintiff brought this breach of contract action seeking, among other things, to retain the 10 percent contract deposit of $99,900. After joinder of issue, plaintiff successfully moved for summary judgment. Defendant appeals.

Defendant argues that it cannot be determined as a matter of law that the death of a party to a real estate contract amounts to a willful breach entitling plaintiff to the return of the down payment. We find no merit to this argument. As this executory contract contains no provision to the contrary (see Gura v. Herman, 227 App.Div. 452, 454, 238 N.Y.S. 230 [1929], affd. 253 N.Y. 618, 171 N.E. 808 [1930]), and does not involve an obligation personal in nature to the decedent (see Spalding v. Rosa, 71 N.Y. 40, 41 [1877]; Cooper v. Dhafir, 211 A.D.2d 860, 860, 621 N.Y.S.2d 200 [1995]), decedent's death did not terminate the contract (see EPTL 11-3.1). Moreover, willfulness is not a factor (see Cipriano v. Glen Cove Lodge # 1458, B.P.O.E., 1 N.Y.3d 53, 62–63, 769 N.Y.S.2d 168, 801 N.E.2d 388 [2003]). "It has long been the rule in New York that a purchaser who defaults on a real estate contract without lawful excuse cannot recover the down payment" (Korabel v. Natoli, 210 A.D.2d 620, 621–622, 619 N.Y.S.2d 833 [1994], lv. denied 85 N.Y.2d 889, 626 N.Y.S.2d 753, 650 N.E.2d 411 [1995] [citation omitted]; see Maxton Bldrs. v. Lo Galbo, 68 N.Y.2d 373, 378, 509 N.Y.S.2d 507, 502 N.E.2d 184 [1986]), as long as the parties "were dealing at arm's length" (Vitolo v. O'Connor, 223 A.D.2d 762, 764, 636 N.Y.S.2d 163 [1996]). This is the result "notwithstanding that a seller's actual damages may be less than a given down payment" (Barton v. Lerman, 233 A.D.2d 555, 555, 649 N.Y.S.2d 107 [1996]). Therefore, absent a legally cognizable excuse for defendant's failure to perform the contract, plaintiff may retain the down payment (see Collar City Partnership I v. Redemption Church of Christ of Apostolic Faith, 235 A.D.2d 665, 666, 651 N.Y.S.2d 729 [1997], lv. denied 90 N.Y.2d 803, 661 N.Y.S.2d 179, 683 N.E.2d 1053 [1997]). Defendant's asserted excuse–the illiquidity of the estate and its inability to obtain financing–is unavailing. "[W]here impossibility or difficulty of performance is occasioned only by financial difficulty or economic hardship, even to the extent of insolvency or bankruptcy, performance of a contract is not excused" (407 East 61st Garage v. Savoy Fifth Ave. Corp., 23 N.Y.2d 275, 278, 296 N.Y.S.2d 338, 244 N.E.2d 37 [1968]). In addition, this contract contains no mortgage contingency clause. Thus, as defendant raised no issue of fact, plaintiff was entitled to summary judgment.

ORDERED that the order is affirmed, with costs.

CARDONA, P.J., CREW III, PETERS and SPAIN, JJ., concur.

⌷ PARALEGAL EXERCISE 12.2

In June, the Browning Agency, a creative advertising agency, contracted with Edith Edwards to send a hot air balloon over Chicago on the Fourth of July as part of an advertising campaign for Edith's Ice Cream Shoppe. High winds on the Fourth of July prevented Browning from sending up the balloon.

Edith sued Browning for breach of contract, alleging that Browning breached by not sending up the balloon. Could Browning successfully maintain that its nonperformance was excused?

1. What was the external event that led to Browning's failure to perform? Was this event expected or unexpected, and did it occur after the contract was formed?
2. Did the occurrence of this event render Browning's performance of its contractual duty impossible or impracticable?
3. Was the risk associated with the occurrence of this event allocated by contract or by custom?
4. Was the nonoccurrence of this event a basic assumption on which the contract was made? ■

⌷ PARALEGAL EXERCISE 12.3

Rona contracted to create a sculpture of a moose for Andy for Christmas. Shortly before Christmas, Rona completed the sculpture and arranged for it to be delivered to Andy. Before the sculpture could be delivered, a thief broke into Rona's studio and stole the sculpture. An extensive search by the police did not locate the sculpture.

Andy sued Rona for breach of contract, alleging that Rona breached by not delivering the sculpture. Could Rona successfully maintain that her nonperformance was excused?

1. What was the external event that led to Rona's failure to perform? Was this event expected or unexpected, and did it occur after the contract was formed?
2. Did the occurrence of this event render Rona's performance of her contractual duty impossible or impracticable?
3. Was the risk associated with the occurrence of this event allocated by contract or by custom?
4. Was the nonoccurrence of this event a basic assumption on which the contract was made? ■

⌷ PARALEGAL EXERCISE 12.4

Gateway Industries of St. Louis contracted to buy twelve new pickup trucks from Good Deal Motors of Detroit. Good Deal contracted with Express Railway to deliver the trucks to St. Louis. Enroute, the train derailed and the trucks were damaged.

Gateway sued Good Deal for breach of contract, alleging that Good Deal breached by not delivering the trucks. Could Good Deal successfully maintain that its nonperformance was excused?

1. What was the external event that led to Good Deal's failure to perform? Was this event expected or unexpected, and did it occur after the contract was formed?
2. Did the occurrence of this event render Good Deal's performance of its contractual duty impossible or impracticable?
3. Was the risk associated with the occurrence of this event allocated by contract or by custom?
4. Was the nonoccurrence of this event a basic assumption on which the contract was made? ▦

▥ PARALEGAL EXERCISE 12.5

Baldwin contracted to sell Cox 2,000 tons of potatoes to be grown on Baldwin's farm in Boise, Idaho. Without any fault on Baldwin's part, a disease destroyed his entire potato crop. Cox sued Baldwin for breach of contract, alleging that Baldwin breached by not delivering the potatoes. Could Baldwin successfully maintain that his nonperformance was excused?

1. What was the external event that led to Baldwin's failure to perform? Was this event expected or unexpected, and did it occur after the contract was formed?
2. Did the occurrence of this event render Baldwin's performance of his contractual duty impossible or impracticable?
3. Was the risk associated with the occurrence of this event allocated by contract or by custom?
4. Was the nonoccurrence of this event a basic assumption on which the contract was made?

Would it make any difference if the contract had not specified that the potatoes were to be raised on Baldwin's farm? ▦

▥ PARALEGAL EXERCISE 12.6

In January, Howard contracted to perform in Roxy's motorcycle stunt show. The first show was scheduled for the end of February. In early February, Howard broke both his legs in a skiing accident. Roxy sued Howard for breach of contract, alleging that Howard breached by not performing in her stunt show. Could Howard successfully maintain that his nonperformance was excused?

1. What was the external event that led to Howard's failure to perform? Was this event expected or unexpected, and did it occur after the contract was formed?
2. Did the occurrence of this event render Howard's performance of his contractual duty impossible or impracticable?
3. Was the risk associated with the occurrence of this event allocated by contract or by custom?
4. Was the nonoccurrence of this event a basic assumption on which the contract was made? ▦

⫼ PARALEGAL EXERCISE 12.7

Brent contracted to sell his car to Susan, who made a $500 down payment. Brent died in a boating accident before the date he was to deliver his car to Susan. When Susan tendered Brent's executor the total purchase price under the contract, the executor refused to deliver Brent's car to Susan.

Susan sued Brent's estate for breach of contract, alleging that Brent breached by not delivering the car. Could Brent's executor successfully maintain that his nonperformance was excused?

1. What was the external event that led to Brent's failure to perform? Was this event expected or unexpected, and did it occur after the contract was formed?
2. Did the occurrence of this event render Brent's performance of his contractual duty impossible or impracticable?
3. Was the risk associated with the occurrence of this event allocated by contract or by custom?
4. Was the nonoccurrence of this event a basic assumption on which the contract was made? ▪

⫼ PARALEGAL EXERCISE 12.8

On January 15, Hudson Bay Pelts Company of Toronto, Canada, contracted to sell 2,400 lamb pelts to American Woolen Company of Philadelphia, Pennsylvania. The contract required Hudson Bay to ship the pelts by railroad from Toronto to Philadelphia on February 20. On February 1, a United States agency outlawed the importation of lamb pelts.

American sued Hudson Bay for breach of contract, alleging that Hudson Bay breached by not delivering the pelts. Could Hudson Bay successfully maintain that its nonperformance was excused?

1. What was the external event that led to Hudson Bay's failure to perform? Was this event expected or unexpected, and did it occur after the contract was formed?
2. Did the occurrence of this event render Hudson Bay's performance of its contractual duty impossible or impracticable?
3. Was the risk associated with the occurrence of this event allocated by contract or by custom?
4. Was the nonoccurrence of this event a basic assumption on which the contract was made? ▪

⫼ PARALEGAL EXERCISE 12.9

Mason Company contracted with Brady to take all the gravel needed for a construction project from Brady's land. After taking 50,000 cubic yards of gravel from Brady's land, the Mason Company discovered that there was not enough gravel on Brady's land without having to dredge and dry gravel that was underwater. Because the cost of dredging and drying the gravel would have been twelve times the cost of buying dry gravel elsewhere, the Mason Company purchased 57,000 cubic yards of gravel from a third party.

Brady sued the Mason Company for breach of contract, alleging that Mason breached by not taking all its gravel requirements from Brady's land. Could Mason successfully maintain that its nonperformance was excused?

1. What was the external event that led to Mason's failure to perform? Was this event expected or unexpected, and did it occur after the contract was formed?
2. Did the occurrence of this event render Mason's performance of its contractual duty impossible or impracticable?
3. Was the risk associated with the occurrence of this event allocated by contract or by custom?
4. Was the nonoccurrence of this event a basic assumption on which the contract was made? ▆

⫼ PARALEGAL EXERCISE 12.10

Weebo Manufacturing Company, a firm specializing in space-age technological equipment, contracted with the Army to develop a heat-sensitive device designed to locate nuclear-powered submarines. Midway through the project, Weebo encountered technical difficulties resulting in unexpectedly heavy production costs far in excess of any profits it would make under the contract. Weebo notified the Army that it could not develop the heat-sensitive device. The Army then contracted with the Space Age Corporation for the development of the heat-sensitive device at a contract price of five times the Weebo contract.

The Army sued the Weebo Company for breach of contract, alleging that Weebo breached by not producing the heat-sensitive device. Could Weebo successfully maintain that its nonperformance was excused?

1. What was the external event that led to Weebo's failure to perform? Was this event expected or unexpected, and did it occur after the contract was formed?
2. Did the occurrence of this event render Weebo's performance of its contractual duty impossible or impracticable?
3. Was the risk associated with the occurrence of this event allocated by contract or by custom?
4. Was the nonoccurrence of this event a basic assumption on which the contract was made? ▆

FRUSTRATION OF PURPOSE

Frustration of purpose involves an unexpected event that destroys the reason for the contract. Even though performance of the contract is still possible, courts may excuse nonperformance on the theory of failure of consideration.

Where, after a contract is made, a party's principal purpose is substantially frustrated without his fault by the occurrence of an event the non-occurrence of which was a basic assumption on which the contract was made, his remaining duties to render performance are discharged, unless the language or the circumstances indicate the contrary. (Restatement (Second) of Contracts § 265 (1981))

Example 12–2

An illustration is the famous English case of *Krell v. Henry,* [1903] 2 K.B. 740 (C.A.). Krell owned a suite of rooms overlooking the parade route for the coronation procession of King Edward VII. Krell contracted to lease his suite to Henry for the purpose of viewing the coronation procession. Shortly before the coronation, the King became ill and the coronation was indefinitely postponed. When Henry refused to pay Krell the balance due on the lease, Krell sued Henry. The court excused Henry's nonperformance. Although the nonhappening of the coronation did not prevent either Krell from renting the suite or Henry from paying Krell the contract price, the postponement of the coronation destroyed the value of the use of Krell's rooms to Henry during the contract period.

With a few minor variations, the analysis used for impossibility and impracticability can be useful in understanding the frustration of purpose cases:

1. What was the external event that led to the promisor's failure to perform? Was this event expected or unexpected, and did it occur after the contract was formed?
2. Did the occurrence of this event render promisor's performance of its contractual duty impossible or impracticable?
3. Did the occurrence of this event substantially frustrate the promisor's principal purpose in making the contract?
4. Was the risk of frustration of purpose associated with the occurrence of this event allocated by contract or by custom?
5. Was the nonoccurrence of this event a basic assumption on which the contract was made?

ⅢＰＡＲＡＬＥＧＡＬ EXERCISE 12.11

The summer Olympic games were scheduled for the week of July 1 in Dallas, Texas. On May 1, in anticipation of the summer Olympic games, the California T-Shirt Company contracted to purchase 500,000 T-shirts bearing the Olympic logo from Channing Enterprises. On May 20, a multinational boycott resulted in cancellation of the summer games. The California T-Shirt Company notified Channing not to ship the T-shirts.

Channing sued California for breach of contract, alleging that California breached by canceling its order. Could California successfully maintain that its nonperformance was excused?

1. What was the external event that led to California's failure to perform? Was this event expected or unexpected, and did it occur after the contract was formed?
2. Did the occurrence of this event render California's performance of its contractual duty impossible or impracticable?
3. Did the occurrence of this event substantially frustrate California's principal purpose in making the contract?
4. Was the risk of frustration of purpose associated with the occurrence of this event allocated by contract or by custom?
5. Was the nonoccurrence of this event a basic assumption on which the contract was made?

▥ PARALEGAL EXERCISE 12.12

In June, XYZ Communications contracted to lease a building from Jackson for five years for the purpose of selling satellite dishes. On December 1, the FCC declared the use of satellite dishes by homeowners illegal. XYZ ceased operating and moved out of the building.

Jackson sued XYZ for breach of contract, alleging that XYZ breached by canceling its lease. Could XYZ successfully maintain that its nonperformance was excused?

1. What was the external event that led to XYZ's failure to perform? Was this event expected or unexpected, and did it occur after the contract was formed?
2. Did the occurrence of this event render XYZ's performance of its contractual duty impossible or impracticable?
3. Did the occurrence of this event substantially frustrate XYZ's principal purpose in making the contract?
4. Was the risk of frustration of purpose associated with the occurrence of this event allocated by contract or by custom?
5. Was the nonoccurrence of this event a basic assumption on which the contract was made?

COULD RESTITUTION BE A CAUSE OF ACTION WHEN THE DEFENDANT'S NONPERFORMANCE OF A CONTRACTUAL DUTY IS EXCUSED?

The "no breach–excuse" response is an admission of nonperformance but a denial of breach. "I am not performing, but my nonperformance is excused." Without a breach of the contract, the plaintiff's remedies for the defendant's breach are unavailable.

Situations arise in which the contract calls for one party to fully perform before the other party is called upon to perform. The first party begins performance (conferring a benefit on the other) when suddenly an unexpected event occurs that terminates his or her duty to continue. The recipient of the benefit is not called upon to perform because the party who began performing must complete his or her performance first. The performance of the contract comes to a standstill. Neither party has breached the contract. What about the performance that has already been conferred by one party on the other? If the recipient of the benefit is able to retain this benefit without compensating the other, will the recipient be unjustly enriched?

The Restatement (Second) of Contracts takes the following position:

> A party whose duty of performance does not arise or is discharged as a result of an impracticability of performance [or] frustration of purpose . . . is entitled to restitution for any benefit that he has conferred on the other party by way of part performance. . . . (Restatement (Second) of Contracts § 377 (1981))

As a general rule when a contractor finds it impossible to complete performance under a construction contract due to the destruction of the structure, the contractor may be entitled to an action of restitution for the value of the work that had been done prior to the destruction.

Example 12–3

Bell owned a building used as a cafe. He hired Carver Air Conditioning Company to install a heating and air conditioning unit in the building. Before Carver could complete the installation, Bell's building was destroyed by fire. The heating and air conditioning unit also was destroyed. Bell refused to pay the contract price.

If Carver sued Bell for breach of contract alleging that Bell breached by not paying, Bell could successfully respond that his nonperformance was excused due to the fire. Therefore, Carver could not maintain a breach of contract cause of action.

Carver could successfully sue Bell in a restitution cause of action for unjust enrichment. Carver conferred a benefit on Bell (the heating and air conditioning unit and the labor involved in the installation) and it would be unjust for Bell to retain the unit and labor without compensating Carver.

In *Stein v. Shaw,* an attorney contracted with a client to file a negligence action on her behalf to recover damages for personal injuries. The client agreed to pay the attorney one-third of any recovery. After the attorney instituted suit and began negotiating a settlement, he was disbarred. The disbarment action was unrelated to this client. The client found herself another attorney, and her suit was ultimately settled for $4,950. Is the disbarred attorney entitled to recover in a breach of contract action? If not, why? Is the disbarred attorney entitled to recover in a restitution action and, if so, how much?

CASE

Stein v. Shaw
Supreme Court of New Jersey (1951)
6 N.J. 525, 79 A.2d 310

VANDERBILT, C. J.

The plaintiff, an attorney at law, entered into a verbal agreement with the defendant to institute a suit in her behalf for the recovery of damages for personal injuries allegedly sustained by another's negligence. Under this agreement the plaintiff was to receive one-third of any recovery. He instituted suit and opened negotiations for a settlement, both of which were pending at the time he was disbarred from the practice of law for reasons not connected in anywise with the prosecution of the defendant's suit. After the plaintiff's disbarment other attorneys were substituted for him and the defendant's suit was subsequently settled for $4,950. The defendant refused to pay the plaintiff and he then commenced this action against her, seeking in the first count to recover $1,028 as the reasonable value of his services and disbursements, and in the second count to recover on his contingent fee contract one-third of the amount of the settlement. On the defendant's motion the trial court dismissed the complaint for failure to state a cause of action. From this judgment the plaintiff appealed to the Appellate Division of the Superior Court and we have certified the appeal here on our own motion.

We are of the opinion that the plaintiff should be permitted to recover in quasi contract for the reasonable value of his services rendered and disbursements made prior to his disbarment, for otherwise the defendant will be unjustly enriched at the expense of the plaintiff. To deprive an attorney of his claim for any and all compensation for services rendered prior to his disbarment when the services are not involved in the unprofessional conduct occasioning disciplinary action, would be inequitable. There is no sound reason in law or morals for permitting the defendant to use the plaintiff's disbarment as an escape from paying him for services rendered or necessary disbursements made by him in her behalf. Article VI, Section II, paragraph 3 of the Constitution imposes on this court the duty to discipline members of the bar for the protection of society, the legal profession and the courts in preserving the due administration of justice in the State, but its exercise does not affect either civil or criminal actions by or against the attorney disciplined by the court.

If the rule were otherwise, the effect of disciplinary action would inevitably be retroactive, which is not the intent or purpose in imposing discipline. The court, moreover, would never know the extent of such retroactive punishment without an undesirable inquiry as to the extent of the attorney's pending business and the monetary value thereof. It is unthinkable that punishment should be inflicted by a court so unintelligently. There are matters, however, which should not be considered by the committees on ethics and grievances appointed by us in the several counties to aid us by investigating complaints against members of the bar and by making presentments to us where the situation requires, nor should such matters be before us in imposing discipline. Our duty of safeguarding the integrity of the bar and of keeping the fountain of justice unpolluted is sufficiently difficult and delicate as it is without further complicating it with any such extraneous matters which should in all fairness be considered in imposing discipline, if the attorney's right to bring suit for services rendered is to be impaired by us. Disbarment is not a form of outlawry. To bring economic considerations into disciplinary proceedings would not only needlessly complicate them, but would in many instances serve to defeat the essential purpose thereof.

We are aware of Davenport v. Waggoner, 49 S.D. 592, 207 N.W. 972, 45 A.L.R. 1126 (S.Dak. 1926) and In re Woodworth, 85 F.2d 50 (2d Cir. 1936) which hold to the contrary, but we cannot subscribe to the theory on which they are premised, that withdrawal from a suit by reason of disbarment constitutes a voluntary abandonment of the contract without just cause. Such is actually not the fact in those cases. The contract was not voluntarily abandoned, it was automatically terminated by operation of law, when the order of the court made further performance impossible. While the plaintiff was disbarred because of his own wrongful acts, so far as this defendant is concerned he is guiltless. It is pure fiction to say that he has intentionally and without cause abandoned his contract with her. While the analogy is not complete, the effect on the client of an attorney's disbarment is the same as that in the case of Justice v. Lairy, 19 Ind.App. 272, 49 N.E. 459 (Ind. App. 1898), where an attorney accepted appointment to the bench and was thereby prohibited from the further practice of law. In either situation the attorney's disability is the result of conduct wholly unrelated to his client's case. In our opinion the situation resulting here from the plaintiff's disbarment is not dissimilar to that when an attorney is incapacitated by reason of death, illness or insanity. In such cases it has been uniformly held that because of his inability to perform the contract is discharged, but that the attorney may nevertheless recover in quasi contract for the reasonable value of the services rendered, 45 A.L.R. 1135, 1158. Nor is recovery in quasi contract here barred by virtue of the express contract for a contingent fee, for as we have indicated that contract was discharged by operation of law when its performance was rendered impossible by the plaintiff's disbarment.

The fact that the defendant was compelled by virtue of the plaintiff's disbarment to retain other counsel to prosecute her claim is, of course, to be considered in determining the reasonable value of the plaintiff's services. In no event, however, should the plaintiff's recovery exceed the amount stipulated for in his express agreement less whatever reasonable sum the defendant paid other counsel to complete the case. While the express contract has been discharged and cannot serve as the measure of recovery, it does operate as a limit on the amount of the recovery in quasi contract, 6 Williston on Contracts (Rev. Ed. 1938) § 1977, p. 5557; Woodward, The Law of Quasi Contracts (1913) § 125, p. 197.

In view of the conclusions we have reached, it becomes unnecessary to consider the other questions raised by the plaintiff. The judgment appealed from is reversed and the cause remanded for further proceedings in accordance with this opinion.

For reversal: Chief Justice VANDERBILT, and Justices CASE, HEHER, OLIPHANT, BURLING and ACKERSON–6.

For affirmance: Justice WACHENFELD–1.

WACHENFELD, J. (dissenting).

In In re Woodworth, D.C., 15 F.Supp. 291, 293, affirmed 85 F.2d 50 (C.C.A. 2, 1936), the court held: "On principle it cannot be doubted that when an attorney makes an agreement to prosecute a case for a fee contingent on success and is disbarred before the fee is earned, he may not collect compensation from his client for the work done. The agreed fee he cannot have, because he has not performed his engagement and the contingency on which the compensation was to rest has not happened. Reasonable compensation in lieu of the fee he cannot have, because his inability to complete his contract has been brought about by his own wrongful conduct."

I subscribe to this reasoning and conclusion and am therefore to affirm.

Adopting this rule would not complicate or bring economic considerations into disciplinary proceedings nor would it defeat their purpose. It would, in my opinion, be an added incentive to professional conduct, which is foreign to disciplinary complaints.

Admittedly, the plaintiff was disbarred because of his own wrongful act, and whether it was with reference to this particular case or not, the result, in my opinion, is the same.

The penalty falls and he can no longer represent his client because of his wrongful conduct. The result of that misconduct should be uniform, not varying with the degree of culpability or its relationship to any particular case.

"His inability to complete his contract has been brought about by his own wrongful conduct."

I would affirm the judgment.

PARALEGAL CHECKLIST

The Defendant's No Breach–Excuse Response to the Plaintiff's Allegation of Breach

❑ Whether the promisor's breach is intentional or unintentional is irrelevant. The law of contracts does not evaluate the mental state accompanying nonperformance.

The fact that the promisee alleges the promisor breached the contract does not make it so. The promisor may respond to the promisee's allegation of breach with "no breach–excuse"—"Although I am not complying with the terms of the contract, my nonperformance is excused." Unlike the "no breach–compliance" response, the promisor admits nonperformance but refers to an external event that occurred after contract formation. This event rendered the promisor's performance impossible or impracticable, so the promisor is excused from performing. The event may be an act of God or a governmental action—the occurrence of which was not recognized in the contract or by custom. The Restatement (Second) of Contracts has folded the term "impossible" into the term "impracticable."

Four questions help determine whether the promisor should be excused from performing due to an intervening impossibility or impracticability:

1. What was the external event that led to promisor's failure to perform? Was this event expected or unexpected, and did it occur after the contract was formed?

2. Did the occurrence of this event render the promisor's performance of its contractual duty impossible or impracticable?

3. Was the risk associated with the occurrence of this event allocated by contract or by custom?

4. Was the nonoccurrence of this event a basic assumption on which the contract was made?

❑ Frustration of purpose may also provide the promisor with a "no breach–excuse" response. Five questions help determine whether the promisor should be excused from performing due to an intervening frustration of purpose:

1. What was the external event that led to the promisor's failure to perform? Was this event expected or unexpected, and did it occur after the contract was formed?

2. Did the occurrence of this event render the promisor's performance of its contractual duty impossible or impracticable?

3. Did the occurrence of this event substantially frustrate the promisor's principal purpose in making the contract?

4. Was the risk of frustration of purpose associated with the occurrence of this event allocated by contract or by custom?

5. Was the nonoccurrence of this event a basic assumption on which the contract was made?

❑ If the promisor's "no breach–excuse" response holds so that the promisee could not successfully maintain his or her breach of contract action, the promisor may seek a restitution cause of action for any benefit that he or she has conferred on the promisee prior to the impracticability or frustration of purpose.

KEY TERM

Supervening external event

REVIEW QUESTIONS

TRUE/FALSE QUESTIONS (CIRCLE THE CORRECT ANSWER)

1. T   F   A successful no breach–excuse response by the defendant to the plaintiff's allegation of breach concludes the breach of contract action on that issue in the defendant's favor.

2. T   F   Although the no breach–excuse response ends the breach of contract action, a possibility of relief for unjust enrichment in a restitution action still exists.

3. T   F   Restitution as it relates to no breach–excuse is a remedy for breach of contract rather than a cause of action.

4. T   F   In a no breach–excuse response, the promisor does not assert that he or she is complying with the terms of the contract.

5. T   F   If the occurrence of an external event prevents the promisor from performing, this nonperformance may be excused even though the external event was not an express term in the contract.

6. T   F   Unexpected events that make nonperformance of the contract impossible may involve illness, physical incapacity, death or destruction, or unavailability of the subject matter of the contract.

7. T   F   Ingmar Borg contracted to rent The Golden Pyramid Restaurant for the purpose of having his daughter's wedding reception and dinner there. Shortly after the contract was signed and before the date for performance, lightning struck the restaurant, damaging its interior. If Borg sued The Golden Pyramid for breach of contract—alleging The Golden Pyramid's failure to provide the restaurant—The Golden Pyramid could successfully respond "no breach–excuse."

8. T   F   Under the Restatement (Second) of Contracts § 261 (1981), a party may be excused from nonperformance of his or her duty if it is impracticable to perform.

9. T   F   Impracticability means the same thing as impracticality.

10. T   F   Under the Restatement (Second) of Contracts, impracticability encompasses impossibility.

11. T   F   A change in the difficulty or expense of performance will render the performance impracticable.

12. T   F   Frustration of purpose involves the occurrence of an unexpected event that destroys the reason for the contract.

13. T   F   Courts may excuse nonperformance if the purpose of the contract is frustrated by the occurrence of an unexpected event even if performance of the contract is not impracticable.

14. T   F   Restitution as a cause of action is not available when nonperformance of the contract is excused.

15. T   F   The no breach–excuse response requires that an unexpected event occurred prior to or contemporaneous with the formation of the contract.

16. T   F   Historically, the no breach–excuse response began as an implied condition in a no breach–compliance response.

17. T   F   Article 2 of the UCC has a section on impracticability but only as it applies to the seller's performance.

18. T   F   For the no breach–excuse response to apply, the risk associated with the occurrence of the unexpected event must have been allocated by contract or by custom.

19. T   F   The no breach–excuse response can only be used if the promisor's performance is impracticable.

FILL-IN-THE-BLANK QUESTIONS

1. _____. The cause of the failure to perform in a no breach-excuse response.

2. _____. When the promisor is unable to perform due to the occurrence of an unexpected event.

3. _____. When the promisor is able to perform—but due to the occurrence of an unexpected event, the cost of performance has become unreasonably high.

4. _____. When the promisor is able to perform—but the purpose of the contract no long exists due to the occurrence of an unexpected event.

5. _____. The cause of action available if the promisor has partially performed—but is excused from completing performance due to the occurrence of an unexpected event.

MULTIPLE-CHOICE QUESTIONS (CIRCLE ALL THE CORRECT ANSWERS)

1. For the no breach-excuse response to apply, the event that led to the promisor's failure to perform must have occurred
   (a) prior to contract formation
   (b) contemporaneous with contract formation
   (c) subsequent to contract formation
   (d) prior to or contemporaneous with contract formation
   (e) Any of the above

2. The no breach-excuse response is based on which of the following?
   (a) An unexpected event
   (b) The act or omission of the promisee
   (c) An express condition precedent
   (d) An implied condition precedent
   (e) A term of the contract that was not in the writing

3. An unexpected event is an event that is
   (a) unpredicted
   (b) unanticipated
   (c) unforeseen
   (d) unscheduled
   (e) unwanted

SHORT-ANSWER QUESTIONS

1. Describe the steps to be taken when evaluating a "no breach-excuse" response when the performance of the contract has become impracticable.

2. Describe the steps to be taken when evaluating a "no breach-excuse" response when the performance of the contract remains doable but the purpose of the contract no longer exists.

3. Describe differences between a "no breach–excuse" response and a "no breach–compliance" response.

4. B. K. George contracted to purchase "Run Away," a racehorse, from Jimmy WhiteEagle. "Run Away" was to be delivered after he competed in the Claremore Downs Futurity. During that race, "Run Away" was injured and had to be put down. If George sues WhiteEagle for breach of contract, alleging WhiteEagle breached by not delivering "Run Away," and WhiteEagle responds no breach–excuse, who will prevail and why?

CHAPTER 13

The Defendant's *No Breach–Justification* Response to the Plaintiff's Allegation of Breach

The defendant's third response to the plaintiff's allegation of breach is "No breach; although I am not complying with the terms of the contract, my nonperformance was justified by your breach of this contract" (see Exhibit 13–1). ("Your breach justified my nonperformance.")

> My nonperformance of the contract was justified by your breach of the contract. Therefore, you are the breaching party and not I.

This response couples the defendant's admission of nonperformance with the claim that the nonperformance was justified by a breach by the plaintiff. Unlike the "no breach–excuse" response, which was based on a supervening external event (an act of God or a governmental regulation), the "no breach–justification" response is based on the action of the other contracting party. The defendant

IN THE DISTRICT COURT OF [NAME] COUNTY
STATE OF [NAME]

[NAME], dba [Name]	)	
	)	
Plaintiff,	)	
	)	
v.	)	Case No. _____
	)	
[NAME], a [Name of State] corporation	))	
	)	
Defendant.	)	

ANSWER OF DEFENDANT [NAME]

Defendant [name] alleges the following in response to the complaint:

1. Defendant admits the allegations of paragraph 1 of the complaint.

2. Defendant admits the allegations of paragraph 2 of the complaint.

3. Defendant admits the allegations of paragraph 3 of the complaint.

4. Defendant admits the allegations of paragraph 4 of the complaint.

5. Defendant denies that all conditions precedent have occurred as alleged in paragraph 5 of the complaint in that payment was conditioned on the Defendant presenting a completed marketing plan and the presented marketing plan was substantially incomplete.

6. Defendant denies the allegations of paragraph 6 that it breached the contract in that Plaintiff's breach by presenting an incomplete marketing plan justified Defendant's not paying.

7. The complaint fails to state a claim against Defendant upon which relief can be granted.

Accordingly, Defendant demands that Plaintiff take nothing by this Action, and that Defendant be awarded costs including reasonable attorney fees.

> [Attorney's name signed]
> [Attorney's name typed]
> Attorney for defendant
> [Bar membership number]
> [Address]
> [Telephone number]

Exhibit 13–1 Answer—Defendant's "No Breach–Justification" Response to the Plaintiff's Allegation of Defendant's Breach

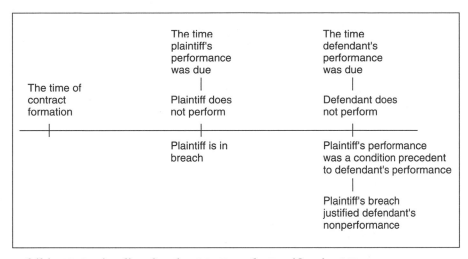

Exhibit 13–2 Timeline for the "No Breach–Justification" Response

is *not* responding "My breach is justified by your breach." The defendant, although not admitting breach, is only admitting non-performance. An admission of nonperformance is not the same as an admission of breach. *The defendant's nonperformance is not a breach.* Because the plaintiff rather than the defendant is the breaching party, the plaintiff cannot maintain a breach of contract action against the defendant (see Exhibit 13–2).

This chapter explores the elements of the justification response. If the defendant established these elements, he or she was justified in not performing the contract and was not in breach. Therefore, the plaintiff cannot maintain a breach of contract action.

Even if the plaintiff cannot maintain a breach of contract action, the plaintiff, who has conferred a benefit on the nonbreaching defendant, could maintain a restitution action against the nonbreaching defendant. This chapter considers restitution as an action for the breaching plaintiff.

THE NO BREACH–JUSTIFICATION RESPONSE UNDER THE COMMON LAW

A careful analysis of the justification response reveals that the defendant must prove the following:

1. Both the plaintiff and the defendant had duties to perform.
2. The plaintiff's performance was a condition precedent to the defendant's performance.
3. The plaintiff was in breach of his or her duty to perform.
4. The magnitude of the plaintiff's breach of his or her duty justified the defendant's nonperformance of his or her duty.

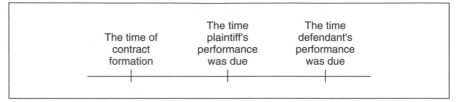

Exhibit 13–3 The Respective Duties for the "No Breach–Justification" Response

The Plaintiff and the Defendant Have Duties to Perform

The first step in the "justification response" is establishing that both the plaintiff and the defendant had duties to perform. The plaintiff must have a duty to perform and must have failed to perform this duty to justify the defendant's claim that his or her nonperformance was justified by the plaintiff's nonperformance of a contractual duty (see Exhibit 13–3).

The Plaintiff's Performance Was a Condition Precedent to the Defendant's Performance

For the defendant to claim a justification response, its performance must be dependent on the plaintiff's performance. If the defendant's performance is independent of the plaintiff's performance, the justification response will fail. Under modern contract law, performances are presumed to be dependent.

▥ PARALEGAL EXERCISE 13.1

Dwayne contracted to paint Robin's portrait for Robin's promise to pay Dwayne $1,000, with $200 down and the balance in $100 weekly installments. Although the painting would take about three weeks, a time was not set for its completion.

Are painting and paying independent or dependent performances? ▦

The defendant's performance must be dependent not only on the plaintiff's performance, but the plaintiff's performance must occur first. The plaintiff's performance must be a condition precedent to the defendant's performance.

Example 13–1

Tom contracted with Gary for the remodeling of Tom's kitchen. The contract required Tom to purchase the materials and Gary to do the carpentry. Tom's buying of the materials is a condition precedent to Gary's duty to remodel. If Tom does not buy materials, Gary will be unable to remodel the kitchen.

⫼ PARALEGAL EXERCISE 13.2

Karen hired Stacy to tutor her in Latin. Is Karen's duty to pay a condition precedent to Stacy's tutoring, or is Stacy's tutoring a condition precedent to Karen's duty to pay? ▪

The Plaintiff Was in Breach

The third step in the "justification response" is establishing that the plaintiff has breached the contract. If the plaintiff has not breached, the defendant's justification response will not succeed.

⫼ PARALEGAL EXERCISE 13.3

The Ace Painting Company contracted to paint Erica's apartment for $1,500. Erica contracted to supply the paint. When Ace arrived to paint Erica's apartment, Erica refused to provide Ace with the paint and demanded that Ace supply the paint. Ace refused and ultimately did not paint Erica's apartment. Erica then hired Russell to paint and paid Russell $2,000.

Erica sued Ace for breach of contract, alleging Ace breached by not painting her apartment. Ace responded, "No breach–justification. My nonperformance (not painting) was justified by your breach (not supplying the paint)."

Did Erica breach the contract by not supplying the paint? Will Ace's justification response succeed? ▪

Entire and Divisible Performances

A contract may require one performance or a number of performances. An **entire contract** is a contract with a single performance.

entire contract
An entire contract is a contract with a single performance.

Example 13–2

The St. Louis Zoo made the following offer to the Ace Transport Company: "The St. Louis Zoo promises to pay you $1,500 for your promise to deliver Flora, an elephant, to the New Orleans Zoo."

A **divisible contract** is a contract with separate or installment performances.

divisible contract
A divisible contract is a contract with separate or installment performances.

Example 13–3

Change the facts in Example 13–2 so the offer reads: "The St. Louis Zoo promises to pay you $1,500–half when Flora is picked up and half when she is delivered–for your promise to deliver Flora to the New Orleans Zoo."

Example 13-4

Change the facts in Example 13–1 by adding a second elephant, Sally. The offer now reads: "The St. Louis Zoo promises to pay you $3,000—half when Flora is delivered to the New Orleans Zoo in the fall and half when Sally is delivered to the same zoo in the spring—for your promise to deliver the two elephants to that zoo."

Whether a performance of a contract is entire (one performance) or divisible (multiple performances) may affect when the plaintiff breached the contract. If the performance is divisible, the plaintiff may breach a later performance, although not an earlier one. If the plaintiff has not breached an early performance, the defendant may not withhold the performance that corresponds to the plaintiff's performance.

Example 13-5

Add the following facts to Example 13–4. Suppose Ace delivers Flora in the fall but refuses to deliver Sally in the spring. Ace has not breached its duty to deliver Flora, but has breached its duty to deliver Sally. If each delivery was to be paid for separately, the Zoo could not refuse to pay for the first delivery because Ace has not breached its duty as to the first delivery.

⏚ PARALEGAL EXERCISE 13.4

The Juniper Lumber Company owns a 100,000-acre forest of oak, maple, and white pine. Juniper hired the Paul Bunyon Company to harvest 20 truckloads of trees from this forest (5 truckloads of oak, 5 of maple, and 10 of white pine) and to deliver them to the Juniper sawmill, a 100 miles away. The contract provided that Juniper would pay by the truckload ($20,000 for each truckload of oak, $15,000 for each truckload of maple, and $10,000 for each truckload of white pine).

Paul Bunyon harvested and delivered the maple and white pine but did not harvest or deliver any oak. Juniper accepted the maple and pine but subsequently refused to pay because it did not receive the oak.

Paul Bunyon sued Juniper for breach of contract. Answer the following questions:

1. What law governs this transaction?
2. Has a contract been formed?
3. If a contract has been formed, is it enforceable?
4. If a contract has been formed and is enforceable, what will Paul Bunyon allege was Juniper's breach?

5. Should Juniper answer Paul Bunyon's allegation of breach with a *no breach—justification* response?
   a. Did both Paul Bunyon (the plaintiff) and Juniper (the defendant) have duties to perform under the contract?
   b. Was Paul Bunyon's performance a condition precedent to Juniper's performance?
   c. Was Paul Bunyon in breach of its duty to perform? To answer this question, answer the following questions:
      1) Was Paul Bunyon's performance entire or divisible?
      2) What effect does your answer to the entire or divisible question have on whether Paul Bunyon could maintain its breach of contract action against Juniper? ■

Waiver of a Breach

Even if the plaintiff breaches the contract, the defendant might not be able to use the plaintiff's breach in its justification response if the defendant waives the breach.

Example 13–6

Albert hired the Countryside Landscape Company to landscape Blackacre for $2,400. When Countryside finished the job after a week, Albert was dissatisfied with what it had done. Countryside offered to redo some of the work, but Albert said that he was so disgusted, he would take it as it was. When Albert received Countryside's bill for $2,400, he refused to pay it.

Countryside sued Albert for breach of contract, alleging that Albert did not pay. Albert responded, "No breach–justification. My not paying was justified by your breach (not performing the work satisfactorily)." Countryside responded by claiming that Albert waived Countryside's breach by accepting the work.

▥ PARALEGAL EXERCISE 13.5

The Quality Builders, Inc., received a contract to build a home for Barry and Susan McQuade for $1,000,000. The contract provided the following payment schedule:

$100,000 upon the signing of the contract

$200,000 upon the completion of the foundation

$200,000 upon the completion of the framing of the house

$200,000 upon the completion of 90 percent of the construction

$200,000 upon the completion of the house and landscaping

$100,000 at 60 days after the completion of the house and landscaping

Although the contract called for Vermont marble in the master bathroom, Quality purchased New Hampshire marble. The marbles were similar but yet different.

Susan McQuade visited the building sight on a daily basis. She noticed stacks of marble labeled New Hampshire marble. Although she knew that the architect had specified Vermont marble, she did not inquire as to why the marble was labeled New Hampshire marble.

Quality incorporated the New Hampshire marble into the master bathroom. Sixty days after the completion of the house and landscaping, the McQuades stated that they would refuse to make the last payment unless the New Hampshire marble was replaced with Vermont marble. Quality refused.

Quality sued the McQuades for breach of contract. Answer the following questions:

1. What law governs this transaction?
2. Has a contract been formed?
3. If a contract has been formed, is it enforceable?
4. If a contract has been formed and is enforceable, what will Quality allege was the McQuades' breach?
5. Should the McQuades answer Quality's allegation of breach with a *no breach—justification* response?
   a. Did both Quality (the plaintiff) and the McQuades (the defendant) have duties to perform under the contract?
   b. Was Quality's performance a condition precedent to the McQuades' performance?
   c. Was Quality in breach of its duty to perform? Have the McQuades waived Quality's breach?

Estoppel

In addition to waiver, the defendant may be estopped (precluded) from claiming that the plaintiff has breached. Unlike waiver, which requires no action by the breaching party, estoppel requires that the breaching party rely on the nonbreaching party's actions.

Example 13–7

Suppose in the landscape example, Albert had watched Countryside perform the work and had stated dissatisfaction only after the work had been completed. Even if Countryside had been in breach, Albert had said nothing. Countryside relied on Albert's inaction. Albert is estopped from later raising Countryside's breach.

⫼ PARALEGAL EXERCISE 13.6

Return to Paralegal Exercise 13.5 and change the facts to be that Susan McQuade asked the builder why the marble was marked New Hampshire rather than Vermont. Also suppose that the builder said that the marbles were similar and that Susan said "OK." Assume that she did not make a demand at that time that New Hampshire marble would not do.

Sixty days after the completion of the house and landscaping, the McQuades stated that they would refuse to make the last payment unless the New Hampshire marble was replaced with Vermont marble. Quality refused.

Quality sued the McQuades for breach of contract. Answer the following questions:

1. What law governs this transaction?
2. Has a contract been formed?
3. If a contract has been formed, is it enforceable?
4. If a contract has been formed and is enforceable, what will Quality allege was the McQuades' breach?
5. Should the McQuades answer Quality's allegation of breach with a *no breach–justification* response?
   a. Did both Quality (the plaintiff) and the McQuades (the defendant) have duties to perform under the contract?
   b. Was Quality's performance a condition precedent to the McQuades' performance?
   c. Was Quality in breach of its duty to perform? Should the McQuades be estopped from arguing that Quality breached its contractual duty by using the New Hampshire marble? ■

The Magnitude of the Plaintiff's Breach Justified the Defendant's Nonperformance

The defendant may not use just any breach by the plaintiff to justify his or her nonperformance. The plaintiff's breach must be of sufficient magnitude. If the contract is a construction contract, the plaintiff's performance must be less than "substantial performance." If the contractor has substantially performed but did not fully perform, the owner will not be justified in nonperforming (not paying).

⫿ PARALEGAL EXERCISE 13.7

Beautiful Homes, Inc., contracted to build a house for the Culvers. Beautiful Homes promised to complete the home in 90 days, and the Culvers were to pay in four installments—25 percent at the time of signing the contract and 25 percent at the end of each month thereafter. At the end of 90 days, Beautiful Homes had the house completed except for exterior painting. Has Beautiful Homes substantially performed the contract? ■

If the contract is for employment rather than for construction, the language changes from "substantial performance" to "immaterial breach." An employee's immaterial breach will not justify the employer's nonperformance (nonpayment), even though the employee has not fully performed.

⫿ PARALEGAL EXERCISE 13.8

The Modern Sign Company hired Alvin to solicit sign orders from businesses in town. The contract provided that Alvin would be paid $500 a month plus commissions. The salary was to be paid at the end of each month. After working for Modern Sign for three weeks, Alvin quit without giving the two weeks' notice required in his contract.

Was Alvin's breach material or immaterial? ▪

⫿ PARALEGAL EXERCISE 13.9

For the following case, *American Outdoorsman, Inc. v. Pella Products, Inc.,* develop a timeline beginning with contract formation. Then answer the following:

1. Who is the plaintiff, who is the defendant, and what does the plaintiff allege as the defendant's breach?
2. What is the defendant's response to the plaintiff's allegation of breach?
3. If the defendant's response is no breach–justification, answer the following:
   a. What duties did American Outdoorsman and Pella Products have under this contract?
   b. Was American Outdoorsman's performance of its duty a condition precedent to Pella's performance of its duty or vice versa?
   c. If American Outdoorsman performance of its duty was a condition precedent to Pella's performance of its duty, did American Outdoorsman breach its duty?
   d. If American Outdoorsman breached its duty to perform, did the magnitude of this breach justify Pella's nonperformance of its duty? ▪

CASE

American Outdoorsman, Inc. v. Pella Products, Inc.

Kansas Court of Appeals (2006)

144 P.3d 81 (Table), 2006 WL 3000779

Before MCANANY, P.J., PIERRON, J., and BRAZIL, S.J.
MEMORANDUM OPINION
PER CURIAM.
Pella Products, Inc., (Pella) appeals from the trial court's award of damages to The American Outdoorsman, Inc. (American Outdoorsman), based on Pella's failure to make payments for advertising under its contract with American Outdoorsman.

In this contract action, American Outdoorsman agreed to run Pella's clothing ads on its program, The American Outdoorsman, for a period of three years starting in May 2002. Pella agreed to pay $600 per week. Pella paid through December 2003. The trial court found that Pella had breached the contract and awarded American Outdoorsman $43,800 plus costs.

Pella contends American Outdoorsman breached the contract when it unilaterally changed networks over which it advertised Pella's products. We disagree. . . .

American Outdoorsman produces a national television show called The American Outdoorsman that covers hunting, fishing, and outdoor activities. To broadcast its television show, American Outdoorsman buys a 30-minute slot on a network and then sells the advertising slots within its show to cover costs. Pella manufactures and markets rugged outdoor clothing.

Under the contract provisions covering the parties' advertising agreement, Pella agreed to purchase a 30-second advertising slot on American Outdoorsman's television show for $600 a week. Specifically, Article III, Paragraph 1, Subparagraph I, of the agreement states that Pella "will purchase and receive one (1) Advertising Spot per Program on a weekly basis for a period of three (3) years from the date the first Advertising Spot shall run on the Program at a cost of $600.00 per week or at a total contract price of $93,600.00." Article I, Paragraph 12 defined the term "program" as follows:

> " 'Program' shall mean The American Outdoorsman television show. The American Outdoorsman is currently broadcast primarily on The Outdoor Channel (the television show is temporarily on America One, and for all times the Program is shown on America One, Advertiser will enjoy advertising at no additional cost but Advertiser acknowledges and understands that The Outdoor Channel is the only channel Advertiser may maintain an expectation of broadcasting). The Program is broadcast as listed hereunder but programming times and dates are subject to change without notification:
>
> "On the Outdoor Channel
> "Tuesdays 9:30 am PST 10:30 am CST 11:30 am EST
> "Wednesday 5:30 pm CST 6:30 pm CST 7:30 pm EST
> "Sunday 6:30 am PST 7:30 am CST 8:30 am EST
>
> "On America One:
> "Saturday 11:00 am EST, CST, PST
> "Sunday 10:00 am EST, CST, PST"

. . . .

American Outdoorsman began broadcasting Pella's ads on its television show in May 2002 and continued running the ads through May 2005. American Outdoorsman broadcast its television show on The Outdoor Channel until the end of 2003. In the late part of 2003, The Outdoor Channel notified American Outdoorsman that their rates would nearly double in 2004. American Outdoorsman would not gain any additional households despite the price increase. After receiving this notification from The Outdoor Channel, Robert D. Fanning, Jr., president of American Outdoorsman, did some research and determined that the number of viewer households could be almost doubled by switching networks.

In January 2004, American Outdoorsman changed the networks over which it broadcast its television show from The Outdoor Channel to The Men's Channel,

Comcast Southeast, Fox Digital, and Fox Midwest. According to Fanning, The American Outdoorsman was aired on the new networks during a block of outdoor shows. This network change allowed American Outdoorsman to broadcast its television show to more than 40 million households, an increase of viewership from The Outdoor Channel by almost 20 million viewer households, and to increase the number of airings from 3 times a week to 10 times a week. As a result of the change in networks, Pella's ads went from being aired 3 times a week to 10 times a week at no additional cost to Pella. American Outdoorsman notified Pella of the change in networks in December 2003.

Pella stopped paying advertising costs under the contract after December 2003. . . .

. . . .

In August 2004, American Outdoorsman sued Pella, claiming breach of contract due to Pella's failure to pay advertising costs under the contract. . . .

Pella answered the petition by claiming that American Outdoorsman had breached the terms of the contract and, thus, was precluded from recovery of damages. . . .

The trial was conducted in this case in July 2005. American Outdoorsman presented testimony from Paul Newsom, the president of an advertising audio and video production company. According to Newsom, he had his own show called Paul Newsom's Great Outdoors which had started out on The Outdoor Channel. Newsom testified however, that he had since moved his show to The Men's Channel. Newsom indicated that The Men's Channel was one of the networks that specialized in outdoor programs. According to Newsom, the value of advertising on The Men's Channel was greater than the value of advertising on The Outdoor Channel based on the number of viewer households.

The day after trial, the trial court issued its findings of fact and conclusions of law from the bench. These findings were later put into a written memorandum decision by the attorney for American Outdoorsman and signed by the trial court. The trial court found that Pella had failed to terminate the contract as required by Article X. In addition, the trial court determined that the specific portion of Article I, Paragraph 12, stating that "... Advertiser [Pella] acknowledges and understands that The Outdoor Channel is the only channel Advertiser may maintain an expectation of broadcasting," was ambiguous. The trial court then stated: "Looking at that ambiguity within the confines of the law as how the contract was drafted, the negotiations between the parties, and looking at the true nature of the agreement of the parties, the Court finds that the agreement of the parties was for the program and not for the channel." The trial court stated that Pella had materially breached the contract by failing to pay American Outdoorsman as required by the contract. The trial court found that American Outdoorsman's change in networks was not a material breach of the contract. Moreover, the trial court stated that even if the change in networks constituted a breach of contract, American Outdoorsman substantially performed all of the important parts of its obligation under the agreement. . . .

THE CONTRACT

First, Pella argues that the trial court erred in awarding damages to American Outdoorsman based upon Pella's failure to make payments under the contract. Pella contends that American Outdoorsman first breached the contract by changing the networks over which it broadcast Pella's ads and was not entitled to recover damages following such breach.

Pella's argument requires this court to interpret the contract that existed between Pella and American Outdoorsman. "The interpretation and legal effect of written instruments are matters of law, and an appellate court exercises unlimited review. Regardless of the construction given a written contract by the trial court, an appellate court may construe a written contract and determine its legal effect. [Citation omitted.]" Unrau v. Kidron Bethel Retirement Services, Inc., 271 Kan. 743, 763, 27 P.3d 1 (2001).

Moreover, Pella's argument requires this court to review the trial court's findings of fact and conclusions of law contained within its memorandum decision. The function of an appellate court is to determine whether the trial court's findings of fact are supported by substantial competent evidence and whether the findings are sufficient to support the trial court's conclusions of law. Substantial evidence is such legal and relevant evidence as a reasonable person might accept as sufficient to support a conclusion. U.S.D. No. 233 v. Kansas Ass'n of American Educators, 275 Kan. 313, 318, 64 P.3d 372 (2003). An appellate court's review of conclusions of law is unlimited. Nicholas v. Nicholas, 277 Kan. 171, 177, 83 P.3d 214 (2004).

TERMINATION CLAUSE

The main problem in this case is that Pella never properly terminated its contract with American Outdoorsman. In its answer to American Outdoorsman's petition, Pella alleged that American Outdoorsman breached the terms and conditions of the contract thereby precluding American Outdoorsman from recovering damages. In its appeal brief, Pella again argues that American Outdoorsman "breached the contract between the parties by changing the networks over which it advertised [Pella's] products and [American Outdoorsman] therefore was not entitled to recover damages following said breach." Nevertheless, Pella never fulfilled the requirements of the termination clause which would have allowed Pella to terminate its required performance of making payments under the contract.

The termination clause of the contract is contained in Article X, Paragraph 1 and states as follows:

> "In the event either Licensee [Pella] or Licensor [American Outdoorsman] fails to perform any of their respective obligations under this Agreement, the other party (i.e., Licensee or Licensor) may terminate this Agreement upon one hundred and eighty (180) days' prior written notice, provided, however, that the nonperforming party shall not have remedied such failure to the other party's reasonable satisfaction with such one hundred and eighty (180) day period."

Under the plain language of this provision, Pella was allowed to terminate the contract in the event that American Outdoorsman failed to perform any of its obligations under the contract. Pella was required to give 180 days' prior written notice of its intent to terminate. During this 180 days, American Outdoorsman would be allowed to cure its failure to perform such obligation to Pella's reasonable satisfaction.

The trial court found that American Outdoorsman was not given 180 days' written notice for its right to cure. The trial court stated that Pella failed to terminate the contract as required by Article X. Moreover, the trial court found that American Outdoorsman continued to air Pella's ads as agreed for the entirety of the three-year contract term.

. . . .

Throughout the case, Pella was never able to provide any evidence establishing that it had given written notice of its intent to terminate the agreement in January 2004. . . . Pella never afforded American Outdoorsmen 180 days to cure any alleged failure to perform its obligations under the contract. As American Outdoorsman points out in its brief, the July 2004 letter never provided it with any sort of indication as to why Pella was no longer honoring the contract. . . . Fanning indicated that he was unaware that Klein objected to the change in networks until after the depositions were taken in this case. Thus, American Outdoorsman was never given an adequate opportunity to cure to Pella's reasonable satisfaction. Particularly, whether there was a problem with American Outdoorsman's performance was a matter peculiarly within the knowledge of Pella. The trial court correctly determined that Pella failed to terminate the contract as required by Article X.

Nevertheless, Pella contends that the termination provision contained in Article X is not the exclusive means of addressing a failure by American Outdoorsman to abide by the terms of the contract. Pointing out that it and American Outdoorsman had other relationships that included website sales and royalties, Pella maintains that it certainly was not required to terminate the entire contract in order to stop making advertising payments following American Outdoorman's unilateral decision to change networks.

Pella fails to cite any authority to support this argument. To accept Pella's argument, this court would essentially have to disregard the termination provision. Nevertheless, when interpreting contracts, an appellate court determines the parties' intent from the instrument's four corners by construing all provisions together and in harmony with each other. See Metropolitan Life Ins. Co. v. Strnad, 255 Kan. 657, 671, 876 P.2d 1362 (1994). Moreover, "[w]here the language of the contract is clear and can be carried out as written, there is no room for construction or modification of the terms. [Citation omitted.]" 255 Kan. at 671. The plain and unambiguous language in the termination provision in this case requires 180 days' prior written notice to terminate when there has been failure by either party "to perform any of their respective obligations" under the agreement. (Emphasis added.) "[C]onstruing all provisions [of the contract] together and in harmony with each other" may be made only by construing the termination clause along with the other provisions of the contract. Otherwise, if this court were to adopt Pella's reasoning, the termination provision would, in effect, be read out of the contract.

Parties to a contract have a right to agree on how the contract will be terminated. A termination provision is binding and will be enforced just as other parts of the contract. See Mosher v. Kansas Coop Wheat Mkt. Ass'n, 136 Kan. 269, 276, 15 P.2d 421 (1932). Pella has not shown why, based upon the circumstances of this case, it would not be required to abide by the termination clause.

MATERIAL BREACH

Instead, Pella's main argument is that American Outdoorsman's change in networks constituted a material breach that relieved it from any future performance under the contract. The rule concerning the first material failure of performance is set forth in Restatement (Second) of Contracts § 237 (1979), as follows: "Except as stated in § 240, it is a condition of each party's remaining duties to render performances to be exchanged under an exchange of promises that there be no uncured material failure by the other party to render any such performance due at an earlier time." Under this section, an uncured material failure of performance, which includes defective performance, is considered a nonoccurrence of a condition that excuses the other party's performance under the contract. Restatement (Second) of Contracts § 237, comment a.

Pella contends that American Outdoorsman materially breached the contract by changing networks. Here, the trial court found that American Outdoorsman's change in networks was not a material breach of the contract. Whether a party breached the contract is a question of fact. See Dutta v. St. Francis Regional Med. Center, Inc., 18 Kan.App.2d 245, 257, 850 P.2d 928 (1993). "A breach is material if the promisee receive[s] something substantially less or different from that for which he bargained. [Citation omitted.]" Almena State Bank v. Enfield, 24 Kan.App.2d 834, 838, 954 P.2d 724 (1998). Restatement (Second) of Contracts § 241 (1979) lists the factors that are significant in determining whether a breach is material, as follows:

"In determining whether a failure to render or to offer performance is material, the following circumstances are significant:
"(a) the extent to which the injured party will be deprived of the benefit which he reasonably expected;
"(b) the extent to which the injured party can be adequately compensated for the part of that benefit of which he will be deprived;
"(c) the extent to which the party failing to perform or to offer to perform will suffer forfeiture;
"(d) the likelihood that the party failing to perform or to offer to perform will cure his failure, taking account of all the circumstances including any reasonable assurances;
"(e) the extent to which the behavior of the party failing to perform or to offer to perform comports with standard of good faith and fair dealing."

Pella also contends that the trial court erroneously found that American Outdoorsman substantially performed its contract obligations. "Substantial performance is the antithesis of material breach. If it is determined that a breach is material, it follows that substantial performance has not been rendered." Almena, 24 Kan.App.2d 834, Syl. ¶ 3. "Whether a party has substantially performed a promise under a contract is a question of fact to be determined from the circumstances of each case. 'Substantial performance' of a contract does not contemplate exact performance of every detail, but rather performance of all important parts." 24 Kan.App.2d 834, Syl. ¶ 4.

In its findings of fact, the trial court stated that the contract between Pella and American Outdoorsman was entered into upon the parties' wish to purchase advertising on the American Outdoorsman's television shows under the terms and conditions of the contract. The trial court found that the January 2004 change in networks allowed American Outdoorsman to broadcast to more households and increase the number of airings each week. The trial court further found that Pella had not made payments for advertising under the contract since December 2003. The trial court stated that American Outdoorsman continued airing Pella's ads as agreed for the entire three-year contract term. Pella never provided American

Outdoorsman with written notice of its intent to terminate or of any alleged breach by American Outdoorsman. The trial court found that American Outdoorsman was not given 180 days' notice for its right to cure.

The trial court's findings are supported by substantial competent evidence. American Outdoorsman continued to run Pella's ads on its television show throughout the term of the contract. American Outdoorsman switched networks 20 months into the 36-month contract. As a result of the January 2004 change in networks, Pella's ads were shown to more viewer households and were given more airings each week. The trial court was correct in determining that American Outdoorsman's change in networks was not a material breach and that American Outdoorsman substantially performed its obligations under the contract.

Similarly, in Walker & Company v. Harrison, 347 Mich. 630, 81 N.W.2d 352 (1957), the Michigan Supreme Court determined that a failure to clean a sign, as required by the terms of a contract between the plaintiff and the defendants, did not constitute a material breach justifying repudiation. Instead, the defendants were entitled to recover damages. In determining that the defendants were not justified in repudiating the contract, the Michigan Supreme Court stated:

> "[T]he injured party's determination that there has been a material breach, justifying his own repudiation, is fraught with peril, for should such determination, as viewed by a later court in the calm of its contemplation, be unwarranted, the repudiator himself will have been guilty of material breach and himself have become the aggressor, not an innocent victim." 347 Mich. at 635.

Here, similar to Walker, Pella was not entitled to terminate the contract due to American Outdoorsman's failure to broadcast on The Outdoor Channel. American Outdoorsman's change in networks did not constitute a material breach and American Outdoorsman substantially performed its obligations under the contract. Pella could not exercise its right to self-help by unilaterally terminating the contract. Unlike the facts of Walker, Pella never filed a claim for damages due to American Outdoorsman's conduct.

Nevertheless, even if American Outdoorsman's network change could be considered a material breach, Pella should not be allowed to assert this breach as a defense when it failed to give American Outdoorsman the opportunity to correct such breach. Farnsworth on Contracts §§ 8.15 and 8.18 (3d ed. 2004), indicates that a party who has materially breached the contract should ordinarily be given time to cure the contract before the contract is terminated. Specifically, Farnsworth on Contracts § 8.15 explains that an injured party is justified in suspending performance under a contract if the breach is material but is not entitled to suspend performance when the breach is immaterial. Farnsworth states that a party who disrupts performance under a contract by suspending in response to an immaterial breach commits a breach itself. Farnsworth on Contracts § 8.18 further explains that a party in breach should be allowed a period of time to cure a material breach before the contract is terminated:

> "Although a material breach justifies the injured party in exercising a right to self-help by suspending performance, it does not necessarily justify the injured party in exercising such a right by terminating the contract. Fairness ordinarily dictates that the party in breach be allowed a period of time—even if only a short one—to cure the breach if it can. If the

party in breach does cure within that period, the injured party is not justified in further suspension of its performance and both parties are still bound to complete their performance."

Farnsworth on Contracts § 8.18 continues that "an injured party that acts precipitously and terminates before it is entitled to do so loses its defense as well as the possibility of claiming damages for total breach, and will itself be liable for damages for total breach."

Thus, before an injured party can terminate a contract for material breach, the party in breach should be given a period of time to cure the alleged breach. Here, the parties contracted for a 180-day period of time to cure any alleged failure of performance under the contract to the other party's reasonable satisfaction before the contract could be terminated. Even if the breach was material in this case, Pella needed to give notice that it intended to terminate and allow American Outdoorsman the opportunity to cure within 180 days. By receiving the benefits of advertising after receiving notice of the network change, an argument could be made that Pella ratified the network change. Consequently, one could argue that Pella waived its argument that American Outdoorsman materially breached the contract and, thus, excused Pella's failure to perform. See Restatement (Second) of Contracts § 247 (1979).

If Pella believed that American Outdoorsman's change in networks constituted a failure of performance under the contract, Pella was required under Article X, Paragraph 1 to give 180 days' prior written notice to allow American Outdoorsman to correct such failure. The trial court's finding that Pella failed to give such written notice is supported by substantial competent evidence in the record. It appears that the trial court properly determined that Pella had failed to terminate the contract as required by Article X, Paragraph 1. Pella's failure to follow the termination clause left it liable for damages under the contract.

. . . .

Affirmed.

THE NO BREACH–JUSTIFICATION RESPONSE UNDER ARTICLE 2 OF THE UCC

Article 2 of the Uniform Commercial Code governs the no breach–justification response for all contracts for the sale of goods. Both the seller and the buyer may use the no breach–justification response.

Seller's Response: "No Breach–Justification"

The buyer who contracts for the sale of goods may breach by

1. repudiating with respect to a part or the whole.
2. failing to make a payment due on or before delivery.
3. wrongfully rejecting the goods.
4. wrongfully revoking acceptance of the goods.

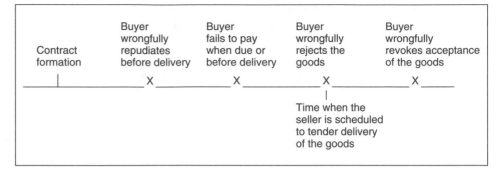

Exhibit 13–4 Types of Buyer's Breaches

See UCC § 2–703. (See Exhibit 13–4.)

If the buyer wrongfully repudiates with respect to a part or the whole or fails to make a payment before delivery, the seller may withhold delivery of the goods and seek a remedy for breach of contract (see UCC § 2–703 for seller's remedies for buyer's breach).

The buyer, however, may seek to change the focus from its own repudiation or nonpayment to the seller's failure to deliver by initiating a breach of contract action (buyer alleges that seller has breached by failing to deliver). The seller deflects the focus back to the buyer's repudiation or nonpayment by responding with "no breach–justification; my nonperformance (not delivering) was justified by your breach (repudiating before delivery or failing to pay when due or before delivery)" (UCC § 2–703).

Example 13–8

On June 1st, the Sarasota Zoo contracted to sell Jules, a manatee, to the Brookline Zoo for $20,000. Delivery was set for September 1st although the contact did not provide when the price would be paid. When June 1st came around, the Brookline Zoo had not paid, so the Sarasota Zoo refused to deliver.

The Brookline Zoo sued the Sarasota Zoo for not delivering. The Sarasota Zoo responded, "no breach–justification; my nonperformance (not delivering) was justified by your breach (not paying)."

1. The Brookline Zoo had a duty to pay and the Sarasota Zoo had a duty to deliver. (UCC § 2–301).
2. Brookline's performance of its duty to pay was a condition precedent to Sarasota's duty to deliver. (UCC § 2–310, comment 2–"[The Seller] is not required to give up possession of the goods until he has received payment, where no credit has been contemplated by the parties.")

3. Brookline breached its duty by not paying.
4. Brookline's breach (not paying) justified Sarasota's nonperformance (not delivering under UCC § 2–703(a)).

> § 2–703. Where the buyer . . . fails to make a payment due on or before delivery . . . , then with respect to any goods directly affected . . . , the aggrieved seller may
>
> (a) withhold delivery of such goods. . . .

Buyer's Response: "No Breach–Justification"

The seller who contracts for the sale of goods may breach by

1. repudiating before delivery.
2. failing to make delivery.
3. sending nonconforming goods.

See UCC § 2–711(1). (See Exhibit 13–5.)

If the seller repudiates before delivery or fails to make delivery, the buyer may cancel the contract and seek a remedy (buyer v. seller for breach of contract) (UCC § 2–711(1)). Cancellation is defined in UCC § 2–106(4) as follows:

> When either party puts an end to the contract for breach by the other and its effect is the same as that of "termination" (in a termination, no breach is present) except that the canceling party also retains any remedy for breach of the whole contract or any unperformed balance.

The seller, however, may seek to change the focus from its own repudiation before delivery or failure to deliver when delivery was due by initiating the breach of contract action (seller alleges that the buyer breached by canceling the contract). The buyer responds, "no breach–justification; my nonperformance (canceling) was justified by your breach (repudiating before delivery or failing to make delivery when delivery was due)."

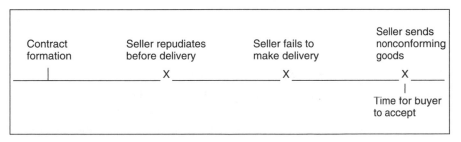

Exhibit 13–5 Types of Seller's Breaches

Example 13-9

On June 1st, the Sarasota Zoo contracted to sell Jules, a manatee, to the Brookline Zoo for $20,000. Delivery was set for September 1st, with payment to be made on or before September 15th. When June 1st came around, Sarasota refused to deliver. The Brookline Zoo then refused to pay.

The Sarasota Zoo sued the Brookline Zoo for breach of contract, alleging that Brookline breached by refusing to pay. Brookline responded, "no breach—justification; my nonperformance (not paying) was justified by your breach (not delivering)."

1. Sarasota had a duty to deliver and Brookline had a duty to pay (UCC § 2–301).
2. Sarasota's performance of its duty to deliver was a condition precedent to Brookline's duty to pay.
3. Sarasota breached its duty by not delivering.
4. Sarasota's breach (not delivering) justified Brookline's nonperformance (not paying).

Sending nonconforming goods may lead to a "no breach–justification" response. Assume that the contract is an entire contract—that is, one shipment. The number of shipments, rather than the number of payments, determines whether a contract is an entire or an **installment contract** (UCC § 2–612(1)). Also assume that the seller ships goods that are nonconforming. The buyer may reject the shipment if the goods fail to conform to the contract in any respect under UCC § 2–601 (unless the seller can cure under UCC § 2–508), and may seek a remedy (UCC § 2–703).

installment contract

An installment contract is one that requires or authorizes the delivery of goods or services in separate lots or increments to be separately accepted.

> Subject to the provisions of this Article on breach in installment contracts (Section 2–612), and unless otherwise agreed under the sections on contractual limitations of remedy (Sections 2–718 and 2–710), if the goods or the tender of delivery fail in any respect to conform to the contract, the buyer may
> a) reject the whole; or
> b) accept the whole; or
> c) accept any commercial unit or units and reject the rest. (UCC § 2–601)

Section 2–601 is known as the perfect tender rule.

Example 13-10

John and Carol ordered a $200 wedding cake from the Elite Bakery to be delivered on April 19 at 5 P.M. Elite prepared the cake and delivered it to John and Carol's reception at 5 P.M. on April 19.

As the cake was being placed on the table by Elite, the bride's mother noticed that the inscription read "John and Alice."

The cake fails to conform to the contract and can be rejected.

But what if the seller, rather than the buyer, were the plaintiff (seller v. buyer for breach of contract) and the seller alleges that the buyer breached by rejecting the shipment? The buyer responds, "no breach–justification; my nonperformance (rejecting the shipment) was justified by your breach (delivering nonconforming goods)."

Now change the facts so that the contract is an installment contract (multiple shipments), rather than an entire contract (one shipment). Also assume that the seller ships goods that are nonconforming. The buyer might be able to reject the shipment under UCC § 2–612(2), cancel the contract and seek a remedy for breach of contract (UCC § 2–711).

(1) An "installment contract" is one which requires or authorizes the delivery of goods in separate lots to be separately accepted, even though the contract contains a clause that "each delivery is a separate contract" or its equivalent.

(2) The buyer may reject any installment which is non-conforming if the non-conformity substantially impairs the value of that installment and cannot be cured . . . , but if the non-conformity does not fall within subsection (3), and the seller gives adequate assurance of its cure, the buyer must accept that installment.

(3) Whenever non-conformity . . . substantially impairs the value of the whole contract, there is a breach of the whole. But the aggrieved party reinstates the contract if he accepts a non-conforming installment without seasonably notifying of cancellation or if he brings an action with respect only to past installments or demands performance as to future installments. (UCC §§ 2–612(2), (3))

Example 13–11

Buyer contracts to buy 300,000 tons of coal to be delivered in three shipments of 100,000 tons each on the first day of three consecutive months. The first shipment is only 75,000 tons. Because this was an installment contract (three deliveries), Buyer cannot reject the shipment unless the shortage substantially impairs the value of that installment and the shortage cannot be cured. Furthermore, if the shortage does not substantially impair the value of the whole contract and if Seller gives adequate assurance of its cure, Buyer must accept the shipment even though it is 25,000 tons short.

But what if the seller, rather than the buyer, were the plaintiff (seller v. buyer for breach of contract) and the seller alleges that the buyer breached by rejecting the shipment? The buyer responds, "no breach–justification; my nonperformance (rejecting the shipment) was justified by your breach (delivering nonconforming goods)." Whether the buyer was justified in rejecting the shipment will be determined by UCC §§ 2–612(2), (3).

PARALEGAL EXERCISE 13.10

Read *Midwest Mobile Diagnostic Imaging, L.L.C. v. Dynamics Corporation of America* and answer the following:

1. What is the choice of law?
2. Was a contract formed and, if so, who were the contracting parties?
3. Was the contract enforceable?
4. Who filed suit against whom and what did the plaintiff allege was the defendant's breach?
5. What was the defendant's response and did this response succeed (and if not, why)?
6. If the plaintiff was successful in maintaining its cause of action, what were the plaintiff's remedies for the defendant's breach?

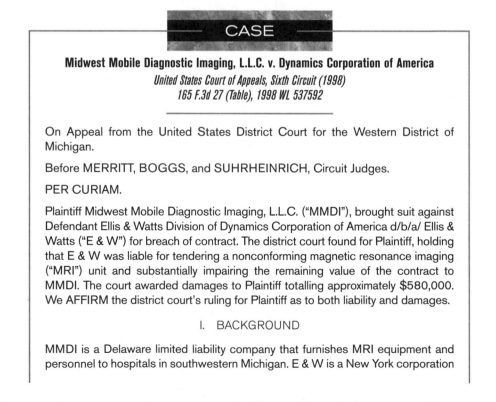

CASE

Midwest Mobile Diagnostic Imaging, L.L.C. v. Dynamics Corporation of America
United States Court of Appeals, Sixth Circuit (1998)
165 F.3d 27 (Table), 1998 WL 537592

On Appeal from the United States District Court for the Western District of Michigan.

Before MERRITT, BOGGS, and SUHRHEINRICH, Circuit Judges.

PER CURIAM.

Plaintiff Midwest Mobile Diagnostic Imaging, L.L.C. ("MMDI"), brought suit against Defendant Ellis & Watts Division of Dynamics Corporation of America d/b/a/ Ellis & Watts ("E & W") for breach of contract. The district court found for Plaintiff, holding that E & W was liable for tendering a nonconforming magnetic resonance imaging ("MRI") unit and substantially impairing the remaining value of the contract to MMDI. The court awarded damages to Plaintiff totalling approximately $580,000. We AFFIRM the district court's ruling for Plaintiff as to both liability and damages.

I.   BACKGROUND

MMDI is a Delaware limited liability company that furnishes MRI equipment and personnel to hospitals in southwestern Michigan. E & W is a New York corporation with its principal place of business in Cincinnati, Ohio. E & W designs and manufactures trailers for mobile medical uses, including MRI systems.

In April 1995, MMDI contacted E & W to negotiate the purchase from E & W of four trailers equipped with MRI scanners. MMDI intended to purchase the scanners directly from the manufacturer, Philips Medical Systems, and have E & W install them in the trailers subject to Philips's specifications and approval. In July 1995, Philips gave E & W the trailer specifications. On August 10, 1995, MMDI and E & W executed a Purchase Agreement for four mobile MRI units. E & W understood that MMDI had commitments to its clients to provide MRI services. Delivery of the MRI units was conditioned on Philips's final approval that the trailers conformed to certain minimum specifications. Philips delivered the first scanner to E & W in September 1995, well before E & W was prepared to install it.

On November 17, 1995, MMDI paid E & W $321,500 for the first trailer. Philips completed its preliminary testing of that trailer on November 27, 1995, and found that it complied with all technical specifications. However, on November 28, 1995, Philips road tested the trailer by moving and then parking the trailer, calibrating the scanner, then moving the trailer again, and finally parking the trailer and recalibrating the scanner. The trailer did not pass the road test, because the unit's side walls had flexed too much. Excessive variance in the wall causes unacceptable "ghosting" in the MRI scans. In response, E & W installed a reinforcing brace or gusset of bare steel beams around the scanner and road tested the trailer on December 11, 1995. The reinforcing brace solved the wall-flexing problem and satisfied all of Philips's technical specifications.

On December 13, 1995, MMDI objected to the reinforcing brace, because MMDI: (1) believed that the brace impeded service access to the magnet; (2) did not approve of the new appearance of the trailer; and (3) felt that the brace would reduce the resale value of the trailer. MMDI refused to accept the trailer with the brace and demanded that E & W return the full purchase price. E & W responded that: (1) the brace solved the flexing problem; (2) the trailer passed Philips's tests; and (3) E & W had fulfilled its contractual obligations. By December 14, 1995, however, E & W began working on an alternatively designed and more aesthetically pleasing brace.

On December 18, 1995, MMDI informed E & W that it would accept the defective trailer as a temporary unit, provided that E & W returned the purchase price and would move forward on an acceptable design for a replacement trailer. E & W did not agree to these conditions, but did continue to work on a new design. When E & W did not agree to MMDI's terms, MMDI canceled the contract, rented a replacement MRI trailer for temporary use, and contracted with another manufacturer for the four permanent MRI trailers it required.

On January 11, 1996, Philips confirmed in writing that the first trailer with the reinforcing brace met "all technical requirements" and could be delivered under "temporary conditions." However, Philips would not fully certify the unit, because the brace impeded access to the scanner.

MMDI filed suit, and the district court granted summary judgment to Plaintiff, holding that E & W was liable for breach by tendering a nonconforming MRI unit and substantially impairing the remaining value of the contract to MMDI. The district court awarded MMDI $384,500 in compensatory damages ($63,000 deposited for the fourth unit and $321,500 for the first unit), and $185,250 in incidental damages for the gross rent of a mobile MRI trailer between December 19, 1995, and April 20, 1996.

II. DISCUSSION

E & W argues that the district court was clearly erroneous in finding that: (1) E & W breached the Purchase Agreement by tendering a nonconforming good; (2) MMDI rightfully rejected E & W's tender of the first trailer with the reinforcing brace; (3) E & W did not provide adequate assurances of cure within a reasonable time and, in fact, did not cure within a reasonable time; and (4) any nonconformity in the first trailer substantially impaired the value of the contract as a whole. E & W's arguments are unpersuasive.

First, we hold that the district court correctly found that a breach occurred as a result of E & W's nonconforming tender. The trailer E & W tendered to MMDI on December 13, 1995, did not conform to the Purchase Agreement because: (1) Philips would not certify it as being in full compliance with the specifications; (2) the brace was not included in the contracted design diagrams; and (3) the reinforcing brace was unsightly and blocked access to the scanner for servicing purposes. Where the time of performance is not specified, a reasonable time is assumed. Mich. Comp. Laws Ann. § 2–309(1). In the present case, the written contract did not have a definite delivery date. When the parties executed the Purchase Agreement, they both expected delivery of the first trailer in October 1995. The parties later changed the delivery date several times and eventually agreed on December 1, 1995 (as found by the district court) or at least at some point in early December 1995.

Pursuant to the "perfect tender rule," a buyer may reject nonconforming goods if they fail in any respect to conform to the contract. Id. § 440.2601 (West 1994). The perfect tender rule, however, is relaxed in installment sales. Id. § 440.2612. An installment sale is a contract for multiple items that permits delivery in separate groups and at different times. Id. § 440.2612(1). Although the MRI units were individual commercial units, the Purchase Agreement between MMDI and E & W was an installment contract, because it provided for delivery of individual units at different times.

Moreover, a buyer may reject any nonconforming installment if the nonconformity substantially impairs the value of that installment and cannot be cured within a reasonable time. Id. § 440.2612(2). However, if the seller gives adequate assurance of curing the nonconformity, the buyer must accept that installment. Id. After the first trailer failed its road test because of the wall-flexing problem, E & W promised to cure the defect and, therefore, was entitled under law to a reasonable amount of time in which to cure the defect. Id. § 440.2612(2). E & W tendered its attempted cure on December 13, 1995, by delivering the trailer with the reinforced brace. This attempted cure substantially breached the Purchase Agreement, because the reinforcing brace: (1) was not included in the original structural design; (2) blocked access to the scanner for servicing; (3) was unsightly for use in a mobile medical unit; and (4) decreased the resale value of the unit. Accordingly, we find that MMDI rightfully rejected the attempted cure.

If the nonconformity in any given installment substantially impairs the value of the whole contract, then there is a breach of the whole. Id. § 440.2612(3). MMDI's purpose in entering into the Purchase Agreement was to obtain, in a timely fashion, the four mobile MRI units that it needed to serve its growing client demand. As the district court reasoned, by failing to cure the initial tender of November 28, 1995, E & W substantially delayed completion of the contract. In addition, loss of even one installment substantially impaired the value of the whole contract to MMDI, because it reduced MMDI's anticipated capacity by at least 25 percent.

The district court awarded MMDI $384,500 in compensatory damages and $185,250 in incidental damages. This latter amount reflects the gross rent that MMDI paid for a replacement MRI unit. E & W argues that the profits earned while using the replacement unit should offset the damage award reflecting the rental payment. Incidental damages include "expenses or commissions in connection with effecting cover and any other reasonable expense incident to the delay or other breach." Id. § 440.2715(1). MMDI covered for E & W's breach by contracting with another company to make the mobile MRI units. Meanwhile, MMDI still had commitments to provide MRI services. To fulfill its commitments, MMDI rented an MRI unit. The rental of a temporary replacement unit was an out-of-pocket expense incidental to covering for E & W's failure to supply a conforming MRI unit. If E & W had performed, MMDI would have made a profit on the conforming unit and would not have incurred $185,250 in rental expense. The fact that MMDI made a profit on the rental unit is immaterial, because MMDI presumably would have made the same profit had E & W performed. However, if E & W had performed, then MMDI would not have incurred the incidental rental expense.

If E & W had shown that MMDI made a greater profit on the rented unit than it would have had on the unit that E & W did not deliver, then E & W might be entitled to some reduction. However, E & W has not shown in this record that MMDI earned a greater profit by using the rented unit or that MMDI enjoyed any savings in pretermitted costs resulting from E & W's breach. Accordingly, we hold that any profits that MMDI made while using the rented MRI should not serve to reduce the amount of its award for the incidental rental expense.

III. CONCLUSION

Because E & W tendered a nonconforming MRI unit, and thereby substantially impaired the remaining value of the contract to MMDI, E & W was liable for breach of contract. Moreover, the district court properly awarded $185,250 as a commercially reasonable expense to MMDI that MMDI incurred while effecting cover incident to E & W's breach. Therefore, we AFFIRM the district court's judgment for MMDI as to both liability and damages.

📖 PARALEGAL EXERCISE 13.11

Reconsider the facts in *Midwest Mobile Diagnostic Imaging, L.L.C. v. Dynamics Corporation of America*. Switch the parties so the plaintiff in the case becomes the defendant and the defendant becomes the plaintiff. Answer the following:

1. What is the choice of law?
2. Was a contract formed and, if so, who were the contracting parties?
3. Was the contract enforceable?
4. Who filed suit against whom and what did the plaintiff allege was the defendant's breach?
5. What was the defendant's response and did this response succeed (and if not, why)? ■

RESTITUTION AS AN ACTION FOR THE BREACHING PLAINTIFF

Because a breach of contract action is an action against a breaching party and since the plaintiff rather than the defendant is the breaching party, if the defendant is successful in its "no breach–justification" response, the plaintiff has no cause of action against the defendant for breach of contract. The breaching plaintiff may, however, maintain a cause of action in restitution against the non-breaching defendant if the plaintiff has conferred a benefit on the defendant and it would be unjust to permit the defendant to retain that benefit without compensating the plaintiff.

The Restatement (Second) of Contracts § 374 (1981), entitled "Restitution in Favor of Party in Breach," provides the following:

(1) Subject to the rule stated in Subsection (2), if a party justifiably refuses to perform on the ground that his remaining duties of performance have been discharged by the other party's breach, the party in breach is entitled to restitution for any benefit that he has conferred by way of part performance or reliance in excess of the loss that he has caused by his own breach.

(2) To the extent that, under the manifested assent of the parties, a party's performance is to be retained in the case of breach, that party is not entitled to restitution if the value of the performance as liquidated damages is reasonable in the light of the anticipated or actual loss caused by the breach and the difficulties of proof of loss.

▥ PARALEGAL EXERCISE 13.12

Bradley, incarcerated for murder, hired Murphy as his legal counsel. Bradley paid Murphy $4,000 as an advance for legal services to be rendered in his defense. Before Murphy could render any legal services, Bradley committed suicide. Bradley's estate demanded that Murphy return the $4,000, and Murphy refused.

If Bradley's estate sues Murphy for breach of contract, what would be the allegation of breach? What would be Murphy's response to this allegation of breach? Could the estate recover in a breach of contract action?

Could Bradley's estate successfully sue Murphy in a restitution action? What benefit did Bradley confer on Murphy? Would it be unjust to permit Murphy to retain this benefit without compensating Bradley's estate? ▪

Today, one of the more important questions dealing with the breaching plaintiff is whether the breaching purchaser of real property can recover payments made to the seller before the purchaser's breach. Although the majority position is that restitution will not be granted, a number of jurisdictions have adopted a minority view allowing recovery and the perceptible trend is away from the rigidity of the majority rule.

If the contract were for the sale of goods, the courts would give restitutionary relief to a breaching seller. Before the enactment of the UCC, the majority of courts treated a breaching buyer of goods the same as a breaching purchaser of real property. In both cases, a majority of courts refused to give the breaching buyer restitutionary relief. Under section 2–718 of the UCC, the breaching buyer has gained some rights. Section 2–718 requires the seller to return to the buyer so much of the deposit or down payment as exceeds the damages that the seller in fact sustains. This reverses pre-Code authority, which generally regarded a buyer's willful refusal to take proper goods as forfeiting the right to the return of the down payment.

Courts are split three ways over whether a contractor who has not substantially performed may recover in a restitution action for benefits conferred on the nonbreaching owner.

- Some courts apparently reject restitution as a cause of action in these cases.
- Some courts permit restitution but only if the contractor's breach was not willful or "voluntary."
- Some courts permit restitution even where the contractor is guilty of a willful breach of court.

If a court does permit the breaching contractor to maintain a restitution action and the contractor's costs exceed the value conferred, the contractor's recovery will be limited to the actual value to the defendant rather than the contractor's cost of construction.

🏛 PARALEGAL CHECKLIST

The Defendant's Response to the Plaintiff's Allegation of Breach—No Breach–Justification

❑ A defendant, by responding "no breach–justification," is saying "although I am not complying with the terms of the contract, my nonperformance was justified by your breach of the contract." As with the "no breach–excuse" response, the defendant admits nonperformance. Unlike the "no breach–excuse" response, however, the defendant is *not* alleging that the reason for nonperformance was an unexpected external event (act of God or governmental action); rather, the defendant is alleging that the reason was an act or omission of the other party. The allegation is, therefore, that the roles should be reversed. The plaintiff is actually the breaching, not the nonbreaching, party.

Carefully analyze a "no breach–justification" response to determine whether the defendant can prove that

1. both the plaintiff and the defendant had duties to perform.
2. the plaintiff's performance was a condition precedent to the defendant's performance.
3. the plaintiff was in breach of his or her duty to perform.
4. the magnitude of the plaintiff's breach of his or her duty justified the defendant's

nonperformance of his or her duty. The common law and Article 2 of the UCC have different articulations of the magnitude, depending on the situation.

❏ If the plaintiff, rather than the defendant, is the breaching party, the plaintiff cannot maintain a cause of action for breach of contract. A breaching plaintiff may, however, maintain a restitution action based on unjust enrichment.

KEY TERMS

Divisible contract

Entire contract

Installment contract

REVIEW QUESTIONS

TRUE/FALSE QUESTIONS (CIRCLE THE CORRECT ANSWER)

1. T F   The defendant's "no breach–justification" response is based on the action of the other contracting party rather than on an external event.

2. T F   An admission of nonperformance is the same as an admission of breach.

3. T F   Under the "no breach–justification" response, the defendant responds that my breach was justified by your breach.

4. T F   An "entire contract" is a contract with a single delivery, whereas a "divisible contract" requires multiple performances.

5. T F   An installment contract under Article 2 of the UCC has one shipment and multiple payments.

6. T F   The defendant may not be able to use the plaintiff's breach in its justification response if the defendant has waived the breach.

7. T F   The defendant's performance must be independent of the plaintiff's performance for the defendant to claim a justification response.

8. T F   The defendant may use any breach by the plaintiff, however small, to justify his or her nonperformance.

9. T F   The contractor's performance in a construction contract must be less than a "substantial performance" to justify an owner's nonpayment.

10. T F   An employee's "immaterial breach" will not justify the employer's nonperformance in an employment contract.

11. T F   If a contract for the sale of goods is not an installment contract, UCC § 2–601 authorizes the buyer to reject the

goods that fail to conform to the contract in any respect (the perfect tender rule).

12.   T   F   If a contract for the sale of goods is an installment contract, the perfect tender rule does not apply.

13.   T   F   In some situations, the seller of goods may have a right to "cure" (correct the nonconformity) if the buyer rejects a nonconforming tender.

14.   T   F   Even though a breaching plaintiff has conferred a benefit on the defendant, the breaching plaintiff may not successfully maintain a restitution cause of action.

FILL-IN-THE-BLANK QUESTIONS

1.   _____.   A contract for the sale of goods with multiple deliveries of goods.

2.   _____.   Defendant admits nonperformance but asserts his or her nonperformance was due to the other party's breach.

3.   _____.   A contract for the sale of goods with a single delivery of goods.

4.   _____.   The rule set forth in UCC § 2–601 authorizing the buyer to reject goods that fail to conform to the contract in any respect.

5.   _____.   The type of condition required for a no "breach–justification" response.

MULTIPLE-CHOICE QUESTIONS (CIRCLE ALL THE CORRECT ANSWERS)

1. Which of the following are installment contracts under Article 2 of the UCC?
    (a) Multiple deliveries
    (b) Multiple payments
    (c) Single payment with multiple deliveries
    (d) Single delivery with multiple payments
    (e) Multiple deliveries with multiple payments

2. The "no breach–justification" response is concerned with which of the following?
    (a) Unanticipated external events
    (b) Mistake in integration
    (c) Mistake in understanding
    (d) The relationship between the plaintiff's and the defendant's conduct
    (e) The parol evidence rule

3. In a sale of goods, what is the standard in UCC § 2–612(2) for the magnitude of the breach?
    (a) Substantial performance
    (b) Material breach

(c) A substantial impairment of the value of this installment
(d) Perfect tender
(e) Immaterial breach

4. In a construction contract, what is the standard for the magnitude of the contractor's breach that justifies the owner in not paying?
(a) A less than substantial performance
(b) Material breach
(c) A substantial impairment of the value of this installment
(d) A less than perfect tender
(e) More than an immaterial breach

5. In an employment contract, what is the standard for the magnitude of the employee's breach that justifies the employer in not paying?
(a) Substantial performance
(b) Material breach
(c) A substantial impairment of the value of this installment
(d) Perfect tender
(e) Immaterial breach

SHORT-ANSWER QUESTIONS

1. Describe the steps to be taken when evaluating a "no breach–justification" response.

2. Distinguish a "no breach–compliance" response from a "no breach–justification" response.

3. Distinguish a "no breach–excuse" response from a "no breach–justification" response.

4. Hiram Novak contracted with Quality Builders for the construction of a family room to be added to his house. After about a third of the construction had been completed, Quality left the job. When Quality demanded *pro rata* payment, Novak refused. Quality sued Novak for breach of contract, alleging nonpayment. Novak responded "no breach–justification."

Apply each step of the "no breach–justification" response to these facts. Who prevails?

CHAPTER 14

The Defendant's *No Breach–Terminated Duty* Response to the Plaintiff's Allegation of Breach

- Condition Subsequent Terminates the Duty
- Consensual Termination of a Duty
- Unilateral Termination of a Duty
- Termination of a Duty by Operation of Law

The defendant's fourth response to the plaintiff's allegation of breach is "No breach; although I am not complying with the terms of the contract, my duty to perform the contract has been terminated" (see Exhibit 14–1).

> My obligation to perform according to the contract no longer exists due to some duty-terminating occurrence. Therefore, I am not in breach.

The "no breach–terminated duty" response couples the defendant's admission of nonperformance with a claim that his or her contractual duty has ended either by agreement or by law and therefore the defendant is not in breach of contract. The terminating event may be a part of the contract (condition subsequent) or external to the contract. If external, the terminating occurrence may be consensual (substitute contract, accord and satisfaction, or novation), unilateral (waiver), or by operation of law (statute of limitations). Because the defendant is not the breaching party, the plaintiff cannot maintain a breach of contract action against the defendant.

Unlike with the "no breach–compliance," "no breach–excuse," and "no breach–justification" responses, a restitution action is not available with the "no breach–terminated duty" response.

IN THE DISTRICT COURT OF [NAME] COUNTY
STATE OF [NAME]

[NAME], dba [Name])	
)	
Plaintiff,)	
)	
v.)	Case No. _____
)	
[NAME], a [Name of State])	
corporation)	
)	
Defendant.)	

ANSWER OF DEFENDANT [NAME]

Defendant [name] alleges the following in response to the complaint:

1. Defendant admits the allegations of paragraph 1 of the complaint.

2. Defendant admits the allegations of paragraph 2 of the complaint.

3. Defendant admits the allegations of paragraph 3 of the complaint.

4. Defendant admits the allegations of paragraph 4 of the complaint.

5. Defendant admits the allegations of paragraph 5 of the complaint.

6. Defendant denies the allegations of paragraph 6 and alleges that after the alleged breach of the agreement and before the filing of this action, Defendant delivered to Plaintiff and Plaintiff accepted $ [dolllars] in full satisfaction of Plaintiff's claim.

7. The complaint fails to state a claim against Defendant upon which relief can be granted.

Accordingly, Defendant demands that Plaintiff take nothing by this Action, and that Defendant be awarded costs including reasonable attorney fees.

[Attorney's name signed]
[Attorney's name typed]
Attorney for defendant
[Bar membership number]
[Address]
[Telephone number]

Exhibit 14–1 Answer—Defendant's "No Breach–Terminated Duty" Response to the Plaintiff's Allegation of Defendant's Breach

CONDITION SUBSEQUENT TERMINATES THE DUTY

A duty may be terminated by the occurrence of a **condition subsequent**. A condition subsequent is a duty-terminating event.

condition subsequent
A condition subsequent is a duty terminating event.

Example 14–1

"I promise to play tennis with you today unless it rains." Rain is the event that ends the duty to play tennis. The promisor has a duty to play tennis up until the time it rains.

CONSENSUAL TERMINATION OF A DUTY

A contractual duty may be terminated by the consent of the contracting parties. Consent will involve a contractual relationship with all the trappings of consideration. Such contracts as the substitute contract, the accord and satisfaction, and the novation illustrate termination by consent. Each is discussed in detail in another part of this text: substitute contract (see Chapter 5); accord and satisfaction (see Chapter 5); and novation (see Chapter 17).

UNILATERAL TERMINATION OF A DUTY

A contractual duty may also be terminated by a unilateral act by the party to whom the duty is owed, the promisee. Such a termination may take the form of a waiver.

TERMINATION OF A DUTY BY OPERATION OF LAW

A contractual duty may also be terminated by operation of law. An illustration is the Statute of Limitations.

⚖ PARALEGAL EXERCISE 14.1

Ultrasound Electronics Company contracted to purchase 25 TVs from Sound Warehouse, a wholesaler, for the 2006 Christmas season. Although the TVs were to be delivered by November 1, 2006, they were actually delivered on January 15, 2007, too late for Christmas.

On March 1, 2010, Ultrasound filed a breach of contract action against Sound Warehouse, alleging as breach the late delivery. If the Statute of Limitations for breach of contract actions is three years, could Sound Warehouse answer the allegation of breach with the "no breach–terminated duty" response? ■

 PARALEGAL CHECKLIST

The Defendant's Response to the Plaintiff's Allegation of Breach—No Breach–Terminated Duty

❏ The defendant who responds "no breach–terminated duty" is saying "although I am not complying with the terms of the contract, my duty to perform the contract has been terminated and therefore I am not in breach." The terminating event may be a term of the contract (condition subse-

quent), or may arise after the contract was formed through consent (substitute contract, accord and satisfaction, novation), by unilateral act (waiver), or by operation of law (statute of limitations).

If the defendant is not a breaching party, the plaintiff cannot maintain an action for breach of contract. Also, the plaintiff cannot maintain a restitution action against the defendant for a benefit conferred.

KEY TERM

Condition subsequent

REVIEW QUESTIONS

TRUE/FALSE QUESTIONS (CIRCLE THE CORRECT ANSWER)

1. T F A restitution action is available with the "no breach–terminated duty" response.

2. T F A contractual duty may be terminated by the consent of the contracting parties.

3. T F Consensual termination of a contractual duty will involve a contractual relationship with all the trappings of consideration.

4. T F A contractual duty may not be terminated by a unilateral act such as waiver by the promisee.

5. T F A novation will terminate a contracting party's duties under the original contract.

6. T F The Statute of Limitations may terminate a party's contractual duty to perform.

7. T F The promisee may be estopped from asserting the promisor's contractual duty to perform.

8. T F When a defendant responds "no breach–terminated duty," the defendant admits nonperformance of a contractual duty.

FILL-IN-THE-BLANK QUESTIONS

1. _____. The type of condition that is a duty-terminating event.

2. _____. A consensual method for terminating a contractual duty.

3. _____. A unilateral method for terminating a contractual duty.

4. _____. An operation of law that terminates a contractual duty.

MULTIPLE-CHOICE QUESTIONS (CIRCLE ALL THE CORRECT ANSWERS)

1. Which of the following defendant responses admits nonperformance of a contractual duty?
   (a) No breach–compliance
   (b) No breach–excuse
   (c) No breach–justification
   (d) No breach–terminated duty
   (e) Admission of breach

2. Which of the following are consensual methods for terminating a contractual duty?
   (a) Estoppel
   (b) Waiver
   (c) Substitute contract
   (d) Novation
   (e) Statute of limitations

SHORT-ANSWER QUESTIONS

1. Distinguish a "no breach–terminated duty" response from a "no breach–compliance" response.

2. Distinguish a "no breach–terminated duty" response from a "no breach–justification" response.

PART VI

Step Six: Plaintiff's Remedies for the Defendant's Breach of Contract

REMEDIES FOR BREACH

Once an enforceable contract has been breached, the nonbreaching party* may successfully maintain an action for breach of contract and is entitled to a remedy for the breach but may not seek punitive damages. In most cases, the nonbreaching party will receive a judgment awarding money damages as a substitute for what was promised. The nonbreaching party will seldom be awarded specific goods or services.

In most cases, the nonbreaching party will be compensated for what he or she expected to receive under the contract (**expectation remedies**, which include expectation damages). This places the nonbreaching party in the position he or she would have been in had the contract been fully performed. Although the nonbreaching party generally fares best with compensation based on lost expectation, compensation based on reliance or restitution may, at times, exceed compensation based on contract expectations.

Reliance remedies (which include reliance damages) for breach of contract will compensate the nonbreaching party for his or her costs incurred while relying on the breaching party's promise. The reliance remedy returns the nonbreaching party to the position he or she was in prior to relying on the breaching party's promise.

Restitution remedies (which include restitution damages) for breach of contract will compensate the nonbreaching party for any benefit that he or she conferred on the breaching party for which it would be unjust to permit the breaching party to retain without compensating the nonbreaching party. The restitution remedy returns the breaching party to the position he or she was in prior to receiving the benefit from the nonbreaching party.

Chapter 15 explores the nonbreaching party's expectation, reliance, and restitution common law remedies for a breach of contract. Chapter 16 introduces the array of UCC Article 2 remedies available to the nonbreaching party.

*The Restatement (Second) of Contracts (1981) refers to the nonbreaching party (in this context) as "the injured party."

expectation remedies (including expectation damages)
Expectation remedies (including expectation damages) place the nonbreaching party in the position he or she would have been in had the contract been fully performed.

reliance remedies (including reliance damages)
Reliance remedies (including reliance damages) place the nonbreaching party back to the position he or she was in prior to relying on the breaching party's promise.

restitution remedies (including restitution damages)
Restitution remedies (including restitution damages) place the breaching party back to the position he or she was in prior to the time the breaching party received the benefit conferred upon him or her by the nonbreaching party. The measure of damages is the reasonable value of the benefit conferred to the breaching party.

The Plaintiff's Common Law Remedies

- Expectation Remedy for Breach of Contract
  Compensatory Damages
  Liquidated Damages
  Injunction and Specific Performance
  Costs and Attorney Fees
- Reliance Remedy for Breach of Contract
- Restitution Remedy for Breach of Contract
- Could Restitution Be a Cause of Action for the Plaintiff When the Defendant Has Breached the Contract?

When an enforceable contract is breached, the nonbreaching party is entitled to an expectation, reliance, or restitution remedy for the breach. This chapter examines these three remedies and why the nonbreaching party may not pursue a restitution action when a breach of contract action is available (see Exhibit 15–1).

EXPECTATION REMEDY FOR BREACH OF CONTRACT

When parties contract, they have expectations about what their *net* gains will be once the contract is performed. The parties have perceptions of the value of what they promise to give and the value of what they are promised in return. Protecting the nonbreaching party's **expectation interest** places the nonbreaching party in the

expectation interest
Protecting the nonbreaching party's expectation interest places the nonbreaching party in the position he or she would have been in had the contract been fully performed by both parties according to the contract.

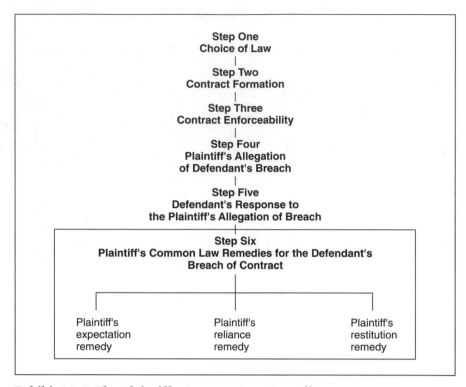

Exhibit 15–1 The Plaintiff's Common Law Remedies

position he or she would have been in had the contract been fully performed according to its terms by *both parties*.

To move the nonbreaching party to the position he or she would have been in had the contract been fully performed requires two calculations. First, the nonbreaching party must receive what he or she expected to receive. Second, the nonbreaching party must give what he or she expected to give. These two calculations represent the two elements of the offer and the two elements of the acceptance (i.e., the mirror image of the offer).

Example 15–1

Offer: "I promise to work for you for four weeks for your promise to pay me $2,000 a week."

Acceptance: "I promise to pay you $2,000 a week for your promise to work for me for four weeks."

The formula for an expectation reads: *[(what the nonbreaching party expected to receive) less (what the nonbreaching party did receive)]*

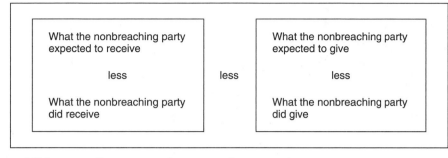

Exhibit 15–2 The Expectation Formula

less [(what the nonbreaching party expected to give) less (what the nonbreaching party did give)].

Exhibit 15–2 is useful in visualizing the expectation remedy formula. The left box is the "receiving" box. The difference between "what the nonbreaching party expected to receive" and "what the nonbreaching party did receive" is what the nonbreaching party must receive to be brought to full performance on the receiving side. The right box is the "giving" box. The difference between "what the nonbreaching party expected to give" and "what the nonbreaching party did give" is what the nonbreaching party must give to be brought to full performance on the giving side.

Example 15–2

In Example 15–1, if the employee completes four weeks of work (full performance) and the employer breaches the contract by not paying (no performance by the employer), the employee may seek $8,000 as an expectation remedy for the employer's breach [($8,000 − $0) less (4 weeks of work − 4 weeks of work)].

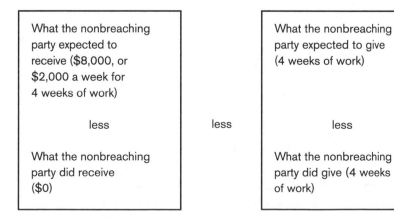

If the employee completes four weeks of work (full performance) and the employer breaches the contract by paying for only three weeks, the employee may seek $2,000 as an expectation remedy for the employer's breach [($8,000 − $6,000) less (4 weeks of work − 4 weeks of work)].

What the nonbreaching party expected to receive ($8,000, or $2,000 a week for 4 weeks of work) less What the nonbreaching party did receive ($6,000, or $2,000 a week for 3 weeks of work)	less	What the nonbreaching party expected to give (4 weeks of work) less What the nonbreaching party did give (4 weeks of work)

If the employee completes three weeks and four days of work (almost full performance) and the employer breaches the contract by not paying for any of the work, the employee may seek $8,000 less the value of one day of work as an expectation remedy for the employer's breach [($8,000 − $0) less (4 weeks of work − 3 weeks and 4 days of work)].

What the nonbreaching party expected to receive ($8,000, or $2,000 a week for 4 weeks of work) less What the nonbreaching party did receive ($0)	less	What the nonbreaching party expected to give (4 weeks of work) less What the nonbreaching party did give (3 weeks and 4 days of work)

If the employee completes three weeks and four days of work (almost full performance) and the employee breaches the contract by paying for only three weeks, the employee may seek $2,000 less the value of one day of work as an expectation remedy for the employer's breach [($8,000 − $6,000) less (4 weeks of work − 3 weeks and 4 days of work)].

What the nonbreaching party expected to receive ($8,000, or $2,000 a week for 4 weeks of work) less What the nonbreaching party did receive ($6,000, or $2,000 a week for 3 weeks of work)	less	What the nonbreaching party expected to give (4 weeks of work) less What the nonbreaching party did give (3 weeks and 4 days of work)

▥ PARALEGAL EXERCISE 15.1

Suppose Andrew contracted to sell Blackacre to Bently for Bently's promise to pay Andrew $200,000. If Andrew receives $0 but gives Bently Blackacre, what should Andrew recover?

What the nonbreaching party expected to receive ($_____) less What the nonbreaching party did receive ($_____)	less	What the nonbreaching party expected to give (_____) less What the nonbreaching party did give (_____)

If Andrew receives $50,000 but gives Blackacre, what are Andrew's expectation damages?

What the nonbreaching party expected to receive ($_____) less What the nonbreaching party did receive ($_____)	less	What the nonbreaching party expected to give (_____) less What the nonbreaching party did give (_____)

If Andrew received $100,000 but gave Blackacre, what are Andrew's expectation damages?

What the nonbreaching party expected to receive ($_____)		What the nonbreaching party expected to give (_____)
less	less	less
What the nonbreaching party did receive ($_____)		What the nonbreaching party did give (_____)

Compensatory Damages

compensatory damages

Compensatory damages are intended to compensate the nonbreaching party for not receiving his or her expectation under the contract.

punitive damages

Monetary awards that are above and beyond compensation for injury and that would punish the breaching party.

The nonbreaching party's damages are **compensatory damages**; that is, damages intended to compensate the nonbreaching party for not receiving his or her expectation under the contract. The nonbreaching party will be brought to full performance, no more and no less. Therefore, punitive damages are not awarded in breach of contract actions. **Punitive damages** are monetary awards that punish the breaching party. The breaching party is not held up to the public as an example of what might happen if a party breaches.

The fact that damages for breach of contract do not include punitive damages is consistent with the fact that the intentions of the breaching party are irrelevant. Intentional and unintentional breaches will result in the same measure of expectation damages. Therefore, a contracting party may find breaching a contract to be in his or her best economic interest. Breaching a contract and paying expectation damages may place the breaching party in a better economic position than performing the contract.

Example 15–3

The ABC Painting Company contracts to paint Smith's house for $3,000. Before beginning to paint, ABC breaches the Smith contract so it could paint the First Bank Building. The First Bank contract is for $12,000. Smith hires Quality Painters for $3,500.

If Smith sues ABC for breach of contract, she will recover $500, the additional amount it would cost her to have her house painted. ABC may be more than willing to pay Smith $500 if it can make substantially more on the First Bank contract.

In some situations, it may be difficult to decide what will place the injured party in the position he or she would have been in had the contract been fully performed. In construction contracts, the issue is whether the injured party is entitled to the cost of replacement (or repair)—or only to the diminished value of the subject of the contract.

Example 15–4

Contractor builds Owner a house but mislocates an interior wall by one foot. After the house is completed, Owner discovers Contractor's error. The mislocation does not change the value of the house. Contractor has breached the contract by not building according to the blueprints.

Is Owner entitled to the cost of relocating the wall or only to the diminished value of the house with the mislocated wall? Unless there was some overriding reason why the house is unacceptable with the mislocated wall, a relocation of the wall will create "economic waste." A court will generally award Owner only the diminished value of the house attributable to the mislocation.

PARALEGAL EXERCISE 15.2

The Allegheny Coal Company leases ranch land from the Bar Z Ranch for the purpose of strip mining coal. The contract provides that Allegheny will reclaim the land (restore the surface) after it completes strip mining. At the end of the lease term, Allegheny leaves the mining site without reclaiming the land. The value of the land is $50 an acre if not reclaimed and $600 an acre if reclaimed. Reclaiming the land will cost $900 an acre.

Should the Bar Z Ranch be entitled to the diminished value of the land or to the cost of reclaiming it? Consider the policy arguments supporting each position. ■

Damages for breach of contract are limited to those that the breaching party could reasonably foresee at the time of the making of the contract as the probable result of such a breach. Foreseeable damages are either general or special damages. The classic case of *Hadley v. Baxendale,* 9 Ex. 341, 156 Eng. Rep. 145 (1854), states the rule of foreseeability:

> Where two parties have made a contract which one of them has broken, the damages which the other party ought to receive in respect of such breach of contract should be such as may fairly and reasonably be considered either arising naturally, i.e., according to the usual course of things, from such breach of contract itself, or such as may reasonably be supposed to have been in the contemplation of both parties, at the time they made the contract, as the probable result of the breach of it.

general damages

General damages arise naturally, that is, according to the usual course of events when a contract is breached. General damages are foreseeable.

General damages "arise naturally, i.e., according to the usual course of things, from such breach of contract itself." In a contract for the lease of grazing land,

1. what are the lessee's normal damages if the lessor breaches by refusing to deliver the land?
2. what are the lessor's normal damages if the lessee breaches by refusing to pay for the leased land?

In a contract for employment,

1. what are the employee's normal damages if the employer breaches by wrongfully discharging the employee?
2. what are the employer's normal damages if the employee breaches by wrongfully leaving the job?

Special damages do not "arise naturally, i.e., according to the usual course of things, from such breach of contract itself." **Special damages** are those that "may reasonably be supposed to have been in the contemplation of both parties, at the time they made the contract, as the probable result of the breach of it." Because they may reasonably be supposed to have been in the contemplation of both parties, they are foreseeable.

special damages

Special damages do not naturally arise from a breach of contract. They are not within the usual course of events when a contract is breached. Special damages become foreseeable when they may reasonably be supposed to have been in the contemplation of both parties at the time of contract formation as the probable result of the breach.

▥ PARALEGAL EXERCISE 15.3

The Hunter Hotel Corporation contracts with Apex Construction Company for renovation of the hotel. The contract provides September 1st as the completion date for the renovation. Apex does not complete the renovation until October 1st, and as a result, the hotel loses a convention that it scheduled during the week of September 15th.

Is the Hunter Hotel entitled to recover the lost profits for the convention? ▨

Whether a nonbreaching party can recover damages for pain and suffering and emotional distress in a breach of contract action is a question of foreseeability. Generally, damages for pain and suffering or for emotional distress are not available in a breach of contract action. In some instances, however, recovery can be awarded for pain and suffering or emotional distress if they were the natural result of the breach (i.e., within the contemplation of the parties at the time the contract was made).

Damages for breach of contract must be shown with reasonable certainty. Damages that are speculative and incapable of being ascertained with reasonable certainty are not recoverable. Although damages must be reasonably certain, mathematical exactness is not required.

▥ PARALEGAL EXERCISE 15.4

Assume in Paralegal Exercise 15.3 that Apex knew at the time of contracting that the Hunter has a convention scheduled for September 15th and

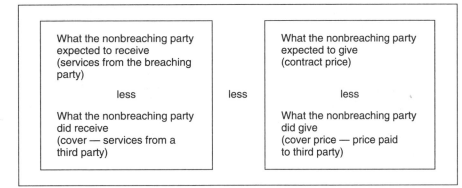

Exhibit 15-3 Employer's Expectation Damages

that if the renovation is not completed before that date, the Hunter will lose the convention and the accompanying profits.

Is the Hunter entitled to recover the lost profits for the convention? ▪

In an employment contract, the nonbreaching employer may need certain services and can attempt to find a substitute employee. Even though the nonbreaching party has found a substitute, he or she may still be entitled to damages. These damages include the difference in cost between what the nonbreaching party expected to pay for the services and what the nonbreaching party did pay, in addition to any expenses incurred in finding the substitute (see Exhibit 15-3).

Example 15-5

The Pink Panther Lounge hired Irma LaRue to sing at the Lounge on Friday and Saturday nights. The contract was for the month of December at a salary of $500 an evening. After appearing for one weekend, Irma quit to perform in Atlantic City. Because this was the Christmas season and most entertainers had engagements, the Lounge hired Melody Layne, who appeared through the month of December at a salary of $700 an evening.

The Lounge is entitled to $200 for each of the remaining Friday and Saturday evenings in December. The Lounge is also entitled to any costs incurred in finding Melody.

In the event of breach, the nonbreaching party has a duty to mitigate the damages. **Mitigation** requires the nonbreaching party to use reasonable means to avoid or minimize damages. Mitigation may take different forms. In some situations, the doctrine prevents

mitigation

Mitigation requires the nonbreaching party to use reasonable means to avoid or minimize damages.

the nonbreaching party from increasing the amount the breaching party must pay.

In a construction contract, the contractor is entitled to the contract price upon completion of the structure. If the owner breaches the contract before the contractor begins to build, the contractor is entitled to its profits (contract price less the expected cost to build the structure). If the owner breaches after the contractor begins to build but before the structure is complete, the contractor is entitled to the contract price less the amount it saved by not having to complete the structure. If the contractor ignores the owner's notice not to complete the structure, the contractor cannot increase the amount due on the contract by continuing to build.

PARALEGAL EXERCISE 15.5

Broken Arrow Construction Company contracts to build a school building for the Oolagah School District for $8,500,000. At the time of contract formation, the contractor estimates that it would cost $8 million in labor and materials to complete the work.

1. Calculate the Construction Company's damages if the School District breaches the contract before the Construction Company begins to build.
2. Calculate the Construction Company's damages if the School District breaches the contract after the Construction Company has begun to build and has spent $1,500,000 on labor and materials and anticipates spending another $6,750,000 to complete the work.
3. Calculate the Construction Company's damages if, instead of stopping the work when the School District wrongfully orders it to do so, the Construction Company completes the school.

In other situations, the doctrine of mitigation requires the nonbreaching party to decrease the amount of damages the breaching party must pay. In an employment contract, a wrongfully terminated employee must attempt to use his or her saved time productively by seeking substitute employment. If the employee does use this saved time by taking another job, the money earned from the new job will be subtracted from the money the employee expected to earn under the original contract. If the employee does not take another job but should have taken it, the money that could have been earned from the new job will be subtracted from the money the employee expected to earn under the original contract.

PARALEGAL EXERCISE 15.6

The *Daily News* hires Brenda under a one-year contract to write the local news. After three months, Brenda is wrongfully discharged. The *Chronicle,* a rival newspaper, learns of Brenda's discharge and offers her a nine-month contract at 90 percent of her salary with the *Daily News.*

In determining Brenda's damages for the *Daily News*'s breach of contract, must her salary with the *Chronicle* be subtracted from her expected salary with the *Daily News* if she accepts the *Chronicle*'s offer?

Must the salary the *Chronicle* offers be subtracted from Brenda's expected salary with the *Daily News* if she does not accept the *Chronicle's* offer?

Liquidated Damages

Liquidated damages are damages included in the contract by the parties at the time of contract formation that will be due in the event of breach. Not all clauses that purport to provide liquidated damages are enforceable. When one of the parties challenges such a clause, the court will evaluate whether the clause is in fact a liquidated damage provision or merely a penalty. Clauses classified as penalties are unenforceable.

A clause is a liquidated damage provision and not a penalty if

1. at the time of contract formation the damages in the event of a breach would be impossible or very difficult to estimate accurately.
2. there was a reasonable endeavor by the parties to fix a fair compensation.
3. the stipulated amount bears a reasonable relation to probable damages and is not disproportionate to any damages reasonably anticipated.

PARALEGAL EXERCISE 15.7

Reliable Property Company owns a 50-unit apartment complex. Reliable hires Felix to repaint apartments as they become vacant, for $300 each. The contract provides that Felix has five days from the date of notice of vacancy to paint each apartment. The contract further provides that Felix will pay Reliable 10 percent of the contract price for each day he is late. Felix finishes painting the first apartment in eight days and is paid $210.

Could Felix successfully sue Reliable for breach of contract and, if so, for how much? Would the following facts be relevant?

1. The apartment rents for $400 a month.
2. The apartment complex has an 85 percent occupancy rate.
3. The apartment was ready by the first of the month.

The bottom portion of the right box in Exhibit 15–4 includes both that which the nonbreaching party has given pursuant to the contract and the nonbreaching party's incidental damages. **Incidental damages** are the nonbreaching party's post-breach expenses incurred to salvage the contract, retrieve or protect the goods, or otherwise mitigate damages (see Exhibit 15–4).

liquidated damages

Liquidated damages are those damages agreed to by the parties at the time of contract formation that will apply to the transaction if a breach occurs.

incidental damages

Incidental damages are awarded to the nonbreaching party for expenses reasonably incurred as a result of the other contracting party's breach. See UCC § 2–710 (Seller's Incidental Damages) and UCC § 2–715(1) (Buyer's Incidental Damages).

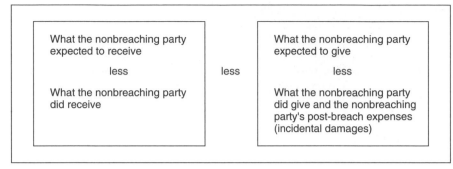

Exhibit 15–4 Incidental Damages

The nonbreaching party who establishes a breach of contract but is unable to prove damages is entitled to nominal damages. **Nominal damages** are a trifling sum awarded when the plaintiff does not prove actual damages. A judgment for nominal damages, while not compensating the nonbreaching party in dollars, clarifies the rights and duties of the parties and may include an award of court costs.

Injunction and Specific Performance

At times, damages may not totally compensate the nonbreaching party for his or her injury. The circumstances may be such that future injuries will occur. An **injunction** orders the breaching party to refrain from further action.

Example 15–6

A research chemist hired by Green Farm Fertilizer Company promises not to work for another farm fertilizer company for two years after she ends her employment with Green Farm. After working for Green Farm for several years, the chemist quits and begins to work for another farm fertilizer company. Although Green Farm is entitled to damages for the chemist's breach of her covenant not to compete, damages will not protect Green Farm from loss of its secrets that the chemist could reveal to her new employer. If the court precludes the chemist from working for the new employer for the remainder of the covenant's term, Green Farm would be better protected. This court order precluding the chemist from working for the new employer is known as an injunction.

Specific performance mandates delivery of the thing. Specific performance is available only when the remedy of damages would be inadequate. If the seller, in a contract for the sale of real property, refuses to convey title, specific performance may be available if the property is unique and thus not easily replaceable in the market.

---

nominal damages

Nominal damages are a token award to the nonbreaching party, given more for clarification of the rights and duties of the parties than for actual monetary compensation. Court costs may be included.

injunction

An injunction is an order issued by a court directing a party to refrain from a specified act.

specific performance

Specific performance is an order issued by a court directing a party to do a specified act.

▥ PARALEGAL EXERCISE 15.8

Blue Grass Stables contracts to sell Neal's Diamond, an outstanding three-year-old thoroughbred and winner of the Triple Crown, to California Meadows, a breeding syndicate. Prior to the delivery date, Blue Grass notifies California Meadows that it has decided to race Neal's Diamond for another year and would not deliver him to the syndicate.

1. Could California Meadows find a substitute horse in the market to replace Neal's Diamond?
2. Would damages (money) be an adequate remedy for California Meadows?
3. Would specific performance be an appropriate remedy? ▦

Specific performance is not available when the breach is the failure to pay money. Money is interchangeable and not unique. Specific performance is also not available in personal service contracts. Involuntary servitude violates the Thirteenth Amendment to the United States Constitution.

▥ PARALEGAL EXERCISE 15.9

Sylvia, a female acid rock group, contracts to give a Fourth of July concert at Woodstock. Early in June, Woodstock notifies Sylvia that its services are no longer needed.

Should Sylvia be entitled to the remedy of specific performance for Woodstock's breach of contract? ▦

Costs and Attorney Fees

The parties might stipulate in the contract who will pay costs in the event of a dispute. **Costs** generally include filing fees, service of process, jury fees, and court officer charges, but not attorney fees. To predetermine who will pay these expenses, the contract might contain a term stating, "the party initiating litigation will pay all costs." Such a term will cause a court to levy the costs against the named party.

If the contract does not include a provision for costs, most courts allocate costs to the losing party. Some states, however, place limitations on this rule. For example, in Illinois, the court may apportion costs to the parties if the case is not decided on all of the issues presented. Because the rules on costs may vary from jurisdiction to jurisdiction, contracting parties must determine prior to drafting a contract which state's law will apply in the event of a breach and who will be assessed costs if the contract does not allocate costs.

Unlike costs, the nonbreaching party in a breach of contract action generally cannot recover its attorney fees from the other, even after winning the judgment. This rule has two general exceptions. First, attorney fees can be recovered if suit is brought under a statute allowing the nonbreaching party to recover attorney fees.

costs
Costs include filing fees, service of process, jury fees, and court officer charges, but not attorney fees.

What the nonbreaching party did give in reliance	less	What the nonbreaching party did receive in reliance

Exhibit 15–5 The Reliance Formula

A statute might include the clause, "Anyone bringing a cause of action under this statute may recover attorney fees, if that party has obtained a favorable judgment."

Second, the parties may allocate attorney fees by contract. The agreement may state, "if litigation arises from this contract, the party obtaining a favorable judgment in such litigation may recover his or her attorney fees from the opposing party." Although most states allow the parties to allocate attorney fees, some, such as California, limit the attorney fees recoverable to "reasonable attorney fees." Because the rules on attorney fees vary from jurisdiction to jurisdiction, the parties must determine prior to drafting the contract which state's law will apply in the event of a breach, whether that state will enforce an allocation of attorney fees, and whether limitation will be placed on the allocation.

RELIANCE REMEDY FOR BREACH OF CONTRACT

The reliance remedy is not concerned with the nonbreaching party's expectations. What the nonbreaching party expected to receive and what the nonbreaching party expected to give are irrelevant when computing damages based on reliance. The important factors are what the nonbreaching party did give and did receive in reliance on the breaching party's promise. The formula for the reliance remedy reads: *[(what the nonbreaching party gave in reliance on the breaching party's promise) less (what the nonbreaching party received in reliance on the breaching party's promise)]* (see Exhibit 15–5).

Example 15–7

If Andrew gave Blackacre (worth $200,000) and received $0, Andrew should receive $200,000 to place him back in the position he was in before he relied on the breaching party's promise.

What the nonbreaching party did give in reliance (Blackacre, worth $200,000 to the nonbreaching party)	less	What the nonbreaching party did receive in reliance ($0)

If Blackacre was worth $250,000 rather than $200,000 and Andrew received $0, he should receive $250,000 to place him back in the position he was in before he relied on the breaching party's promise.

What the nonbreaching party did give in reliance (Blackacre, worth $250,000 to the nonbreaching party)	less	What the nonbreaching party did receive in reliance ($0)

On the other hand, if Blackacre was only worth $150,000, Andrew should receive $150,000 if his reliance interest, rather than his expectation interest, were to be protected.

What the nonbreaching party did give in reliance (Blackacre, worth $150,000 to the nonbreaching party)	less	What the nonbreaching party did receive in reliance ($0)

▥ PARALEGAL EXERCISE 15.10

Mary Oliver, a financial consultant in New York City, is hired by the Golden Gate Investment Company of San Francisco for $80,000 a year for three years. Mary stays for a week in San Francisco at her own expense, finding a place to live. She also spends $5,000 moving her household goods. When she reports to work, she finds that new management has taken over the investment company and her services are no longer needed. Fortunately for Mary, she is able to return to her old job in New York City at $78,000 a year.

Could Mary successfully sue Golden Gate for breach of contract and, if so, for how much? Consider both Mary's expectation and reliance remedies. ■

RESTITUTION REMEDY FOR BREACH OF CONTRACT

The restitution remedy, like the reliance remedy, is not concerned with what the nonbreaching party expected to receive and what that party expected to give. The restitution remedy also is not concerned with what the nonbreaching party gave or received in reliance on the breaching party's promise. Rather, the restitution remedy is concerned with the benefit that the nonbreaching party conferred on the breaching party and what the nonbreaching party received for conferring that benefit. The measure of damages is the reasonable value of the benefit conferred to the party receiving the benefit, that is, the breaching party (see Exhibit 15–6).

| What benefit the nonbreaching party conferred on the breaching party | less | What the nonbreaching party received for the benefit conferred |

Exhibit 15–6 The Restitution Formula

Example 15-8

If Andrew gave Bently Blackacre—worth $200,000 to Andrew but worth only $150,000 to Bently—and Bently did not pay Andrew the $200,000 contract price, Andrew's restitution remedy is only $150,000, the reasonable value of Blackacre to Bently.

| What benefit the nonbreaching party conferred on the breaching party (Blackacre, worth $150,000 to Bently) | less | What the nonbreaching party received for the benefit conferred ($0) |

If Bently had paid Andrew $25,000 for Blackacre, Andrew could recover $125,000, the reasonable value of Blackacre to Bently ($150,000) less the amount Bently already paid Andrew for Blackacre ($25,000).

| What benefit the nonbreaching party conferred on the breaching party (Blackacre, worth $150,000 to Bently) | less | What the nonbreaching party received for the benefit conferred ($25,000) |

Although the expectation remedy is generally greater than the restitution remedy, instances do exist in which the restitution remedy exceeds expectation. This may occur when the breaching party breaches a contract that was unfavorable to the nonbreaching party. The nonbreaching party is taken off the hook.

Example 15-9

The Sunset Nursery Company contracts to landscape the Zenith Mall for $50,000. Sunset spends several weeks grading the land for trees and sod. The work takes longer than Sunset expected due to the lack of spring rains and the hot summer that baked the soil. Zenith becomes impatient and fires Sunset without cause. At the time of the termination, Sunset has spent the equivalent of $40,000 on the job and would have spent an additional $20,000 to complete it. The reasonable value of Sunset's work to Zenith is also $40,000.

Zenith breaches the contract by firing Sunset without cause. Sunset is entitled to a restitution remedy for Zenith's breach of contract. Sunset's measure of damages is the reasonable value of its work to Zenith, that is, $40,000. Had Sunset sought to protect its expectation interest, it would have recovered two-thirds of the contract price ($33,333) (two-thirds of the work was completed), or less than the value of its work.

In determining a restitution recovery, two factors come into play:

1. Was the nonbreaching party to pay money?
2. Did the nonbreaching party fully perform?

If the nonbreaching party was to pay money and has partially performed (i.e., has paid some money), the nonbreaching party is entitled to restitution of the money paid.

⫟ PARALEGAL EXERCISE 15.11

Alexander contracts to build a barn for Herman for $100,000. Herman pays Alexander $15,000 in advance. Alexander, however, does not begin to build the barn. If the barn had been built, it would have been worth only $75,000.

When Herman sues Alexander for breach of contract, how much should he recover to protect his expectation interest?

How much should he recover to protect his restitution interest? ▪

If the nonbreaching party was to perform services and did partially perform, then the nonbreaching party is entitled to the value of the services performed as measured by the reasonable value of the services to the breaching party. The nonbreaching party may recover the reasonable value of the services to the breaching party even though the reasonable value exceeds the prorated contract price.

Example 15–10

A Client hires an Attorney to handle his divorce for $1,500. The divorce turns out to be more complicated than the Attorney originally thought, and the Attorney devotes substantial time to the case. Before the Attorney can procure the divorce, the Client wrongfully discharges the Attorney. If the Attorney computes his time in billable hours, he would charge $2,500 as of the time of his discharge.

The Attorney is entitled to a restitution remedy for breach of contract of $2,500, the reasonable value of his services even though this exceeds the $1,500 contract price.

If the nonbreaching party has fully performed the services, then the contract price limits recovery.

Example 15–11

If the Client discharges the Attorney after the Attorney procures the divorce, the Attorney is entitled to only the contract price, $1,500, even though the reasonable value of his services is $2,500.

This rule contains an anomaly. The nonbreaching party may recover more than the contract price for less than full performance but no more than the contract price for full performance.

PARALEGAL EXERCISE 15.12

Fields, seeking a divorce from her husband, hires Bailey as her attorney. The parties agree upon a flat legal fee of $2,500 for the completed property settlement and the divorce decree. After Bailey spends substantial time preparing the case, Fields reconciles with her husband and refuses to pay Bailey. The case turns out to be more complicated than Bailey had originally thought, and had she charged by billable hour, her fee for work performed prior to the reconciliation would easily have been $4,000.

How much should Bailey recover from Fields in an action for breach of contract? Consider both Bailey's expectation and restitution interests. ■

In *Sullivan v. O'Connor,* the court discusses the injured party's expectation, reliance, and restitution remedies. Ms. Sullivan, a patient, contracts with Dr. O'Connor, a surgeon, for plastic surgery on her nose. The surgery fails to enhance her beauty and improve her appearance. The surgery in fact disfigures and deforms her nose and causes her pain and suffering beyond what she expects. Ms. Sullivan sues Dr. O'Connor for both breach of contract and negligence. The jury did not find Dr. O'Connor negligent but did find that he breached his contract with Ms. Sullivan. As you read the case, consider the following questions:

1. Was a contract formed between Dr. O'Connor and Ms. Sullivan?
2. Was the contract enforceable?
3. What did Ms. Sullivan allege was Dr. O'Connor's breach?
4. Which response did Dr. O'Connor raise to negate Ms. Sullivan's allegation of breach? Was Dr. O'Connor successful?
5. Referring to the diagrams in Exhibit 15–7 on damages (see p. 473), answer the following questions:
   a. What did Ms. Sullivan expect to give?

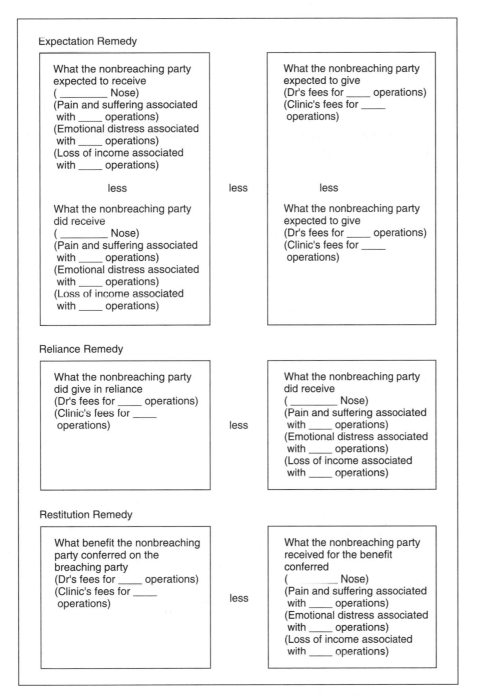

Exhibit 15-7 Measuring Expectation, Reliance, and Restitution Damages in *Sullivan v. O'Connor*

  b. What did Ms. Sullivan give?

  c. What did Ms. Sullivan expect to receive?

   What kind of nose?

   Pain and suffering for how many operations?

   Emotional distress for how many operations?

   Loss of income associated with how many operations?

  d. What did Ms. Sullivan receive?

   What kind of nose?

   Pain and suffering for how many operations?

   Emotional distress for how many operations?

   Loss of income associated with how many operations?

6. What were Ms. Sullivan's expectation damages?

7. What were Ms. Sullivan's reliance damages?

8. What were Ms. Sullivan's restitution damages?

9. Were the expectation, reliance, and restitution damages theoretically the same?

10. Did Ms. Sullivan's attorney ask for all the damages to which she was entitled?

CASE

Sullivan v. O'Connor
Supreme Judicial Court of Massachusetts (1973)
363 Mass. 579, 296 N.E.2d 183

Before TAURO, C. J., and REARDON, QUIRICO, KAPLAN and WILKINS, JJ.

KAPLAN, Justice.

The plaintiff patient secured a jury verdict of $13,500 against the defendant surgeon for breach of contract in respect to an operation upon the plaintiff's nose. The substituted consolidated bill of exceptions presents questions about the correctness of the judge's instructions on the issue of damages.

  The declaration was in two counts. In the first count, the plaintiff alleged that she, as patient, entered into a contract with the defendant, a surgeon, wherein the defendant promised to perform plastic surgery on her nose and thereby to enhance her beauty and improve her appearance; that he performed the surgery but failed to achieve the promised result; rather the result of the surgery was to disfigure and deform her nose, to cause her pain in body and mind, and to subject her to other damage and expense. The second count, based on the same transaction, was in the conventional form for malpractice, charging that the defendant had been guilty of negligence in performing the surgery. Answering, the defendant entered a general denial.

  On the plaintiff's demand, the case was tried by jury. At the close of the evidence, the judge put to the jury, as special questions, the issues of liability under the two counts, and instructed them accordingly. The jury returned a verdict for the plaintiff on the contract count, and for the defendant on the negligence count. The judge then instructed the jury on the issue of damages.

As background to the instructions and the parties' exceptions, we mention certain facts as the jury could find them. The plaintiff was a professional entertainer, and this was known to the defendant. The agreement was as alleged in the declaration. More particularly, judging from exhibits, the plaintiff's nose had been straight, but long and prominent; the defendant undertook by two operations to reduce its prominence and somewhat to shorten it, thus making it more pleasing in relation to the plaintiff's other features. Actually the plaintiff was obliged to undergo three operations, and her appearance was worsened. Her nose now had a concave line to about the midpoint, at which it became bulbous; viewed frontally, the nose from bridge to midpoint was flattened and broadened, and the two sides of the tip had lost symmetry. This configuration evidently could not be improved by further surgery. The plaintiff did not demonstrate, however, that her change of appearance had resulted in loss of employment. Payments by the plaintiff covering the defendant's fee and hospital expenses were stipulated at $622.65.

The judge instructed the jury, first, that the plaintiff was entitled to recover her out-of-pocket expenses incident to the operations. Second, she could recover the damages flowing directly, naturally, proximately, and foreseeably from the defendant's breach of promise. These would comprehend damages for any disfigurement of the plaintiff's nose—that is, any change of appearance for the worse—including the effects of the consciousness of such disfigurement on the plaintiff's mind, and in this connection the jury should consider the nature of the plaintiff's profession. Also consequent upon the defendant's breach, and compensable, were the pain and suffering involved in the third operation, but not in the first two. As there was no proof that any loss of earnings by the plaintiff resulted from the breach, that element should not enter into the calculation of damages.

By his exceptions the defendant contends that the judge erred in allowing the jury to take into account anything but the plaintiff's out-of-pocket expenses (presumably at the stipulated amount). The defendant excepted to the judge's refusal of his request for a general charge to that effect, and, more specifically, to the judge's refusal of a charge that the plaintiff could not recover for pain and suffering connected with the third operation or for impairment of the plaintiff's appearance and associated mental distress.

The plaintiff on her part excepted to the judge's refusal of a request to charge that the plaintiff could recover the difference in value between the nose as promised and the nose as it appeared after the operations. However, the plaintiff in her brief expressly waives this exception and others made by her in case this court overrules the defendant's exceptions; thus she would be content to hold the jury's verdict in her favor.

We conclude that the defendant's exceptions should be overruled.

[The court found Dr. O'Connor had contracted to provide Ms. Sullivan with a beautiful nose and had breached his contract.]

If an action on the basis of contract is allowed, we have next the question of the measure of damages to be applied where liability is found. Some cases have taken the simple view that the promise by the physician is to be treated like an ordinary commercial promise, and accordingly that the successful plaintiff is entitled to a standard measure of recovery for breach of contract—"compensatory" ("expectancy") damages, an amount intended to put the plaintiff in the position he would be in if the contract had been performed, or, presumably, at the plaintiff's election, "restitution" damages, an amount corresponding to any benefit conferred by the plaintiff upon the defendant in the performance of the contract disrupted by the defendant's breach. See Restatement: Contracts § 329 and comment a, §§ 347, 384(1). Thus in Hawkins v. McGee, 84 N.H. 114, 146 A. 641, the defendant doctor was taken to have promised the plaintiff to convert his damaged hand by means of an operation into a good or perfect hand, but the doctor so operated as to damage the hand still further. The court, following the usual expectancy formula, would have asked the jury to estimate and award to the plaintiff the difference between the value of a good or perfect hand, as promised, and the value of the hand after the operation. (The same formula would apply, although the dollar result would be less, if the operation had neither worsened nor improved the condition of the hand.) If the plaintiff had not yet paid the doctor his fee, that amount would be deducted from the recovery. There could be no recovery for the pain and suffering of the operation, since that detriment would have been incurred even if the operation had been successful; one can say that this detriment was not "caused" by the breach. But where the plaintiff by reason of the operation was put to more pain than he would have had to endure, had the doctor performed as promised, he should be compensated for that difference as a proper part of his expectancy recovery. It may be noted that on an alternative count for malpractice the plaintiff in the *Hawkins* case had been nonsuited; but on ordinary principles this could not affect the contract claim, for it is hardly a defense to a breach of contract that the promisor acted innocently and without negligence. The New Hampshire court further refined the *Hawkins* analysis in McQuaid v. Michou, 85 N.H. 299, 157 A. 881, all in the direction of treating the patient-physician cases on the ordinary footing of expectancy. See McGee v. United States Fid. & Guar. Co., 53 F.2d 953 (1st Cir.) (later development in the *Hawkins* case); Cloutier v. Kasheta, 105 N.H. 262, 197 A.2d 627; Lakeman v. LaFrance, 102 N.H. 300, 305, 156 A.2d 123.

Other cases, including a number in New York, without distinctly repudiating the *Hawkins* type of analysis, have indicated that a different and generally more lenient measure of damages is to be applied in patient-physician actions based on breach of alleged special agreements to effect a cure, attain a stated result, or employ a given medical method. This measure is expressed in somewhat variant ways, but the substance is that the plaintiff is to recover any expenditures made by him and for other detriment (usually not specifically described in the opinions) following proximately and foreseeably upon the defendant's failure to carry out his promise. Robins v. Finestone, 308 N.Y. 543, 546, 127 N.E.2d 330; Frankel v. Wolper, 181 App.Div. 485, 488, 169 N.Y.S. 15, affd., 228 N.Y. 582, 127 N.E. 913; Frank v. Maliniak, 232 App.Div. 278, 280, 249 N.Y.S. 514; Colvin v. Smith, 276 App.Div. 9, 10, 92 N.Y.S.2d 794; Stewart v. Rudner, 349 Mich. 459, 465–473, 84 N.W.2d 816. Cf. Carpenter v. Moore, 51 Wash.2d 795, 322 P.2d 125. This, be it noted, is not a "restitution" measure, for it is not limited to restoration of the benefit conferred on the defendant (the fee paid) but includes other expenditures, for example, amounts paid for medicine and nurses; so also it would seem according to its logic to take in damages for any worsening of the plaintiff's condition due to the breach. Nor is it an "expectancy" measure, for it does not appear to contemplate recovery of the whole difference in value between the condition as promised and the condition actually resulting from the treatment. Rather the tendency of the formulation is to put the plaintiff back in the position he occupied just before the parties entered upon the agreement, to compensate him for the detriments he suffered in reliance upon the agreement. This kind of intermediate pattern of recovery for breach of contract is discussed in the suggestive article by

Fuller and Perdue, The Reliance Interest in Contract Damages, 46 Yale L.J. 52, 373, where the authors show that, although not attaining the currency of the standard measures, a "reliance" measure has for special reasons been applied by the courts in a variety of settings, including noncommercial settings. See 46 Yale L.J. at 396–401.

For breach of the patient-physician agreements under consideration, a recovery limited to restitution seems plainly too meager, if the agreements are to be enforced at all. On the other hand, an expectancy recovery may well be excessive. The factors, already mentioned, which have made the cause of action somewhat suspect, also suggest moderation as to the breadth of the recovery that should be permitted. Where, as in the case at bar and in a number of the reported cases, the doctor has been absolved of negligence by the trier, an expectancy measure may be thought harsh. We should recall here that the fee paid by the patient to the doctor for the alleged promise would usually be quite disproportionate to the putative expectancy recovery. To attempt, moreover, to put a value on the condition that would or might have resulted, had the treatment succeeded as promised, may sometimes put an exceptional strain on the imagination of the fact finder. As a general consideration, Fuller and Perdue argue that the reasons for granting damages for broken promises to the extent of the expectancy are at their strongest when the promises are made in a business context, when they have to do with the production or distribution of goods or the allocation of functions in the market place; they become weaker as the context shifts from a commercial to a noncommercial field. 46 Yale L.J. at 60–63.

There is much to be said, then, for applying a reliance measure to the present facts, and we have only to add that our cases are not unreceptive to the use of that formula in special situations. We have, however, had no previous occasion to apply it to patient-physician cases.

The question of recovery on a reliance basis for pain and suffering or mental distress requires further attention. We find expressions in the decisions that pain and suffering (or the like) are simply not compensable in actions for breach of contract. The defendant seemingly espouses this proposition in the present case. True, if the buyer under a contract for the purchase of a lot of merchandise, in suing for the seller's breach, should claim damages for mental anguish caused by his disappointment in the transaction, he would not succeed; he would be told, perhaps, that the asserted psychological injury was not fairly foreseeable by the defendant as a probable consequence of the breach of such a business contract. See Restatement: Contracts, § 341, and comment a. But there is no general rule barring such items of damage in actions for breach of contract. It is all a question of the subject matter and background of the contract, and when the contract calls for an operation on the person of the plaintiff, psychological as well as physical injury may be expected to figure somewhere in the recovery, depending on the particular circumstances. The point is explained in Stewart v. Rudner, 349 Mich. 459, 469, 84 N.W.2d 816. Cf. Frewen v. Page, 238 Mass. 499, 131 N.E. 475; McClean v. University Club, 327 Mass. 68, 97 N.E.2d 174. Again, it is said in a few of the New York cases, concerned with the classification of actions for statute of limitations purposes, that the absence of allegations demanding recovery for pain and suffering is characteristic of a contract claim by a patient against a physician, that such allegations rather belong in a claim for malpractice. See Robins v. Finestone, 308 N.Y. 543, 547, 127 N.E.2d 330; Budoff v. Kessler, 2 A.D.2d 760, 153 N.Y.S.2d 654. These remarks seem unduly sweeping. Suffering or distress resulting from the breach going beyond that which was envisaged by the treatment as agreed, should be compensable on the same ground as the worsening of the patient's condition because of the breach. Indeed it can be argued that the very suffering or distress "contracted for"—that which would have been incurred if the treatment achieved the promised result—should also be compensable on the theory underlying the New York cases. For that suffering is "wasted" if the treatment fails. Otherwise stated, compensation for this waste is arguably required in order to complete the restoration of the status quo ante.

In the light of the foregoing discussion, all the defendant's exceptions fail: the plaintiff was not confined to the recovery of her out-of-pocket expenditures; she was entitled to recover also for the worsening of her condition, and for the pain and suffering and mental distress involved in the third operation. These items were compensable on either an expectancy or a reliance view. We might have been required to elect between the two views if the pain and suffering connected with the first two operations contemplated by the agreement, or the whole difference in value between the present and the promised conditions, were being claimed as elements of damage. But the plaintiff waives her possible claim to the former element, and to so much of the latter as represents the difference in value between the promised condition and the condition before the operations.

Plaintiff's exceptions waived.

Defendant's exceptions overruled.

COULD RESTITUTION BE A CAUSE OF ACTION FOR THE PLAINTIFF WHEN THE DEFENDANT HAS BREACHED THE CONTRACT?

A nonbreaching party does not have the luxury of selecting between a breach of contract action and a restitution action. (The restitution action should not be confused with the restitution remedy for a breach of contract action.) If a contract has been formed and is enforceable and if the defendant has breached, the nonbreaching party has no choice but to pursue a breach of contract action. If the nonbreaching party ignores the breach of contract action and pleads a restitution action, the breaching party can defend the restitution action by claiming the existence of an enforceable contract that has been breached.

But why would a breaching party want to defend a restitution action by stating that he or she breached the contract? The answer may be found in the baggage that accompanies each cause of action. Each cause of action has its own attributes. The difference may include: the Statute of Limitations, costs and attorney fees, and the simplicity of the issues to be litigated.

Example 15-12

The ABC Corporation contracts with the Washington County Sheriff's Department to provide video cameras in all deputy sheriff patrol vehicles. ABC installs the cameras, but the Sheriff's Department refuses to pay. The contract provides that in the event of breach, the breaching party will pay one-half of the nonbreaching party's attorney's fees. Under a state statute, attorney fees may be awarded by the court in a restitution cause of action.

Although ABC would like to sue the Sheriff's Department in a restitution action and seek all of its attorney's fees, it would be unsuccessful because a cause of action for breach of contract could be maintained. A contract exists between ABC and the Sheriff's Department. The contract is enforceable. The Sheriff's Department breached the contract and ABC has a cause of action for breach of contract. A restitution cause of action can only be maintained when a breach of contract cause of action cannot be maintained. Therefore, ABC has no choice but to claim its remedies under a breach of contract action. ABC could recover only one-half of its attorney's fees.

ABC may, however, plead both breach of contract and restitution as alternative causes of action. If the breach of contract action survives the trial, the restitution action ceases to exist. If the breach of contract action does not survive trial, the restitution action could be maintained.

PARALEGAL CHECKLIST

Plaintiff's Common Law Remedies for the Defendant's Breach of Contract

☐ Once an enforceable contract has been breached, the nonbreaching party may successfully maintain an action for breach of contract and *seek a remedy for the breach.* The remedies may compensate the nonbreaching party: (1) for what it expected to receive under the contract (expectation); (2) for costs incurred while relying on the breaching party's promise (reliance); *or* (3) for any benefit conferred by the nonbreaching party on the breaching party that would result in an unjust result if retained by the breaching party without compensating the nonbreaching party (restitution).

☐ Although the nonbreaching party generally fares best when seeking compensation based on lost expectations, compensation based on reliance or restitution may exceed compensation based on contract expectations. The paralegal must, therefore, analyze for the supervising attorney what the nonbreaching party could receive under each remedy to produce the largest award.

1. Evaluate the expectation remedy to determine how the nonbreaching party will be placed at the point of full performance by considering the following questions:

   a. What will it take to give the nonbreaching party what he or she expected to receive; and what will it take to have the nonbreaching party give what he or she expected to give?

  (1) What has the nonbreaching party already received? Anything that has been received must be subtracted from what the nonbreaching party expected to receive. Otherwise, the nonbreaching party will get more than he or she expected to receive.

  (2) What has the nonbreaching party already given? Anything that has been given must be subtracted from what the nonbreaching party expected to give. Otherwise, the nonbreaching party will be required to give more than he or she expected to give. Incidental damages are included as something that the nonbreaching party gave.

b. How can the injured party be brought up to full performance, no more and no less (compensatory damages)? Punitive damages are not awarded in breach of contract actions.

c. What damages could the breaching party reasonably foresee at the time of contract formation as the probable result of such a breach? Damages are limited to those foreseeable. Foreseeable damages are either general or special damages.

  (1) General damages arise naturally from the breach itself—they can be expected to occur when the contract is breached. The damages will vary depending on how the contract is breached.

  (2) Special damages do not arise naturally when a contract is breached but may reasonably be supposed to have been in the contemplation of both contracting parties and are, therefore, foreseeable.

d. How can damages for breach of contract be shown with reasonable certainty? Damages that are speculative and incapable of being ascertained with reasonable certainty are not recoverable. Although damages must be reasonably certain, mathematical exactness is not required.

e. How can the nonbreaching party meet the duty to mitigate the damages? The nonbreaching party must use reasonable means to avoid or minimize damages (mitigation).

  (1) The mitigation doctrine prevents the nonbreaching party from increasing the amount the breaching party must pay.

  (2) The nonbreaching party is required, under the mitigation doctrine, to decrease the amount of damages the breaching party must pay.

f. If the nonbreaching party can establish breach—can the nonbreaching party prove damages? If not, the nonbreaching party is entitled to nominal damages. Nominal damages clarify the parties' rights and duties.

g. What other protection is available if damages do not totally compensate the nonbreaching party for his or her injury?

  (1) Consider an injunction, which may protect the nonbreaching party from future injuries.

  (2) Look at the availability of specific performance if the performance is unique and therefore not easily replaceable on the market.

    (a) Specific performance is not available when the breach is the failure to pay money. Money is interchangeable and therefore not unique.

    (b) Specific performance is not available in a personal service contract. Involuntary servitude is unconstitutional.

h. At the time of contract formation, did the parties stipulate what the damages would be in the event of breach? Such a provision will be enforceable as a liquidated damage provision and not as a penalty if
   (1) at the time of contract formation the damages in the event of a breach would be impossible or very difficult to estimate accurately.
   (2) there was a reasonable endeavor by the parties to fix a fair compensation.
   (3) the amount stipulated bears a reasonable relation to probable damages and is not disproportionate to any damages reasonably anticipated.
i. Did the contracting parties stipulate in the contract who will pay costs? Costs generally include filing fees, service of process, jury fees, and court officer charges, but not attorney fees. If the parties have not allocated costs in the contract, the court may allocate costs to the losing party. Contracting parties may allocate attorney fees by contract. Limitations may be placed on both the allocation of costs and attorney fees, depending on the jurisdiction.

2. The court, when evaluating the reliance remedy, will place the nonbreaching party back to the time prior to his or her reliance on the promisor's promise.
   a. Therefore, ask the following questions:
      (1) What did the nonbreaching party give in reliance on the promise?
      (2) What did the nonbreaching party receive in reliance on the promise?
   b. The nonbreaching party's expectations (what would have been given or received) are irrelevant because the nonbreaching party is not being moved forward to the time when performance would have been completed by both sides.

3. The restitution remedy will place the nonbreaching party back to the time prior to conferring the benefit on the breaching party.
   a. Therefore, ask the following questions:
      (1) What benefit did the nonbreaching party confer on the breaching party?
      (2) What did the nonbreaching party receive for conferring this benefit?
   b. The nonbreaching party's expectations (what he or she would give or receive) are irrelevant because the nonbreaching party is not being moved forward to the time when performance would have been completed by both sides.
   c. Two factors come into play in determining a restitution remedy
      (1) Whether the nonbreaching party was to pay money?
      (2) Whether the nonbreaching party fully performed?
         (a) If the nonbreaching party was to pay money and has partially performed, he or she is entitled to restitution of the money paid.
         (b) If the nonbreaching party was to perform services and has partially performed, he or she is entitled to the value of the services performed (measured by the reasonable value of the services to the breaching party). The nonbreaching party may recover the reasonable value of the services to the breaching party even though the reasonable value exceeds the prorated contract price.
         If the nonbreaching party has fully performed the services, the contract price limits recovery. Therefore, the nonbreaching party may

recover more than the contract price for less than full performance but no more than the contract price for full performance.

4. A nonbreaching party may not choose between breach of contract and restitution actions. If an enforceable contract has been breached, the nonbreaching party has no choice but to pursue a breach of contract action. If the nonbreaching party ignores the breach of contract action and pleads a restitution action, the breaching party can defend the restitution action by claiming the existence of an enforceable contract. Whether a defendant finds this strategy beneficial may depend on the Statute of Limitations, costs and attorney fees, and other issues to be litigated.

KEY TERMS

Compensatory damages	Mitigation
Costs	Nominal damages
Expectation remedies	Punitive damages
Expectation interest	Special damages
General damages	Specific performance
Incidental damages	Reliance remedies
Injunction	Restitution remedies
Liquidated damages	

REVIEW QUESTIONS

TRUE/FALSE QUESTIONS (CIRCLE THE CORRECT ANSWER)

1. T   F   The nonbreaching party is entitled to a remedy for the breach of an enforceable contract.

2. T   F   A remedy for breach of contract may involve expectation, reliance, or restitution interests.

3. T   F   Courts give the breaching party what he or she expected to receive when an expectation interest is being protected.

4. T   F   Courts require the nonbreaching party to give what he or she expected to give when an expectation interest is being protected.

5. T   F   The reliance interest concerns the nonbreaching party's expectations.

6. T   F   What the nonbreaching party expected to receive and expected to give must be considered when computing damages based on the reliance interest.

7. T   F   The restitution interest is not concerned with what the nonbreaching party expected to receive and expected to give.

8. T   F   The restitution interest is concerned with what the nonbreaching party gave or received in reliance on the breaching party's promise.

9. T   F   The restitution interest is concerned with the benefit that the nonbreaching party conferred on the breaching party and what the nonbreaching party received for conferring that benefit.

10. T   F   The restitution remedy measures damages by considering the reasonable value of the benefit conferred to the breaching party.

11. T   F   When the expectation interest is protected, the nonbreaching party will be placed in the position he or she would have been in had the contract been fully performed according to its terms.

12. T   F   Damages for breach of contract include incidental damages.

13. T   F   Damages for breach of contract include punitive damages.

14. T   F   The intentions of the breaching party are relevant when computing damages for breach of contract.

15. T   F   Intentional and unintentional breaches yield the same measure of expectation damages.

16. T   F   A contracting party will never find that breaching a contract will be in his or her best economic interest.

17. T   F   The breaching party is held up to the public as an example of what might happen to a party who breaches.

18. T   F   Determining what will place the injured party in the position he or she would have been in had the contract been fully performed often is not achievable with mathematical precision.

19. T   F   Damages for breach of contract are limited to those that the breaching party could reasonably foresee, when the contract was made, as a probable result of breach.

20. T   F   Only general damages are foreseeable.

21. T   F   General damages arise naturally while special damages do not.

22. T   F   Damages for pain and suffering or for emotional distress are never available in a breach of contract action.

23. T   F   Damages that are speculative and incapable of being ascertained with reasonable certainty are not recoverable for breach of contract.

24. T   F   The nonbreaching party has a duty to mitigate the damages in the event of a breach.

25. T   F   Although the nonbreaching party is required by the doctrine of mitigation to prevent increasing damages, he or she is not required to decrease the damages the breaching party must pay.

26. T   F   A nonbreaching party who establishes a breach of contract but is unable to prove damages is entitled to nominal damages.

27.   T   F   A judgment for nominal damages compensates the nonbreaching party in dollars.

28.   T   F   A judgment for nominal damages clarifies the rights and duties of the parties and may include an award of court costs.

29.   T   F   An injunction is a court order directing the breaching party to refrain from a specified act and is designed to prevent future injuries to the nonbreaching party.

30.   T   F   Specific performance is available to a nonbreaching party who prefers it as compensation for his or her injury rather than accepting damages.

31.   T   F   Specific performance may be available in a contract for the sale of real property if the property is unique.

32.   T   F   Specific performance is not available when the breach is a failure to pay money.

33.   T   F   Specific performance is available in personal service contracts if the service is unique.

34.   T   F   The nonbreaching employer in an employment contract may not be entitled to damages even though he or she has found a substitute employee.

35.   T   F   Liquidated damages are those imposed on the parties by the court.

36.   T   F   Parties to a contract may agree upon what damages will be in the event of a breach and incorporate this agreement in a provision known as a liquidated damage clause.

37.   T   F   All contract provisions that purport to be liquidated damage clauses are enforceable.

38.   T   F   Liquidated damage clauses that are classified by the court as penalties are unenforceable.

39.   T   F   Parties to a contract may not include a provision regarding who will pay costs if litigation ensues.

40.   T   F   Most courts will allocate costs to the losing party in a contractual dispute in which the contract does not include a provision for costs.

41.   T   F   Costs in a breach of contract case usually include attorney fees.

42.   T   F   Attorney fees may not be allocated by contract.

43.   T   F   A nonbreaching party may choose between a breach of contract action and a restitution action.

44.   T   F   A restitution action is the same thing as a restitution remedy for a breach of contract action.

FILL-IN-THE-BLANK QUESTIONS

1. _____. Damages that place the nonbreaching party in a position he or she would have been in had both parties fully performed according to the terms of the contract.

2. _____. Damages based on what the nonbreaching party did give and did receive in reliance on the breaching party's promise.

3. _____. Damages based on the benefit that the nonbreaching party conferred on the breaching party and what the nonbreaching party received for conferring that benefit.

4. _____. Damages intended to compensate the nonbreaching party for not receiving his or her expectation under the contract.

5. _____. Damages that the breaching party could reasonably foresee, at the time of the making of the contract, as a probable result of the breach.

6. _____. Damages that "arise naturally, i.e., according to the usual course of things, from such breach of contract itself."

7. _____. Damages that "may reasonably be supposed to have been in the contemplation of both parties, at the time they made the contract, as the probable result of the breach of it."

8. _____. Action that the aggrieved party must take after a breach of contract to limit the damages that will arise due to the breach.

9. _____. Damages that clarify the rights and duties of the parties but do not compensate the nonbreaching party in dollars.

10. _____. A court order directing the breaching party to refrain from a specified act.

11. _____. A remedy whereby a court directs a party to do a specified act.

12. _____. Damages agreed to by the parties, at the time of contract formation, that will apply to the transaction if a breach occurs.

13. _____. Expenses incurred in litigation that generally include filing fees, service of process, jury fees, and court officer charges, but not attorney fees.

MULTIPLE-CHOICE QUESTIONS (CIRCLE ALL THE CORRECT ANSWERS)

1. Naomi contracted to sell Greenacre to Watson for $1,500,000. Watson paid Naomi $100,000, and Naomi delivered Greenacre. The reasonable value of Greenacre to Naomi was $1,300,000. The reasonable value of Greenacre on the open market was $1,600,000. Watson refused to pay the balance. In a breach of contract action, Naomi is entitled to recover which of the following amounts?
   (a) $1,600,000
   (b) $1,500,000
   (c) $1,400,000
   (d) $1,300,000
   (e) $1,200,000

2. Naomi contracted to sell a Greenacre to Watson for $1,500,000. Watson paid Naomi $100,000 and was to pay an additional $400,000 before Naomi had a duty to deliver Greenacre. Watson never paid the $400,000, so Naomi never delivered Greenacre. The reasonable value of Greenacre to Naomi was $1,300,000. The reasonable value of Greenacre on the open market was $1,600,000. Watson refused to pay the balance. In a breach of contract action, Naomi is entitled to recover which of the following amounts?
   (a) $1,600,000
   (b) $1,400,000
   (c) $1,300,000
   (d) $1,200,000
   (e) $ 0

3. Naomi contracted to sell Greenacre to Watson for $1,500,000. Watson paid Naomi $100,000, and Naomi delivered Greenacre. The reasonable value of Greenacre to Naomi was $1,300,000. The reasonable value of Greenacre on the open market was $1,600,000. Watson refused to pay the balance. If Naomi seeks to protect her reliance interest in a breach of contract action, she is entitled to recover which of the following amounts?
   (a) $1,600,000
   (b) $1,500,000
   (c) $1,400,000
   (d) $1,300,000
   (e) $1,200,000

4. Naomi contracted to sell Greenacre to Watson for $1,500,000. Watson paid Naomi $100,000, and Naomi delivered Greenacre. The reasonable value of Greenacre to Naomi was $1,300,000. The reasonable value of Greenacre on the open market was $1,600,000. The reasonable value of Greenacre to Watson was $1,700,000. Watson refused to pay the balance. If Naomi seeks to protect her restitution interest in a breach of contract action, she is entitled to recover which of the following amounts?
   (a) $1,600,000
   (b) $1,500,000
   (c) $1,400,000
   (d) $1,300,000
   (e) $1,200,000

5. Delana contracted to refinish an antique dining room table for Cornelia for $950. After Cornelia made a $200 down payment, Delana refused to work on the table. Cornelia found another furniture restorer to refinish the table, but it cost her $1,500. The restoration increased the value of the table by $2,000. It will cost $1,000 in attorney's fees for Cornelia to successfully maintain her

breach of contract action. If Delana sues Cornelia for breach of contract, she could recover which of the following amounts?

(a) $2,500
(b) $2,400
(c) $1,750
(d) $ 750
(e) $ 200

SHORT-ANSWER QUESTIONS

1. Complete the expectation damages diagram and discuss.

2. Complete the reliance damages diagram and discuss.

3. Complete the restitution damages diagram and discuss.

CHAPTER 16

The Plaintiff's Remedies under Article 2 of the UCC

- Seller's Remedies for Buyer's Breach (UCC §§ 1–106(1) & 2–703)

  Before the Buyer Accepts the Goods (UCC §§ 2–706, 2–708(1), & 2–708(2))

  After the Buyer Accepts the Goods—Action for the Price (UCC § 2–709)

  Liquidated Damages (UCC § 2–718(1))

- Buyer's Remedies for Seller's Breach (UCC §§ 1–106(1), 2–711, 2–714, & 2–717)

  Before the Buyer Accepts the Goods (UCC § 2–711(1))

  After the Buyer Accepts the Goods—Damages for Breach with Regard to Accepted Goods (UCC § 2–714)

  Liquidated Damages (UCC § 2–718(1))

- Statutory Liquidated Damages

When a contract is for the sale of goods, the remedies for breach are found in Articles 1 and 2 of the UCC. Section 1–106(1) states the overarching intent of the Code remedies:

> (1) The remedies provided by this Act shall be liberally administered to the end that the aggrieved party may be put in as good a position as if the other party had fully performed but neither consequential or special nor penal damages may be had except as specifically provided in this Act or by other rule of law.

Unlike common law remedies for breach of contract where the aggrieved party may recover for an injury to its expectation, reliance, and restitution interests, the Code almost always limits recovery to an expectation interest (see Exhibit 16–1).

Section 1–106(1) clearly states that compensatory damages are limited to compensation, unless the Code or other rule of law states

489

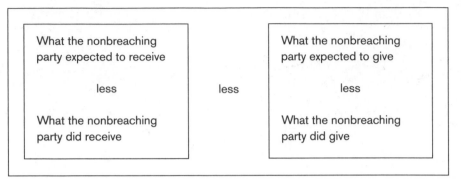

Exhibit 16–1 Expectation Remedy Formula

differently. As was true with the common law damages for breach of contract, punitive damages cannot be awarded. But unlike common law damages for breach of contract where consequential (special) damages may be awarded if they were foreseeable, they may not be awarded for the breach of a contract for the sale of goods unless the Code states differently.

The specific remedy formulations for breach of a sale of goods contract are found in Part 7 of Article 2. Part 7 is divided between the seller's remedies and the buyer's remedies. The seller's remedies for the buyer's breach are grouped between sections 2–703 and 2–710, with section 2–703 being the index to the seller's remedies. The buyer's remedies for the seller's breach are grouped between sections 2–711 and 2–716, with section 2–711(1) being the index for the buyer's remedies before the buyer accepts the goods and section 2–714 being the index for the buyer's remedies after the buyer accepts the goods.

SELLER'S REMEDIES FOR BUYER'S BREACH (UCC §§ 1–106(1) & 2–703)

Applying section 1–106(1) to the seller's remedies for the buyer's breach, the expectation remedy formula becomes the following (see Exhibit 16–2):

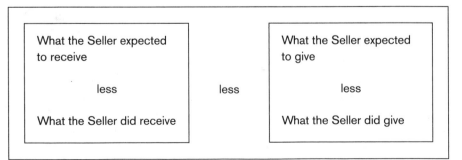

Exhibit 16–2 The Seller's Expectation Remedy Formula

Section 2–703 indexes explicit seller's remedies for the buyer's breach.

> Where the buyer wrongfully rejects or revokes acceptance of goods or fails to make a payment due on or before delivery or repudiates with respect to a part or the whole, then with respect to any goods directly affected and, if the breach is of the whole contract (Section 2–612), then also with respect to the whole undelivered balance, the aggrieved seller may
>
> (a) withhold delivery of such goods;
> (b) stop delivery by any bailee as hereafter provided (Section 2–705);
> (c) proceed under the next section respecting goods still unidentified to the contract;
> (d) resell and recover damages as hereafter provided (Section 2–706);
> (e) recover damages for non-acceptance (Section 2–708) or in a proper case the price (Section 2–709);
> (f) cancel. (UCC § 2–703)

Section 2–703 forms the "wheel's hub" for seller's remedies, with sections 2–704 through 2–710 radiating out as spokes (e.g., section 2–703(d) is developed in section 2–706; the first half of section 2–703(e) is developed in section 2–708; and the second half of section 2–703(e) is developed in section 2–709). All three sections (2–706, 2–708, and 2–709) incorporate section 2–710 (incidental damages) by reference.

> Incidental damages to an aggrieved seller include any commercially reasonable charged, expenses or commissions incurred in stopping delivery, in the transportation, care and custody of goods after the buyer's breach, in connection with return or resale of the goods or otherwise resulting from the breach. (UCC § 2–710)

Section 2–703(a) through (d) and the first half of (e) apply before the buyer accepts the goods. The second half of (e) applies after the buyer accepts the goods (see Exhibit 16–3).

Before the Buyer Accepts the Goods (UCC §§ 2–706, 2–708(1), & 2–708(2))

When the buyer breaches before accepting the goods, the seller may resell the goods and recover damages for any loss incurred (section 2–706) (assuming the seller has goods to resell) or may recover damages for nonacceptance of the goods or repudiation (section 2–708). The fact that the seller resells does not limit the seller to the section 2–706 measure of damages. The seller may resell and not calculate damages under section 2–706, and instead recover damages under section 2–708.

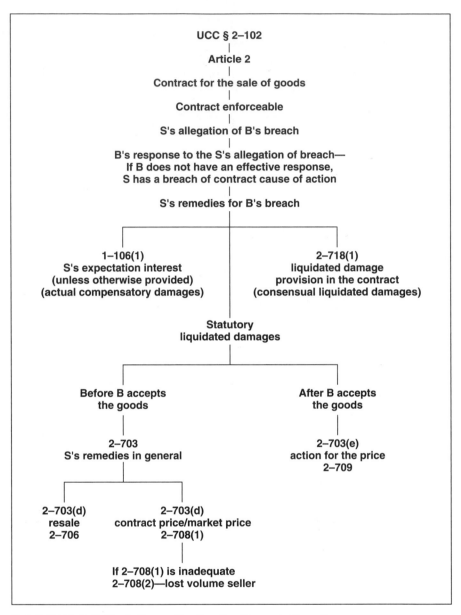

Exhibit 16-3 Seller's Remedies for the Buyer's Breach

Damages after Resale (UCC § 2–706)

When the buyer breaches before accepting the goods and the seller is left with the goods, the seller must decide whether to sell them to a third party. Generally, the seller would like to sell the goods (thus creating contract #2) and recover any loss suffered by not receiving

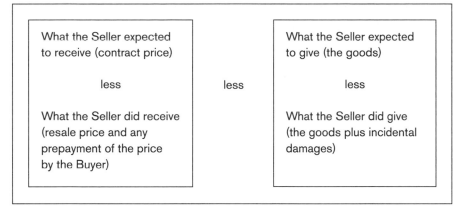

Exhibit 16-4 Seller's Remedy under UCC § 2-706

full performance (generally full payment) under the original bargain (contract #1). Section 2-706(1) authorizes the seller to resell and recover damages (see Exhibit 16-4).

(1) Under the conditions stated in Section 2-703 on seller's remedies, the seller may resell the goods concerned or the undelivered balance thereof. Where the resale is made in good faith and in a commercially reasonable manner the seller may recover the difference between the resale price and the contract price together with any incidental damages allowed under the provisions of this Article (Section 2-710), but less expenses saved in consequence of the buyer's breach. (UCC § 2-706(1))

Example 16-1

The Sail & Sea Shipbuilding Company contracted to build a yacht for Anthony in return for Anthony's promise to pay $100,000. As Sail & Sea was completing the yacht, Anthony changed his mind and notified Sail & Sea that he no longer wanted the yacht (breach by anticipatory repudiation). Sail & Sea then sold the yacht to Karen for $75,000. (Sail & Sea spent $60,000 in building the yacht, and the market price for the yacht was $85,000.) After Anthony's breach, Sail & Sea spent $2,000 in extra storage and transportation charges.

Sail & Sea is entitled to recover $27,000 in damages for breach of contract under section 2-706.

What Sail & Sea expected to receive (contract price) ($100,000) less What Sail & Sea did receive (resale price) ($75,000)	less	What Sail & Sea expected to give (the goods) (the yacht) less What Sail & Sea did give (the goods plus incidental damages) (the yacht + $2,000)	

⬛ PARALEGAL EXERCISE 16.1

Change the facts in Example 16–1 to be that Anthony contracted to pay $95,000, the market price was $100,000, Karen paid $100,000, and Sail & Sea's extra storage and insurance expenses were $1,000. Calculate Sail & Sea's damages under UCC § 2–706. ▨

Damages for Nonacceptance or Repudiation (UCC §§ 2–708(1) & (2))

Whether or not the seller resells, the seller is still entitled to measure its damages under section 2–708(1). Section 2–708(1) states a general damage formula—the market price/contract price differential. This formula is applicable to all situations where the buyer breaches and has not accepted the goods (see Exhibit 16–5).

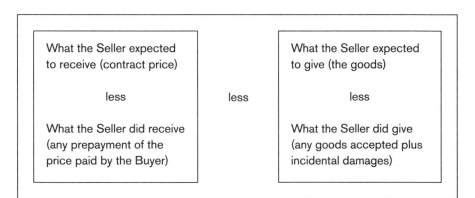

Exhibit 16–5 Seller's Remedy under UCC § 2–708(1)

(1) Subject to subsection (2) and to the provisions of this Article with respect to proof of market price (Section 2–723), the measure of damages for non-acceptance or repudiation by the buyer is the difference between the market price at the time and place for tender and the unpaid contract price together with any incidental damages provided in this Article (Section 2–710), but less expenses saved in consequence of the buyer's breach.

Example 16–2

Sail & Sea is entitled to recover $17,000 in damages for breach of contract under section 2–708(1).

What the Seller expected to receive (contract price) ($100,000)		What the Seller expected to give (the goods) ($85,000 as measured by the market price of the yacht)
less	less	less
What the Seller did receive (any prepayment of the price by the Buyer) ($0)		What the Seller did give (any goods accepted plus incidental damages) ($0 + $2,000)

☰ PARALEGAL EXERCISE 16.2

In Paralegal Exercise 16.1, add the fact that Anthony paid Sail & Sea $20,000 as a down payment at the time of contract formation. Calculate Sail & Sea's damages using UCC § 2–708(1). ▪

Under UCC § 2–708(1), the seller would recover the difference between the contract price and the market price. If the measure of damages as calculated in subsection (1) is inadequate, the seller may explore a third damage formula. Section 2–708(2) applies to situations where a seller is referred to as a "lost volume seller"; the damage calculation for this seller is measured by the seller's profit on the original contract (see Exhibit 16–6). Section 2–708(2) often becomes important when the contract price, market price, and resale price are the same (or similar) and the seller's damages under sections 2–706 and 2–708(1) would be only incidental damages.

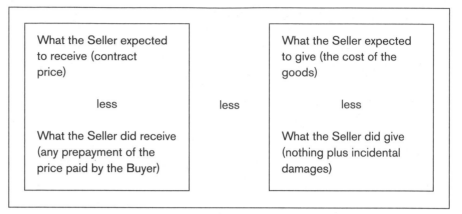

Exhibit 16–6 Seller's Remedy under UCC § 2–708(2)

(2) If the measure of damages provided in subsection (1) is inadequate to put the seller in as good a position as performance would have done then the measure of damages is the profit (including reasonable overhead) which the seller would have made from full performance by the buyer, together with any incidental damages provided in this Article (Section 2–710), due allowance for costs reasonably incurred and due credit for payments or proceeds of resale. (UCC § 2–708(2))

Example 16–3

Sail & Sea is entitled to recover $27,000 in damages under section 2–706, $17,000 in damages under section 2–708(1), and $37,000 under section 2–708(2).

What Sail & Sea expected to receive (contract price) ($100,000)	less	What Sail & Sea expected to give (the cost of the goods) ($65,000, the cost of the yacht)
less		less
What Sail & Sea did receive (any prepayment of the price by the buyer) ($0)		What the Seller did give (nothing plus incidental damages) ($0 + $2,000)

⫼ PARALEGAL EXERCISE 16.3

Using the facts from Paralegal Exercises 16.1 and 16.2, calculate Sail & Sea's damages using section 2–708(2). Would this be an appropriate case for section 2–708(2)? ▪

After the Buyer Accepts the Goods—Action for the Price (UCC § 2–709)

When buyer breaches after accepting the goods, the seller no longer has the goods to resell—so section 2–706 is inapplicable. Section 2–708(1) will give the seller only the difference between the contract price less the market price. The seller does not recover his or her costs for either manufacturing the goods or buying the goods for resale. Under section 2–708(2), the seller recovers the contract price *less* costs (i.e., profits), but not the costs.

The seller, however, may have an action for the price under section 2–709(1). The price (the contract price) would include the seller's cost to buy or manufacture the goods plus the seller's anticipated profits for those goods (see Exhibit 16–7).

> (1) When the buyer fails to pay the price as it becomes due the seller may recover, together with any incidental damages under the next section, the price
>   (a) of goods accepted or of conforming goods lost or damaged within a commercially reasonable time after risk of their loss has passed to the buyer; and
>   (b) of goods identified to the contract if the seller is unable after reasonable effort to resell them at a reasonable price or the circumstances reasonably indicate that such effort will be unavailing. (UCC § 2–709(1))

What the Seller expected to receive (contract price) less What the Seller did receive (any prepayment of the price paid by the Buyer)	less	What the Seller expected to give (the goods) less What the Seller did give (the goods plus incidental damages)

Exhibit 16–7 Seller's Remedy under UCC § 2–709

Example 16–4

The Sail & Sea Shipbuilding Company contracted to build a yacht for Anthony in return for Anthony's promise to pay $100,000. At the time of contract formation, Anthony paid $20,000 as a down payment. When the yacht was delivered, Anthony accepted delivery but refused to pay. Sail & Sea may recover $80,000 under section 2–709(1).

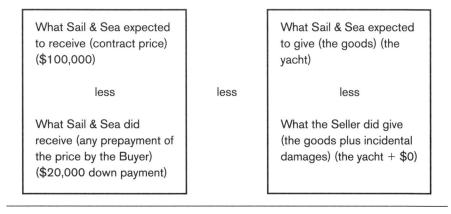

Liquidated Damages (UCC § 2–718(1))

Section 2–718(1) authorizes the buyer and seller to agree at the time of contracting to forego the calculation of damages under Articles 1 and 2 and instead stipulate what damages would be in the event of a subsequent breach.

> (1) Damages for breach by either party may be liquidated in the agreement but only at an amount which is reasonable in light of the anticipated or actual harm caused by the breach, the difficulties of proof of loss, and the inconvenience or nonfeasibility of otherwise obtaining an adequate remedy. A term fixing unreasonably large liquidated damages is void as a penalty. (UCC § 2–718(1))

BUYER'S REMEDIES FOR SELLER'S BREACH (UCC §§ 1–106(1), 2–711(1), 2–714, & 2–717)

Applying section 1–106(1) to the buyer's remedies for the seller's breach, the expectation remedy formula becomes *[(what the buyer expected to receive) less (what the buyer did receive)] less [(what the buyer expected to give) less (what the buyer did give)]* (see Exhibit 16–8).

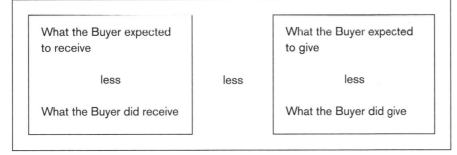

Exhibit 16–8 The Buyer's Expectation Remedy Formula

Unlike the index for the seller's remedies for the buyer's breach that appears in one location (section 2–703), the index for the buyer's remedies for the seller's breach (section 2–711(1)) only covers situations occurring before the buyer has accepted the goods. Section 2–714(1) deals with the buyer's remedies after the buyer has accepted the goods (see Exhibit 16–9).

Section 2–717 permits the buyer to deduct from the price damages resulting from the seller's breach.

> The buyer on notifying the seller of his intention to do so may deduct all or any part of the damages resulting from any breach of the contract from any part of the price still due under the same contract. (UCC § 2–717)

Before the Buyer Accepts the Goods (UCC § 2–711(1))

Section 2–711(1) provides an index of the buyer's remedies when the seller breaches before the buyer accepts the goods. Section 2–711(1) is the hub and sections 2–712 and 2–713 are the spokes that develop the buyer's remedies before the buyer accepts the goods.

> (1) Where the seller fails to make delivery or repudiates or the buyer rightfully rejects or justifiably revokes acceptance then with respect to any goods involved, and with respect to the whole if the breach goes to the whole contract (Section 2–612), the buyer may cancel and whether or not he has done so may in addition to recovering so much of the price as has been paid
>   (a) "cover" and have damages under the next section as to all the goods affected whether or not they have been identified to the contract; or
>   (b) recover damages for non-delivery as provided in this Article (Section 2–713). (UCC § 2–711(1))

Both sections 2–712 and 2–713 refer to the buyer's incidental damages.

> (1) Incidental damages resulting from the seller's breach include expenses reasonably incurred in inspection, receipt, transportation

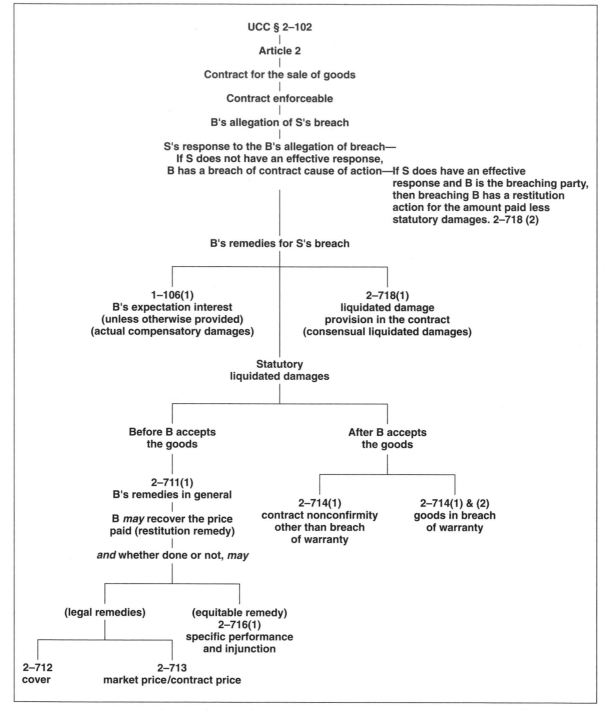

Exhibit 16–9 Buyer's Remedies for the Seller's Breach

and care and custody of goods rightfully rejected, any commercially reasonable charges, expenses or commissions in connection with effecting cover and any other reasonable expense incident to the delay or other breach. (UCC § 2–715(1))

Section 1–106(1) states

(1) The remedies provided by this Act shall be liberally administered to the end that the aggrieved party may be put in as good a position as if the other party had fully performed *but neither consequential or special . . . damages may be had except as specifically provided in this Act. . . .*

Both sections 2–712 and 2–713 authorize the buyer to recover his or her consequential damages as provided in section 2–715(2).

(2) Consequential damages resulting from the seller's breach include
  (a) any loss resulting from general or particular requirements and needs of which the seller at the time of contracting had reason to know and which could not reasonably be prevented by cover or otherwise, and
  (b) injury to person or property primarily resulting from any breach of warranty. (UCC § 2–715(2))

Ⅲ PARALEGAL EXERCISE 16.4

Why is the buyer entitled to consequential damages for the seller's breach but the seller is not entitled to consequential damages for the buyer's breach? ▪

Cover (UCC § 2–712)

When the seller fails to deliver or repudiates, or the buyer rightfully rejects or justifiably revokes its acceptance of the goods, the buyer must decide whether to purchase substitute goods from another seller. Section 2–712 provides the buyer with the opportunity to **cover**, that is, the right to obtain goods as a substitute for those that the seller had contracted to deliver (see Exhibit 16–10). The buyer may cover but is not required to cover.

cover

Cover is a substitute performance.

(1) After a breach within the preceding section the buyer may "cover" by making in good faith and without unreasonable delay any reasonable purchase of or contract to purchase goods in substitution for those due from the seller.
(2) The buyer may recover from the seller as damages the difference between the cost of cover and the contract price together with any incidental or consequential damages as hereinafter defined (Section 2–715), but less expenses saved in consequence of the seller's breach.
(3) Failure of the buyer to effect cover within this section does not bar him from any other remedy. (UCC § 2–712)

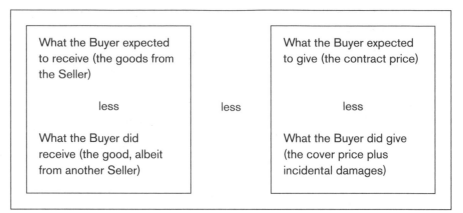

What the Buyer expected to receive (the goods from the Seller)		What the Buyer expected to give (the contract price)
less	less	less
What the Buyer did receive (the good, albeit from another Seller)		What the Buyer did give (the cover price plus incidental damages)

Exhibit 16–10 Buyer's Remedy under UCC § 2–712

Example 16–5

The Browning Fruit Company contracted to purchase one carload of Mason green jars (one-third pints, one-third quarts, and one-third half gallons) from the Silas Glass Company for $17,500. Silas failed to delivery any of the jars.

Although the market prices for the jars had increased to $21,000 by the time Browning learned of Silas's breach, Browning was able to purchase substitute jars from the Sunshine Glass Company for $20,000. To effect the purchase, Browning spent an extra $1,000 on transportation. Under section 2–712, Browning is entitled to purchase the substitute and recover $3,500 in damages from Silas.

What Browning expected to receive (the goods from the Seller) (carload of jars from Silas)		What Browning expected to give (the contract price) ($17,500)
less	less	less
What Browning did receive (the goods from another Seller) (carload of jars from Sunshine)		What Browning did give (the cover price plus incidental damages) ($20,000 plus $1,000)

What the Buyer expected to receive (the goods)		What the Buyer expected to give (the contract price)
less	less	less
What the Buyer did receive (some or none of the goods)		What the Buyer did give (prepaid price, if any, plus incidental damages)

Exhibit 16–11 Buyer's Remedy under UCC § 2–713

PARALEGAL EXERCISE 16.5

Change the facts in Example 16–5 so the original contract price, market price, and cover price are all $17,500. Calculate Browning's damages under section 2–712(2). ■

Damages for Nondelivery or Repudiation (UCC § 2–713)

Whether or not the buyer covers, the buyer is still entitled to measure its damages for the seller's nondelivery or repudiation under section 2–713 (see Exhibit 16–11).

(1) Subject to the provisions of this Article with respect to proof of market price (Section 2–723), the measure of damages for nondelivery or repudiation by the seller is the difference between the market price at the time when the buyer learned of the breach and the contract price together with any incidental and consequential damages provided in this Article (Section 2–715), but less expenses saved in consequence of the seller's breach.

(2) Market price is to be determined as of the place for tender or, in cases of rejection after arrival or revocation of acceptance, as of the place of arrival. (UCC § 2–713)

Example 16–6

The Browning Fruit Company contracted to purchase one carload of Mason green jars (one-third pints, one-third quarts, and one-third half gallons) from the Silas Glass Company for $17,500. Silas failed to deliver any of the jars.

Although the contract price was $17,500, the market price at the time Browning learned of the breach had increased from $17,500 to $21,000. Browning was able to purchase substitute jars from the Sunshine Glass Company for $20,000. To effect the purchase, Browning spent an extra $1,000 on transportation.

Under section 2–713, Browning is entitled to the difference between the market price at the time when it learned of the breach and the contract price together with any incidental and consequential damages—but less expenses saved in consequence of the Silas breach. Therefore, Browning can recover $4,500 in damages from Silas.

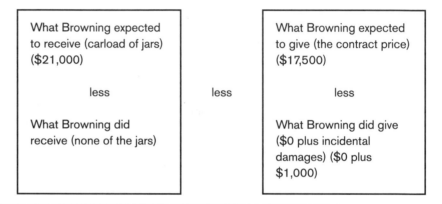

▥ PARALEGAL EXERCISE 16.6

Using the facts from Example 16–6, calculate Browning's damages using section 2–713. ▨

Specific Performance (UCC §§ 2–716(1) & (2))

In rare cases, the goods may be such that the buyer is unable to cover. Sections 2–716(1) and (2) authorize the buyer to seek specific performance.

(1) Specific performance may be decreed where the goods are unique or in other proper circumstances.
(2) The decree for specific performance may include such terms and conditions as to payment of the price, damages, or other relief as the court may deem just. (UCC §§ 2–716(1) & (2))

Specific performance may be decreed when a good is "unique," when it is the only one of its kind, when it is superior to all others goods, or when it is different enough from other goods to make it noteworthy. Specific performance may also be decreed when the good is not unique but there are "other proper circumstances." The question under section 2–716(1) is "what is the commercial feasibility for finding a replacement?"

Example 16-7

In 1974, John Z. DeLorian formed DeLorian Motor Company. After building and testing numerous prototypes, the DMC-12, the first and only model of the DeLorian, began production in 1981. The DMC-12 was only produced for three years (1981–1983). Only 8,583 vehicles were manufactured, not counting the prototypes and test cars (1981–6,539 cars; 1982–1126 cars; and 1983–918 cars). Today, a DeLorian is valued from $15,000 to $40,000.

John Swift, the owner of a 1981 DMC-12, contracted to sell it to Elizabeth Benson-White for $25,000. On the date set for delivery, John refused to part with his vehicle.

Elizabeth sued John for breach of contract, seeking specific performance. John moved for summary judgment under UCC § 2–716(1), claiming that his 1981 DMC-12 was not unique. The court would sustain John's motion since Elizabeth could not demonstrate an inability to cover.

PARALEGAL EXERCISE 16.7

Using the facts in Example 16–7, take the facts one step further. The DeLorian Motor Company built two 24K gold-plated cars for an American Express Christmas catalog. One still remains. Later, two more were assembled but were not as highly regarded as the original two.

If the original gold-plated DMC-12 that was still intact was the subject of the contract and John refused to deliver, would Elizabeth be successful in a breach of contract action seeking specific performance? ▪

After the Buyer Accepts the Goods—Damages for Breach with Regard to Accepted Goods (UCC § 2–714)

Section 2–714 deals with the remedies available to the buyer after the goods have been accepted and after the time for revocation of acceptance has passed (see Exhibit 16–12 and Exhibit 16–13). The breach may involve a nonconformity of tender, including breach of warranty.

(1) Where the buyer has accepted goods and given notification (2–607(3)) he may recover as damages for any nonconformity of tender the loss resulting in the ordinary course of events from the seller's breach as determined in any manner which is reasonable.

(2) The measure of damages for breach of warranty is the difference at the time and place of acceptance between the value of the goods accepted and the value they would have had if they

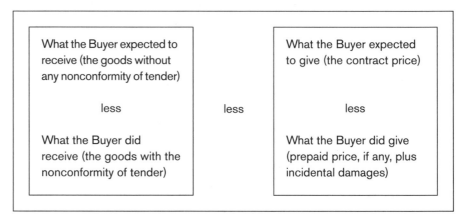

Exhibit 16–12 Buyer's Remedy for Breach of Warranty under UCC §§ 2–714(1) & (2)

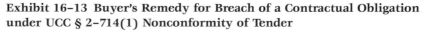

Exhibit 16–13 Buyer's Remedy for Breach of a Contractual Obligation under UCC § 2–714(1) Nonconformity of Tender

had been as warranted, unless special circumstances show proximate damages of a different amount.

(3) In a proper case any incidental and consequential damages under the next section may also be recovered. (UCC § 2–714)

Liquidated Damages (UCC § 2–718(1))

At the time of contracting, the parties may have an opportunity to create a liquidated damage provision, thus diverting the remedies away from those formulas found in the Code.

(1) Damages for breach by either party may be liquidated in the agreement but only at an amount which is reasonable in light of the anticipated or actual harm caused by the breach, the

difficulties of proof of loss, and the inconvenience or nonfeasibility of otherwise obtaining an adequate remedy. A term fixing unreasonably large liquidated damages is void as a penalty. (UCC § 2–718(1))

STATUTORY LIQUIDATED DAMAGES

Section 1–106(1) stated the overarching intent of the Code remedies—placing the nonbreaching party in the position he or she would have been in had the contract been fully performed. The section 1–106(1) formula is the common law expectation formula: *[(what the nonbreaching party expected to receive) less (what the nonbreaching party did receive)] less [(what the nonbreaching party expected to give) less (what the nonbreaching party did give)]*. The Article 2 remedies (2–706, 2–708, 2–709, 2–712, 2–713, 2–714, and 2–716) provide the formulas for calculating expectation damages. Section 2–718(1) authorizes the contracting parties to scrap these formulas and consent to their own predispute computation of potential damages. Taking the liquidated damages discussion one step further, are these Article 2 damage formulas in fact statutory liquidated damage formulas? Put another way, could a seller or a buyer use an Article 2 damage formula even though the damages so calculated do not approximate the seller's or buyer's actual damages?

In *Tongish v. Thomas*, Tongish contracted to grow and sell its sunflower seeds to the Decatur Coop Association. Decatur Coop then sold Tongish's future seeds to Bambino Bean Company.

When the price for sunflower seeds increased substantially, Tongish breached his contract with the Coop and sold instead to Thomas, another buyer. Tongish delivered his seeds to Thomas and a balance remained due. Tongish sued Thomas for breach of contract, seeking the amount due (action for the price—UCC § 2–709). The Coop intervened seeking damages against Tongish for breach of contract. Should the remedy be based on the buyer's actual loss of profit or the difference between the market price and contract price?

CASE

Tongish v. Thomas
Supreme Court of Kansas (1992)
251 Kan. 728, 840 P.2d 471

McFARLAND, Justice:
This case presents the narrow issue of whether damages arising from the non-delivery of contracted-for sunflower seeds should be computed on the basis of K.S.A. 84-1–106 or K.S.A. 84-2–713. That is, whether the buyer is entitled to its

actual loss of profit or the difference between the market price and the contract price. The trial court awarded damages on the basis of the buyer's actual loss of profit. The Court of Appeals reversed the judgment, holding that the difference between the market price and the contract price was the proper measure of damages (Tongish v. Thomas, 16 Kan.App.2d 809, 829 P.2d 916 [1992]). The matter is before us on petition for review.

The pertinent facts are as follows. Denis Tongish entered into a contract on April 28, 1988, with the Decatur Coop Association (Coop) where Tongish agreed to grow 160 acres of sunflower seeds, said crop to be purchased by Coop at $13 per hundredweight for large seeds and $8 per hundredweight for small seeds. By agreement, the acreage was subsequently reduced to 116.8 acres. The crop was to be delivered in increments of one-third by December 31, 1988, March 31, 1989, and May 31, 1989.

Coop had a contract to deliver the seeds purchased to Bambino Bean & Seed, Inc. Coop was to be paid the same price it paid the farmers less a 55 cent per hundredweight handling fee. Coop's only anticipated profit was the handling fee.

In October and November 1988, Tongish delivered sunflower seeds to Coop. In January, a dispute arose over the amount of dockage charged against Tongish's seeds. Tongish's seeds were of higher quality than those of many other farmers selling to Coop, and Coop's practice of commingling seeds prior to sampling was disadvantageous to Tongish. This was resolved by Coop issuing an additional check to Tongish reflecting a lower dockage charge.

Due to a short crop, bad weather, and other factors, the market price of sunflower seeds in January 1989 was double that set forth in the Tongish/Coop contract. On January 13, Tongish notified Coop he would not deliver any more sunflower seeds.

In May 1989, Tongish sold and delivered 82,820 pounds of sunflower seeds to Danny Thomas for approximately $20 per hundredweight. Tongish was to receive $14,714.89, which was $5,153.13 more than the Coop contract price. Thomas paid for approximately one-half of the seeds. Tongish brought this action to collect the balance due. Thomas paid the balance of $7,359.61 into court and was ultimately dismissed from the action.

Meanwhile, Coop intervened in the action, seeking damages for Tongish's breach of their contract. Following a bench trial, the district court held that Tongish had breached the contract with no basis therefor. Damages were allowed in the amount of $455.51, which was the computed loss of handling charges. Coop appealed from said damage award. The Court of Appeals reversed the district court and remanded the case to the district court to determine and award damages pursuant to K.S.A. 84-2–713 (the difference between the market price and the contract price).

The analyses and rationale of the Court of Appeals utilized in resolving the issue are sound and we adopt the following portion thereof:

> The trial court decided the damages to Coop should be the loss of expected profits. Coop argues that K.S.A. 84-2–713 entitles it to collect as damages the difference between the market price and the contract price. Tongish argues that the trial court was correct and cites K.S.A. 84-1–106 as support for the contention that a party should be placed in as good a position as it would be in had the other party performed. Therefore, the only disagreement is how the damages should be calculated.

The measure of damages in this action involves two sections of the Uniform Commercial Code: K.S.A. 84-1–106 and K.S.A. 84-2–713. The issue to be determined is which statute governs the measure of damages. Stated in another way, if the statutes are in conflict, which statute should prevail? The answer involves an ongoing academic discussion of two contending positions. The issues in this case disclose the problem.

If Tongish had not breached the contract, he may have received under the contract terms with Coop about $5,153.13 less than he received from Danny Thomas. Coop in turn had an oral contract with Bambino to sell whatever seeds it received from Tongish to Bambino for the same price Coop paid for them. Therefore, if the contract had been performed, Coop would not have actually received the extra $5,153.13.

We first turn our attention to the conflicting statutes and the applicable rules of statutory construction. K.S.A. 84-1–106(1) states:

> The remedies provided by this act shall be liberally administered to the end that the aggrieved party may be put in as good a position as if the other party had fully performed but neither consequential or special nor penal damages may be had except as specifically provided in this act or by other rule of law.

If a seller breaches a contract and the buyer does not 'cover,' the buyer is free to pursue other available remedies. K.S.A. 84-2–711 and 84-2–712. One remedy, which is a complete alternative to 'cover' (K.S.A. 84-2–713, Official comment, ¶ 5), is K.S.A. 84-2–713(1), which provides:

> Subject to the provisions of this article with respect to proof of market price (Section 84-2–723), the measure of damages for nondelivery or repudiation by the seller is the difference between the market price at the time when the buyer learned of the breach and the contract price together with any incidental and consequential damages provided in this article (Section 84-2–715), but less expenses saved in consequence of the seller's breach.

Neither party argues that the Uniform Commercial Code is inapplicable. Both agree that the issue to be determined is which provision of the UCC should be applied. As stated by the appellee: 'This is really the essence of this appeal, i.e., whether this general rule of damages [K.S.A. 84-1–106] controls the measure of damages set forth in K.S.A. 84-2–713.' However, Tongish then offers no support that K.S.A. 84-1–106 controls over K.S.A. 84-2–713. The authority he does cite (M & W Development, Inc. v. El Paso Water Co., 6 Kan.App.2d 735, 634 P.2d 166 [1981]) is not a UCC case and K.S.A. 84-2–713 was not applicable.

The statutes do contain conflicting provisions. On the one hand, K.S.A. 84-1–106 offers a general guide of how remedies of the UCC should be applied, whereas K.S.A. 84-2–713 specifically describes a damage remedy that gives the buyer certain damages when the seller breaches a contract for the sale of goods.

The cardinal rule of statutory construction, to which all others are subordinate, is that the purpose and intent of the legislature govern. State ex rel. Stephan v. Kansas Racing Comm'n, 246 Kan. 708, 719,

792 P.2d 971 (1990); Cedar Creek Properties, Inc. v. Board of Johnson County Comm'rs, 246 Kan. 412, 417, 789 P.2d 1170 (1990); and Stauffer Communications, Inc. v. Mitchell, 246 Kan. 492, Syl. ¶ 1, 789 P.2d 1153 (1990). When there is a conflict between a statute dealing generally with a subject and another statute dealing specifically with a certain phase of it, the specific statute controls unless it appears that the legislature intended to make the general act controlling. State v. Wilcox, 245 Kan. 76, Syl. 1, 775 P.2d 177 (1989). The Kansas Supreme Court stated in Kansas Racing Management, Inc. v. Kansas Racing Comm'n, 244 Kan. 343, 353, 770 P.2d 423 (1989): 'General and special statutes should be read together and harmonized whenever possible, but to the extent a conflict between them exists, the special statute will prevail unless it appears the legislature intended to make the general statute controlling.'

K.S.A. 84-2–713 allows the buyer to collect the difference in market price and contract price for damages in a breached contract. For that reason, it seems impossible to reconcile the decision of the district court that limits damages to lost profits with this statute.

Therefore, because it appears impractical to make K.S.A. 84-1–106 and K.S.A. 84-2–713 harmonize in this factual situation, K.S.A. 84-2–713 should prevail as the more specific statute according to statutory rules of construction.

As stated, however, Coop protected itself against market price fluctuations through its contract with Bambino. Other than the minimal handling charge, Coop suffered no lost profits from the breach. Should the protection require an exception to the general rule under K.S.A. 84-2–713?

In Panhandle Agri-Service, Inc. v. Becker, 231 Kan. 291, 292, 644 P.2d 413 (1982), a farmer agreed to sell 10,000 tons of alfalfa to the buyer for $45 per ton. At the time the seller breached the contract, the market price was $62 per ton. 231 Kan. at 293 [644 P.2d 413]. The court found, pursuant to K.S.A. 84-2–713, that the damages amounted to $17 per ton or the difference between the market price and the contract price. The court stated: 'We find nothing which would justify the trial court in arriving at damages using loss of business profits which are consequential damages.' 231 Kan. at 298 [644 P.2d 413].

In Baker v. Ratzlaff, 1 Kan.App.2d 285, 564 P.2d 153 (1977), the seller contracted to sell all the popcorn planted on 380 acres for $4.75 per hundredweight. The seller breached, and the trial court found that the market price for popcorn was $8 per hundredweight when the buyer learned of the breach. The court held that the proper measure of damages would be the difference between the market price and the contract price as provided in K.S.A. 84-2–713. 1 Kan.App.2d at 290 [564 P.2d 153].

Neither Panhandle nor Baker involved a conflict between the two UCC provisions. The difference between the market price and the contract price placed the nonbreaching party in as good a position as that party would have been if the contract had been performed. The decisions can be distinguished from this case, however, in that Coop protected itself against market price fluctuations with the Bambino contract.

There is authority for appellee's position that K.S.A. 84-2–713 should not be applied in certain circumstances. In Allied Canners & Packers, Inc. v. Victor Packing Co., 162 Cal.App.3d 905, 209 Cal.Rptr. 60 (1984), Allied contracted to purchase 375,000 pounds of raisins from Victor for 29.75 cents per pound with a 4 percent discount. Allied then contracted to sell the raisins for 29.75 cents per pound expecting a profit of $4,462.50 from the 4 percent discount it received from Victor. 162 Cal.App.3d at 907–08 [209 Cal.Rptr. 60].

Heavy rains damaged the raisin crop and Victor breached its contract, being unable to fulfill the requirement. The market price of raisins had risen to about 80 cents per pound. Allied's buyers agreed to rescind their contracts so Allied was not bound to supply them with raisins at a severe loss. Therefore, the actual loss to Allied was the $4,462.50 profit it expected, while the difference between the market price and the contract price was about $150,000. 162 Cal.App.3d at 908–09 [209 Cal.Rptr. 60].

The California appellate court, in writing an exception, stated: 'It has been recognized that the use of the market-price contract-price formula under Section 2–713 does not, absent pure accident, result in a damage award reflecting the buyer's actual loss. [Citations omitted.]' 162 Cal.App.3d at 912 [209 Cal.Rptr. 60]. The court indicated that section 2–713 may be more of a statutory liquidated damages clause and, therefore, conflicts with the goal of section 1–106. The court discussed that in situations where the buyer has made a resale contract for the goods, which the seller knows about, it may be appropriate to limit 2–713 damages to actual loss. However, the court cited a concern that a seller not be rewarded for a bad faith breach of contract. 162 Cal.App.3d at 912–14 [209 Cal.Rptr. 60].

In Allied, the court determined that if the seller knew the buyer had a resale contract for the goods, and the seller did not breach the contract in bad faith, the buyer was limited to actual loss of damages under Section 1–106. 162 Cal.App.3d at 915 [209 Cal.Rptr. 60].

The similarities between the present case and Allied are that the buyer made a resale contract which the seller knew about. (Tongish knew the seeds eventually went to Bambino, although he may not have known the details of the deal.) However, in examining the breach itself, Victor could not deliver the raisins because its crop had been destroyed. Tongish testified that he breached the contract because he was dissatisfied with dockage tests of Coop and/or Bambino. Victor had no raisins to sell to any buyer, while Tongish took advantage of the doubling price of sunflower seeds and sold to Danny Thomas. Although the trial court had no need to find whether Tongish breached the contract in bad faith, it did find there was no valid reason for the breach. Therefore, the nature of Tongish's breach was much different than Victor's in Allied.

Section 2–713 and the theories behind it have a lengthy and somewhat controversial history. In 1963, it was suggested that 2–713 was a statutory liquidated damages clause and not really an effort to try and accurately predict what actual damages would be. Peters, *Remedies for Breach of Contracts Relating to the Sale of Goods Under the Uniform Commercial Code: A Roadmap for Article Two,* 73 Yale L.J. 199, 259 (1963).

In 1978, Robert Childres called for the repeal of Section 2–713. Childres, *Buyer's Remedies: The Danger of Section 2–713,* 72 Nw.U.L.Rev. 837 (1978). Childres reflected that because the market price/contract price remedy 'has been the cornerstone of Anglo-American damages' that it has been so hard to see that this remedy 'makes no sense whatever when applied to real life situations.' 72 Nw.U.L.Rev. at 841–42.

In 1979, David Simon and Gerald A. Novack wrote a fairly objective analysis of the two arguments about section 2–713 and stated:

> For over 60 years our courts have divided on the question of which measure of damages is appropriate for the supplier's breach of his delivery obligations. The majority view, reinforced by applicable codes, would award market damages even though in excess of plaintiff's loss. A persistent minority would reduce market damages to the plaintiff's loss, without regard to whether this creates a windfall for the defendant. Strangely enough, each view has generally tended to disregard the arguments, and even the existence, of the opposing view.' Simon and Novack, *Limiting the Buyer's Market Damages to Lost Profits: A Challenge to the Enforceability of Market Contracts,* 92 Harv.L.Rev. 1395, 1397 (1979).

Although the article discussed both sides of the issue, the authors came down on the side of market price/contract price as the preferred damages theory. The authors admit that market damages fly in the face 'of the familiar maxim that the purpose of contract damages is to make the injured party whole, not penalize the breaching party.' 92 Harv.L.Rev. at 1437. However, they argue that the market damages rule discourages the breach of contracts and encourages a more efficient market. 92 Harv.L.Rev. at 1437.

The *Allied* decision in 1984, which relied on the articles cited above for its analysis to reject market price/contract price damages, has been sharply criticized. In Schneider, *UCC Section 2–713: A Defense of Buyers' Expectancy Damages,* 22 Cal.W.L.Rev. 233, 266 (1986), the author stated that *Allied* 'adopted the most restrictive [position] on buyer's damages. This Article is intended to reverse that trend.' Schneider argued that by following Section 1–106, 'the court ignored the clear language of Section 2–713's compensation scheme to award expectation damages in accordance with the parties' allocation of risk as measured by the difference between contract price and market price on the date set for performance.' 22 Cal.W.L.Rev. at 264.

Recently in Scott, *The Case for Market Damages: Revisiting the Lost Profits Puzzle,* 57 U.Chi.L.Rev. 1155, 1200 (1990), the *Allied* result was called 'unfortunate.' Scott argues that Section 1–106 is 'entirely consistent' with the market damages remedy of 2–713. 57 U.Chi.L.Rev. at 1201. According to Scott, it is possible to harmonize Sections 1–106 and 2–713. Scott states, 'Market damages measure the expectancy ex ante, and thus reflect the value of the option; lost profits, on the other hand, measure losses ex post, and thus only reflect the value of the completed exchange.' 57 U.Chi.L.Rev. at 1174. The author argues that if the nonbreaching party has laid off part of the market risk (like Coop did) the lost profits rule creates instability because the other party is now encouraged to breach the contract if the market fluctuates to its advantage. 57 U.Chi.L.Rev. at 1178.

We are not persuaded that the lost profits view under *Allied* should be embraced. It is a minority rule that has received only nominal support. We believe the majority rule or the market damages remedy as contained in K.S.A. 84-2–713 is more reasoned and should be followed as the preferred measure of damages. While application of the rule may not reflect the actual loss to a buyer, it encourages a more efficient market and discourages the breach of contracts." Tongish v. Thomas, 16 Kan.App.2d at 811–17 [829 P.2d 916].

At first blush, the result reached herein appears unfair. However, closer scrutiny dissipates this impression. By the terms of the contract Coop was obligated to buy Tongish's large sunflower seeds at $13 per hundredweight whether or not it had a market for them. Had the price of sunflower seeds plummeted by delivery time, Coop's obligation to purchase at the agreed price was fixed. If loss of actual profit pursuant to K.S.A. 84-1–106(1) would be the measure of damages to be applied herein, it would enable Tongish to consider the Coop contract price of $13 per hundredweight plus 55 cents per hundredweight handling fee as the "floor" price for his seeds, take advantage of rapidly escalating prices, ignore his contractual obligation, and profitably sell to the highest bidder. Damages computed under K.S.A. 84-2–713 encourage the honoring of contracts and market stability.

. . . .

The judgment of the Court of Appeals reversing the district court and remanding the case for the determination and award of damages pursuant to the provisions of K.S.A. 84-2–713 is affirmed. The judgment of the district court is reversed.

PARALEGAL CHECKLIST

The Plaintiff's Remedies under Article 2 of the UCC

❏ If the contract is for a sale of goods, the Articles 1 and 2 remedies of the UCC apply. Section 1–106(1) states the general expectation formula that runs throughout the Code: *[(what the nonbreaching party expected to receive) less (what the nonbreaching party did receive)] less [(what the nonbreaching party expected to give) less (what the nonbreaching party did give)].* This formula calculates actual damages. Punitive damages are not awarded under the Code.

1. Article 2 provides a number of damage formulas for the breach of a contract for the sale of goods. While these formulas may at times approximate actual damages, they are in fact statutory liquidated damages. That is, the plaintiff is entitled to the product of the calculation whether or not the calculation approximates actual damages.

Article 2 of the UCC is divided between seller's damages for buyer's breach (2–703) and buyer's damages for seller's breach if the seller's breach occurs before the buyer accepts the goods (2–711(1)) and the seller's breach occurs after the buyer accepts the goods (2–714).

2. The analysis of the seller's remedies for the buyer's breach begins with section 2–703.

   a. When the buyer breaches *before* accepting the goods, the seller may:

      1) resell the goods and recover damages (2–703(d) and 2–706);

      2) recover damages for non-acceptance of the goods (regardless of whether the seller resells) (contract price less market price plus incidental damages) (2–703(e) and 2–708(1)); or

      3) recover profits expected on the first contract as a lost volume seller (contract price less costs plus incidental damages) (2–703(e) and 2–708(2)).

   b. When the buyer breaches *after* accepting the goods, the seller may bring an action for the price plus incidental damages (2–703(e) and 2–709). The price includes the cost to manufacture or purchase and expected profits.

3. The analysis of the buyer's remedies for the seller's breach begins with section 2–711 or section 2–714.

   a. When the seller breaches *before* the buyer accepts the goods, the buyer may:

      1) cover (buy substitute goods) and recover damages (cover price less contract price plus incidental damages (2–711(1) and 2–712);

      2) recover damages for non-delivery (market price less contract price plus incidental damages) (2–711(1) and 2–713(1)); or

      3) obtain specific performance in the proper case (2–711(2)(b) and 2–716).

   b. When the seller breaches *after* the buyer accepts the goods, the buyer may recover damages for the nonconformity of tender or the breach of warranty (2–714).

   c. In either case, the buyer, upon notifying the seller of his or her intention to do so, may deduct the damages from any outstanding price (2–717).

KEY TERM

Cover

REVIEW QUESTIONS

TRUE/FALSE QUESTIONS (CIRCLE THE CORRECT ANSWER)

1. T F Section 1–106(1) authorizes expectation, reliance, and restitution damages under the Code.

2. T F The remedies for breach of a contract for the sale of goods must be analyzed under Articles 1 and 2 of the UCC and not with common law principles.

3. T F The seller's remedies for the breaching buyer are indexed in 2–703.

4. T   F   All of the buyer's remedies for the seller's breach are indexed in 2–711.

5. T   F   The remedy computations in Article 2 of the UCC produce statutory liquidated damage rather than actual damages.

6. T   F   Both the aggrieved buyer and the aggrieved seller may recover incidental damages under Article 2.

7. T   F   If the buyer breaches before accepting the goods and the seller still has the goods in its possession, the seller must resell and recover damages (contract price less resale price).

8. T   F   If the buyer breaches before accepting the goods and the seller resells the goods, the buyer must calculate its damages based on the contract price less the resale price plus incidental damages.

9. T   F   If the buyer breaches before accepting the goods, the seller may recover either the difference between the contract price and the market price or the difference between the contract price and the costs of either manufacturing or purchasing the goods.

10. T   F   If the buyer breaches after accepting the goods, the seller may recover the unpaid contract price.

11. T   F   The seller may recover consequential damages in the event the buyer breaches.

12. T   F   If the seller breaches, all the buyer's remedies in general are indexed in 2–711.

13. T   F   If the seller breaches after the buyer accepts the goods, the buyer's remedies are limited to those associated with breach of warranty.

14. T   F   If the seller breaches before the buyer accepts the goods, the buyer may cover.

15. T   F   If the buyer covers, the buyer is not entitled to damages based on cover price less contract price.

16. T   F   If the buyer covers, the buyer must calculate its damages using 2–712 and may not use 2–713.

17. T   F   The aggrieved buyer always has the option of pursuing specific performance.

18. T   F   Specific performance is a form of self-help and requires no court intervention.

19. T   F   The aggrieved buyer will find its remedies indexed in 2–703.

20. T   F   The nonbreaching party may use either the general expectation formula referenced in 1–106(1) or one of the explicit remedy formulas found in Article 2 of the UCC.

21. T   F   The aggrieved buyer may recover punitive damages for an intentional breach by the seller.

22. T   F   The remedy sections in Article 2 are statutory liquidated damages rather than actual damages.

FILL-IN-THE-BLANK QUESTIONS

1. _____. The interest the Code protects: expectation, reliance, or restitution.

2. _____. The Article 1 section that states the overarching theory of Code remedies.

3. _____. The Article 2 section that indexes the seller's remedies for the buyer's breach.

4. _____. The Article 2 section that indexes the buyer's remedies when the seller breaches before the buyer accepts the goods.

5. _____. The Article 2 section for the seller's remedy of resale.

6. _____. The Article 2 section for the seller's remedy for the buyer's nonacceptance of the goods.

7. _____. The Article 2 section for the seller's action for the unpaid price.

8. _____. The Article 2 section for the buyer's remedy for accepted goods that do not comport with warranty.

9. _____. The Article 2 section for the buyer's right to cover.

10. _____. The Article 2 section for the buyer's right to incidental damages.

11. _____. The Article 2 section for the seller's right to incidental damages.

12. _____. The technical name for substitute goods.

MULTIPLE-CHOICE QUESTIONS (CIRCLE ALL THE CORRECT ANSWERS)

1. The aggrieved seller may resell the goods and recover damages under which of the following sections of the UCC?
   a. 1–106(1)
   b. 2–706
   c. 2–708(1)
   d. 2–709
   e. 2–711(1)

2. The aggrieved buyer may cover and recover damages under which of the following sections of the UCC?
   a. 1–106(1)
   b. 2–706
   c. 2–708(1)
   d. 2–712
   e. 2–713

3. A lost volume seller may recover its expected profits under which of the following sections of the UCC?
   a. 1–106(1)
   b. 2–706

   c. 2–708(1)
   d. 2–708(2)
   e. 2–709

4. If the buyer breaches after accepting the goods, the seller may have an action for the price under which of the following sections of the UCC?
   a. 1–106(1)
   b. 2–706
   c. 2–708(1)
   d. 2–708(2)
   e. 2–709

5. The aggrieved seller's incidental damages are defined in which of the following sections of the UCC?
   a. 2–710
   b. 2–706
   c. 2–708(1)
   d. 2–708(2)
   e. 2–715

6. The aggrieved buyer's incidental damages are defined in which of the following sections of the UCC?
   a. 2–710
   b. 2–706
   c. 2–708(1)
   d. 2–708(2)
   e. 2–715

7. If the goods are unique or in other proper circumstances, the aggrieved buyer may seek specific performance under which of the following sections of the UCC?
   a. 2–711
   b. 2–712
   c. 2–713
   d. 2–714
   e. 2–716

SHORT-ANSWER QUESTIONS

1. Distinguish the following: actual damages, liquidated damages, and statutory liquidated damages. Give an example of each.

2. Discuss the remedy options open to an aggrieved seller when the buyer breaches before accepting the goods.

3. Discuss the remedy options open to an aggrieved buyer when the seller breaches before the buyer accepts the goods.

PART VII

Third-Party Interests

BEYOND THE TWO CONTRACTING PARTIES

The first six parts of this book have explored the consensual relationship between the two contracting parties. Part Seven (Chapter 17) moves beyond these two parties.

CHAPTER 17

Third-Party Interests

- Third-Party Beneficiary Contracts
- The Assignment of Contractual Rights and Delegation of Contractual Duties
  - *Assignment*
  - *Delegation*
  - *Assignment and Delegation*
  - *Substituting and Releasing a Contracting Party: The Novation*
- Third Party's Interference with Existing Contractual Rights

Chapter 17 moves beyond the two contracting parties to explore three types of third-party interests: third-party beneficiary contracts; assignment of contractual rights and delegation of contractual duties (including the novation); and tortious interference with existing contractual rights.

THIRD-PARTY BENEFICIARY CONTRACTS

A **third-party beneficiary contract**, as its name suggests, is a contract for the benefit of a third party who is not a contracting party. Historically, courts held that a party who was not a contracting party was not in **privity of contract** with either contracting party and could not maintain a breach of contract cause of action against the promisor who breached his or her promise. Privity issues took two forms: vertical privity and horizontal privity. A buyer in a distribution chain would lack **vertical privity** if he or she did not buy directly from the party who breached his or her promise. A nonbuyer

third-party beneficiary contract

A third-party beneficiary contract is a contract for the benefit of a third party. This party is neither the offeror nor offeree.

privity of contract

Privity of contract is a relationship that must exist before a party can successfully maintain a breach of contract action. See horizontal privity and vertical privity.

vertical privity

Vertical privity of contract is the relationship that must be established by a legislature or a court before an injured purchaser of a product can successfully sue a remote seller in a breach of contract action for a breach of warranty. The remote seller did not contract directly with the injured purchaser, but one or more intermediate sellers were involved in the distribution of the product.

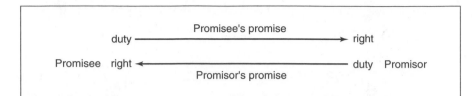

Exhibit 17–1 Contractual Rights and Duties in a Bilateral Contract

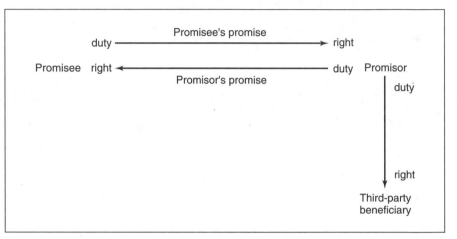

Exhibit 17–2 Contractual Rights and Duties in a Third-Party Beneficiary Contract

horizontal privity

Horizontal privity of contract is the relationship that must be established by a legislature or court before an injured user of a product, although not contracting with the seller of the product, can successfully sue the seller in a breach of contract action for a breach of warranty.

would lack **horizontal privity** even if he or she were injured or adversely affected by the subject of the contract.

Most courts now agree that a contract made for the benefit of a third-party beneficiary may be enforced by that third party if that party is more than an incidental beneficiary.

In a bilateral contract, each contracting party has a duty associated with his or her promise and a right associated with the other party's promise (see Exhibit 17–1).

In a third-party beneficiary contract, the two contracting parties have duties and rights. The third-party beneficiary has only contractual rights but no contractual duties (see Exhibit 17–2).

The following contract between Abigail and Fleet Street Press illustrates a typical third-party beneficiary contract.

Example 17–1

Abigail, a mystery writer, promises to write a new mystery for her publisher, Fleet Street Press, if Fleet Street promises to put the royalties in trust for her godchild. Tracy, the third-party beneficiary, owes no duty to either Abigail or to Fleet Street. Abigail owes a duty to Fleet Street to write, and Fleet Street owes both Abigail and Tracy a duty to pay Tracy. Because Fleet Street owes a duty to Tracy, Tracy has a right to have Fleet Street perform this duty.

The following diagram illustrates the parties' rights and duties:

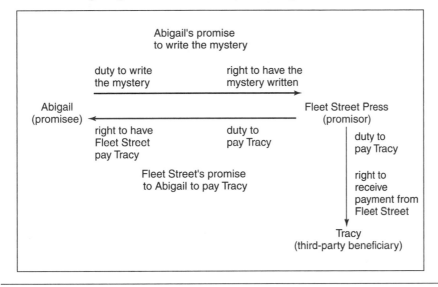

A third-party beneficiary contract is subject to the same rules of contract formation as any other contract. The consideration for Abigail's promise to write is Fleet Street's promise to pay Tracy. The consideration for Fleet Street's promise to pay Tracy is Abigail's promise to write.

Third-party beneficiaries come in three forms: donee, creditor, and incidental. A **donee beneficiary** receives a gift.

Example 17–2

In the Abigail/Fleet Street example, Tracy is a donee beneficiary. Prior to the third-party beneficiary contract, neither Abigail nor Fleet Street had a duty to give Tracy Abigail's royalties.

A **creditor beneficiary** has a right to receive something that arose prior to the third-party beneficiary contract. The promisor's performance of his or her duty extinguishes the third-party beneficiary prior right.

Example 17–3

Change the Abigail/Fleet Street example. Add the fact that Tracy had lent Abigail money in a prior transaction. Now add the third-party beneficiary transaction so Abigail promises to write the mystery for

donee beneficiary

A donee beneficiary is a third-party beneficiary to a contract who receives a gift under the contract.

creditor beneficiary

A creditor beneficiary is a third-party beneficiary to a contract who received a right under the contract when it was formed to discharge a prior obligation that the promisee had with the third-party beneficiary.

Fleet Street Press for Fleet Street's promise to Abigail to pay Tracy to satisfy Abigail's debt. Tracy would be a creditor beneficiary of the Abigail/Fleet Street Contract.

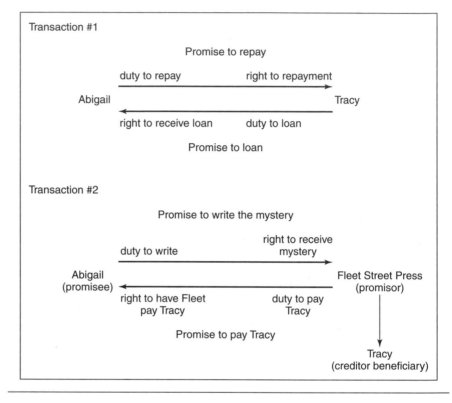

intended beneficiary

An intended beneficiary is a third-party donee or creditor beneficiary. The Restatement (First) of Contracts uses the terms "donee" and "creditor beneficiary." The Restatement (Second) of Contracts uses the term "intended beneficiary."

incidental beneficiary

An incidental beneficiary is a third-party beneficiary to a contract who is neither a creditor nor a donee beneficiary. An incidental beneficiary receives a windfall if the contract is performed, but has no enforceable rights under the contract if it is not performed.

The Restatement (Second) of Contracts has moved away from the creditor-donee beneficiary distinction. **Intended beneficiary** is the Restatement's term for a third-party beneficiary who has an enforceable right.

An **incidental beneficiary** is a third-party beneficiary who is neither a creditor nor a donee, and therefore has no enforceable rights under the contract. To determine whether a beneficiary has a right to enforce the contract, use the "intent to benefit" test, which examines who the promisee intended to receive the performance of the contract. If the *promisee* intended to benefit the third party, the third party is a protected beneficiary with enforceable contractual rights.

⫿ PARALEGAL EXERCISE 17.1

Uncle Bill promised his nephew, George, that if George would quit smoking cigarettes for one year, Uncle Bill would buy George a new Corvette. George quit smoking for a year.

    1. What are the rights and duties between Uncle Bill and George?

2. Is the Chevrolet Motor Company a donee, creditor, or incidental beneficiary of this contract?

3. What are the rights and duties between Uncle Bill and the third-party beneficiary? ▇

▥ PARALEGAL EXERCISE 17.2

Alan contracted to sell Greenacre to Graham for Graham's promise to pay $250,000 according to the following plan: $10,000 to Alan's nephew Calvin as a graduation gift; $100,000 to Charge-It Credit Company as full payment of Alan's last month's charges; and $140,000 to Benton, a broker, to invest for the benefit of Alan's mother, Margaret.

1. What are the rights and duties between Alan and Graham?
2. Are Calvin, Charge-It Credit Company, and Margaret donee, creditor, or incidental beneficiaries?
3. What are the rights and duties between Graham and the third-party beneficiaries? ▇

The distinction between intended (creditor and donee) beneficiaries and incidental beneficiaries is important when considering breach of implied warranties in a contract for the sale of goods.

Example 17-4

An automobile with a defective wheel was manufactured by Ford Motor Company and sold to Friendly Motors, a dealership. Friendly sold the Ford to Stanley. When Stanley was out on a Sunday drive with his girlfriend, Josephine, the wheel collapsed and the car crashed. Both Josephine and Stanley were injured.

Although Stanley could sue Friendly on his contract with Friendly, could Stanley sue Ford, the deep pocket up the distribution chain? Was Stanley a third-party beneficiary of the Ford Motor Company/ Friendly Motors contract? Because the three parties are in the distribution chain (as either buyers or sellers), the question is whether Stanley will be barred from suing Ford Motor on the ground that he was not in vertical privity of contract with the Ford Motor Company. The vertical nonprivity plaintiff is a buyer in the distribution chain who did not buy directly from the defendant.

Unlike Stanley, who was a buyer, Josephine was not contractually related to either Friendly or Ford. She was not in the distribution chain. The question is whether Josephine is in horizontal privity of contract with Friendly Motors. The horizontal nonprivity plaintiff is not a buyer in the distribution chain but one who consumes, uses, or is affected by the goods.

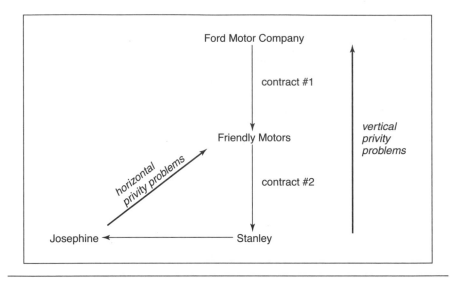

The "privity of contract" language can be translated into donee and incidental beneficiary. A third party who is in privity of contract is a donee beneficiary and has contractual rights. A third party who is not in privity of contract is an incidental beneficiary and has no contractual rights.

Because the subject matter of this illustration is a sale of goods, the Uniform Commercial Code applies. Unfortunately, the Code is silent as to the first question—whether Stanley can sue up the distribution chain. After the enactment of the Code, many courts viewed this legislative silence as an indication that such a suit is prohibited due to a lack of vertical privity of contract.

Recently, a number of courts have abrogated at least a part of the vertical privity requirement. The abrogation has been piecemeal based on the injury sustained by the aggrieved party. Products can cause three different types of injury: personal injury, property damage, and economic loss. Personal injury and property damage have traditionally been compensated under the tort actions of strict liability and negligence. Economic loss has traditionally been compensated in a breach of contract action. Some courts, therefore, found the abrogation of vertical privity for breach of warranty cases involving economic loss a reasonable evolutionary step. Other courts have gone further and have abrogated vertical privity for breach of warranty cases involving personal injury.

The second question—whether Josephine can sue the last seller in the distribution chain—is addressed in the Code. Section 2–318 offers the states a selection among three alternatives. Alternative A extends a seller's express and implied warranty liability to family and household members and guests in the buyer's home if it is reasonable to expect that such person may use, consume, or be affected by the goods.

Alternative A

A seller's warranty whether express or implied extends to any natural person who is in the family or household of his buyer or who is a guest in his home if it is reasonable to expect that such person may use, consume or be affected by the goods and who is injured in person by breach of the warranty. A seller may not exclude or limit the operation of this section.

Alternative B extends the seller's express and implied warranty liability to any person who may reasonably be expected to use the goods. Alternative B expands coverage to persons beyond the buyer's family, household, or guests.

Alternative B

A seller's warranty whether express or implied extends to any natural person who may reasonably be expected to use, consume or be affected by the goods and who is injured in person by breach of the warranty. A seller may not exclude or limit the operation of this section.

Alternative C is the broadest of the three and expands coverage to business entities.

Alternative C

A seller's warranty whether express or implied extends to any person who may reasonably be expected to use, consume or be affected by the goods and who is injured by breach of the warranty. A seller may not exclude or limit the operation of this section with respect to injury to the person of an individual to whom the warranty extends.

⫼ PARALEGAL EXERCISE 17.3

Is Josephine a donee or incidental beneficiary in the Stanley/Friendly Motors contract? Is the answer the same under the three alternatives of UCC § 2–318? ▪

In *Coombes v. Toro Co.,* The Toro Company manufactured a three-wheel utility vehicle which was distributed by Turf Products Corporation and purchased by a golf course. Coombes, an employee of a golf course sued The Toro Company, the manufacturer, and Turf Products Corporation, the seller, for personal injuries incurred when he was using the vehicle (see Exhibit 17–3).

1. Does Coombes have a horizontal or vertical privity problem when he sues Turf and Toro?
2. Is Coombes a donee, creditor, or incidental beneficiary of the Toro/Turf contract and of the Turf/golf course contract?
3. Why did the court use UCC § 2–318?
4. Which alternative of UCC § 2–318 was enacted in Connecticut?
5. Did the court correctly apply the facts to the law?
6. Would the result have been the same if Connecticut had enacted either of the other alternatives to section 2–318?

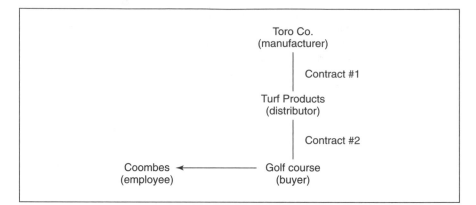

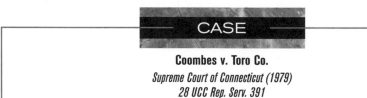

Exhibit 17–3 *Coombes v. Toro Co.*

CASE

Coombes v. Toro Co.
Supreme Court of Connecticut (1979)
28 UCC Rep. Serv. 391

DUPONT, J.

Plaintiff is bringing this action to recover for personal injuries allegedly incurred when, in the course of his employment, the engine of a "three wheel utility vehicle" which he was operating stalled and the brakes failed. As a result, the vehicle rolled backwards down an incline and the plaintiff was thrown to the ground and struck by the vehicle when it overturned. The defendants are The Toro Company which manufactures this model and the Turf Products Corporation which distributes and sells it. The plaintiff-employee was a member of the maintenance crew of a golf course which purchased the vehicle for use by its workers. The action is grounded in negligence, strict tort, and breach of warranty. The defendants have moved to strike that part of the third count which sounds in breach of statutory warranty. The parties have agreed that those portions of the Motion to Strike relating to other counts need not be addressed by the court.

Defendants argue that the complaint does not state a claim upon which relief can be granted because, inter alia, count three does not allege that plaintiff is within the category of individuals protected by § 42a-2–318. Resolution of this issue in favor of the defendants is dispositive of the other claims of the Motion to Strike.

The provision governing third-party beneficiaries, CGS § 42a-2–318, was adopted in 1959 and amended in 1965. It is significant to note that although more expansive alternatives to the statute have existed since 1966,[1] the

---

1. Alternative B extends warranties to "any natural person who may reasonably be expected to use, consume or be affected by the goods and who is injured in person by the breach of warranty." Alternative C extends to "any person who may reasonably be expected to use, consume or be affected by the goods and who is injured by the breach of warranty." 1A Uniform Laws Annotated 52–53 (1976).

Connecticut legislature has maintained its adherence to Alternative A. The sentence pertaining to the neutrality in the statute apparently refers to developing tort law. See J. White & R. Summers, Uniform Commercial Code § 11-3 at 330-31 (1972 ed).

The Supreme Court has not yet considered whether an employee is covered by § 42a-2-318. However, in the only Superior Court case on point, Chen v. Reliable Rubber & Plastic Machinery Co., 5 CLT #7 at 13 [25 UCC Rep 1274], September 18, 1978, the court held that an employee is not an intended beneficiary. The court relied heavily on the availability of a cause of action in strict tort. Furthermore, the majority of states which like Connecticut, have adopted Alternative A and which have considered the issue at hand have decided that the section does not extend to employees.[2]

The plaintiff urges that the spirit of various Connecticut warranty decisions should encourage the court to extend coverage to employees. The cases cited were decided under tort principles, however. It has been recognized that "an action based on strict liability is to be distinguished from liability on breach of warranty or simple negligence." De Felice v. Ford Motor Co., 28 Conn Supp 164, 168, 255 A2d 636 (1969), citing Rossignol v. Danbury School of Aeronautics, Inc., 154 Conn 549, 227 A2d 418 [4 UCC Rep 305] (1967). As a result, the import of plaintiff's cited decisions is limited.

Plaintiff also suggests that the Chen decision concerning employee coverage is not well reasoned because it is not in accord with the Connecticut decisions extending warranties and does not follow the rationale of jurisdictions which have included employees. As indicated above, however, the warranty decisions were made in accord with tort principles and the majority of Alternative A jurisdictions have denied coverage.

Motion to strike that portion of Count 3 relating to a cause of action in breach of warranty under § 42a-2-318 granted.

---

2. The following Alternative A states have not extended the warranties to employees: Alaska, Georgia, Maryland, North Carolina, Ohio, Oklahoma, Tennessee, and West Virginia. The following Alternative A states have extended the warranties to employees: Arkansas, Florida, Maine, and Pennsylvania. 1A Uniform Laws Annotated 74-77 (1976) and 10-11 (Supp 1979).

Third-party beneficiary rights depend on the existence and enforceability of a contract between the contracting parties. If a contract has not been formed, a third-party beneficiary does not exist. If a contract exists but the contract is unenforceable, the third-party beneficiary cannot enforce the contract.

Example 17-5

Mickie contracted to sell Brent her car for Brent's promise to pay the purchase price to Mickie's debtor, Kathy. Mickie misrepresented the car's mileage as 50,000, instead of the correct mileage of 150,000. If Brent disaffirms the contract due to the misrepresentation, Brent no longer has a duty to pay Kathy.

Contracting parties are generally free to make a subsequent agreement to discharge or modify duties to the beneficiary if the beneficiary consents. If, however, the beneficiary does not consent, he or she may still be able to enforce the contract despite efforts by the contracting parties to discharge or modify their duties. The trend is to allow both creditor and donee beneficiaries to enforce the contract when the beneficiary has learned of the contract and has relied on it or brought suit to enforce the contract before receiving notification of the discharge or modification. The equal treatment of creditor and donee beneficiaries in the Restatement (Second) of Contracts supports this trend.

Example 17–6

Sneed owed Sanders $200. Sneed contracted with Johnson for Johnson to pay Sanders the $200 Sneed owed Sanders. Sneed notified Sanders that Johnson would pay his debt. Later Sneed, in exchange for Johnson's loaning Sneed his lake cabin over Labor Day weekend, released Johnson from his duty to pay Sanders. Ignorant of Sneed's attempted discharge of Johnson's duty, Sanders sued Johnson for $200. Johnson remained liable to Sanders because Sanders learned of the contract and brought suit to enforce it before receiving notice of the attempted discharge.

THE ASSIGNMENT OF CONTRACTUAL RIGHTS AND DELEGATION OF CONTRACTUAL DUTIES

After a contract has been formed, it may become advantageous for one of the parties to either sell his or her contractual rights or delegate his or her contractual duties. This section introduces assignment and delegation. Rights are assigned. Duties are delegated.

Assignment

An **assignment** is the transfer of a contractual right. The **assignor** is the original promisee and is the party who transfers the contractual right. The **assignee** is the party to whom the contractual right is transferred.

The promisor may also be called an obligor. The **obligor** (promisor) is the party who owes the contractual duty associated with the contractual right. The promisee may be called the original obligee. The original **obligee** (promisee) is the party to whom the contractual right was originally owed (see Exhibit 17–4).

assignment

An assignment is the transfer of a contractual right.

assignor

The assignor is the promisee in the original contract who transfers his or her contractual right to a third person.

assignee

The assignee is the third party (not one of the original contracting parties) to whom a contractual right is transferred.

obligor

The obligor (promisor) is the contracting party who owes the contractual duty associated with the contractual right.

obligee

The obligee (promisee) is the contracting party with the contractual right to whom is owed the contractual duty.

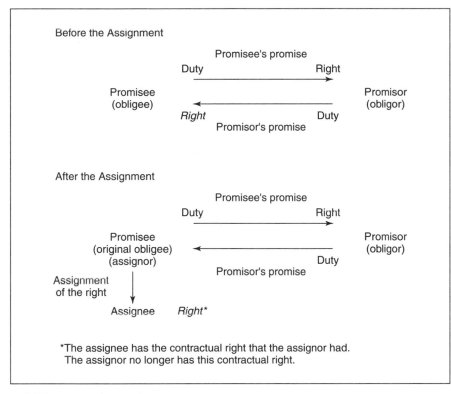

Before the Assignment

Promisee's promise

Duty → Right

Promisee (obligee) ←— Promisor (obligor)

Right   Duty
Promisor's promise

After the Assignment

Promisee's promise

Duty → Right

Promisee (original obligee) (assignor) ←— Promisor (obligor)

Duty
Promisor's promise

Assignment of the right ↓

Assignee   Right*

*The assignee has the contractual right that the assignor had. The assignor no longer has this contractual right.

Exhibit 17–4 The Assignment

Example 17-7

Corner Store sells a VCR to Sylvia on $300 credit. Under this contract, Corner Store has a duty to deliver the VCR to Sylvia and a right to have Sylvia pay $300. Sylvia has a duty to pay Corner Store $300 and a right to receive delivery of the VCR. Because Corner Store lacks the assets to finance its credit sales, it sells its right to payment to Friendly Finance Company. Friendly pays Corner Store in exchange for Corner Store's right to have Sylvia pay $300. Once Sylvia is notified of the assignment, she will have a duty to pay Friendly Finance. She will no longer have a duty to pay Corner Store.

In this transaction, Corner Store, the promisee, is the original obligee and the assignor. Sylvia is the obligor. Friendly Finance is the assignee.

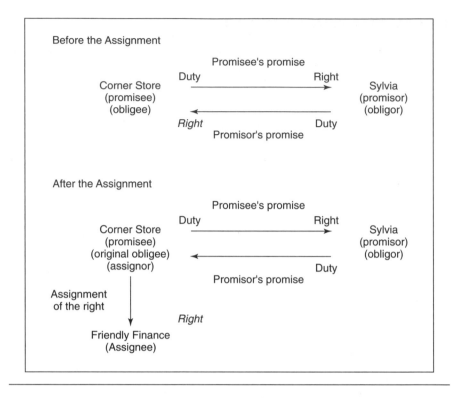

Before the Assignment

Promisee's promise

Corner Store
(promisee)
(obligee)

Duty ──────────────→ Right

Sylvia
(promisor)
(obligor)

Right ←────────── Duty

Promisor's promise

After the Assignment

Promisee's promise

Corner Store
(promisee)
(original obligee)
(assignor)

Duty ──────────────→ Right

Sylvia
(promisor)
(obligor)

←────────── Duty

Promisor's promise

Assignment
of the right

Right

Friendly Finance
(Assignee)

Although many rights can be assigned, not all rights may be assigned. Whether a right is assignable depends on whether the transfer of the right will materially alter the duty of the obligor (promisor), the party who must perform the duty associated with that right.

▥ PARALEGAL EXERCISE 17.4

The law firm of Peabody, Anderson & Grable, hired Samantha Stevenson as their legal assistant. The contract had a one-year term. After working for the Peabody firm for several months, Samantha was notified that the firm had transferred its right to her work to O'Sullivan & Mead. Was Samantha's contract assignable? ■

Whether the transfer of the right will materially alter the duty of the obligor is not the only factor determining whether a contractual right can be assigned. A court may place great weight on a well-drafted term in the contract prohibiting the assignment of a contractual right. A court may also refuse to enforce an assignment where a special relationship exists between parties. Also many states have statutes that prohibit or limit certain types of assignments.

An assignee takes the assigned-rights subject to any defense that the obligor could have set up against the assignor-obligee at the time of the assignment. Common defenses include lack of consideration, misrepresentation, fraud, and duress.

PARALEGAL EXERCISE 17.5

A-1 Motors sold a used Volvo to Andre for $4,500. The sale was a credit sale. A-1 assigned its right to Andre's payment to Consumer Credit. Several days after Andre took possession of the Volvo, he discovered that it had a cracked block and therefore was in breach of the implied warranties of merchantability. The seriousness of this defect in the vehicle would have justified Andre in withholding his time payments.

Must Andre pay Consumer Credit? ■

Delegation

A **delegation** of a contractual duty is an authorization to another party to perform the contractual duty. The **delegator** is the original promisor and is the party who delegates the contractual duty. The original promisor is also called the original obligor. The **delegatee** is the party who is authorized by the delegator to perform the contractual duty. The delegatee is the new promisor and is the new obligor. The promisee is the obligee (see Exhibit 17–5).

delegation
A delegation is the empowering of another by the obligor to perform the obligor's contractual duty.

delegator
The delegator is the promisor in the original contract who delegates his or her contractual duty to a third party.

delegatee
The delegatee is the third party (not one of the original contracting parties) who is empowered by the delegator to perform the delegator's contractual duty.

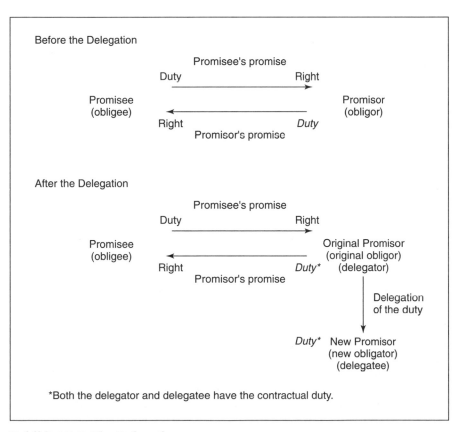

Exhibit 17–5 The Delegation

Example 17–8

Tony had a contract with the *Evening Gazette* to deliver newspapers. Because Tony's paper route was quite lucrative, he sold it to Michael. Tony delegated his duty to deliver newspapers to Michael.

The act of delegating a duty does not terminate the duty on the part of the delegator. Delegation only increases the number of parties who have the duty.

Example 17–9

Barnes delegated his duty to clean Dell's garage to Roberts.
If Roberts fails to perform, Dell could receive performance from Barnes.

As was the case with assignment, not all duties may be delegated. Whether a duty is delegable depends on whether the delegation of the duty will materially alter the right of the obligee (the promisee), the party who has the right associated with that duty. The obligee may have a substantial interest in requiring the original obligor to perform, especially when the performance is "personal," involving qualities such as character, reputation, taste, or skill.

Example 17–10

Showtime hired the Blue Notes to perform at its club. The Blue Notes could not delegate its duty to perform. Its performance is "personal" because it involves unique talent.

⫼ PARALEGAL EXERCISE 17.6

Under Paralegal Exercise 17.4, could Samantha delegate her duty to work for the firm? ▪

Even general rules have exceptions. In *Rossetti v. City of New Britain,* 163 Conn. 283, 303 A.2d 714 (1972), the architectural firm of Rossetti, DiCorcia, and Mileto, a partnership, contracted with the city of New Britain to design a police station and circuit court building. DiCorcia left the partnership and assigned all of his rights and delegated all of his duties to the new partnership, Rossetti and Mileto. This included the contract to design the New Britain police station and circuit court building.

The City ultimately terminated the contract with Rossetti and Mileto and hired another architect for the project. Rossetti and Mileto sued the City for breach of contract. In *Rossetti,* the court addressed the City's claim that the original partnership's duty was not delegable.

> As to the defendant's claim concerning the nonassignability of personal service contracts, it is indeed the general rule that contracts for personal services cannot be assigned. To be technically accurate, it is not the benefits that are nonassignable; rather, it is the duties which are nondelegable. Performance, in other words, cannot be delegated to another. 4 Corbin, Contracts, p. 439; 6 Am.Jur.2d, Assignments, § 11. Thus if a specific artist is hired to paint a picture, the artist cannot delegate his duty of performing. See LaRue v. Groezinger, 84 Cal. 281, 24 P. 42; 6 Am.Jur.2d, Assignments, § 13. Personal performance is of the essence. Agreements to render professional services as a physician or lawyer fall within this rule. Deaton v. Lawson, 40 Wash. 486, 82 P. 879; Corson v. Lewis, 77 Neb. 446, 109 N.W. 735. Whether a duty is personal such that it cannot be delegated, however, is a question of the intention of the parties to be ascertained from the contract, its nature, and the attending circumstances. Clearly, a contract to render architectural services could be one where personal performance is of the essence. Smith v. Board of Education, 115 Kan. 155, 222 P. 101. The claims of proof, by which the charge is to be tested, do not support such a conclusion in the case at bar. The defendant's contention is that the contract was personal to the Rossetti, DiCorcia, and Mileto partnership. From the claims of proof, however, it is clear that all dealings were with the plaintiff. He was the person in charge of and responsible for the contract. There was nothing offered to show an intent that the plaintiff's partners could not delegate whatever duties they had to the plaintiff. We cannot say that the court erred in its charge in this respect. Id. at 718–19.

Assignment and Delegation

Contracting parties often assign and delegate in one transaction.

Example 17–11

Kelly Collins, a professional photographer, has a contract to photograph all of the Fashion Statement's models for one year. Six months into the contract, Kelly decided to move to Milano, Italy. Kelly delegated her duty to photograph all of the Fashion Statement's models for the remainder of the year to Amanda Campbell. Kelly also assigned her right to payment to Amanda. Assuming that Fashion Statement has no objection to the delegation, the Kelly/Amanda transaction is both an assignment and a delegation.

When an assignment and a delegation take place in the same transaction, the transaction is termed an assignment. When analyzing a transaction labeled an assignment, care must be taken to determine whether the transaction also includes a delegation. Note in an assignment, the assignor (original promisee) no longer has the right to receive the promisor's performance. In a delegation, however, the delegator (original promisor) still has the duty to perform.

Substituting and Releasing a Contracting Party: The Novation

novation

A novation is a contract that discharges a party to the contract, sometimes an obligor and sometimes an obligee, and substitutes a new party in his or her place.

A time may come when one of the original contracting parties would like to be replaced by a party who had not been a party to the original contract. This transaction is called a "novation." A **novation** is a contract between one or both of the original contracting parties and a third party that substitutes the third party in the place of one of the original contracting parties and discharges that party. Often parties attempt a novation but fail to discharge the original contracting party. Substitution without discharge is not a novation.

If the new party is a substitute for the promisor (obligor), the new promisor's duties may be the same as, or different from, those of the original promisor. If the new party is a substitute for the promisee (obligee), the new promisee's rights may be the same as, or different from, those of the original promisee.

As a substituted contract, a novation replaces the original contract. The end result of a novation is the immediate discharge of one of the original contracting parties and the creation of a new duty. A novation does not exist until the discharge has been accomplished. Because the novation is substituted for the original contract and the duties in the original contract are terminated, a party is unable to maintain a breach of contract action under the original contract.

A novation may be a simple novation or a compound novation. A simple novation begins with one original contract. In a simple novation (the substitute contract) a new promisor (obligor) is substituted for an original promisor or a new promisee (obligee) is substituted for an original promisee.

Example 17–12

Bank One loaned Amanda $10,000. Subsequently, Stephanie, Amanda's aunt, promised Bank One that she would pay the bank the amount owed by Amanda if Bank One promised to discharge Amanda's debt. Bank One promised.

The original contract was between Bank One and Amanda. Bank One promised to loan for Amanda's promise to repay. As to

Amanda's promise to repay, Amanda is the promisor (has a duty to repay) and Bank One is the promisee (has a right to repayment).

The novation (the substitute contract) was between Bank One and Stephanie. Bank One promised Stephanie to substitute Stephanie for Amanda and to discharge Amanda. Stephanie promised Bank One to pay Amanda's debt. Under this simple novation, Stephanie is substituted for Amanda as the promisor (has a duty to repay).

Example 17–13

Adam loaned Megan $10,000. Subsequently, Adam married Sarah. Adam promised Megan that he would discharge her debt to him if she promised to pay Sarah the amount she owed him. Megan promised Adam.

The original contract was between Adam and Megan. Adam promised to loan for Megan's promise to repay. As to Megan's promise to repay, Megan is the promisor (has a duty to repay) and Adam is the promisee (has a right to repayment).

The novation (the substitute contract) was between Adam and Megan. Adam promised Megan to discharge her from her duty to pay him. Megan promised Adam that she would pay Sarah. Under this simple novation, Sarah is substituted for Adam as the promisee (has a right to repayment).

The compound novation may begin with one original contract, which is executory on both sides. That is, at the time of making the novation, both parties had duties outstanding and both parties were promisors and promisees. As with the case of a simple novation, a third party becomes involved. The third party assumes both the duties and rights of one of the original contracting parties.

Example 17–14

Adam promised to deliver a tractor to Ben for Ben's promise to pay Adam $1,000. Subsequently, Adam promises Ben and Carol to deliver a bulldozer to Carol and to discharge Ben's duty to pay him $1,000 if Ben promises to discharge Adam's duty to deliver the tractor to him and if Carol promises to pay $2,000 to Adam. Ben and Carol promise.

The original contract was between Adam and Ben. Adam promised to deliver a tractor to Ben for Ben's promise to pay $1,000. As to

Adam's promise to deliver, Adam is the promisor (has the duty to deliver) and Ben is the promisee (has the right to receive delivery). As to Ben's promise to pay, Ben is the promisor (has the duty to pay) and Adam is the promisee (has the right to receive payment).

The novation (the substitute contract) was among Adam, Ben, and Carol. Adam promised both Ben and Carol to deliver the bulldozer to Carol in exchange for Ben's promise to discharge him from his duty to deliver the tractor to him and for Carol's promise to pay him $2,000. Under this compound novation, Carol is substituted for Ben as both promisor (promise to pay) and promisee (right to receive the bulldozer). Adam is discharged from his duty to deliver the tractor to Ben and Ben is discharged from his duty to pay Adam.

The compound novation may also begin with two original contracts with one party being common to both. In the novation (the substitute contract), the three parties to the original contracts agree that the party common to both contracts shall drop out.

Example 17–15

Anthony contracted with Best Construction for Best to provide materials and remodel Anthony's restaurant. Best subcontracted with the Century Lumber Company for Century to supply the materials. Century supplied the materials and Best incorporated some of these materials into Anthony's restaurant. For some reason, the construction stopped. Anthony promised Best and Century that he would discharge Best from its duty to complete the remodeling and he would pay Century what Best owed Century for the materials if Best promised to discharge Anthony from his duty to pay Best and Century promised to discharge Best from Best's duty to pay Century. When Anthony, Best, and Century promised, a novation was formed, Anthony's duty to pay Best was discharged, and Best's duties to Anthony and Century were discharged. Anthony now has a duty to pay Century for the materials supplied.

THIRD PARTY'S INTERFERENCE WITH EXISTING CONTRACTUAL RIGHTS

In most states, one who interferes with the contractual relationship of others may be liable for harming their contractual relationship. The cause of action is known as "tortious interference with a contract."

The party claiming interference can maintain this cause of action by demonstrating the following elements:

1. An enforceable contract existed.
2. The party inducing the breach knew of the contract.
3. The interfering party intentionally induced the breach.
4. The interfering party induced the breach unjustifiably.
5. The party claiming interference was damaged by the breach.

The first element, an enforceable contract, is demonstrated by the information in Chapters 2 through 5 and 7 through 9.

The second element, knowledge of the contract, can be established by proving that the interfering party had either actual or constructive knowledge of the contract. Constructive knowledge means that the party who interfered knew facts that would cause a reasonable person to believe that a contract existed.

The third element, that the interfering party intentionally induced the breach, requires a showing that the interfering party acted intentionally to induce a breach. The inducement may include threats, coercion, or economic persuasion. Some jurisdictions do not require actual breach of contract. These jurisdictions require only that the party somehow disrupt the contractual relationship. Generally, a party acts intentionally if he or she acts with the purpose of bringing about a particular result. Some courts reject the intent requirement and demand only a showing that the party interfering knew his or her acts would result in a breach.

The fourth element is a showing that the party inducing the breach was unjustified in his or her actions. Generally, courts do not consider the breaching of a contract for personal gain to be "justified." Some courts go a bit further and require that the act be wrongful, malicious, or unjust, which indicates an interpretation stronger than "unjustified."

The fifth and final element is a showing that the party complaining of the interference was damaged by the interference. The most traditional aspects of harm are those damages related to the breaching of a contract.

The courts have applied various remedies in tortious interference of contract cases. One remedy is injunctive relief. The injunction forces a party to cease any activities that are designed to result in a breach of contract. If a breach has already occurred, an injunction may be of little consequence. Courts, however, will frequently award a traditional measure of contract damages. Some courts will also award punitive damages.

▥ PARALEGAL EXERCISE 17.7

Carriers, Inc., delivered the *Times* newspaper to subscribers. The *Post,* a rival newspaper, liked the job that Carriers was doing so much that it hired

Carriers to deliver its newspaper to its subscribers. The Carriers/*Post* contract stated that Carriers must deliver all the newspapers that the Post printed.

Recently, the *Post* doubled its production, thereby placing a heavy burden on Carriers. Because of the increased burden, Carriers informed the *Times* that it might have to cancel its contract with them. Unfortunately, Carriers was the only delivery company in town and the *Times* did not have its own delivery system.

Will the *Times* be successful in its suit against the *Post* for tortiously interfering with its contract? If so, what should be the remedy? ■

The following cases, *R. C. Hilton Associates, Inc. v. Stan Musial & Biggie's, Inc.* and *Ahern v. Boeing Co.,* add perspective on how courts deal with the tortious interference issue. Check each case for the five elements necessary for maintaining the action.

CASE

R. C. Hilton Associates, Inc. v. Stan Musial & Biggie's, Inc.
United States Court of Appeals, Eleventh Circuit (1983)
702 F.2d 907

Before GODBOLD, Chief Judge, RONEY, Circuit Judge, and PITTMAN*, District Judge.
GODBOLD, Chief Judge:
A real estate broker, R. C. Hilton Associates, Inc., brought this action to recover a commission on the sale of a hotel. Initially Hilton's agent visited the hotel to determine whether it was for sale. An agent of Stan Musial & Biggie's, Inc. (Musial), the owner, advised Hilton that the hotel might be for sale for $4.25 million, net to owner. Musial stated that it did not intend to pay any sales commission and that Hilton would have to make arrangements for its commission with the buyer. Hilton subsequently initiated discussions between Musial and Edward Stern. After a short period of negotiations (in which Hilton did not participate) Stern agreed to purchase the hotel for $4.12 million. No commission was paid to Hilton.

Hilton brought suit against Musial and Stern in Florida state court. The defendants removed the case to federal court based on diversity.

The complaint contains three counts: (1) a breach of contract action against Musial; (2) a claim of tortious interference with a business contract against Stern; and (3) an unjust enrichment claim against Musial for the value of services rendered. The case was referred to a United States Magistrate acting as a special master pursuant to Fed.R.Civ.P. 53. After a nonjury trial the magistrate made findings of fact and conclusions of law and recommended that judgment be entered against Hilton on all counts. The district court adopted and confirmed the magistrate's findings and conclusions. We affirm.

The district court ruled that Hilton had neither an express nor implied contract with Musial. [Discussion of count one is omitted.]

---
* Honorable Virgil Pittman, U.S. District Judge for the Southern District of Alabama, sitting by designation.

Hilton seeks recovery from Stern for malicious interference with a "business contract." The district court concluded: "Although a claim for tortious interference may be based upon a contractual agreement which is not legally enforceable, no recovery is allowed if there is no contractual relationship at all." On appeal Hilton argues that the existence of a contract is not necessary in order to recover for tortious interference with a "business relationship." Even assuming that the court should have liberally interpreted Hilton's claim for tortious interference with contract as a claim for tortious interference with business relationship, see Smith v. Ocean State Bank, 335 So.2d 641 (Fla. App. 1976), Hilton has failed to establish its right to recover.

To establish a claim for tortious interference with business relationship the plaintiff must prove:

> the existence of a business relationship under which the plaintiff has legal rights; an intentional and unjustified interference with that relationship by the defendant; and damage to the plaintiff as a result of the breach of the business relationship.

> Fearick v. Smugglers Cove, Inc., 379 So.2d 400, 403 (Fla. App. 1980).

> Initially, the broker had the burden of establishing an advantageous relationship with the seller. A broker can not recover for his services unless they were rendered at the express or implied request of his employer and a contract for services will not be implied unless the vendor knows or has reasonable grounds to believe that they were rendered with the expectation of receiving payment therefor.

Retzky v. J. A. Cantor Associates, Inc., 192 So.2d 24, 26 (Fla. App. 1966). Hilton failed to prove that its services were rendered at the express or implied request of Musial. Having failed to establish an advantageous relationship with the seller, Hilton's tort claim against Stern fails.

Hilton also seeks recovery from Musial under an unjust enrichment theory. [Discussion of count three is omitted.]

In the present case Musial clearly informed Hilton that it did not intend to pay a sales commission. Thus, Hilton's services could not reasonably be "given and received in the expectation of being paid for. . . ."

AFFIRMED.

CASE

Ahern v. Boeing Co.
United States Court of Appeals, Eleventh Circuit (1983)
701 F.2d 142

Before HILL, KRAVITCH and HENDERSON, Circuit Judges.

KRAVITCH, Circuit Judge:

Appellants appeal from summary judgment granted to appellee by the district court. We conclude that the district court, 539 F.Supp. 1210, applied an incorrect legal standard to the facts of this case; therefore we reverse and remand for trial on the merits.

In 1976, "A & O," a partnership in which appellants were partners, entered into an agreement with Scientific Energy Engineering, Inc., ("SEE") covering the testing, production, sales, and leasing aspects of an incinerator device. A prototype of the incinerator was installed for testing on appellants' property. In May 1977, the agreement was modified to grant appellants the exclusive marketing rights to the incinerator. The agreement as modified did not contain an express durational provision, but did contain references to termination upon default of either of the parties.

SEE and A & O subsequently experienced some difficulties in their relationship, and SEE filed a state court action in September 1978, seeking declaratory relief and damages. While the state action was pending, SEE entered into negotiations with Boeing Company regarding the incinerator. On June 7, 1979, Boeing executed an option agreement with SEE and its principals, which gave Boeing an option to acquire the marketing rights to the incinerator and other products. Boeing exercised the option and on February 14, 1980, Boeing, SEE, and its principals entered into a marketing agreement. Appellants contend that this agreement directly interfered with the exclusive marketing rights that SEE had granted them.

On April 24, 1980, the state trial court entered a final declaratory judgment and declined to award SEE damages. The court found that the joint venture agreement granted certain marketing rights to the appellants, but that the contract was terminable at will by either party upon thirty-days' notice. Shortly after the state court judgment was entered and after the contract with Boeing had taken effect, SEE notified the appellants that it was terminating the marketing agreement with A & O. Appellants then filed this action in Florida state court seeking compensatory and punitive damages against Boeing for alleged tortious interference with the business relationship between A & O and SEE. The case was removed to federal district court pursuant to 28 U.S.C. §§ 1332 and 1441. After discovery was concluded, Boeing moved for summary judgment, and the district court granted the motion.

Under Florida law, to establish a cause of action for tortious interference, a party must demonstrate:

1. the existence of an advantageous business relationship under which that party has legal rights;
2. an intentional and unjustified interference with that relationship by the defendant; and
3. damage to the plaintiff as a result of the interference with the business relationship.

Unistar Corporation v. Child, 415 So.2d 733, 734 (Fla. 3d Dist.Ct.App. 1982); Wackenhut Corporation v. Maimone, 389 So.2d 656, 657 (Fla. 4th Dist.Ct.App. 1980); Lake Gateway Motor Inn v. Matt's Sunshine Gift Shops, Inc., 361 So.2d 769, 771 (Fla. 4th Dist.Ct.App. 1978). The Florida courts have determined that "an action will lie where a party tortiously interferes with a contract terminable at will." Unistar Corporation, 415 So.2d at 734. Thus, where the plaintiff shows "an intentional and unjustified interference with an existing business relationship which causes damage to the plaintiff," a prima facie case is established, and the burden then shifts to the defendant to justify its actions. Id. at 734–35. "If the defendant can prove that the interference was lawful competition—a privilege which the courts recognize when the contract is terminable at will—the defendant will not be found to have committed the tort of wrongful business interference." Id. at 735 (citing Insurance Field Services, Inc. v. White & White Inspection and Audit Service, Inc., 384 So.2d 303 (Fla. 5th Dist.Ct.App. 1980); W. Prosser, *Handbook of the Law of Torts* § 129, at 932, 946 (4th ed. 1971)).

The district court focused upon this privilege of competition in granting Boeing's motion for summary judgment. The court found that Boeing was motivated by no ill will toward A & O, but only by competitive interests, a finding we do not dispute. The court, however, concluded that Florida law protects interference with at-will contracts as long as the motivation for that interference is deemed "proper." The trial court in its opinion and order granting summary judgment, stated:

> that where, as here, there is a contract terminable at will and part of defendant's motivation for interfering with that contract was to advance defendant's business interests, the interference is privileged as competition and is therefore justified as a matter of law.

We believe that the judge erred in her reading of the Florida case law. In the recent trilogy of cases cited above, the Florida courts ruled that the plaintiffs had not established the requisite unjustified interference with their business relationships. In none of the cases did the defendant actually enter into a contract that interfered with the existing at-will contract of the plaintiff. In *Lake Gateway Motor Inn,* the plaintiff was a gift shop operator who had an at-will contract with the motel. The motel notified the plaintiff that it was exercising its rights to terminate the contract upon thirty-days' notice. The gift shop operator then negotiated with a possible successor, but that successor also held discussions with the motel. The successor found that the motel would contract with him if he paid the motel the amount due the gift shop operator under the "buy-out" clause of the at-will contract. The court found no tortious interference because the successor and the motel had not entered into a contract interfering with the gift shop's operation. The privilege of competition, the court held, protects solicitation for future business, not interference with existing contracts. The court summarized its reasoning as follows:

> Assuming all alleged actions of the successor were as bad as the appellee paints them, (although this is disputed) said successor went to the motel and solicited a take over of the gift shop, having heard it was to be available. Such competition seems to us to be par for the course in the free enterprise system. Can not the IBM salesman solicit this court to change over from a Xerox copier? *Of course he can, unless he suggests to us that we violate a contract with Xerox in so doing.*
>
> *In the case at bar, there is no proof that the successor operator sought to persuade the motel to break a contract or strip his predecessor of some legal rights.*

Lake Gateway Motor Inn, 361 So.2d at 772 (emphasis added).

The district court concluded that the determining factor under Florida law is the motivation of the alleged tortfeasor. Motivation is *not,* however, the guiding star in the constellation of Florida's common law of tortious interference. The case law clearly demonstrates that mere self-interested and competitive solicitation will not constitute tortious interference with an at-will contract, so long as the third party does not induce the breach of or interference with that existing contract.

Viewing the facts in the light most favorable to the nonmoving party as we must in reviewing a grant of summary judgment, Northwest Power Prods., Inc. v. Omark Indus., Inc., 576 F.2d 83, 85 (5th Cir. 1978), cert. denied, 439 U.S. 1116, 99 S.Ct. 1021, 59 L.Ed.2d 75 (1979), we conclude that appellants have alleged a prima facie case showing that Boeing went much further than the mere solicitation that would be protected under Florida's privilege of competition. We hold, therefore, that appellants are entitled to present their case to a jury. The order of the district court granting summary judgment is REVERSED, and the case REMANDED for trial.

PARALEGAL CHECKLIST

Third-Party Interests

❑ A paralegal must sometimes be concerned with parties other than those contracting. These parties include third-party beneficiaries, assignees, delegatees, and third parties who interfere with existing contractual rights (tortfeasors). Regardless of the situation, the first step in an analysis requires the paralegal, with the supervision of an attorney, to determine the existence of a contract. Without a contract, there can be no third-party beneficiary, assignee, delegatee, or tortfeasor. Use the following guidelines to evaluate whether a contract exists.

1. Who does the contract benefit? A third-party beneficiary contract is a contract for the benefit of a third party.
   a. Is the third party a donee or a creditor beneficiary? A donee or a creditor beneficiary has enforceable contractual rights. An incidental beneficiary has no enforceable contractual rights. The Restatement (Second) of Contracts does not distinguish between donee and creditor beneficiaries but identifies both as intended beneficiaries. Focus on the intent of promisor to determine whether a beneficiary is an intended beneficiary.
   b. Does the third party have rights and duties under the contract? A third-party beneficiary has only contractual rights (no duties) under the contract.
   c. Is there a third-party beneficiary who can enforce the contract? A third-party beneficiary's rights depend on the existence and enforceability of a contract between the contracting parties.
      (1) If a contract has not been formed, a third-party beneficiary does not exist.
      (2) If a contract exists but is unenforceable, the third-party beneficiary cannot enforce the contract.
   d. Can the beneficiary enforce the contract? Contracting parties are generally free to make a subsequent agreement to discharge or modify duties to the beneficiary if the beneficiary consents. If the beneficiary does not consent, he or she may be able to enforce the contract despite efforts by the contracting parties to discharge or modify their duties. The trend is to allow both creditor and donee beneficiaries to enforce the contract when the beneficiary has learned of the contract and has relied on it or has brought suit to enforce the contract before receiving notification of the discharge or modification.

2. Did the parties retain their contractual rights and duties? After a contract has been formed, the parties may either sell contractual rights or delegate contractual duties.
   a. Was there an assignment of contractual rights? An assignment of a contract is the transfer to another of the rights due under the terms of the contract.
      (1) Many, although not all, rights can be assigned. Whether a right is assignable depends on whether the transfer of the right will materially alter the duty of the obligor—the party who must perform the duty associated with that right.
      (2) An assignee takes the assigned right subject to any defense that the obligor could have raised against the assignor-obligee at the time of the assignment.
   b. Was there a delegation of a duty? A delegation of a duty is an authorization to another party to perform the duty.
      (1) The party who delegates the duty is the delegator and the party who is authorized to perform the duty is the delegatee. The party who has the right to receive performance of the duty is the obligee.
      (2) The act of delegating a duty does not terminate the duty on the part of the delegator. Delegation only increases the number of parties who have the duty.
      (3) Not all duties may be delegated. Whether a duty is delegable depends on whether the delegation of the duty will materially alter the right of the obligee. The obligee may have a substantial interest in requiring the original obligor to perform.
   c. Has there been a novation? A novation occurs when one of the original contracting parties is replaced by a party who was not a party to the original contract. A novation is a contract that discharges a party to the contract, sometimes an obligor and sometimes an obligee, and substitutes a new party in his or her place.
      (1) If the new party is an obligor, the obligor may have the same or different duties as the original obligor. If the new party is an obligee, the new obligee may have the same or different rights as the original obligee.
      (2) Although novations come in different forms, what is critical is that a third party, one who was not a party to the original contract, must be added and either the original obligor or the original obligee must be discharged.
      (3) As a substitute contract, a novation replaces the original contract. Because the novation is substituted for the original contract and the duties in the original contract are terminated, a party is unable to maintain a breach of contract action under the original contract.
3. Has there been interference in the contract by a third party? One who interferes with the contractual relationship of others may be liable for harming this relationship. The cause of action is known as "tortious interference with a contract." A party claiming interference must be able to answer the following questions affirmatively:
   a. Did an enforceable contract exist?
   b. Did the party inducing the breach know of the contract?
   c. Did the interfering party intentionally induce the breach?
   d. Did the interfering party induce the breach unjustifiably? and
   e. Was the party claiming interference damaged by the breach of contract?

KEY TERMS

Assignee

Assignment

Assignor

Creditor beneficiary

Delegatee

Delegation

Delegator

Donee beneficiary

Horizontal privity

Incidental beneficiary

Intended beneficiary

Novation

Obligee

Obligor

Privity of contract

Third-party beneficiary contract

Vertical privity

REVIEW QUESTIONS

TRUE/FALSE QUESTIONS (CIRCLE THE CORRECT ANSWER)

1. T　F　A third-party beneficiary contract is a contract made for the benefit of a third party.

2. T　F　A contract made for the benefit of a third-party beneficiary may not be enforced by that third party.

3. T　F　In a third-party beneficiary contract all three parties have both rights and duties.

4. T　F　A third-party beneficiary contract is subject to the same rules of contract formation as any other contract.

5. T　F　Under classical common law and the Restatement (First) of Contracts (1932), there are three types of third-party beneficiaries.

6. T　F　If a party contracts to give a third party a gift, the third party is an incidental beneficiary.

7. T　F　If a party contracts to discharge a prior obligation that the promisee had with a third party, the third party is a creditor beneficiary.

8. T　F　A beneficiary who is neither a creditor nor a donee beneficiary is an incidental beneficiary.

9. T　F　An incidental beneficiary has enforceable rights under the contract.

10. T　F　There is no distinction between intended and incidental beneficiaries when considering breach of implied warranties in a contract for the sale of goods.

11. T　F　The "vertical" nonprivity plaintiff is a buyer in the distribution chain who did not buy directly from the defendant.

12. T F   The "horizontal" nonprivity plaintiff is not a buyer in the distribution chain but one who consumes, uses, or is affected by the goods.

13. T F   A third party who is in privity of contract is a donee beneficiary and has contractual rights.

14. T F   A third party who is not in privity of contract is an incidental beneficiary and has no contractual rights.

15. T F   Even if the contracting parties cannot enforce the contract, the third-party beneficiary can enforce it.

16. T F   Contracting parties are free to make a subsequent agreement to discharge or modify duties to the beneficiary without consent of the beneficiary.

17. T F   Contracting parties may delegate their rights and assign their duties.

18. T F   An assignment of a contract is a transfer to another of the rights due under the terms of the contract.

19. T F   All rights may be assigned.

20. T F   A right will not be assignable if the transfer of the right will materially alter the duty of the obligor, the party who must perform the duty associated with that right.

21. T F   A court may refuse to enforce an assignment when there is a well-drafted term in the contract prohibiting the assignment of a contractual right.

22. T F   A court will not take into account a special relationship between the parties when deciding whether to enforce an assignment.

23. T F   A delegation of a duty is an authorization to another party to perform the duty.

24. T F   Not all duties may be delegated.

25. T F   Whether a duty is delegable depends on whether the delegation of the duty will materially alter the right of the obligee, the party who has the right associated with that duty.

26. T F   A party who was not a party to the original contract may not replace one of the original contracting parties.

27. T F   A novation is a contract that discharges a party to the contract and substitutes a new party in place of the original party.

28. T F   A party may still maintain a breach of contract action under the original contract when a novation has been substituted for the original contract.

29. T F   Novations may be simple or compound.

30. T F   A novation is not created if the new contract merely adds the third party without discharging the original obligor.

31. T F   In most states, one who interferes with the contractual relationship of others will not be liable for harming their contractual relationship.

32.　T　F　In most states, one who interferes with the contractual relationship of others may be sued for tortious interference with a contract.

33.　T　F　Courts may offer injunctive relief in tortious interference of contract cases in which a third party is engaged in activities designed to result in breach of a contract.

34.　T　F　Courts frequently award a traditional measure of contract damages in tortious interference of contract cases.

35.　T　F　Courts never award punitive damages in tortious interference of contract cases.

FILL-IN-THE-BLANK QUESTIONS

1. _____. A contract made for the benefit of a party other than the two contracting parties.

2. _____. The party who has contractual rights but no contractual duties in a third-party beneficiary contract.

3. _____. The party who will receive a gift under a third-party beneficiary contract.

4. _____. The third party who benefits when a party contracts to discharge a prior obligation that the promisee had with the third party.

5. _____. The term used by the Restatement (Second) of Contracts for the third-party beneficiary who has an enforceable right.

6. _____. A beneficiary who is neither a creditor nor a donee beneficiary.

7. _____. A nonprivity plaintiff who is a buyer in the distribution chain who did not buy directly from his or her seller's seller.

8. _____. A nonprivity plaintiff who is not a party in the distribution chain but who consumed, used, or was affected by the goods.

9. _____. The transfer to another of the rights due under the terms of the contract.

10. _____. An authorization to another party by the obligor to perform the obligor's contractual duty.

11. _____. A contract between one or both of the original contracting parties and a third party.

12. _____. A novation that substitutes a new obligor for the original obligor or a new obligee for the original obligee.

13. _____. A novation that may involve one original contract in which a new contract replaces an executory contract where one party to the new contract was a party to the original contract, *or* two original contracts with one party being common to both contracts.

14. _____. The cause of action that may be filed against one who interferes with the contractual relationship of others.

MULTIPLE-CHOICE QUESTIONS (CIRCLE ALL THE CORRECT ANSWERS)

1. Aunt Jean promised to give her car to Tommy if Tommy would promise to drive his sister Charlotte to school every morning. This transaction illustrates which of the following?
   (a) A donee beneficiary
   (b) A creditor beneficiary
   (c) An incidental beneficiary
   (d) An assignment
   (e) A delegation

2. Harvey borrowed $500 from Charlie. Sarah borrowed $500 from Harvey and promised him that she would repay the $500 to Charlie. The second transaction illustrates which of the following?
   (a) A donee beneficiary
   (b) A creditor beneficiary
   (c) An incidental beneficiary
   (d) An assignment
   (e) A delegation

3. Adam promised to loan $10,000 to Bridget for Bridget's promise to repay the loan at 8 percent interest. Cary promised Bridget to loan her the $10,000 if she would promise to substitute Cary for Adam and to release Adam from his obligation to loan her the $10,000. Bridget promised Cary. The second transaction illustrates which of the following?
   (a) A donee beneficiary contract
   (b) A creditor beneficiary contract
   (c) An assignment of a right
   (d) A simple novation with substitution of promisors (obligors)
   (e) A simple novation with substitution of promisees (obligees)

SHORT-ANSWER QUESTIONS

1. Discuss how courts determine whether a third-party beneficiary has a right to enforce the contract (i.e., whether the beneficiary is a donee or incidental beneficiary).

2. Describe the difference between a party who is a vertical nonprivity plaintiff and one who is a horizontal nonprivity plaintiff.

3. Describe the difference between an assignment and a delegation.

4. List four basic variations of novations.

5. Define the two essential elements of a novation.

6. List the elements that a party claiming interference with a contractual relationship must demonstrate.

Briefing Cases and Analyzing Statutes

Textbooks for paralegals usually include court opinions and this textbook is no exception. Court opinions begin with litigation initiated by an aggrieved party who files a complaint or petition in the office of the clerk of the trial court. This court is often named the district court, but not in all cases—for example, in New York the trial court is the Supreme Court. At trial, both questions of fact (i.e., was the light red or green?) and issues of law (i.c., should a minor have the right to disaffirm a contract and, if so, when?) are determined. Questions of fact are resolved by the jury unless the trial is without a jury (bench trial)—in which case questions of fact are resolved by the judge. Issues of law are decided by the judge.

If a party appeals, alleging an error committed by the trial court, an appellate court will review for the alleged error. The review of questions of fact carries a much higher standard of review as compared with the review of issues of law; questions of fact, therefore, are generally not appealed. Since most published state court opinions are from an appellate court, they generally deal exclusively with issues of law.

Court structures differ from state to state. Some states have a two-tier judicial system—a trial court and one appellate court. Some have three tiers—a trial court, an intermediate appellate court, and a higher appellate court. Some have more complicated systems (e.g., some types of cases are appealed to an intermediate appellate court while others are appealed directly to the higher appellate court; or all cases are appealed to the higher appellate court and that court either retains or transfers the case to an intermediate appellate court).

Not all opinions have the same precedental value. An opinion from a state's highest court has more precedental value than an opinion from that state's intermediate appellate court. The justices of the highest court have the final word and intermediate appellate court judges may feel reluctant to forge new precedent, knowing that their decisions may not be upheld by the highest court.

With a few exceptions (e.g., New York), most state trial court opinions are not published. Federal trial court (United States District Court) opinions may be published if the federal district court judge deems publication appropriate.

Textbooks for paralegals often include statutory material. Both judicial opinions and statutes are the primary authority and are used extensively in preparing a client's case for most forms of dispute resolution—litigation being only one of these. Even when preparing only to negotiate, for example, knowing the law (relevant judicial opinions and statutes) is essential.

HOW TO BRIEF A CASE

Students must dissect assigned cases to be able to participate in and follow the class discussion. One outline form for dissecting judicial opinions is called a "brief." Some instructors require students to read their written briefs in class. Most assume that students have written a brief prior to class. The information generated in a brief is usually the focal point for classroom discussion.

Many instructors give students guidance on how to brief for their class. Students may find it convenient to use the following briefing format as the starting point, refining it to conform to each instructor's suggestions. This format uses the headings "Case Name," "Pre-Trial Facts," "Action," "Decision(s)," "Issue," "Rule," "Application," and "Conclusion."

Case Name

The case name, jurisdiction, court, year, and page in the casebook are written in this order.

Example A-1

Laredo Hides Co. v. H&H Meat Prods. Co. (TX Civ. App. 1974) p. 2

Use *A Uniform System of Citation* as the guide to case names.

Pre-Trial Facts

State the key facts. Omit non–key facts.

> "A fact in an opinion is a key fact when the result in the opinion would have been different if that fact had been altered." W. Statsky & R. Wernet, Case Analysis and Fundamentals of Legal Writing 164 (1977).

Cardinal Rule #1.	During the prelitigation stage, do not refer to the disputants as plaintiff and defendant.
Cardinal Rule #2.	Do not write an excessively long brief.
Cardinal Rule #3.	Do not include extraneous material in the "Action."
Cardinal Rule #4.	An "Issue" must contain both fact and rule components.
Cardinal Rule #5.	An "Issue" must be stated in a single sentence.
Cardinal Rule #6.	A brief must contain the rule and application and not just a conclusion.
Cardinal Rule #7.	Do not just restate the court's opinion.
Cardinal Rule #8.	Do not disregard the court's rationale and go your own merry way.

Exhibit A–1 Cardinal Rules

For many courses, the key facts are prelitigation facts—those facts that led to the lawsuit. The filing of the lawsuit is discussed under "Action," and the various judicial decisions for that case are discussed under "Decisions." The brief, under this format, follows events in chronological order.

At the prelitigation stage, neither a plaintiff nor a defendant exists. Do not, therefore, refer to a plaintiff or to a defendant in the statement of the facts. Refer to the disputants by name. Referring to the disputants as plaintiff and defendant at the prelitigation stage violates **Cardinal Rule #1** (see Exhibit A–1).

The statement of facts should be long enough to trigger an accurate recollection of the case but short enough to represent a substantial condensation of the court's statement of the facts. The entire brief should be no longer than one page (if at all possible). An excessively long brief violates **Cardinal Rule #2.**

Action

The action step covers who is suing whom, the name of the action, and the nature of the relief requested.

Example A–2

Laredo Hides sued H&H for breach of contract seeking specific performance and damages.

The "who is suing whom" designates the disputants by name rather than "plaintiff sued defendant."

The "name of the action" or "cause of action" is separated from the "remedy." For example, breach of contract is a cause of action; specific performance is a remedy; negligence is a cause of action; damages is a remedy.

Remember, the "Action" step in the brief is the entry into the trial court. The trial court is where the lawsuit is initiated (by complaint or petition) and the trial held. Including extraneous material in "Action" violates **Cardinal Rule #3.**

Decision(s)

The decision step involves highly technical material that flows in chronological order.

Look ahead to what the appellant is alleging as the trial court's error. The appellant will complain that the trial court erroneously sustained the opposing counsel's demurrer, motion for summary judgment, motion for judgment not withstanding the verdict (judgment n.o.v.), or motion for a new trial—or erroneously overruled his or her own demurrer or motion. Begin the "Decision(s)" section of the brief with a statement regarding this procedural move (that is, error asserted). Follow with the trial court's resolution of this procedural move, the outcome of the case, and who appealed.

Next, consider the first appellate court and how the case was resolved on appeal. If the case has been appealed to a still higher court, who appealed and how was the case resolved?

Begin each sentence with the name of the court followed by what that court did. Do this for each court.

Example A-3

The District Court (without a jury) sustained Smith's motion for summary judgment. Jones appealed. The Texas Court of Civil Appeals reversed and remanded the case for trial.

Issue

The issue has two components:

(1) The key facts to which the rule will be applied
(2) The applicable rule

An issue that omits either the fact or the rule component violates **Cardinal Rule #4.**

State the issue in one sentence in question form. An issue not stated in one sentence violates **Cardinal Rule #5.**

Work enough facts into the issue so that the brief still means something two weeks after the case is briefed.

If the case involves several issues, state the issue, rule, application, and conclusion for the first issue. Repeat these steps for subsequent issues.

Rule

The rule is the legal statement that governs the resolution of the issue. The rule may emanate from the United States Constitution, a state constitution, or the Bill of Rights—or from a statute, an ordinance, an administrative regulation, or a prior case (case law). Because the rules form the structure for the substantive or procedural area being studied, students must think about how these rules relate to one another.

Application

Apply the rule to the facts. By the time the application step is reached (because this is an appellate case, it will emphasize the law rather than the facts), the application in most cases is straightforward.

Conclusion

The conclusion returns to the issue and states how the issue is resolved based on this set of facts. A brief that states only a conclusion and omits the rule and application violates **Cardinal Rule #6.**

In briefing, do not merely rewrite the court's opinion. Think about what is said and put it into the briefing format in your own words. Some judicial opinions have shortcomings. Astute briefing identifies these shortcomings. A brief that merely restates the court's opinion violates **Cardinal Rule #7.**

Do not rewrite the court's opinion to the extent that the brief no longer follows the court's rationale. (If the opinion is resolved by common law, for example, do not use the Uniform Commercial Code in the brief.) A brief that disregards the court's rationale and goes its own merry way violates **Cardinal Rule #8.**

Once the brief is completed, consider what you would have done if you had been the court. Specifically:

1. Is the court deciding the appropriate issue?
2. Is the court using the appropriate rule?
3. Is the application of rule to facts correct?
4. Based on social and economic needs of the community, is the rule sound? Should a different rule be promoted? If so, what would it be and why?

Postscript

A memorandum of law is organized around the "Issue," "Rule," "Application," and "Conclusion" format of briefs. Begin with the issue. The issue would be followed by the rule, the application of rule to facts, and the conclusion for that issue.

If the memorandum has more than one issue, begin the next section with the next issue, continuing in this manner until all issues are covered. As students develop their briefing technique, they are also developing their writing technique.

HOW TO ANALYZE CONSTITUTIONS, STATUTES, REGULATIONS, AND OTHER RULES

Law in the form of constitutions, statutes, regulations, executive orders, and ordinances comes into existence focusing not on one dispute but on a number of pending and hypothetical disputes or concerns. It is created in a deliberate process. Hearings are often held to gain information to enable the drafter or drafters to fully comprehend the problem and write a law that will apply to a range of situations. As a result, the law often appears cumbersome because it aims not at one target but at multiple targets.

As you research constitutional provisions, statutes, and other rules, you must dissect them in order to understand them thoroughly. The following outline uses a decision tree approach. This approach is helpful in identifying the various components of the law and how they relate to one another. Does all the language of a statute apply to each problem governed by the statute? If not, which phrases apply and which do not?

Your initial task is to find the elements of the law that apply to the problem. The simplest form of law will have all the elements arranged linearly with no choice between elements.

Example A-4

The Uniform Commercial Code § 2–201(2) provides:

> (2) Between merchants if within a reasonable time a writing in confirmation of the contract and sufficient against the sender is received and the party receiving it has reason to know its contents, it satisfies the requirements of subsection (1) against such party unless written notice of objection to its contents is given within 10 days after it is received.

A writing satisfies the requirements of section (1) of 2–201 against the party receiving it if the following conditions are met:

1. The writing was sent between merchants.
2. The writing was received within a reasonable time.

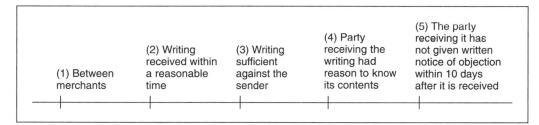

Exhibit A–2 Decision Tree of a Statute with No Disjunctives

3. The writing is sufficient against the sender.
4. The party receiving the writing had reason to know its content.
5. The party receiving the writing has not given written notice of objection to the writing's contents within 10 days after receiving it.

A decision tree of 2–201(2) would be a straight line because there are no choices within the statute (see Exhibit A–2). All elements of the statute must be satisfied for it to be applicable.

To develop a decision tree that has a number of choices, divide the statute by using the word "or." Each "or" indicates a branching of the tree. Choose one branch or the other. Since "or" is disjunctive, only one branch is used when resolving a dispute. By applying the facts to each decision as the tree branches, the appropriate path through the statute is found.

Example A-5

The Uniform Commercial Code § 2–104(1) defines the term "merchant" when used in transactions that involve a sale of goods.

"Merchant" means a person who deals in goods of the kind or otherwise by his occupation holds himself out as having knowledge or skill peculiar to the practices or goods involved in the transaction or to whom such knowledge or skill may be attributed by his employment of an agent or broker or other intermediary who by his occupation holds himself out as having such knowledge or skill.

This definition uses "or" eight times. Since "or" is disjunctive, some phrases in this statute will be applicable to some problems and some to others. The trick is to identify which phrases apply to which problems. Tracing the various branches in section 2–104(1) shows that a person could be a merchant if he or she fits into one of eleven different scenarios (see Exhibit A–3):

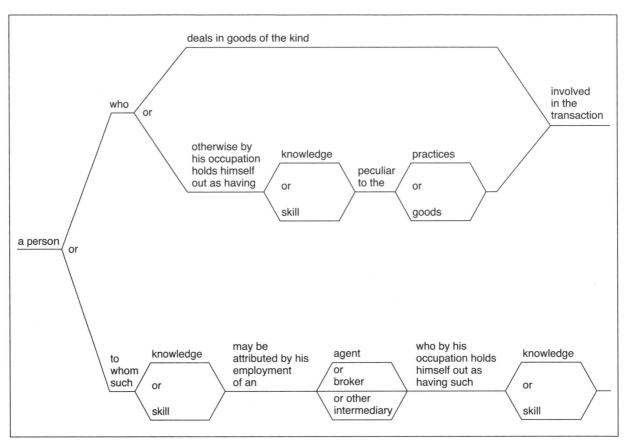

Exhibit A–3 Decision Tree of a Statute with Disjunctives

1. He or she is a person who deals in goods of the kind involved in the transaction;
2. He or she is a person who by his or her occupation holds himself or herself out as having knowledge peculiar to the practices involved in the transaction;
3. He or she is a person who by his or her occupation holds himself or herself out as having knowledge peculiar to the goods involved in the transaction;
4. He or she is a person who by his or her occupation holds himself or herself out as having skill peculiar to the practices involved in the transaction;
5. He or she is a person who by his or her occupation holds himself or herself out as having skill peculiar to the goods involved in the transaction;
6. He or she is a person to whom such knowledge may be attributed by his or her employment of an agent who by his or her occupation holds himself or herself out as having such knowledge;

7. He or she is a person to whom such knowledge may be attributed by his or her employment of a broker who by his or her occupation holds himself or herself out as having such knowledge;

8. He or she is a person to whom such knowledge may be attributed by his or her employment of another intermediary who by his or her occupation holds himself or herself out as having such knowledge;

9. He or she is a person to whom such skill may be attributed by his or her employment of an agent who by his or her occupation holds himself or herself out as having such skill;

10. He or she is a person to whom such skill may be attributed by his or her employment of a broker who by his or her occupation holds himself or herself out as having such skill; or

11. He or she is a person to whom such skill may be attributed by his or her employment of another intermediary who by his or her occupation holds himself or herself out as having such skill.

Glossary

A

abrogated An abrogated law has been repealed or nullified by a constitution, the legislature, or through the evolution of case law.

acceptance An acceptance is the offeree's manifestation of assent to the terms of the offer.

accord An accord is a contract to pay a stated amount to discharge a prior obligation that is either uncertain as to its existence or amount. Satisfaction (performance) of the accord contract is required before the duties under the original contract are terminated.

account stated An account stated is the debtor's and creditor's manifestation of assent to a stated sum as an accurate computation of an amount due the creditor.

acknowledgment form The acknowledgment form is the seller's acceptance form.

action An action is a shorthand phrase for cause of action, that is, the theory upon which relief should be granted.

actual knowledge Actual knowledge is valid objective knowledge based upon known facts rather than guesses or theories.

additional term When two forms are exchanged, an additional term is a substantive boilerplate term that appears in the second form but not in the first form.

adhesion contract An adhesion contract (contract of adhesion) is a contract formed by one party imposing his or her will upon an unwilling or even unwitting party.

affirmance Affirmance is the manifestation, by a contracting party who has the power to avoid the contract, of a willingness to continue with the performance of the contract.

agreement An agreement is the actual bargain of the parties as found in their language, course of dealing, usage of trade, and course of performance. Whether an agreement has legal consequences is determined by the law of contracts.

ambiguity An ambiguity occurs when a word has two different meanings. The ambiguity may be patent (apparent on its face) or latent (apparent only in light of surrounding circumstances).

anticipatory repudiation Anticipatory repudiation is a shorthand phrase for "breach by anticipatory repudiation." It is a party's refusal to perform a contractual duty made prior to the time the performance is due.

assignee The assignee is the third party (not one of the original contracting parties) to whom a contractual right is transferred.

assignor The assignor is the promisee in the original contract who transfers his or her contractual right to a third person.

assignment An assignment is the transfer of a contractual right.

assumpsit Assumpsit, a common law form of action, was one of the forerunners to the modern breach of contract and restitution actions. The term "assumpsit" meant an undertaking. Assumpsit was divided into Special Assumpsit and General (common or indebitatus) Assumpsit. An action of Special Assumpsit was brought on an express promise. An action of General Assumpsit was brought on an implied in fact or an implied by law promise.

auction with reserve In an auction with reserve, the auctioneer may withdraw the property at any time until he or she announces the completion of the sale. The potential bidders are the offerors.

auction without reserve In an auction without reserve, the auctioneer is the offeror and the bidders are the offerees.

avoidability of damages Avoidability of damage refers to the losses that occur after a breach of contract that are preventable by the nonbreaching party. A court ordinarily will not compensate an injured party for a loss that he or she could have prevented by an appropriate effort.

B

bargain   A bargain is an agreement between the parties.

bargained-for terms   The bargained-for terms in a preprinted form are those terms that are supplied by the party on the form and have not been preprinted.

beneficiary   A beneficiary is the recipient of a contractual promise.

between merchants   Between merchants means that both parties to the transaction (the buyer and the seller) are chargeable with the knowledge or the skill required to be a merchant for a particular Code section.

bilateral contract   A bilateral contract is a contract consisting of a promise by the offeror and a reciprocal promise by the offeree.

boilerplate terms   Boilerplate terms are the fixed terms in a preprinted form and are not bargained-for. Boilerplate terms may be either substantive terms (warranty, disclaimer, credit, arbitration, risk of loss, choice of law, and choice of forum) or procedural terms ("only my terms shall apply" and "this is not an acceptance unless you agree to all of our terms").

breach by anticipatory repudiation (anticipatory breach)   A breach by anticipatory repudiation is a notice that the promisor will not perform in the future.

breach by nonperformance (breach by failure to perform)   A breach by failure to perform is the usual breach and arises when the time for the promisor's performance has come and gone without the promisor performing.

C

capacity   Capacity is the legal ability a party has to contract. Some parties, such as minors and the mentally incapacitated, have only limited capacity and therefore have, under some circumstances, the right to disaffirm their contracts.

cause of action   A cause of action is the theory upon which relief should be granted. The cause of action should be distinguished from the remedy sought if the cause of action could be maintained. Breach of contract is a cause of action; damages is a remedy for breach of contract.

certainty   Certainty is the requirement that contract terms must be discernible to provide the basis for determining breach and the appropriate remedy.

choice of law   Choice of law is the determination of which law applies where more than one state is involved in a transaction, where conflicting laws exist within a state, or where federal law may preempt state law.

cognitive test   The traditional common law test whereby a contracting party may disaffirm a contract if his or her mind was so affected by mental disease or defect as to render him or her wholly and absolutely unable to comprehend and understand the nature of the transaction.

collateral illegality   Collateral illegality is an illegal act that occurred during the performance of the contract although not contemplated as a part of the performance of the contract when the contract was formed.

common law   Common law has several meanings. The common law is the body of law and jurisprudential theory that originated and developed in England. Common law, as distinguished from law created by legislative enactment, is derived from custom and usage and from judicial decisions recognizing and enforcing custom and usage.

compensatory damages   Compensatory damages are intended to compensate the nonbreaching party for not receiving his or her expectation under the contract.

concealment   Concealment is an act intended or known to be likely to keep another party from learning a fact.

condition   A condition is a contingency.

condition precedent   A condition precedent is a duty-creating event. An event external to the contract can be a condition precedent to the performance of a contracting party. An event internal to the contract, such as the performance by one party, can be a condition precedent to the performance by the other.

condition subsequent   A condition subsequent is a duty-terminating event.

conditional promise   A conditional promise is another name for promise with a condition precedent. The promisee does not have a duty to perform until the event occurs.

consequential damages   Consequential damages do not flow directly from an act but from the consequences or results of that act. See UCC § 2–715(2) (Buyer's Consequential Damages).

consideration   A contract has two "considerations"— consideration for the promisor's promise and consideration for the promisee's promise or performance. Consideration is the "price" sought by the promisor for his or her promise and the "price" sought by the promisee for his or her promise or performance.

consideration for the promisee's promise or performance   Consideration for the promisee's promise or performance is the "price" sought by the promisee for his or her promise.

consideration for the promisor's promise   Consideration for the promisor's promise is the "price" sought by the promisor for his or her promise.

constructive contract   A constructive contract is not a contract because the transaction lacks the elements of a contract. A court, however, might use this terminology to impose recovery under a restitution cause of action.

constructive knowledge   Constructive knowledge is inferred or deduced rather than based upon known facts.

contract   A contract is the total legal obligation that results from the parties' agreement. It may consist of an exchange of promises (bilateral contract) or an exchange of a promise for a performance (unilateral contract).

costs   Costs include filing fees, service of process, jury fees, and court officer charges, but not attorney fees.

counterclaim   A counterclaim is a claim the defendant has against the plaintiff that arises out of the same transaction that is the basis for the claim that the plaintiff has against the defendant.

counteroffer   A counteroffer is an offer made by the offeree to the offeror that deals with the subject matter of the original offer but with some variation in terms.

course of dealing   A course of dealing is a sequence of previous acts and conduct between the contracting parties, which can be regarded as establishing a common basis of understanding for interpreting their expressions and other conduct.

cover   Cover is a substitute performance.

creditor beneficiary   A creditor beneficiary is a third-party beneficiary to a contract who received a right under the contract when it was formed to discharge a prior obligation that the promisee had with the third-party beneficiary.

cure   Cure is the correction of performance to meet contract specifications.

D

damages   Damages are compensation awarded by a court to a party who has suffered loss or injury to rights or property.

deep pocket   Deep pocket is an expression used to designate a party with substantial assets or insurance.

definite expression of acceptance   When the offeree responds to the offeror's preprinted form with his or her own preprinted form, the offeree manifests a definite expression of acceptance when the offeree's form accepts the offeror's "bargained-for" terms.

delegatee   The delegatee is the third party (not one of the original contracting parties) who is empowered by the delegator to perform the delegator's contractual duty.

delegation   A delegation is the empowering of another by the obligor to perform the obligor's contractual duty.

delegator   The delegator is the promisor in the original contract who delegates his or her contractual duty to a third party.

detrimental reliance   Detrimental reliance is conduct by a party that was induced by another party making a promise and would result in an injury if compensation is denied.

different term   When two forms are exchanged, a different term is a substantive boilerplate term that appears in both forms—but one is not the mirror image of the other.

disaffirm   A contracting party disaffirms a contract when that party notifies the other contracting party that he or she will no longer be bound by the contract's terms.

divisible contract   A divisible contract is a contract with separate or installment performances.

donee beneficiary   A donee beneficiary is a third-party beneficiary to a contract who receives a gift under the contract.

duress   Duress is the use of any wrongful act or threat to influence a party to contract. Duress has two forms: duress by actual physical force and duress by threat.

duress by actual physical force   This form of duress occurs when a person using physical force compels a party to assent to the contract, even though that party did not intend to contract.

duress by threat   This form of duress occurs when a person improperly threatens a party to induce assent to a contract, when the threatened party has no reasonable alternative but to assent. Duress by threat includes "economic duress."

duty   "Duty" is the correlative of "right." When one party has a duty, another will have a corresponding right. Duty means that which is owed to a party.

E

economic duress   A party subjected to economic duress is wrongfully threatened with severe economic loss if he or she does not enter the proposed contract.

emancipation   Emancipation occurs when a court no longer considers the person a minor even though the person's chronological age would fall within the definition of a minor.

entire contract   An entire contract is a contract with a single performance.

estoppel   Estoppel is the judicial preclusion of a party's assertion of a position inconsistent with his or her prior actions or promise.

excuse   Excuse is the term used to indicate that the promisor is exempted by an unforeseen external event from performing under a contract.

executory contract   An executory contract is one that has not been fully performed by both parties.

expectation remedies (including **expectation damages**)   Expectation remedies (including expectation damages) place the nonbreaching party in the position he or she would have been in had the contract been fully performed.

expectation interest   Protecting the nonbreaching party's expectation interest places the nonbreaching party in the position he or she would have been in had the contract been fully performed by both parties according to the contract.

express promise   An express promise is a promise stated either orally or in writing.

F

federal preemption   The doctrine derived from the Supremacy Clause of the United States Constitution ("This Constitution, and the laws of the United States which shall be made in pursuance thereof; and all treaties made, or which shall be made, under the authority of the United States, shall be the supreme law of the land; and the judges in every state shall be bound thereby, anything in the Constitution or laws of any State to the contrary notwithstanding") whereby any federal law takes precedence over any conflicting state law.

forbearance   Forbearance means refraining from taking action.

forfeiture   Forfeiture is the loss of a right.

forum state   The forum state is the state in which the case is filed (the state hearing the case).

fraud in the factum   Fraud in the factum involves the very character of the proposed contract.

fraud in the inducement   Fraud in the inducement is a false representation or concealment of fact, that should have been disclosed, that deceives and is intended to deceive another party to the contract.

frustration of purpose   Frustration of purpose occurs when an unexpected event destroys a party's underlying reason for contracting. Even though performance of the contract is still possible, courts may excuse nonperformance on the theory of failure of consideration.

G

gap fillers   Those contract terms supplied by Article 2 of the UCC (sale of goods) that supplement the express terms of the contracting parties.

general damages   General damages arise naturally, that is, according to the usual course of events when a contract is breached. General damages are foreseeable.

good faith   Good faith in the case of a merchant means honesty in fact and the observance of reasonable commercial standards of fair dealing in the trade. In the case of a nonmerchant, good faith means honesty in fact in the conduct or transaction concerned.

gratuitous promise (Gift Promise)   If a promisor makes a gratuitous promise, the promisor does not seek consideration for his or her promise.

guarantor   A guarantor is a party whose duty is conditioned on the failure of another party's performance.

H

horizontal privity   Horizontal privity of contract is the relationship that must be established by a legislature or court before an injured user of a product, although not contracting with the seller of the product, can successfully sue the seller in a breach of contract action for a breach of warranty.

hybrid transactions   Contracts that are for both the sale of goods and the sale of services.

I

illusory promise   An illusory promise is a statement that is less than a commitment to do or refrain from doing something. Therefore, an illusory promise is a misnomer because it is not a promise.

implied by law (implied in law) promise   The implied by law promise is neither express nor implied in fact. It is a legal fiction, not a promise, which represents the court's label attached to the set of facts to reach a desired result.

implied in fact promise   An implied in fact promise is a promise that is inferred from conduct rather than expressed orally or in writing.

implied promise   An implied promise may be either an implied in fact or implied by law promise. The facts must be evaluated to determine whether the promise can be inferred from conduct or whether the promise is merely a legal fiction.

impossibility   Impossibility results from the occurrence of an unexpected event that renders a party incapable of performing his or her contractual duties.

impracticability   Impracticability results from the occurrence of an unexpected event that renders the performance of a contractual duty extremely difficult or expensive to perform.

incidental beneficiary   An incidental beneficiary is a third-party beneficiary to a contract who is neither a creditor nor a donee beneficiary. An incidental beneficiary receives a windfall if the contract is performed, but has no enforceable rights under the contract if it is not performed.

incidental damages   Incidental damages are awarded to the nonbreaching party for expenses reasonably incurred as a result of the other contracting party's breach. See UCC § 2–710 (Seller's Incidental Damages) and UCC § 2–715(1) (Buyer's Incidental Damages).

indefinite promise   An indefinite promise is a statement that appears to be a promise but omits terms essential to enable the courts to determine an appropriate remedy in the event the "promise" is breached.

injunction   An injunction is an order issued by a court directing a party to refrain from a specified act.

insolvent   Insolvent may be defined differently depending on the context. A person may be insolvent when he or she has ceased to pay his or her debts in the ordinary course of business; cannot pay his or her debts as they become due; or is insolvent within the meaning of the federal bankruptcy law (the sum of the debts is greater than the fair valuation of all of the debtor's property).

installment contract   An installment contract is one that requires or authorizes the delivery of goods or services in separate lots or increments to be separately accepted.

integration   An integration is the final written form of a contract.

intended beneficiary   An intended beneficiary is a third-party donee or creditor beneficiary. The Restatement (First) of Contracts uses the terms "donee" and "creditor beneficiary." The Restatement (Second) of Contracts uses the term "intended beneficiary."

interstate transaction   A transaction spanning several states. Also known as a multistate transaction.

J

justification   A promisor may be justified in not performing his or her contractual duties if the promisor was freed from performing due to a prior breach by the promisee.

K

knowledge   A person "knows" or has "knowledge" of a fact when he or she has actual knowledge of it.

L

lapse   Lapse is the termination of the offer through the offeree's failure to accept it within the time specified in the offer or, if no time is specified, then within a reasonable time.

last shot doctrine   A common law doctrine that provides where the acceptance of an express offer is implied from the offeree's performance (e.g., acceptance of the shipment and paying), the offeree, by performance, has accepted the offeror's terms.

latent ambiguity   A latent ambiguity is a miscommunication between the promisor and the promisee and occurs when a term has a double meaning.

liquidated damages   Liquidated damages are those damages agreed to by the parties at the time of contract formation that will apply to the transaction if a breach occurs.

M

mailbox (posting) rule   The rule of determining when an acceptance sent from a distance is effective. Under the mailbox (posting) rule, acceptance is effective when sent.

manifestation   A manifestation is a demonstration that could be readily perceived by a third party.

manifestation of assent   Manifestation of assent is the modern phrase that refers to the objective theory of contracts law.

meeting of the minds   Meeting of the minds is an outdated phrase that refers to the subjective theory of contract law.

merchant   A merchant as used in Article 2 of the UCC is defined in section 2–104 and its comment 2 and may be either a merchant who has specialized knowledge as to the goods, specialized knowledge as to the business practices, or specialized knowledge as to both the goods and the business practices. The business practices are those practices discussed in a specific code section. Therefore, a party may have specialized knowledge as to some business practices but not others—or may have specialized knowledge as to the goods but not as to specialized business practices and therefore may be a merchant for one Code section but not another.

minors (infants)   A minor is a person under the legal age. In most states the legal age is 18. A minor may be referred to as an infant in older cases and statutes.

mirror image   Mirror image means that the offeree must accept the offer without changing it.

misrepresentation   A misrepresentation is an assertion that is not in accord with the facts.

mistake   Mistake may take one of five forms: (1) mistake in judgment; (2) mistake in the performance of the contract; (3) mistake in understanding the terms of the contract (mistake: misunderstanding); (4) mistake in a basic assumption of fact; and (5) mistake in the integration of the contract.

mistake in a basic assumption of fact   A mistake in a basic assumption of fact involves a situation where the contracting parties believe they were bargaining for something different from what they actually did contract for.

mistake in integration   A mistake in integration occurs when a party makes a clerical error in writing the terms of the contract.

mistake in judgment   A mistake in judgment occurs when a party makes an erroneous assessment regarding how beneficial the contract will be.

mistake in the performance of the contract   A mistake in the performance of the contract occurs when a party makes an error by overperforming his or her contractual duty. The overperformance may include an overpayment.

mistake: misunderstanding   A mistake in understanding the terms of a contract occurs when, at the time of contract formation, both contracting parties use the same manifestations, but the parties do not attach the same meaning to these manifestations.

mistake of fact   A mistake of fact is a belief that is not in accordance with the facts.

mistake of law   A mistake of law is a belief that is not in accordance with the law.

mitigation   Mitigation requires the nonbreaching party to use reasonable means to avoid or minimize damages.

modification   Under classical contract theory, modification of a contract is itself a contract and must follow the same rules of contract formation required for the original contract.

motion in limine   Motion in limine is a preliminary request to limit evidence or testimony as specified by agreement of the parties or by order of the court.

mutual mistake   Mutual mistake is a mistake that both parties share at the time they reduced their agreement to writing.

mutual mistake of fact   Mutual mistake of fact occurs when the parties to a contract have a common intention but the writing does not reflect that intention due to their misconception of the facts.

mutual releases   Mutual releases will terminate the parties' duties to perform their contractual duties.

N

necessaries   Necessaries are those articles that the minor actually needs and must supply for himself or herself because the person who has the duty to provide these articles either cannot or will not provide them.

no breach–compliance   The defendant responds to the plaintiff's allegation of breach—"I am complying with the terms of the contract."

no breach–excuse   The defendant responds to the plaintiff's allegation of breach—"Although I am not complying with the terms of the contract, my nonperformance was excused, and therefore I have not breached the contract."

no breach–justification   The defendant responds to the plaintiff's allegation of breach—"Although I am not complying with the terms of the contract, my nonperformance was justified by your breach of this contract, and therefore I have not breached the contract."

no breach–terminated duty   The defendant responds to the plaintiff's allegation of breach—"Although I am not complying with the terms of the contract, my duty to perform the contract has been terminated, and therefore I have not breached the contract."

nominal damages   Nominal damages are a token award to the nonbreaching party, given more for clarification of the rights and duties of the parties than for actual monetary compensation. Court costs may be included.

nondisclosure A nondisclosure occurs when one party withholds information from another.

notice A person has "notice" of a fact when he or she has actual knowledge of a fact, has received a notice or notification of a fact, or, in light of all the facts and circumstances known to him or her at the time in question, has reason to know that a fact exists.

novation A novation is a contract that discharges a party to the contract, sometimes an obligor and sometimes an obligee, and substitutes a new party in his or her place.

O

objective standard The objective standard is the reasonable person's standard. It is based on manifestations that could be reasonably interpreted by hypothetical third persons watching the transaction.

obligee The obligee (promisee) is the contracting party with the contractual right to whom is owed the contractual duty.

obligor The obligor (promisor) is the contracting party who owes the contractual duty associated with the contractual right.

offer An offer is a manifestation of willingness to enter into a bargain, which justifies another person in understanding that his or her assent to that bargain is invited and will conclude it.

offer for a bilateral contract In an offer for a bilateral contract, the offeror makes a promise to entice the offeree to make a promise (a promise for a promise).

offer for a unilateral contract In an offer for a unilateral contract, the offeror makes a promise to entice the offeree to perform (a promise for a performance).

offeree An offeree is the party whom the offeror invites to accept the offer.

offeror An offeror is the party who extends the offer to the offeree.

officious Officious means to act in a meddlesome manner, interfering in the affairs of another by conferring an unnecessary or unwanted benefit.

offset An offset is a deduction of the amount awarded to the defendant from the amount awarded to the plaintiff.

option contract An option contract is a contract that negates the promisor's power to revoke the offer. An option contract has the same requirements as the main contract—promisor's promise, consideration for the promisor's promise, promisee's promise or performance, and consideration for the promisee's promise or performance.

P

pari delicto *Pari delicto* means equal fault. When parties are not *in pari delicto,* they do not share fault equally.

parol evidence rule The parol evidence rule is a substantive rule of contracts law that limits the terms of a contract in final written form to those in the writing. Prior or contemporaneous parol evidence cannot be used to add to or contradict terms in the final writing. Parol evidence, however, can be used to interpret terms in the final writing.

parol terms Parol terms are terms that are oral or, if written, are not in the final writing.

partial integration A partial integration is a contract that has only some of its terms in final written form.

party autonomy rule The court deference to the parties' own choice of applicable law.

patent ambiguity A contract term suffers from a patent ambiguity when the ambiguity is apparent from the face of the writing.

performance Performance must be distinguished from promise. A performance is an act or omission (doing or not doing something). A promise is the unequivocal assurance that something will or will not be done.

person A person includes an individual and an organization. See UCC § 1–201(30).

plain meaning Plain meaning is the meaning that reasonable people would give to a word or phrase.

posting (mailbox) rule The rule of determining when an acceptance sent from a distance is effective. Under the posting (mailbox) rule, acceptance is effective when sent.

predominant factor test The test used to resolve whether a hybrid transaction should be treated under Article 2 of the UCC (sale of goods) or under the common law (sale of a service).

preemption doctrine Under the federal preemption doctrine, state law must give way to federal law when federal law either expressly regulates the matter or when a particular subject is regarded as being beyond the bounds of state action.

preexisting duty A preexisting duty is that which is already owed to a party before a promise is made to perform that duty to that party.

preliminary negotiation Preliminary negotiations include all discussions of the parties that occur prior to the offer.

privity of contract Privity of contract is a relationship that must exist before a party can successfully maintain a breach of contract action. See **horizontal privity** and **vertical privity.**

promise A promise is a manifestation of intention to act or refrain from acting in a specified way, which justifies a promisee's understanding that the promisor has made a commitment. A promise is an unequivocal assurance that something will or will not be done.

promisee A promisee is the party to whom a promise is made.

promisor A promisor is the party who makes the promise.

promissory estoppel Promissory estoppel is the preclusion of an assertion by the promisor that is inconsistent with a previously made promise upon which the promisee has relied.

puffing Puffing is an expression of opinion by a seller not intended as a representation of fact.

punitive damages Monetary awards that are above and beyond compensation for injury and that would punish the breaching party.

purchase order The purchase order is the buyer's offer form.

Q

quantum meruit *Quantum meruit* is a common count (a standard allegation) in an action of assumpsit for work and labor. It is based on an implied assumpsit or promise on the part of the defendant to pay the plaintiff as much as is reasonably deserved for his or her labor.

quantum valebant *Quantum valebant* is a common count (a standard allegation) in an action of assumpsit for goods sold and delivered. It is based on an implied assumpsit or promise on the part of the defendant to pay the plaintiff as much as the goods sold by the plaintiff and delivered to the defendant were reasonably worth.

quasi contract A quasi contract is an implied by law or constructive contract. A quasi contract is not a contract but is a restitution cause of action based on unjust enrichment.

R

ratification Ratification is the confirmation (affirmation) of the contract.

reasonable person A reasonable person is a hypothetical (not one of the contracting parties), rational person who can objectively interpret a set of facts.

reasonable person's standard (reasonable man's standard) The reasonable person's standard is an objective rather than a subjective standard. The inquiry is how a reasonable person, having observed the transaction, perceived the transaction. The inquiry is not whether the parties mentally viewed the transaction in a common fashion. For example, if the parties dispute whether an offer was made, the legal conclusion will be that an offer was made if a reasonable person would conclude from the disputants' manifestations that an offer was made. The reasonable person's standard is used in modern contract law.

reformation Reformation is a judicial remedy designed to revise a writing to conform to the real agreement or intention of the parties.

rejection Rejection is the offeree's manifestation of nonacceptance of the offer.

release A release is the intentional relinquishment of a right.

reliance Reliance may be a cause of action (the basis of a claim), a remedy (the relief sought) for a breach of contract or a reliance cause of action, or a tool to circumvent an obstacle to a breach of contract cause of action (e.g. reliance may circumvent a lack of consideration, a lack of an express option contract, and a lack of a writing required by the Statute of Frauds). Reliance is based on the aggrieved party reasonably relying on the promisor.

reliance cause of action A reliance cause of action uses reliance as the basis of the plaintiff's complaint (or claim).

reliance interest Protecting the nonbreaching party's reliance interest places the nonbreaching party back to the position he or she was in prior to relying on the breaching party's promise.

reliance remedies (including **reliance damages**) Reliance remedies (including reliance damages) place the nonbreaching party back to the position he or she was in prior to relying on the breaching party's promise.

remedy A remedy is the relief sought if a cause of action can be maintained.

renunciation A renunciation is the abandonment of a right.

repentance Repentance is a feeling of remorse or regret concerning one's actions.

repudiation   Repudiation is the refusal to accept a right or to perform a duty.

rescission   A rescission is the abrogation of a contract. Rescission usually involves returning the parties to their pre-contract positions.

Restatements of the Law   The Restatements are an attempt by the American Law Institute (ALI) to codify the common law of the various states into black letter law with commentary and examples. At times, the Restatements go beyond the common law and present the ALI's view of what the law should be.

restitution   Restitution may be either a cause of action (the basis of a claim) or a remedy (the relief sought) for a breach of contract or restitution cause of action. Both forms of restitution are based on unjust enrichment.

restitution cause of action   A restitution cause of action uses unjust enrichment as the basis of the plaintiff's complaint (or claim).

restitution interest   Protecting the nonbreaching party's restitution interest places the breaching party back to the position he or she was in prior to receiving the benefit conferred upon him or her by the non-breaching party.

restitution remedies (including **restitution damages**)   Restitution remedies (including restitution damages) place the breaching party back to the position he or she was in prior to the time the breaching party received the benefit conferred upon him or her by the nonbreaching party. The measure of damages is the reasonable value of the benefit conferred to the breaching party.

revocation   Revocation is the offeror's manifestation to withdraw the offer.

right   "Right" is the correlative of "duty." When one party has a right, another will have a corresponding duty. Right means that which is due a party.

S

satisfaction   Satisfaction is the performance of the accord contract. Once the accord contract has been performed, the original contractual duties are terminated.

seal   An emblem or symbol affixed to a document to authenticate a signature.

seasonable expression of acceptance   When pre-printed forms are exchanged, a seasonable expression of acceptance refers to the fact that the second form must have been sent within a reasonable time after receiving the first form.

setoff   Setoff is a claim the defendant has against the plaintiff that arises independent of the claim the plaintiff has against the defendant.

sham consideration   Sham consideration is feigned or pretended consideration.

signature   A signature is any symbol made by a party with a present intention to authenticate the writing as that of the signer.

special damages   Special damages do not naturally arise from a breach of contract. They are not within the usual course of events when a contract is breached. Special damages become foreseeable when they may reasonably be supposed to have been in the contemplation of both parties at the time of contract formation as the probable result of the breach.

specific performance   Specific performance is an order issued by a court directing a party to do a specified act.

Statute of Frauds   The Statute of Frauds is a statute forbidding enforcement of certain types of contracts unless they are in writing. Under the Statute of Frauds, for example, a contract for the sale of goods for the price of $500 or more and a contract that cannot be fully performed within one year from the time of its formation must be in writing.

Statute of Limitations   A Statute of Limitations provides for a specified period of time within which a cause of action must be brought.

subjective standard   The subjective standard refers to a party's thinking or mental state rather than manifestations. The subjective standard is commonly referred to as the meeting of the minds.

substitute contract   A contract between the original contracting parties that replaces the original contract.

supervening external event   A supervening external event is an event that occurs after contract formation and before full performance of the contract.

surety   A surety is one who, by contract, is liable for the obligations of another.

T

third-party beneficiary   A third-party beneficiary is a party who will be benefited by the performance of a contract. A third-party beneficiary may be a donee, creditor, or incidental beneficiary. An incidental beneficiary has no enforceable rights under the contract.

third-party beneficiary contract   A third-party beneficiary contract is a contract for the benefit of a third party. This party is neither the offeror nor offeree.

total integration   A contract is totally integrated if all of the contractual terms are in final written form.

trade usage   Trade usage gives a word or phrase the meaning of the trade that is different from its plain meaning.

U

unconscionability   A contract or contract term is unconscionable if, at the time of contract formation, one party imposed an unreasonably favorable contract or term on the other party who lacked a meaningful choice.

undue influence   Undue influence involves unfair persuasion by a party who is either in a position of dominance or in a position of trust and confidence. Undue influence requires neither threats nor deception, although one or the other is often present.

unenforceable contract   An unenforceable contract is a contract that the court will not implement.

Uniform Commercial Code   A comprehensive compilation of rules drafted by the American Law Institute and the National Conference of Commissioners on Uniform State Laws that includes a number of topics including sale of goods and which becomes the law of a given state upon enactment by that state's legislature and signature of the governor.

unilateral contract   A unilateral contract is a contract consisting of a promise by the offeror and a reciprocal performance by the offeree.

unjust enrichment   Unjust enrichment is the underlying theory for a restitution remedy for breach of contract or a restitution cause of action. Unjust enrichment occurs when the plaintiff has conferred a benefit on the defendant and it would be unfair to permit the defendant to retain the benefit without compensating the plaintiff.

usage   Usage is a habitual or customary practice.

V

vagueness   A term suffers from vagueness if it lacks a precise meaning.

vertical privity   Vertical privity of contract is the relationship that must be established by a legislature or a court before an injured purchaser of a product can successfully sue a remote seller in a breach of contract action for a breach of warranty. The remote seller did not contract directly with the injured purchaser, but one or more intermediate sellers were involved in the distribution of the product.

void contract   A void contract is an agreement that has no legal effect as a contract.

voidable contract   A voidable contract is a contract in which one or both parties have the power to avoid the legal relationship created by the contract or to ratify the contract and thus extinguish the power of avoidance.

volitional test   The more modern test which supplements the cognitive test so a person may disaffirm a contract when, due to mental disease or defect, he or she is unable to act in a reasonable manner and the other party had reasons to know of the mental disease or defect.

W

waiver   Waiver is the intentional or voluntary relinquishment of a right.

Index

An f after a page number indicates a figure.